D1126441

Elements of Electronic Communications

Elements of Electronic Communications

Joseph J. Carr

Reston Publishing Company, Inc., Reston, Virginia
A Prentice-Hall Company

Library of Congress Cataloging in Publication Data

Carr, Joseph J.
Elements of electronic communications.

Bibliography: p.
1. Telecommunication. 2. Radio. 3. Electronics.
I. Title.
TK5101.C2987 621.38′0413 77-15939
ISBN 0-87909-206-8

To Julian Brown, "Uncle Julian"
who filled a void in my life for many years

Reston Publishing Company, Inc.
A Prentice-Hall Company
Reston, Virginia 22090

10 9 8 7 6 5 4 3 2 1

Printed in the United States of America

Contents

Preface

That electronic communications has ch
secret, and this observation is not partict
three-quarters of a century ago, in the
pulsating spark of the shipboard radic
dollar business employing thousands (
nicians. The amateur and professional
communications, now ordinary, that v
generation ago. Synchronous satellites
only to relay voice communications, bu
nals as well.

Despite complexity of modern coı
have not changed very much—and tha
here, you should be able to go on to
Commission license examinations and
communications electronics. Also, you
nications as your hobby. Although thi
those aspiring to ham radio, it is exce
tionship is mutual—amateur radio is e:
in electronic communications. Buildin
radio station will give you experience,
able but necessary quality that no boo
about this hobby can be obtained
League, 225 Main Street, Newington, (

Preface

That electronic communications has changed the world we live in is no secret, and this observation is not particularly astute or clever. What started three-quarters of a century ago, in the form of an ozone stench and the pulsating spark of the shipboard radiotelegrapher, is now a multibillion dollar business employing thousands of engineers, operators, and technicians. The amateur and professional alike participate daily in feats of communications, now ordinary, that would have created a furor only a generation ago. Synchronous satellites orbit the earth and are used not only to relay voice communications, but computer data and television signals as well.

Despite complexity of modern communications equipment, the basics have not changed very much—and that is the subject of this book. From here, you should be able to go on to pass the Federal Communications Commission license examinations and do quite well earning your living in communications electronics. Also, you could use electronics and communications as your hobby. Although this book is not especially written for those aspiring to ham radio, it is excellent preparation. In fact, the relationship is mutual—amateur radio is excellent preparation for a profession in electronic communications. Building and operating your own amateur radio station will give you experience, insight, and "savvy"—that inexplicable but necessary quality that no book will ever give. More information about this hobby can be obtained from The American Radio Relay League, 225 Main Street, Newington, Connecticut, 06111.

JOSEPH J. CARR

1
Fundamentals of Electricity

1.1 THE ATOM

All matter is composed of building blocks called *atoms*. Each atom is composed of still smaller particles that are not unique to any particular chemical element. Three major particles are known; these are called electrons, protons, and neutrons. The first two of these carry equal, but opposite polarity, electric charges. The electron carries a negative (−) charge that is equal in magnitude to the positive (+) charge on the proton. The neutron carries no electric charge, so it is said to be electrically neutral.

The physical and chemical properties of any element are determined by the makeup of its atoms. In particular are the number of protons and electrons used to make up the atom. Figure 1.1(a) shows a model of the structure of the simplest atom, that of the element hydrogen. We now know that this particular model is oversimplified, but it remains sufficiently valid for discussions at this level.

The central core of the atom, called the *nucleus,* contains positively charged protons and electrically neutral neutrons. The masses of the protons and neutrons are very nearly identical, so the nucleus has a mass that reflects the total number of both protons and neutrons. In hydrogen there is but one proton.

In an electrically neutral atom there is only one electron for each proton. In the hydrogen atom, therefore, there is a single electron orbiting about the nucleus. Helium, on the other hand, has two protons in the nucleus, so it has two orbital electrons. Again, we see electrical neutrality, because there are exactly as many electrons as there are protons.

The distance between the nucleus and the orbital electrons is not arbitrary, but is subject to some specific restrictions. The reasons that this is true are beyond the scope of this book, but are taken up in a subject called "quantum mechanics" (a branch of physics). For our purposes let us say that there are only certain allowable distances and that these form imaginary shells around the nucleus. Each shell has a maximum electron holding capacity. Any electrons in excess of that magic number must go into the next higher shell until it, in turn, is full of electrons. The first shell, that nearest the nucleus, can hold only two electrons. If an atom has

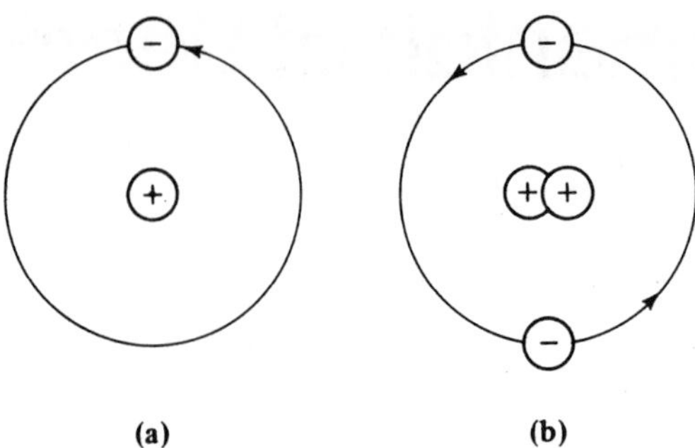

Figure 1.1 The atom of hydrogen has one electron and one proton, while the atom of helium has two electrons and two protons.

more than two electrons, more than one shell will be needed. The element lithium, for example, has three electrons and three protons. Two of the electrons completely fill the first shell, so the third is forced to enter the second shell. This shell is filled when it contains eight electrons, while the third shell can accommodate up to eighteen electrons.

Atoms in which the electrons are tightly bound to the nucleus do not give them up easily. In those materials it takes a relatively large amount of energy to break loose any electrons. Other materials, notably acids and metals, have weakly bound outer electrons. In that type of material it takes very little additional energy to strip free large numbers of electrons. Even the random motion of atoms caused by thermal agitation at room temperature is sufficient to cause large numbers of free electrons. In the absence of any external forces, these electrons drift about almost aimlessly inside of the material until they find some atom in need of an electron to complete its complement and restore electrical neutrality. An atom that has fewer than its normal quantity of electrons is called a *positive ion,* whereas one in which there is an extra electron present is a *negative ion.*

1.2 STATIC ELECTRICITY

Some materials give up electrons if merely rubbed hard by certain other materials. An electrical charge then exists on the surface of the materials. This is the source of the static charges built up on your body when you walk across a rug, pet a cat, or slide across your car seat. One of the two touching surfaces takes on a positive charge, while the other takes on a negative charge.

Surrounding any electrical charge is an electric field. When such fields are stationary, and do not move, the field is said to be electrostatic. If, on the other hand, the charges move, then an electrical current is said to exist.

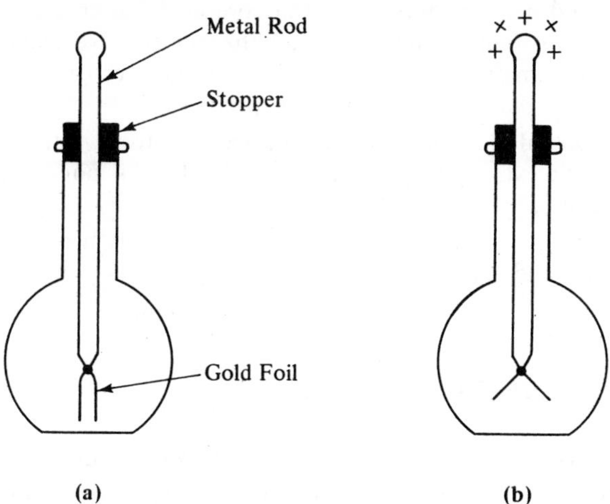

Figure 1.2 The electroscope **(a)** uncharged, and **(b)** charged.

An electroscope (See Figure 1.2) is a simple instrument used to detect the presence of a static electric charge. When there is no charge nearby, we find the gold leaves hanging limp. Application of an electric charge, whether positive or negative, will cause the foil pieces to spread apart. This occurs because the two pieces each receive a charge of the same polarity. A fundamental fact to commit to memory is that *unlike charges attract* and *like charges repel each other.* (See Figure 1.3.)

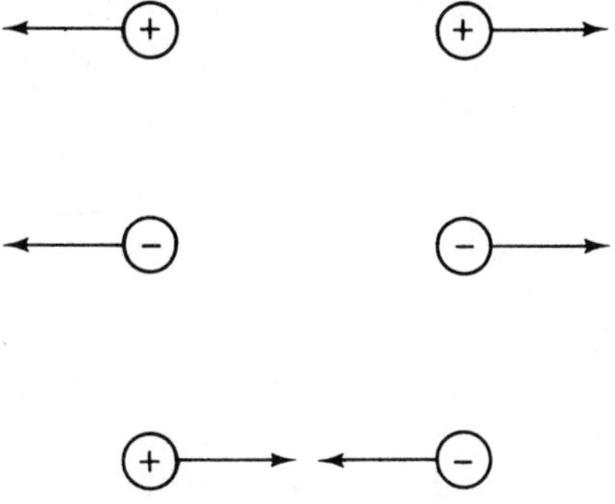

Figure 1.3 *Like* charges repel, and *unlike* charges attract each other.

Review. Before proceeding on to the material of the next section, let us take a moment to quickly review the high points of the preceding material.

1. Atoms are the building blocks of matter, and are composed of negatively charged particles called electrons, positively charged particles called protons and electrically neutral (no charge) particles called neutrons.

2. Protons and neutrons form a central core in the atom called the nucleus. Electrons are found orbiting around the nucleus. Neutrons and protons have approximately the same weight, but the electron is roughly 1850 times lighter than either neutrons or protons.
3. Loosely bound electrons can become free electrons with the application of very little extra energy. If static electric charges move, then an electric current exists.
4. "Like" charges (+ and +, or − and −) repel each other, while unlike charges (− and +) attract each other.

1.3 ELECTRIC CURRENT

If free electrons travel in the same general direction, an electric current is said to exist. Normal motion of free electrons due to thermal and other forms of energy inside the material is random, and not so well ordered that it could be called an electrical current. An external force, however, can cause a large number of electrons to migrate in the same general direction, and that is what constitutes the electrical current.

In the electronics field we say that electron flow is from negative to positive. Do not become confused when you hear some people loudly and vehemently defend the notion that just the opposite is true. In physics courses, and those electrical courses intended mostly for electricians, they often teach it that way. This does not reflect a fundamental ignorance of electrical theory, but the fact that current flow is defined in two different ways. In both cases, however, it is electrons that actually move. The problem with directional flow began in the eighteenth century when early investigators into electrical phenomena, such as Benjamin Franklin, discovered two polarities and arbitrarily assigned (+) and (−) polarities. In electronics work we assign the (−) symbol to the terminal of the battery or other source that has the *excess of electrons*. The (+) terminal has a deficiency of electrons. Nature seems to love equilibrium, so the electrons flow from the area of excess (−) to the areas of deficiency (+). This seems to make good sense in light of the fact that an area with an excess of the negative electrons has a net charge that is negative, justifying use of the (−) symbol. Similarly, the (+) symbol for the terminal with a deficiency seems justified by the fact that there is a net positive charge at that terminal. The other fields assign a (−) symbol for a deficiency and a (+) symbol for an excess. When speaking to electronics people, or taking examinations intended for electronics people (i.e., the FCC license exams), use the electronics definition—current flows from *negative to positive*.

Electrons cannot flow in an "orderly manner" without some external

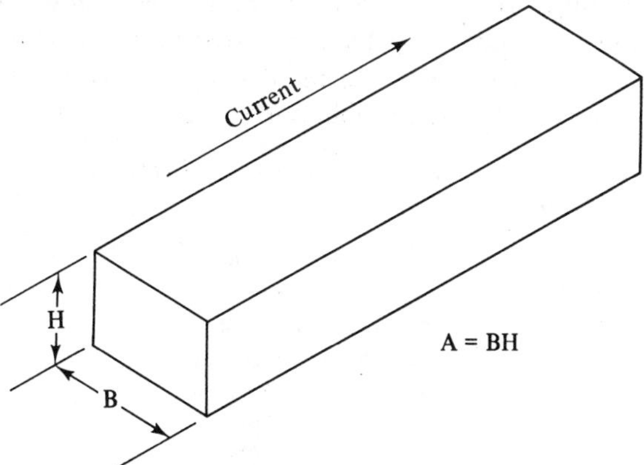

Figure 1.4 Electrical resistance of a conductor is directly proportional to the length and resistivity, and *inversely* proportional to the cross-sectional area.

force's being applied. This force is called various names including "electromotive force" (EMF), "electric(al) potential," "potential difference," "potential," or "voltage." All are correct and may be used interchangeably. Voltage tends to set electrons in motion, thereby setting up an electric current. *Resistance* is a property of materials that tends to oppose the flow of electric current. It is a function of the cross-sectional area, temperature, and a property called *resistivity,* which is specific to the particular material in which the current is flowing. The exact relationship between the factors affecting resistance is that resistance is inversely proportional to the cross-sectional area, and directly proportional to resistivity and length. (See Figure 1.4.) In mathematical form:

$$R = \rho \times \frac{L}{A} \tag{1-1}$$

where ρ (Greek letter "rho") is resistivity.
L is the length.
A is the cross-sectional area.

The units for resistivity are "meter-ohms" if metric units are used for L and A, or "ohms/circular mil foot" if feet are used for length and circular mils are used for cross-sectional area.

Not all materials are good electrical conductors. Some materials, like metals, contain large numbers of free electrons, and these can produce large values of electrical current flow with very little applied force. Other materials, though, have tightly bound outer electrons, and consequently are not able to support an electrical current flow. These materials are called "insulators," examples of which are listed in the chart of Figure 1.5. Since insulators have few free electrons, it takes an extremely large value of voltage to produce any appreciable current flow in those materials.

An "insulator" has few free electrons, whereas a "conductor" has many free electrons.

Conductors	Insulators
Carbon	Dry air
Acids	Ceramics
Metals	Dry wood
	Glass
	Rubber
	Resins

Figure 1.5 Some common conductors and insulators.

1.4 THE "PLUMBING ANALOGY" OF ELECTRICITY

The flow of electricity has often been likened to the flow of water in a hydraulic system. Indeed, the word "current" seems to have come from the fact that Benjamin Franklin and his early colleagues viewed electricity as some kind of strange, unseen, fluid phenomenon.

We know that electrons flow from a region where they are in excess to a region where they are deficient in numbers. This is analogous to the water system of Figure 1.6. Notice that the level in the right-hand container is lower than the level of water in the left-hand container. The difference between the two fluid heights is the potential difference of the system, so is analogous to voltage—the potential energy of electrical systems. The actual forces applied to the two containers are gravitational, so there will be a potential difference only when the heights are unequal. Under that condition water (i.e., current) will flow from the left side to the right side until the water levels in the two containers are equal. This will, then, make the potential difference zero, so the flow of water ceases. This is also true of electrical circuits. A battery, for instance, is dead when the potential difference between the terminals is zero—or 0 volts, if you prefer.

An even stronger version of the plumbing analogy brings in the concept of an electric circuit, because it is a closed loop. We can visualize such a system to have a pump that supplies the pressure (potential) to force water through the pipes of a hydraulic "circuit," which returns to the suction side of the pump. This is very much like the situation existing

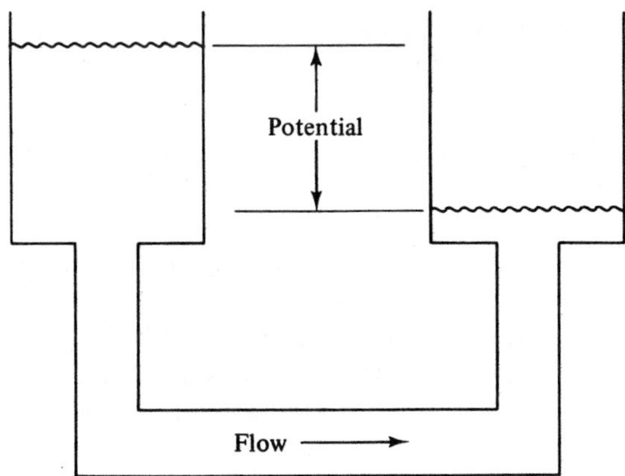

Figure 1.6 Electrical current flow is analogous to water flow in a plumbing system.

when a battery, or other electrical source, forces electrons through an electrical circuit. The pump is similar in function to an electrical generator, which maintains a potential difference so long as it is turning.

We know that voltage, or EMF, is much like a pressure in a hydraulic system; both are examples of forces, or force differences. Furthermore, we can see how the flow of water is similar to the flow of electrons through an electrical circuit. But where is the analogy to electrical resistance? The plumbing analogy would not hold up unless it also provided some property similar to electrical resistance, which it fortunately does: the constriction of the pipe walls. A pipe, or any other hydraulic conduit, can allow only some specific amount of water to flow past for any given value of applied pressure. Similarly, only a certain amount of electrical current will flow for a set voltage. In both cases, the degree of opposition offered is inversely proportional to the diameter of the conductor or pipe.

1.5 UNITS OF ELECTRICITY

Electrical current is measured in units called "amperes," often abbreviated simply "amps." One ampere is defined as the passage of a certain quantity of electrical charge past a point in some unit of time—the second. This electrical charge is called the "coulomb" and represents a charge equal to the sum of charges on 6.28×10^{18} electrons. One ampere, then, is the flow of one coulomb of charge per second, or

$$I = \frac{Q}{t} \qquad (1\text{-}2)$$

where I is the current in amperes.
Q is the electrical charge in coulombs.
t is time in seconds.

(Note that the electrical charge on a single electron is equal to 1.6×10^{-19} coulomb.)

The ampere has a magnitude that is quite suitable for many practical applications, but may be too unwieldy in others. Smaller units are often required, so we also must use the *milli*ampere and the *micro*ampere. The milliampere (mA) is equal to 10^{-3} (that is 0.001) ampere, while the microampere (μA) is equal to 10^{-6} (0.000001) ampere. Figure 1.7 gives some of the more common prefixes used in conjunction with basic electrical units.

The unit of electrical resistance is the "ohm." One ohm can be defined as the resistance of a column of mercury (or some other material) with specific dimensions, but for our purposes we shall use the old definition: One ohm is the resistance that will allow the passage of one ampere of current when a potential of one volt is applied.

(Prefix)-Units	*Multiply Units by:*
Giga–	1,000,000,000 (10^9)
Mega–	1,000,000 (10^6)
Kilo–	1,000 (10^3)
Milli–	.001 (10^{-3})
Micro–	.000001 (10^{-6})
Pico–	.000000001 (10^{-9})

Example. .000001 ampere equals 1 "μA" or microampere

Figure 1.7 Metric prefixes for electrical units.

1.6 OHM'S LAW

Ohm's law describes the relationship between the three basic electrical parameters: voltage, current, and resistance. Stated as a formula that you are expected to remember, Ohm's law is given by

$$E = IR \tag{1-3}$$

where E is the electrical potential in volts.
I is the electrical current in amperes.
R is the resistance in ohms.

We can obtain other forms of Ohm's law by doing a little algebra on the basic equation. These are

$$I = \frac{E}{R} \qquad R = \frac{E}{I} \tag{1-4}$$

"Conductance" is another electrical parameter that is seen occasionally. It is merely the reciprocal of resistance, and is measured in a unit called the "mho" (which is merely "ohm" spelled backwards). While the resistance is a measure of a circuit's opposition to the flow of current, conductance is a measure of its *ability* to conduct current. Conductance is given by

$$G = \frac{1}{R} \tag{1-5}$$

where G is the conductance in mhos.
R is the resistance in ohms.

Ohm's law example. Suppose that an electrical circuit passes a 10-mA (0.01-A) current through a resistance of 1250 Ω. What is the applied voltage?

$$E = I \times R$$
$$E = (0.01)(1250) \tag{1-6}$$
$$E = 12.5 \text{ V}$$

1.7 SIMPLE ELECTRICAL CIRCUITS

Before we can discuss circuits in any detail, there must be established some means for graphic communication. To that end, electronics people use schematic symbols to represent electrical circuitry. Resistors, for example, are represented by Figure 1.8a and batteries by Figure 1.8b.

(a) (b) **Figure 1.8** Schematic symbols for **(a)** resistor, and **(b)** battery.

If no polarity marking is used on the battery symbol, you are usually safe in assuming that the short bar is the negative end of the battery.

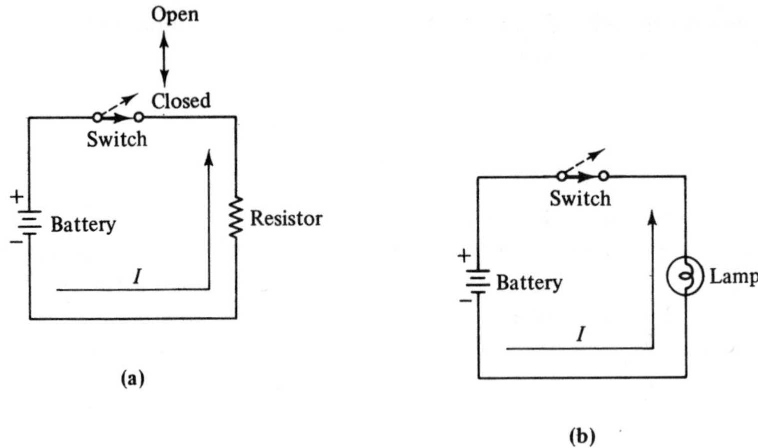

Figure 1.9 The concept of an *electrical circuit.*

Figure 1.9 shows two simple electrical circuits. When the switch is closed the circuit is "completed," so we find that the electrons can flow from the negative terminal of the battery, through the resistor and connecting wires, to the positive pole of the battery. When the switch is open, this path is broken, so no current will flow.

Not all electrical circuits use actual "resistors" as the path for electrons, or "load." A flashlight, for example, uses an incandescent lamp instead of a resistor. Although the component and its schematic symbol may not look like a resistor, it is functionally the same, as far as Ohm's law is concerned.

1.8 ELEMENTARY ELECTRICAL COMPONENTS

Batteries are devices that store electrical energy in the form of chemicals. This energy can be released in the form of an electric current if certain chemical reactions take place inside of the cell. The individual cell can only produce a voltage on the order of 1.25–2.00 V. Greater voltages require the combination of several cells; such combinations are called "batteries." The simple 1.5-V flashlight "battery" is not really a battery, but is, instead, a cell.

Batteries and cells (see Figure 1.10) come in many different forms and styles. Even those in ordinary, everyday use are often quite different from each other. The battery in your automobile, for example, is a lead-acid storage battery. It is called a "storage battery," because it is capable of being recharged after it runs down. It can, therefore, "store" charge for later use. The main advantage of the lead-acid battery is that it can produce enormous amounts of current—it takes up to several hundred amperes to start a large V-8 automobile engine on a cold morning. The two disadvantages to the lead-acid battery, however, are that it is very heavy and that acid may spill. It is necessary to operate the lead-acid battery in one position only (upright), or the acid will spill out and eat anything it touches. Some modern lead-acid batteries are totally sealed and are considered "serviceless." (The "water level" does not need constant checking.) These may sometimes be operated in adverse positions.

Another form of battery is the dry cell. Most common of these are the carbon-zinc cells and batteries used in flashlights, transistor radios, and so forth. Other forms of dry cell are the mercury, alkaline, and nickel-cadmium ("ni-cad"). All of these have their own advantages, and may be found in portable communications equipment if suited for some particular service. The mercury battery, for example, has the ability to maintain very nearly the same terminal voltage throughout most of its lifetime. This makes it useful for voltage standards in test equipment and those portable applications where the terminal voltage is critical. The alkaline type has a larger current capacity and life expectancy than the carbon-zinc type. Although it is somewhat more expensive than carbon-zinc cells, it is often specified because it is capable of a lower cost in the long run in that fewer battery changes are required. The ni-cad battery is relatively lightweight and is rechargeable. This makes it very desirable for use in portable communications equipment.

One method for specifying batteries and cells is by the ampere-hour rating. This is the number of amperes drawn times the hours. For example, a battery that is rated at 80 A-h (as a lead-acid auto battery might be) can supply up to 80 A for one hour, or almost any other combination of current and time that equals 80 A-h. This is why you can only crank your engine for a few minutes before the battery dies. Let us say you have a

Figure 1.10 Some types of batteries.

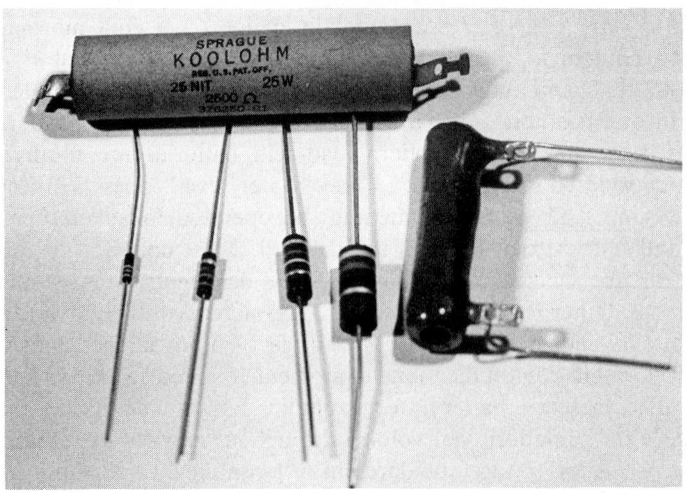

Figure 1.11 Electrical resistors.

400+ cu. in. engine that wants 300 A to crank. If the battery is rated at 80 A-h, the total cranking time will be less than 0.27 h, or about 15 min.

Smaller batteries and cells used in communications equipment provide many fewer ampere-hours than does the automobile battery. The common ni-cad, for example, is available in standard cell sizes: AA, C, and D. These will be rated at 1.3 or 1.36 V depending upon type. The ampere-hour ratings are 0.5 A-h (500 mA-h) for the AA penlight size, 2 A-h for the "C" size, and 4 A-h for the "D." Be aware that some manufacturers offer lower ratings in the same size. This is especially true of those that are offered primarily to the consumer or hobbyist trade. Industrial ni-cad batteries, however, are available in the larger ratings, and these should be used for communications applications unless the equipment manufacturer says otherwise. The ni-cad cells can be purchased separately in either end connector or solder tab versions, or they may be obtained already "put-up" in module cases that will produce terminal voltages of 13.6 or 6.8 V dc (or some whole number multiple of 1.36) at an A-h rating equal to that of the size cells used.

Resistors (see Figure 1.11) are devices that are found at certain points in electrical circuits to form a bulk or lump resistance that is needed for some specific purpose. Most resistors are marked with their resistance value (and perhaps tolerance) with either numerals printed on the body of the resistor or color-coded bands of paint. Size is the factor that determines the power rating of most resistors. Since the resistor color code will be used almost daily in your electronics career, it is wise to spend some time right now to memorize it (see Figure 1.12).

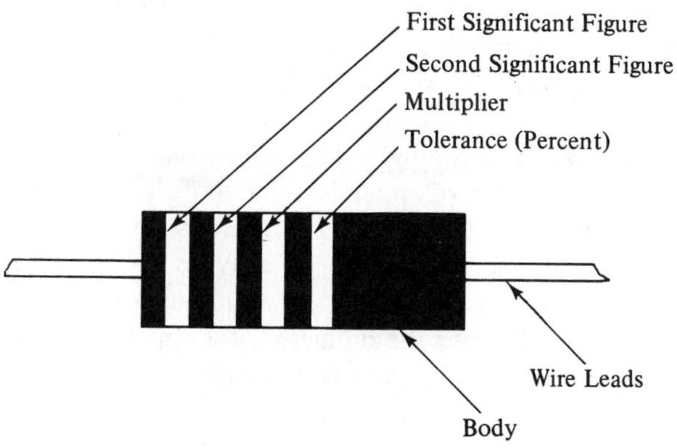

Color	Number	Multiplier Value	Tolerance
Black	0	— (none) —	–
Brown	1	10	–
Red	2	100	–
Orange	3	1000	–
Yellow	4	10,000	–
Green	5	100,000	–
Blue	6	1,000,000	–
Violet	7	10,000,000	–
Gray	8	100,000,000	–
White	9	1,000,000,000	–
Gold	–	0.1	5%
Silver	–	0.01	10%
No Color	–	–	20%

Note that color bands are closer to one end of the resistor than the other. First figure is color closest to an end.

Example: A resistor has colors, from left to right, yellow-violet-orange-gold. This is a 4 (yellow) 7 (violet) x 1000-ohm resistor. The tolerance band of this 47,000 resistor indicates the true value to be ± 5% of 47k. The actual value then will lie between 44,650 and 49,350 ohms.

Figure 1.12 The resistor color code—memorize it.

1.9 ELECTRICAL CONDUCTORS

Not all conducting materials are equally good. Silver, for example, is one of the best electrical conductors, followed by copper, gold, aluminum, and so forth. Silver is rarely used in practical work, even though it is the best conductor, because it is expensive and it will tarnish easily when exposed to air. Aluminum is a relatively good conductor, although poorer than either silver or copper, and is reasonably cheap—much more so than either of the other metals. Although aluminum is used extensively in house wiring and power transmission lines, it is rarely used in electronics, because it cannot be easily soldered. Copper is a bit more costly than aluminum, but is used extensively in electronics. The reasons for this are that copper is a better conductor than aluminum, is easy to solder, and is not too unmanageably expensive. Incidentally, an aluminum conductor must have a diameter equal to 1.25 times the diameter of a copper conductor rated to carry the same current. It is, however, much lighter than the copper equivalent.

Gold is prohibitively expensive for common use in electronic circuits, but there are cases where it is used because it will not tarnish in air, or even in sea water. There are instances where treasure hunters have recovered Spanish coins and artifacts from sunken shipwrecks that were still bright and gold-colored after almost 500 years of immersion in salt water. Copper and silver artifacts, on the other hand, were heavily encrusted with corrosion. In electrical circuits the corrosion (a metal oxide) is an insulator, so it will have a high resistance. In relay contacts, switch contacts, and socket terminals that are in high-reliability applications, gold is used to prevent tarnish from causing an open circuit. In most such cases, the gold is too soft for good mechanical strength, as well as ridiculously expensive, so the terminal is made either gold-filled or gold-plated over a copper, nickel, or steel base metal structure.

PROBLEMS

1. The electrical charge of a neutron is __________.
2. What are the respective electrical charges of the proton and electron?
3. A stationary electric charge accumulated on an object is called ________ electricity.
4. Like charges ________ each other, and ________ charges attract.
5. "Electromotive force" and "electrical potential difference" are alternate ways of denoting __________.
6. A certain material has a resistivity of 9.56. What is the electrical resistance, in ohms, of a piece of wire made from this material if the wire is 10 feet long and has a cross-sectional area of 1.5 circular mils?
7. List several conductors of electricity.
8. List several electrical insulators.
9. How many electrons does it take to have one coulomb of electrical charge?

10. A charge of 10-coulombs is delivered through an electrical circuit in 1-sec. How much electrical current flows?
11. How many microamperes (μA) are there in 1 mA?
12. Express 0.00150 A in μA.
13. Express 0.02 A in milliamperes (mA).
14. What is the unit of electrical resistance?
15. What is the unit for conductance?
16. What is the equivalent resistance if the conductance is 2500 micromhos (μmhos)?
17. How many mhos are equivalent to 100 Ω?
18. Find the voltage if we have a 1000-Ω resistor passing a current of 250 mA.
19. Find the resistance if there is a current of 50 mA and a voltage of 150 V.
20. The metal ________ is used to make tarnish-resistant relay and switch contacts in high-reliability equipment.
21. A potential of 1000 V is applied to a resistance of 10,000 Ω (10 k Ω, or simply 10 k). What current will flow?
22. Find the voltage if 120 mA is flowing in a 50-Ω resistance.
23. A resistor has the following color bands: BROWN-BLACK-RED-SILVER. What are its resistance and tolerance?
24. A resistor has the following color bands: BROWN-GREEN-YELLOW-GOLD. What are its resistance and tolerance?
25. What is the resistance if the color code is ORANGE-WHITE-ORANGE?
26. A 47,000-Ω resistor has no color band for tolerance. Its *measured* resistance is 45,803 Ω. Is it within tolerance?

2
Direct Current Circuits

2.1 SOME REVIEW

In Chapter 1 we learned about Ohm's law. It was stated that voltage is proportional to the current in amperes and the resistance in ohms. In mathematical form,

$$E = IR \tag{2-1}$$

If we know two of the three basic variables, the third can be calculated by rearranging the equation.

2.2 ELECTRICAL POWER—WATTS

Power can be defined as the time rate of doing work. You can have a large reservoir of free electrons, but unless a voltage is present to push the electrons through a circuit, no work is performed. Alternatively, you could have a battery or power supply capable of producing a large voltage, but unless it is connected to a circuit, so that current can flow, there will be no work done. In both cases we find that no work is done unless both a current and voltage are present. Power, the time rate of electrical work, is measured in a unit called the "watt." One watt of electrical power is developed when a potential of one volt pushes a current of one ampere through a resistance of one ohm. Power, then, is expressed by

$$P = E \times I \tag{2-2}$$

where P is the power in watts.
E is the potential in volts.
I is the current in amperes.

We can find several other useful formulas for calculating power by plugging in the equivalent expressions from Ohm's law for E and I. For example, since $I = E/R$, we can substitute E/R for I, and this yields

$$P = EI$$
$$P = (E)(E/R) \qquad (2\text{-}3)$$
$$P = E^2/R$$

Similarly, since $E = IR$, we can also substitute IR for E, and get

$$P = EI$$
$$P = (IR)I \qquad (2\text{-}4)$$
$$P = I^2R$$

The three power formulas commonly used, then, are

$$P = EI = \frac{E^2}{R} = I^2R \qquad (2\text{-}5)$$

Figure 2.1 shows a graphical device for remembering the most commonly used electrical formulas.

As was true with the other electrical units, we find the watt either too large or too small in many practical situations. For circuits that consume very low amounts of electrical power we find the *milliwatt* (mW) and microwatt (μW) more applicable, in that they result in more manageable numbers. Of course, you can use watts if you prefer, but there may be an

$E =$	$I =$
IR, $\frac{W}{I}$, $\sqrt{(WR)}$	$\frac{E}{R}$, $\frac{W}{E}$, $\sqrt{\left(\frac{W}{R}\right)}$
Volts	Amperes
$W =$	Ω (Ohms)
EI, I^2R, $\frac{E^2}{R}$	$\frac{E}{I}$, $\frac{E^2}{W}$, $\frac{W}{I^2}$
Watts	Ohms

Figure 2.1 The electrical relationships.

unwieldy number of significant zeros. On the other end of the power range, we find many television, international shortwave, and even some Navy communications transmitters rated in *megawatts* (mW)—millions of watts.

Electrical energy is measured in units of power per unit of time. The basic unit is the watt-second or "joule" (1 J = 1 W-s). Both of these units are the same; only the names are different. The terms, however, are synonymous. The power companies are in the business of selling energy, rather than "power" as implied by their names. They commonly use larger units in the form of watt-hour or kilowatt-hours.

Any time that power is dissipated in a load, there must be some work performed. That work might be in the form of a turning motor shaft, light and heat output from an incandescent lamp, or the generation of a radio or television signal in a transmitter. Any power dissipated by a load that is not turned into some other kind of work will usually produce additional heat as its work. This is why an electric motor will heat up, often to the point of destruction, if the bearings seize or any other force causes the rotation to cease. The power that had been used to turn the motor and its mechanical load now shows up as heat work. The incandescent lamp is another example of a device that produces both some form of work and some of heat. In an ordinary lamp the light output is the useful work, while the heat is work wasted because of inefficient operation.

Power Problem Examples

1. How much power is dissipated in a resistance of 100 Ω if a current of 1 mA is flowing?

$$\begin{aligned} P &= I^2R \\ P &= (0.001)^2(100) \\ P &= (0.001)(0.001)(100) \\ P &= 0.0001 \text{ W} = 0.1 \text{ mW} = 100\ \mu\text{W} \end{aligned} \qquad (2\text{-}6)$$

2. How much power is dissipated when 75 V causes a current of 2.2 A to flow?

$$\begin{aligned} P &= EI \\ P &= (75)(2.2) \\ P &= 165 \text{ W} \end{aligned} \qquad (2\text{-}7)$$

3. How much power is dissipated by applying a potential of 280 V across a 4700-Ω resistance?

$$\begin{aligned} P &= E^2/R \\ P &= (280)^2/(4700) \\ P &= (280)(280)/4700 \\ \text{P} &= 16.7 \text{ W} \end{aligned} \qquad (2\text{-}8)$$

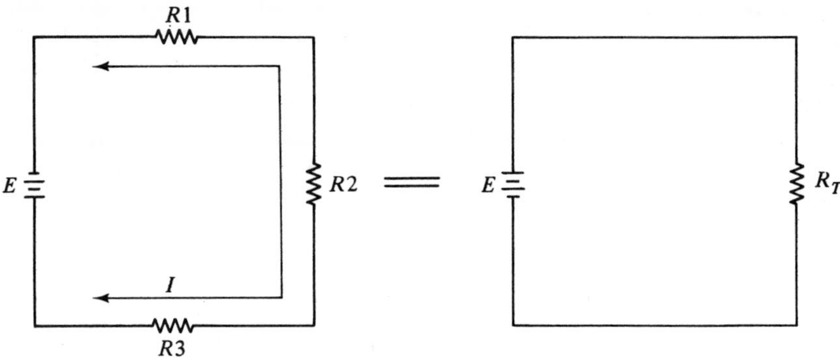

Figure 2.2 Reduction to an equivalent circuit.

2.3 SERIES AND PARALLEL CIRCUITS

Once we have more than one component in a circuit, we find that it has become less easy to make simple statements on the circuit operation based solely on Ohm's law and the power formulas without first making some apparent circuit modifications.

Figure 2.2 shows a simple series circuit containing three resistors labeled $R1$, $R2$, and $R3$. A *series* circuit is one in which the *full amount* of current leaving one terminal of the battery must flow through *each* and *every* element of the circuit. The currents in all three resistors, then, are equal. The total resistance seen by the battery is equal to the sum of the individual resistances in the circuit, or

$$R_T = R1 + R2 + R3 + \ldots + R_n \tag{2-9}$$

The voltage applied to a series circuit will be divided among the various resistors of the circuit in a manner that reflects their percentage of the total resistance, R_T.

A *parallel* circuit is a multibranch circuit, such as Figure 2.3, in

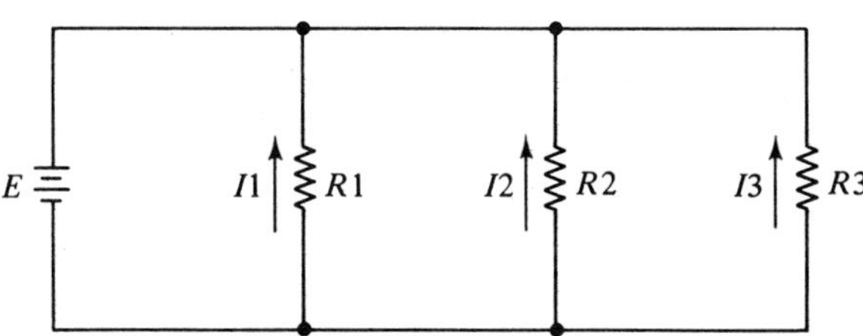

Figure 2.3 Three branch parallel circuit.

which the total terminal voltage applied by the battery is across each and every element in the circuit. In that type of circuit the current from the battery splits into two or more paths (one for each circuit branch), and then rejoins the main stream at the other battery terminal.

The total resistance seen by the battery across a parallel circuit is less than the resistance of the smallest individual element making up the circuit. This total resistance is given by

$$R_T = \frac{1}{\dfrac{1}{R1} + \dfrac{1}{R2} + \dfrac{1}{R3} + \ldots + \dfrac{1}{R_n}}$$

or, in the special case where there are only two resistors in parallel,

$$R_T = \frac{R1R2}{R1 + R2} \tag{2-11}$$

Both of these expressions should be learned well.

One further case of a simple dc circuit is a combination of the two preceding types: the series-parallel circuit of Figure 2.4. Circuits actually encountered in day-to-day electronics work are usually more like the series-parallel than either of the two simpler cases. In the examples in the

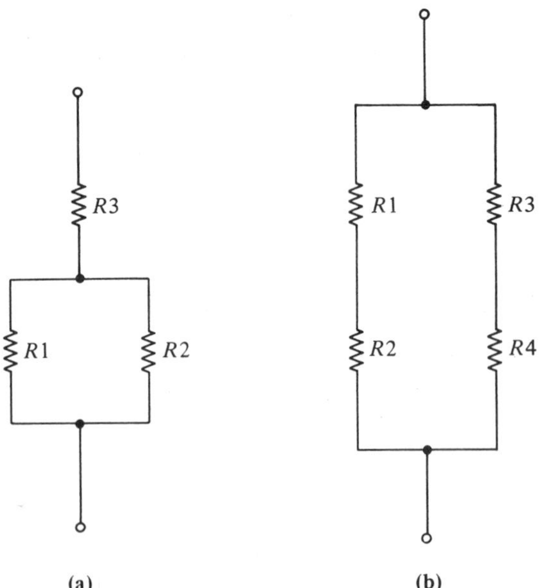

Figure 2.4 The series-parallel circuit.

figure there are two of the almost endless varieties of possible series-parallel circuits.

In Figure 2.4(a) we see that $R1$ and $R2$ are in parallel. Their total combination resistance, R_t is added to $R3$ to find the total circuit resistance R_T.

The other series-parallel circuit, Figure 2.4(b) has a configuration in which two series branches, $(R1 + R2)$ and $(R3 + R4)$, form a parallel circuit.

2.4 KIRCHOFF'S LAWS

Physicist Kirchoff formulated two laws that are of immense help in analyzing electrical circuits. These are the current law and the voltage law.

(1) Kirchoff's current law states that the algebraic sum of all currents entering and leaving a point in a circuit must be zero, whereas (2) Kirchoff's voltage law states that the algebraic sum of all voltage drops and rises around a circuit must be zero.

Kirchoff's laws are illustrated in Figure 2.5. At Figure 2.5(a) we see the current law. I1 is the total current drawn from the battery. When the current reaches the junction it will split into two components, $I2$ and $I3$. The total current, according to Kirchoff's current law, obeys the relationships

$$I1 = I2 + I3$$

or (2-12)

$$I1 - I2 - I3 = 0$$

For our purposes, it is wise to label all currents entering a point as positive (+) and all currents leaving the same point as negative (−). This is an arbitrary convention used mainly to keep our results consistent when we are solving difficult circuit problems.

The current in any particular branch of a parallel circuit can be calculated from a simple formula called the *current divider equation:*

$$I_{R1} = \frac{R2}{R1 \times R2} \times I1 \quad \text{(Refer to Figure 2.5)} \tag{2-13}$$

Note that the denominator contains the sum of all resistances in the parallel circuits. The numerator contains all of the resistances *except* the one for which you want to know the current flow. For example, suppose that you had five resistors ($R1$–$R5$) in parallel and wanted to know the current in, say, $R3$. The current divider equation would then be

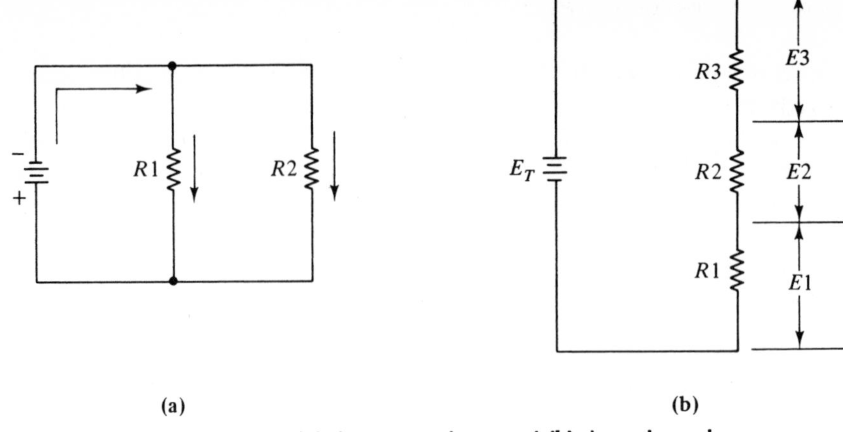

Figure 2.5 Kirchoff's law. **(a)** the current law, and **(b)** the voltage law.

$$I_{R3} = \frac{R1 + R2 + \quad + R4 + R5}{R1 + R2 + R3 + R4 + R5} \times I_{\text{total}} \qquad \text{(2-14)}$$

Kirchoff's voltage law is illustrated in Figure 2.5(b). The current flowing in the resistors causes voltage drops that can be calculated from Ohm's law. Kirchoff's voltage law merely states that the sum of all these voltage drops is equal to the sum of the voltage rises (i.e., batteries or other sources of energy). For this particular circuit:

$$E_T = E1 + E2 + E3$$

or

$$E_T - E1 - E2 - E3 = 0 \qquad \text{(2-15)}$$

A voltage divider equation can be used to find the voltage drop across any particular resistor; for example,

$$E1 = \frac{R1}{R1 + R2 + R3} \times E_T \qquad \text{(2-16)}$$

You may substitute any of the other resistors in the circuit for the $R1$ term in the numerator to find their respective voltage drops.

2.5 POWER TRANSFER

Up until now we have considered all batteries and other voltage-current sources to be ideal—a convention to which simplicity and ease of explanation will force us to return after a brief digression to admit the truth. Such an ideal source could theoretically deliver an infinite current, since it would have an internal resistance of zero ohms. That is *not* the case in real circuits. Real sources, the kind that you can make or buy, all exhibit a certain amount of internal resistance, shown in R_i in Figure 2.6. The maximum voltage available across any value load resistor is less than the open circuit (load disconnected) terminal voltage of the source. If the internal resistance of the source is known, then you can calculate the actual output voltage using the voltage divider equation with R_L in the numerator and $R_i + R_L$ in the denominator.

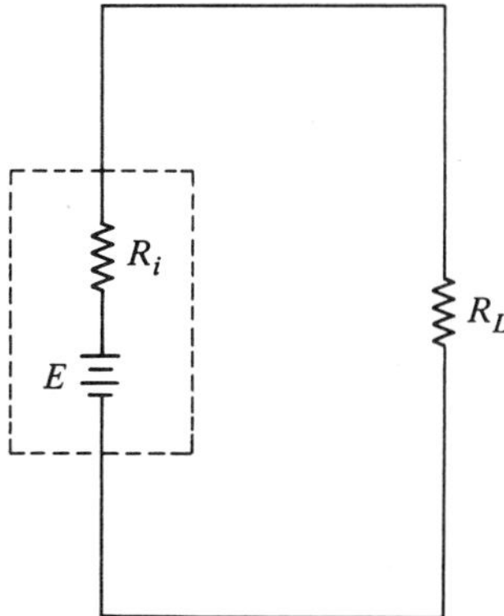

Figure 2.6 Internal resistance of electrical sources reduces the voltage available to external loads.

The internal resistance also limits the current output from the power supply. I_{max} is that current that will flow if R_L is zero ohms (a dead short). If this value and the open circuit voltage are known, then R_i can be computed by using Ohm's law. Of course, it is necessary for you to realize that this should be done only as a "thought experiment," not with real power supplies. Shorting the output could create a disastrous short circuit current that will burn up the supply. A better technique is to find R_i analytically and apply Ohm's law. For example, if you measure the open-circuit voltage, and then remeasure the output voltage after a known value of R_L is connected, you will have E_{R_L}, E_T, and R_L, so you may use the current divider equation to solve for R_i. The short-circuit current is then found by Ohm's law using $I_{max} = E_T/R_i$.

A fundamental theorem in electricity to remember is that the maximum power transfer between the source and the load occurs *only* if the internal resistance is equal to the load resistance; in other words, when $R_i = R_L$. This is a very important concept, and you *will see it again.*

Problem Examples

1. Calculate the total resistance of the circuit in Fig. 2.7.

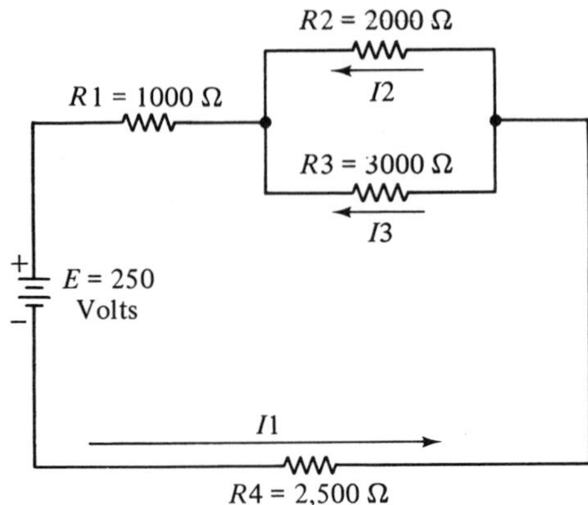

Figure 2.7 Calculate the total resistance.

$$R_T = R1 + \frac{R2R3}{R2 + R3} \quad R4$$

$$R_T = (1000) + \frac{(2000)(3000)}{(2000) + (3000)} + (2500) \qquad (2\text{-}17)$$

$$R_T = 3500 + \frac{6 \times 10^6}{5 \times 10^3}$$

$$R_T = 4700\ \Omega$$

2. In the same circuit as in Problem 1, find current $I1$.

$$I = E/R_T$$

$$I = 250/4700 \qquad (2\text{-}18)$$

$$I = 0.053$$

3. Now find currents $I2$ and $I3$, using the current divider equation.

$$I2 = I1 \times \frac{R3}{R2 + R3}$$

$$I2 = (0.053) \times (3000/5000)$$
$$I2 = (0.053) \times 3/5 \qquad (2\text{-}19)$$
$$I2 = 0.0318\ \text{A}$$

and
$$I3 = I1 \times \frac{R2}{R2 + R3}$$

$$I3 = (0.053) \times (2000/5000)$$
$$I3 = (0.053) \times 2/5 \qquad (2\text{-}20)$$
$$I3 = 0.0212\ \text{A}$$

4. Calculate the voltage drop across $R4$, using the voltage divider equation. (*Note:* The parallel combination $R2R3$ is equal to 1200 Ω).

$$E_{R4} = \frac{(2500)}{(1000) + (1200) + (2500)} \times 250\ \text{V} \qquad (2\text{-}21)$$

$$E_{R4} = 0.532 \times 250\ \text{V}$$
$$E_{R4} = 133\ \text{V}$$

5. Calculate the power dissipated in resistor $R4$.

$$P = E^2/R = (133)^2/2500 = 7.08\ \text{V} \qquad (2\text{-}22)$$

6. Calculate the total resistance of a parallel circuit that has the following resistors: 47 k, 27 k, 100 k, 10 k and 220 k.

$$R_T = \frac{1}{\dfrac{1}{47{,}000} + \dfrac{1}{27{,}000} + \dfrac{1}{100{,}000} + \dfrac{1}{10{,}000} + \dfrac{1}{220{,}000}}$$

$$R_T = 5{,}785\ \Omega \qquad (2\text{-}23)$$

2.6 FUSING

Fuses are placed in electrical circuits and equipment in order to provide protection from short circuits and overload conditions. Because their main use is *protection,* you must never attempt to defeat the purpose of any fuse or circuit breaker. The consequences of such actions are always potentially serious, and may lead to either destruction of the equipment or injury (including loss of life) to humans.

Figure 2.8 shows several types of fuse and circuit breaker. The glass, cylindrical type of fuse is that most commonly used in commercial communications equipment. The circuit breaker is a "resetable" fuse, in that it opens the circuit when an overload occurs, but can be reset for normal operation once the short or overload is cleared.

The degree of protection offered by any fusing device depends upon

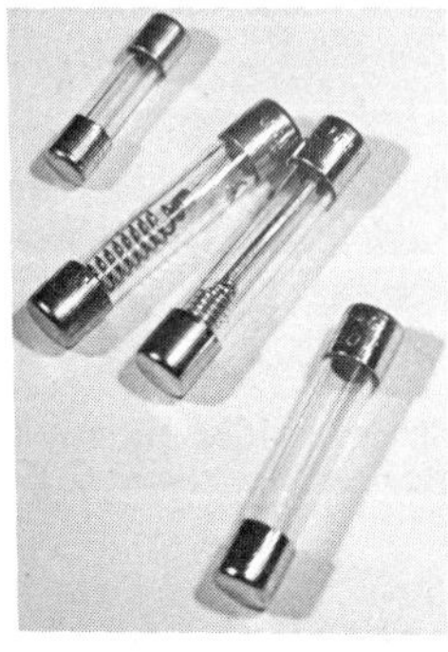

Figure 2.8 Examples of typical fuses used in electronic equipment.

two factors: its current rating and its circuit placement. For most common, ordinary applications in communications, the rating of the fuses is specified by the equipment manufacturer. It is not wise to operate a piece of equipment with any other rating unless instructed to do so by the manufacturer.

Figure 2.9 shows the proper placement of a fuse in a circuit. It should be located between one terminal of the voltage source and the circuit it is to protect. Physically, it should be located as close as possible to the power supply, or the power entrance point to the equipment. The idea is to have the fuse blow, and remove power from the circuit, when a short occurs.

Fuses do not *cause* trouble, they *indicate* trouble. Any blown fuse, especially if the glass is smoked up, should always be regarded with suspicion. An experienced electronics technician will investigate to see if there is a cause, even if the equipment seems to operate normally when a new fuse is installed.

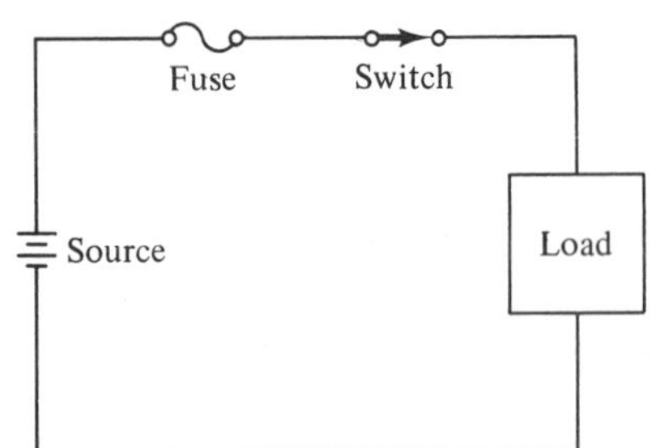

Figure 2.9 Correct placement of a circuit's fuse.

2.7 METERS IN ELECTRICAL CIRCUITS

Meters are instruments used to measure current and voltage in electrical circuits. Ammeters, milliammeters, and microammeters are used to measure current, whereas voltmeters are used to measure potential differences. The manner in which meters are connected into the circuit is critical. Recall that voltage is the difference in potential *between two points* in a circuit. Consequently, you must connect a voltmeter (see Figure 2.10) in parallel with the component or section across which you want to know the voltage.

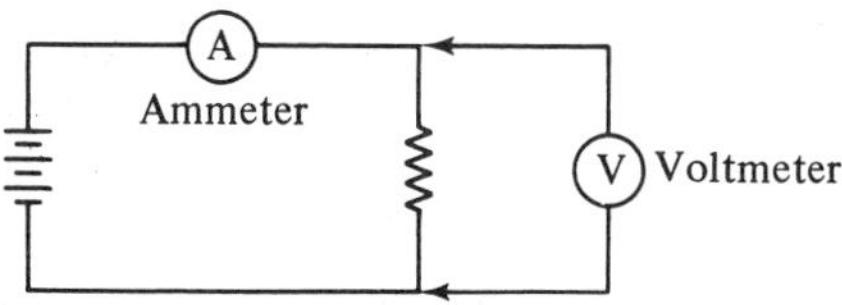

Figure 2.10 Ammeters are connected in series with the load, while voltmeters are connected in parallel—do not confuse these!

Alternatively, we connect an ammeter (or other current meter) in series with the circuit under test. Note that these respective connections require an ammeter to have a very low resistance and a voltmeter to have a very high resistance to prevent loading of the circuit, errors, and damage to the instrument. It is absolutely essential that meters be connected into the circuit correctly, or destruction of the meter, and possibly the circuit, will result. If you make the mistake of connecting in parallel a milliammeter, its destruction will be so rapid that your reflexive action of reaching for the on-off switch will be far too slow to keep the instrument from burning up. Note well that most electronics lab instructors and employers do not look kindly on the person who burns up test equipment.

PROBLEMS

1. The unit of electrical power is the ______________.
2. One watt is defined as one ampere flowing under a pressure of ______ volt(s).
3. How many watts are dissipated if a potential of 100 V creates a current flow of 0.68 A?
4. Find the current if a potential of 560 V causes a power dissipation of 90 W.
5. Find the power if a potential of 80 V is applied across a 120-Ω resistor.
6. Find the power if a current of 150 mA flows through a 560-Ω resistor.
7. Find the power dissipated in a 12-k resistor if a current of 50 mA is flowing.
8. What is the total resistance if there are four 100-Ω resistors connected in series?
9. What is the resistance between points *A* and *B* in Figure 2.11?
10. What is the resistance between points *A* and *B* in Figure 2.12?

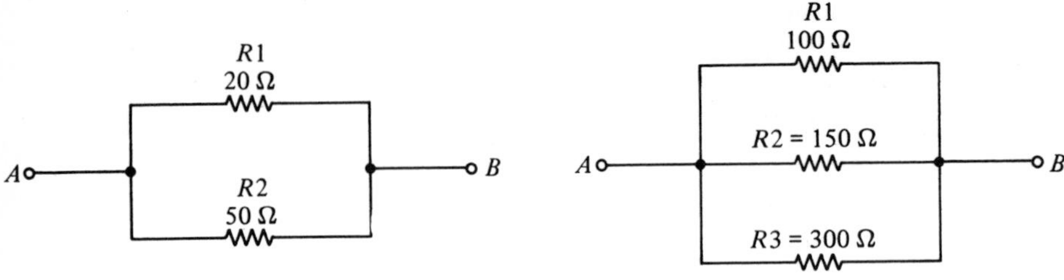

Figure 2.11

Figure 2.12

11. Find the total resistance in the circuit shown in Figure 2.13.

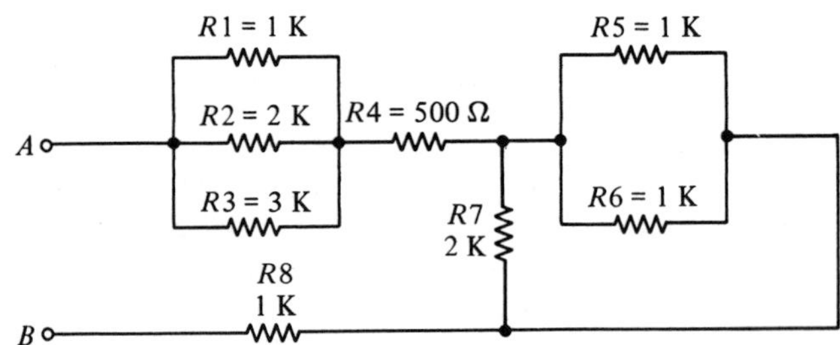

Figure 2.13

12. What is the voltage drop across $R2$ in Figure 2.14?
13. In Figure 2.14, how much current will flow in $R3$ if $R2$ is 1000 Ω?
14. In Figure 2.14, how much power is dissipated by resistor $R1$?
15. How much voltage appears across points A and B in Figure 2.15?
16. In Figure 2.15, how much voltage is dropped across $R1$?

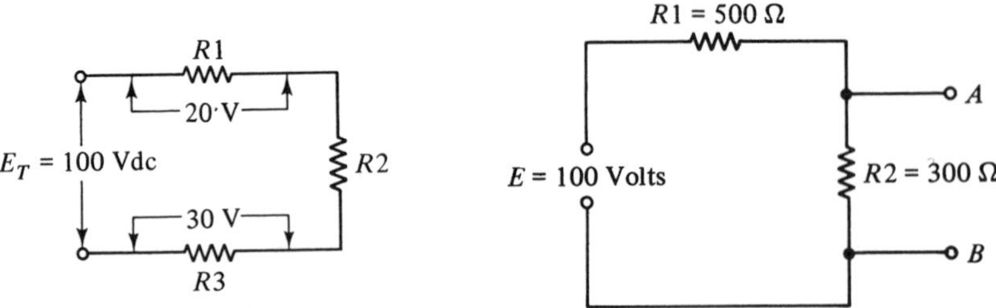

Figure 2.14

Figure 2.15

17. Assume that a parallel circuit of two resistors exists. $R1 = 1$ k and $R2 = 750$ Ω. What current will flow in $R2$ if the total current drawn by the combination is 120 mA? (*Hint:* use the current divider equation.)

18. How much current will flow in $R1$ of Question 17?

19. A fuse should be connected in _______ with the circuit it is supposed to protect.

20. A 1.5-V battery has an internal resistance of 3 Ω. What value of external resistor will maximize power transfer?

21. A voltmeter is connected in _________ with the load.

22. A voltmeter ideally has a (high) (low) internal resistance.

23. An ammeter is connected in _________ with the load.

24. An ammeter ideally has a (high) (low) internal resistance.

25. A blown fuse may be temporarily replaced with a penny or by a fuse of higher value. Yes or no?

3
Magnetism

3.1 MAGNETIC BASICS

Magnetism is a force with which almost everybody is familiar. Its application in our daily lives is both immense and diverse. One of the most readily recognized forms of magnetism is the permanent magnet, such as the bar magnet of Figure 3.1. Magnetism, like electricity, is "polarized." The two opposite types of magnetism are designated "north" and "south." These terms are drawn from geomagnetism (the earth's magnetic field), because the earth's north pole attracts the "north" end of a bar magnet.

The difference between magnetic and nonmagnetic materials is in the alignment of certain regions of magnetic force within the material called *domains*. In most materials, the magnetic field generated by each moving proton is exactly cancelled by the magnetic field of an electron associated with the proton. In materials such as iron, cobalt, nickel (etc.), however, the atoms form magnetic domains that possess a certain moment. In the nonmagnetized state [Figure 3.1(b)] these domains take on a random orientation in which the magnetic moments tend to cancel each other. When the material becomes magnetized, as in Figure 3.1(c), the domains are aligned in the same general direction, so their respective fields tend to support each other. The result is that they add together to produce a larger, stronger, overall field.

Magnetic forces can be represented by "flux lines," which leave the north pole and enter the south pole of the magnet. The total number of flux lines in any given magnet is denoted by the symbol ϕ (Greek letter phi). The unit for flux is the Maxwell, which represents one flux line. Flux density, on the other hand, is denoted by the letter B, and is defined as the number of flux lines per unit of area. If the unit of area is the square centimeter, then the unit for B is gauss. In other cases, we simply use "flux per square inch."

As was true of electric charges, we find that magnetic opposites attract each other, but like poles repel. Flux lines are continuous loops that never intersect each other. When flux lines are brought in close proximity (see Figure 3.2) to each other, they generate repulsion forces that tend to deform their shape. In this way we may visualize flux lines as imaginary elastic bands that may be deformed to almost any shape.

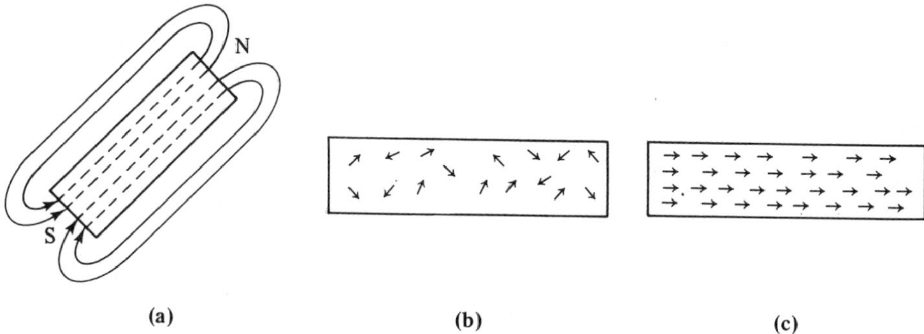

Figure 3.1 (a) A bar magnet, (b) Unmagnetized material and (c) Magnetized material.

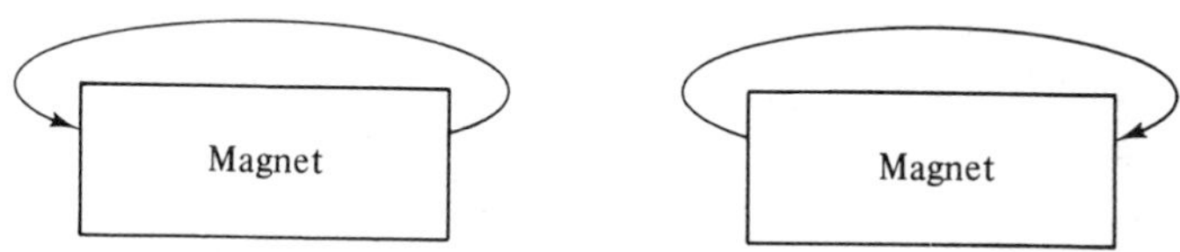

Figure 3.2 Magnetic poles, like electrical poles, obey the rule that like poles attract, and opposite poles (shown) *repel.*

3.2 ELECTROMAGNETISM

Electric current and magnetism are inseparable by virtue of their natures. Although static electricity produces no magnetism, it has been found that any electrical charge set in motion does generate a magnetic field perpendicular to its line of travel. When viewed from the perspective in which the electron is traveling toward you, flux lines of the magnetic field generated by the electron will surround the charge and will have a polarity in a clockwise direction. (See Figure 3.3.)

The left-hand rule for magnetism (see Figure 3.4) allows us to visualize this situation. If your left hand is used to grasp the charge-carrying conductor (do not actually perform this experiment, because charge-carrying conductors can be lethal) so that your thumb points in the direction of current flow, the fingers will point in the direction of the magnetic field.

We can also use the left-hand rule to predict the direction of current flow if we know the direction of the magnetic field. Although some textbooks call this the left-hand rule for current flow, it is actually nothing more than an application of the left-hand rule for magnetism.

The magnetic field surrounding a current-carrying wire can be concentrated, and thereby strengthened, by the mere expedient of forming the wire into a coil as in Figure 3.5. The strength of the magnetic field is

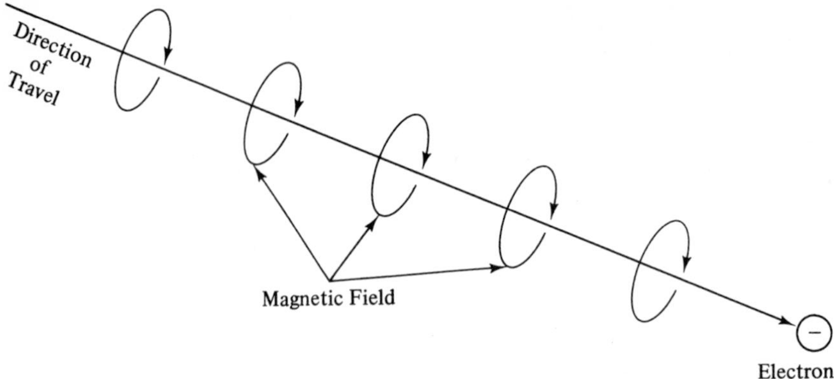

Figure 3.3 Magnetic lines of force in an electric circuit are *concentric* to the direction of an electron's travel.

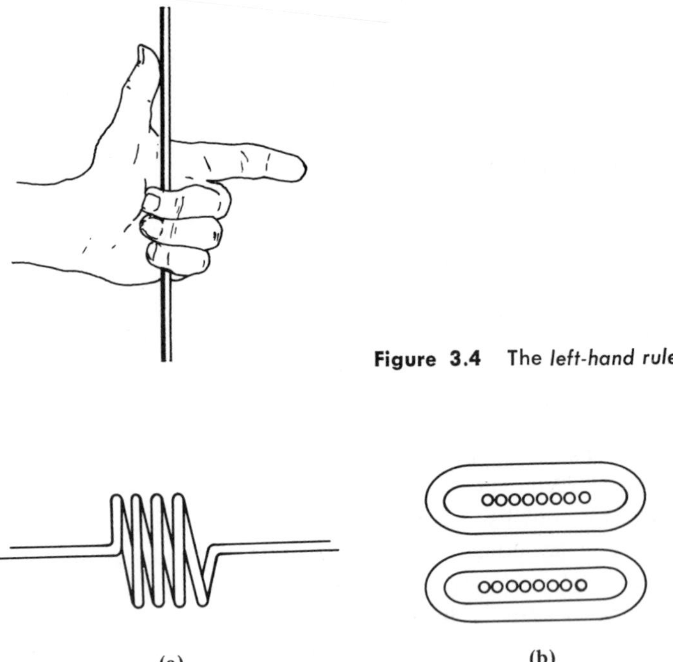

Figure 3.4 The *left-hand rule.*

Figure 3.5 Coiling a current-carrying wire enhances the magnetic effects.

increased, because all of the flux lines from the coil must flow through the interior of the coil. We can control the intensity of the field by varying the number of turns in the coil and by setting the intensity of the current flowing in the coil. The value of the magnetic field thus generated is given by

$$F = NI \tag{3-1}$$

where F is the magnetomotive force (MMF) in ampere-turns.
N is the number of turns.
I is the current in amperes.

Another unit of MMF is the Gilbert, which for our purposes may be defined as $N \times I \times 1.26$, where N and I are as above. Also of occasional use is an expression of MMF per unit of coil length—symbolized by the letter H, a measure of ampere-turns/inch.

Example. A certain electromagnet generates a force of 150 ampere-turns and is 2 in. long. Find the value of H.

$$H = \text{ampere-turns/length} \tag{3-2}$$

$$H = 150/2$$

$$H = 75$$

3.3 ELECTROMAGNETIC CORE EFFECTS

Looping a current-carrying wire into a coil increases the magnetic effects in the core of the coil by concentrating the flux lines in a small area. A further increase can be realized by using a ferromagnetic material, such as soft iron, as the core material, instead of air. This does not actually create additional flux lines out of nowhere, but simply allows more of the existing flux to pass through the central region of the coil. The flux density, therefore, increases dramatically if we slip a piece of iron into the core of an air-core electromagnet. A certain coil, for example, may have a flux density of 7500 with an air core, but close to 1,000,000 with an iron core.

The measure of a magnet's ability to increase flux density is its permeability. This property of materials is symbolized by the Greek letter μ (lowercase "mu"), and is equal to the ratio of flux density to field intensity

$$\mu = \frac{B}{H} \tag{3-3}$$

The permeability of air is defined as unity (1), so all materials can be compared against air as the standard. The soft iron core used as our example may have permeability figures ranging between several hundred and several thousand. Most common materials, including many metals, have permeabilities close to that of air, so they will not exhibit any magnetic properties. Certain other materials, such as brass, have quite the opposite property; they have less permeability than air.

"Reluctance" is that property which keeps some materials from being easily magnetized. Materials that are highly permeable have a low reluctance, and those with low values of permeability have a high reluctance. Reluctance is expressed by

$$\mathcal{R} = \frac{F}{\phi} = \frac{\text{MMF (flux lines)}}{\text{\# flux lines}} \tag{3-4}$$

Once again, we use air as the standard, and assign it a reluctance value of unity.

One might easily become confused and mistake "permeance" for permeability. These are actually reciprocal relationships that can be found from

$$P = \frac{1}{\mathcal{R}} \tag{3-5}$$

where P is permeance and the other symbol is as above.

Permeability can also be called "permeance per unit of volume."

3.4 THE B-H CURVE AND HYSTERESIS LOOPS

The magnetization caused by changing the value of H does not cause flux density B to change in a linear manner, as might be hoped by those striving for perfect order. Figure 3.6 shows a typical graph of flux density vs field intensity (B vs H). This latter parameter can be varied easily by changing the current through the coils of an electromagnet. At low values of H only those domains most easily magnetized will become aligned, so the slope of the B-H curve is shallow. As the field increases, however, more and more of the domains become aligned, so the slope of the curve rises. At point C we find that most of the domains have been aligned, and that further increases in current through the coils produce little or no increase in flux. The electromagnet is said to be "saturated" at that point.

Most materials do not demagnetize in the same manner in which they became magnetized. If that actually occurred, we would find that the B-H curve for demagnetization overlays the magnetization curve (Figure 3.6). What actually happens is that the magnetic domains exhibit a certain

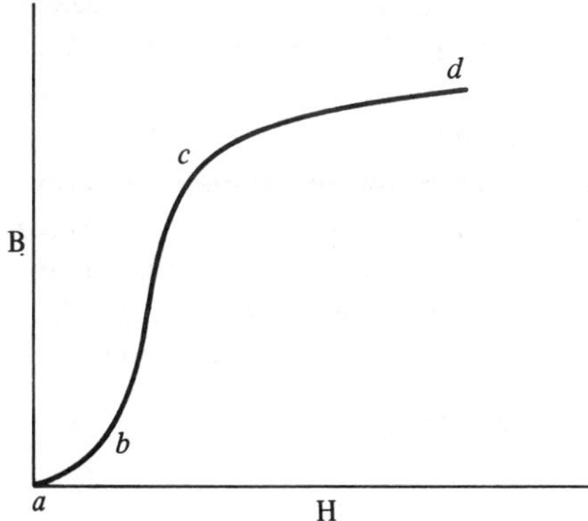

Figure 3.6 Flux density versus field intensity curve.

kind of "magnetic inertia" (for want of a better word), which causes them to resist changes in their state of alignment. If the current that caused a material to become magnetized is turned off, the magnetic force will drop, but not all the way back to zero; some residual magnetism will remain. If the current through the coil is reversed, rather than turned off, we find that even then the demagnetization curve differs from the magnetization curve. This is due to a certain amount of magnetic "hysteresis" in the core. Figure 3.7 shows a typical hysteresis curve or "loop." This curve is generated by magnetizing the core, then reversing the electromagnet current in an effort to demagnetize the core. The dotted line shows the *B-H* characteristic when the material is initially magnetized from a nonmagnetic

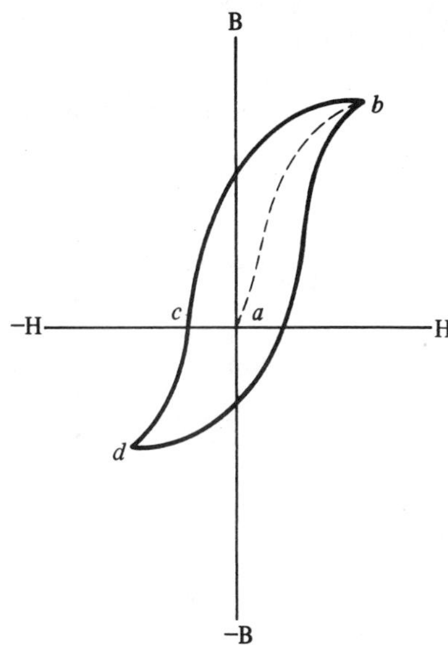

Figure 3.7 The hysteresis loop.

condition. The current through the coil of the electromagnet is increased until saturation is reached. The current flow is then reversed. The *B-H* curve generated does not follow the original section (*a-b*), but follows a new path (*b-c*). This is true because the current is having to work against the magnetic field existing in the core. After a certain amount of magnetizing force has been applied, we find that the flux density drops to zero. If the current is allowed to increase further, we find the core again becoming magnetized, but in the opposite direction. When it has saturated in this new direction, we can again reverse the current flow and increase its level until point *B* is again reached.

3.5 APPLICATIONS OF MAGNETISM

The effects of magnetism find a number of practical uses, even in everyday life. Geomagnetism, for example, attracts the needle of a compass, so we can easily find directions relative to the north pole. In a similar manner, the needle of a compass that is close to an electromagnet is deflected according to the strength and direction of the current flowing in the magnet's coil. This is the basic phenomenon on which we build a whole class of measuring instruments called "meters."

Large, multikilowatt electromagnets are used in scrap yards, steel plants, and other industrial sites to lift large masses of ferrous metals such as iron and steel. Tiny electromagnets, on the other hand, are often used as relays in electronic equipment. These devices are remotely controlled switches. Figure 3.8 details a simple type of relay using an electromagnet. The actual electromagnet is an iron-core coil which, when energized by an electrical current, produces a magnetic field that attracts the armature plate. This is mechanically connected to an insulated link that drives a set

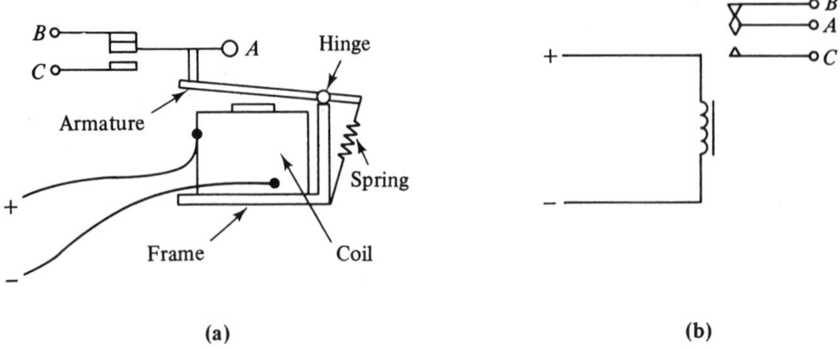

Figure 3.8 A magnetic relay.

of simple switch contacts. Normally, with the coil unenergized, contact *A* rests against contact *B*. When power is applied to the relay magnet coil, this connection is broken, and a new connection between *A* and *C* is established. Removing the current causes the magnetic field to collapse, and this allows the spring to pull the armature back to its rest position.

PROBLEMS

1. The north pole of the earth's magnetic field attracts the south pole of a bar magnet.
2. The unit of magnetomotive force is the ______________.
3. The ability of a magnetic core to increase flux density is given by its ______________.
4. The symbol for permeability is ______________.
5. Permeance is the reciprocal of ______________.
6. The unit for magnetic flux is the ______________.
7. Find *H* if the MMF is 250 ampere-turns and the coil is 4 in. long.
8. A graph of flux density vs field intensity is called a ______________.
9. Permeability is a measure of ______________.
10. The two segments of the curve of Question 8 do not overlay each other because of magnetic ______________.

4
Alternating Currents

4.1 WHAT IS ALTERNATING CURRENT?

Until now we have allowed ourselves to keep matters simple by considering only direct current (dc) situations. Direct current is the type of current available from batteries. In this chapter we shall introduce the concept of alternating current (ac).

Figure 4.1 shows the waveforms of direct current plus four common types of alternating current. If a dc source [Figure 4.1(a)] is turned on, the voltage and current rise to a certain level, and remain there until the source is turned off. Unless somebody actually reverses the wires from the source, direct current will flow in only one direction. An ac sinewave, the type of ac waveform available from the power mains, is shown in Figure 4.1(b). When the current is turned on, it rises to a maximum, but somewhat more gradually than the dc waveform. After it reaches its maximum, it then begins to diminish until it reaches zero again. It then *reverses direction* and repeats the process. It rises to a peak, and then diminishes back to zero. A graphical convention is used in Figure 4.1(b), in which the current flow in one direction is designated "positive," and it is graphed above the zero-volts baseline. The flow in the opposite direction is deemed "negative," and it is graphed below the zero baseline. It is important to realize that the flow conventions in alternating current do not violate the dictum that current flows from negative to positive. It is the polarity of the source that changes.

Figures 4.1(c) through 4.1(e) are other types of alternating current. These are waveforms that are frequently found in electronic circuits, but are shown here mostly for interest. They will be covered in more depth in a later chapter. Most ac circuits that we shall discuss, such as the ac power mains, audio amplifiers, or a radio transmitter, deal with the sine wave. It is also the simplest ac waveform, so we can treat it extensively without becoming too mathematical.

We know that electricity can be generated in a number of different ways. The nature of the source will determine the waveform, whether it is dc, a sine wave, or one of the other ac shapes. Direct current can be obtained from electrochemical effects (batteries), from photoelectric effects (solar cells), or mechanically (generators). Alternating current, on the

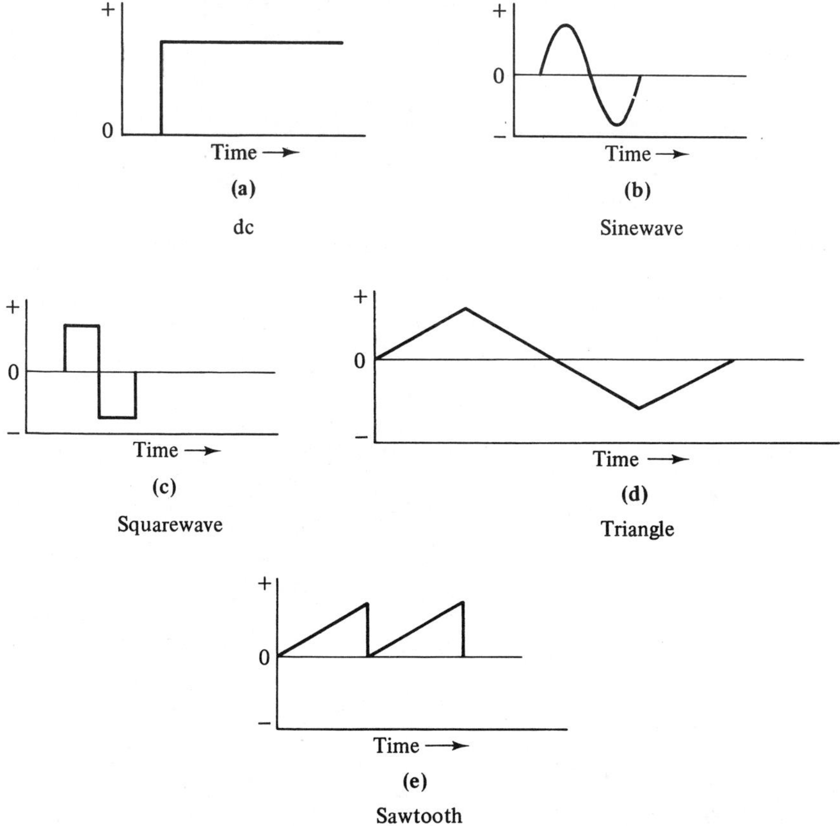

Figure 4.1 Electrical waveforms (a) dc, (b) sinewave, (c) squarewave, (d) triangle and (e) sawtooth.

other hand, is generated electronically (oscillator circuits, of which more later), and mechanically (ac generators, also called *alternators*).

4.2 AC GENERATORS AND ALTERNATORS

In the chapter on magnetism we learned that a moving electron generates a magnetic field perpendicular to its direction of travel. It is also true that a moving magnetic field can generate an electric current. If a magnet in proximity to an electrical conductor is set in motion, or if the conductor is set in motion relative to a stationary magnet, such as is done in Figure 4.2, we have a situation in which an electrical current is generated. In Figure 4.3(a) we have a simplified drawing of an ac alternator. Although the

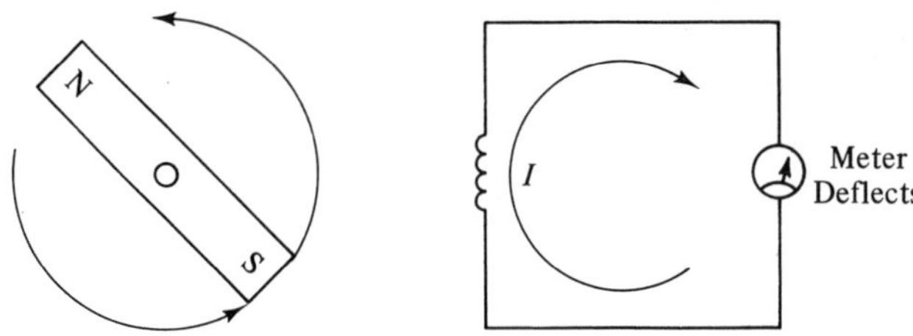

Figure 4.2 A coil in a moving magnetic field shows a current flow.

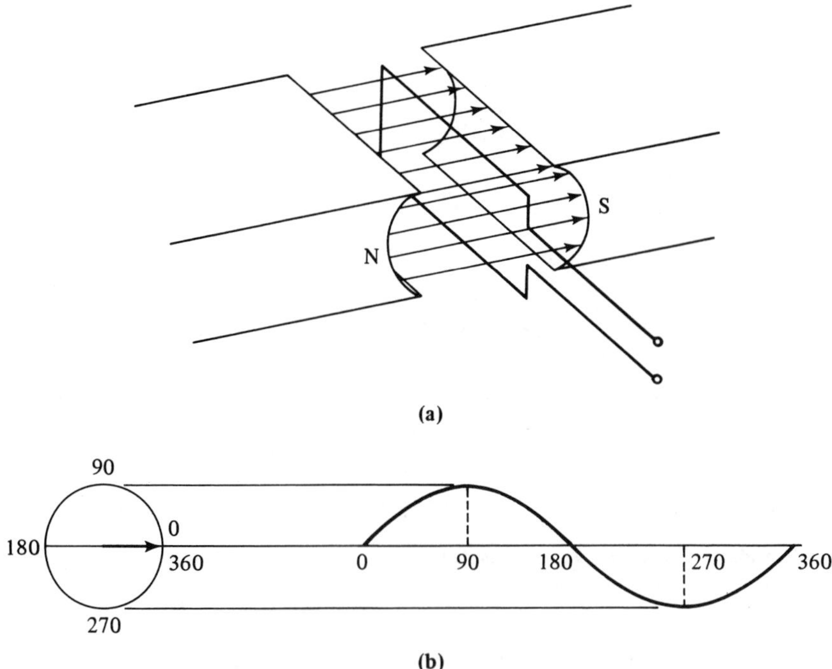

Figure 4.3 An ac generator **(a)** mechanism of coil in a magnetic field, **(b)** produces a sinewave.

figure shows but one loop of wire, a real alternator might have as many as thousands of turns of wire. The rotating coil of wire is called the *armature,* and is turned by any of several means: steam turbines, falling water, gasoline or diesel engines, or even windmills. Figure 4.3(b) shows the ac sinewave generated by the alternator of Figure 4.3(a). When the loop of wire is horizontal, it cuts no flux lines, so no current is generated. When the coil begins to swing upward to the position shown in the drawing, it cuts more and more flux lines, sc a larger and larger current is generated. When the

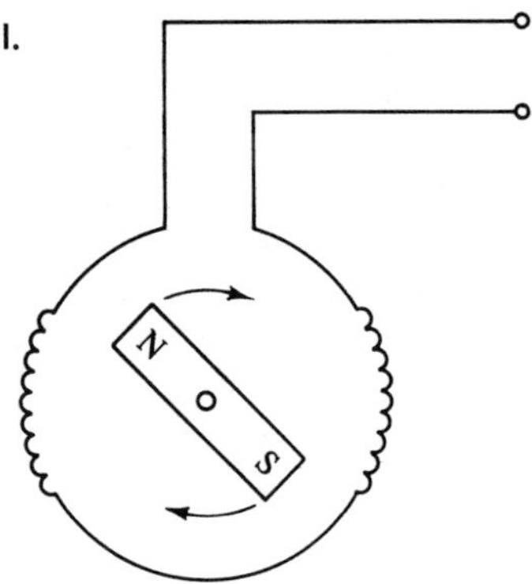

Figure 4.4 Moving magnet inside of a stator coil.

coil is at the 90-deg position, the current and voltage generated are at a maximum. As the coil swings past the 90-deg point, however, it encounters weaker and weaker flux, so the current diminishes as the coil swings. When the coil reaches the 180-deg point, it is once again horizontal, so no current is generated. When the coil swings past the 180-deg point, it encounters more and more flux, so the current output again builds up. But now the situation is a little different; the polarity of the current is reversed. Note that sides *A* and *B* are now reversed. The negative current flow will build to a maximum at 270-deg and then diminish to zero at 360-deg of rotation. This brings the coil back to its starting point, so we can say that the 360-deg end point of one sine wave is the 0-deg starting point of another.

Alternators such as that in Figure 4.3 have the disadvantage of requiring elaborate mechanical slip rings to collect the current induced into the loops of wire by the magnetic field. Since either the coil or the magnet may, in theory, be the moving part, many alternators, such as that in Figure 4.4, use a rotating permanent magnet inside a fixed, stationary coil, usually called a "stator winding." Interestingly enough, alternators used in most automobiles use a stator coil such as that shown in Figure 4.4, but the rotating magnet is actually an iron-core electromagnet called the "field coil." Although this may seem at first to be a case of worst of both worlds, there is a good reason for the design. Current to the field coil can be switched on and off by the car's regulator to control the charging of the battery by the alternator.

4.3 FEATURES OF THE SINE WAVE

In Figure 4.3 we showed that the time axis of the sine wave can be calibrated in degrees, because it can be represented by a vector sweeping out the rotational path of the armature. We shall use the degrees notation in most discussions, but we shall introduce notation using units of time shortly.

Various amplitude features of the sine wave are shown in Figure 4.5. A pure sine wave is symmetrical about the baseline, so what is said here about the positive half of the waveform applies equally well to the negative half. "Peak voltage" is measured from the zero-volts baseline to the highest point on the sine wave (at 90 deg). "Peak-to-peak" voltage is measured from the highest point on the positive portion of the sine wave to the highest point of the negative half. This makes the peak-to-peak voltage of a sine wave equal to twice the peak voltage. In other words,

$$E_{\text{p-p}} = 2 \times E_{\text{peak}} \tag{4-1}$$

The voltage amplitude marked "rms" is the root-mean-square voltage. This amplitude level can be defined in terms of the amount of direct current required to do an equivalent amount of work. One simple way to measure this is to allow alternating current to heat some resistor, and then record the temperature. The resistor is allowed to cool back down to room temperature, and is then connected across a precisely calibrated dc power supply. The voltage of the dc supply is then turned up until the resistor is at the same temperature that existed under ac heating. The voltage at which this occurs is equal to the rms voltage of the ac waveform.

A few older rms voltmeters used a scheme similar to this in which two identical resistors were used. The ac waveform heated one, while an internal voltage source (dc) heated the other. Either thermistors or thermocouples were used to automatically measure the temperature. The

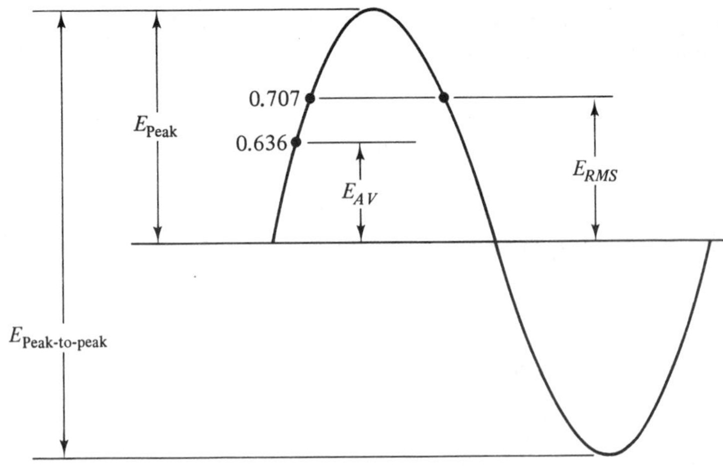

Figure 4.5 Relationships on the ac sine wave curve.

value of the voltage applied from the internal dc source was automatically adjusted to keep the difference in temperature between the two resistors zero. When equilibrium was established, the voltage output from the internal supply was read.

When you hear someone say that the power mains deliver (approximately) 110 volts, ac, it is the rms voltage that he is quoting. For a sine wave (only), the rms voltage is equal to

$$E_{rms} = \frac{E_{peak}}{(2)^{1/2}} \tag{4-2}$$

which is the same as

$$E_{rms} = (1/1.414) \times E_{peak}$$
$$E_{rms} = 0.707 \times E_{peak} \tag{4-3}$$

The *average* voltage of a sine wave is

$$E_{ave} = 0.636 \times E_{peak} \tag{4-4}$$

Note that some people erroneously call rms the average voltage, but in reality, the two are slightly different. Be aware that these sine wave values will show up on certain types of electronic or communications examinations that you may be asked to take. Even though you may not use them in the daily work in electronics, it is wise to commit them to memory, because they will pop up from time to time.

The voltage and current represented by an ac sine wave are continuously changing. The instantaneous voltage or current is the amplitude that exists at any given point in time. It can be found from

$$e = \mathrm{E} \sin \theta \tag{4-5}$$

where e is the instantaneous voltage (or current).
E is the maximum voltage (or current).
θ is the angle through which the sine wave has rotated at the instant in time at which you want to know the voltage.

To find instantaneous values of current, substitute i and I for e and E, respectively.

Example. A certain sine wave has a peak voltage of 100 V. What is the instantaneous voltage when the sine wave has rotated through 60 deg?

From a trig table, or an electronic calculator, we find that sin 60 = 0.866, so

$$e = E \sin 60$$

$$e = (100)(0.866) \tag{4-6}$$

$$e = 86.6 \text{ V}$$

4.4 FREQUENCY, PERIOD, AND PHASE

"Frequency" is the rate of occurrence of an event, so it is measured in "events per unit of time." For an ac sine wave, the event is the cycle, defined as one complete excursion from zero through the positive amplitude peak, back to zero, through the negative peak, and back to zero again—in other words, the complete sine wave. The frequency of ac is the number of cycles per second. This is written as the number of "hertz," because 1 Hz = 1 cps.

"Period," on the other hand, is the length of time required for the sine wave to complete one cycle. Period is measured in seconds, milliseconds, or microseconds. Since the period is the reciprocal of frequency, it may be computed from

$$\text{Time (seconds)} = \frac{1}{\text{Frequency (Hz)}} \tag{4-7}$$

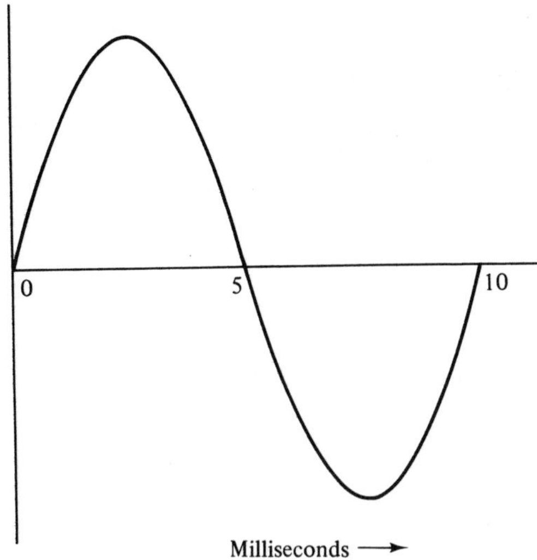

Figure 4.6 Sine wave period.

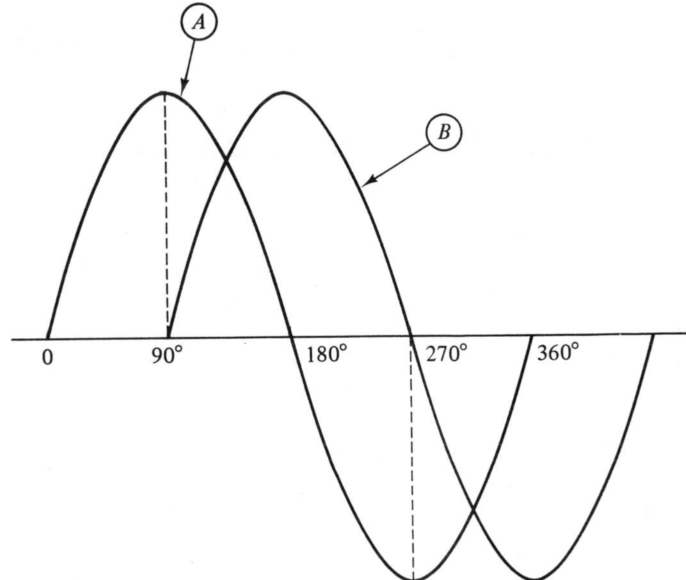

Figure 4.7 *Phase* is the time relationship between two sine waves.

Example. The sine wave in Figure 4.6 has a period of 10 milliseconds (10 ms), or 0.010 s. It has a frequency of

$$F = 1/(0.01) = 100 \text{ Hz} \tag{4-8}$$

"Phase" is the time relationship between two sine waves. The two sines might be two voltages, two currents, or a current and a voltage. Phase angles are generally measured in degrees or radians, one of the sine waves being used as the reference point. In Figure 4.7 we use curve A as the reference. Notice that it has completed 90 deg of its excursion before the second sine wave (B) begins. Thus, we could say that A leads B by 90 deg, or that B lags A by 90 deg. The "phase angle" is 90 deg.

PROBLEMS

1. An ac generator has two pole-pairs, and it rotates at 1800 r/min. If the pole-pairs are positioned at right angles to each other, what frequency ac is produced?
2. The peak voltage of an ac sine wave is 140 V. What is the peak-to-peak voltage, if it is assumed that the sine wave is pure?
3. In the preceding question, what is the rms value of the sine wave?

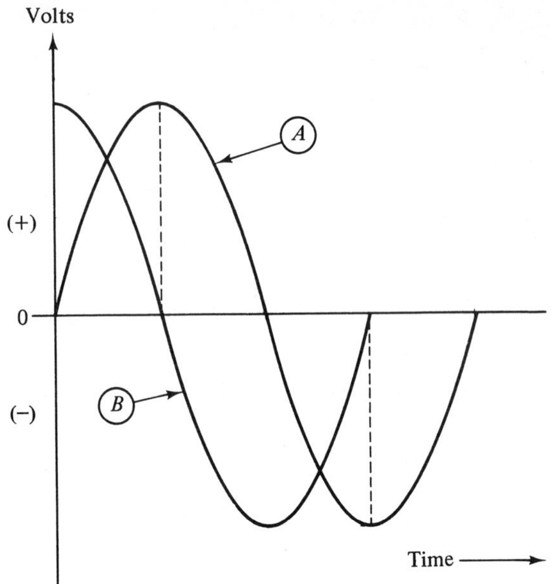

Figure 4.8

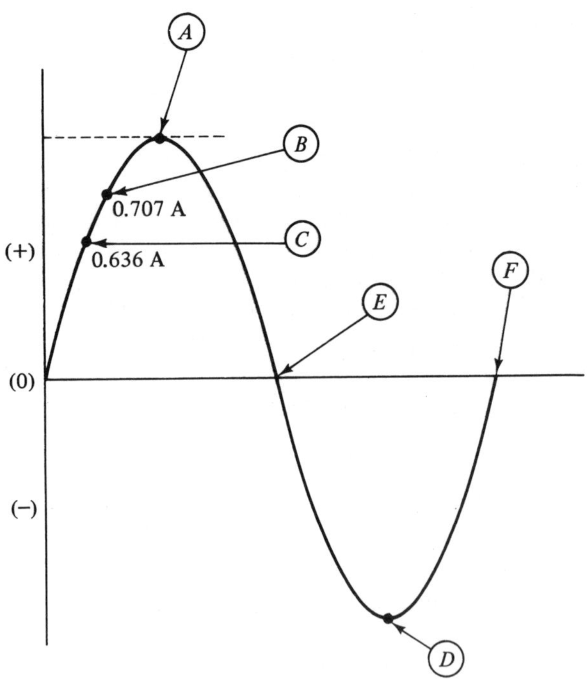

Figure 4.9

4. Find the peak voltage if the rms voltage is 250 V.
5. An ac sine wave heats a test resistor the same amount as 100 V dc. What is the rms value of the sine wave?
6. Suppose that an ac sine wave has an rms value of 70.7 V. What is the instantaneous voltage as it passes through the 136-deg point?
7. Determine the instantaneous voltage at $\theta = 64$ deg if the peak amplitude is 150 V, and the waveform is a sine.
8. Find the frequency of an ac waveform that has a period of 150 ms.
9. Find the period if the frequency is 150 μs.
10. Find the period of a 60-Hz sine wave.
11. Find the period of a 1000-Hz waveform.
12. What is the phase angle between the waveforms shown in Figure 4.8?
13. How many milliseconds (ms) are there in 1500 microseconds?
14. Point *A* in Figure 4.9 represents the ____________ voltage.
15. Point *D* in Figure 4.9 represents the ____________ voltage.
16. The voltage represented by *A–D* is the ____________ voltage.
17. Point *B* represents ____________.
18. Point *C* represents ____________.
19. Point *E* occurs at ____________ degrees.
20. Point *F* occurs at ____________ degrees.

5
Inductance, Inductors, and Transformers

5.1 INDUCTANCE OF WIRES

"Inductance" is a property of electrical conductors that tends to oppose *changes* in the flow of electrical currents. Since this property is related to the magnetic field, we find that it increases when we form the wire into a coil. Also, the amount of inductance increases proportionally to the number of turns in the coil.

As current flows through the coil, a magnetic field is generated concentric to the axis of the wire. The magnetic field of each loop in the coil tends to cut across adjacent loops. See Figure 5.1. Recall that a changing magnetic field cutting across a conductor induces a current into that conductor. Lenz's law tells us that such a current will have a direction (i.e., polarity) that tends to oppose the change in primary current. The voltage drop generated by this current is called "counterelectromotive force," which is usually abbreviated "CEMF." The CEMF exists only when the current through the coil is either increasing or decreasing.

Inductance is symbolized by the letter L and is measured in units called "henrys." One henry is the amount of inductance that causes a 1-V CEMF when the current is changing at a rate of 1-A per second. The inductance of any particular (cylindrical) coil can be approximated by

$$L\mu_{\mathrm{H}} = \frac{r^2 n^2}{9r + 10w} \tag{5-1}$$

where L is the inductance in henrys.
r is the radius in inches.
n is the number of turns.
w is the length in inches.

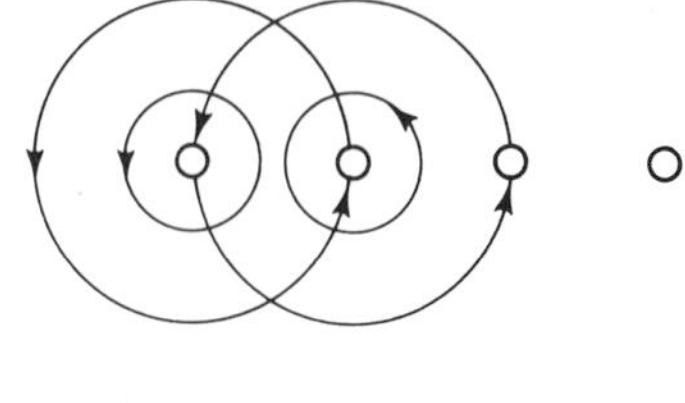

Figure 5.1 The magnetic field surrounding each loop in a coil cuts across adjacent loops.

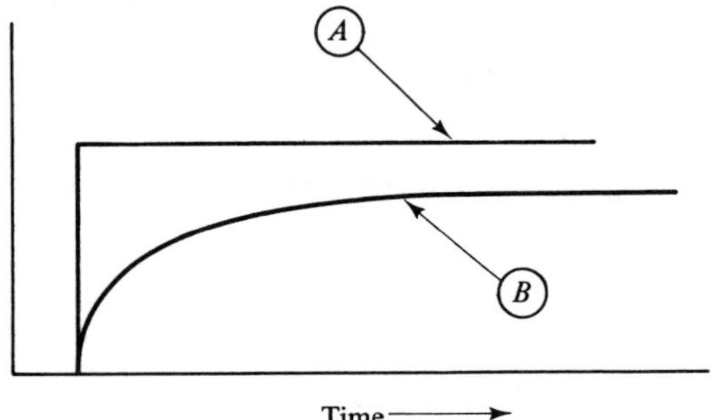

Figure 5.2 When a step-function voltage is applied to an inductor, the current does not rise immediately, but rises exponentially.

5.2 INDUCTIVE TIME CONSTANT

The opposition to the flow of current caused by inductance causes a funny thing to happen when a voltage is applied suddenly to the circuit. If you apply a voltage suddenly to a resistance, both the current and the voltage rise almost immediately to the level dictated by Ohm's law. This is shown in Figure 5.2(a). In an inductive circuit, however, the CEMF opposes changes in current flow, so we shall observe a rise such as that shown in Figure 5.2(b). It takes a certain amount of time for the current to build up to its final value. This can be expressed as the "time constant" of the inductive circuit. The time constant is defined as the length of time required for the current to increase to 63.2 percent of its final value. Consider the circuit in Figure 5.3(a). In this circuit we have an inductor L in series with a resistor R. The resistance might be a fixed resistor, or it might be the ohmic resistance of the wires forming the coil. Note that

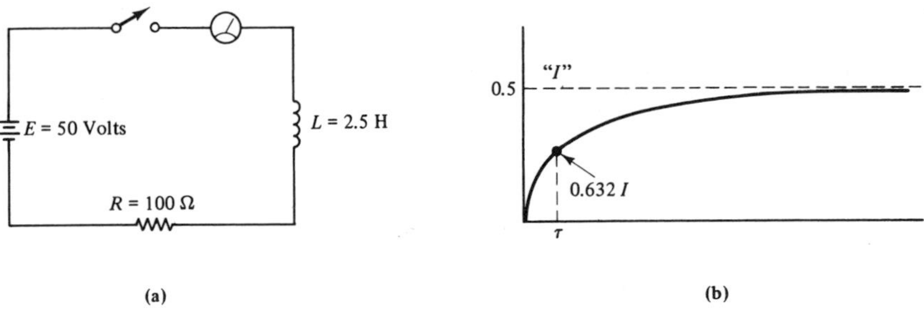

Figure 5.3 (a) R-L circuit, (b) The time constant is the period it takes to rise to 63.2% of its final value.

ideal inductors do not have series resistance, only real inductors have resistance. One might tend to think that Ohm's law applies in this circuit, as needed it would, were it not for the inductor. By Ohm's law,

$$I = E/R = 50/100 = 0.5 \text{ A} \tag{5-2}$$

If the circuit were only resistive, the current would immediately go to that value when the switch was closed. Instead, it crawls up slowly, eventually approaching the 0.5-A level. The time constant can be found from

$$\tau = \frac{L}{R} \tag{5-3}$$

where τ is the time in seconds for I to reach 63.2 percent of its final value.
L is the inductance in henrys.
R is the resistance in ohms.

In the example, given, then,

$$\tau = 2.5 \text{ H}/100 \ \Omega = 0.025 \text{ s} = 25 \text{ ms} \tag{5-4}$$

Theoretically, current in an RL circuit will never actually reach Ohm's law levels (i.e., the 0.5-A level in this case), but will approach that level as an asymptote. We normally accept an inductor as "fully charged" after a period equal to five time constants ($5L/R$).

5.3 ENERGY STORED IN AN INDUCTOR

It requires a certain amount of work to form the magnetic field surrounding an inductor. This action stores a certain potential energy in the magnetic field, which will be returned to the coil as an electric current when the current from the source, which sustains the field, ceases to flow. The energy stored in the field is

$$U = \tfrac{1}{2}LI^2 \tag{5-5}$$

where U is the energy in joules, or watt-seconds.
L is the inductance in henrys.
I is the current in amperes.

When the current through the coil ceases to flow, the stored energy is dumped back into the circuit. The decay curve for an RL circuit resembles the charging curve, but is inverted and is the mirror image of the charging curve. In some instances we will observe a large voltage spike generated when the switch in an RL circuit is opened. A simplistic explanation of this phenomenon is that the open switch makes the circuit look like it contains an extremely high resistance. This, of course, will cause the time constant to become very, very short. Since the energy stored in the magnetic field around the coil tends to diminish far more rapidly than it formed, the voltage across the coil tends to be very large. This phenomenon is usually called "inductive kick."

5.4 BEHAVIOR OF INDUCTORS

The type of inductance that we have been discussing is known as "self-inductance." It is created by the magnetic field of each loop in the coil inducing current into adjacent loops. There is, however, also an inductance created by bringing two coils into close enough proximity for flux lines from one or both to cut across the other. Under these conditions a varying magnetic field created by a changing current in one coil will induce a current and CEMF in the other. The amount of mutual inductance is given by

$$M = k\,(L1 \times L2)^{1/2} \tag{5-6}$$

where M is the mutual inductance in henrys.
$L1$ is the self-inductance of one coil.
$L2$ is the self-inductance of the second coil.
k is a constant called the "coefficient of coupling."
the $^{1/2}$ superscript denotes that we want the square root of the quantity inside the brackets.

The constant k requires some explanation. It is the percentage of flux lines, expressed as a decimal, from one coil which cuts across the other coil. Constant k will always have a value between zero and unity (0–1). If, for example, 78 percent of the flux lines from one coil cuts across the other, the coefficient of coupling is $k = 0.78$.

Figure 5.4 illustrates how coupling between two coils can be varied. Figure 5.4(a) has the coils at right angles to each other, so none of the flux lines intersect turns of the opposite coil, and $k = 0$. As the coil is rotated [Figure 5.4(b)], however, more and more lines cut the second coil, so k will take on values between 0 and 1. In the last case, Figure 5.4(c), the coils are in close proximity, and parallel, so that all flux lines from one will cut the other. The value of k in that case is unity. Actually, that is "possible" only in ideal coils. Because of small imperfections, we shall never find a coil with a k value of unity. It is, however, possible to find coils in which $k = 0.99+$.

In cases where you want to minimize mutual inductance, often the case in communications and other electronic equipment, some means must be provided to prevent the flux from one coil's cutting others. If some tiny amount of coupling can be tolerated, it is possible to mount the coils at right angles to each other, with as much distance between them as possible. In cases where even lesser values of k are required, it may be necessary to place one or both coils inside shielded metal enclosures. Another tactic is to use a coil geometry in which external flux is naturally minimized. Such a shape is the doughnut, or "toroid." This type of coil concentrates so much of the flux inside of the core that it is possible for toroidal inductors to be stacked on top of each other, separated by only a thin insulator, without a great deal of interaction.

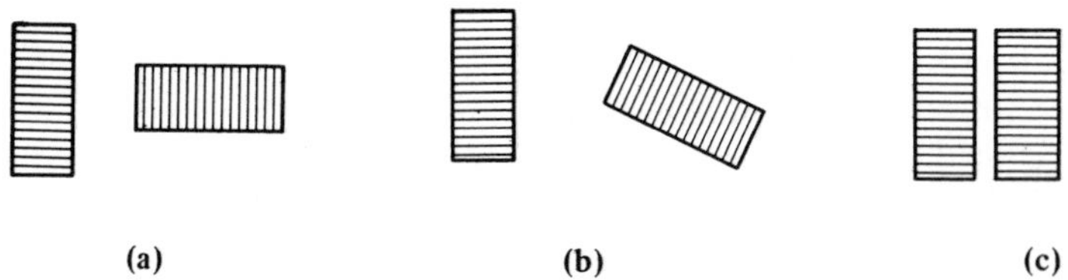

Figure 5.4 Coupling is minimum when coil orientation is 90° (a), and maximum when the coils are parallel (c).

Inductors in series combine their respective values exactly like resistors, provided only that there is no mutual inductance between them. In that case, illustrated in Figure 5.5(a),

$$L_t = L1 + L2 + L3 + \ldots + L_n \tag{5-7}$$

In those cases where there is some mutual inductance we may still use this formula, but the mutual inductance is multiplied by a factor of two, and is then treated as if it were one additional inductor in the circuit. The formula becomes

$$L_t = L1 + L2 + L3 + \ldots + L_n + 2M \tag{5-8}$$

where M is the mutual inductance.

Noncoupled inductors in parallel can be combined to find the total inductance much after the fashion of resistors in parallel. The equation is of the same form as the resistive equations:

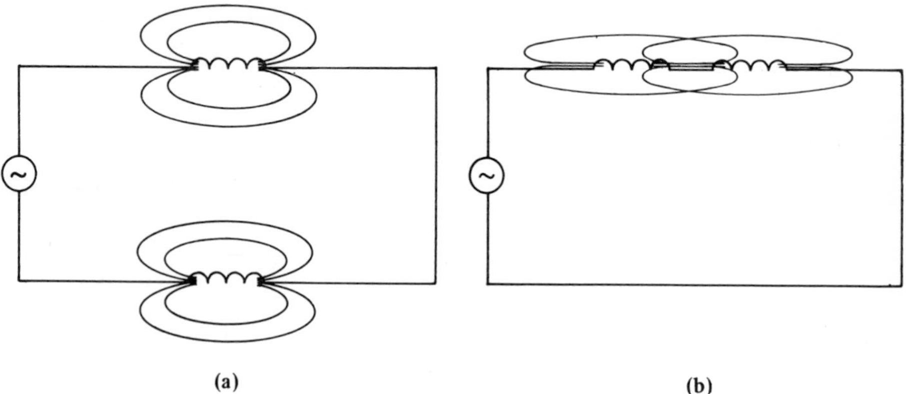

Figure 5.5 **(a)** Coils without interaction, **(b)** coils interacting.

$$L_t = \frac{1}{\frac{1}{L1} + \frac{1}{L2} + \frac{1}{L3} + \ldots + \frac{1}{L_n}} \tag{5-9}$$

and in the special case of only two parallel inductors in parallel:

$$L_t = \frac{L1 \times L2}{L1 + L2} \tag{5-10}$$

We are going to evade the issue of *coupled* coils in parallel, because they tend to be a little messy.

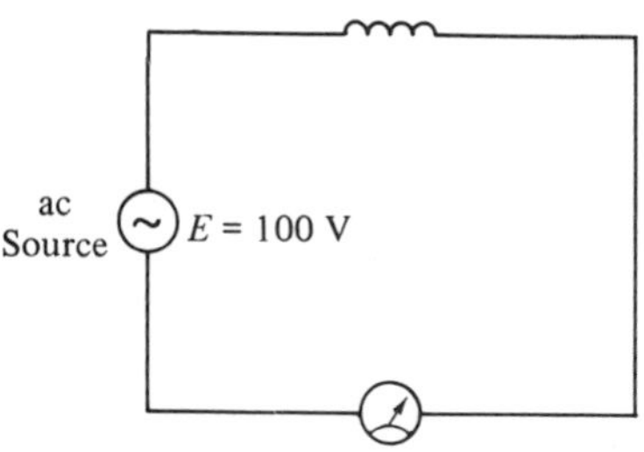

Figure 5.6 Coil in an ac circuit.

5.5 INDUCTIVE REACTANCE

We have seen how the inductor behaves when subjected to a "step function" voltage—a voltage applied suddenly. The current in such a case will rise exponentially until it approaches the steady state value dictated by

Ohm's law. But what happens in such a circuit (see Figure 5.6) when ac sine waves are applied? For a brief instant after a sine wave is applied, there will be a behavior that resembles the step function behavior, but this reaches an equilibrium very rapidly. The ac sine wave is constantly changing, and it is *change* in current flow that the inductor opposes. This implies, then, that the inductor will constantly oppose the flow of alternating current. The measure of this opposition to ac is called "inductive reactance" and is measured in ohms, just like resistance. Inductive reactance is symbolized by X_L. You may guess that the L subscript implies that there is at least one more form of reactance, and that is correct—capacitive reactance will be dealt with shortly. The value of X_L is given by

$$X_L = 2\pi f L \tag{5-11}$$

where X_L is the inductive reactance in ohms.
f is the frequency in hertz.
L is the inductance in henrys.
π is the constant 3.14 (approximately).

You may also see this relationship written as

$$X_L = \omega L \tag{5-12}$$

where $\omega = 2\pi f$.

Example. A 500-millihenry (mH) choke is connected to a source of alternating current that has a frequency of 2 kHz. What is the reactance of this coil?

$$X_L = (2)\ (3.14)\ (2000)\ (0.5)$$
$$X_L = (6.28)(1000) = 6280\ \Omega \tag{5-13}$$

Inductive reactance can be plugged into Ohm's law formulas to make an "Ohm's law" for inductors, provided that there is no resistance in the circuit. For instance, if the coil in the above example were subjected to a 100-V (rms) potential, the current flowing would be

$$I = E/X_L = (100)/(6280) = 0.0159\ \text{A} \tag{5-14}$$

In this case we merely substituted X_L for R in the normal Ohm's law equation for current. Note that this can be done only if there is no resistance or capacitance in the circuit. In that case, we would use "impedance" instead of reactance, but more of that shortly.

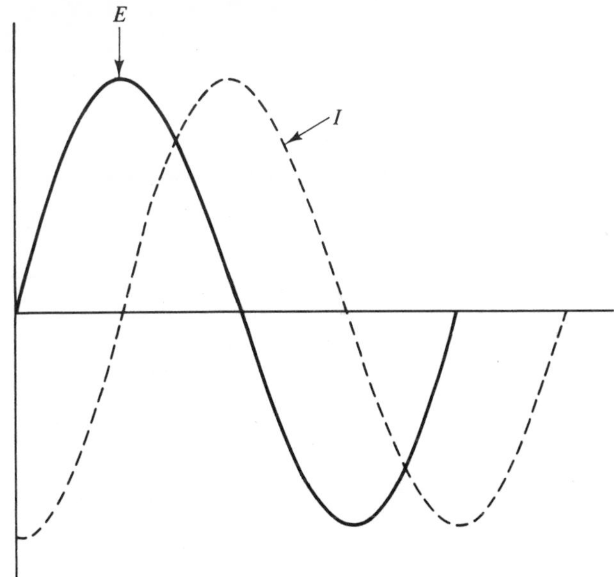

Figure 5.7 Inductive circuits cause current to lag voltage by 90°.

5.6 PHASE SHIFT CAUSED BY INDUCTANCE

When ac is applied to an inductor, we observe that the voltage across the inductor follows the applied voltage, but the current runs into opposition, and is thereby delayed a small amount. In a pure (i.e., "ideal") inductance, the current will lag behind the applied voltage by a factor of 90 deg of the sine wave. That is to say, the sine wave voltage will have completed 90 deg of its cycle before the current begins to flow. The time relationship of current and voltage in an inductive circuit is shown in Figure 5.7. In RL circuits, the phase angle between I and E will be less than 90 deg, and reduces to zero as L approaches zero henrys.

5.7 IMPEDANCE IN RL CIRCUITS

Consider a circuit such as that shown in Figure 5-8, where we have opposition to the flow of current from both resistance and reactance. The total opposition to the flow of current in this type of circuit is called *impedance,* symbolized by the letter Z. Impedance has components of both resistance and reactance, but takes into account the phase angle between current and voltage.

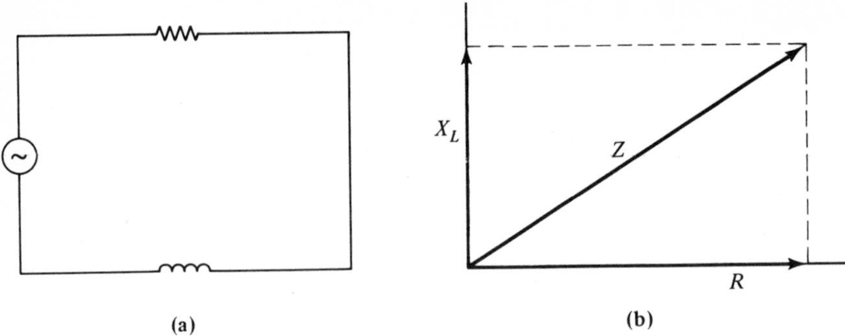

Figure 5.8 (a) R-L circuit, (b) vector relationships. Impedance is the resultant of resistance and reactive components.

Figure 5.8(b) shows a vector diagram representing impedance. Since resistive circuits have a phase angle of 0 deg, we can set the reference point by drawing the resistance vector from the origin to the 0 deg point. The pure reactance (X_L) vector is then drawn along the 90-deg line, as shown. The impedance Z is the resultant of these two vectors. Note that all vectors have two parts, a magnitude (length) and a direction (angle referenced to the R vector). The magnitude of the impedance vector is given by

$$Z = (R^2 + X_L^2)^{1/2} \tag{5-15}$$

where Z is the impedance in ohms.
R is the resistance in ohms.
X_L is the reactance in ohms.
the ½ superscript indicates that we want the square root of the quantity.

Although you will often see the magnitude of the impedance listed alone, it is never technically correct to give only the magnitude without the phase angle. In practice, however, we often only need the magnitude, so the practice is tolerated. When you want the phase angle, it is given by

$$\theta = \arctan\left[\frac{X_L}{R}\right] \tag{5-16}$$

this is also written as $\theta = \tan^{-1}(X_L/R)$.

Example. In the circuit of Figure 5.8(a): Let $R = 10$ k, $X_L = 6$ k; find Z.

$$\begin{aligned} Z &= (10{,}000^2 + 6000^2)^{1/2} \\ Z &= ((1 \times 10^4)^2 + (6 \times 10^4)^2)^{1/2} \\ Z &= (1.36 \times 10^8)^{1/2} \\ Z &= 11{,}166\ \Omega \end{aligned} \tag{5-17}$$

5.8 INDUCTOR CORE MATERIALS

Although we touched briefly on iron core coils in the chapter on magnetism, we have been assuming that all inductors use an air core up until now. Winding an inductor over an iron core greatly increases its inductance compared with the same coil wound over an air core. Once our requirement for inductance exceeds a few millihenrys, it is no longer practical to use air core coils. They become too large and cumbersome. For values between a few hundred microhenrys to just under one henry, cores of powdered iron or "ferrite" are used. Coils with inductance values over one henry are usually wound over soft-iron cores. Of course, there is nothing absolute about these ranges, and examples of the various cores will be found outside the normal range. See Figure 5.9.

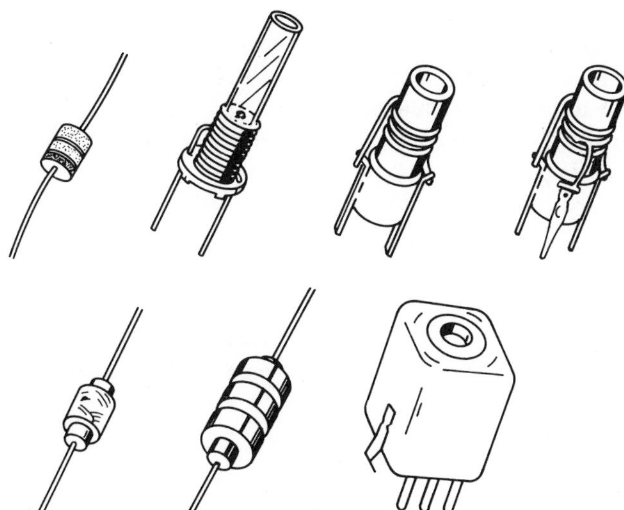

Figure 5.9 Examples of coils.

In many applications we require inductance values in the low, or even fractional, microhenry range. In those coils the inductance is so low that only a part of one turn is needed. This makes it difficult to be precise in constructing the coil. A brass core, however, *reduces* the inductance of a given coil relative to its air core value. We may then use more turns of wire over a brass core to build a coil that is equivalent to partical turn coils. Both brass and powdered brass are used to make these low-inductance-value coils. In a few cases, where very high frequencies (VHF) and ultra high frequencies (UHF) are involved, the inductance of a straight piece of wire is sufficient. Tuning is accomplished on a coarse basis by trimming the wire length.

5.9 TYPES OF INDUCTORS

Figure 5.10 shows the schematic symbols for several types of inductors. The simple fixed inductor with an air core is shown in Figure 5.10(a), while the iron-core version is shown in Figure 5.10(b). The powdered iron core is symbolized by a dotted line, as shown in Figure 5.10(c). Iron-core coils are used at low ac frequencies up to several kilohertz. Powdered iron cores are found in applications from several kilohertz to well into the megahertz region. It is unusual, however, to find a single powdered iron composition formula competent over the entire range. Instead, they are rated in frequency ranges. Air and brass core coils are used from the high frequency (several megahertz—30 megahertz, roughly) to the VHF region. Here again there is enough overlapping of frequency ranges to preclude the use of an absolute rule.

Adjustable inductance is often needed in communications equipment. Figure 5.10(d) shows a tapped coil in which several values of inductance can be selected by choosing the correct taps. A continuously variable coil,

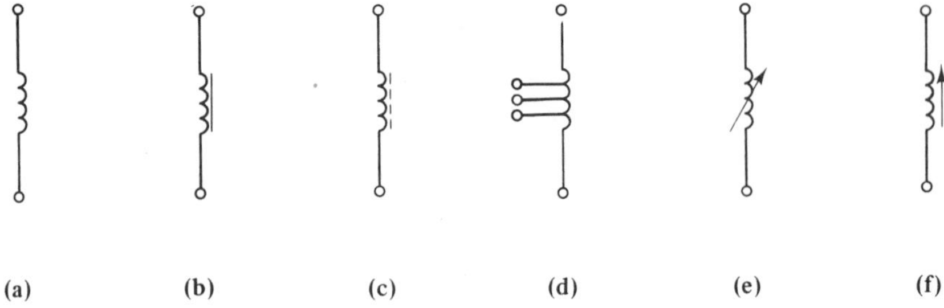

Figure 5.10 Schematic symbols for coils. **(a)** air core, **(b)** iron core, **(c)** powdered iron core, **(d)** tapped air core, **(e)** variable air core and **(f)** variable ("slug-tuned") powdered iron core.

often called a "rotary inductor," is shown in Figure 5.10(e). In that type of coil a mechanism is employed which slides a variable tap along the uninsulated turns of the coil to select any value of inductance that is within the range of the coil. Such inductors are sometimes found in medium- to high-power radio transmitters. Figure 5.10(f) shows one of the more common forms of variable inductor. In that type of coil, the powdered iron or brass core is threaded and mates with similar threads inside of the coil form. Inductance is varied as more or less of the core penetrates the air core of the coil form. Inductance in an iron or ferrite coil such as this is maximum when all of the core is inside of the coil, and minimum when none of the core is inside of the coil. See Figure 5.11.

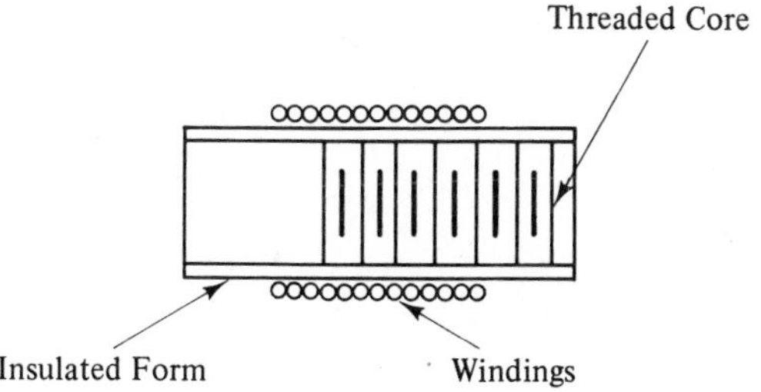

Figure 5.11 Construction of a slug-tuned, powdered iron core coil.

Figure 5.12 "Pie-wound" coil.

5.10 CHOKES

Chokes are coils that are used to offer high impedance to ac frequencies in the high range, and low impedance to dc or low-frequency ac. Iron-core chokes are used when the ac to be blocked is low in frequency (up to several kilohertz), and RF chokes are used to block radio frequency ac signals. Most RF chokes (abbreviated RFC) are wound using the "pie" technique as shown in Figure 5.12. Of course, "blocking" in this sense is

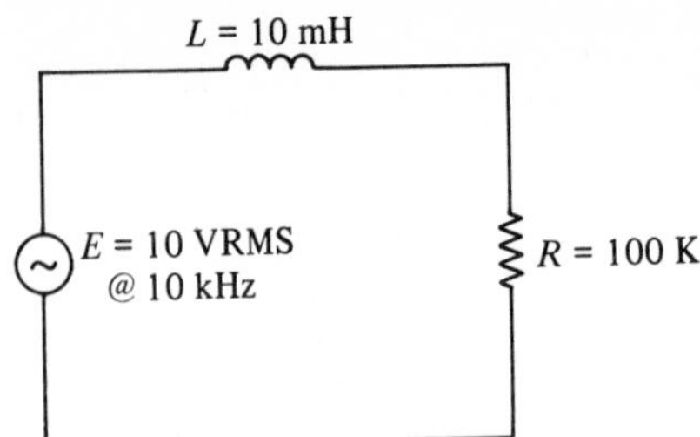

Figure 5.13 Find the reactance of L at 10-mHz, and the voltage drop across L at 10-mHz.

only a relative term. Consider the circuit in Figure 5.13. At a frequency of 10 mHz the coil has a reactance of

$$X_L = (2)(3.14)(10^7)(0.010) \tag{5-18}$$

$$X_L = 628{,}000\ \Omega$$

At 10 mHz, the voltage across the resistor would be

$$E_R = \frac{(10\text{V})\ (1 \times 10^5)}{6.28 \times 10^5 + 1 \times 10^5} \tag{5-19}$$

$$E_R = (10\ \text{V})\ (0.137)$$

$$E_R = 1.37\ \text{V}$$

At 25 mHz, however, the voltage is much lower (if equal input voltages are assumed), because X_L increases to $1.57 \times 10^6\ \Omega$, but the resistance has remained the same. At even higher frequencies the voltage is even lower. At dc, however, only the resistance offers any opposition to the flow of current.

5.11 GENERAL TRANSFORMER THEORY AND CONSTRUCTION

A "transformer" is a device that can be used to step voltage up or down, or change an impedance level in a circuit. In its simplest form a transformer consists of two mutually coupled coils. One coil is connected to a load, while the other is connected to an ac source. The coil that is connected to the ac is called the "primary," and the coil connected to the load is called the "secondary." When ac flows through the primary winding, it

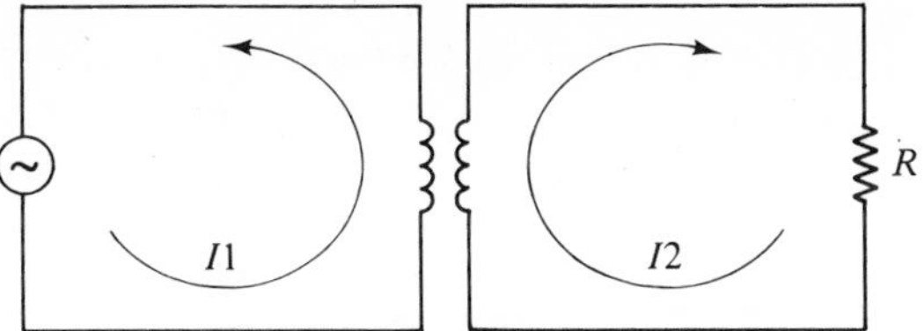

Figure 5.14 The basic transformer.

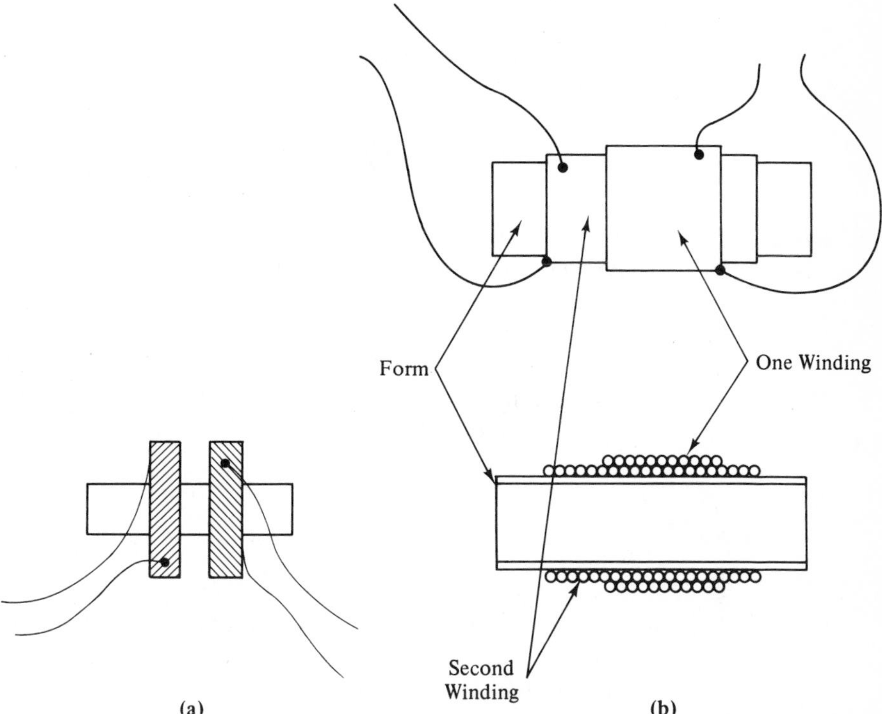

Figure 5.15 (a) Air-core separated windings and (b) overlapping windings.

sets up a magnetic field that cuts the windings of both primary and secondary (see Figure 5.14). This induces a CEMF into the secondary winding, and gives rise to current *I*2, which flows into the load. Since the CEMF has a polarity opposite the applied voltage, current *I*2 will flow in a direction opposite to that of *I*1.

There are almost as many ways to build a transformer as there are applications for transformers. A single, air-core transformer, usually limited to higher frequencies, is shown in Figure 5.15(a). Here we have primary and secondary windings sharing a common core in close proximity. Another popular technique is to wind one coil directly over the other. Of course, both of the windings are insulated from each other.

5.12 VOLTAGE, CURRENT, AND POWER RATIOS IN TRANSFORMERS

The voltage ratio of primary to secondary is directly proportional to the turns ratio. That is to say,

$$\frac{N_p}{N_s} = \frac{E_p}{E_s} \tag{5-20}$$

where N_p is the number of turns in the primary.
N_s is the number of turns in the secondary.
E_p is the voltage applied to the primary.
E_s is the voltage appearing across the secondary.

This equation can be rearranged to find any of the variables that may be unknown. For example, to find the secondary voltage,

$$E_s = \frac{E_p N_s}{N_p} \tag{5-21}$$

Example. A certain transformer has 150 turns of wire in its primary, and 1800 turns in its secondary winding. (1) What is the turns ratio? (2) If 110 V ac is applied to the primary, what secondary voltage can be expected?

(1) The turns ratio is

$$N_p/N_s = 150/1800 = 1/12 = 1{:}12 \tag{5-22}$$

(2) The secondary voltage is

$$E_s = \frac{(110)\ (1800)}{(150)} \tag{5-23}$$

$$E_s = 1{,}320 \text{ V}$$

The current ratio of a transformer is *inversely proportional* to the turns ratio:

$$\frac{I_p}{I_s} = \frac{N_s}{N_p} \tag{5-24}$$

In the case of the transformer used in our example let us assume a load resistance that will draw 120 mA when 1320 V is applied. The primary current is found from

$$I_p = \frac{I_s N_s}{N_p} \tag{5-25}$$

$$I_p = ((0.120)(1800))/(150)$$

$$I_p = 1.44 \text{ A}$$

Notice that an increase in secondary voltage results in a decreased secondary current. This is necessary because the transformer is a passive device, and supplies no power of its own to the circuit: it merely *transfers* power. Power in the secondary, then, will be equal to the power in the primary if the transformer is ideal:

$$I_p E_p = I_s E_s \tag{5-26}$$

Unfortunately, real transformers have certain losses, so the efficiency of real transformers is actually less than 100%. The efficiency is given by

$$\frac{P_p}{P_s} \times 100 = \text{percentage of efficiency} \tag{5-27}$$

Be aware that efficiencies on the order of 95–99.9 percent are not uncommon.

5.13 IMPEDANCE TRANSFORMATION

The impedance reflected across a transformer can be computed from

$$\frac{Z_p}{Z_s} = \left[\frac{N_p}{N_s}\right]^2 \tag{5-28}$$

It is a fundamental electrical principle that maximum power transfer occurs when the impedance of the load matches—that is to say, equals—the impedance of the source. A transformer is often used to effect a match between two circuits in order to facilitate the most efficient transfer of power.

Rearranging Eq. (5-28) gives us another expression that is useful for finding the impedance reflected across the primary by a fixed load:

$$Z_p = Z_s(N_p/N_s)^2 \tag{5-29}$$

Example. Consider a transformer as shown in Figure 5.16. It has a turns ratio of 22:1, and is connected with its secondary across a 4-Ω load resistance. The reflected impedance is

$$\begin{aligned} Z_p &= (4)(22/1)^2 \\ Z_p &= (4)(484) \\ Z_p &= 1936\ \Omega \end{aligned} \tag{5-30}$$

An alternate, and often useful, form of the equation is gained by taking the square root of both sides:

$$(Z_p/Z_s)^{1/2} = \frac{N_p}{N_s} \tag{5-31}$$

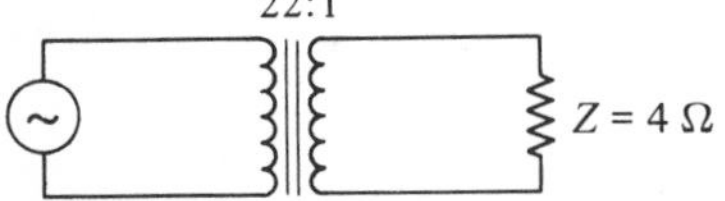

Figure 5.16 The impedance across the secondary is reflected to the primary.

Example. What turns ratio is required to match a 20-Ω source to a 50-Ω load?

$$\begin{aligned} (N_p/N_s) &= (20{,}000/50)^{1/2} \\ (N_p/N_s) &= (400)^{1/2} \\ (N_p/N_s) &= 20 = 20{:}1 \end{aligned} \tag{5-32}$$

5.14 TRANSFORMER LOSSES

The magnetic field generated by the current in the primary induces a current into the secondary. If an iron core is used, the primary also induces a current into the core. In that case the core acts as a single-turn secondary. Large circulating currents are thus set up in the core, which rob the transformer of available power, and thereby reduce efficiency.

The core currents are called "eddy currents." These can be reduced significantly by using a laminated core (see Figure 5.17) instead of a solid iron core. In this type of construction, thin sheets of soft iron are clamped together to form the core. Individual sheets are insulated from each other by a coating of lacquer. Such transformers and chokes have inductance values comparable with solid-core coils, but have greatly reduced eddy current losses.

In the chapter on magnetism we learned that most materials resist changes in their magnetic state. Power lost overcoming this tendency is called *hysteresis loss*. One technique used to overcome this form of loss is to tailor the metallurgy of the core to the application. For lower frequencies, soft iron is used, but alloys are needed as frequency is increased.

All transformer windings have a dc resistance in addition to their inductive reactance. A certain amount of power is lost in heating up this resistance. This power is equal to I^2R and is usually called *copper loss*. The remedy is to increase the diameter of the wire used to wind the transformer. This is a fine solution, so long as it does not result in a transformer that is too bulky. A reasonable trade-off (engineering jargon for "compromise") is to keep the X_L/R ratio greater than 10.

"Flux leakage" is a type of loss that occurs because not all flux lines generated by the primary current cut across the turns of the secondary. "External induction" is loss brought about when flux leaking from a transformer cuts across electrical conductors external to the transformer. The solution for both problems lies in designing the geometry of the transformer to minimize the existence of flux outside of the core area. Toward this end, toroidal transformers work best.

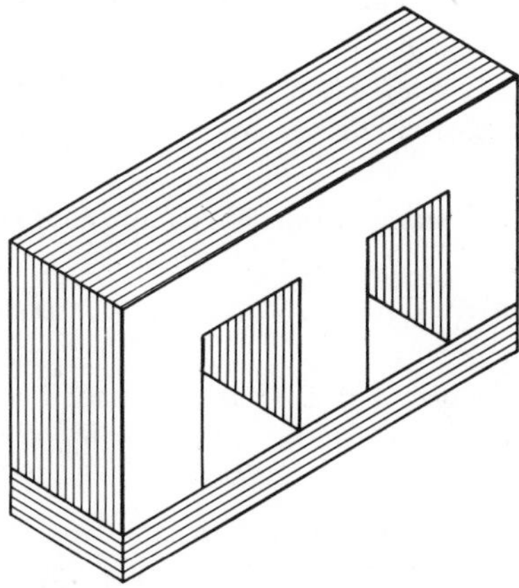

Figure 5.17 A laminated core reduces eddy-current losses.

5.15 AUTOTRANSFORMERS

"Autotransformers" are a class in which the secondary and primary are portions of the same coil. An example is shown in Figure 5.18. The coil is tapped at A, and this point forms the common. Source current flows in winding section A-B, while secondary current is induced in segment A-C.

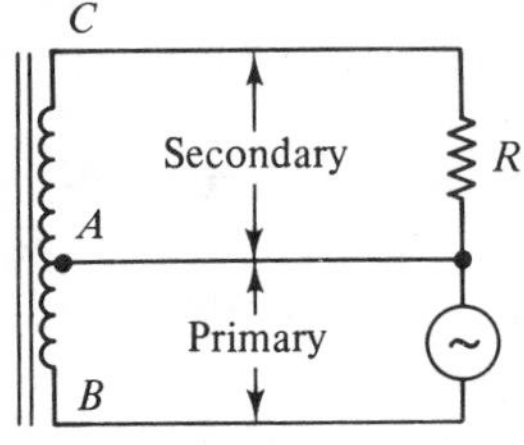

Figure 5.18 An auto transformer.

PROBLEMS

1. Briefly define inductance.
2. The magnetic field surrounding a wire is ______ to the wire.
3. According to Lenz' law, the magnetic field surrounding a current-carrying conductor will itself generate a current in the conductor. What property does this current possess?
4. The voltage drop created by this current is called ________.
5. CEMF can exist *only* when current is changing. True or false?
6. The unit of inductance is the ________.
7. One henry is the inductance that causes ________ CEMF when the current is changing at a rate of 1 A/s.
8. The symbol for inductance is ________.
9. A cylindrical coil has a radius of 1 in., a length of 4 in., and has 150 turns of wire. What is its inductance in μH?
10. The time constant of an RL circuit is defined as the time required (in seconds) for the current to rise to ______ percent of its final, Ohm's law, value.
11. What is the time constant of an RL circuit consisting of a 2-H coil and a 100-Ω resistor?
12. An inductor in an RL circuit is said to be fully charged after ________ time constants.
13. What is the time constant if $L = 0.1$ H, and $R = 10\ \Omega$?
14. How much energy is stored by a 5-H inductor that is fully charged when 3 A are flowing?
15. What is another commonly accepted name for the units in the answer to Question 14?
16. The phenomenon called "inductive kick" occurs when ____________.

17. "Self-inductance" is the phenomenon in which the magnetic field of a coil induces a current ____________.

18. "Mutual inductance" is the phenomenon in which the magnetic field of one coil induces current ______________.

19. A 150-μH coil and a 250-μH coil are coupled. The value of the constant k is 0.05. Find the mutual inductance.

20. Two 0.5-mH coils are oriented at a perfect right angle with respect to each other. What is the theoretical coefficient of coupling? Assume that the coils are ideal.

21. Two series-connected coils are oriented at right angles to each other. If $L1 = 200\ \mu$H and $L2 = 1$ mH, what is the total inductance?

22. What is the total inductance of the combination in Question 21 if the coils are reoriented to have a coefficient of coupling of 0.65?

23. Find the total inductance if there are two 150-μH coils in parallel. Assume $k = 0$.

24. Find the total inductance if there are three 150-μH coils connected in parallel. $k = 0$ for all cases.

25. The unit for inductive reactance is ______________.

26. The symbol for inductive reactance is ______________.

27. Compute the inductive reactance of a 500-mH coil at 1000 Hz.

28. Compute the inductive reactance of a 100-μH coil at 100 kHz.

29. A 10-V, 5-kHz signal is applied to a 1-mH coil. How much current will flow?

30. The symbol ω (lowercase Greek letter omega) is the symbolic representation of what quantity?

31. In a circuit containing only pure inductance, what is the phase angle betwen current and voltage?

32. In an inductive circuit current ________ voltage.

33. What is the magnitude of the impedance if $R = 100\ \Omega$ and $X_L = 500\ \Omega$?

34. A transformer has 100 turns in the primary and 2000 turns in the secondary. What will the secondary voltage be if 110 V is applied to the primary?

35. A transformer has 1000 turns in the primary and 50 turns in the secondary. If the primary winding draws 1.2 A, how much secondary current is being drawn?

36. What is the reflected impedance across the primary if the secondary is connected to a 100-Ω resistor, and the turns ratio is 5:1?

37. Name three types of transformer losses.

38. Power lost heating the wires forming the primary and secondary is proportional to I^2R, and is called ______________.

39. Eddy current losses are reduced by the use of ______________.

40. Some coils and transformers use a ______________ to prevent external induction, or linkage, losses.

6
Capitance and Capacitors

6.1 ELEMENTARY CAPACITORS

A capacitor is an electronic component that can store electrical energy in an electrostatic field set up between two conductive plates placed opposite and parallel to each other. These devices are also sometimes called by the obsolete term, "condensors."

Figure 6.1 shows a basic form of a simple parallel plate capacitor. Also shown are the two commonly seen schematic symbols for a capacitor. In Figure 6.1(a) we have the elementary form of capacitor, consisting of

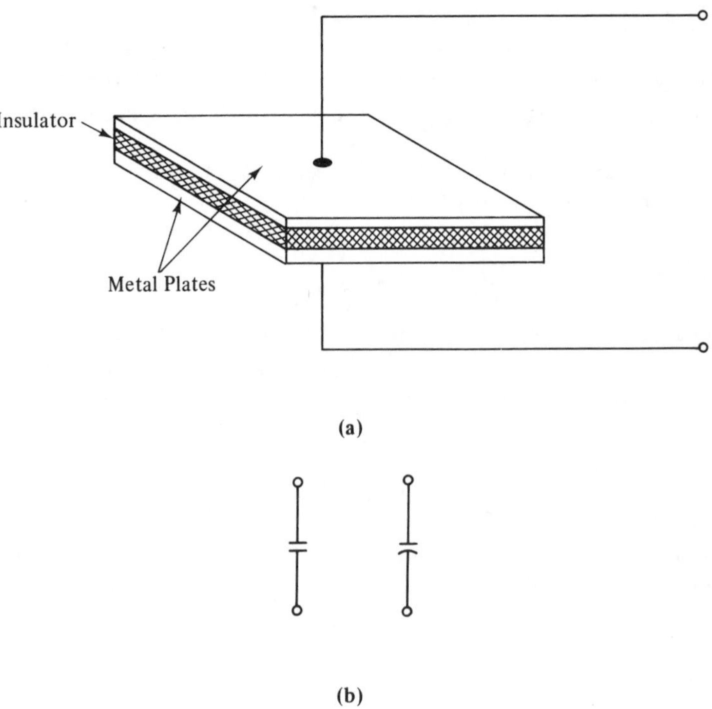

Figure 6.1 (a) Parallel plate capacitor and (b) schematic symbols.

two metallic plates with a piece of insulating material sandwiched between them. When a voltage is applied across a capacitor, it sets up an electrostatic field in the space between the plates. Energy is stored in this field, and can be dumped back into the circuit in the form of an electric current if the right circumstances occur. See Figure 6.2.

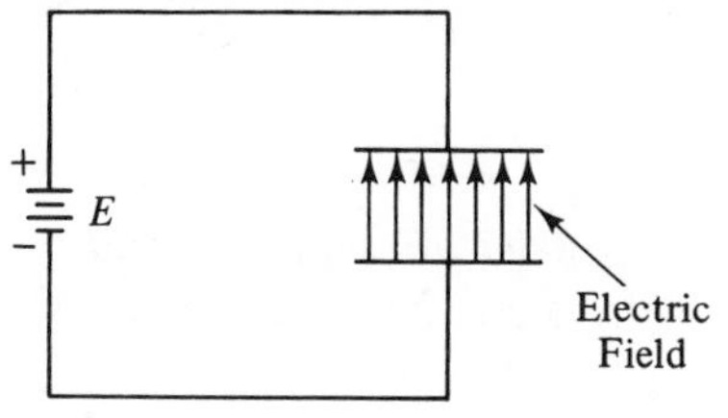

Figure 6.2 Energy is stored in the electric field between the plates.

6.2 ENERGY STORAGE IN A CAPACITOR

The energy storage ability of a capacitor is called its *capacity* or *capacitance*. The unit for capacitance is the farad, which is calculated from

$$C = \frac{Q}{E} \tag{6-1}$$

where C is the capacitance in farads.
Q is the stored electric charge in coulombs.
E is the potential across the capacitor.

From Eq. (6-1) it may be seen that a basic definition of the unit "farad" can be formed. One fared is the capacitance that will store a one-coulomb charge when one volt is applied. The alternative unit for the farad is coulomb per volt.

The size of the farad is, however, too large for most practical applications. More commonly we shall use subunits such as the microfarad (abbreviated "μF," "mFd," "μFd,'" or "mF") and the picofarad ("pF" or "pFd"). The microfarad is equal to 10^{-6} farad (0.000001), and the picofarad is equal to 10^{-12} farads (0.000000000001) or 10^{-6} μF. You will also see occasionally the obsolete term "micromicrofarads" (mmF) instead of the picofarad. The mmF and the pF, however, are identical numerically.

Example. What is the capacitance of a parallel plate capacitor that stores 0.0025 C when a potential of 10 V is applied?

$$C = Q/E = (0.0025)/(10) = 0.00025\ \text{F} = 250\ \mu\text{F} \tag{6-2}$$

The actual *amount* of energy stored in the electric field of a capacitor is measured in joules, or "watt-seconds," and is found from

$$W \text{ (energy)} = \tfrac{1}{2}CV^2 \tag{6-3}$$

where Energy is in watt-seconds or joules.
C is the capacitance in farads.
V is the applied voltage.

Example. What is the voltage applied across a 16 μF capacitor that has been charged to 50 W? (Rearrange the energy equation to solve for V.)

$$V = (2W/C)^{1/2}$$

$$V = ((2)(50)/(1.6 \times 10^{-5}))^{1/2} \tag{6-4}$$

$$V = 2500 \text{ V} = 2.5 \text{ kV}$$

6.3 DETERMINING CAPACITANCE

The value of any given capacitor is a function of several different factors. It is, for instance, directly proportional to the area of the opposing plates, and inversely proportional to the separation between them. Capacitance can be computed from

$$C = \frac{kKA}{d} \tag{6-5}$$

where A is the plate area.
d is the spacing between the plates.
K is the dielectric constant of the insulating material used.
k is the units constant.

The units constant k is dependent upon which system of measure is used—MKS, cgs, or English, and whether the answer is to be in farads, microfarads, or picofarads. If A and d are in inches and the capacitance is to be expressed in picofarads, then the value of k is 0.225, making the formula

$$C = \frac{0.225KA}{d} \tag{6-6}$$

The dielectric constant K represents a property of materials that tends to either ease the way for, and concentrate, or reduce the electrostatic field lines. Figure 6.3 gives the approximate values for this constant for several materials often used as capacitor dielectrics. A vacuum is the reference, so it has been assigned a value of $K = 1$ (unity). Dry air, often listed erroneously as the reference material, has a constant very nearly equal to that of a vacuum, so it is often taken as the reference in lab experiments for determination of capacitance. The actual value of K for air is 1.006, so only a tiny error is introduced into the calculations.

Dielectric Constants

Vacuum	1
Dry air	1+
Glass	2 – 4
Paper	2 – 3
Mica	7 – 8
Ceramic	20 – 2000
Aluminum Oxide	7 – 12

Figure 6.3 Dielectric constants of common materials.

In most experimental determinations of capacitance the other errors are so great as to overshadow the error in dielectric constant. Notice that materials such as ceramic have a constant that is very high. Because of this it is possible to use ceramic to make capacitors that are very small for a given capacitance value.

Example. Two square plates that measure 10 in. on a side are separated by a distance of 0.25 in. Assuming that they are perfectly parallel, and that K for air is unity, find the capacitance.

$$C = \frac{(0.225)(1)(10)(10)}{(0.25)} \tag{6-7}$$

$$C = 90 \text{ pF}$$

6.4 LOSSES IN CAPACITORS

Compared with certain other electronic components, the capacitor has relatively few important losses. This is especially true at dc and low ac frequencies. One form of loss, however, is a series resistance, which is caused by any of several factors. Leakage currents can flow through the dielectric. Although the dielectric is an insulator, we must be mindful of the fact that no insulator is perfect, and that all types of insulator will conduct some small amount of current if a sufficiently high potential is applied. Another source of leakage current is dirt film on the plates of the capacitor, its leads, across the physical dielectric, or on the capacitor body. All of these resistances, from whatever source, are lumped together under the term "equivalent series resistance," or "ESR." Normally, however, one will not see the ESR quoted for most capacitors unless they are intended for use in either very-high-voltage or very-high-impedance circuits.

Another class of loss, not so easily put aside, is the hysteresis loss of the electrostatic field in the dielectric. The forces generating this field tend to deform the orbital paths of the electrons in the atoms of the dielectric. In ac circuits these atoms are continually deforming in step with the applied ac waveform. The motion thus set up generates a certain amount of heat energy, which is power robbed from the circuit. In most practical capacitors this effect is negligible at dc and low-frequency ac. As the frequency is increased, however, more and more heat is generated, and the capacitor becomes less useful. Different dielectric materials exhibit this effect in differing degrees. Paper capacitors become almost useless above frequencies of a few megahertz, while air and some ceramic types are useful to almost 1000 MHz.

One last form of loss is the series inductance. All electrical conductors exhibit a certain amount of inductance, and that includes the metal plates and lead wires of a capacitor. The amount of series inductance in any particular type of capacitor is a limiting factor at high ac frequencies, and is mostly dependent upon the geometry of the capacitor's construction.

6.5 CAPACITOR RATINGS

There are three types of ratings given to most capacitors, and these are most important in selecting a capacitor for any specific electronic job. One of these, of course, is the capacitance rating. Another is the working voltage (WVDC or VDC) rating. WVDC is defined as the maximum voltage at which the capacitor will operate normally, without damage. All types of insulator have a voltage/thickness rating. At higher potentials they may well break down and become relatively good conductors. Each possible type of dielectric insulator is tested and assigned a voltage rating per mil of thickness. Dry air, for example, is given a rating of about 3000 V/mil.

One other rating often applied to capacitors is the temperature coefficient. Thermal expansion of the plates and dielectric, along with other phenomena, causes the capacitance to vary somewhat with temperature changes. Nominal capacitance is usually measured at room temperature, which is taken to be 25°C. The temperature coefficient tells us how many parts per million (ppm) we can expect the nominal value to shift per degree centigrade of temperature change.

Color codes are used in addition to printing for marking capacitors as to their ratings. Several standardized systems for markings are used by U.S. manufacturers, and these are shown in Figure 6.4. For some applications, almost any capacitor will do, but in others the precise ratings become critical. Consequently, it is wise to learn the coding system.

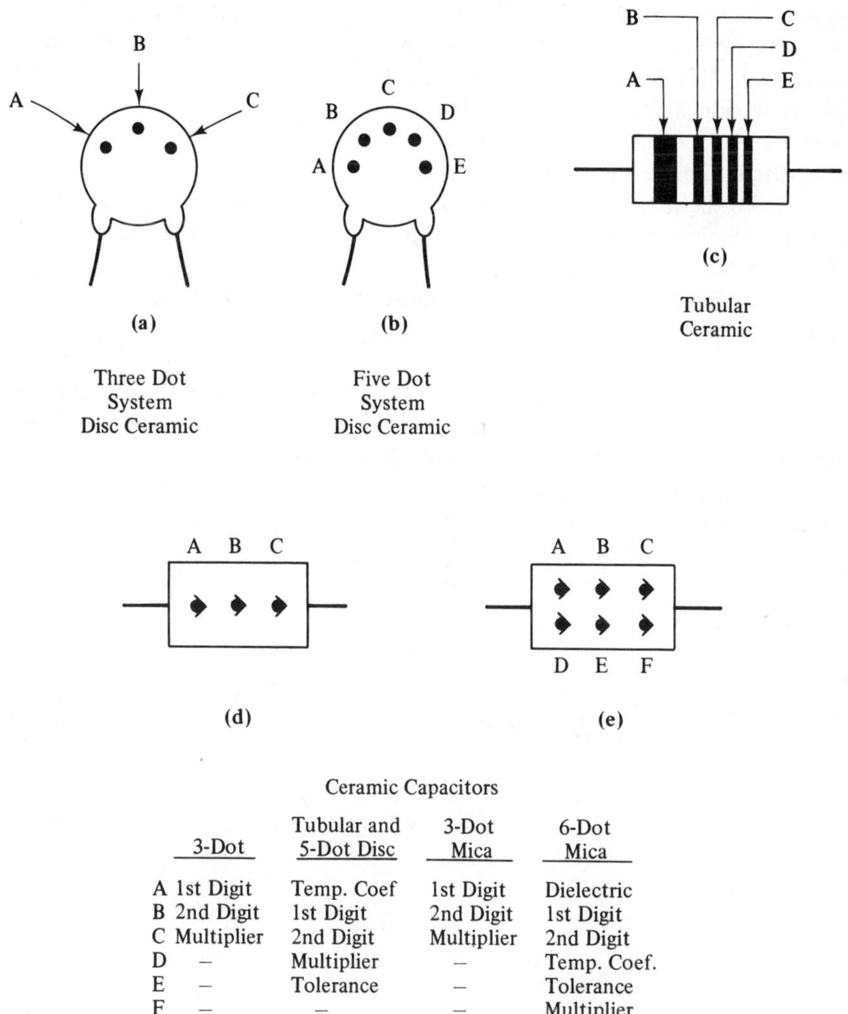

Ceramic Capacitors

	3-Dot	Tubular and 5-Dot Disc	3-Dot Mica	6-Dot Mica
A	1st Digit	Temp. Coef	1st Digit	Dielectric
B	2nd Digit	1st Digit	2nd Digit	1st Digit
C	Multiplier	2nd Digit	Multiplier	2nd Digit
D	–	Multiplier	–	Temp. Coef.
E	–	Tolerance	–	Tolerance
F	–	–	–	Multiplier

Figure 6.4 Capacitor color code.

6.6 TYPES OF CAPACITORS

Figure 6.5 shows a collection of several different types of capacitors often used in communications equipment. In some instances the differences are only in case style, but in others there are major differences in dielectric type, and, therefore, in range of permitted applications.

Paper capacitors still find some application, even though they are an older type, and not without fault. Adding to their decline in popularity is the existence of newer types that have the best properties of the paper type at lower cost and fewer of the bad features. Most paper capacitors are made by sandwiching a piece of waxed paper between two sheets of metal foil. This assembly is then wrapped up into a tight little cylinder and placed inside a cardboard tube. The ends of the tube are then sealed in wax, or the assembly is encapsulated in a plastic container. Even though a plastic body is evident, the capacitor is still a paper type.

Both the nature of the dielectric and the high series inductance of the paper capacitor make it less useful above frequencies on the order of a few megahertz. In most cases where they were previously used, paper capacitors have been replaced with those with a mylar dielectric. In fact, it is usually wise practice to use mylars when one is replacing faulty capacitors in electronic equipment.

Mica is another popular capacitor dielectric material. It can operate at frequencies much higher than paper capacitors. Most mica capacitors are of either the old "postage-stamp" type, or the more modern "dipped" type. Where temperature control is a big factor, the temperature coefficient of a special type called the "silvered mica" is easily appreciated.

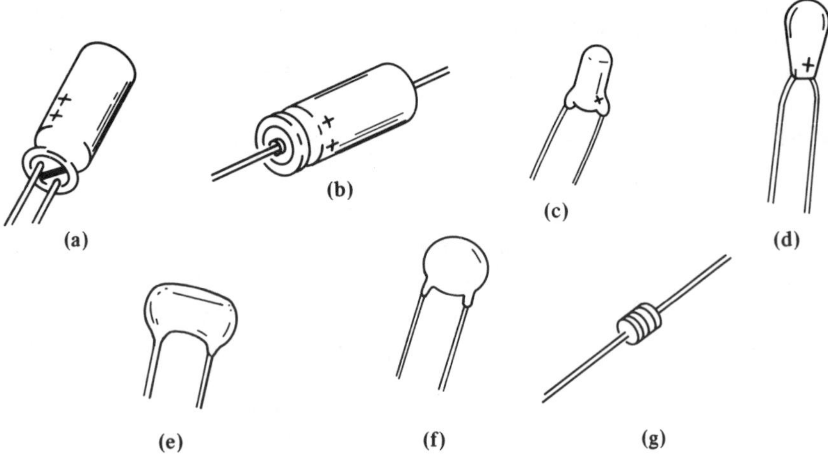

Figure 6.5 Fixed capacitors.

Ceramic capacitors can be made in very small packages for any given value of capacitance. Certain tiny ceramic capacitors can be operated at dc potentials well over 1000 V. Manufacturers can produce ceramic dielectrics with almost any practical temperature coefficient. Ceramic capacitors are usually supplied in either disc or tubular package styles.

Wherever larger values of capacitance are required, it may be necessary to use an electrolytic capacitor in order to keep weight and physical size within reasonable bounds. These capacitors use an aluminum foil coated on one side with an aluminum oxide. Both sides of the foil are then immersed in an electrolyte. Although such capacitors are extremely limited in operating-frequency range (few can operate over a few hundred kilohertz), they find extensive application in low-frequency ac and in dc circuits. One cautionary note, however, may be in order regarding electrolytic capacitors. They are polarity-sensitive. You will note that most of them have one end marked with the positive (+) symbol and the other with the negative (−) symbol. In dc circuits and those ac circuits where the peak amplitude is an appreciable fraction of the WVDC rating, this polarity sensitivity can cause problems. If the capacitor is connected either backwards in a dc circuit, or into an ac circuit, then the current flow will be excessive and may cause the capacitor to explode.

Figure 6.6 shows several types of variable capacitor. The compression variable of Figure 6.6(a) is a special type of mica capacitor in which a screwdriver adjustment is used to either squeeze together, or allow to separate, the plates of the capacitor and the mica insulator. Capacitance is maximum when the plates and mica sheets are fully compressed. Minimum capacitance, then, occurs when the compression is also minimum.

A simple air variable capacitor is shown in Figure 6.6(b). In this type of capacitor there are two sets of intermeshed, parallel plates. One set, called the *stator,* is stationary, whereas the other, called the *rotor,* can be moved in or out of the assembly to increase or decrease the total opposing plate area. Capacitance is maximum when the two sets of plates are fully meshed, and minimum when they are completely unmeshed.

Piston capacitors are another type of variable. The dielectric of a piston capacitor may be either ceramic or air, but the basic form is the same. Two cylinders are formed so that one can slip inside of the other, leaving room for the dielectric. The capacitance of the piston capacitor is a function of the percentage of the movable piston inside of the fixed cylinder.

Figure 6.6(d) shows a larger variable capacitor, such as might be used where high voltages are present. It can withstand those potentials because of the spacing between plates. Note that the area of the plates for a given capacitance must be increased to compensate for the larger plate-plate spacing.

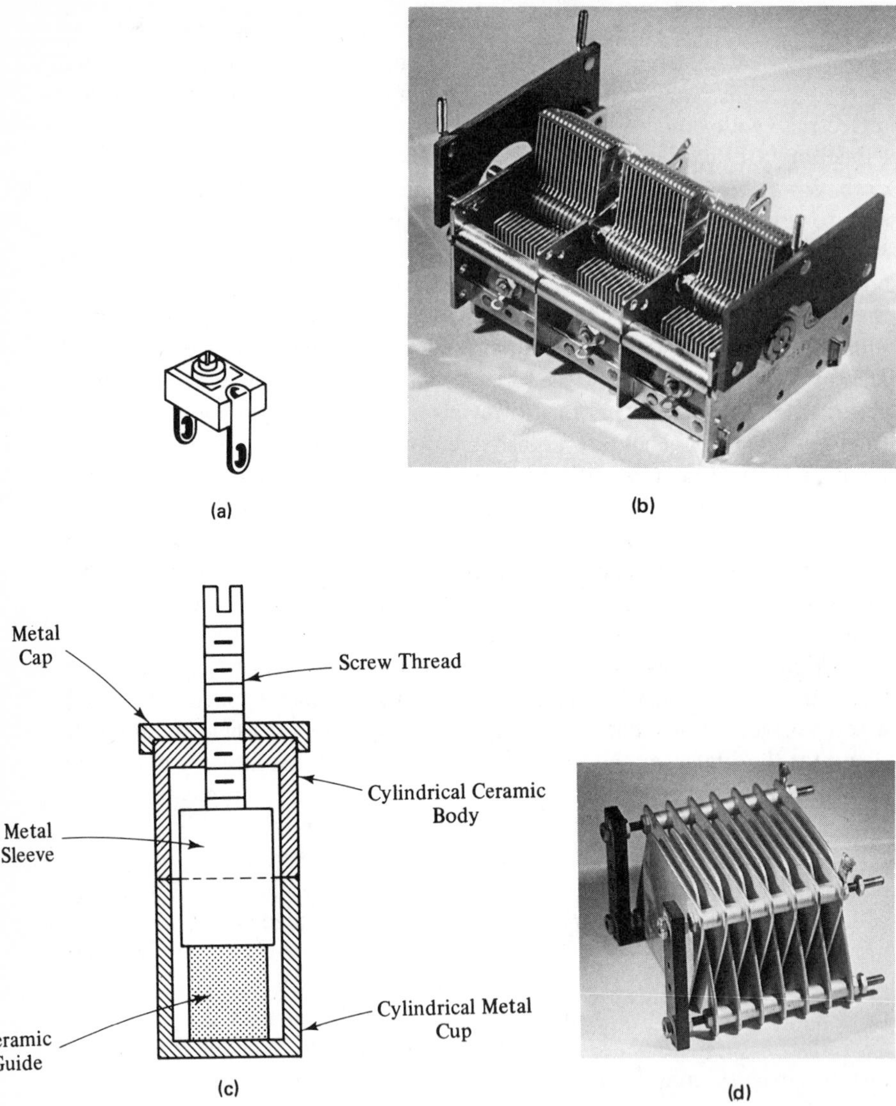

Figure 6.6 (a) compression capacitor, (b) air variable, (c) piston and (d) transmitting capacitor.

We sometimes find small-value variable capacitors used in conjunction with larger-value fixed or variable capacitors, so that precisely specified values of capacitance may be obtained. Capacitors used to trim the value of a combination of capacitors are called, not inappropriately, "trimmer" capacitors.

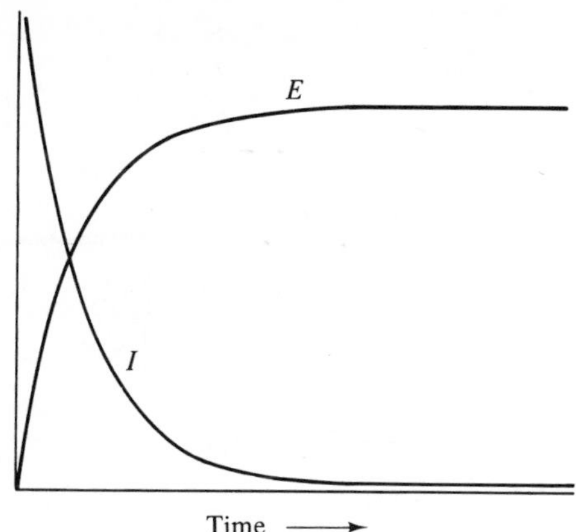

Figure 6.7 Relationship beween voltage and current when the switch is closed, applying dc to a capacitor.

6.7 CHARGING A CAPACITOR

In Figure 6.2 we showed a capacitor connected across a voltage source. If an ammeter had been connected in that circuit, we would have observed a brief, but high-value, flow of current at the instant that the capacitor was connected. Shortly afterwards, we would have noticed that the current flow had dropped to zero. What causes this current? After all, there is no direct connection between the two sets of plates making up the capacitor. When the battery is first connected, electrons on the plate of the capacitor connected to the positive side of the battery are attracted into the battery by its positive potential at that point. This creates a deficiency of electrons on the (+) side of the capacitor. When this occurs, electrons from the negative side of the capacitor sense a positive potential, so will rush to the capacitor in an attempt at neutralizing the deficiency. When as many electrons are drawn to the (−) plate of the capacitor as were removed from the (+) plate, the current ceases to flow.

Figure 6.7 shows the voltage and current waveforms for a capacitor during charging. Note that the current springs to its maximum almost immediately when the connection is made. The voltage, on the other hand, rises exponentially to its maximum. This indicates that capacitors tend to oppose any change in voltage, a situation exactly opposite that of the inductor.

6.8 CAPACITIVE TIME CONSTANT

The time constant of a capacitor is defined as the period required for it to charge to 63.2 percent of its fully charged voltage. (See Figure 6.8). Alternatively, if the capacitor is already fully charged, the time constant is the

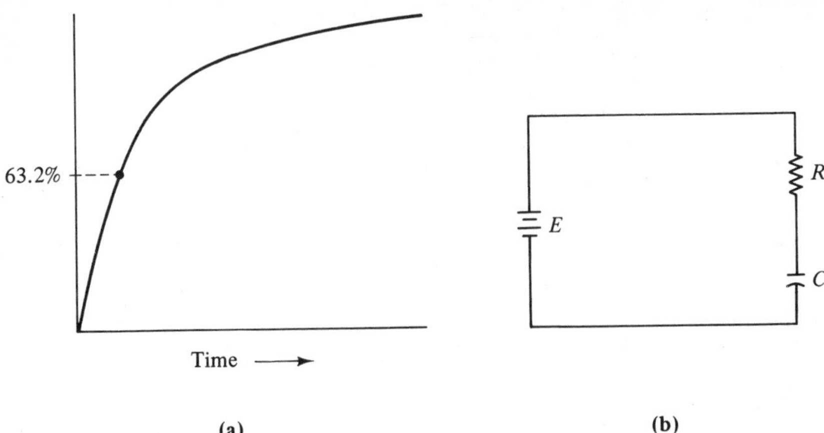

Figure 6.8 The time constant of a capacitor is the period required to charge a capacitor to 63.2% of its final voltage **(a)** in an RC circuit **(b)**.

time required for it to discharge to 36.8 percent of its fully charged value. Both methods for defining and measuring time constant result in the same figure. In a resistor-capacitor (RC) circuit the time constant is

$$\tau = RC \qquad (6\text{-}8)$$

where τ is the time in seconds.
R is the resistance in ohms.
C is the capacitance in farads.

Example. Find the time constant of an RC network consisting of a 0.1-μF capacitor and a 10-kΩ resistor.

$$\begin{aligned} \tau &= RC \\ \tau &= (1 \times 10^4)(1 \times 10^{-7}) \\ \tau &= 1 \times 10^{-3}\text{ s} \\ \tau &= 0.001\text{ s or 1 ms} \end{aligned} \qquad (6\text{-}9)$$

6.9 CAPACITORS IN SERIES AND PARALLEL COMBINATIONS

Capacitors in series combination (Figure 6.9) have a total capacitance less than the capacitance of the smallest capacitor in the network. They com-

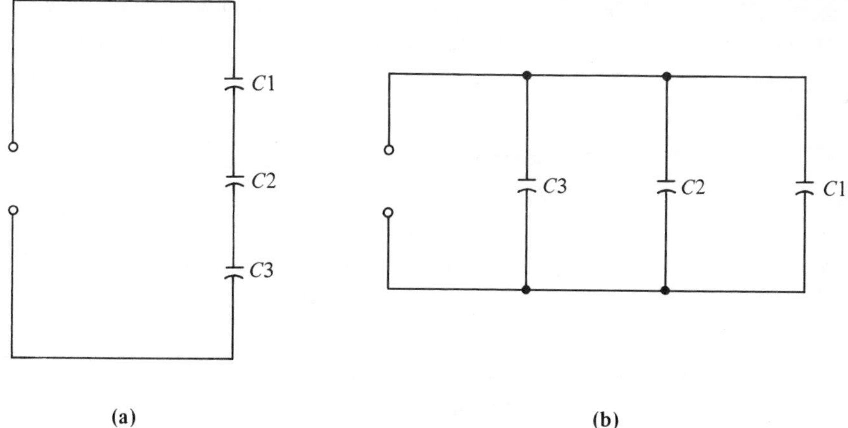

Figure 6.9 **(a) Capacitors in series and (b) capacitors in parallel.**

bine their values in the same manner as resistors in parallel. The general formula is

$$C_t = \frac{1}{\frac{1}{C1} + \frac{1}{C2} + \frac{1}{C3} + \ldots + \frac{1}{C_n}} \tag{6-10}$$

Alternatively, for the special case of only two capacitors in series:

$$C_t = \frac{C1C2}{C1 + C2} \tag{6-11}$$

In circuits such as Figure 6.9(b), where there are several capacitors in parallel, we can compute the total capacitance by adding together the individual values:

$$C_t = C1 + C2 + C3 + \ldots + C_n \tag{6-12}$$

Unless all capacitors in the parallel combination have the same voltage rating, we must use the voltage rating of the capacitor with the *lowest* rating. In other words, the lowest individual rating is the WVDC rating of the entire circuit. In the series circuit we can, with but few limitations, merely add the respective WVDC ratings to find the WVDC rating of the combination.

Example. Four capacitors are connected in parallel: 0.01 μF/600 WVDC,

0.02 μF/600 WVDC, 0.02 μF/400 WVDC, and 0.005 μF/600 WVDC. What is the total capacitance of the combination?

$$C_t = C1 + C2 + C3 + C4$$
$$C_t = 0.01 + 0.02 + 0.02 + 0.005\ \mu\text{F} \tag{6-13}$$
$$C_t = 0.055\ \mu\text{F}$$

What is the voltage rating of the combination? *Answer:* 400 WVDC.

Example. A series combination consists of two 0.1 μF/600 WVDC capacitors. Find the total capacitance and working voltage of the combination.

The working voltage is

$$600 + 600 = 1200\ \text{WVDC} \tag{6-14}$$

The capacitance is

$$C_t = \frac{(0.1)(0.1)}{(0.1) + (0.1)}$$
$$C_t = (0.01)/(0.2) \tag{6-15}$$
$$C_t = 0.05\ \mu\text{F}$$

6.10 CAPACITORS IN AC CIRCUITS

A capacitor offers opposition to changes in applied voltage. Since ac is continuously changing, that opposition is continuous. Opposition such as this is known as capacitive reactance (X_c) and is measured in ohms. The value of X_c is given by

$$X_c = \frac{1}{2\pi f C} \tag{6-16}$$

where X_c is the capacitive reactance in ohms.
f is the frequency in hertz.
C is the capacitance in farads.

Notice that capacitive reactance is *inversely proportional* to frequency. This is in contrast with the inductive reactance, which is directly proportional to frequency.

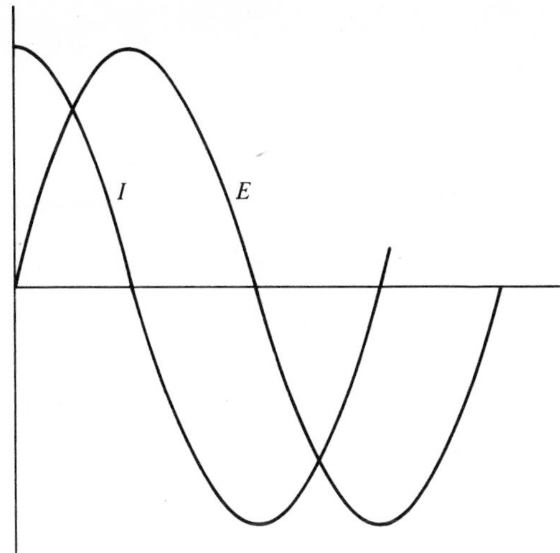

Figure 6.10 In a capacitive circuit the voltage lags behind the current by 90°.

Example. What is the reactance of a 0.15 μF capacitor in a circuit operated at 2500 Hz?

$$X_c = \frac{1}{(2)(3.14)(2500)(1.5 \times 10^{-7})} \qquad (6\text{-}17)$$

$$X_c = 425\ \Omega$$

Figure 6.10 shows the waveform relationships between voltage and current in a capacitive circuit. Since a capacitor opposes changes in voltage, we observe that the current waveform has gone through 90 deg of its excursion before the voltage waveform even begins. This tells us that the current in a capacitive circuit leads the voltage by 90 deg—exactly the opposite of the situation in an inductive circuit. In fact, there are some interesting properties of a circuit in which there are both capacitive and inductive reactance, and they both have the same magnitude. This will be treated more extensively in Chapter 8.

Impedance in a capacitive circuit is a composite of the resistance and the capacitive reactance. (See Figure 6.11.) We can graph the vectors for R and X_c in exactly the same manner as in the inductive circuits of the last chapter. In the capacitive circuit, however, we place the X_c vector at the -90-deg position with respect to the resistance vector at the origin. This is necessary because of the -90-deg phase angle between the two vectors. The magnitude of the resultant impedance vector is

$$Z = (R^2 + X_c^2)^{1/2} \qquad (6\text{-}18)$$

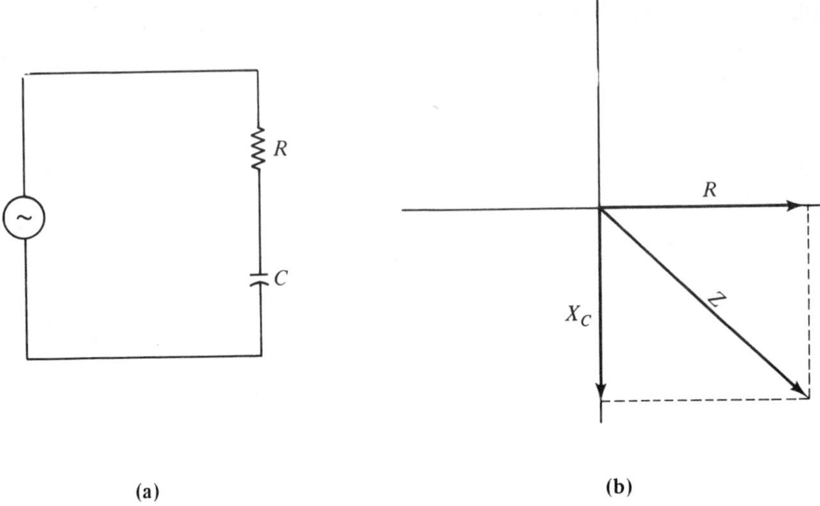

Figure 6.11 (a) RC circuit and (b) vector relationships.

Example. In the previous example we had a certain capacitor with a reactance of 425 Ω. If there is a certain 600 Ω series resistance in the circuit with that capacitor, what is the impedance?

$$Z = ((600)^2 + (425)^2)^{1/2}$$

$$Z = (540{,}625)^{1/2} \tag{6-19}$$

$$Z = 735\ \Omega$$

PROBLEMS

1. A capacitor stores energy in a(n) _______________ between two parallel conductor plates.
2. "Capacitance" is a measure of the _______________ of a capacitor.
3. The unit of capacitance is the _______________.
4. 1 pF = _______________ F.
5. How much energy is stored in a 16-μF capacitor charged to 7.07 kV?
6. A capacitor is charged to 50 Ws and has a voltage of 2 kV. What is its capacitance?
7. Find the capacitance of a parallel plate capacitor if the area is 400 in^2 and the separation is 0.05 in.
8. The time constant of an *RC* network is given by _______________.
9. The time constant is defined as the time required to charge the capacitor to __________ percent of its fully charged level.

10. The time constant may also be defined as the time required to discharge a fully charged capacitor to ________ percent of the fully charged potential.

11. Find the time constant of a circuit with a 0.1-μF capacitor and a 10-kΩ resistor.

12. Find the time constant if $C = 1$ μF and $R = 1$ MΩ.

13. Find the time constant if $C = 100$ μF and $R = 100$ Ω.

14. Four capacitors, $C1$ through $C4$, are connected in parallel. What is the total capacitance if $C1 = 0.01$ μF, $C2 = 0.02$ μF, $C3 = 0.1$ μF, and $C4 = 0.01$ μF?

15. Two 0.01-μF/600-WVDC capacitors are connected in series. What is the total capacitance?

16. In Question 15, what is the total WVDC rating?

17. The unit of capacitive reactance is the ____________.

18. The symbol for capacitive reactance is ____________.

19. What is the capacitive reactance of a 0.001-μF capacitor if the frequency is 10 kHz?

20. In a capacitive circuit the current ____________ voltage.

21. Find X_c if $f = 10^6$ Hz and $c = 10$ pF.

22. Find the impedance if $R = 600$ Ω, and $X_c = 100$ Ω.

23. Find the impedance if the resistance is 0 Ω, and the capacitive reactance is 1000 Ω.

7
AC Circuits

7.1 REACTIVE CIRCUITS: RLC ELEMENTS IN SERIES

Behavior of complex ac circuits may appear difficult to understand, but that is really only an illusion. If we dissect the circuit into smaller, easier to analyze, segments, then we can solve some fairly awesome problems.

Consider the circuit of Figure 7.1. Here we have a series combination of a capacitor, an inductor, and a resistor. Since it is a series network, the currents in all of the elements are equal and in phase with each other. The voltage drops, however, are out of phase. The impedance of the circuit is given by

$$Z = (R^2 + (X_L - X_c)^2)^{1/2} \tag{7-1}$$

For the circuit in question, then

$$\begin{aligned} X_L &= (2)(3.14)(1000)(0.5) \\ X_L &= 3142\ \Omega \end{aligned} \tag{7-2}$$

and

$$\begin{aligned} X_c &= 1/(2)(3.14)(1000)(2.5 \times 10^{-8}) \\ X_c &= 6366\ \Omega \end{aligned} \tag{7-3}$$

Therefore, the impedance is

$$\begin{aligned} Z &= ((5000)^2 + (3142 - 6366)^2)^{1/2} \\ Z &= 5949\ \Omega = 5950\ \Omega \end{aligned} \tag{7-4}$$

In this type of circuit we can calculate the impedance using the standard impedance formula by setting the reactance term equal to $(X_L - X_c)$. In this particular case the capacitive reactance is only partially cancelled by the inductive reactance, so the circuit appears slightly capacitive. In Figure 7.2 we can see how this convention can reduce the complexity of our analysis. In order to ascertain the phase angle of the voltage across each component, however, we must consider each element

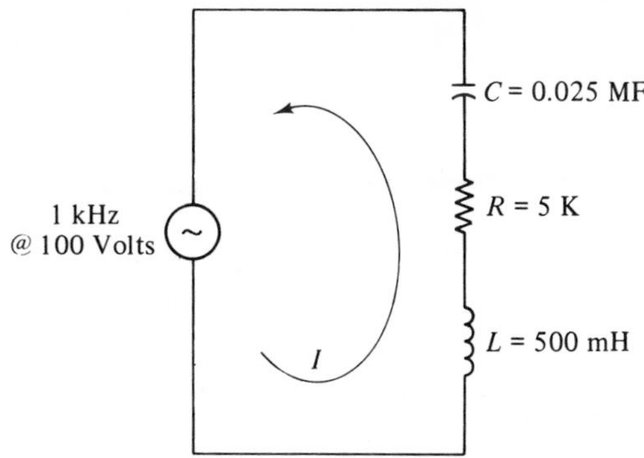

Figure 7.1 Complex ac circuit.

separately. In Figures 7.2 and 7.3 we can see the individual vector relationships. The phase angle of the voltage across the resistor is, of course, zero. Across the inductor, it is out of phase and has an angle of

$$\theta = \arcsin \frac{X_L}{Z'}$$

$$\theta = \arcsin (3142)/(5905) \tag{7-5}$$

$$\theta = 32.15 \text{ deg}$$

Please note that we could have used any trigonometric function that is valid for this right triangle. For example, it is also true that

$$\theta_L = \arctan \frac{X_L}{R}$$

$$\theta_L = \arctan (3142)/(5000) \tag{7-6}$$

$$\theta_L = 32.15 \text{ deg}$$

In fact, for this particular problem, the latter formula would have been quicker, so it is thus preferred. In a similar manner we can compute the phase angle across the capacitor:

$$\theta_c = \arctan X_c/R$$

$$\theta_c = \arctan (6366)/(5000) \tag{7-7}$$

$$\theta_c = 51.85 \text{ deg}$$

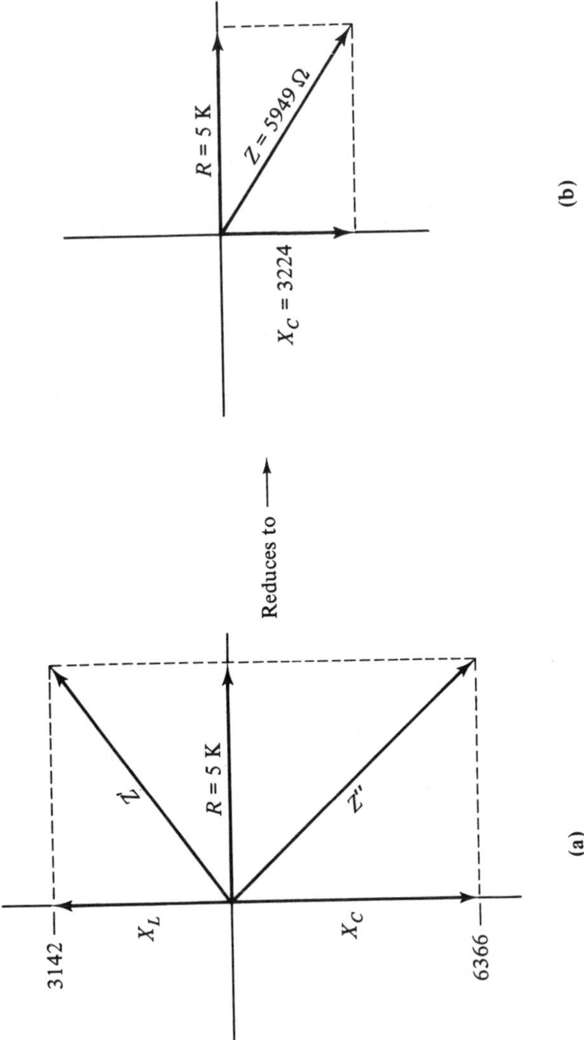

Figure 7.2 **(a)** Vector diagram of Figure 7.1 circuit reduces to **(b)** when reactances are combined.

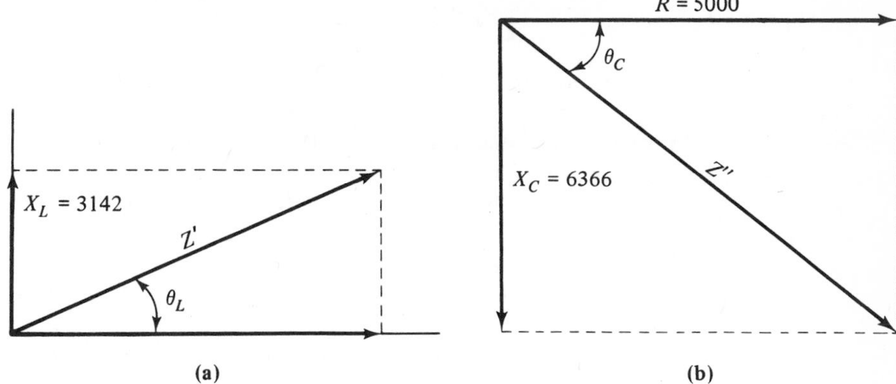

Figure 7.3 Individual vector relationships.

Let us assume that the ac potential across this network has an amplitude of 100 volts, rms. Find the voltage drop across each component. The first step is to calculate the current:

$$I = E/Z = 100/5950 = 0.017 \text{ A} \tag{7-8}$$

The voltage across the resistor is

$$E = IR = (0.017)(5000) = 85 \text{ V} \tag{7-9}$$

The voltage across the inductor is

$$E = IX_L = (0.017)(3142) = 53.4 \text{ V} \tag{7-10}$$

The voltage across the capacitor is

$$E = IX_c = (0.017)(6366) = 108 \text{ V} \tag{7-11}$$

Lest you think that some magic has been wrought here, let us calculate the applied voltage (100 V) from the individual voltage drops. In a simple resistive circuit we would merely sum the individual drops according to Kirchoff's voltage law. But in a reactive circuit we must apply the right-triangle rule used for impedance, etc.:

$$E_t = (E_r^2 + (E_L - E_c)^2)^{1/2}$$

$$E_t = ((85)^2 + (53.4 - 108)^2)^{1/2} \tag{7-12}$$

$$E_t = 100 \text{ V}$$

7.2 POWER IN REACTIVE CIRCUITS

We learned that in simple dc circuits the power was the product of the current and the voltage, or $P = EI$. In the reactive circuit, some energy is dumped back into the circuit each half-cycle. In that case, we find that there exists an apparent power, as measured from voltmeters and ammeters, and a "true power," which is somewhat less. From our previous formula

$$P_{\text{apparent}} = EI \tag{7-13}$$

But true power must take into account the phase angle, so the correct formula becomes

$$P_{\text{true}} = EI \cos \theta \tag{7-14}$$

Example. Find the true power in the circuit of Fig. 7.4.

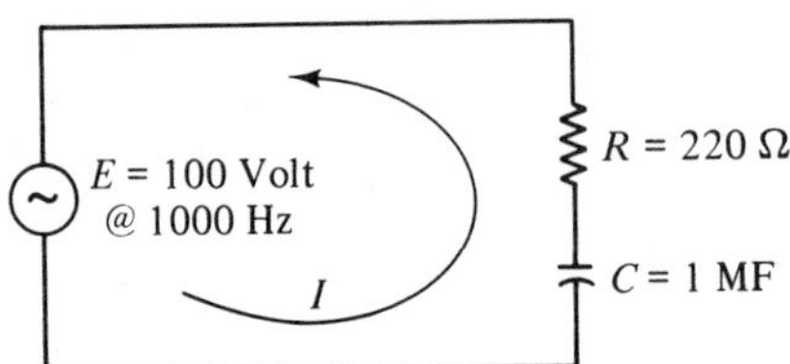

Figure 7.4 Find the true power.

First, calculate the reactance of the capacitor, which in this case happens to be 159 Ω. The impedance is

$$Z = (220^2 + 159^2)^{1/2}$$
$$Z = 271\ \Omega \tag{7-15}$$

Current through the network is

$$I = E/Z = 100/271 = 0.37\text{ A} \tag{7-16}$$

The apparent power is

$$P = EI = (100)(0.37) = 37\text{ W} \tag{7-17}$$

and, since $\cos \theta = R/Z$,

$$P = EI(R/Z) = (100)(0.37)(220/271) = 30\text{ W} \tag{7-18}$$

"Power factor" is the decimal fraction by which you must multiply apparent power to find true power. This is equal to the cosine of the phase angle, so

$$\text{P.F.} = \cos\theta$$
$$\text{P.F.} = R/Z \qquad (7\text{-}19)$$

and also,

$$\text{P.F.} = \frac{\text{true power}}{\text{apparent power}} \qquad (7\text{-}20)$$

The power factor represents lost power, in our example 7 W, so it is desirable to minimize the power factor in circuits that carry large currents. Most power companies, for example, use capacitors mounted at intervals on their poles to cancel some of the inductive reactance caused by inductive machinery owned by customers, and by the inductance of the lines themselves. It is their attempt at reducing the power factor as much as possible.

7.3 THE J-OPERATOR

When sine waves are in quadrature (90 deg out of phase) we may use the so-called "j-operator" to simplify equations and calculations. You may have studied this same operator in algebra under the heading "imaginary numbers." In that context the symbol i was used, and you learned that it was equal to $(-1)^{1/2}$, or the square root of minus one. In electronics we use the same operator, but under the symbol j to avoid confusion with the symbols for current, i and I.

The effect of multiplying a vector by the j-operator is to rotate it through 90 deg. Consider a situation in which we graph real numbers along the vertical and horizontal axes of a Cartesian coordinate system. If a vector is drawn parallel to the X-axis, but is then multiplied by the j-operator, it will wind up parallel to the Y-axis. The $+j$-operator will cause the vector to rotate +90 deg (counterclockwise), while the $-j$-operator will cause a rotation of −90 deg (clockwise). (See Figure 7.5.)

We can use the j-operator to represent the various values existing in an ac RLC circuit. A circuit in which a resistance of 150 Ω is connected in series with an inductive reactance of 85 Ω could be written as $R + jX_L = 150 + j85$. We may also use the j-operator to designate the voltages across certain circuit elements. Suppose that, in the same circuit as above, a current of 2 A is flowing:

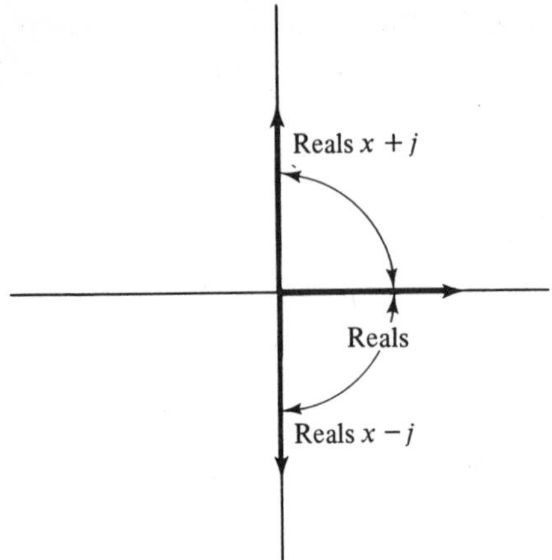

Figure 7.5 The j-operator.

$$\begin{aligned} E_R &= (2)(150) \\ E_R &= 300 \text{ V} \\ E_L &= (2)(85) \\ E_L &= 170 \text{ V} \end{aligned} \tag{7-21}$$

This is written as $E = 300 + j170$. If the inductive reactance were replaced by a capacitive reactance of, say, 50 Ω, and the voltage were then adjusted to maintain the 2-A current flow, we could write the term for the total opposition to current as $150 - j50$, and the voltage drops as $300 - j100$. In circuits that contain both types of reactance, we algebraically add the two reactance terms. For example, assume a circuit with a 150-Ω resistance, a 100-Ω inductive reactance, and a 60-Ω capacitive reactance. This can be written as

$$150 + (j100 - j60)$$

or, in a more simplified form,

$$150 + j40$$

Since the sign of the j-operator is positive, we may safely conclude that the circuit is slightly inductive, and so will have inductive properties. Note that we cannot use j-operator notation for impedance, but we do make use of the magnitudes from j-operator notation to make impedance calculations. (See Figure 7.6.) For the above circuit:

$$\begin{aligned} Z &= ((150)^2 + (40)^2)^{1/2} \\ Z &= 155\ \Omega \end{aligned} \tag{7-22}$$

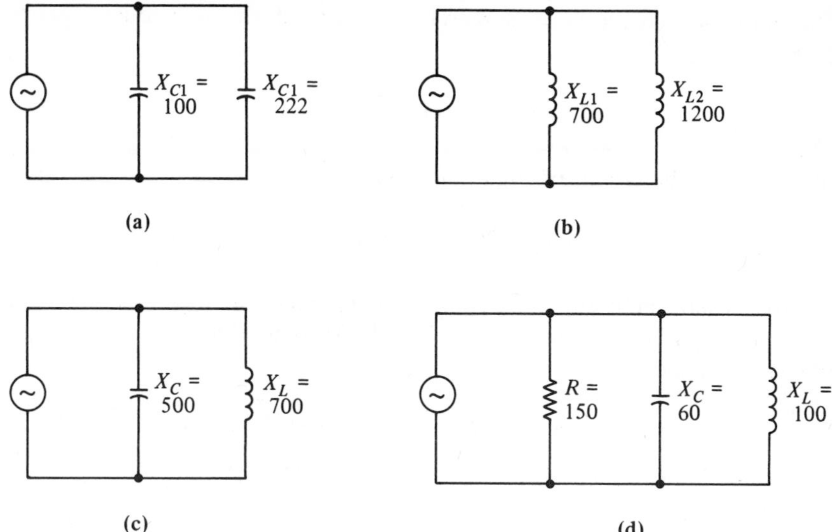

Figure 7.6 Parallel ac circuits.

7.4 PARALLEL AC CIRCUITS

Before proceeding too far into parallel ac circuits, we should digress a moment to introduce some new terminology. Recall from our basic discussion that conductance (G) is the reciprocal of resistance, and is measured in units called "mhos." Two additional reciprocal relationships are susceptance (B) and admittance (Y). Susceptance is defined as the reciprocal of reactance, so it is found from

$$B = \frac{1}{X} \tag{7-23}$$

Admittance is the reciprocal of impedance, so it is found from

$$Y = \frac{1}{Z} \tag{7-24}$$

Consider Figure 7.6(a), where we have two capacitive reactances in parallel. Their respective susceptances are

$$\begin{aligned} B1 &= 1/X_{c1} = 1/100 = 0.01 \\ B2 &= 1/X_{c2} = 1/220 = 0.0045 \end{aligned} \tag{7-25}$$

The combined susceptance is merely the sum of the individual susceptances, or

$$B_t = 0.01 + 0.0045 = 0.0145 \tag{7-26}$$

Similarly, for the circuit of Figure 7.6(b),

$$B_t = 1/700 + 1/1200 = 0.0014 + 0.0008 = 0.0022 \tag{7-27}$$

In cases where there are two opposite susceptances, as might be found in RLC or LC circuits [Figure 7.6(c)], we take their *difference* to find the total susceptance.

$$B_t = (1/X_L) - (1/X_c) = 1/700 - 1/500 \tag{7-28}$$

$$B_t = 0.0014 - 0.002 = -0.00057$$

Since this is a parallel circuit, the voltages across the respective elements will be in phase, but the currents in them will be out of phase. The capacitor in our example has the lowest reactance, so it will draw the greatest amount of current. The circuit, therefore, has capacitive properties—a fact confirmed by the minus symbol preceding the susceptance value.

If we want to find the reactance of a parallel combination such as this, we need only take the reciprocal of the susceptance:

$$X = 1/B \tag{7-29}$$

$$X = 1/(-0.00057)$$

$$X = -1754\ \Omega$$

In Figure 7.6(d) we have a network consisting of a resistance, a capacitance, and an inductance in parallel. The conductance of the resistive branch is

$$G = 1/R = 1/150 = 0.0067\ \Omega \tag{7-30}$$

Combining the two reactive branches to find susceptance, we obtain

$$\begin{aligned} B &= 1/X_L - 1/X_c \\ B &= 1/100 - 1/60 \\ B &= 0.01 - 0.0167 \\ B &= -0.0067 \text{ mho} \end{aligned} \tag{7-31}$$

The admittance is

$$Y = (G^2 + B^2)^{1/2}$$
$$Y = ((0.0067)^2 + (0.0067)^2)^{1/2} \tag{7-32}$$
$$Y = 0.0095 \text{ mho}$$

The impedance, therefore, is found from

$$Z = 1/Y$$
$$Z = 1/(0.0095) \tag{7-33}$$
$$Z = 105 \text{ mhos}$$

This method of analysis may also be applied to circuits such as that in Figure 7.7. This type of circuit is more nearly like the circuits actually encountered in real-life electronics work.

To find the impedance of such a circuit we must first find the admittance. In this type of circuit we use a formula derived from our basic definitions. Recall that $G = 1/R$ and that $R = E/I$. This also means that $G = I/E$. In ac circuits $E = IZ$ and $I = E/Z$, so

$$G = I/E = I/IZ = (E/Z)/(IZ/1)$$
$$G = (1/IZ)(E/Z) \tag{7-34}$$
$$G = E/IZ^2$$

But $E = IR$, so

$$G = R/Z^2 \tag{7-35}$$

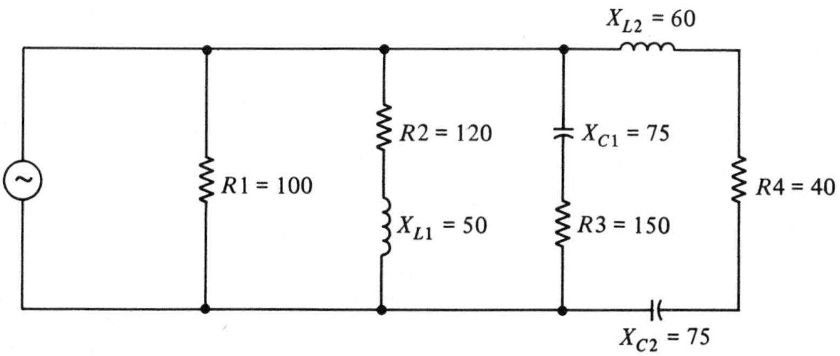

Figure 7.7 Find the impedance.

Equation (7-35) is the one needed to solve circuits such as that in Figure 7.7. A similar derivation gives us

$$B = X/Z^2 \text{ for admittance} \tag{7-36}$$

The first branch of the circuit is pure resistance, so its conductance is

$$G = 1/R1 = 1/100 = 0.01 \text{ mho} \tag{7-37}$$

In the second branch, two steps are required, because there is a reactance and a resistance. The impedance of the branch is

$$Z2 = ((120)^2 + (50)^2)^{1/2}$$

$$Z2 = 130\ \Omega$$

so

$$\begin{aligned} G2 &= 120/130^2 \\ G2 &= 0.007 \text{ mho} \\ B2 &= 50/130^2 \\ B2 &= 0.003 \text{ mho} \end{aligned} \tag{7-38}$$

For the third branch

$$Z3 = ((150)^2 + (75)^2)^{1/2}$$

$$Z3 = 168\ \Omega$$

so

$$\begin{aligned} G3 &= 150/168^2 \\ G3 &= 0.005 \text{ mho} \\ B3 &= 75/168^2 \\ B3 &= 0.003 \text{ mho} \end{aligned} \tag{7-39}$$

In the more complex fourth branch,

$$Z4 = ((40)^2 + (60 - 75)^2)^{1/2}$$

$$Z4 = 43\ \Omega$$

so

$$\begin{aligned} G4 &= 40/43^2 \\ G4 &= 0.022 \text{ mho} \\ B4 &= -15/43^2 \\ B4 &= -0.008 \text{ mho} \end{aligned} \tag{7-40}$$

The total admittance for the circuit of Figure 7.7 is

$$Y = ((G1 + G2 + G3 + G4)^2 + (B1 + B2 + B3 + B4)^2)^{1/2}$$

$$Y = ((0.01 + 0.007 + 0.005 + 0.022)^2 +$$

$$(0 + 0.003 + 0.003 - 0.008)^2 \qquad (7\text{-}41)$$

$$Y = ((0.044)^2 + (-0.002)^2)^{1/2}$$

$$Y = 0.0441 \text{ mho}$$

Impedance, then, is

$$Z = 1/Y \qquad (7\text{-}42)$$

$$Z = 1/0.0441$$

$$Z = 22.67\ \Omega$$

PROBLEMS

1. A series circuit has the following elements: $R = 100\ \Omega$, $X_L = 75\ \Omega$, and $X_c = 50\ \Omega$. Find the magnitude of the impedance.
2. Find the phase angle of the circuit in Question 1 (see Figure 7.8).
3. The circuit of the previous two questions is ____________.
4. Find the equivalent inductive reactance X_L.
5. If the circuit in Question 1 has 10 V impressed across it, what current will flow?
6. The voltage across the resistor will be ____________.
7. Find the voltage across the capacitor.
8. Find the voltage across the inductor.
9. Find the true power if $E = 100$ V, $Z = 100\ \Omega$, and the phase angle (θ) is 38 deg.
10. What is the power factor in Question 9?
11. Use j-operator notation for a circuit in which the resistance is 100 Ω, and the capacitive reactance is 75 Ω.
12. In a circuit we have $R = 500\ \Omega$, $X_c = 400\ \Omega$, and $X_L = 450\ \Omega$. Write j-operator notation for this circuit.
13. The reciprocal of reactance is ____________.
14. The mathematical description of susceptance is ____________.
15. The reciprocal of impedance is ____________.
16. Admittance is given by ____________.

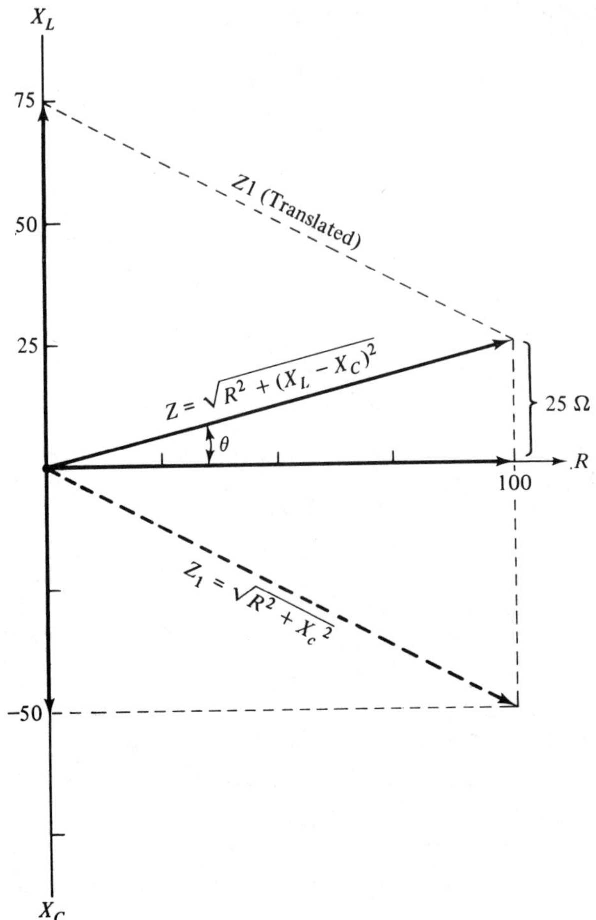
X_L
75
50
25
$Z1$ (Translated)
$Z = \sqrt{R^2 + (X_L - X_C)^2}$
θ
25 Ω
R
100
$Z_1 = \sqrt{R^2 + X_c^2}$
−50
X_C

Figure 7.8

8
Resonance and Resonant Circuits

8.1 RESONANCE

An ac network is said to be resonant at a particular frequency if, at that frequency, the inductive and capacitive reactances are equal. In that condition

$$X_L = X_c$$
$$2\pi f L = \frac{1}{2\pi f C} \tag{8-1}$$

From this relationship we can derive a formula for predicting the resonant frequency of an LC network.

$$\begin{aligned} (2\pi f L)(2\pi f C) &= 1 \\ 4\pi^2 f^2 LC &= 1 \\ f^2 &= 1/(4\pi^2 LC) \\ f &= 1/(2\pi(LC)^{1/2}) \end{aligned} \tag{8-2}$$

Consider the implications of resonance from the viewpoint of reactance vectors. In a series network consisting of an inductance and a capacitance, we know that the total reactance is equal to $(X_L - X_c)$. But at the resonant frequency where the reactances are numerically the same this quantity is equal to zero. Any voltage applied to that circuit will cause an infinite current to flow. Fortunately, all real circuit components and signal sources have resistance, and that tends to limit the current to some finite value. It frequently happens, however, that the finite value is still high enough to cause permanent damage to the coil. (See Figure 8.1.)

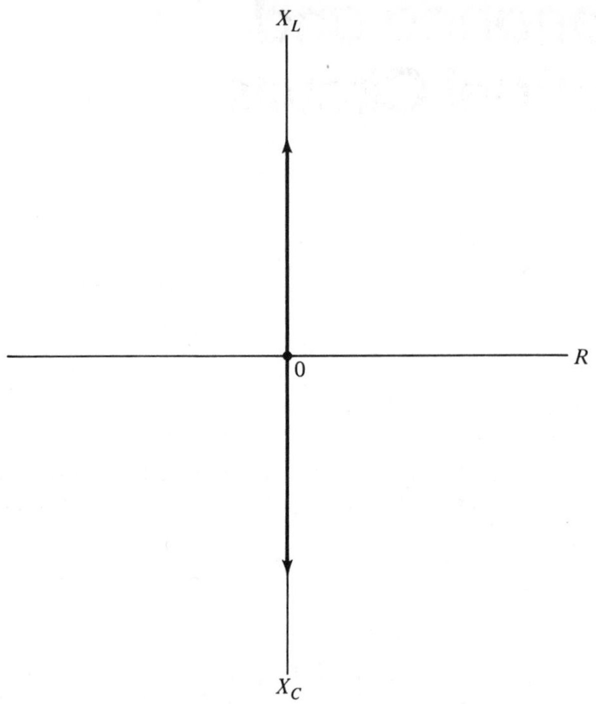

Figure 8.1 Resonance exists when the two types of reactance are equal.

Example. Calculate the resonant frequency of an LC circuit consisting of a 300-pF capacitor and a 100-μH coil.

Our formula is

$$f = \frac{1}{2\pi(LC)^{1/2}} \tag{8-3}$$

where f is the frequency in hertz.

L is the inductance in henrys.

C is the capacitance in farads.

so

$$f = \frac{1}{(2)(3.14)((1 \times 10^{-4})(3 \times 10^{-10}))^{1/2}} \tag{8-4}$$

$$f = 918{,}880 \text{ Hz}$$

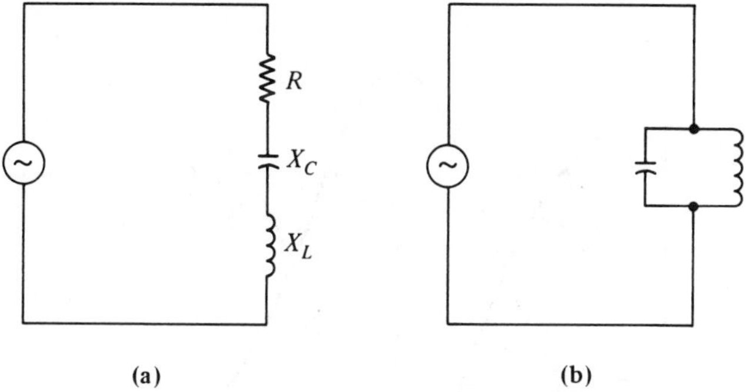

Figure 8.2 **(a)** Series-resonant circuit and **(b)** parallel resonant circuit.

8.2 SERIES AND PARALLEL RESONANT CIRCUITS

In Figure 8.2 we see examples of both series and parallel resonant circuits. Although their respective resonant frequencies can be computed from the same equation, they have properties and characteristics that are quite different.

In the series resonant circuit of Figure 8.2(a) the currents through all of the elements are equal and in phase with each other. The voltage drops, however, are out of phase. At resonance the impedance will reduce to

$$Z = (R^2)^{1/2} = R \tag{8-5}$$

because the term $(X_L - X_c)$ is equal to zero.

The impedance of a series resonant circuit varies with frequency in the manner of Figure 8.3, curve A. It will be at its minimum value when the generator frequency is the resonant frequency, and will increase as the frequency of the generator is varied away from the resonant frequency of the circuit. The voltage drops across the coil and the capacitor in a series-resonant circuit, even though their algebraic sum is zero, may be quite high. Their values are determined by $E = IX$.

In a parallel resonant circuit the voltages across the components are in phase, but the currents in the respective branches are out of phase. On one half of the ac cycle the magnetic field across the coil builds up and then collapses, only to repeat itself on the next alternation. This causes a current to be induced into the circuit by the CEMF cutting the coil. The resultant current is used to charge the capacitor. When the polarity reverses, the charge stored in the capacitor discharges through the coil, thereby reinforcing the magnetic field. This process continues and creates an oscillatory process that stores energy alternately in the magnetic field

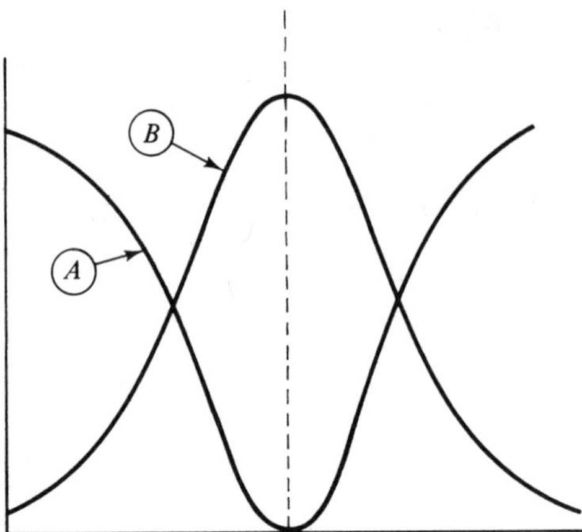

Figure 8.3 (a) Impedance in a series-resonant circuit and (b) impedance in a parallel resonant circuit.

of the inductor and then in the electrostatic field of the capacitor. In an ideal "tank circuit" (another name for LC resonant circuits), this process would continue indefinitely. In fact, one should be able to disconnect the generator altogether once the oscillatory current is established, and electrons should continue to flow. This property of tank circuits is called the "flywheel effect." Unfortunately, this form—like all other forms—of perpetual motion is impossible. The oscillatory current of the tank circuit sees a resistance in the coil wires of the inductor and in the conductors making the connection to the capacitor. Resistance creates I^2R losses, and they tend to dampen the oscillation, causing each successive cycle to be smaller than the preceding cycle. After a few oscillations the amplitude has reduced to zero, and the current ceases to flow.

One property of parallel resonance that differs markedly from the series resonant tank is the behavior of the impedance. In an ideal, resistanceless, tank the current is 180 deg (the sum of two 90-deg phase shifts) out of phase with the current from the generator. This means that the algebraic sum of the tank and generator currents is precisely zero. An ammeter placed in series between the generator output and the tank circuit will read 0 A. The impedance of the perfect parallel resonant tank is

$$Z = E/I$$
$$Z = \mathrm{E/O} \tag{8-6}$$
$$Z = \infty$$

In real tank circuits the impedance at resonance (curve B in Figure 8.3) is very high. As the generator is tuned away from resonance, the cancellation of the generator line current by the tank current is less complete until, at points well removed from resonance, there is no appreciable cancellation at all.

Approximate calculations in parallel resonant circuits can be performed by using the formula.

$$Z_p = \frac{X_L X_c}{X_L - X_c} \tag{8-7}$$

This formula works only if the dc resistance is very small compared with the magnitude of the reactances. In circuits that have an appreciable resistive component

$$Z_p = \frac{1}{R^2 + (X_L - X_c)^2} \tag{8-8}$$

8.3 DECIBELS

The "bel" and "decibel" (1/10-bel) are often used to represent the ratio between two power levels, two voltages, or two currents. The decibel is often used in electronic communications work because it offers more convenient numbers to manipulate.

The full elegance of decibel notation is realized when one is computing gains and losses in electronic systems. The decibel gives us a single number by which a ratio between two numbers is realized. For power, the decibel is given by

$$\text{dB} = 10 \log_{10} \frac{P1}{P2} \tag{8-9}$$

where P1 is one power level.
$P2$ is the second power level.
Both power levels must be expressed in the same units (i.e., watts, milliwatts, or microwatts).

For voltage and current ratios

$$\text{dB} = 20 \log_{10} \frac{E1}{E2} \tag{8-10}$$

and

$$\text{dB} = 20 \log_{10} \frac{I1}{I2} \tag{8-11}$$

Example. A certain amplifier requires a driving power of 0.5 W at its input to produce an output level of 100 W. What is the gain of this amplifier expressed in decibels?

$$\begin{aligned} dB &= 10 \log_{10} (100/0.5) \\ dB &= 10 \log_{10} (200) \qquad (8\text{-}12) \\ dB &= 23 \text{ dB} \end{aligned}$$

Example. The potential applied to the input of a certain passive network is 50 V. At the output, however, only 5 V is measured. What is the gain of this circuit, expressed in decibels?

$$\begin{aligned} dB &= 20 \log_{10} (5/50) \\ dB &= 20 \log (0.1) \qquad (8\text{-}13) \\ dB &= -20 \text{ dB} \end{aligned}$$

Note that a negative gain (−20 dB) is the same as a loss. In this case a loss of ten is expressed as −20 dB.

Sometimes we see special decibel notation in which an arbitrary, or seemingly so, reference is chosen. These are often specified under certain conditions that are relevant for some particular application. For example, signal levels in radio circuits are often expressed in "dBm," which means power decibels referenced to 1 mW developed in a 50-Ω load. Also used in some cases is the dBmV, which is the voltage notation used in certain TV receiver antenna systems. 0 dBmV is 1 mV across a 75-Ω load. This is also quoted as 1000 μV across 75 Ω, but that is the same thing.

Example. A signal level of +14 dBm in a 50-Ω load represents a power level of

$$14 = 10 \log_{10} \frac{P1}{0.001} \qquad (8\text{-}14)$$

$$1.4 = \log_{10} (P1/0.001)$$

Antilog 1.4 = 25, so

$$\begin{aligned} 25 &= P1/0.001 \\ P1 &= (0.001)(25) \qquad (8\text{-}15) \\ P1 &= 0.025 \text{ W} \end{aligned}$$

Table 8.1

Power Ratio	Decibel Equivalent	Voltage or Current Ratio	Decibel Equivalent
2:1	3 dB	2:1	6 dB
10:1	10 dB	10:1	20 dB
100:1	20 dB	100:1	40 dB
1000:1	30 dB	1000:1	60 dB
$0.707 = 1:(2)^{1/2}$	−1.5 dB	$0.707 = 1:(2)^{1/2}$	−3 dB

There are a number of common power and voltage ratios that show up frequently enough to warrant memorization. These are given in Table 8.1.

8.4 Q AND BANDWIDTH

Ideally, a tank circuit will react only to signals at its resonant frequency, and will reject all others. In Figure 8.3, however, we see the actual situation that exists with regard to real tank circuits. In both types of tank circuit the curves have a certain slope which is a function of circuit Q—figure of merit. Q is given by

$$Q = \frac{X_L}{R} \text{ or } \frac{X_c}{R'} \qquad (8\text{-}16)$$

and this is a means for judging and comparing coils, capacitors, and tank circuits. Q is inversely proportional to the series resistance of either the coil or the capacitor. It is usually the coil that has the poorest Q, so it will determine the Q of the tank circuit.

At high frequencies Q will decrease even further because of "skin effect." In ac circuits, current does not flow through the entire cross-sectional area of the conductor but, instead, tends to flow only on the surface of the wire. Skin effect is zero at dc and increases with frequency. Since skin effect has the tendency to reduce the effective area of the conductor, it increases actual resistance, thereby decreasing the Q.

Figure 8.4 shows the dependence of bandwidth on tank Q. When Q is very high the sides of the curve are steep, and only those frequencies very close to resonance are affected by the tank. As Q drops, however, the amplitude of the voltage developed (or if a series circuit, the current) drops and an increased number of frequencies adjacent to resonance are affected. The "bandwidth" of a tank circuit represents the group of frequencies around resonance that develops similar voltages in a parallel tank

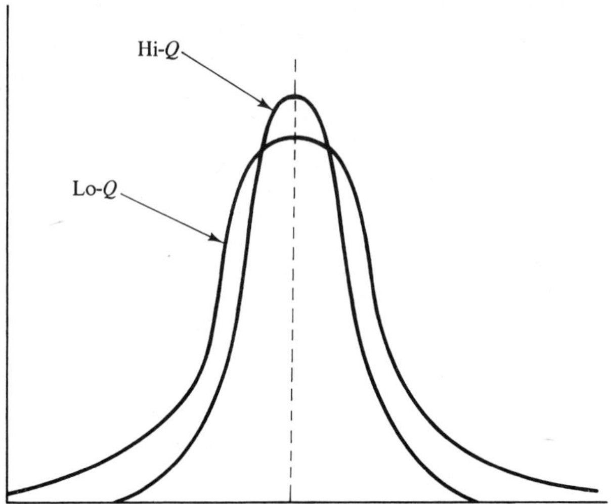

Figure 8.4 High-Q and low-Q produces different bandpass curves.

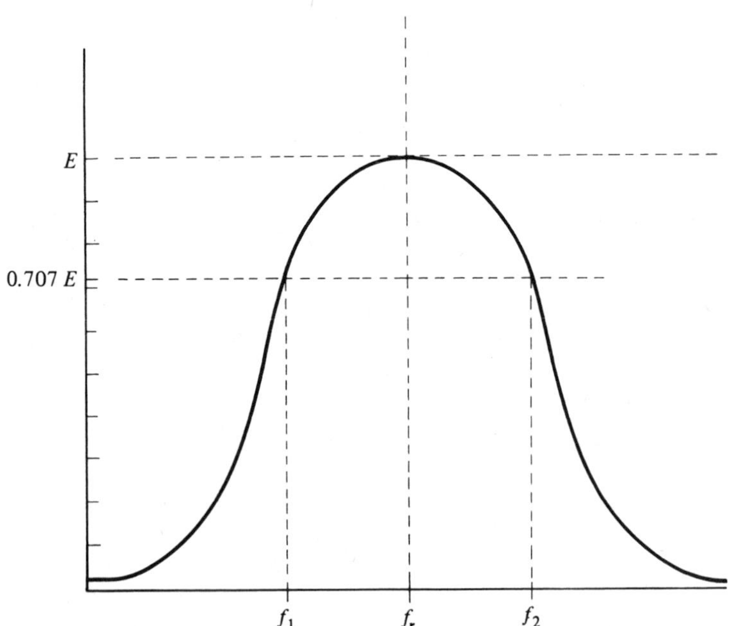

Figure 8.5 Bandwidth is measured between half-power points.

or currents in a series tank. If we want to have some meaningful expression for bandwidth, we must establish conventions as to cutoff points, as in Figure 8.5. Normally, the bandwidth is taken as $(f2 - f1)$, where $f1$ and $f2$ are the frequencies at which the voltage across the tank drops to 0.707 of its value at resonance. Another way of saying this is that the voltage is 3 dB down, or the "half-power points."

$$\text{B.W.} = \frac{F_r}{Q} \tag{8-17}$$

where B.W. is the bandwidth of the tank in hertz, and represents $f2 - f1$.
F_r is the frequency of resonance.

Example. An LC tank circuit is resonant at 3000 kHz, and has a 20-kHz bandwidth. What is the Q?

$$Q = F_r/\text{B.W.} = 3000/20 = 150 \tag{8-18}$$

8.5 TUNED TRANSFORMERS

Figure 8.6 shows a tuned transformer in which the primary is nonresonant, but the secondary is tuned to some specific frequency. As the frequency of the ac generator is varied we shall note that no ac voltage appears across the secondary until the resonant frequency is approached. This type of

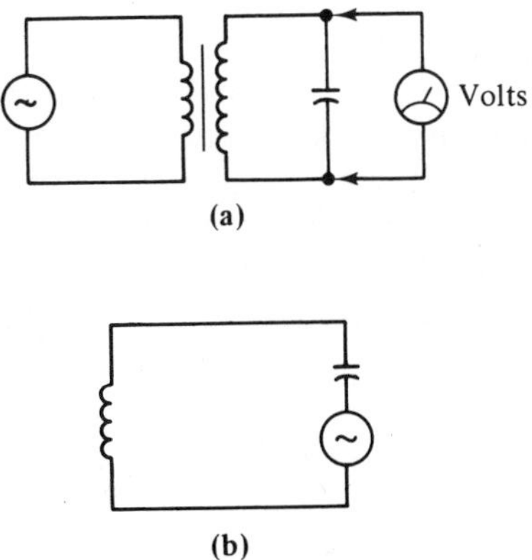

Figure 8.6 Tuned transformer appears to be parallel resonant (a) but is actually a series-resonant (b) circuit.

circuit may appear, on first glance, to be parallel resonant; in actuality it is series-resonant. A true parallel resonant tank must have the voltage source impressed across both L and C elements simultaneously. In this case, though, the voltage is induced across each turn of the coil, and that places the source effectively in series with the secondary inductor. This is shown more clearly in Figure 8.6(b).

Figure 8.7 shows another type of tuned transformer that has both primary and secondary tuned. In this case the primary is parallel resonant, while the secondary is series resonant as before. The response curve of the

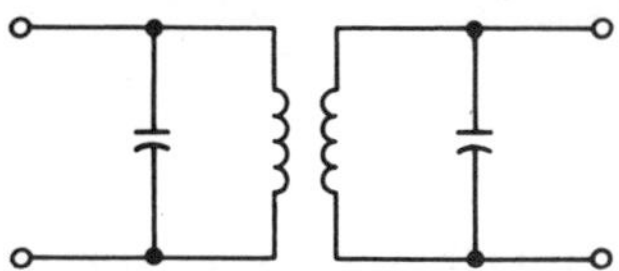

Figure 8.7 Transformer with both primary and secondary tuned.

transformer will resemble those of Figure 8.8, provided that both tanks are resonant at the same frequency. If coupling between the primary and secondary is loose, that is, if only a small fraction of the primary flux cuts the secondary, response bandwidth is narrow. This is the curve in Figure 8.8(a). As coupling is tightened, the response begins to broaden. When it is extremely tight [Figure 8.8(c)], there is a dip in circulating current right at the point of resonance. This type of circuit produces a double-humped response curve that has a dip at resonance. A double-tuned transformer will exhibit a response curve such as that in Figure 8.8(b) at the point where "critical" coupling has been reached. Critical coupling is the amount of coupling immediately before the point where the dip would appear.

The degree of coupling can be used to control the bandwidth of a tuned tank circuit. If it is necessary to reject signals relatively close to the resonant frequency, we can use a transformer that is loosely coupled. If, on the other hand, we want to pass a relatively broad group of frequencies close to resonance we can select a degree of coupling appropriate to the required bandwidth. In certain FM broadcast receivers, for example, it is necessary to pass a band of frequencies from (F_r − 100 kHz) to (F_r + 100 kHz). In that case we would use over-critically coupled transformers.

8.6 SIMPLE FILTERS

A filter is a circuit designed to either stop, or pass, a certain group, or band, of frequencies. The tuned transformers of the previous section are examples of a particular class of simple filters, because they pass only those frequencies close to the resonant point. (See Figure 8.9.)

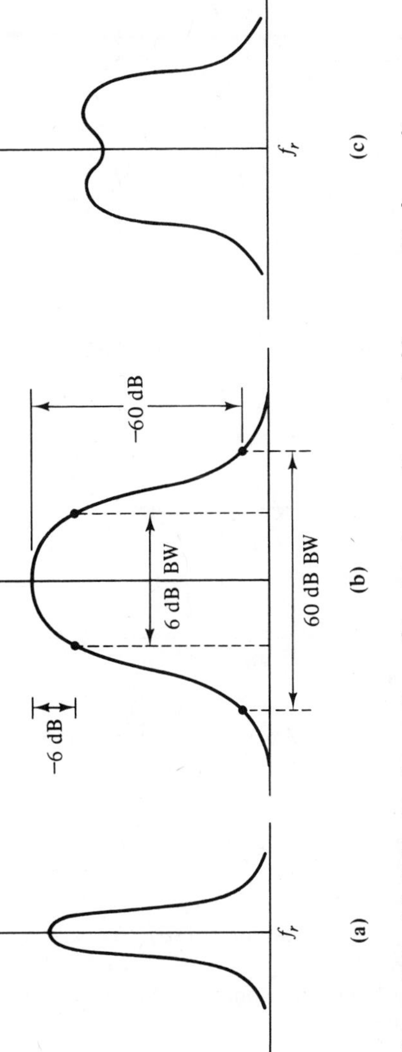

Figure 8.8 **(a) Sub-critical coupling, (b) critical coupling and (c) over-critical coupling.**

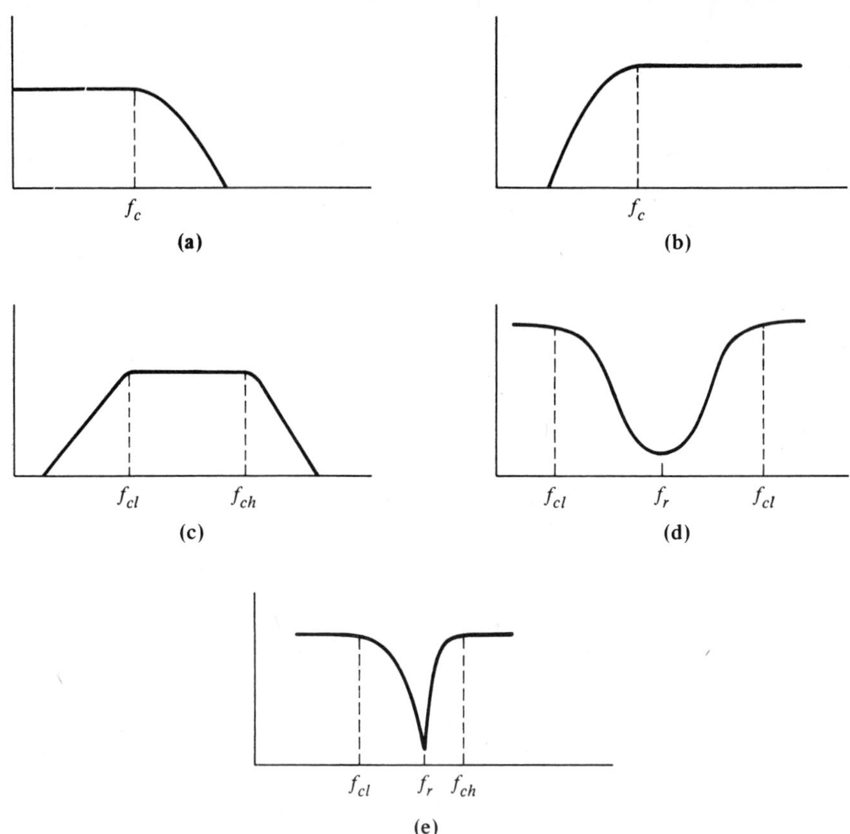

Figure 8.9 Filter response characteristics: **(a)** low pass, **(b)** high pass, **(c)** bandpass, **(d)** band reject and **(e)** notch.

In general, there are several basic classes of elementary frequency sensitive filter:

1. *Low pass.* These will pass only those frequencies lower than a certain cutoff frequency (f_o).
2. *High pass.* These will pass only those frequencies higher than a certain cutoff frequency (f_o).
3. *Bandpass.* Will pass only those frequencies that are between a high and low cutoff frequency.
4. *Bandstop.* This filter will pass all frequencies except those that lie between the high and low cutoff frequencies.

Figure 8.10 shows a simple low-pass filter of the "constant-*k*" family. It gets its name from the fact that the product $X_L X_c$ is always a constant, regardless of frequency. The series inductor has a reactance that increases as frequency increases. This causes it to attenuate the higher frequencies more than it does the low frequencies. In parallel, across the line, is a capacitor. Capacitive reactance, of course, drops with increasing frequency. Since it is shunted across the line, it offers little attenuation to frequencies less than the cutoff frequency, but considerable attenuation to higher frequencies. The component values for the low-pass filter of Figure 8.10 can be approximated from

$$L = \frac{2R}{\omega_c}$$
$$C = \frac{2}{\omega_c R} \qquad (8\text{-}19)$$

where R is the source and load resistances—they must be equal for these simplified formulas to work.
L is the inductance in henrys.
C is the capacitance in farads.
ω_c is the quantity $2\,\pi f_c$ (cutoff frequency).

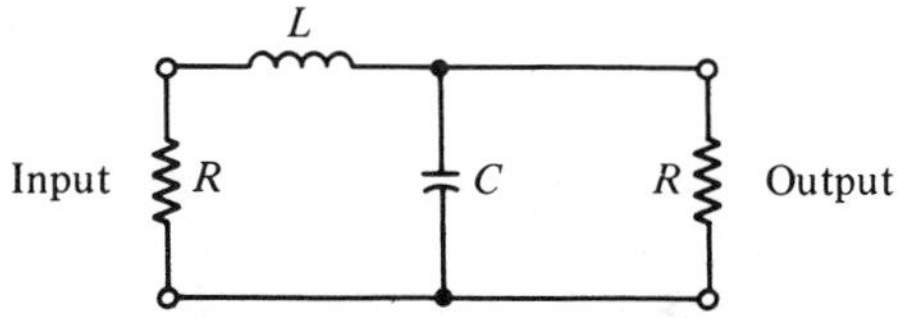

L
Input R C R Output

Figure 8.10 **Constant-*k* low pass filter.**

Exactly the opposite circuit is used in Figure 8.11 to form a high-pass filter, also of the constant-*k* variety. In this case the capacitor is in series with the signal path, and the inductor is in shunt. The cutoff frequency *LC* values are found approximately by

$$L = \frac{R}{2\omega_c}$$
$$C = \frac{1}{2\omega_c R} \qquad (8\text{-}20)$$

where the symbols have the same meaning as before.

The steepness of the cutoff slope is sometimes important in specifying filter properties. If, for instance, there is a strong local signal just above the cutoff frequency, f_c, and that signal must be attenuated, then response

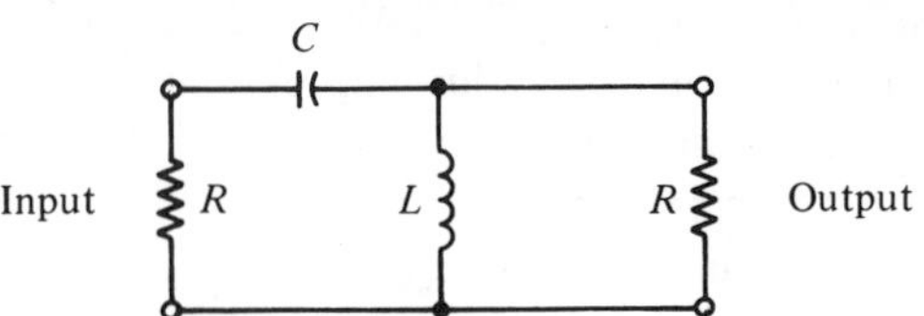

Figure 8.11 Constant-*k* high pass filter.

curves with steep sides are needed. Use of high-Q components and multiple filter sections increases the slope of the sides.

So far, all of our filter examples have been unbalanced with respect to ground, so as to keep our discussion simple. In many cases, however, a balanced filter is needed. An example of a balanced constant-k filter is shown in Figure 8.12.

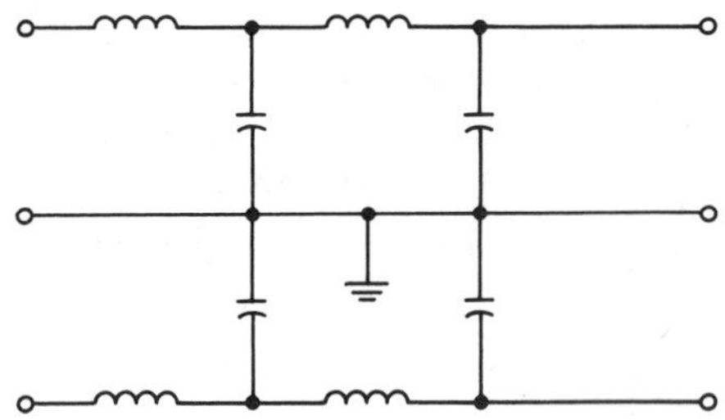

Figure 8.12 Balanced constant-*k* filter.

If sharp cutoff is required, or where a particular frequency must be nulled, in addition to low- or high-pass properties, then an "m-derived" filter (see Figure 8.13) would be used. In the low-pass, *m*-derived filter of

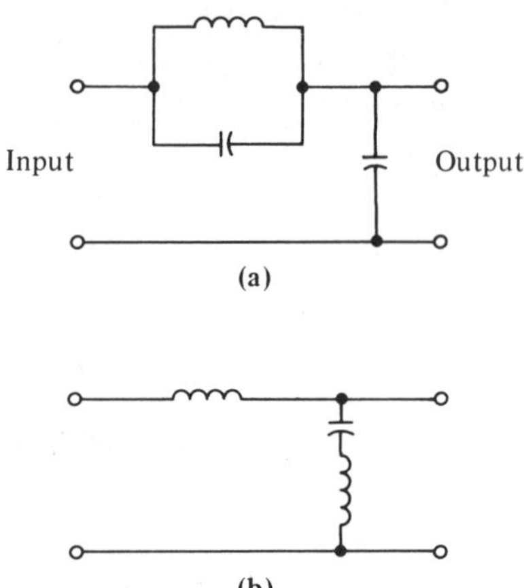

Figure 8.13 *M*-derived filters.

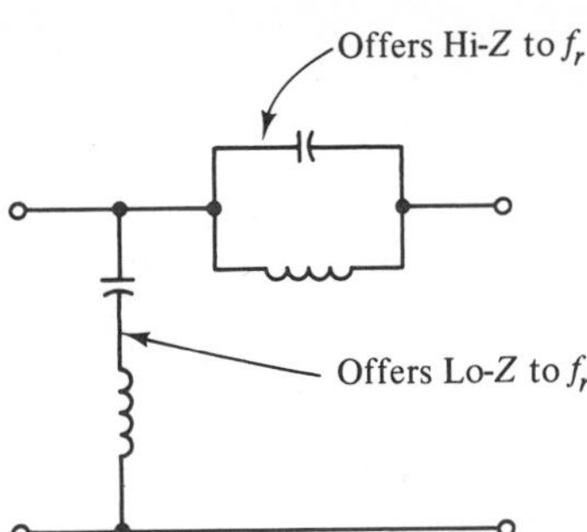

Figure 8.14 Wavetrap.

Figure 8.13, a parallel resonant trap prevents transmission of its resonant frequency. In the formation of high-pass designs it is merely necessary to reverse the roles of the respective components.

Filters that pass only a certain limited band of frequencies can become quite complex above the level of the simple tuned transformer. The *shape factor* of a bandpass filter is the ratio of the bandwidth at −6 dB from center frequency, to the bandwidth at −60 dB down from center frequency.

Simple bandstop filters, or wavetraps, are formed by shunting series tank circuits across a signal line, or by placing parallel resonant tanks in series with the line. Figure 8.14 shows an example of a wavetrap that uses both techniques to provide high attenuation of the undesired frequency.

Real filters tend to be a little more complex than the simple filters presented here. Most will at least have more than a single section, and can be classified according to form. For examples, see Figure 8.15.

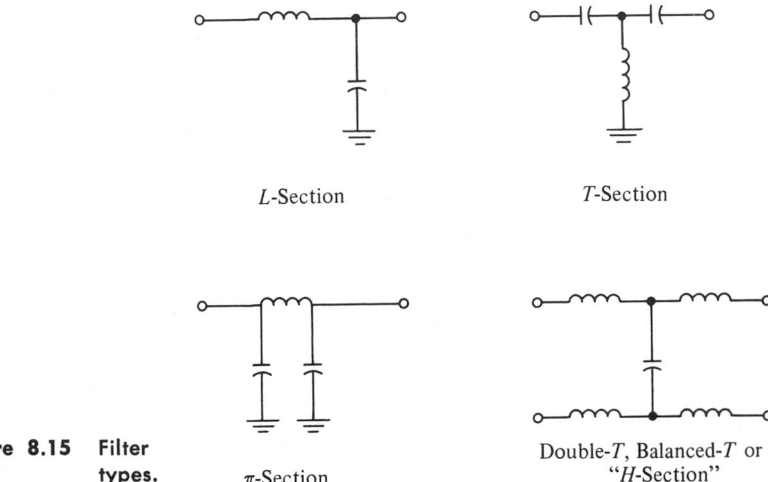

Figure 8.15 Filter types.

PROBLEMS

1. Resonance is a condition in which ________.
2. What is the resonant frequency of a parallel combination consisting of a 100-mH inductor, and a 560-pF capacitor?
3. What is the resonant frequency of a combination consisting of $L = 50$ μH, and $C = 100$ pF?
4. What are the impedance and phase angle of a series circuit in which $R = 1$ k, $X_c = 10$ k, and $X_L = 10$ k?
5. The curve marked A in Fig. 8.16 is for ________ resonant circuits.
6. The peak of curve A would be ________ if $R =$ infinity.
7. Curve B in Fig. 8.16 is for ________ resonant circuits.
8. The line current to a series resonant circuit is ________ at F_r.
9. A generator connected across a parallel resonant circuit is tuned across the band from below to above the resonant frequency, while line current readings are taken. The current at the resonant frequency is ________.
10. If the test of Question 9 were made while the line voltage was monitored, what would the voltage be at the resonant frequency?
11. Assume a parallel resonant tank circuit in which there is no appreciable resistance ($R = 0$). What is the impedance at a frequency near resonance where $X_c = 500\ \Omega$ and $X_L = 525\ \Omega$?
12. What is the gain, expressed in decibels, of a circuit in which the power output is 1000 W, and the input power is 5 W?
13. What loss exists if the input is 500 W and the output is 50 W?

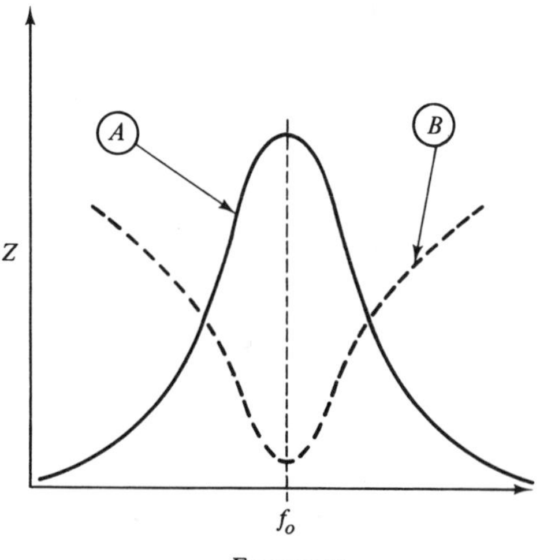

Figure 8.16

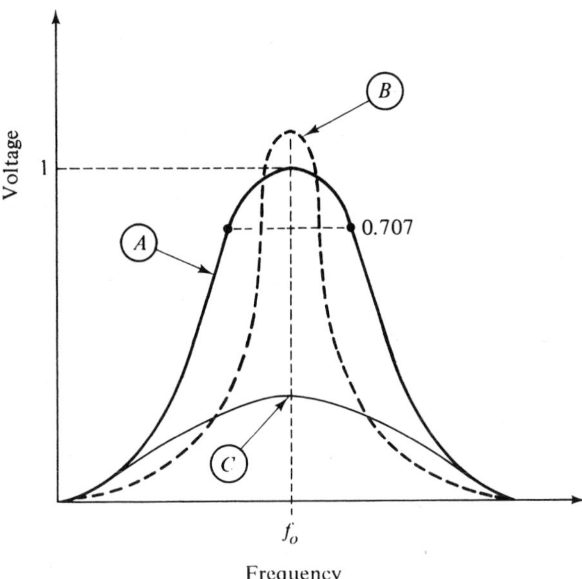

Figure 8.17

14. What is the voltage gain if $E_{in} = 100$ mV and $E_{out} = 10$ V?
15. Express the above answer in decibels.
16. What is the equation for decibel notation of current ratios?
17. O dBm refers to a power level of ________ in a 50 Ω load.
18. What power level is equivalent to −20 dBm?
19. A 2:1 power ratio represents ________ dB.
20. A 10:1 voltage ratio represents ________ dB.
21. A low-Q curve is ________ in Fig. 8.17.
22. A high-Q curve is ________ in Fig. 8.17.
23. A medium-Q curve is ________ in Fig. 8.17.
24. The point on curve A marked "0.707" is ________ dB down from the peak.
25. The Q is also called the ________.
26. Find the Q if $X_L = 2000$ Ω and $R = 100$ Ω.
27. Find the bandwidth of a 10-mHz tank circuit if the Q is 500.
28. Find the Q if the bandwidth of a 455-kHz tank circuit is 25 kHz.
29. Find the Q if the center frequency of a tank circuit is 1 mHz and the bandwidth is 5 kHz.
30. A notch filter rejects ________.
31. A bandpass filter rejects ________.

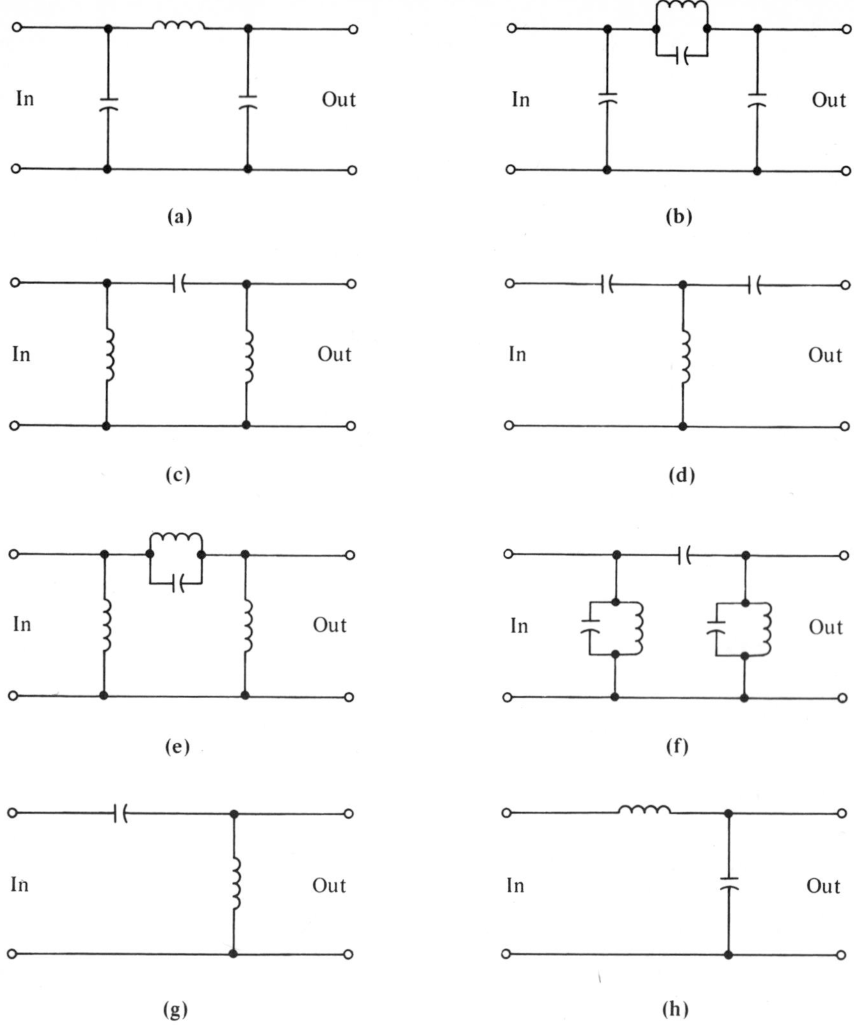

Figure 8.18

32. A low-pass filter rejects ________.

33. A high-pass filter rejects ________.

34. The circuit in Fig. 8.18(a) is a ________.

35. The circuit in Fig. 8.18(b) is a ________.

36. The circuit in Fig. 8.18(c) is a ________.

37. The circuit in Fig. 8.18(d) is a ________.

38. The circuit in Fig. 8.18(e) is a ________.

39. The circuit in Fig. 8.18(f) is a ________.

40. The circuit in Fig. 8.18(g) is a ________.
41. The circuit in Fig. 8.18(h) is a ________.
42. In a constant-*k* filter the product ________ is always constant.
43. The parallel resonant trap of the *m*-derived filters ________ F_r.
44. ________ sides are a characteristic of the *m*-derived filter.
45. Bandstop filters are also called ________.
46. The shape factor is the ratio of the filter ________ at dB and 60 dB down from F_r.

9
Vacuum Tubes

9.1 VACUUM TUBE BASICS

Vacuum tube amplifiers have been with us for many decades. From around the turn of the present century until only a few years ago, "electronics"—as opposed to "electricity"—meant vacuum tube circuits. Since the transistor and related semiconductor devices have come of age, however, the vacuum tube has slowly faded into the background so much that many electronics people who receive their training in current technical schools will not study the vacuum tube. This chapter is included because there is a large amount of electronic communications equipment still in service that uses vacuum tube technology. Most designers of electronic equipment in the past have tended to be a little conservative with new technology. In fact, one rather well-known electrical engineering professor—who is professionally as up to date as tomorrow's newspaper—makes the claim that "state of the art" and "unreliable" are synonyms. Electronic design engineers did not take to the transistor as quickly as they might have. Even after the problems of the early devices were, for the most part, solved many designers used them haltingly, in "hybrid" designs consisting of both tubes and transistors. Much of the communications equipment manufactured in the mid- to late 1960s was of the hybrid variety. Even though it is now more than a decade later, much of that equipment is still in at least occasional use.

If engineers of ten years ago seemed a little slow to appreciate the transistor, the designers in their grandfathers' youth were excited about the introduction of vacuum tubes—if they could make the darn things work with anything like reliability. Even though the tubes presented demonstrable advantages over existing equipment, they were not too reliable in the early days. The amplifying vacuum tube was invented by American Lee DeForest in the early years of this century. Certain vacuum tube principles were, however, known in the latter part of the previous century.

Edison Effect. When Thomas Alva Edison was conducting some of his many electric lamp experiments in the last quarter of the nineteenth century, he observed and recorded a number of interesting phenomena. One of these, which bears his name, is the "Edison effect." This was noted, or discovered if you prefer, during experiments that were designed to eliminate, or at least reduce, the blackening of the insides of Edison's electric lamps. One method that was tried involved placing an extra electrode inside of the lamp's glass bulb along with the filament. Edison noted a small current flow to that electrode whenever a positive potential was applied to it. Since a positive potential attracts electrons, we may assume that a source of free electrons must somehow be connected with the glowing filament.

Thermionic Emission of Electrons. The source of the free electrons inside of a lamp is the electrically heated wire. When an electric current is passed through a conductor, a certain amount of heat is generated. In the case of the lamp filament this heating is so intense that red-to-white light is given off. The color of the light is dependent upon the filament's temperature, which, in turn, is dependent upon the current flowing.

When an electrical conductor is heated, its free electrons take on additional kinetic energy. This follows, in fact, from one of the physical definitions of "temperature." Increased kinetic energy means that the velocity of the individual electrons is increased.

Imagine the situation inside such a metallic conductor. The free electrons will be moving rapidly, and in all directions. They will, of course, bump into each other, creating millions of collisions per second. Out of all of these helter-skelter electrons, a few, only a few percent actually, will have both the direction of travel and the velocity to escape when they are near the hot surface of the filament.

The electrons that escape from the filament surface form a *space charge* (see Figure 9.1) in the immediate vicinity of the filament. When Thomas Edison introduced a positively charged electrode into the glass envelope, it was the space charge electrons that were attracted to form the *Edision effect current.*

Thermionic emission of electrons is this same phenomenon, in which surface electrons boil off because of the conductor's being heated. Thermionic emission, then, is responsible for the current on which vacuum tube operation depends.

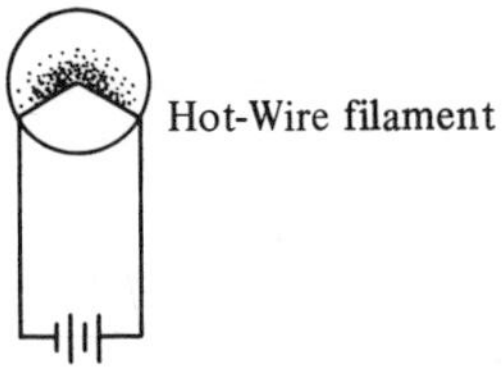

Hot-Wire filament

Figure 9.1 Thermionic emission from a hot wire in a vacuum.

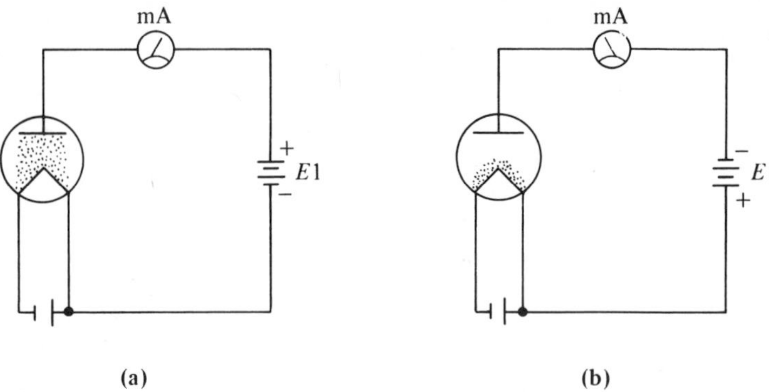

Figure 9.2 The Edison effect.

9.2 THE VACUUM TUBE DIODE

An Englishman named Fleming used the Edison effect to produce a diode (*di*—two, *ode*—electrode, or two-electrode tube) tube. Fleming's tube used an incandescent filament (one of the electrodes) as a source of thermionic electrons, and Edison's extra electrode as an electron collector. When positively biased with respect to the filament [as is Figure 9.2(a)], this "anode" will collect the space charge electrons, and a current will be registered on the milliammeter.

When battery $E1$ is reversed, however, the anode is negative with respect to the filament. This negative charge on the anode repels the negatively charged electrons, so they are driven back toward the filament. In this case, no current will be registered on the milliammeter—it will read zero.

This tells us that Fleming's diode will pass electrical current in only one direction. It may be a little difficult to see the usefulness of this at this point, but it proves to be among our more useful phenomena—more of that later.

The electrode that collects electrons is called the *anode* or *plate*. The electrode that emits electrons is called the *cathode*. In our simple example the cathode was an incandescent (i.e., "gives off light when heated") filament. This is an example of a *directly heated cathode*.

An indirectly heated cathode is shown in Figure 9.3. The physical construction is shown as a cut-away drawing in Figure 9.3(a), while the schematic symbol is shown in Figure 9.3(b).

Any cathode material will emit electrons when heated. From a theoretical point of view, it does not matter where the heat comes from. You could, for example, extend the cathode out of the glass vacuum tube envelope so that it may be heated with a cigarette lighter, but that is

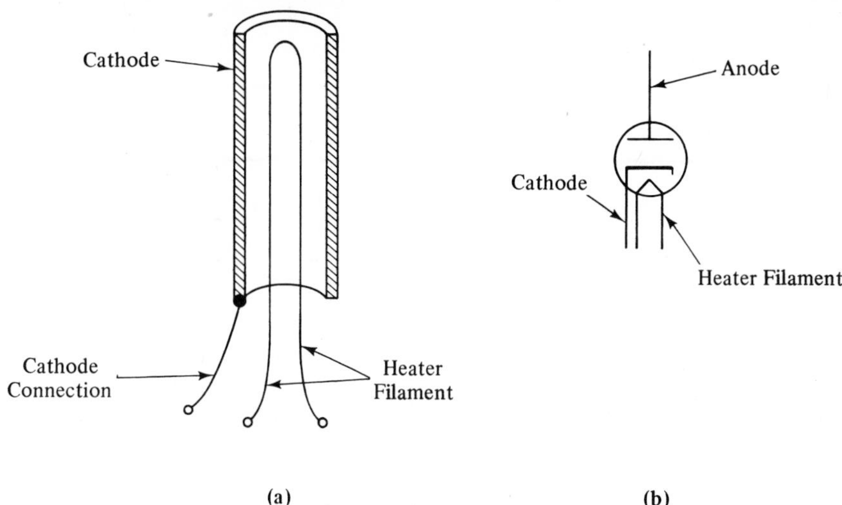

Figure 9.3 The indirectly heated cathode.

totally impractical. In real vacuum tubes the heat is generated by an electrical current in an incandescent filament. Keep in mind that the current in the filament is used solely to *heat* the cathode—it does not supply the anode electrons—any heat source would create the anode current from free electrons within the cathode material.

In Figure 9.3 we have the cathode heated indirectly from an incandescent filament. The actual cathode structure is a hollow cylinder of thoriated (i.e., coated with a thorium oxide) tungsten. Inside this structure is a filament not unlike those described earlier. It is the incandescence of this filament that causes the red-to-white hot glow inside the tube.

Diode Operation. Consider a circuit such as that in Figure 9.4(a). You may recognize this as being similar to Figure 9.2, except that supply voltage E_B is variable from 0 VDC to some positive potential. Figure 9.4(b) shows the anode current-vs-anode voltage curve for a typical diode. Note that the plate current is zero when the plate voltage is also zero. It is also true that plate current is zero when the potential on the plate is negative with respect to the cathode. Current will register on meter $M1$ only when E_B is positive with respect to the cathode.

Before proceeding further, let us consider some basic terminology. In the discussion of vacuum tube circuits several different voltages are mentioned with some regularity. These have been traditionally given letters to designate their usage. The *A* voltage is the filament supply. It typically ranges from about 1.5 V to over 100 V, but 6 V and 12 V are

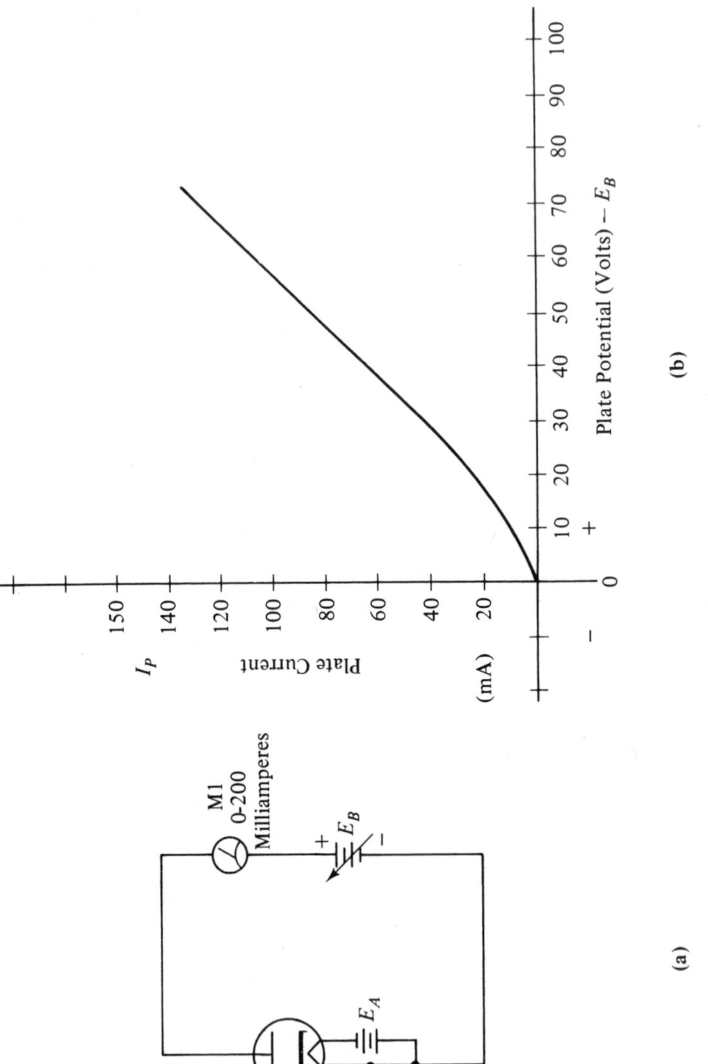

Figure 9.4 **(a)** Diode circuit with variable plate voltage and **(b)** diode characteristic curve.

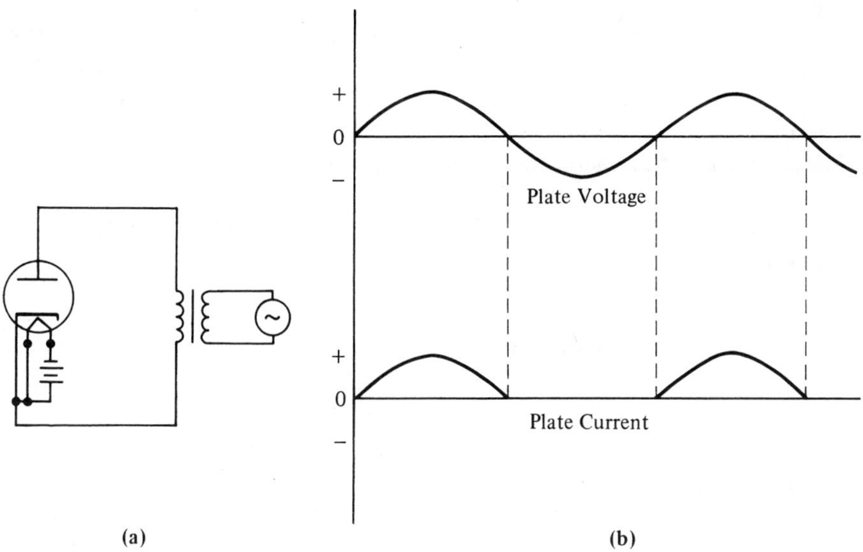

Figure 9.5 **(a)** The battery replaced by an ac source. **(b)** Plate current only flows when the plate voltage is positive.

probably the most common. The potential connected between the plate and cathode is usually called the *B* supply. It ranges from a low of around 12 V in car radios of the late 1950s to several kilovolts in high-powered transmitters. In a short while, we shall introduce another electrode, which is called a "grid." The voltage applied to the grid is usually designated the *C* supply.

The graph in Figure 9.4(b) is the relationship I_p vs E_B. In the upper ranges, this curve is what we might expect—it is a straight line. The *plate resistance* is the quantity

$$R_p = \frac{E_B}{I_p} \tag{9-1}$$

Notice, however, that the plate current is not linear in the low range—where plate voltage becomes low. At these potentials only those electrons which have the greatest kinetic energy will reach the plate. At slightly higher potentials electrons with lower kinetic energy levels will reach the plate. At about 25 Volts, however, all emitted electrons will reach the plate and the curve straightens out. In this region the diode is almost perfectly linear.

Figure 9.5 shows a diode that has the B battery replaced by a transformer and ac generator. The transformer is connected so that the secondary voltage is impressed across the diode's anode and cathode. The graph in Figure 9.5(b) shows the voltage that is applied to the anode—with respect to the cathode. Also shown is the plate current existing at these various plate voltages. Whenever the plate voltage is positive, plate current will flow. Also, note that the shape of the current curve is very nearly the same as that of the plate voltage.

On negative peaks of the ac voltage applied to the plate, on the other hand, no flow of current exists. This action follows from the diode's passing current in only one direction, and is called "rectification."

9.3 TRIODE VACUUM TUBES

The range of applications enjoyed by the diode is severely limited by the fact that the diode cannot amplify signals. One definition of amplification is the control of a large current or voltage by a much smaller current or voltage. Lee DeForest was the first to devise a practical amplifying vacuum tube. He did this neat trick by inserting a third element, called a *grid,* into the space between the cathode and anode of Fleming's diode. This new type of tube had three electrodes, or elements as they are sometimes called, so it is called a *triode.*

Figure 9.6(a) shows a triode vacuum tube. The grid is a control element, and is often called the *control grid.* It might be an actual mesh, or grid of fine wires, but is more often a wire that encircles the cathode. The grid may be viewed as an electrically porous element placed in the

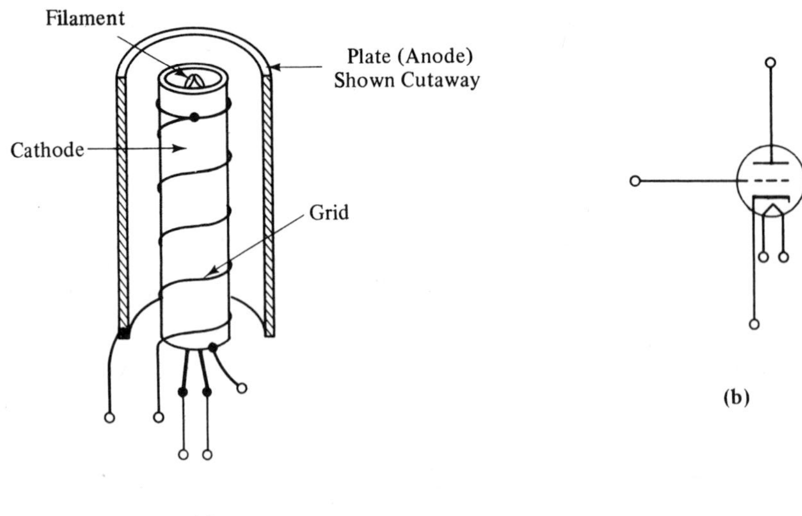

Figure 9.6 Triode construction.

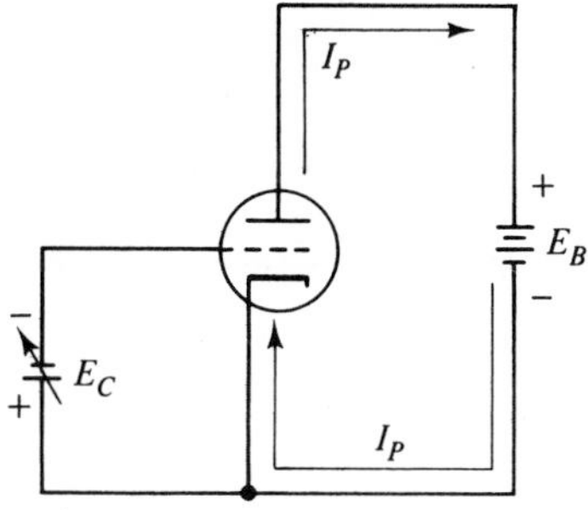

Figure 9.7 Triode circuit.

E_A Not Shown, but is Assumed to Exist

path of electrons flowing between the plate and the cathode. The proper schematic symbol is shown in Figure 9.6(b).

Let us assume, first, that no voltage is applied to this grid. In that case, electrons attracted to the high positive potential on the plate will pass right through spaces in the grid to strike the plate in the normal manner. Next, let us consider a case where the grid voltage E_c is *not* zero.

A triode in which $E_c \neq 0$ is shown in Figure 9.7. The grid, in this case, is negatively biased, so it will oppose the flow of negatively charged electrons from cathode to anode. At low negative values of grid voltage only a small retarding effect is apparent on the electron stream. As E_c becomes more negative, however, fewer and fewer electrons make it to the plate. At some particular value of E_c, no electrons will pass to the plate, and the triode is said to be cut off.

At $E_c = 0$, the triode tube acts very nearly like the diode discussed earlier. Positive values of E_c, however, will increase plate current to a point where the tube may well be destroyed.

Now let us consider how a triode is able to amplify. Recall that amplification means that we want to be able to control a large voltage with a smaller voltage. Study Figure 9.8. The circuit in Figure 9.8 shows a triode connected as a practical voltage amplifier. Resistor R_L is the *load,* and is used to develop the output signal voltage. Voltage E_c is the dc grid bias, while voltage E_g is the ac input signal voltage. The total voltage applied to the grid will be the algebraic sum of E_c and E_g.

If E_g is zero, then E_c is the total control over the plate current. The value of plate current I_p under this condition will be constant, and is a static current. Alternating current voltage E_g is in series with E_c, so it will either add or subtract its value to that of E_c, depending upon polarity. The voltage applied to the grid of $V1$, then, is $(-E_c \pm E_g)$.

The bias voltage creates a certain value of current I_p flowing in the

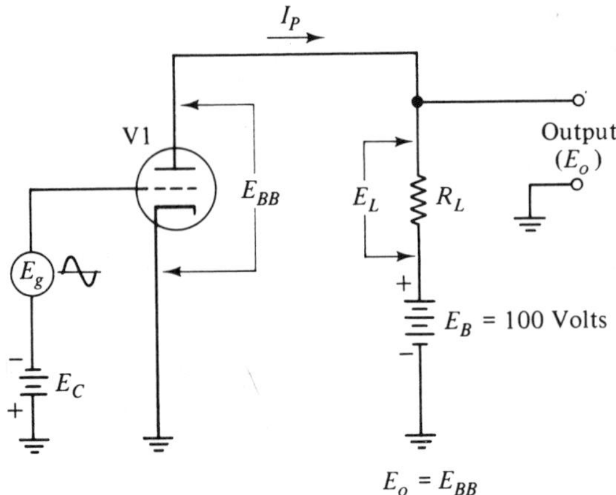

Figure 9.8 Voltage amplifier circuit.

plate circuit. This current also flows in the load resistor R_L, causing voltage drop E_L to appear across the load resistor. The actual voltage seen by the triode's plate-cathode circuit, then, will be something less than E_B. It will actually be

$$E_{BB} = E_B - E_L \tag{9-2}$$

Grid bias voltage E_c is set so that plate current I_p is in the middle of its straight-line portion. This is the region of *linear operation.*

If E_g is allowed to swing positive, then the total grid voltage will become less negative. Plate current I_p, then, must increase, thereby increasing E_L. Under this circumstance E_o and E_{BB} will decrease. This tells us that the signal voltage output waveform will be decreasing or "negative going."

Voltage E_o, then, becomes lower as E_g goes positive, and will become greater as E_g goes negative. Although the output waveform E_o is thus *inverted* (it is said to be 180 deg out of phase), it has the same shape and is much larger than E_g.

Voltage E_g can increase in a positive direction until either it exceeds $-E_c$, or until E_{BB} drops to zero. In the first case, if E_g overcomes $-E_c$ so much that the voltage applied to the grid is positive, then plate current I_p increases sharply. In that case, the shape of the output waveform no longer resembles the input waveform, and the output is said to be *distorted.*

Similarly, distortion also occurs if E_{BB} is allowed to drop to zero, before E_g reaches its positive peak. In that case the tube is said to be *saturated.* No further increase in grid voltage will cause an increase in plate current. In either case, the output will be distorted, and the amplifier

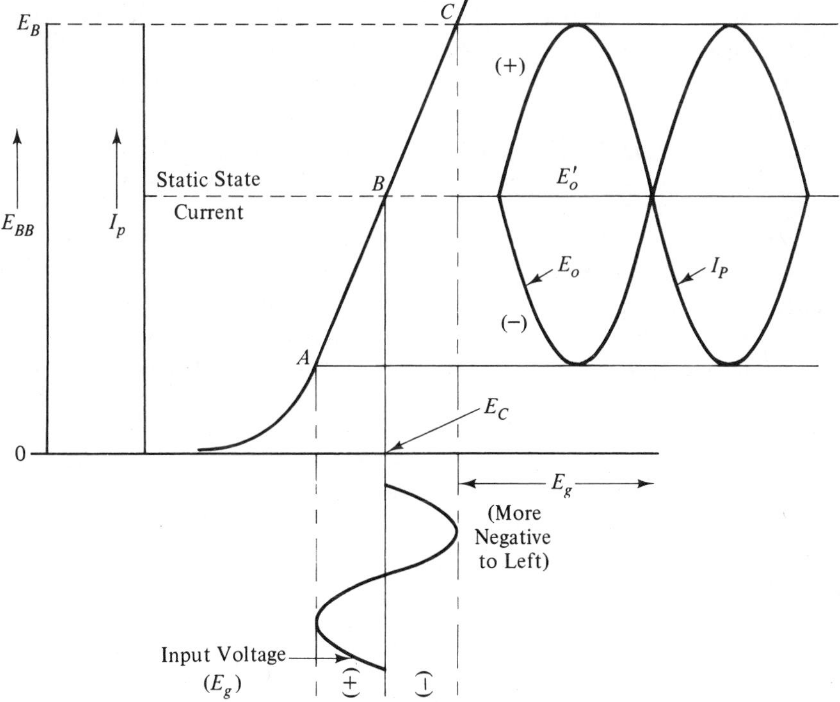

Figure 9.9 Characteristic curves.

is said to be operating in a *nonlinear* manner.

There are certain limitations and constraints placed on vacuum tube operation, especially if linearity—the absence of distortion—is a desirable factor. The value of the grid bias voltage E_c, for example, must be set so that it is approximately in the center of the linear, or "straight-line," portion of the characteristic curve (see Figure 9.9). The input voltage may be allowed to swing positive and negative only enough to prevent E_o from trying to exceed E_B—it can not, but when it tries, distortion results—or from dropping to a point where the curve is not linear. In either region distortion results and that is bad. These limitations make it highly desirable to keep the tube operating only between points *A* and *C* in Figure 9.9.

9.4 TETRODE VACUUM TUBES

High amplification in triodes requires the placement of the control grid very close to the cathode. This, unfortunately, produces a few problems. One is the fact that close proximity of the two electrodes increases the probability of their accidentally shorting together. It also tends to reduce the voltage level that may exist between them without arcing. Another of the problems is that it tends to increase interelectrode capacitance, thereby deteriorating the tube's performance at high frequencies. It must also be noted that close grid-cathode spacing requires much higher plate current.

These problems can be partially overcome by making the four-element, or "tetrode," vacuum tube. (See Figure 9.10.) In this design a second, but positively biased, grid is placed in the space between the control grid and the plate. The advantages of this construction include higher amplification at a given plate current and lower interelectrode capacitance.

In the normal tetrode, the plate and control grid voltages are much the same as they were in the triode. The plate is made positive with respect to the cathode, while the control grid is biased negative with respect to the control grid. The screen grid, placed between the control grid and the plate, is biased with a positive potential, but usually less so than the plate.

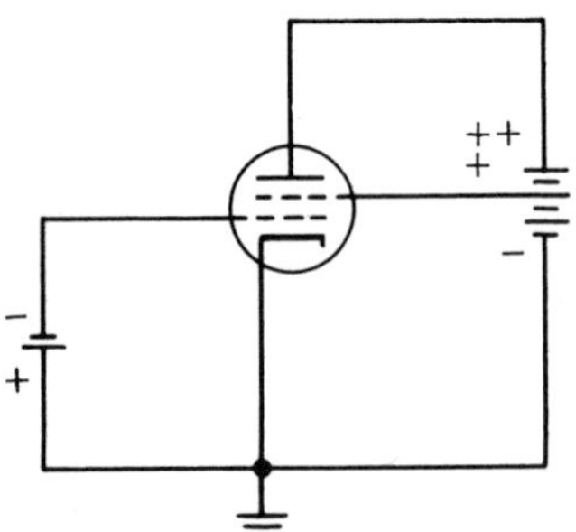

Figure 9.10 Tetrode vacuum tube.

9.5 PENTODE VACUUM TUBES

The five-element "pentode" vacuum tube was invented in response to certain limitations and problems in both triode and tetrode designs. It seems that electrons attracted to the plate are accelerated through quite a large potential, so they therefore acquire a large kinetic energy that is proportional to the combined effects of plate and screen grid potentials. This acceleration is even greater in tetrodes than in triodes, because of the positively charged screen grid. In fact, a common alternate name for the screen grid is "accelerator grid." (See Figure 9.11.) When electrons acquire sufficient kinetic energy, they are capable of striking the plate with such force that a few electrons in the plate material are dislodged into the space between the plate and the screen grid. This is called *secondary emission* of electrons. Some of these electrons have sufficient kinetic energy

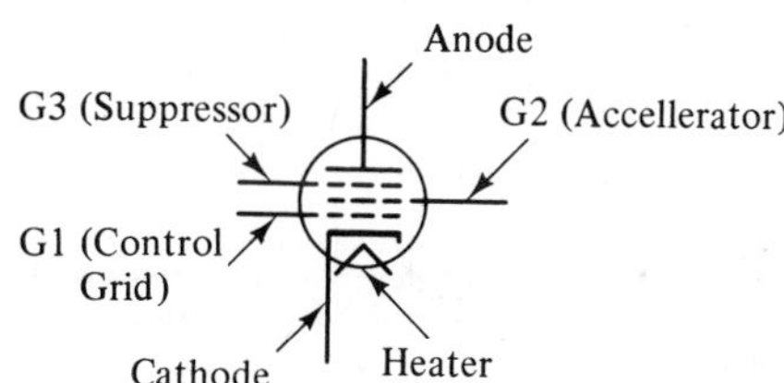

Figure 9.11 Pentode vacuum tube.

to be impelled into the region where they can be attracted by the positively charged screen grid. Of course, this constitutes a reverse current flow to the screen grid. Other electrons have less kinetic energy after emission from the plate, so they remain near the plate, and are attracted back to the plate by its positive potential. This creates a slight variation in plate current that is not caused by a corresponding variation in grid voltage. This is another form of distortion. In addition to the nonlinearity caused by secondary emission, there is also the possibility that the reverse screen current will cause the total screen current to exceed the ratings of the tube, thereby causing burnout of the device.

The problem of secondary emission is reduced in severity by placement of a grid electrode between the screen grid and the anode, and giving it a slight negative, or zero, bias. Electrons displaced by secondary emission are typically lower in kinetic energy than are the primary cathode electrons. The secondary electrons, then, can be repelled by a tiny voltage on the third grid (called a "suppressor grid"), and so are forced back to the plate. Primary electrons, on the other hand, have sufficient kinetic energy to overcome the weak negative field of the suppressor, so will continue on towards the plate.

The suppressor grid may be biased at either a zero potential, or it may be given some specific negative bias. In many circuits the suppressor grid is tied to the cathode, so it will have the same bias. In fact, there are many tubes in which the suppressor is tied to the cathode internally.

Several factors make the pentode desirable for a wide range of applications. One is the particularly high amplification factor evident in the pentode design. Most pentodes have amplification factors much higher than do triodes and tetrodes operated at similar plate potentials. This allows a great deal of voltage gain in a relatively small package. Another valuable benefit is the extremely low values of interelectrode capacitance present in pentodes. These are made lower by the fact that the control grid sees several capacitances effectively in series, and that makes the total capacitance lower. In many circuits the tube's interelectrode capacitance is so high as to require external circuitry to compensate for its effects. This is called *neutralization,* about which more will be said later. In many

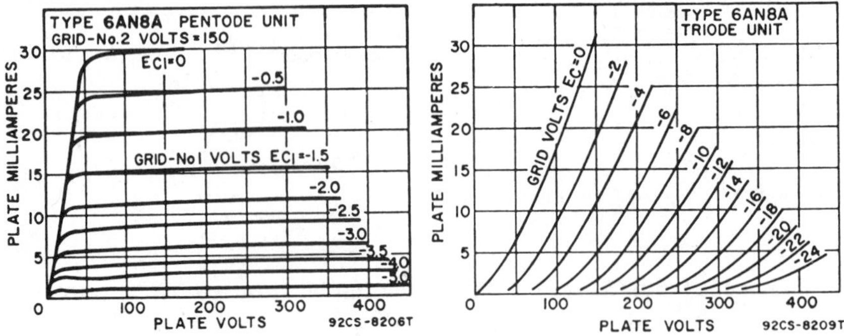

Figure 9.12 Family of characteristic curves for pentode and triodes.

circuits pentodes will operate satisfactorily without neutralization, whereas a triode or tetrode would not.

On the debit side, however, is the fact that the pentode plate resistance tends to be very high—values between 50 kΩ and 1MΩ are common. This makes the pentode a little more difficult to match, almost forcing the use of transformer or RC-coupling techniques.

Figure 9.12 shows two sets of vacuum tube characteristic curves from the type 6AN8A vacuum tube. This tube was selected for our example because it is actually a dual tube that has a triode and a pentode in the same glass envelope. This affords us the opportunity to study both types in a setting where we may more easily appreciate their respective differences.

Notice that each family of curves actually contains several characteristic curves for each tube. These are taken at different values of grid bias voltage. Note that the E_c values for the triode are much higher than those in the case of the pentode. This is a consequence of the lower gain factor for the triode.

If you examine the graph of plate current-vs-grid bias voltage it will be found that there are two types of pentode vacuum tube: remote cutoff and sharp cutoff.

The respective I_PE_B curves for these two varieties are shown in Figure 9.13. The sharp-cutoff pentode has a plate current characteristic that drops sharply to zero at some specific and relatively low value of negative grid bias. The other type of pentode is the remote-cutoff type, which is also sometimes called a "variable-mu" pentode. Notice that its plate current does not drop sharply to zero, but approaches zero in a more gradual manner. In general, it takes a very high negative bias voltage to force the plate current to zero in a remote-cutoff pentode.

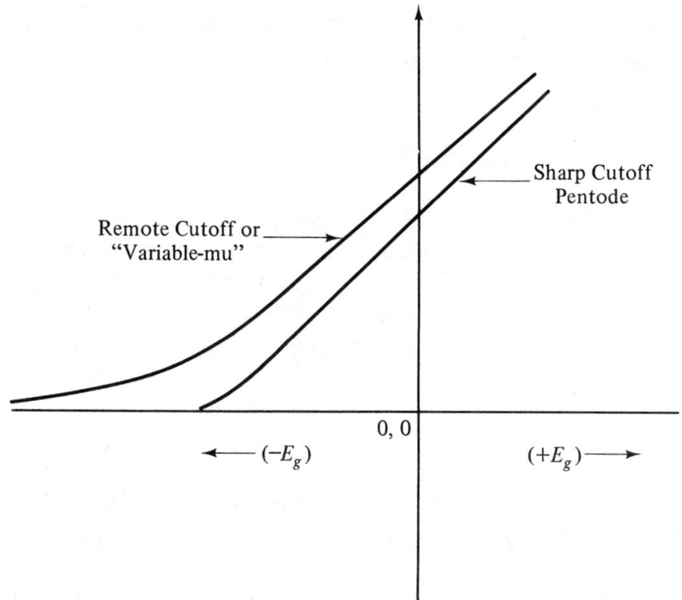

Figure 9.13 Curves of sharp and remote cutoff tubes.

9.6 BEAM POWER TUBES

According to one way of thinking, it is proper to call any large vacuum tube a "power tube." This is often justifiable because such tubes are quite able to handle large currents at high voltages; hence they are high power. There is, however, a distinct class of power tubes used in radio transmitters, and these are called "beam power tubes" after their internal structure.

Before we deal with the beam power construction, let us first consider some problems of power generation. The main limiting factor is heat. No vacuum tube, or any other device for that matter, is perfect—that is, nothing will be 100 percent efficient. The difference between the dc power consumed from the power supply and the signal power delivered to an external load is given up as heat in the plate structure of the tube. This is partially what causes the tube's glass envelope to heat up to an unbearable temperature after only a few moments of operation. The rest of the heat, incidentally, comes from the filament.

Example. A vacuum tube is operated in a low-power radio transmitter at a plate potential of 1000 V dc and a plate current of 200 mA (0.2 A).

If the transmitter delivers 150 W of RF signal power to a perfect antenna, how much power is dissipated as heat in the anode?

$$\begin{aligned}\text{Anode heat} &= (E_B \times I_p) - \text{power delivered to load}\\ &= (1000 \times 0.2) - 150 = 200 - 150 = 50\text{ W}\end{aligned}$$

The plate dissipation rating of a vacuum tube is the amount of heat, in watts, that the tube can dissipate in normal operation without damage. It must, however, be pointed out that this means *continuous* operation. Tubes are frequently operated in excess of their plate dissipation ratings for short periods, even though this might mean shorter reliable life expectancy.

Radio transmitters can be found that have any of the three different types of power vacuum tubes: triodes, tetrodes, and power pentodes. Examples of the triode power tube include the old 833A and newer types such as the 3-400, 3-500, or 3-1000. Popular tetrodes include the 4-400, 4-1000, 4CX250, 4CX2500, etc. The type 813B is an example of a power pentode.

Most modern transmitters that use the tetrode type of power tube are actually using *beam* power tubes. An example of beam power tube construction is shown in Figure 9.14. This type of power tube uses a set of electron beam forming plates, or beam deflection plates, to bunch the electrons together and more effectively direct them toward the plate.

The beam power tube operates at better efficiency and higher power gain than the other types of power tube. They also possess a better third-order distortion figure. The low-power, but very popular, type 6146B is an example of a beam power tube—and a tetrode at that.

The data sheet for a small beam power tube is shown in Figure 9.15.

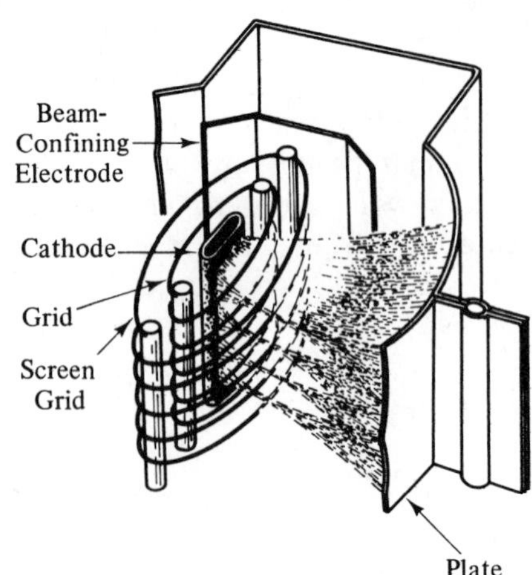

Figure 9.14 Construction of the beam power tube (*Courtesy* RCA).

Class A_1 Amplifier

MAXIMUM RATINGS (Design-Maximum Values)

Plate Voltage	275	volts
Grid-No.2 (Screen-Grid) Voltage	275	volts
Plate Dissipation	12	watts
Grid-No.2 Input	2	watts
Bulb Temperature (At hottest point)	250	°C

CHARACTERISTICS (Triode Connection)

Plate Voltage	250	volts
Grid-No.1 Voltage	—12.5	volts
Amplification Factor	9.5	
Plate Resistance (Approx.)	1970	ohms
Transconductance	4800	μmhos
Plate Current	49.5	mA
Grid-No.1 Voltage (Approx.) for plate current of 0.5 mA	—37	volts

TYPICAL OPERATION

Same as for type 6V6GTA within the limitations of the maximum ratings.

MAXIMUM CIRCUIT VALUES

Grid-No.1-Circuit Resistance:		
For fixed-bias operation	0.1	megohm
For cathode-bias operation	0.5	megohm

Vertical Deflection Amplifier (Triode Connection)°

For operation in a 525-line, 30-frame system

MAXIMUM RATINGS (Design-Maximum Values)

DC Plate Voltage	275	volts
Peak Positive-Pulse Plate Voltage#	1100	volts
Peak Negative-Pulse Grid-No.1 (Control-Grid) Voltage	275	volts
Peak Cathode Current	115	mA
Average Cathode Current	40	mA
Plate Dissipation	10	watts
Bulb Temperature (At hottest point)	250	°C

MAXIMUM CIRCUIT VALUE

Grid-No.1-Circuit Resistance, for cathode-bias operation	2.2	megohms

° Grid No.2 connected to plate.

Pulse duration must not exceed 15% of a vertical scanning cycle (2.5 milliseconds).

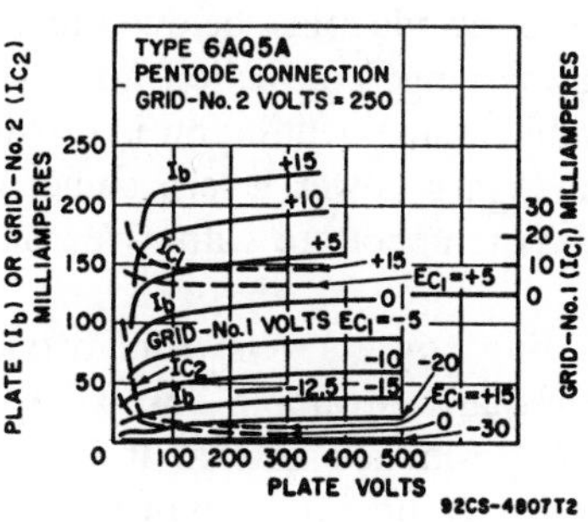

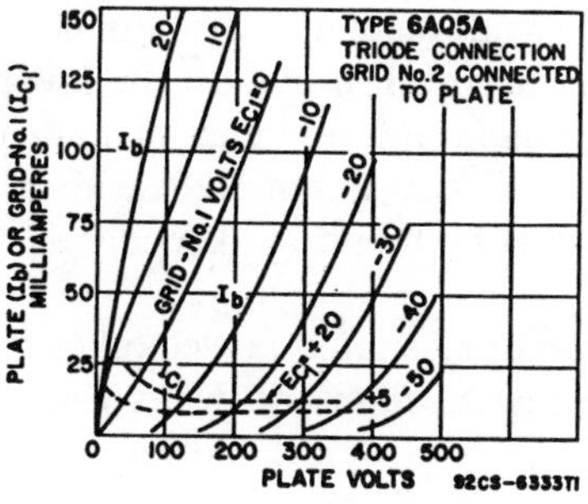

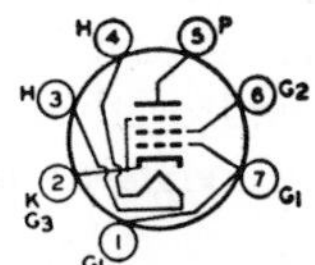

BEAM POWER TUBE 6AQ5A

5AQ5, 12AQ5

Miniature type used as output amplifier primarily in automobile receivers and in ac-operated receivers and, triode-connected, as a vertical-deflection amplifier in television receivers. **Outlines section,** 5D; requires miniature 7-contact socket. Within its maximum ratings, the performance of this type is equivalent to that of larger types 6V6 and 6V6GTA. Types 5AQ5 and 12AQ5 are identical with type 6AQ5A except for heater ratings.

	5AQ5	6AQ5A	12AQ5	
Heater Voltage (ac/dc)	4.7	6.3	12.6	volts
Heater Current	0.6	0.45	0.225	ampere
Heater Warm-up Time (Average)	11	11	—	seconds
Heater-Cathode Voltage:				
Peak value	±200 max	±200 max	±200 max	volts
Average value	100 max	100 max	100 max	volts

Direct Interelectrode Capacitances (Approx.):		
Grid No.1 to Plate	0.4	pF
Grid No.1 to Cathode, Heater, Grid No.2, and Grid No.3	8	pF
Plate to Cathode, Heater, Grid No.2, and Grid No.3	8.5	pF

Figure 9.15 6AQ5A vacuum tube specifications.

9.7 RECEIVING TUBES VS TRANSMITTING TUBES

There is no *real* distinction between receiving and transmitting tubes except power level. It would be rare, for example, to find a 4-1000, which has a plate dissipation rating of 1000 W, in a receiver circuit. For the rest of the tubes, whether they are used in receivers or transmitters is purely a matter of function and choices made by the designer. The same tube might well be used in both types of instrument. One popular single-sideband transceiver uses 6AU6 tubes in both receiver and transmitter sections. In general, it is common vernacular to call small tubes used in low-power, voltage-amplifier types of circuits "receiving tubes," whereas power-generating types are called generically by the term "transmitting tubes." This should not, however, lead you to be surprised when you find a small voltage-amplifier tube in a transmitter circuit.

One way of classifying different types of power tube is the means by which heat is dissipated. There are several different methods for heat removal in transmitter tubes. For low- to medium-power tubes in the under 200 W range, it is often sufficient to use convection air cooling. The problem in any type of power tube is to keep the temperature of the glass envelope and vacuum seals around the electrode pins below the range where damage will occur. In the low-power range convection air currents are often sufficient, provided that adequate cabinet ventilation is provided. Where ventilation is not sufficient, or at higher power levels, some other means must be found for keeping the glass temperature within reasonable bounds.

Glass or ceramic power tubes boasting power levels from two hundred to several thousand watts usually require an ample dose of forced air cooling. A powerful blower or fan is positioned so that it blows air across the tube. Some tubes in this class can be operated in an Eimac air-system socket, which has a glass chimney surrounding the tube. Air is forced up through the socket from beneath the chassis, past the glass envelope, and out the top of the socket. This has the added advantage of keeping the seals around the pins of the tube cool enough to prevent breakage.

In really high-power transmitter tubes, those over about five or 10 kW, water cooling is used. These high-level tubes are built with a water jacket encasing the outside of the tube. The water jacket is connected through some plumbing to a water pump and a radiator. The amount of heat generated in these tubes is a little fantastic. More than a few 5- to 10-kW radio stations use heat from the transmitter to keep the transmitter blockhouse warm during cold weather.

9.8 OTHER MATTERS TO CONSIDER

In this section we shall discuss matters such as the definitions of amplification factor (used on an intuitive level so far), plate resistance, plate impedance, and transconductance.

Amplification factor is the ability of the tube to amplify small signals. It is usually denoted by the lowercase Greek letter μ (mu). Amplification factor, or μ, is given by

$$\mu = \left.\frac{\Delta E_B}{\Delta E_c}\right|_{I_p\ =\ \text{constant}} \tag{9-3}$$

The Greek letter Δ (delta) is used to represent a concept that you will see often in electronics, in lieu of the more correct notation from the mathematics of calculus. It is used to denote a "small change in . . . ." It should be noted that the change should be very small, and that the formula is not totally correct unless the change approaches, but is not equal to, zero. In that more nearly ideal case we would use calculus notation and write

$$\mu = \left.\frac{dE_B}{dE_c}\right|_{I_p\ =\ \text{constant}} \tag{9-4}$$

It is also important that plate current be held constant when this measurement is made. The other terms in the equation are the familiar plate voltage E_B and negative grid bias E_c.

It is possible to use amplification factor to compute the approximate cutoff voltage for a vacuum tube at any given plate voltage. The equation is

$$-E_{co} = \frac{E_B}{\mu} \tag{9-5}$$

where E_{co} is the grid voltage necessary to effect cutoff.
E_B is the plate voltage.
μ is the amplification factor.

Plate resistance and *plate impedance* are related terms, but are different in that one is a quasi-static dc process and the other is an ac process. Many who are less discerning than they should be are often tempted to look upon these as one and the same. Plate *resistance* is defined as

$$R_p = \frac{E_B}{I_p} \tag{9-6}$$

where R_p is the plate resistance.
E_B is the plate voltage (dc).
I_p is the plate current (dc).

Since direct current is specified for the measurement of plate resistance, it is the static opposition to the flow of current from the cathode to the plate. Plate impedance, on the other hand, is defined in terms of alternating current, so it can be called a *dynamic* measure of the same thing.

It must be noted, however, that plate resistance varies a great deal with plate voltage level, but the plate impedance is much more constant, especially in the all-important linear region of the characteristic curve. The formula for plate impedance is

$$r_p = \frac{\Delta e_b}{\Delta i_p}\bigg|_{E_C\,=\,\text{constant}} \tag{9-7}$$

Note the use of lowercase letters in the plate impedance formula. This is a general convention when one is trying to denote an ac case of something that could be either ac or dc.

Transconductance, or *mutual conductance* as it is often called, is a superior method for measuring vacuum tube performance. It is defined as a change in plate current for a given change in grid voltage:

$$g_m = \frac{\Delta i_p}{\Delta e_c}\bigg|_{E_B\,=\,\text{constant}} \tag{9-8}$$

The unit of transconductance g_m is the mho, or more conveniently in real cases, the micromho (μmho).

Example. A 0.5-V change in grid voltage produces a 4-mA (0.004-A) change in plate current. What is the transconductance?

$$g_m = \frac{0.004}{0.5} \tag{9-9}$$

$$g_m = 0.01 \text{ mho} = 10{,}000\text{-}\mu\text{mho}$$

There is one equation, or expression, that relates amplification factor, plate impedance, and transconductance:

$$\mu = g_m \times r_p \tag{9-10}$$

One last fact that should be mentioned is that all current in both the plate and the screen grid of a vacuum tube also must flow in the cathode. In other words,

$$I_{\text{cath}} = I_{\text{plate}} + I_{\text{screen}} \tag{9-11}$$

This equation may seem to be useless at this point, but you are advised to remember it. A very popular type of examination question, both in electronics courses and in F.C.C. or company exams, involves calculating a current in cathode, plate, or screen using what at first glance seems too little information. For instance, you may be given the plate current, plus the cathode resistance and the voltage across that resistance, and you may be asked to find the screen current. In that case you would use Eq. (9-11) as demonstrated in the following example.

Example. An amplifier stage has a plate current of 100 mA, and a voltage drop of 10.6 V across a 100-Ω cathode resistor. Find the screen current.

$$\begin{aligned}
I_{\text{cath}} &= I_{\text{plate}} + I_{\text{screen}} \\
I_{\text{screen}} &= I_{\text{cath}} - I_{\text{plate}} \\
I_{\text{screen}} &= ((10.6)(100)) - 0.1 \text{ A} \\
I_{\text{screen}} &= 0.106 - 0.1 \text{ A} \\
I_{\text{screen}} &= 0.006 \text{ A} = 6 \text{ mA}
\end{aligned}$$

PROBLEMS

1. Thermionic emission is the boiling off of _______ from a metal surface heated to incandescence.
2. If a positively charged electrode is inserted into an evacuated glass envelope containing a thermionic emitter element such as a glowing filament wire, it attracts a flow of electrons (current). This is named the _______.
3. Electrons that escape from a thermionic surface form a cloud called a _______.
4. The electron current in a vacuum tube is due to _______ from a filament or cathode.
5. A two-electrode vacuum tube is called a ___________.

6. The person usually credited with the invention of the diode is ______.
7. The positively charged electrode in a vacuum tube is called either the ______ or the ______.
8. A diode passes current in ______.
9. A diode (will) (will not) conduct when the plate is negative with respect to the cathode.
10. An electrode is fashioned in such a way that a cylindrical metal sleeve is heated by a glowing filament at its axis. This is called an ______ cathode.
11. A typical cathode material for a structure such as that described in Question 10 is ______.
12. The *A* supply powers the ______.
13. The *B* supply powers the ______.
14. The *C* supply is used with diodes. True or false?
15. What is the plate resistance if the plate current is 12 mA and the *B*+ supply is 15 VDC?
16. The ______ is the type of vacuum tube that has three internal electrodes.
17. The simplest tube that will amplify is the ______.
18. The inventor credited with the triode is ______.
19. The third element forming the triode is called a ______.
20. A grid is a porous (electrically) element located ______.
21. If a high negative voltage exists between the grid and the cathode, such that the cathode is more positive than the grid, plate current will be ______.
22. A triode acts like a diode if ______.
23. Linearity is a measure of ______.
24. High amplification in a triode requires ______.
25. A four-element vacuum tube is called a ______.
26. The fourth element is called a ______ or ______.
27. The screen grid in a tetrode is biased with a ______ voltage.
28. One function of the screen grid is ______ of the electron stream from cathode to plate.
29. Electrons accelerated by the screen sometimes acquire sufficient kinetic energy to dislodge electrons from the anode. True or false?
30. The phenomenon of Question 29 is called ______.
31. An implication of secondary emission is ______ current flow to the screen grid.
32. A ______ is sometimes used to reduce the effects of secondary emission.
33. A vacuum tube having a suppressor grid, a fifth element, is called a ______.
34. The suppressor grid is placed ______.
35. Give two additional advantages of the pentode.
36. What is a normal range for pentode plate resistance?
37. Two different types of pentode are ______ and ______.
38. Another name for the remote cutoff pentode is ______.

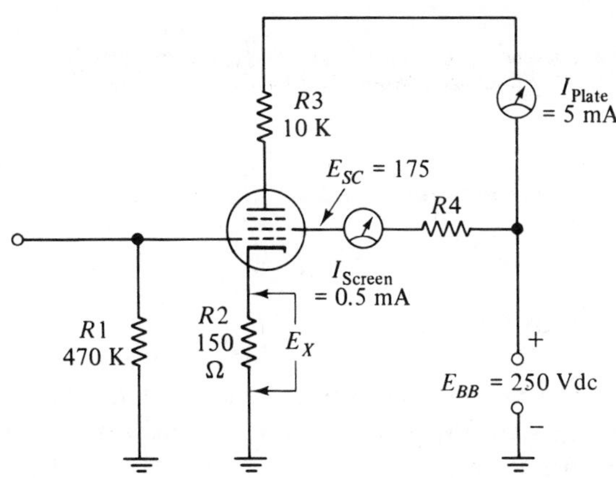

Figure 9.16

39. A radio transmitter with a vacuum tube final amplifier delivers 2500 W to a 50-Ω antenna. If the plate voltage is 5.5 kV, and plate current is 1.2 A, how much heat is dissipated?
40. What is the efficiency of the transmitter in Question 39?
41. The amount of heat that a vacuum tube anode can safely handle is given by the ____________ rating.
42. A ____________ is sometimes used to cool power tubes operated at high power levels.
43. The expression $\Delta E_B/\Delta E_c$ (I_p = constant) gives the ____________.
44. What is the approximate cutoff voltage if $u = 200$ and the plate voltage is 350 VDC?
45. What is the plate resistance if there is a current of 1.2 mA flowing in the plate when 200 V dc is applied?
46. A grid voltage change of 0.25 V causes a plate current change of 5 mA. What is the mutual conductance?
47. Find the mutual conductance if the amplification factor is 200 and the plate impedance is 150 kΩ.
48. Refer to Figure 9.16. Find E_x.
49. Refer to Figure 9.16. Find the value of $R4$.

10 Semiconductor Basics

10.0 INTRODUCTION

The transistor was not actually invented until the late 1940s, but it had been recognized as theoretically possible for about ten years. Solid-state, or semiconductor, diodes were known as early as pre-World War I days when a natural mineral crystal called "Galena" was used as the detector in radio "crystal sets." The semiconductor diode is a blood relative and precursor to the transistor, but it took metallurgy that grew out of World War II research efforts to stimulate the development of reliable, manufactured semiconductor diodes. Once that hurdle was out of the way, scientists at Bell Laboratories were able to make the world's first working transistor.

Today we find that semiconductor devices have all but eliminated vacuum tubes in the design of electronic apparatus. Transistors and diodes are used extensively in electronics equipment, so much so that it is proper to claim the almost total eclipse of vacuum tubes in new designs.

10.1 SOLID-STATE BASICS

The study of solid-state electronic devices must necessarily begin with a simple model of atomic structure, as developed in Chapter 1. You should recall that an atom is composed of a nucleus containing positively charged protons and uncharged particles called neutrons. The nucleus is surrounded by a cloud of negatively charged particles called electrons. The electrons orbit about the nucleus in shells, that is to say at fixed distances from the nucleus. Electroneutrality requires that the number of negatively charged electrons exactly equal the number of positively charged protons. This will allow the positive charges to exactly cancel the negative charges, leaving the atom electrically neutral.

Chemical reactions and electrical currents are possible, however, because in some atoms the outer-shell electrons are less tightly bound. A shell becomes tightly bound only if a certain critical number of electrons is present in that shell. In the first shell, that nearest the nucleus, we find that two electrons exactly fill the shell, and that makes them tightly bound. The next shell is completely filled by eight electrons, and the third shell by eighteen.

A filled shell does not easily give up electrons. If the outermost shell is not filled, however, the outer electrons are relatively loosely bound, so can be more easily freed. Look at carbon, for example. It has six electrons. Two will completely fill the innermost shell, leaving four in the second shell. Since the second shell is completely filled by eight electrons, it will easily give up electrons when only four are present. This is why carbon will conduct electricity and why it is chemically active. Those outer electrons that are available for chemical and electrical activity are called *valence* electrons.

Semiconductors are elements that are neither good conductors of electricity nor good insulators. Examples of semiconductors often used to make solid-state electronic devices are germanium (Ge) and silicon (Si). Germanium has an atomic number of 32. There are two electrons in the first shell, eight in the second shell, and 18 in the third shell, leaving four electrons in the fourth, and outermost, shell.

Silicon has an atomic number of 14. In this atom there are two electrons filling the first shell and eight in the second, for a total of ten. This leaves four electrons in the third (outermost) shell. Both of these elements have four valence electrons, so are *tetravalent*.

Semiconductors such as Ge and Si form covalent bonds with nearby atoms in an attempt at simulating the stable octet (eight-electron) outer shell. Figure 10.1 shows this arrangement, which is typical of the class of semiconductors that we are considering. Each tetravalent atom shares each of its four valence electrons with adjacent atoms. Each bond contains two electrons, one contributed by each of the two bonded atoms. Figure

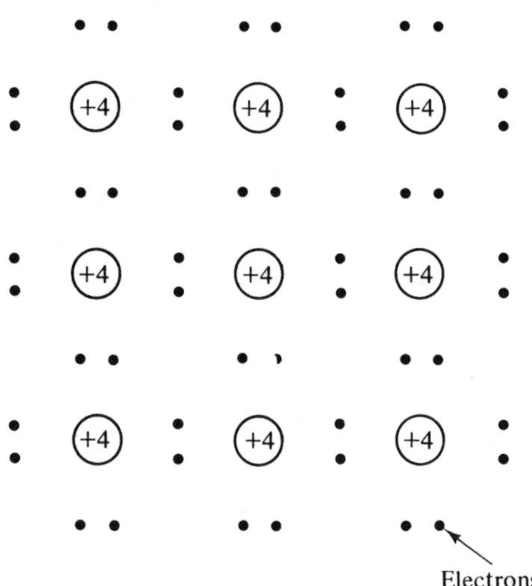

Figure 10.1 Crystal structure in a tetravalent semiconductor.

10.1 shows only a limited, two-dimensional, picture; in reality, the crystal structure of any semiconductor material extends for millions of atoms in all three directions.

10.2 CONDUCTION OF ELECTRICAL CURRENTS IN SEMICONDUCTORS

Semiconductors ordinarily make poor electrical conductors because there are few free electrons. But what if some other material is introduced into the crystal structure as an impurity? Suppose, for example, that the semiconductor crystal, either Ge or Si, were doped with a pentavalent (five valence electrons) impurity such as arsenic, antimony, or phosphorous. Each of these has five valence electrons, but is, in itself, completely neutral electrically—no rules are violated. The situation inside the tetravalent crystal in that case will look something like Figure 10.2. The pentavalent atom fits right into the structure, forming covalent bonds with the tetravalent atoms. Since there are five valence electrons in the impurity atom, there will be one excess electron for each impurity atom. These excess electrons are then available as free electrons to form a flow of electric current. Of course, we show only one pentavalent atom to make the graphics simpler, but in reality there would be millions. A material doped with a pentavalent material to gain excess electrons is known as an "*N*-type" semiconductor.

Another type of semiconductor is the *P*-type material, which is doped in a slightly different manner to create a deficiency of electrons.

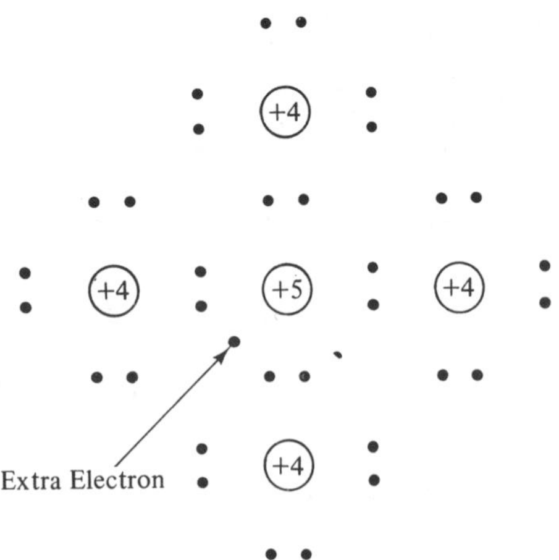

Figure 10.2 Adding a pentavalent impurity creates *N*-type semiconductor material by creating an excess of electrons.

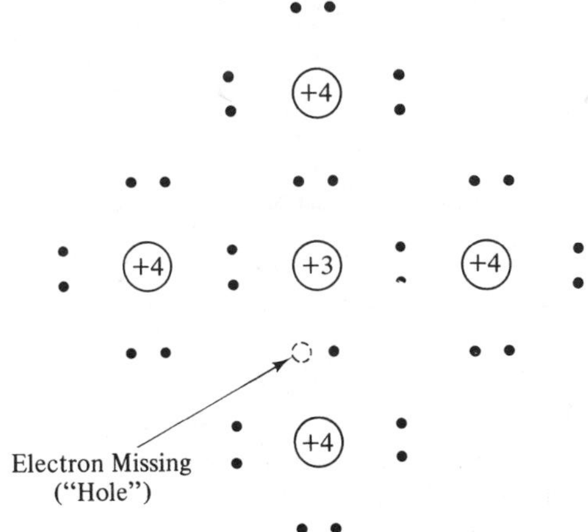

Figure 10.3 A trivalent impurity combines with the tetravalent semiconductor atoms leaving "holes,"—places where electrons should be but aren't.

This is done by adding a trivalent impurity to the structure. Examples of suitable dopants are boron, aluminum, and indium. The *P*-type structure is shown in Figure 10.3.

The spot in a covalent bond where an electron is missing is called a "hole." This concept frequently gives students of electronic fundamentals a great deal of trouble, and that is unfortunate, because it is really simple. The difficulty may possibly be due to the fact that many textbooks tell students that holes flow, and that is simply not true—electrons flow. An electron may fill the hole, but only at the expense of creating a hole elsewhere in the crystal. This may make it appear that the hole traveled from its original location to the location where the new hole was created. A hole is nothing more than a place where an electron should be but is not. Holes give the *appearance* of flowing through the mechanism shown in Figure 10.4. Suppose that, at the instant power is applied, there is a hole at atom *A*. The voltage field generated by the external power supply acts as a force, and breaks loose an electron from atom *B*. This electron drifts over to be captured by electron-deficient atom *A*. This will fill the hole at *A,* but creates one at *B*. The hole did not physically *move*. How could it? It does not have physical reality. Suppose that a short time later an electron breaks loose from atom *C* and drifts so that it is captured by *B* to fill the hole. This will create a hole at *C,* but fills one at *B*. Again, we see the appearance of movement, in this case from atom *B* to atom *C*. If, over a period of time, similar actions occur several more times, the hole will wind up at atom *F*.

Although several different electrons actually did the moving, there

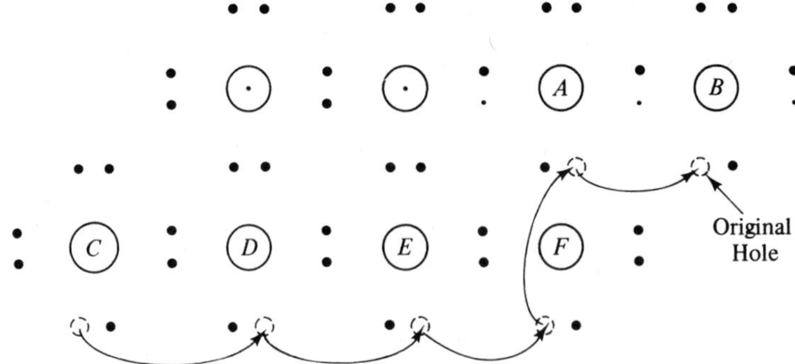

Figure 10.4 Holes don't actually move; electrons move and give the illusion of hole movement.

is the *appearance of hole movement* over a meandering path from atom *A* to atom *F*. Averaged over a large number of atoms in a given piece of material, we would see what we might think is the movement of positively charged holes from right to left in the drawing.

You will frequently see holes actually referred to as "positive carriers" and electrons as "negative carriers." For the electron it is easy to see how this label is justified, because they are real things—they actually exist. Furthermore, they carry a negative charge. Negative carriers, or electrons if you prefer, are the dominant carriers in *N*-type semiconductor material.

P-type semiconductor material has far more holes, or so-called "positive carriers." Although there is no real, physical, particle with a positive electrical charge in this case, the absence of an electron unbalances the associated atom, leaving it with a net electrical charge of +1 unit. This is because there will be one more proton than electron in the bonded pair, thereby giving the atom the appearance of a positive charge.

Keep in mind the fact that electrons flow from negative to positive. In a *P*-type material connected across an electrical potential, such as a battery, holes migrate from positive to negative—just the opposite from electrons, further justifying our considering them as positively charged "particles."

10.3 THE *P-N* JUNCTION

A single piece of *P*- or *N*-type semiconductor material is of little interest or use in electronic devices, but a *junction* (see Figure 10.5) consisting of one section of each type of material has properties and characteristics that are of immense use and interest in electronics. This junction may con-

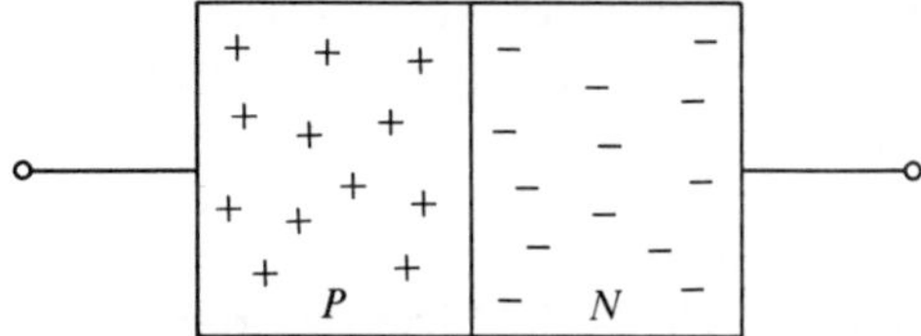

Figure 10.5 A *P-N* junction.

sist of either Si or Ge material, but in most newer devices Si is predominant.

Figure 10.6 shows the behavior of a *P-N* junction where an electric potential is applied across its ends. In Figure 10.6(a) we see the case where the battery is connected so that its positive end is to the *N*-type material end of the *P-N* junction. Negative carriers present in the *N*-type material are attracted toward the positive terminal of the battery. Similarly, electrons from the battery's negative terminal enter the opposite end of the junction to fill many of the holes. The appearance, often given as gospel in elementary texts, is that positive carriers from the *P*-type end of the junction entered the battery. In any event, a zone is created at the interface between the two types of material that is devoid of carrers. This region near the *P-N* boundary is called a *depletion zone,* and it contains very few carriers.

Under conditions where a large depletion zone exists [Figure 10.6(a)] the semiconductor material will have a very high electrical resistance, so little or no current will flow across the junction. Actually, there

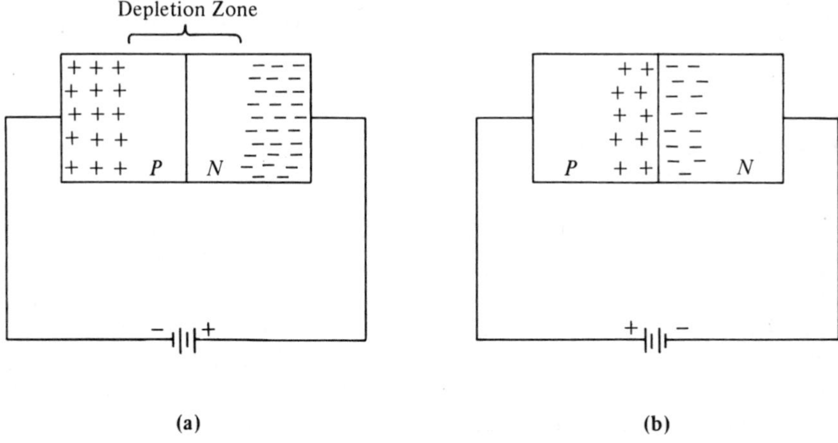

Figure 10.6 **(a)** Reverse biasing a *P-N* junction creates a wide depletion zone in which no charge carriers exist. **(b)** Forward biasing the *P-N* junction destroys the depletion zone and allows current flow across the junction.

will be, in most cases, some very tiny, minute current flowing across the junction, and this is called a *leakage current.* Designers of solid-state devices go to great lengths to reduce or eliminate cross-junction leakage currents. Leakage current is also called *reverse current.*

The alternative case, in which the battery connections have been reversed, is shown in Figure 10.6(b). In this case we find the carriers closer to the barrier between *P*- and *N*-type materials. Positive carriers are repelled toward the barrier by the positive terminal of the battery, while electrons are repelled toward the barrier by the negative terminal of the battery. This causes the depletion zone to disappear, and some electrons and holes will neutralize each other when the electrons cross the barrier. If an electron crosses the barrier to fill a hole, then a current is flowing.

If a *P-N* junction has voltage applied so that no current can flow, it is said to be *reverse-biased.* A junction that is biased in just the opposite manner, so that current will flow, is said to be *forward-biased.*

10.4 SOLID-STATE DIODES

A solid-state diode (see Figure 10.7) consists of a single *P-N* junction. Like their vacuum tube counterparts, solid-state diodes pass current in only one direction. The relationship between voltage applied and current flow for a solid-state diode is shown in Figure 10.7(a), and the test circuit for generating this curve is shown in Figure 10.7(b).

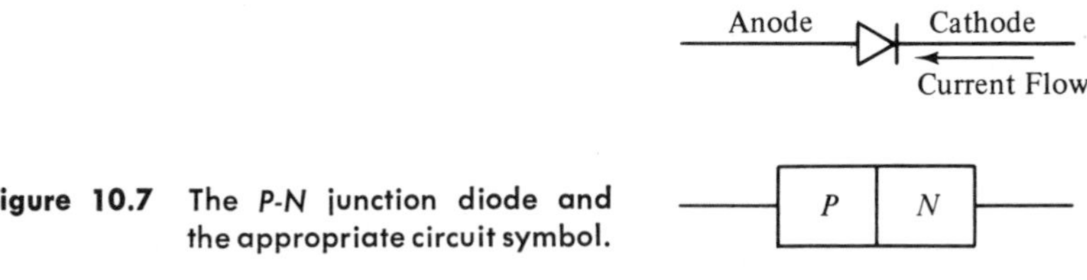

Figure 10.7 The *P-N* junction diode and the appropriate circuit symbol.

In one position of switch *S*1, the voltage applied to the anode (*P*-side) of the diode is negative, so no current will flow. Under this condition, the diode is reverse-biased.

The alternate switch position applies a positive voltage to the anode, and that causes carriers of both polarities to be repelled toward the junction. In this case the diode is forward-biased, so current will flow.

A good rule of thumb to remember for almost all *P-N* junction diodes is that the electron current flow is in the direction opposite the direction of the arrow. Commit that convention to memory: Current flows *against* the arrow.

Notice that the current-vs-voltage relationship of Figure 10.8(a) is

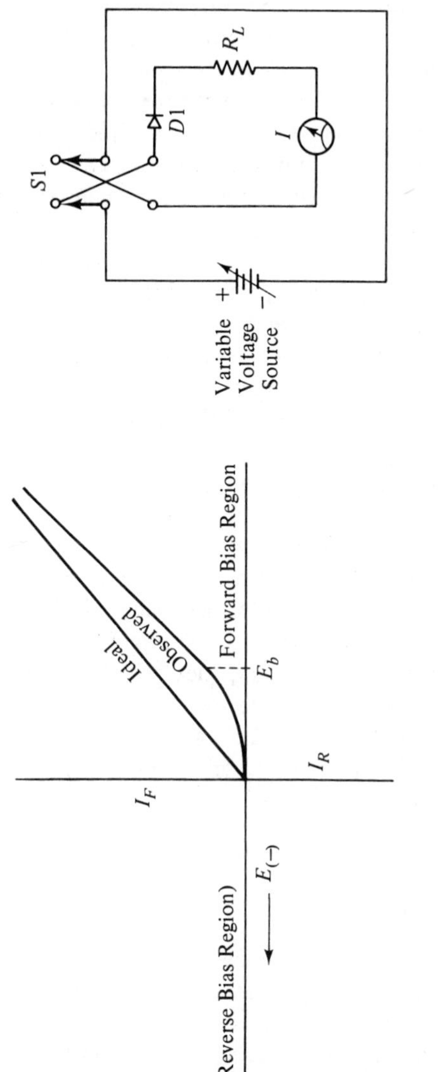

Figure 10.8 (a) Current *versus voltage* characteristic of ideal and real *P-N* junction diodes. (b) Circuit used to create the I-vs-E curve.

not linear at low values of applied voltage. For any given type of semiconductor material there is a critical value of applied voltage required before linearity can be achieved. Below that critical level there is a great deal of nonlinearity. The value of this voltage is dependent upon the type of material. This voltage, shown as E_b in the figure, will be approximately 0.2 to 0.3 V for germanium devices, and 0.6 to 0.7 V for silicon. These figures are for a forward-biased *P-N* junction diode. Remember these values, because they will become important to you when you are studying transistor and diode circuits, or when you are troubleshooting electronic circuits containing these devices.

Other parameters of interest are the *peak forward voltage, peak forward current, peak reverse voltage* (p.r.v.), and the *leakage current*. All of these parameters, except p.r.v., are fairly ordinary, so they need not be amplified upon here. The peak reverse voltage, also called the *peak inverse voltage* (p.i.v.), is the maximum reverse bias potential that may be applied to the diode for any period of time without causing permanent damage to the diode. It is generally true that destruction of the diode will occur if the p.i.v. is exceeded for any length of time.

Diodes are used in many different applications in electronic communication equipment. In general, however, a diode designed to be optimum in one application or type of operation will not do well in other applications. Signal diodes, for example, are meant to be used primarily in low-level modulation, demodulation, clamping, or switching uses. If they are used as power supply rectifiers, they will burn out immediately. Rectifier diodes, on the other hand, are designed to handle much higher applied voltages and forward current levels. They are almost useless for most signal applications, because they are too slow (low frequency) and have too much leakage current.

10.5 SIMPLE TRANSISTORS

Transistors are amplifying devices made from semiconductor materials. The simple bipolar transistor is often likened to a pair of diodes connected back to back. The story is much more complex, however, as may be seen if you attempt to obtain anything resembling "transistor action" by so connecting a pair of signal diodes.

The basic transistor consists of three sections of semiconductor material, as shown in Figure 10.9. There are two types shown here, called *NPN* and *PNP*. Both consist of a central region of one type of semiconductor material sandwiched between two other regions of the opposite type of material. An *NPN,* for example, has two *N*-type regions sandwiching a region of *P*-type material. In the *PNP* transistor just the opposite situation obtains; there is an *N*-type central region between two *P*-type sections.

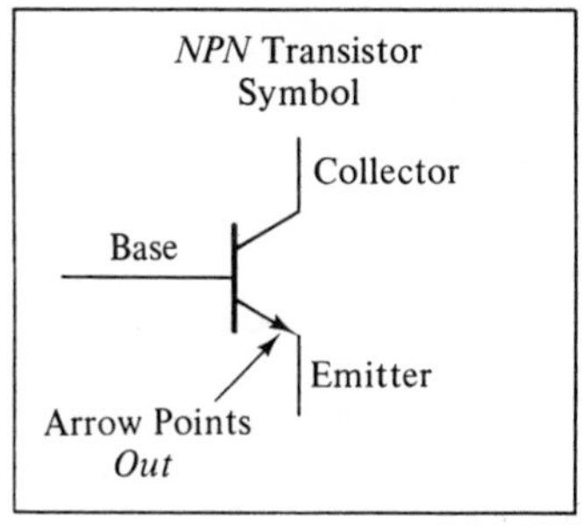

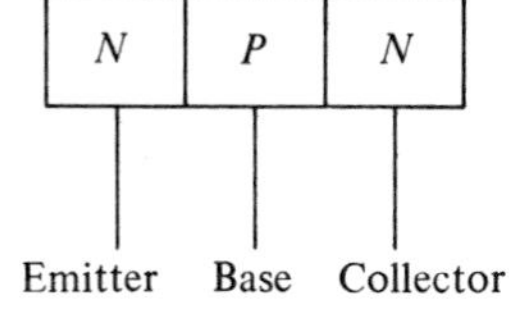

(a)

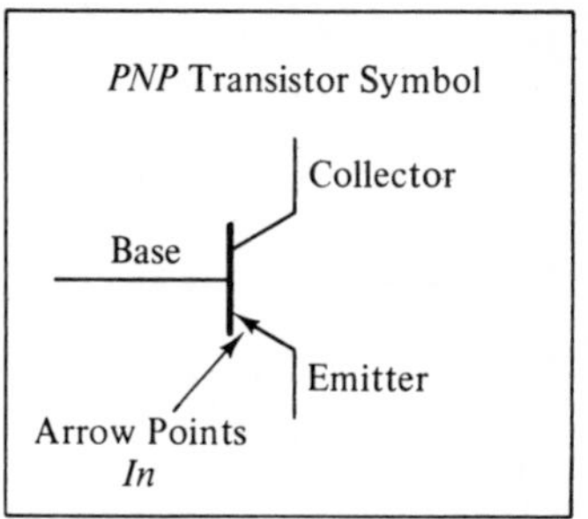

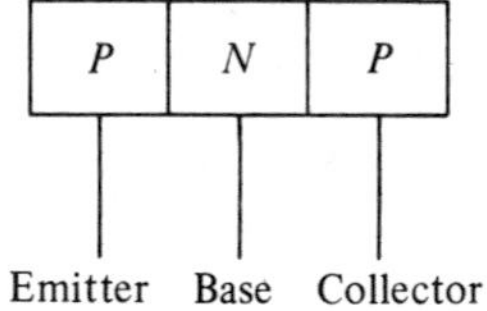

Memory Aid for Arrow Direction
P-N-P ⇒ Points i*N*

(b)

Figure 10.9 (a) Structure and circuit symbol for *NPN* transistor. (b) Structure and circuit symbol for *PNP* transistor. (*Note memory aid for remembering which symbol goes to the PNP transistor: "PNP-arrow Points iN."*)

The central region is called the *base,* and it controls the activities of the entire transistor. The two end sections are called the *emitter* and the *collector,* respectively. You may be tempted to think of these regions as being interchangeable because of the apparent symmetry in the picture. This was true in a very limited sense in the early days of transistors, but today's transistors use a physical geometry that is like our illustration electrically, but is quite different physically. The picture is merely an idealization, or graphical model, of the actual situation.

Figure 10.10 shows an *NPN* transistor biased properly for normal operation. The base-emitter junction is forward-biased, and the collector is made positive with respect to the emitter. Current will flow into the base region because the b-e junction is forward biased. Although the actual circuit action is a little bit more complex, we may describe the operation of a transistor by claiming that electrons attracted into the base from the emitter pass across the base region to the collector region. The base region is extremely thin, so the electrons from the emitter will be attracted (i.e., "collected") by the positive potential from the collector bias. In most cases approximately 95–99 percent of the emitter current will pass through the base region to the collector. Only about 1–5 percent of the emitter current

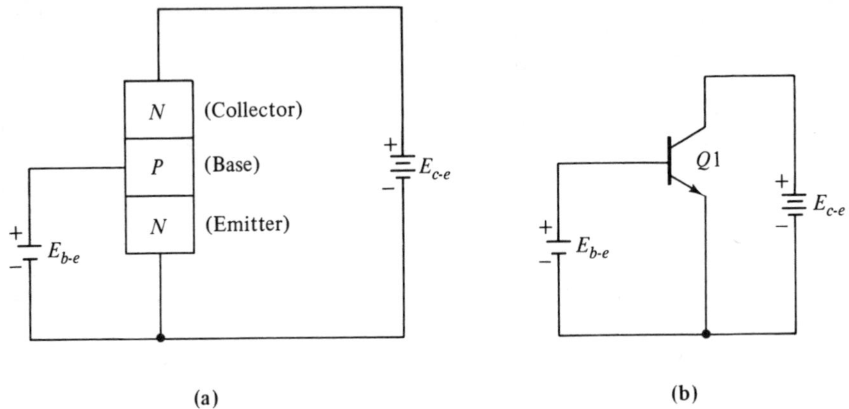

Figure 10.10 **(a)** Circuit for a forward biased *NPN* transistor. **(b)** As it appears in a circuit diagram.

will flow into the base bias battery, E_{be}. This, then, gives us a mechanism for amplification—in this case the control of a large current by a small current.

Suppose that we modified the previous circuit to include a series-connected signal source in the base-emitter circuit. An example is shown in Figure 10.11. The input signal is a sine wave, so its amplitude will alternately add to, or subtract from, the current created by E_{be}.

On positive excursions of the input sine wave the collector-emitter current will increase, but on negative alternations of the input signal collector current decreases. Since I_b is always very much less than I_c, we can rightfully claim that the transistor is a current amplifier.

Before you fix in your mind that a transistor is a current amplifier, and not a voltage amplifier, remember Ohm's law. There is an $E = IR$

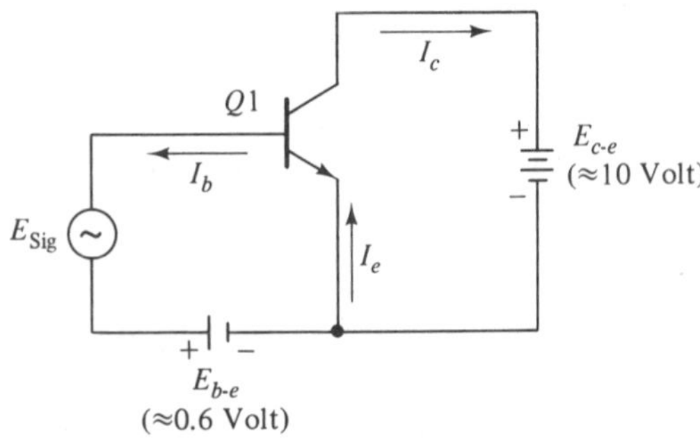

Figure 10.11 Current flow in the forward biased *NPN* transistor. *PNP* circuits are similar, but flow is reversed.

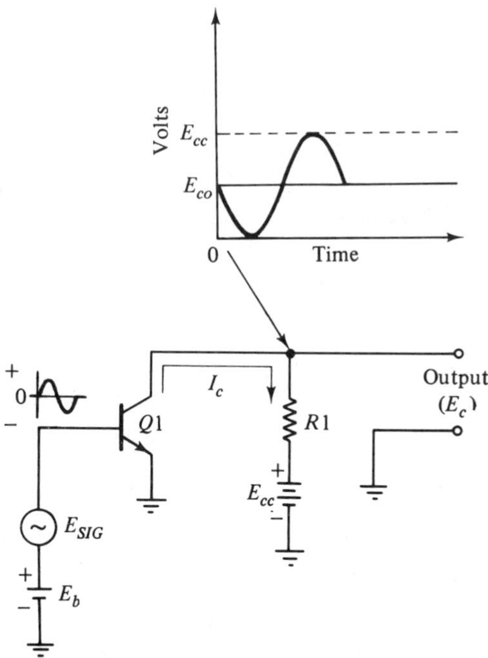

Figure 10.12 Transistor as a voltage amplifier.

relationship between current and voltage, so we can create an output *signal voltage* from the transistor's collector current by including a resistance, as in Figure 10.12. In this circuit we have a resistor R_i in series with the collector-emitter voltage. Again, let us assume that E_{sig} is a sine wave voltage. As E_{sig} increases, so does collector current I_c. The voltage drop across R_i is equal to I_cR_i, and by Kirchoff's law, $E_c + E_{ri} = E_{cc}$. Since the battery voltage E_{cc} is fixed, output voltage E_c must go down as increasing collector current forces E_{ri} to increase. In this case, we have a small voltage controlling a large voltage, so the transistor *acts as if it were a voltage amplifier*. Do not let much of what you read in electronics literature about transistors being current amplifiers lead you to believe that they cannot amplify voltage levels as well. They will, as demonstrated here, act as a voltage amplifier if suitable external circuitry is provided.

We have been discussing the *NPN* transistor, but we can apply the same ideas to the *PNP* transistor if the battery polarities are reversed. In a *PNP* transistor amplifier the collector is more negative than either the emitter or base. This is exactly the opposite of the *NPN* case discussed above.

In the circuit of Figure 10.12 it was necessary to pick a value of base bias that would create a collector current that dropped approximately half of the E_{cc} supply across a resistance R_i when the signal input voltage was zero. This allows E_c to vary from 0 V when E_{sig} is maximum to E_{cc} when E_{sig} is minimum. This is shown on the graph in Figure 10.12(b). A bias network is used to set the value of E_b that will produce a resting, or "quiescent," value of E_c that is equal to approximately ½ E_{cc}. Examples of typical transistor bias networks are shown in Figure 10.13. Notice that standard practice makes it advisable to provide bias through a network from the main collector supply instead of through a separate battery. This is both economic and convenient.

Figure 10.13(a) and 10.13(b) show one of the simplest types of bias network. In Figure 10.13(a) bias resistor *R*2 sets the quiescent base current, and is connected directly to the E_{cc} supply. An alternative scheme, shown in Figure 10.13(b), is supposedly a little more stable. It takes the dc for the bias resistor from the collector of the transistor.

A superior system is shown in Figure 10.13(c). Here we have base bias derived from the E_{cc} supply through a voltage divider consisting of resistors *R*2 and *R*3. This circuit also shows the use of emitter stabilizer resistor *R*4. It is used to improve thermal performance, and may be used with any of the bias schemes.

Examples of bias networks suitable for a *PNP* transistor are shown in Figures 10.13(d) and 10.13(e). The former is merely a reverse-polarity version of Figure 10.13(c), which is perfectly permissible, since the *PNP* and *NPN* transistors are of opposite polarities. In fact, all three of the previous bias networks may be used with *PNP* transistors if the polarity of the collector battery is reversed.

The circuit in Figure 10.13(e) is for use with *PNP* transistors when the only power supply available is positive with respect to ground. This is frequently the situation in mobile communications equipment in vehicles where the negative post of the battery is grounded to frame and the positive post forms the hot side of the auto electrical system. There is no reason why the *PNP* transistor cannot be operated from a negative-ground power supply. The only requirement as far as the transistor is concerned is that the base and collector be more negative than the emitter. This criterion may be easily met by making the emitter more positive than the base and collector terminals.

In the example of Figure 10.13(e) the collector of *Q*1 is connected to ground through resistor *R*1. The voltage drop across *R*1 is both the collector potential *and the output signal.* Voltage divider *R*2-*R*3 is designed to place a positive potential on the base of *Q*1 that is approximately 0.7 V lower than the positive potential on the emitter. This makes the base 0.7 V negative with *respect to the emitter.* The collector voltage will take on some quiescent value when the signal voltage is zero, but will vary as E_{sig} also varies.

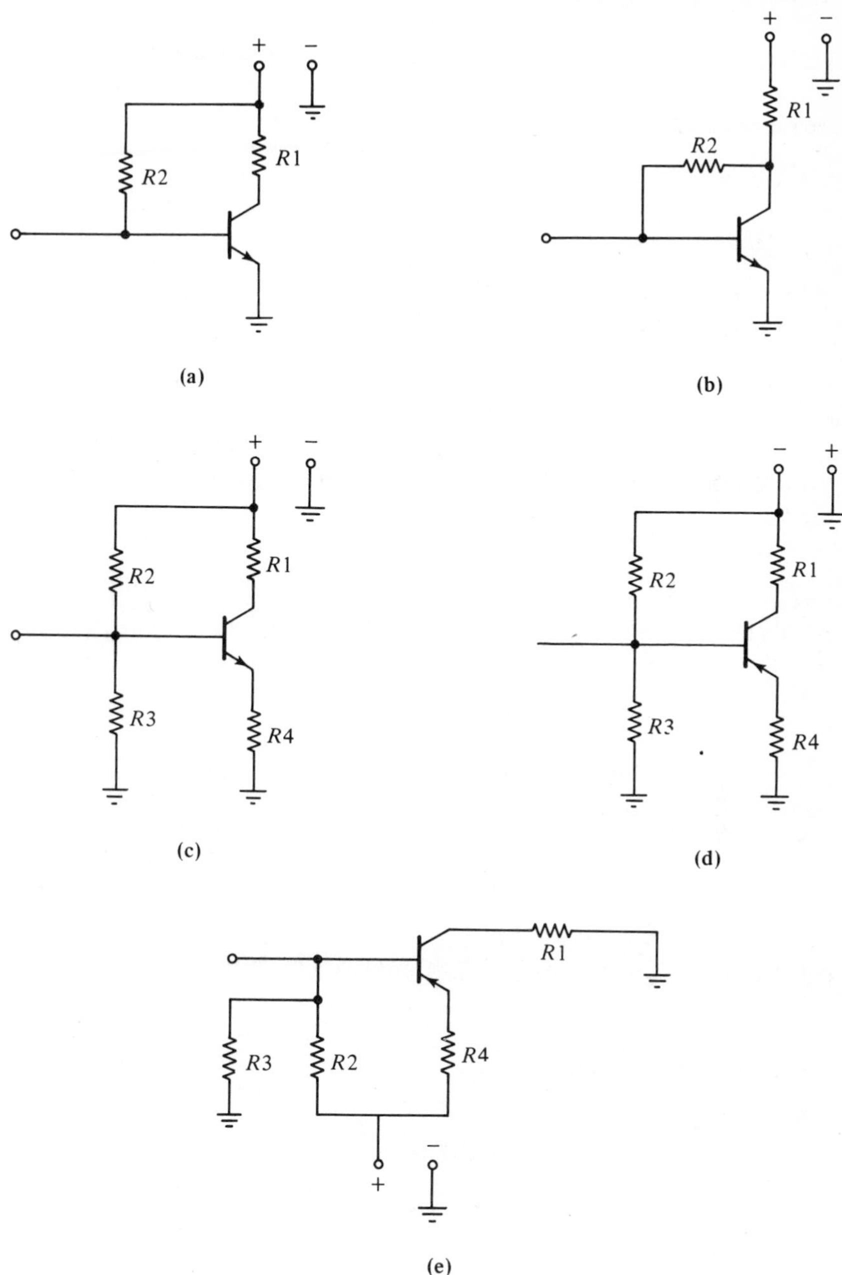

Figure 10.13 Methods for resistor biasing transistors from the collector-emitter power supply.

10.6 TRANSISTOR GAIN

There are several popular ways to denote transistor current gain, but only two are of interest to us here: alpha and beta. Alpha can be defined as the ratio

$$\alpha = \frac{I_c}{I_e} \tag{10-1}$$

where I_c is the collector current.
I_e is the emitter current.

α usually has a value less than unity (1), with values between 0.7 and 0.99 being the typical range.

The other representation of transistor gain, and the one that seems more often favored over the others, is the beta (β) which is defined as the ratio

$$\beta = \frac{I_c}{I_b} \tag{10-2}$$

where I_c is the collector current.
I_b is the base current.

Alpha and beta are related to each other, and one can use the equations below to compute one when the other is known.

$$\alpha = \frac{\beta}{1 + \beta} \tag{10-3}$$

$$\beta = \frac{\alpha}{1 - \alpha} \tag{10-4}$$

Example. What is the alpha of a transistor that has a beta of 120?

$$\begin{aligned} \text{Alpha} &= \frac{\beta}{1 + \beta} \\ &= \frac{120}{1 + 120} \qquad (10\text{-}5) \\ &= 120/121 \\ &= 0.99 \end{aligned}$$

The values given above are for static dc situations. In ac terms you will see ac alpha (h_{fb}) defined as

$$h_{fb} = \frac{\Delta I_c}{\Delta I_e} \tag{10-6}$$

and ac beta (h_{fe}) is defined as

$$h_{fe} = \frac{\Delta I_c}{\Delta I_b} \tag{10-7}$$

10.7 FREQUENCY CHARACTERISTICS

Transistors, like most other electron devices, operate only over a certain specified frequency range. Here are three basic cutoff frequencies that may interest us: alpha, beta, and the gain-bandwidth product.

The alpha cutoff frequency F_{ab} is the frequency at which the ac current gain h_{fb} drops to a level 3 dB below its low-frequency (usually 1000-Hz) gain. This is the frequency at which $h_{fb} = 0.707 h_{fbo}$, where h_{fbo} is the ac current gain at 1000 Hz.

The beta cutoff frequency is similarly defined as the frequency where the ac beta, h_{fe}, drops 3 dB relative to its 1000-Hz value. In general, this frequency is lower than the alpha cutoff, but is considered somewhat more representative of a transistor's performance.

The frequency specification that seems to be quoted most often is the gain-bandwidth product, which is given the symbol F_t. This parameter is usually accepted only for transistors operated in the manner of Figure 10.13. It is defined as

$$\text{Gain} \times \text{bandwidth} = h_{fe} \times F_o \tag{10-8}$$

where h_{fe} is the ac beta.
F_o is the frequency at which gain is measured. The value of F_t quoted in specification sheets is the frequency at which h_{fe} drops to unity.

If the beta cutoff frequency F_{ae} is known, then the gain-bandwidth product may be approximated from

$$F_t = F_{ae} \times h_{feo} \tag{10-9}$$

It must be recognized, however, that this is an approximation that may not hold up in every case. Also, you can often get away with assuming that F_o is approximately equal to, but usually slightly less than, the alpha cutoff frequency.

10.8 TRANSISTOR AMPLIFIERS

Transistors can be used in the three basic amplifier configurations shown in Figure 10.14. We have already briefly touched upon the first of these [Figure 10.14(a)], but have not really discussed its basic properties. It is called the "common emitter circuit."

Common Emitter Circuits. The first type of transistor amplifier is called the "common emitter configuration," because the emitter terminal of the transistor is common to both the input and the output circuits. Input signal voltage is applied between the base and the emitter, while output voltage is taken between the collector and the emitter.

The common emitter circuit is able to offer both current and voltage gain through the mechanism described earlier in this chapter, in which the output voltage is developed across a load resistor. The values of gain are, of course, different for current and voltage. The current gain, for example, is approximately equal to beta (h_{fe}). The voltage gain, on the other hand, is approximately equal to the current gain multiplied by the ratio R_L/R_e; in other words,

$$A_v = \frac{R_L(h_{fe})}{R_e} \tag{10-10}$$

The impedance levels at input and output terminals are also quite different. The output impedance is approximately equal to R_L, whereas the input impedance Z_{in} is approximately $R_e \times h_{fe}$.

Common Collector Circuits. Figure 10.14(b) shows the common collector transistor amplifier configuration. This circuit is more popularly known as the "emitter follower." In this type of circuit, input signal is applied across the base-collector junction, while output is taken across the emitter collector path. The voltage gain of the common collector circuit is approximately unity or a little less. The current gain, however, is considerably greater, being on the order of 100 or so, because it is given by $h_{fe} + 1$.

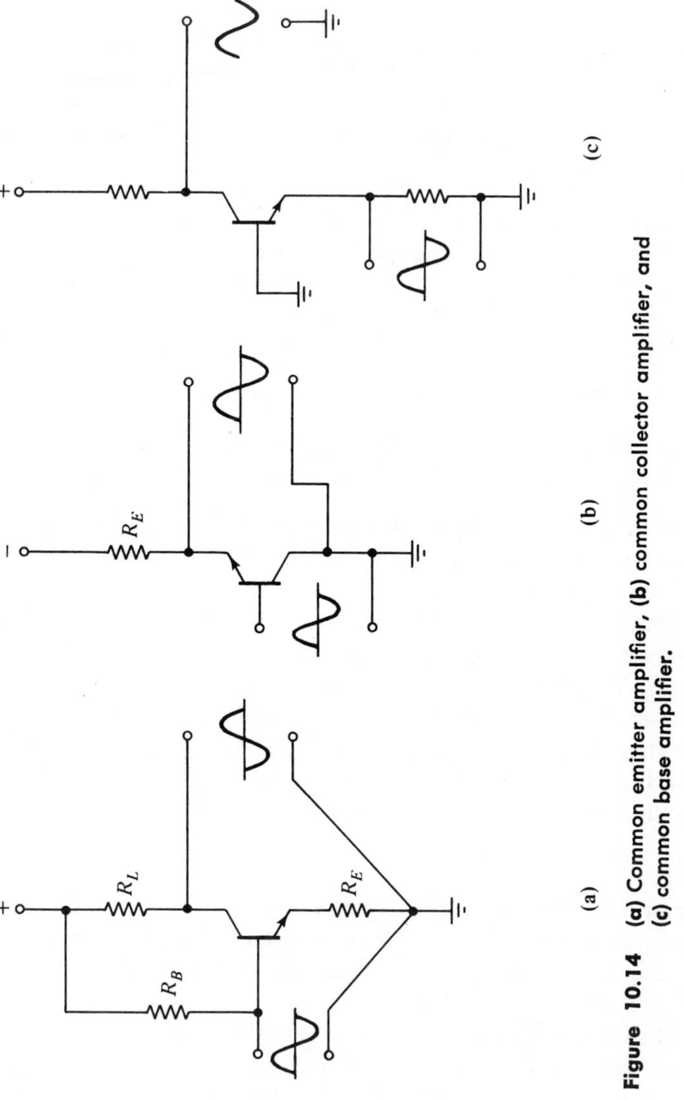

Figure 10.14 **(a)** Common emitter amplifier, **(b)** common collector amplifier, and **(c)** common base amplifier.

Table 10.1. Properties of the Common Emitter, Common Collector, and Common Base Amplifier Configurations.

	Common Emitter	Common Collector	Common Base
Voltage Gain	High	Low ($\approx$1 or less)	High (>100)
Current Gain	High	High ($\beta + 1$)	Low (<1)
Z_{in}	Medium ($\approx$1 K)	High (>100 K)	Low
Z_{out}	Medium to High (50 K)	Low (<100 Ω)	High (>500 K)
Phase Inversion ?	Yes	No	No

Note that the input and output signals in this type of amplifier are in phase with each other. There is no voltage phase inversion as was true in the common emitter case.

There are two basic applications for the common collector, or emitter follower, circuit. These are high-to-low impedance transformation and buffering. The first of these is possible because of the fact that the input impedance is (h_{fe}) times higher than the emitter resistance, while the output impedance is merely the emitter resistance. In the second application we find emitter followers used to provide isolation between input and output so that load variations will not affect the preceding stages.

Common Base Circuits. The common base, or "grounded base," circuit is shown in Figure 10.14(c). In this circuit the input signal is applied across the base-emitter junction, while the output is taken across the collector-base junction.

The common base circuit is used mostly at high frequencies, because it usually requires no neutralization. The gain properties of this configuration are opposite those of the emitter follower. In this circuit we have unity (or less) current gain and a high voltage gain.

Table 10.1 gives a synopsis of key properties for the three categories of transistor amplifiers. Notice that the common emitter circuit is unique in that it offers both high voltage gain *and* high current gain. It is also the only class to offer voltage phase inversion.

10.9 FIELD EFFECT TRANSISTORS

The field effect transistor is a relative newcomer to electronics, yet one persistent legend in the industry claims that the FET theory had been known at least a decade prior to the invention of the bipolar transistor—in the mid- to late 1930s—but poor metallurgical technique prevented construction of a working model until many years later.

There are two basic types of FET: the junction FET (JFET) and the insulated gate FET (IGFET). The latter is also known as the metal oxide semiconductor FET or MOSFET.

JFET Operation. Figure 10.15(a) shows an idealized diagram of a JFET. The channel is a bar of silicon doped to be either *P*-type or *N*-type material. Diffused into the channel are two emitter regions made of the type of semiconductor material that is opposite that used in the channel. The two emitter regions are electrically connected together. Ohmic contacts connect the two ends of the channel (labeled "drain" and "source"), and the emitters (labeled "gate") to the outside-world electrodes.

P-channel and *N*-channel JFET devices behave similarly theoretically, but are not interchangeable in the circuit unless some design changes are made. The respective symbols for the *N*- and *P*-channel devices are shown in Figures 10.15(b) and 10.15(c). In the discussion to follow we shall treat only the *N*-channel, but reversal of the supply voltage polarity makes it also valid for the *P*-channel device.

Figure 10.16 shows an *N*-channel JFET connected to the correct voltage sources. The drain is made positive with respect to the source, so a current will flow through the channel material. The emitters (i.e., gate) form junctions with the channel, but are normally reverse-biased, so they will not conduct current.

If gate voltage E_g is zero, then current will flow through the channel, subject only to the limiting effect of the channel resistance. When E_g is made negative, however, depletion zones are created in the channel regions adjacent to the emitter junctions, narrowing the effective channel through which electrons may flow, and thereby reducing the cross-sectional area. This will raise the channel resistance. A high channel resistance will, of course, reduce the channel current I_{ds}.

This phenomenon is called the "pinch effect." The value of gate voltage that causes the channel to completely pinch off the flow of current is called, handily enough, the "pinch-off voltage." Amplification takes place by controlling current I_{ds} with gate voltage E_g, through the mechanism of pinching in the channel. The JFET, then, can be described as a transconductance amplifier not too unlike the vacuum tube. Although

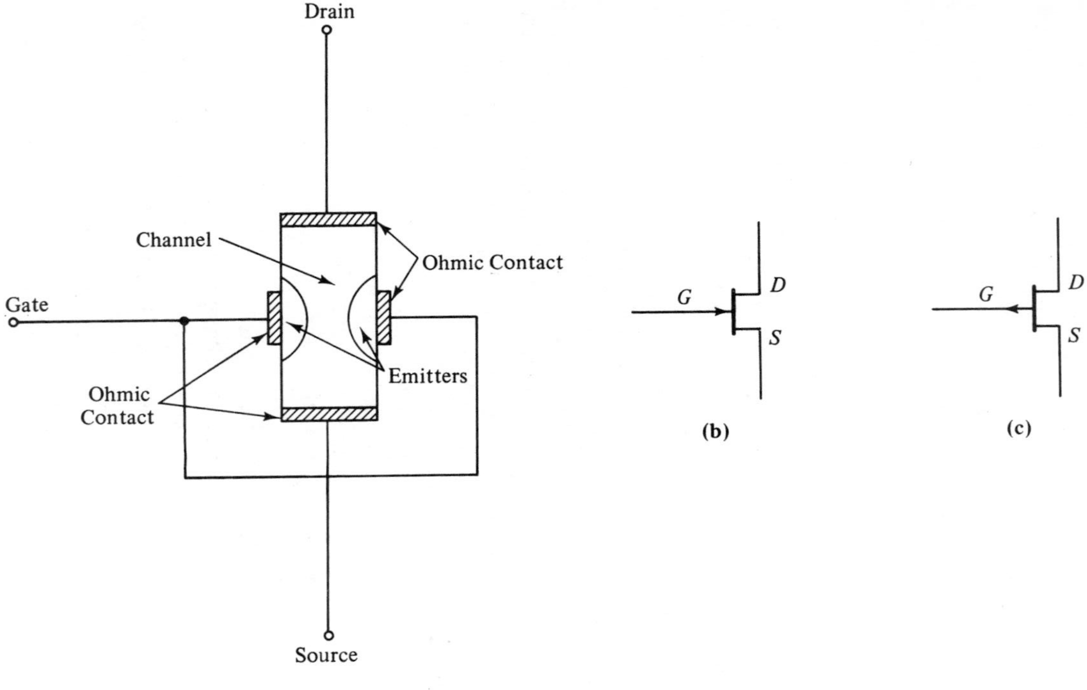

Figure 10.15 **(a)** Structure of a junction field effect transistor. **(b)** Circuit symbol for an *N*-channel JFET. **(c)** Circuit symbol for a *P*-channel JFET.

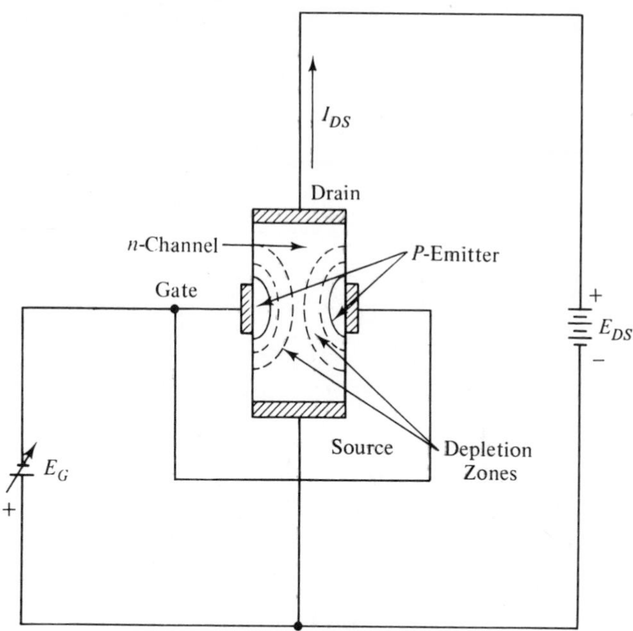

Figure 10.16 The emitter structure creates a depletion zone in the channel. The width of this zone depends upon the reverse bias between the gate (emitter structure) and determines the channel resistance.

totally dissimilar in actual operation, both the vacuum tube and the JFET can be described by using the same type of formula. For the JFET this formula is

$$g_m = \frac{\Delta I_c}{\Delta E_g} \tag{10-11}$$

A typical JFET amplifier sage is shown in Figure 10.17. A load resistor R_L is connected between the supply voltage and the JFET drain terminal. The output signal voltage is developed across this resistor by the drain-source current.

Bias for the JFET is developed by two different methods in this example, although only one would probably be used in any given real circuit. The first method is battery E_g, in which the (+) terminal is grounded and the (−) terminal is connected through a resistor to the JFET gate terminal. This method is not the most popular because of the need for an external battery.

The alternate method is to use a resistor such as R_s to place the

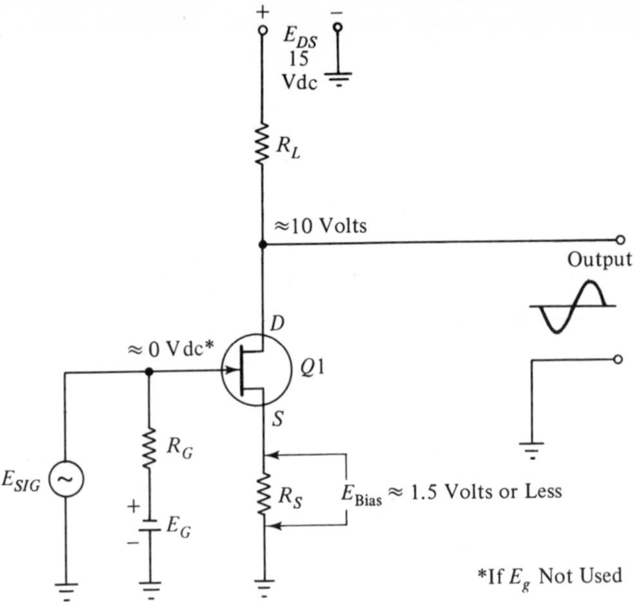

Figure 10.17 JFET as a voltage amplifier.

source terminal at a voltage, E_{bias}, that is slightly positive with respect to ground. The gate is at near-ground potential, even though resistor R_g tends to have a high value. Little voltage is developed across R_g, because the gate current is very tiny. For proper operation we want the gate to be more negative than the source. This is actually accomplished by making the source more positive than the gate. This is called *source bias* or *self-bias* and is analogous to the technique in vacuum tube circuits called *cathode bias*.

The JFET used as a voltage amplifier, as in Figure 10.17, has several interesting and useful properties. We have, for example, voltage phase reversal between input and output. Another property is the relationship between input and output impedances. The output impedance figures tend to be in the same range as those of the pentode vacuum tube—on the order of 100 kΩ to 1 mΩ—which make the JFET particularly useful in situations where the driving impedance is high.

MOSFET (IGFET) Devices. The basic MOSFET structure is shown in Figure 10.15(a). There is a difference between this type of FET and the JFET discussed previously. In the MOSFET there is no emitter forming the gate, but there is an ohmic contact used as the gate. This gate is separated from the channel by an extremely thin metal oxide insulator. The gate is able to affect happenings in the channel through the use of the electrostatic field created in the channel when a potential is impressed across the gate-channel terminals.

There are two basic types of MOSFET, enhancement and depletion types. In an enhancement mode MOSFET there is no current path through the channel when the gate voltage is zero. When a positive voltage is applied to the gate, conduction in the channel is enhanced, so current will flow from source to drain. The depletion mode FET operates in a manner similar to that of the JFET. When the gate potential is zero, there will be a low channel resistance, which is pinched off as the gate potential goes more negative. Some MOSFET devices will operate in either mode. For *N*-channel devices with this ability a negative gate potential causes depletion mode operation, and positive gate voltages cause enhancement mode. The channel resistance is a trade-off between the two at zero gate voltage.

The FET structure for both MOSFET and JFET, is usually formed on a substrate of semiconductor material of a type opposite that of the channel. In the *N*-channel type of FET, then, we have a *P*-type substrate. The channel and the substrate form a *P-N* junction that must be kept either at zero bias, or at a reverse bias. If this "diode" becomes forward-biased, it is probable that the device will be destroyed.

Another accidental destruction mechanism for MOSFET devices is the breakdown of the gate insulator due to excessive applied voltage. Static electricity collected on your body, tools, or workbench (etc.) can and does destroy MOSFET devices. When installing or handling these devices you must be grounded so that static electricity on your body is drained off harmlessly. Most susceptible MOSFETs come packaged in such a way as to prevent damage. Some are packed with a shorting ring binding all leads together. This ring is not cut off or removed until the device is installed in the circuit. Others are packed with the leads stuck into a piece of black, conductive foam. It should not be removed until installation into a circuit is imminent.

Follow these rules when working with MOSFET devices or circuit cards containing MOSFETs:

1. Connect together via wires your body (wristband electrode), tools, soldering irons, work surface (metal cookie sheet or piece of aluminum sheet nailed to the bench), the circuit, and the MOSFET.
2. Connect all of these together and earth them through a single 1-MΩ/2-W resistor. This provides a reasonable path to ground for static charges, and a resistance that is high enough to prevent injury to you if you should come in contact with a high potential. Connecting yourself accidentally to *110 Vac* while grounded, for example, probably would be fatal.

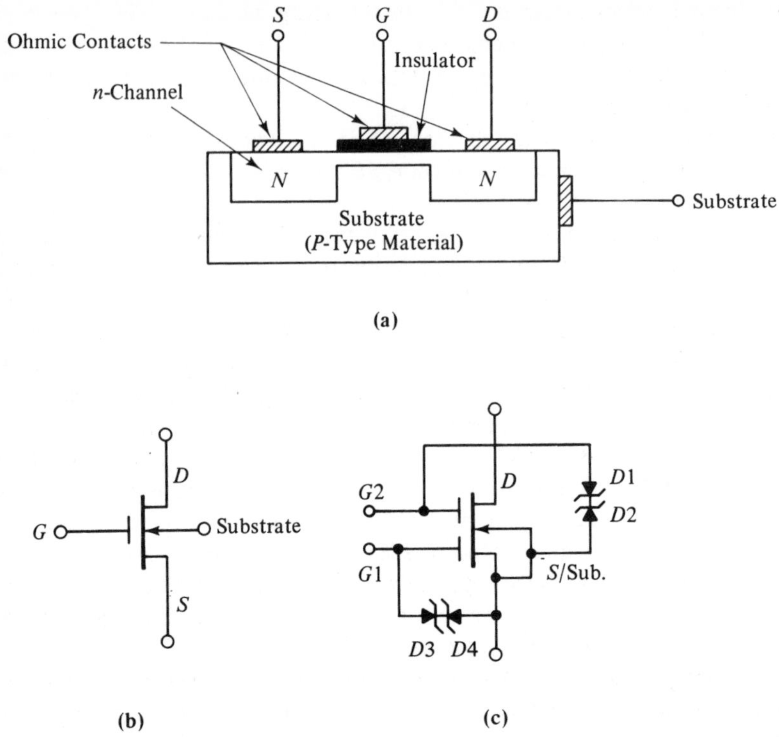

Figure 10.18 (a) Structure of a MOSFET, (b) Circuit symbol for a common MOSFET, (c) Circuit symbol for a diode-protected dual gate MOSFET.

The circuit symbol for a MOSFET such as discussed above is shown in Figure 10.18(b). A diode-protected, dual-gate, MOSFET symbol is shown in Figure 10.18(c). The diodes, which are discussed in the next section, are used to shunt excess voltages around the delicate gate insulator. Diode-protected, also called diode-clamped, MOSFETs can usually survive ungrounded handling. JFET devices, incidentally, require no special handling procedures.

10.10 ZENER DIODES

A special class of semiconductor devices used extensively in electronic communications equipment is the zener diode. Figure 10.19(a) shows the current-vs-voltage graph of the zener diode. When the zener diode is forward-biased it behaves very much like any solid-state diode. At some

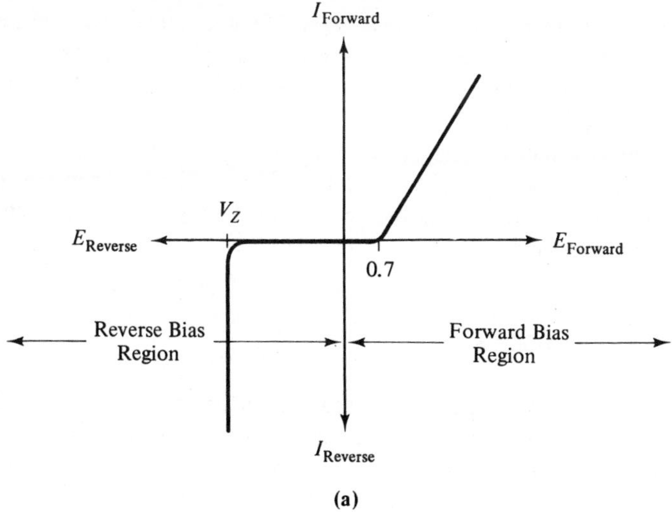

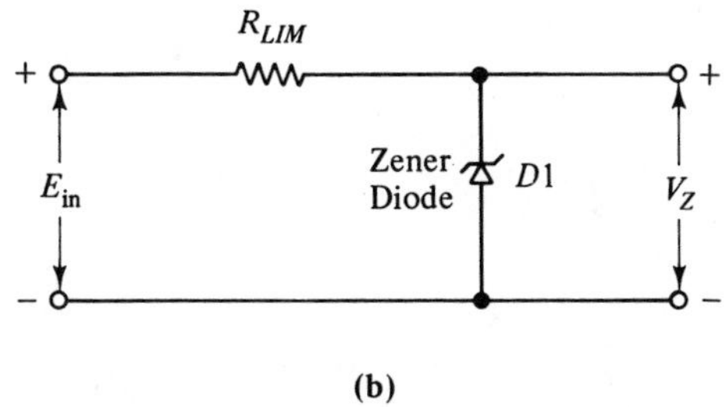

Figure 10.19 (a) I versus E characteristic for a zener diode. (b) Normal circuit operation of a zener diode voltage regulator.

potential around 0.6–0.7 V the current flow increases abruptly. The difference between ordinary diodes and the zener diodes is in the reverse-bias region.

When a regular diode becomes reverse-biased there will be no current flow. The zener, however, operates like a regular diode at reverse-bias potentials between 0 V and some particular reverse potential marked V_z in Figure 10.19(a). At that point there is an abrupt increase in reverse current flow. If the reverse voltage tries to increase, it will be clamped at V_z.

The clamping of input voltage to V_z allows use of the reverse-biased zener as either a voltage limiter or voltage regulator. Both applications would use a circuit like that of Figure 10.19(b). The limiter application occurs when E_{in} normally varies between 0 V and some potential less than V_z. If it attempts to exceed V_z, it is clamped. The zener diode ($D1$) is used to prevent possible damage to circuits following the limiter should E_{in} try to exceed its limits.

Voltage regulator applications are usually found in power supplies. In that case E_{in} is usually higher than V_z and may vary over a considerable range. The zener diode clamps the voltage to the level of V_z, and this level is reasonably constant.

10.11 TUNNEL DIODES

The tunnel diode is a unique device that, unfortunately, cannot be properly described without resorting to some very complicated ideas called "quantum mechanics." We can, however, describe the gross operation in a brief discussion.

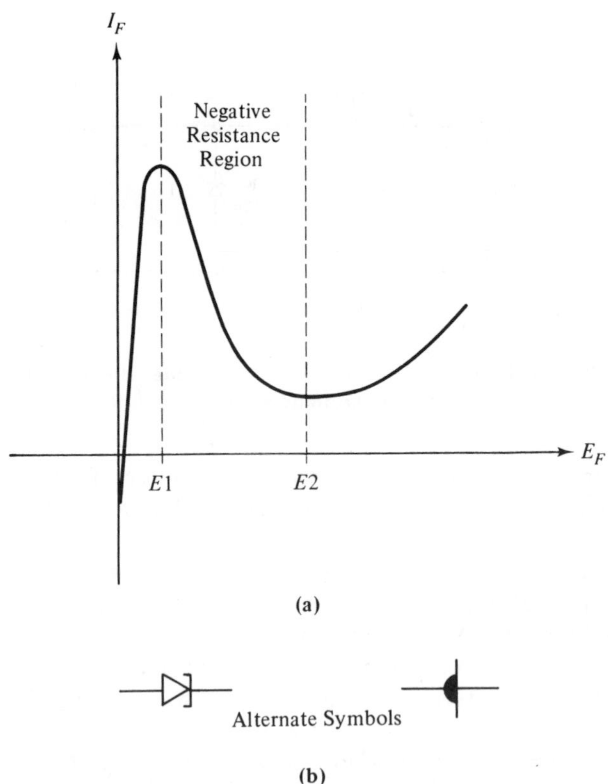

Figure 10.20 (a) I versus E characteristic for a tunnel diode. (b) Alternate circuit symbols for a tunnel diode.

The characteristic curve for the tunnel diode is shown in Figure 10.20(a). At potentials less than *E*1, the tunnel diode operates much like any forward-biased diode or *P-N* junction. In this region forward current increases as forward voltage also increases—the device obeys Ohm's law. Over a range of forward bias between *E*1 and *E*2, however, forward currant *decreases* as voltage *increases*. This is a property usually called *negative resistance*.

The tunnel diode can be made to switch, amplify, and oscillate (generate signals) if it is biased into the negative resistance region of its characteristic curve.

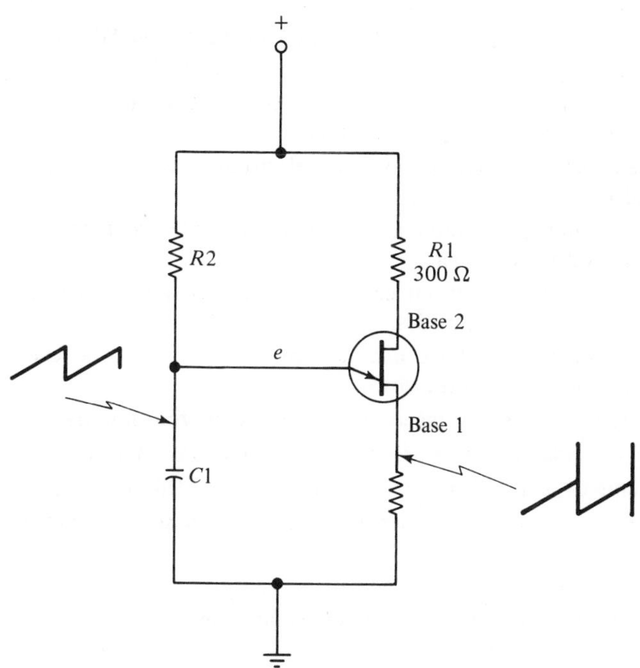

Figure 10.21 Unijunction transistor (UJT) relaxation oscillator.

10.12 THE UNIJUNCTION TRANSISTOR (UJT)

Figure 10.21 shows a unijunction transistor (UJT) and a typical circuit. The UJT is constructed much like a JFET(but with a critical difference. Instead of drain and source, the contacts at the ends are called "base 1" and "base 2."

Current conduction from *B*1 to *B*2 is limited unless the emitter-base junction becomes forward-biased. At that point the junction conduction increases dramatically. The circuit in Figure 10.21 is called a "UJT relaxation oscillator." There will be little $B1$-$B2$ conduction until the base-emitter voltage reaches a critical breakover point. This voltage is controlled by the charge on capacitor $C1$, which is charged from the power supply through resistor $R2$. The emitter voltage rises slowly until the breakover point is reached. At that time the b-e resistance drops suddenly, discharging $C1$. The waveform across $C1$ will be nearly a sawtooth, especially if the value of $R2$ is high.

PROBLEMS

1. A natural semiconductor diode used in pre-World War I-era crystal set radio receivers used a ____________ crystal.
2. Two examples of semiconductor elements used in the construction of transistors are ____________ and ____________.
3. These elements have four valence electrons in each atom. Such atoms are said to be ____________.
4. Silicon and germanium atoms in a crystal lattice form ____________ bonds with each other.
5. A semiconductor crystal can be turned into *N*-type material by adding ____________ impurities.
6. Pentavalent atoms have five valence electrons. Name a few examples of such atoms used in transistors.
7. Current carriers in a piece of *N*-type silicon are primarily ____________.
8. *P*-type semiconductors are doped with trivalent impurities.
9. Examples of trivalent impurities commonly used are ____________.
10. The positive carriers associated with *P*-type semiconductors are called ____________.
11. Describe a "hole."
12. The flow of holes in a *P*-type semiconductor is ____________ the flow of electrons.
13. A hole has an effective electric charge of ____________ unit(s).
14. Refer to Figure 10.22. The diode is ____________-biased.

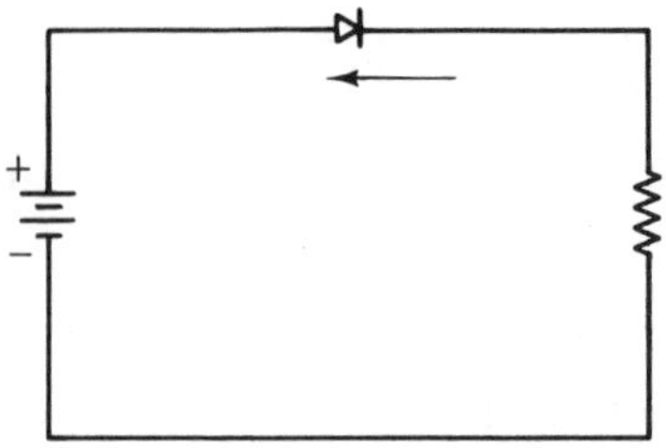

+
−

Figure 10.22

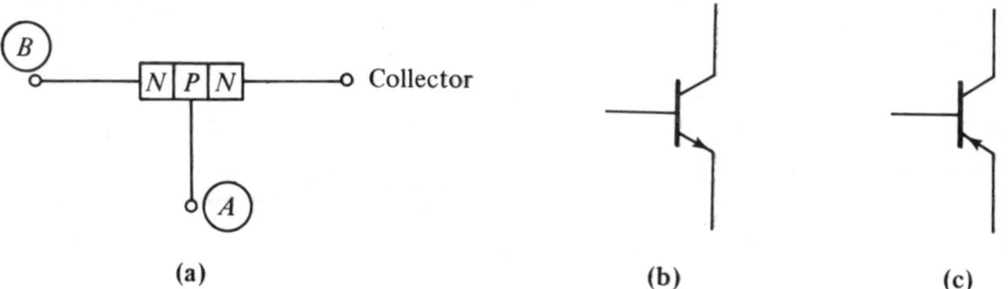

Figure 10.23

15. A reverse-biased *P-N* junction has a ____________ in the region where the *P*- and *N*-type materials are joined.
16. A *P-N* junction with a wide depletion zone has a ____________ resistance.
17. A minute flow of current across a reverse-biased *P-N* junction is called ____________ current.
18. A solid-state diode is basically a *P-N* junction. True or false?
19. Current flow in the circuit of Figure 10.22 is correct as shown. True or false?
20. Normal forward bias of a germanium *P-N* junction creates a voltage drop of ____________ V.
21. If the *P-N* junction in Question 20 were made of silicon instead of germanium, the drop would be ____________ V.
22. P.R.V. (also called p.i.v.) is the highest ____________ voltage that a *P-N* junction can tolerate.
23. Identify the two unnamed sections of Figure 10.23(a).
24. The symbol in Figure 10.23(b) represents a ____________ transistor.
25. The symbol in Figure 10.23(c) represents a ____________ transistor.
26. Current flow in a transistor amplifier is controlled by the ____________.
27. The following normal voltages are found on a transistor: collector, +3; emitter, +14; base, +13.4. The transistor is a ____________-type.
28. The following normal voltages are found on a transistor: collector, +10; base, +0.7; emitter, 0. The transistor is a ____________.
29. Only about ____________ percent of the emitter current in an *NPN* transistor passes out of the base terminal.
30. The bipolar (*NPN* or *PNP*) transistor is basically a ____________ amplifier.
31. An emitter resistor is sometimes used to improve ____________.
32. The relationship I_c/I_e represents ____________.
33. Compute the alpha gain if the collector current is 900 μA and the emitter current is 0.99 mA.
34. Beta gain is 60, and collector current is 100 mA. Find the base current.

35. Alpha is given as 0.95; find the beta gain.
36. Beta is 150; find the alpha gain.
37. $\Delta I_c / \Delta I_b$ represents ________.
38. F_{ab}, the alpha cutoff, is the frequency where alpha drops ________ from its 1000-Hz value.
39. Beta cutoff is usually ________ than alpha cutoff.
40. Beta cutoff is defined as the frequency at which the beta gain drops ________ relative to its 1000-Hz value.
41. A transistor has an F_t of 100 MHz. What is the value of h_{fe} at 5 MHz?
42. The h_{fe} of the above transistor at 100 MHz is ________.
43. In a common-emitter amplifier the ________ is part of both input and output circuits.
44. The current gain in a common-emitter amplifier is approximately equal to ________.
45. The common-emitter amplifier can operate as both a current and a ________ amplifier.
46. A common emitter amplifier has a 2.7-kΩ collector load resistor and a 560-Ω emitter resistor. If the ac beta gain (h_{fe}) is 90, what is the approximate voltage gain?
47. Find the approximate input impedance if $h_{fe} = 150$, and $R_e = 1000\ \Omega$.
48. In a common-collector circuit the ________ is part of both input and output circuits.
49. The voltage gain of a common-collector circuit is ________.
50. What is the current gain of a common-collector circuit?
51. In a common-emitter voltage amplifier the input and output signal are ________ phase with each other.
52. In a common-collector voltage amplifier the input and output signals are ________ with each other.
53. In a common-base voltage amplifier the input and output signals are ________ with each other.
54. Another name for the common-collector circuit is ________.
55. Give two applications for the emitter follower.
56. In a common-base amplifier the current gain is approximately ________.
57. A common-base amplifier exhibits ________ gain.
58. A transistor in which a single emitter is fused into a source-drain semiconductor channel is called a ________.
59. Reverse bias applied between the gate and source terminals of a JFET creates a ________ in the channel.
60. A large depletion zone creates a ________ channel resistance.
61. In a *P*-channel JFET the drain is made more (negative) (positive) than the source.

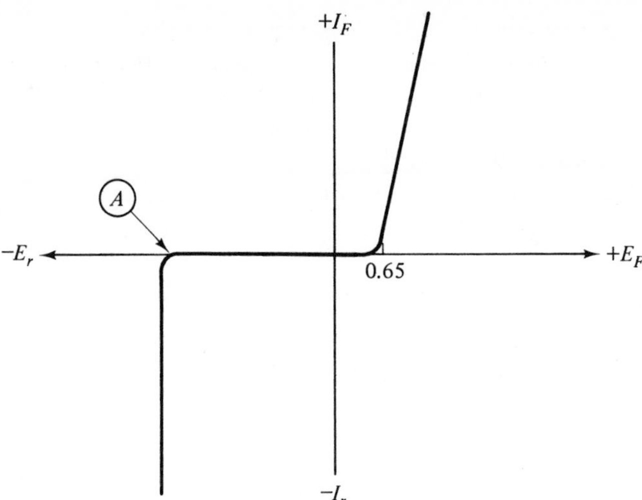

Figure 10.24

62. The source-gate voltage that reduces current flow in the channel to zero is called the _______ voltage.
63. What is the transconductance of a JFET if a 0.5-V change in gate voltage causes a 1-mA change in drain current?
64. The characteristics of a JFET are similar to those of a _______ vacuum tube.
65. The input impedance of a JFET is typically _______.
66. An FET with a thin insulating layer of a metal oxide or glass material between a gate electrode and the semiconductor channel material is called a _______ or an _______.
67. There are two basic operating modes for MOSFET devices. These are called _______ and _______.
68. Enhancement mode MOSFETs are normally (on) (off) when $E_g = 0$.
69. The foundation of semiconductor material on which JFET and MOSFET devices are made is called the _______.
70. The *P-N* junction between the channel and the substrate must be kept _______, or the device will be destroyed.
71. The characteristic curve in Figure 10.24 is for a _______.
72. The point in Figure 10.24 marked *A* is called _______.
73. Special precautions must be taken when one is handling unprotected MOSFETs because _______ on your tools, body, etc. can damage the gate insulator.
74. _______ and _______ are examples of field effect transistors that may be handled in ordinary ways.

75. A diode sometimes used for voltage regulation is the _______.

76. A _______ diode is sometimes used to generate UHF or microwave signals because of its negative-resistance capability.

77. A unijunction transistor used to generate a sawtooth waveform is in a _______ oscillator circuit.

78. A diode that is normally reverse-biased is the _______.

11
Basic Amplifiers

11.1 TYPES OF AMPLIFIERS

There are several methods for classifying amplifiers, in addition to the obvious method of accounting for whether they use bipolar transistors, FETs, or tubes. Two principal classification systems are based on the transfer function and the conduction angle, respectively.

Under the first method there are four basic categories: voltage, current, transconductance, and transresistance.

A voltage amplifier typically has a transfer function that relates the output voltage that is expected for any given value of input voltage, and the voltage gain (A_v). The transfer function for such an amplifier is

$$E_{out} = A_v \times E_{in} \qquad (11\text{-}1)$$

Voltage amplifiers tend to have very high input impedances so as to prevent loading of the previous stages. Similarly, a true voltage amplifier has a very low output impedance. An ideal voltage amplifier has an infinite input impedance and an output impedance of zero, but, of course, ideal amplifiers of any description exist only in our mind. (See Table 11.1.)

Table 11.1. Properties of Voltage, Current, Transconductance, and Transresistance Amplifiers.

	Voltage Ampl.	Current Ampl.	gm	Transresistance
Transfer Function	$E_o = A_v E_{in}$	$I_o = A_i I_{in}$	$I_o = \text{gm}\, E_{in}$	$E_o = R_x I_{in}$
R_{in}	Very High	Very Low	High	Very Low
R_{out}	Very Low	Very High	High	Very Low

Current amplifiers have a transfer function that is very similar to that of the voltage amplifier. In a current amplifier the output current is related to the input current and a gain factor:

$$I_{out} = A_i \times I_{in} \tag{11-2}$$

The input impedance of the current amplifier must be very low so as to not impede the flow of input current. The output impedance, on the other hand, must be very high so that variations in external load impedance will not affect the output current.

We discussed the transconductance amplifier g_m under the vacuum tube and FET discussions. Such amplifiers have a transfer function that relates an output current to an input voltage and a property called *transconductance*. The transfer function follows from the definition of transconductance:

$$g_m = \frac{\Delta I_{out}}{\Delta E_{in}} \tag{11-3}$$

So the transfer function is

$$I_{out} = g_m \times E_{in} \tag{11-4}$$

Since the transconductance amplifier usually follows a voltage source, it must have a high input impedance. Similarly, the g_m amplifier must have a very high output resistance so that it will act as a current source.

11.2 AMPLIFICATION CLASSES—CONDUCTION ANGLE

One of the most commonly applied methods for categorizing amplifiers is by the *amplification class*. This method of designating amplifiers is used with both tube and transistor circuits, and is based solely on conduction angle.

The conduction angle is defined as the length of time, as measured in degrees over a single cycle of the input waveform, that collector (or plate) current flows. The following classes are established:

Class A. Class A amplifiers are those in which the collector or plate current flows over the entire 360 deg of the input cycle.

Class B. In this class of amplifier the collector or plate current flows over only 180 deg of the input cycle.

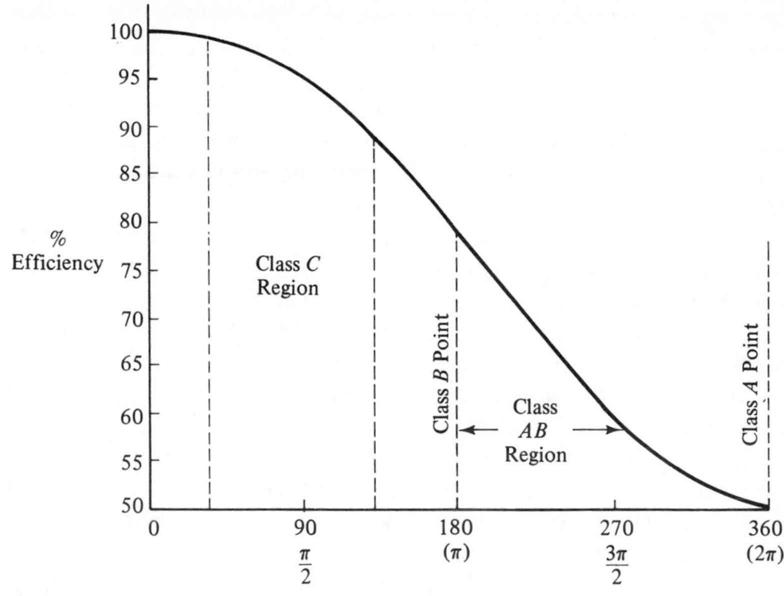

Figure 11.1 Percentage efficiency versus conduction angle.

Class C. Current flows in the collector or plate for something less than 180 deg of the input cycle, with 120 deg being a popular value.

Class AB. Actually this is a subclass or a trade-off between class A and class B. In the class AB amplifier the collector or plate current flows somewhat longer than 180 deg of the input cycle, but less than the full 360 deg of the class A amplifier.

The relative efficiencies of the various amplifier classes may be seen in Figure 11.1, where we have a graph of plate circuit efficiency-vs-conduction angle. Efficiency is the relationship

$$\frac{\text{DC input power}}{\text{Output power}} \times 100 = \frac{E_b I_p}{P_{out}} \times 100 \qquad (11\text{-}5)$$

The second expression is given in the notation of vacuum tubes.

Unfortunately, efficiency is not the sole criterion to be considered in the design of radio amplifier stages. We may, for example, also be required to pay attention to linearity. This is a measure of the degree to which the output signal resembles the input signal. If only one tube or transistor is used in the stage, good linearity is possible only in the class A amplifier. Two other classes, B and AB, will prove to be linear if two tubes or transistors are used in a special circuit, which we will discuss shortly—these are called "push-pull" amplifiers. Class C amplifiers are not suited at all to linear operation, but will generate the most power in any given configuration.

Efficiency becomes important, however, where amplifier design is considered because the power lost ($P_{dc} - P_{out}$) is given up as heat in the anode or collector. If the heat lost is greater than the rated heat dissipation of the device, we will expect a shortened life expectancy at least, and immediate destruction of the device at worst. For any given output power level, then, class A stages will require more dc power and will operate hotter than classes B, C, or AB.

Before proceeding further with our discussion of amplifier classes, we shall digress a moment to describe radio frequency (RF) amplifiers. This will give us an application on which to hang our discussion of the classification system.

Figure 11.2(a) shows the schematic of an RF amplifier using a vacuum tube as the active element. This circuit uses an untuned input circuit in which the input signal E_{in} is impressed across grid resistor R_g. Bias for the amplifier tube is provided by a C supply, such as a battery. Capacitors $C1$ and $C2$ are used to block dc potentials so that they will not appear across either input or output terminals. The plate circuit is tuned by a parallel resonant tank circuit consisting of coil $L1$ and capacitor $C3$. Capacitors $C4$ and $C5$ are used to provide a low-impedance path to ground for the RF signals, but not for dc potentials.

The waveforms for the class A amplifier are shown in Figure 11.2(b). The negative bias voltage E_c is set at a value about halfway between cutoff and zero bias. The maximum allowable peak value for E_{in} will be E_c. If this is kept true, then bias will just approach zero on positive peaks of E_{in}, and just approach cutoff on negative peaks. For a class A amplifier the important point is that plate current flows over the entire 360 deg of input signal waveform E_{in}.

The efficiency figures given in Table 11.1 are theoretical maximums, and actual attainable efficiency may be from none to these values, depending upon the situation. A class A amplifier will only approach 50 percent efficiency if operated at certain optimum dc potentials, and if the load impedance matches the plate impedance of the tube. The former requirement is seldom met, so we find most class A power amplifiers operating at about 20 to 30 percent efficiency. Typically, a class A amplifier, optimally matched to the load, that is required to generate 25 W of RF or audio power will require almost 100 W of dc power from the supply.

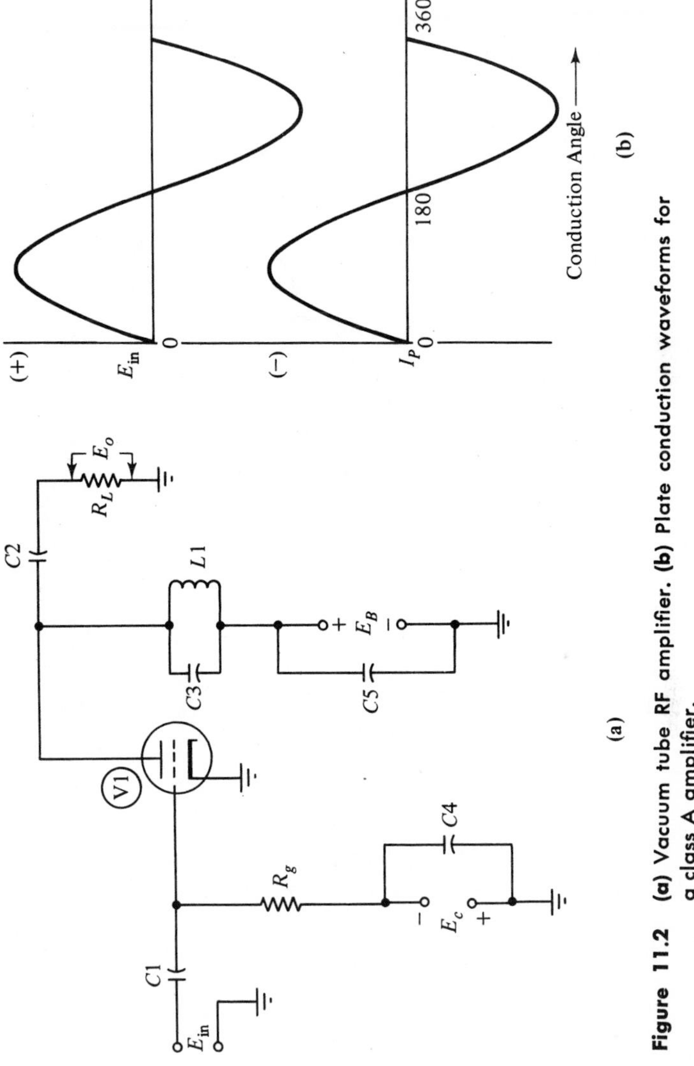

Figure 11.2 **(a) Vacuum tube RF amplifier. (b) Plate conduction waveforms for a class A amplifier.**

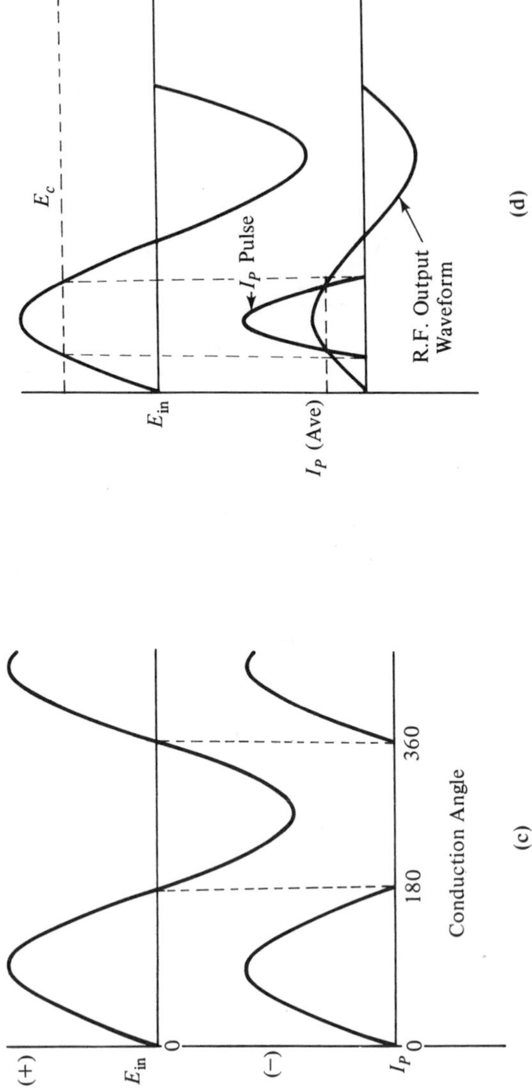

Figure 11.2 (cont.) **(c)** Plate conduction waveforms for a class B amplifier. **(d)** Plate conduction waveforms for a class C amplifier.

If the load impedance is much higher than the output impedance, then very little power is generated, but the output voltage is maximized. Since most class A amplifiers are operated in this manner, we usually think of the class A amplifier as a voltage amplifier. Be aware, though, that there are many examples of class A power amplifiers, such as the audio output stages of radio communications receivers—especially mobile units.

It is also a fact that class A amplifiers are usually operated over a straight portion of the characteristic curve, so they are *linear amplifiers.* An amplifier is linear if it produces little or no distortion in the output signal. Class A amplifiers draw current all of the time. Even when the input voltage is zero, we find current drain. In that case the drain will be approximately one-half the full drain. A class A amplifier therefore generates relatively large amounts of heat energy. The grid circuit of a class A amplifier does not draw any current, so no power is required from the source [$P = E_{in}I_{in} = E_{in}\ (0) = 0$]. This means that the stages driving a class A amplifier need not be power amplifiers, but may be voltage amplifiers.

Figure 11.2(c) shows the waveforms associated with the class B amplifier. In this case a high-mu tube is used with zero dc bias on the grid. Low-mu tubes may also be used, but may require some value of negative grid bias, especially if plate current runaway proves to be a problem. In this latter case, current will flow over a slightly different conduction angle. In either case, however, input voltage E_{in} must drive the tube hard into the region where the grid will draw current. This, of course, means that the driving source must be a power amplifier or power source; otherwise the grid will be starved for current.

The class B amplifier is not linear, but it can be made linear if a push-pull circuit (of which, more later) is used. The class B amplifier can be used to generate RF pulses, however, and the tube can be worked harder than was true in the class A case.

There are two versions, or subclasses, of the class AB amplifier. These stages are biased higher than class A stages so that current does not flow over the entire cycle of the input signal. Class AB_1 amplifiers are not driven hard enough for the input signal to overcome the negative grid bias, and produce an input current. The other subclass, class AB_2, *is* driven hard enough to produce a grid current, but only on the small excursion of the input signal's peak.

The conduction situation for a class C amplifier is shown in Figure 11.2(d). This class of amplifier has a very high negative bias, so plate current flow will occur only over a very small portion of the input waveform's positive peak. The dc plate current flows in a pulse at the peak of this waveform. In the tuned plate of the circuit of Figure 11.2(a) there will be a "flywheel effect" that will make the output waveform a sine wave again. Flywheel effect results from the collapse of the magnetic field around coil $L1$, and tends to fill in the missing half of the output waveform. This is not to say that the class C amplifier is linear; it is decidedly *nonlinear,* but it will produce a sine wave RF output. Class C amplifiers are normally used in radiotelegraph, FM, and some types of AM transmitters. They cannot be used for single sideband (SSB) or TV video applications.

11.3 NEGATIVE FEEDBACK AMPLIFIERS

Many aspects of amplifier performance can be improved by providing *negative* or *degenerative feedback.* The block diagram of this idea is shown in Figure 11.3. Among the benefits of the feedback amplifier are improved stability and lower distortion.

Negative feedback, also called degenerative feedback, is a sample of the output signal, fed back to the input of the amplifier, 180 deg out of phase with the input signal. As a general rule, the transfer function of a negative feedback amplifier takes into account the inverse of the transfer function of the feedback path.

The gain of the feedback amplifier is less than the gain of the amplifier without feedback. The open-loop feedback (A_{vol}) gain is typically very high, but the closed-loop gain, A_v, is found from

$$A_v = \frac{A_{vol}}{1 + (A_{vol})\,B} \tag{11-6}$$

and represents the gain with the feedback path connected.

Details of various feedback loops vary somewhat with amplifier type, so only the generic type has been given here. Other types will be discussed in different chapters.

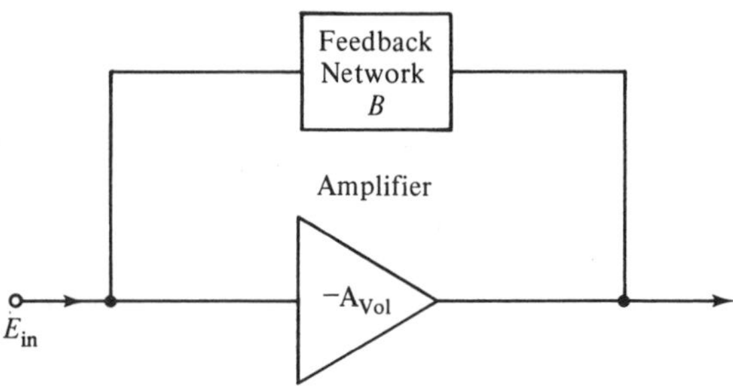

Figure 11.3 Principle of a feedback amplifier.

11.4 CASCADE AMPLIFIERS

The gain that is attainable in any one amplifier stage is limited by a number of factors. Amplifiers can, however, be connected so that the output of one becomes the input signal driving the input of the next. Amplifier stages connected in this manner are said to be in *cascade*.

In some cases the overall gain of the cascade chain will be the gain of one stage multiplied by the gain of the next, and so on. In other words, $A_{v(\text{total})} = A_{v1} \times A_{v2} \times \ldots \times A_{vn}$. In many cases, however, there is some mutual interaction between stages in cascade that tends to reduce gain to some figure less than the products of the individual gains.

11.5 AMPLIFIER COUPLING

Some method for coupling between amplifiers in cascade must be provided. In fact, two stages not properly coupled will most probably not work at all. It is also necessary to couple the last amplifier in the cascade chain to its external load. Several different coupling techniques are in common use. These are direct, transformer, and resistance. The last method is called "capacitor coupling" by some authorities. There is also a technique, not much in evidence anymore, called choke or impedance coupling.

Direct Coupling. Of the several methods for coupling, direct coupling is probably the simplest to implement. Figure 11.4 shows an example of a direct-coupled cascade amplifier. In this type of circuit the operating point of transistor *Q*1 is set so that the collector voltage is the same as the potential required as the base voltage by transistor *Q*2. Although only two stages are shown here, there might actually be almost any number in cascade.

A direct-coupled amplifier is often called a "dc amplifier" not because of the initials for "direct-coupled," but because it will pass signals of frequencies down to dc (0 Hz). A small dc potential perturbing the input of such an amplifier will create a change in the output voltage.

Although you will certainly find examples of direct-coupled amplifiers using vacuum tubes in communications equipment, the technique has been most popular in the design of transistorized equipments. In the transistor circuits the voltage difference requirements are smaller, so the technique has improved in popularity.

Frequency response refers to the range of frequencies that an amplifier will pass at approximately the same gain. This is usually measured as "so many kilohertz between those points where the gain has dropped

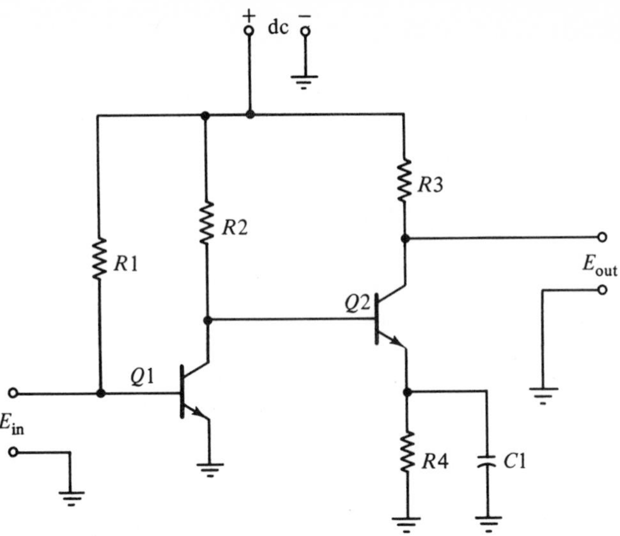

Figure 11.4 Direct-coupled cascade amplifier.

3 dB." In a direct-coupled amplifier frequency response is limited mostly by the properties of the transistors used.

Transformer Coupling. Figure 11.5 shows two examples of transformer coupling in a two-stage cascade amplifier. Transistor $Q1$ is used as a driver stage to build up the signal to the level required by the base circuit of transistor $Q2$. Transformer $T1$, then, is used as an *interstage coupling transformer.*

Transformer $T2$ is used to match the output load resistance R_L to the impedance of the $Q2$ collector circuit. Recall that maximum power transfer occurs only when the source impedance and the load impedance are matched. In this case, the stage is operating as a power amplifier, so impedance matching becomes important, even critical. The relationship between the two impedances is given by

$$\left(\frac{Z_{pri}}{Z_{sec}}\right)^{1/2} = \frac{N_{pri}}{N_{sec}} \tag{11-7}$$

where Z_{pri} is the impedance of the primary as reflected from the secondary.
Z_{sec} is the impedance of the load R_L.
N_{pri} is the number of turns in the primary.
N_{sec} is the number of turns in the secondary.

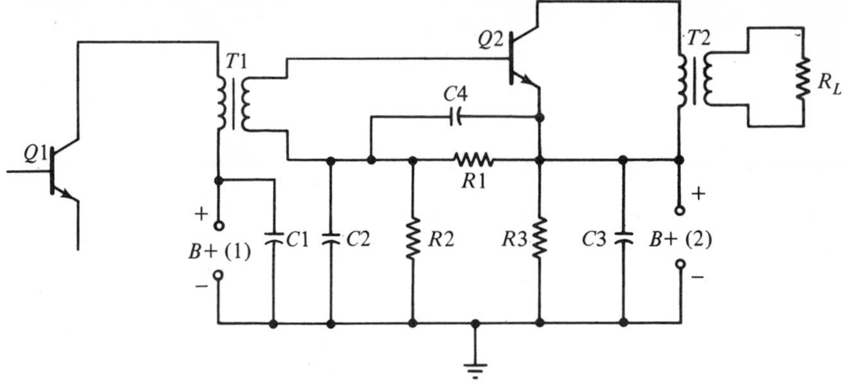

Figure 11.5 Transformer coupled amplifier.

Transformer coupling is not without problems, however. Most immediately, we notice that transformer coupling is much more expensive than other types. It is also sometimes true that good transformers are hard to obtain in turns ratios that most nearly meet the requirements of the circuit. Another problem is that the magnetic field surrounding the transformer may be coupled to other circuits. Similarly, other magnetic fields in the circuit may be coupled into the amplifier via the transformer. A common occurrence of this problem is the 60-Hz field surrounding power transformers coupling into an audio amplifier via the interstage coupling transformer. This induces a 60-Hz hum into the coupling transformer. This can be partially eliminated by the use of electrostatic shields in each transformer, but that adds to cost. The frequency response of transformer-coupled amplifiers is a little less than with other types of coupling. Transformers have a relatively poor frequency response unless you can afford the cost of high-quality units.

Resistance Coupling. Resistance coupling, such as that shown in Figure 11.6, is used mostly for coupling together voltage amplifier stages. The gain of stage *V*1 is partially dependent upon the value of the plate resistance R_p. In general, up to a certain limit, the higher the value of the plate resistance, the higher the voltage gain of the stage. It is, however, also necessary to consider the grid resistance of the stage following (R_g). The grid resistor should be larger than the plate resistance by a factor of at least two, but in standard practice designers like to see the grid resistance greater than five times the plate resistance.

There are two different paths for current in almost all types of amplifier stage: one each for ac and dc voltages. The dc path has been discussed at length in previous chapters, so it will only be given here in general form. For stage $V1$ in Figure 11.6, the dc path is from ground through the cathode and plate of $V1$, plate resistance R_p, the $B+$ supply, and back to ground. The ac path, however, is slightly different. AC signals pass through capacitor $C1$ to resistor R_g and the grid of $V2$, but dc is blocked by $C1$. In a similar manner, capacitors $C2$ and $C3$ will pass the ac signals, but will block dc. These latter capacitors are called "bypass capacitors" because they bypass ac signals around the $B+$ and $C-$ power supplies.

In the transistor circuit of Figure 11.5, capacitors $C1$–$C4$ are used for bypassing, so they are considered part of the ac circuit. Transformers $T1$ and $T2$, on the other hand, are part of both ac and dc circuits. The primary of transformer $T1$ is part of the dc path in the collector circuit of transistor $Q1$. The secondary of $T1$, however, is in the dc path of the $Q2$ base circuit. The primary of transformer $T2$ is part of the dc path of the $Q2$ collector circuit, yet its secondary is not part of any dc path, so is solely in the ac path.

In any circuit where capacitors are used to block dc, but pass ac, there are rules to follow regarding their values. The reactance of the capacitor must be low (i.e. 1/10) relative to the impedance at dc. Capacitor $C1$ in Figure 11.6, for example, must have a value such that its reactance at the lowest frequency to be amplified is one-tenth of the parallel combination of R_p and R_g. In a similar manner, X_{c2} at the lowest frequency to be amplified must be one-tenth of the impedance of the dc $B+$ supply. These rules are not actually absolute, but are generally taken to be good engineering practice.

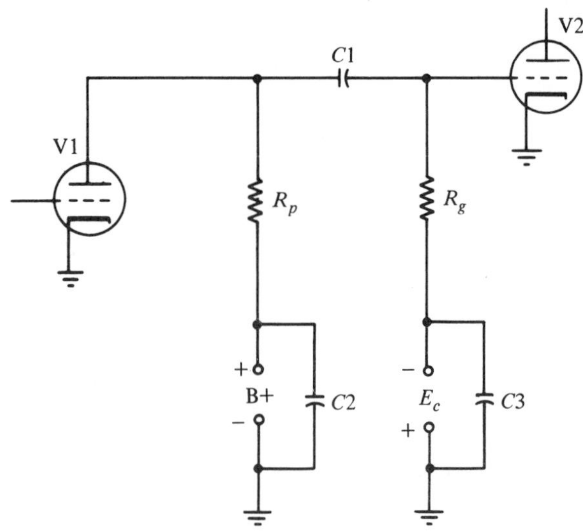

Figure 11.6 Resistance coupling.

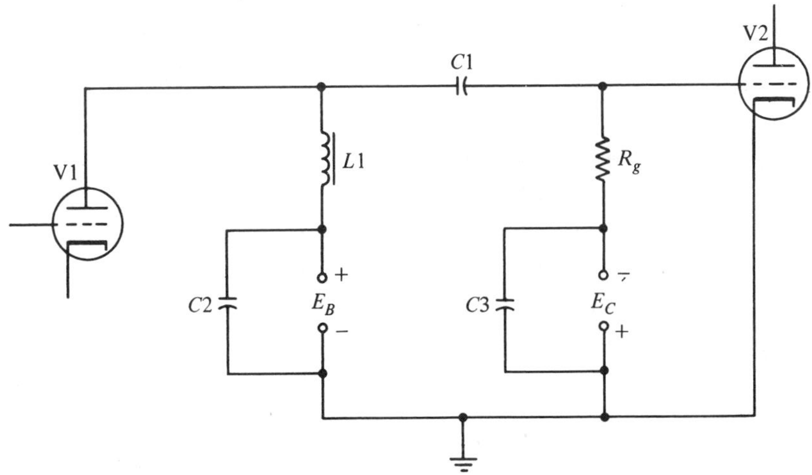

Figure 11.7 Choke or impedance coupling.

Choke Coupling. An example of choke or "impedance" coupling is shown in Figure 11.7. The only real advantage to this circuit is that the peak ac signal voltage developed across inductor $L1$ is greater than it would be if resistance coupling were used. In fact, E_{peak} approaches the value of $B+$ in Figure 11.7, but only ½ $B+$ in circuits such as that in Figure 11.6. This, of course, results in a much higher stage gain, but not without some penalty. The inductor $L1$ suffers from almost all of the defects suffered by transformers. As a result, impedance coupling is not very popular in modern equipment designs.

PROBLEMS

1. An ideal voltage amplifier has an ________ input impedance.
2. Collector current flows over ________ degrees of the input cycle in a class A amplifier.
3. Collector current flows over ________ degrees of the input cycle in a class B amplifier.
4. Collector current flows over ________ degrees of the input cycle in a class C amplifier.
5. The conduction angle of a class AB amplifier is less than ________ degrees but greater than ________ degrees.
6. A class A amplifier has a dc input to the plate of 150 W and an RF output power of 38 W. What is the efficiency?
7. A ________ amplifier is linear, but requires only a single transistor.

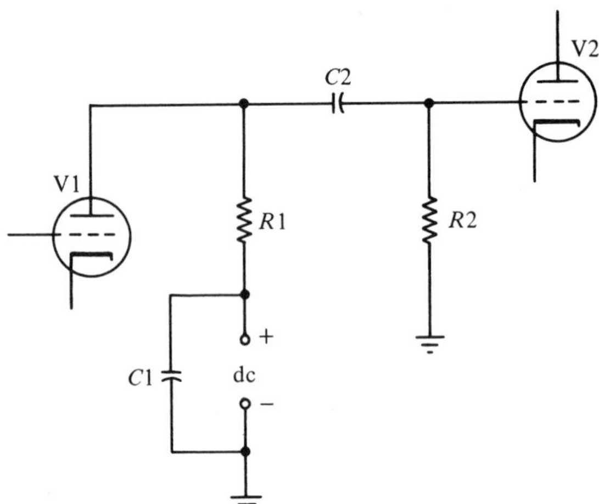

Figure 11.8

8. Power lost between input power and signal output power converts to ________ in the anode.
9. The peak driving voltage that may be applied to a class A amplifier is ________.
10. The maximum efficiency of a class A amplifier is ______ percent.
11. A class A amplifier in which the load resistance is much greater than the plate resistance is usually called a ________ amplifier.
12. If an amplifier stage draws grid current, then only ________ may be used as driver source.
13. Zero-bias class B amplifier stages require ________ triodes.
14. A class AB_1 amplifier (does) (does not) draw grid current.
15. A class AB_2 amplifier (does) (does not) draw grid current.
16. An RF output sine wave is produced from dc plate current pulses due to a ________ in the plate tank circuit of a class C amplifier.
17. Amplifier performance can often be improved by ________ feedback.
18. Another name for negative feedback is ________ feedback.
19. The open-loop gain A_{vol} of an amplifier is 1000, and the feedback factor B is 0.01. Find the closed-loop gain of the amplifier.
20. An amplifier with an output impedance of 2500 Ω is to be coupled through a transformer to a 10-Ω load. What turns ratio is required?
21. An example of ________ coupling is shown in Figure 11.8.
22. The purpose of $C2$ in Figure 11.8 is ________.
23. The purpose of $C1$ in Fig. 11.8 is ________.
24. In general, the reactance of a bypass capacitor should be ________ of the impedance being bypassed.
25. In resistance-coupled stages the peak ac output voltage is limited to ________.

12
Power Supplies

Most electronic circuits require direct current power sources for proper operation. In our examples previous to this chapter we have shown batteries as the power supply, but that is not the usual case in real communications equipment, except for the portable models.

The usual commercial power available in the United States is 60-Hz, 115-V ac. The function of the dc power supply circuit is to convert this readily available ac power to a dc level appropriate to the use intended. A power transformer is used to reduce or increase the voltage level as appropriate. The actual conversion of the ac to smooth dc is the function of a circuit called the rectifier-filter.

12.1 RECTIFIERS

The one major difference between alternating current and direct current is that ac flows in both directions, while dc flows in only one direction. A *rectifier* is a device that will allow current to flow in only one direction, so it will convert ac to dc. You should recall that vacuum tube and solid-state diodes possess this property, so they are used in the conversion. There is also such a thing as a mechanical rectifier, but they are no longer in widespread use. Although most of the illustrations in this chapter show solid-state diodes, most of the circuits are also suitable for use with vacuum tube devices. In fact, some older textbooks usually used the vacuum tube version because solid-state rectifiers had not achieved the maturity to be popular. In those days the solid-state diodes had a limited voltage and current capacity, so they could only be used in the lowest-powered supplies.

Halfwave Rectifiers. Figure 12.1 shows a simple halfwave rectifier circuit. Transformer *T*1 changes the 115-V ac power from the mains to the level required. In general, but by no means universally, it is proper to state that power transformer power supplies feeding vacuum tube circuits step the voltage up. Whereas those feeding transistor circuits are step-down.

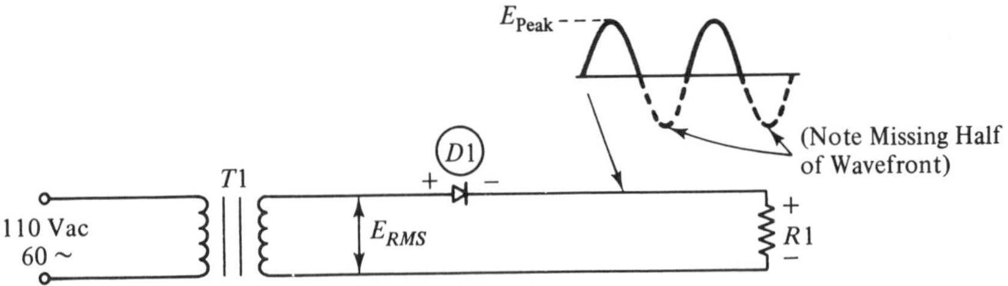

Figure 12.1 A halfwave rectified power supply.

Diode $D1$ will conduct only when its anode is positive with respect to the cathode. This fact shows up in the waveform of Figure 12.1, in which only one alternation of the ac cycle is passed through the rectifier. This is a so-called "single-hump" waveform. On alternate half-cycles the anode of diode $D1$ will be negative with respect to the cathode, so diode $D1$ will be reverse-biased—and no current will pass. This portion of the waveform shows up in Figure 12.1 as the missing hump, which produces a gap, because the negative alternation is cut out. The output of a halfwave rectifier is not pure dc, but is called "pulsating direct current." The pulsation or "ripple" frequency of a halfwave rectified sine wave is 60 Hz, or the same as the line.

Pulsating dc is almost as useless in electronic circuits as sine wave ac. A filter circuit following the rectifier must be used to smooth out the pulsations to produce a nearly pure dc waveform. This filtering process is necessary in all rectifier power supplies, but in the halfwave type of supply it is especially troublesome, and more difficult to completely eliminate. Because of these problems it is rare to find a halfwave rectifier in commercial electronics equipment, or any other equipment where the purity of the dc supply is important. Its primary use is in consumer electronics devices such as radio and television receivers. A widely used alternative is the fullwave rectifier of Figure 12.2.

The transformer for a fullwave rectifier circuit is center-tapped on the secondary. Such transformers are often rated in catalogs and specification sheets as having a certain number of volts center-tapped, or in the volts-0-volts manner. A typical transformer, for example, might be rated at 350-0-350 volts, or "700 volts center-tapped."

With reference to Figure 12.2, on one half of each alternation, point A will be positive with respect to the center tap, and point B will be negative. On the second half of each alternation the situation reverses, making A negative and B positive.

When point A is positive, diode $D1$ conducts. The current flow in this case is from the center tap through resistor $R1$, from minus to plus, to diode $D1$, and the point A end of the transformer, through the transformer

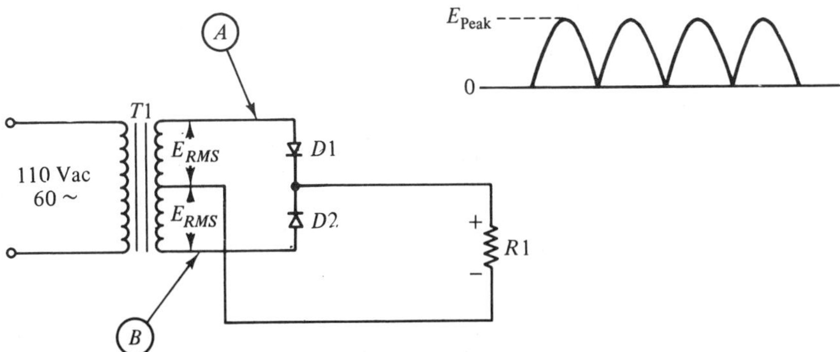

Figure 12.2 Fullwave rectification.

secondary back to the center tap. This current flow path is shown in Figure 12.3(a). On the second half-cycle, diode *D*1 is reverse-biased, but diode *D*2 becomes forward-biased. The current flow path switches from that of Figure 12.3(a) to that of Figure 12.3(b). Notice that the direction of current flow through load resistor *R*1 *does not change.* In both cases, regardless of whether it is *D*1 or *D*2 that is conducting, the direction of current flow through the load is the same. This produces the characteristic double-humped fullwave output waveform of Figure 12.2(b). In this case the second half of the alternation (negative side of the ac input waveform) is flipped over. The pulsation, or ripple, frequency in a fullwave rectifier power supply is twice that of the ac power mains, or 120 Hz in the United States. This higher ripple frequency is the reason why fullwave rectifier power supplies are less difficult to filter than are halfwave supplies.

The regular fullwave rectifier power supply utilizes only half of the transformer secondary winding because of the necessity for a center tap. The fullwave supply of Figure 12.4 offers the advantages of both fullwave

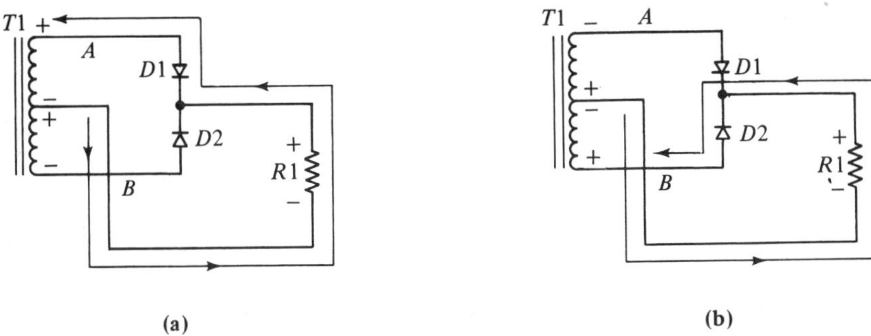

Figure 12.3 Current flow on alternate halves of the ac cycle in a fullwave power supply.

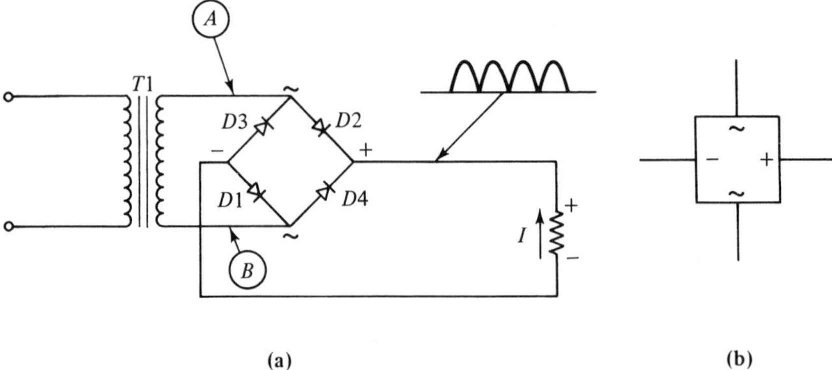

Figure 12.4 **(a)** Fullwave bridge rectification, **(b)** circuit symbol for a bridge rectifier stack.

rectification and the full use of secondary winding voltage. The disadvantage to this circuit is that it will allow only half the current that would be available from the same transformer in a regular fullwave circuit. This is due to the fact that a transformer is a passive device, so it will not generate power. If the output voltage is doubled, then the current must be halved, if the power is to remain constant. Of course, a transformer that is conservatively rated (e.g., those that meet military specifications), then this limit may be pushed. That is, however, considered poor practice outside of amateur activities. Another disadvantage, although a minor one, is the fact that the fullwave "bridge" rectifier of Figure 12.4 requires two additional rectifier diodes.

On one alternation of each ac sine wave point *A* will be positive and point *B* will be negative. Under this set of conditions diodes *D*1 and *D*2 will be forward-biased, and both *D*3 and *D*4 will be reverse-biased. Current flow will be from point *B*, through diode *D*1, resistor *R*1, diode *D*2, and back to the transformer secondary at point *A*.

On the second half of each ac cycle the situation reverses, and point *A* becomes negative while point *B* is positive. The reversal of transformer polarity causes diodes *D*1 and *D*2 to become reverse-biased, while *D*3 and *D*4 are forward-biased. The current flow will be from point *A*, through diode *D*3, through resistor *R*1 in the same direction as previously was the case, through diode *D*4, and back to the transformer via side *B*.

The ripple frequency of the fullwave bridge is also 120 Hz, the same as for the ordinary fullwave rectifier. This type of rectifier is very popular in communications equipment. In many cases, especially in equipment of more recent design, the four diodes will be encapsulated in an epoxy package to form a single component, shown as the inset at Figure 12.4. The symbols (−) and (+) designate the dc output sides of the bridge, while either the letters "AC" or the sine wave symbol ∿ designates the two points where ac transformer connections are made.

Advantages of the fullwave bridge rectifier include the higher ripple frequency of fullwave rectification, greater output voltage for a given size of transformer, and the use of encapsulated rectifier diodes. Disadvantages include the availability of only half of the output current, and slightly higher cost because of the extra diodes needed.

12.2 RECTIFIER RATINGS

Regardless of the type of rectifier diode used, there will be certain critical ratings on the device, and these must be observed. We learned in Chapter 10 that diodes have a peak inverse voltage (p.i.v.) or peak reverse voltage (p.r.v.) that is defined as the maximum reverse bias potential that can be sustained without damage. In solid-state and mercury vapor rectifier circuits, exceeding the p.i.v. for even a short time can cause permanent damage, but for high-vacuum diodes damage is less likely, although it is seen occasionally.

Another rating often quoted is the peak forward current. This is defined as the maximum forward current that can be sustained for a very short period of time—usually 1/60 s. This is also called the surge current or peak surge current. The peak forward current will usually have a much higher value than the normal or rms forward current and should never be taken as the working current. The rms current rating is the working current.

Occasionally you will also see a peak forward voltage rating. Very often, though, specification sheets for solid-state diodes delete this rating, since it is more important in vacuum tubes than in semiconductor types. The reason why this is deleted is that for most solid-state diodes the p.i.v. rating is the ruling factor.

12.3 RECTIFIER TYPES

High-vacuum rectifiers are little more than regular vacuum tube diodes with forward voltage, current, and p.i.v. ratings suitable for power rectifier service.

High-vacuum rectifiers are used in power supplies from only a few watts up to several hundred watts. A few types are known that can operate into the low kilowatt range, however. The chief disadvantage of this type of rectifier is that there is a relatively high forward voltage drop between plate and cathode. This means that a higher transformer secondary voltage is required for any given dc voltage level. An advantage of the high-vacuum rectifier is that it is relatively troublefree and long lasting.

Mercury vapor rectifiers are not, strictly speaking, *vacuum* tubes, because some mercury is introduced into the glass envelope by the manufacturer. When the tube filament is heated, this mercury vaporizes, and is then ionized by the plate-cathode potential. Ionized mercury gives off blue light, and that is the trademark of the mercury vapor rectifier.

A mercury vapor tube has a low forward voltage drop compared with high-vacuum types. It is also able to withstand relatively high forward voltages, and can pass rather substantial amounts of current without damage. Depending upon type number, these tubes can handle from several hundred to several thousand milliamperes of forward current. Mercury vapor tubes, then, have been popular in medium- to high-powered equipment such as industrial induction heaters and radio transmitters.

On the debit side, however, are two major problems. One is that mercury vapor tubes are somewhat intolerant of excessive peak inverse voltages. The other major problem is that these tubes generate not inconsiderable amounts of radio frequency noise called "hash." This could interfere with the signals that are being processed by the equipment, or with signals in nearby equipment. Where this hash proves to be a problem, it is common to use an L-C lowpass filter in the plate circuit of the mercury vapor tube to eliminate, or at least partially suppress, the noise.

Solid-state rectifiers are heavy-duty semiconductor diodes and have largely replaced both high-vacuum and mercury vapor rectifiers in modern equipment. In fact, even some older equipment may use solid-state rectifiers, because many manufacturers have offered their customers retrofit kits that allow replacement of the older-style rectifiers with newer solid-state devices, although often at the expense of some circuit modifications.

The first solid-state rectifiers were rather poor affairs compared with types available today. For years, diodes used as rectifiers were limited to forward currents of as little as 500 mA, at as little as 400 V (p.i.v.). Figure 12.5 shows several types of power supply diodes that might be used in rectifier service. In almost every instance you will find that the cathode end of the device is marked. The case style shown in Figure 12.5(a) is called the "top hat" rectifier, and is probably the oldest type known. The cathode end is made larger by use of an enlarged cover plate. Far more common these days is the molded epoxy type of case shown in Figure 12.5(b). The cathode end is designated by a band of paint on one end. A variation of the epoxy package offered by some manufacturers is a rounded, or bullet-shaped, package. The rounded end designates the cathode end. In some epoxy diodes the polarity will be given by the diode symbol —▶|— or a variation painted on the case. The high-power diode

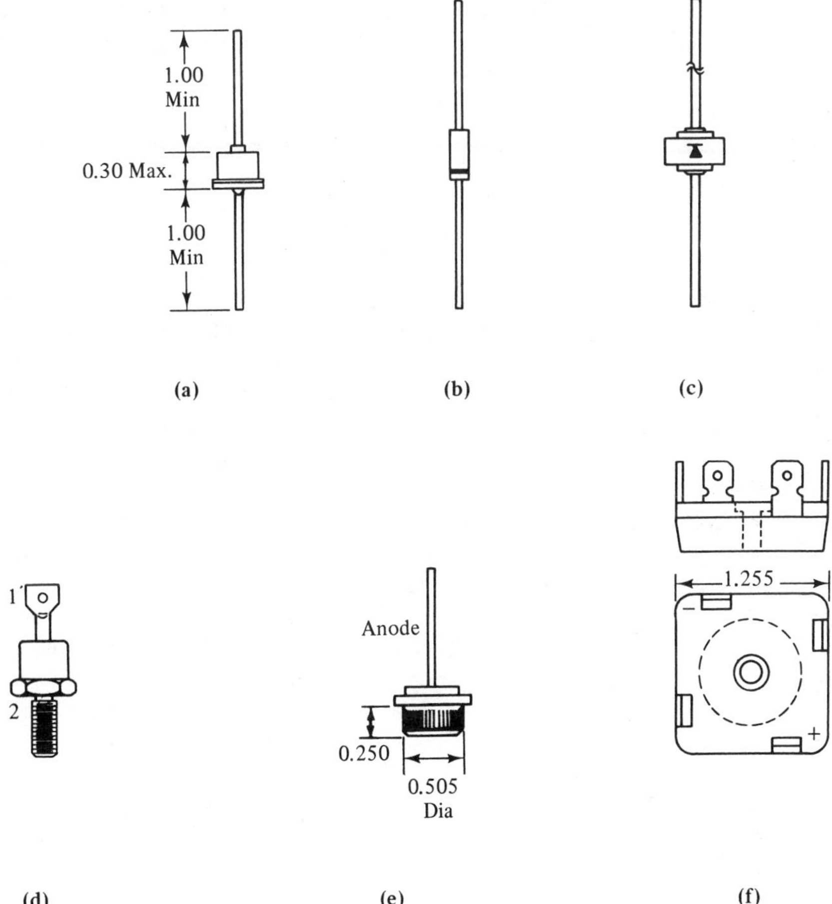

Figure 12.5 Diode styles.

of Figure 12.5(c) is an example of this type of marking. This particular rectifier is an axial lead rectifier.

Stud-mounted and press-fit rectifier diodes are shown in Figures 12.5(d) and 12.5(e), respectively. The stud-mounted type is generally mounted to a metal heat sink, being attached by its stud and a nut. It is important when one is thus mounting *any* solid-state device to use a small amount of silicone heat transfer grease between the two contact surfaces, and to be sure that the device-mounting hardware is torqued down tight.

The press-fit case is usually mounted to a heat sink or other metal surface by pressing its body into an exact-fit hole made in the surface. Both types of power diode are sometimes made available in reverse polarity versions. In most diodes that use these package styles the end that mounts to the heat sink is the cathode. If there is a letter "R" on the case, or following the type number (e.g., 1N3913R), then one should suspect that the diode is a reverse polarity type. Failure to observe this can result in destruction of the diode or associated circuitry.

12.4 POWER SUPPLY RIPPLE AND FILTERING

The waveforms in Figures 12.1 through 12.4 show that the dc output from a rectifier is anything but pure dc. The pulsating dc has humps, called the "ripple component," and is not at all smooth. Electronic circuits usually require relatively pure dc in order to guarantee proper operation. A filter circuit is used to remove the ripple and generate this pure dc.

One type of very simple filter scheme using only one capacitor is shown in Figure 12.6(a). This type of filter is usually found in certain types of solid-state power equipment (such as power supplies and high fidelity amplifiers) where there is a requirement for low voltage and high current. Capacitor values for $C1$ are typically into the several thousand microfarad range.

The voltage waveforms for this circuit are shown in Figure 12.6(b). During positive-going excursions of each half-cycle, capacitance $C1$ charges to a level of the peak voltage. This is, of course, also the peak

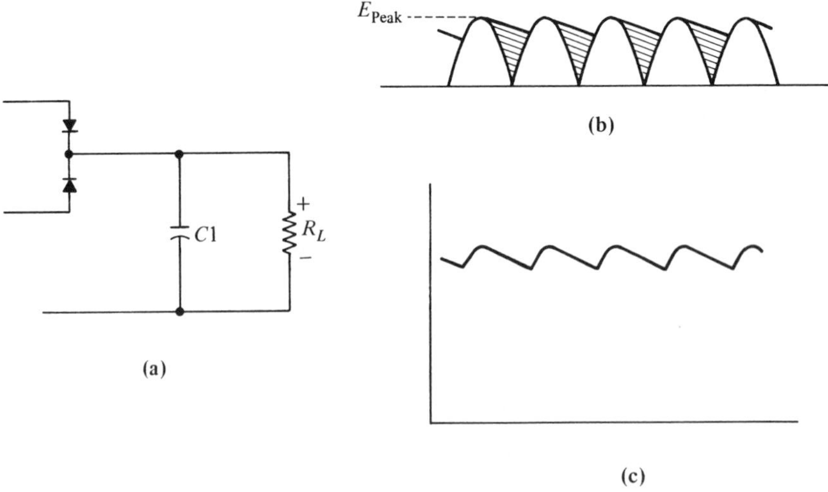

Figure 12.6 (a) Symbol for a capacitor filter, (b) Composite of waveforms affecting R_L, (c) waveform across output (R_L) as seen on an oscilloscope.

voltage of the ac sine wave. During the downward, or negative-going, excursion—after the peak is passed—capacitor $C1$ partially discharges. The energy that is dumped back into the circuit at that time partially fills in the shaded area of the graph. To resistor R_L, however, the individual humps are not seen, but instead, a waveform such as Figure 12.6(c). This last waveform shows that the ripple has been reduced a considerable amount. This level of ripple may be satisfactory for many electronic applications—such as audio power amplifiers, for example. If additional ripple reduction is required, however, then additional filter stages will probably produce better results than simply increasing the value of the lone capacitor.

Different types of filter, even different versions of the same design, vary in effectiveness. The *ripple factor* is a measure of filter effectiveness, and is defined as

$$\text{R.F.} = \frac{E_{\text{ripple}}}{E_{\text{dca}}} \tag{12-1}$$

where E_{ripple} is the rms value of the ripple at the input of the filter.
E_{dca} is the average value of the dc output voltage.

Another method for expressing the ripple factor is to call it the ratio of input to output ripple component.

There is a different equation for expressing ripple factor for each different type of filter circuit. For the simple capacitor filter of Figure 12.6(a) the equation is

$$\text{R.F.} = \frac{1}{208 R_L C1} \tag{12-2}$$

This equation is valid only if halfwave rectification is used, and reflects the 60-Hz ripple frequency. In the case where fullwave rectification is used, there is a 120-Hz ripple frequency, so the following equation is used:

$$\text{R.F.} = \frac{1}{416 R_L C1} \tag{12-3}$$

It should be obvious that we can reduce the ripple factor only by increasing either the load resistance R_L or the value of capacitor $C1$. But the load resistance is set mostly by factors outside of the power supply, so it is not easily controlled. Capacitance $C1$, on the other hand, can be made almost any value that we select—even though quite large values are

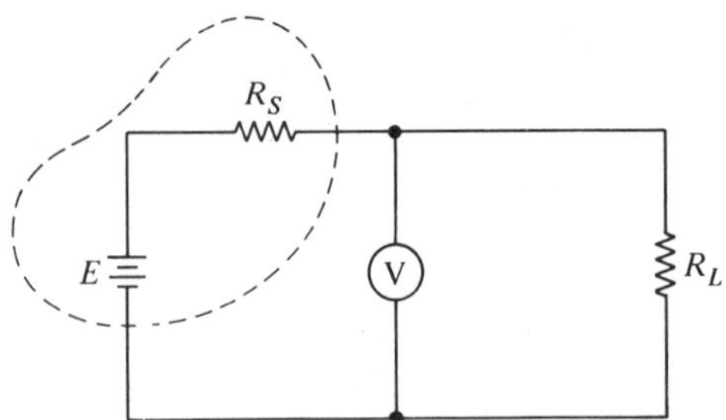

Figure 12.7 Power supply internal resistance causes poor output voltage regulation by ordinary voltage divider action.

needed. This partially accounts for the large capacitor values found in these power supplies.

Power Supply Regulation. All power sources have a certain internal resistance. In our discussions so far we have conveniently avoided this topic by assuming that all power supplies are ideal—a rather presumptuous assumption, as it turns out. The real situation is more like the model shown in Figure 12.7. We will define voltage source E as "perfect." The resistance R_s is the internal impedance of a real supply as might be seen from the outside. An ideal voltage source would exhibit a value of zero ohms for the source resistance R_s. Furthermore, the perfect supply would have the same output voltage regardless of whether the supply were connected to a load, or were left open-circuited. All real supplies have a value of source resistance equal to

$$R_s = \frac{E}{I_s} \tag{12-4}$$

where R_s is the internal resistance of the power supply in ohms.
E is the voltage measured across the output if the load R_L is disconnected.
I_s is the current that would flow if R_L were shorted out.

(*Note: Do not actually attempt to perform this experiment—it may burn out the supply. Few real supplies will tolerate a direct short across the output terminals.*)

In a real power supply the source resistance, that is to say the internal resistance of the power supply, must be taken into account because it produces a voltage drop, and limits the current available to the value of I_s. The output voltage when any load—such as R_L—is connected will be a fraction of the open terminal voltage E equal to

$$E_o = \frac{ER_L}{R_s + R_L} \qquad (12\text{-}5)$$

Obviously, the nearer the source resistance is to zero, the higher the output voltage. Maximum *power transfer* occurs, however, when the source resistance is equal to the load resistance ($R_s = R_L$).

Power supply regulation is a measure, given as a percentage, describing the difference between open terminal and loaded output voltages. It is defined as

$$\text{Percentage of regulation} = \frac{E - E_o}{E} \times 100 \qquad (12\text{-}6)$$

If there is a high-value capacitor, such as $C1$ in Figure 12.6(a), it will appear to the outside world that there is a low internal resistance, so regulation will be better than would be the case if the capacitor were removed. This is due to the fact that the capacitor will tend to dump its charge back into the circuit when E_o drops badly, yet it will also resist changes that would tend to increase E_o. The regulation provided by the large value of filter capacitance is far from perfect, and may not be acceptable in all cases, but it is better than no regulation at all.

RC Pi-section Filters. The filter circuit shown in Figure 12.8 offers some degree of improvement over the single-capacitor filter circuit. The function of $C1$ in this circuit is similar to its function in the previous case.

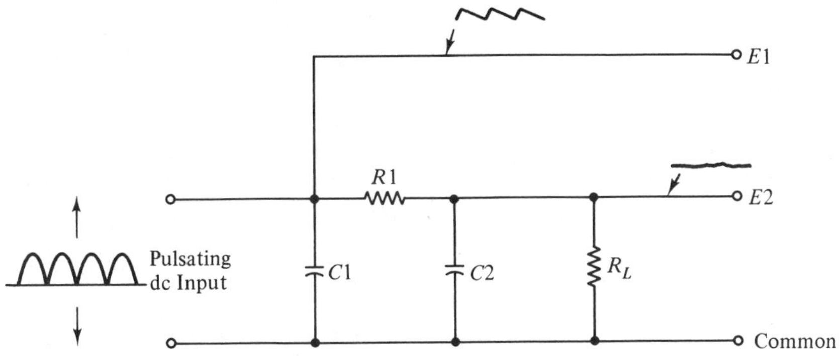

Figure 12.8 Two section RC filter.

Additionally, we have added filtering due to $R1C2$. The reactance of capacitor $C2$ at the ripple frequency must be very low relative to the value of resistor $R1$. This will make the circuit act as an averager, or a lowpass filter with a cutoff frequency less than the ripple frequency.

Two voltages are available from the power supply circuit of Figure 12.8. Potential $E1$ will be higher than $E2$, but will also have a higher ripple component. We find that $E1$ is typically used for power stages, such as audio power amplifiers, where low impedance requires a high current capability, and low stage gain offers some immunity from the higher ripple component. Potential $E2$ would go to stages that present lower current demands, but which also need the extra ripple reduction offered by the additional filter section. The ripple factor on $E2$ will be approximately

$$\text{R.F.} = \frac{1}{(4 \times 10^5)(C1C2R1R_L)} \tag{12-7}$$

in fullwave circuits, and

$$\text{R.F.} = \frac{1}{(10^5)(C1C2R1R_L)} \tag{12-8}$$

in the halfwave case.

Clearly, since all other terms except the constants are the same in both equations, the ripple factor in the halfwave case will be several times larger than the ripple factor in the fullwave case.

Although the RC pi-section filter reduces the ripple quite a bit, it does increase the apparent internal resistance of the power supply (as seen from the $E2$ terminal), because resistor $R1$ is effectively in series with the source resistance. This tends to deteriorate regulation of $E2$. Because of this fact it is usually the case that the RC filter is used only where current drain is relatively constant, or where excursions of output voltage as load current changes can be tolerated.

Choke Input L-section Filters. Figure 12.9 shows an L-section filter with an inductive input. Recall from Chapter 5 that an inductor opposes changes in current flow. Inductor $L1$ tends to average out changes in the load current, which in real circuits could be due to changes in load resistances or input voltage.

The ripple factor for an L-section filter such as that given in Figure 12.9 is dependent upon the capacitors and the input inductor. If $C1$ were temporarily deleted, the ripple factor would be

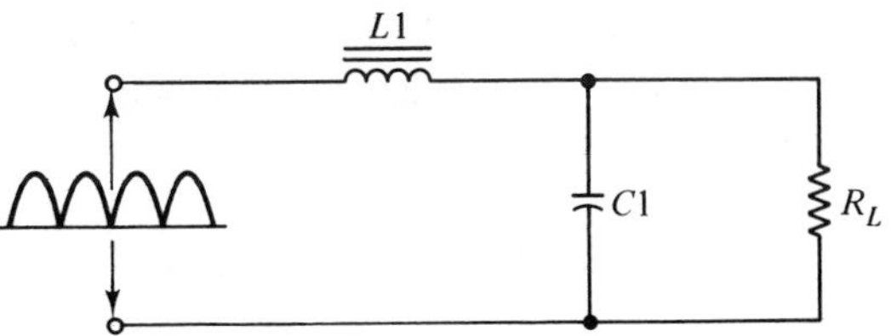

Figure 12.9 Choke input filter.

$$\text{R.F.} = \frac{R_L}{3.2 \times 10^{3}{}_{L}} \tag{12-9}$$

Since R_L appears in the numerator, we may reasonably expect the ripple factor of such a circuit to be dependent upon load current, and that is not a good situation. By adding capacitor $C1$, however, we completely eliminate dependence on load current. The total ripple factor for Figure 12.9 is given if we multiply Eq. (12-9) by Eq. (12-3):

$$\text{R.F.} = \frac{R_L}{3.2 \times 10^3 L} \times \frac{1}{416CR_L}$$

$$\text{R.F.} = \frac{1}{(1.3 \times 10^6)LC} \tag{12-10}$$

Notice that the R_L terms are cancelled, leaving the final ripple factor equation [Eq. (12-10)] without any dependence on ripple factor. This makes the choke-input, L-section filter desirable where a changing load resistance is reflected to the power supply as a changing load current requirement.

One limitation placed on the inductive input filter is that it should not be used with halfwave rectifiers. High rates of change in the current waveform creates an inductive kick voltage spike that could overcome the insulation on the choke, or destroy certain other components. The value of the choke should be

$$L_{(\text{Hy})} \geq \frac{R_L}{1000} \tag{12-11}$$

You should be aware that some authorities use a value of 1100 in the denominator of Eq. (12-11).

Example. A power supply with a choke-input filter is providing an output potential of 500 V, and the current load varies between 100 mA and 250 mA. What value inductor should be supplied?

By Ohm's law we know that the load resistance varies as the load current varies, so

$$R_{L(1)} = E/I1$$
$$R_{L(1)} = 500/0.1 = 5000\ \Omega$$
$$R_{L(2)} = E/I2$$
$$R_{L(2)} = 500/0.25 = 2000\ \Omega$$

Since $R_{L(1)}$ is greater, we shall use it in Eq. (12-11).

$$L \geqq R_{L(1)}/1000$$
$$L \geqq 5000/1000$$
$$L \geqq 5\ \mathrm{H}$$

We can use the desired ripple factor to find a suitable value for capacitor $C1$. Suppose the specification was for a ripple factor of 0.05. From Eq. (12-10) we can calculate

$$C = \frac{1}{(1.3 \times 10^6)(\mathrm{R.F.})L}$$

$$C = 3.1 \times 10^{-6}\ \mathrm{F}$$

$$C = 3.1\ \mu\mathrm{F}$$

Since 4 μF is the nearest higher standard value, most would use it rather than trying to find an exact value of capacitor, so let $C1 = 4\ \mu$F.

Several L-section filters may be cascaded to obtain even better ripple reduction. Each additional L-section reduces ripple factor by approximately X_c/X_L. In the previous problem $X_c = 330\ \Omega$ and $X_L = 3800\ \Omega$, so this ratio is $330/3800 = 0.09$. Since the ripple factor of one section was defined as 0.05, the ripple factor with two identical sections would be 0.05×0.09, or approximately 0.005.

Inductive Pi-section Filters. A popular variation on the inductive filter theme is the pi-section, or "capacitor-input," filter of Figure 12.10. The ripple factor of this circuit is given by

$$\mathrm{R.F.} = \frac{(1.4)(X_{c1})(X_{c2})}{(X_L)(R_L)} \tag{12-13}$$

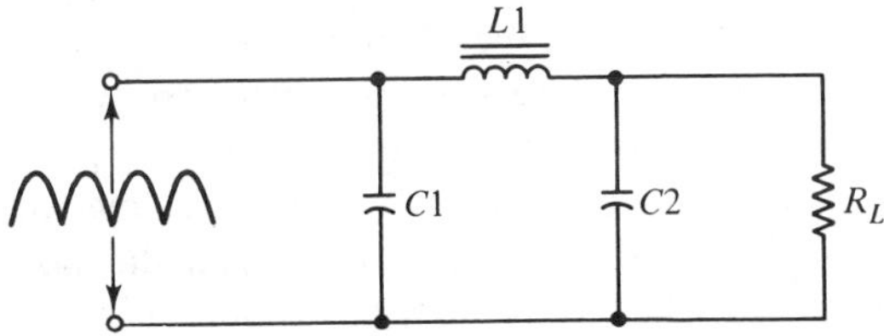

Figure 12.10 Pi-section filter.

Examples. In the problem given earlier we found the value of the capacitor to be 4 μF, the inductor was 5 Hy, and the load resistance varied between 2 kΩ and 5 kΩ. Assuming that $C1 = C2 = 4\ \mu$F, find R.F. at both R_L limits. (Note that $X_L = 3.8$ kΩ, and $X_c = 330\ \Omega$, as before.)

At $I_o = 100$ mA:

$$\text{R.F.} = \frac{(1.4)(330)(330)}{(3800)(5000)} = 0.008$$

At $I_o = 250$ mA:

$$\text{R.F.}' = \frac{(1.4)(330)(330)}{(3800)(2000)} = 0.02$$

The ripple factor, then, varies with the load current. The ripple reduction is not as good as the two-stage, L-section filter, but then again, only one inductor is needed.

Figure 12.11 shows a practical radio transmitter power supply using vacuum tube rectifiers. This is a fairly typical inductive input filter network.

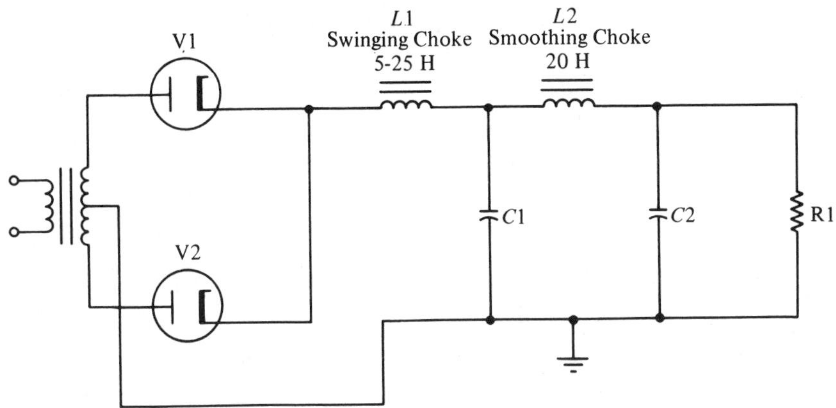

Figure 12.11 Two-section choke filter using swinging and smoothing chokes.

Input choke $L1$ is a special type of iron-core inductor designed with no air gap in the core material. Its inductance will vary with current flow, because the core will saturate at relatively low current levels. At heavy current loads the typical *swinging* choke will have a low inductance, on the order of 4 or 5 H. At higher current levels, on the other hand, the inductance climbs to a higher value, on the order of 20 to 25 H. All other chokes in the circuit, which do *not* exhibit variable inductance, are called *smoothing chokes.* A smoothing choke is an ordinary iron-core choke.

Power Supply Capacitors. Filter capacitors used in a power supply must be fairly high-valued—up to several thousand microfarads, depending upon the case. Because of this fact it is almost mandatory that they be electrolytic types, or, if less than about 25 μF, oil-filled. They also must have a working voltage in excess of the highest voltage expected in the circuit.

Filter capacitors may be connected in series, as in Figure 12.12, in order to increase the working voltage rating. The capacitance of the series combination will, of course, be less than the capacitance of the smallest capacitor in the chain. By the usual capacitor-in-series formula,

$$C_{\text{total}} = \cfrac{1}{\cfrac{1}{C1} + \cfrac{1}{C2} + \cdots + \cfrac{1}{C_n}}$$

The total working voltage is the sum of all working voltages if all of the

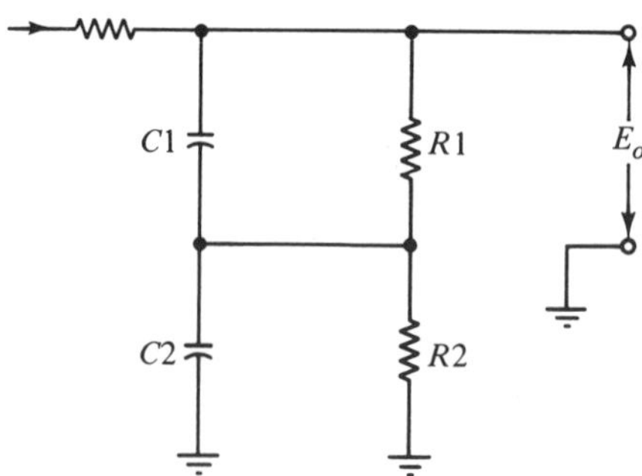

Figure 12.12 Connecting filter capacitors in series increases the overall working voltage, although at the expense of lower total capacitance. $R1$ and $R2$ are for voltage equalization.

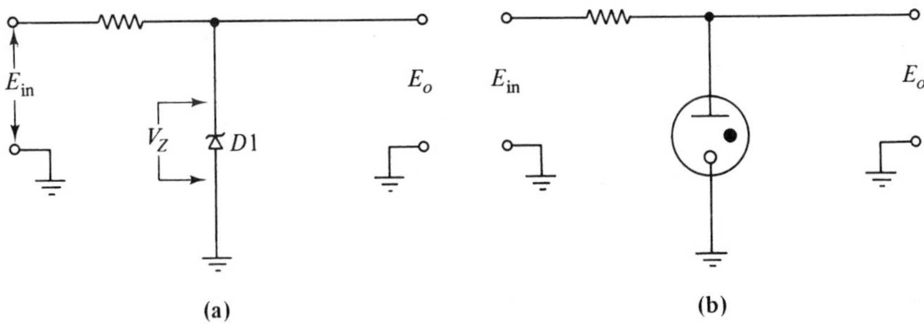

Figure 12.13 **(a)** Zener diode shunt regulator, **(b)** VR tube shunt regulator.

capacitors have identical capacitance ratings—in fact, it is wise to use the same ratings for all capacitors in the stack.

A resistor is shown connected across each capacitor in the series stack. These are used to equalize the voltage drops across $C1$ and $C2$. For most transmitter power supplies in the low- to medium-power range these resistors will have a value between 25 kΩ and 100 kΩ.

12.5 POWER SUPPLY REGULATORS

The output of any power supply will vary because of load and input voltage changes. There are some electronic circuits, however, that are not able to tolerate any voltage changes. An oscillator circuit in a transmitter is one such circuit. A regulator is an electronic circuit that will stabilize the output voltage of a power supply.

One of the simplest voltage regulators is the zener diode shunt regulator of Figure 12.13(a). In this circuit diode $D1$ is connected across the power supply output lines, and is used to clamp the output voltage to the value of the zener potential of the diode. Resistor $R1$ is used to limit the current through the zener diode to a safe level.

Zener diodes are available in relatively high voltage ratings, but for the most part are limited to low voltage applications. In most higher voltage applications a gas regulator tube is used instead. An example of this is the circuit in Figure 12.13(b). Gas regulator tubes are sometimes given two different number designations. One is the regulator type number and follows the usual U.S. type numbering forms. Typical numbers are OA2, OA3, OB2, etc. ("O" because the filament voltage is zero—there is no filament). The alternate numbering system uses the letters "VR"—for "voltage regulator"—followed by the nominal voltage to which the tube regulates. A VR-105, for example, regulates to 105 V, while a VR 150 regulates to 150 V. These cold-cathode regulator tubes glow a color

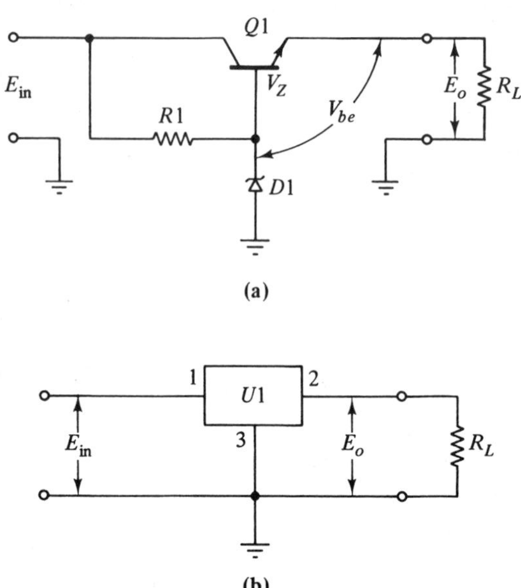

Figure 12.14 **(a)** Series-pass transistor increases the current handling capability of a zener diode regulator. **(b)** Three-terminal IC voltage regulator.

that is dependent upon the type of gas used in the tube and the applied voltage. Most, when operated at their normal current level, glow either violet or orange.

Solid-state Regulators. New electronic equipment, meaning less than ten years old, most likely use a solid-state, active regulator such as those shown in Figures 12.14(a) and 12.14(b). The circuit in Figure 12.14(a) uses a zener diode to hold the base voltage of a series-pass transistor ($Q1$) at a constant value. The output voltage will be approximately equal to $(V_z - V_{be})$. If E_o reduces, then V_{be} rises, increasing the forward bias on the transistor. This causes greater collector-emitter current to flow, and that raises the voltage drop across the load—E_o goes up. Alternatively, if E_o goes up because of reduced load requirements, then V_{be} is reduced, so the load receives less current. That will, of course, reduce output voltage E_o. Between these two mechanisms the output voltage tends to stabilize around the figure given by the expression $(V_z - V_{be})$. One way of viewing the function of series-pass transistor $Q1$ is as an electronically variable resistor.

In more recent equipment you will see *integrated circuit* regulators in which all of the circuitry is contained within a single solid-state device. Some of these are rather complex devices with many pins, and are very flexible. Others, however, have only three terminals: E_{in}, E_{out}, and ground, or common. While less flexible in that they deliver only one voltage, they are a cheap and easy-to-implement way of obtaining voltage regulation. An example is given in Figure 12.14(b). Note that these IC regulators are usually packaged in a transistor case, so they take up very little room inside the equipment. It is not unusual to find all of the regulation for each printed circuit board in a piece of equipment on the board it serves.

PROBLEMS

1. A device used to convert ac to dc is called a ________.
2. One desirable property of a rectifier is that it ________.
3. The output of a rectifier is not *pure dc,* but is ______ dc.
4. The ripple frequency of a halfwave rectifier is ________.
5. The ripple frequency of a fullwave rectifier is ________.
6. A simple fullwave rectifier power supply requires a ________ transformer.
7. The waveform shown in Figure 12.15 is the unfiltered output of a ________ rectifier.

Figure 12.15

8. The circuit in Figure 12.16 represents ________.

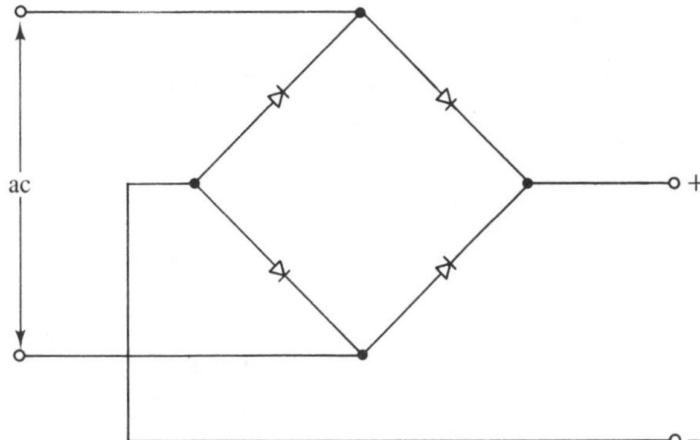

Figure 12.16

9. For any given transformer the circuit in Question 8 provides ________ the output voltage as a regular fullwave rectifier.
10. The ripple frequency of a bridge rectifier is ________.
11. The maximum *reverse bias* potential that may safely be applied to a rectifier is called the ________.
12. List two or more disadvantages to the high vacuum type of rectifier tube.
13. A transmitter has a pair of 866A rectifier diode tubes. It is noted that they are blue in color when turned on. What type of rectifier is the 866A?
14. List several advantages to the mercury vapor rectifier.
15. List two *disadvantages* of the mercury vapor rectifier.
16. The rectifier tubes in Figure 12.17 are mercury vapor types. What is the purpose of $L1/C1$ and $L2/C2$?

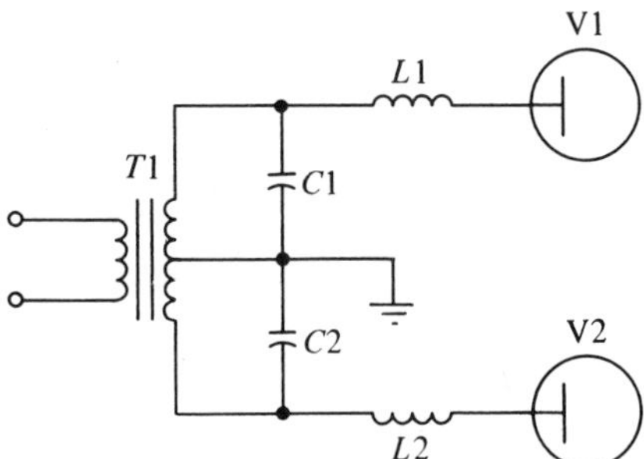

Figure 12.17

17. A ________ is used to smooth out power supply ripple and make the output nearly pure dc.
18. A fullwave rectifier is filtered by a single 1000-μF capacitor across the dc output. If the load is 100 Ω, what is the ripple factor?
19. Find the internal impedance of a battery if the open circuit voltage is 1.36 VDC and the short circuit current is 560 mA.
20. If the battery in Question 19 were connected to a 20-Ω load, the voltage across the load would be ________.
21. Find the percentage of regulation in Question 20.
22. If a battery or power supply has a 10-Ω internal resistance, maximum power transfer will occur with a ______-Ω load.
23. The filter circuit shown in Figure 12.18 is a(n) ________.

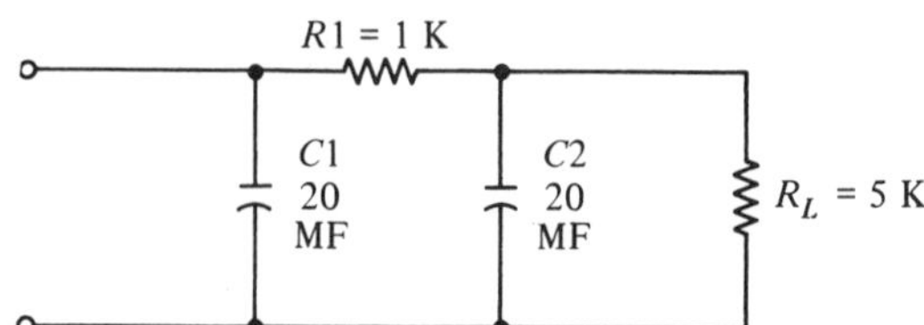

Figure 12.18

24. If the circuit in Figure 12.18 is connected to a halfwave rectifier, the ripple factor is ________.
25. What would the ripple be in Question 24 if the rectifier were a fullwave type?
26. In a choke input filter the inductor averages ________ in the ripple.
27. An L-section filter consists of a 10-H choke and a 4-μF capacitor. What is the ripple factor if this filter is driven by a fullwave rectifier?
28. An inductive input filter should not be used with ________.
29. The reason for not using inductive input filters on halfwave rectifiers is ________.
30. The minimum value for an inductor will be ________ if the load resistance is 3300 Ω.
31. What is the load resistance if a 300-VDC supply delivers 200 mA?
32. A supply with a 2500-Ω load and a 10-H choke is to have a ripple factor of 0.01. What value of capacitor is needed in an L-section filter?
33. A pi-section inductive filter consists of an 8-H choke and two 4-μF capacitors. The load resistance is 5-kΩ. What is the ripple factor?
34. A ________ changes inductance depending upon current flow.
35. The inductance of a swinging choke is highest at ________ current levels.
36. What are several types of capacitor suitable for use as power supply filters?
37. Three 60-μF/450-WVDC capacitors are connected in series. What is the effective capacitance?
38. In Question 37, what is the working voltage rating of the combination?
39. A type of diode used for voltage regulation is the ______ diode.
40. Another shunt regulator device is the ________.
41. A series-pass transistor is used in a regulator circuit. If the zener voltage is +5.6 VDC, and $V_{be} = 0.6$ VDC what is the output voltage?
42. The curve in Figure 12.19 is for a ________.
43. The nominal regulation voltage of a VR-105 tube is ________.

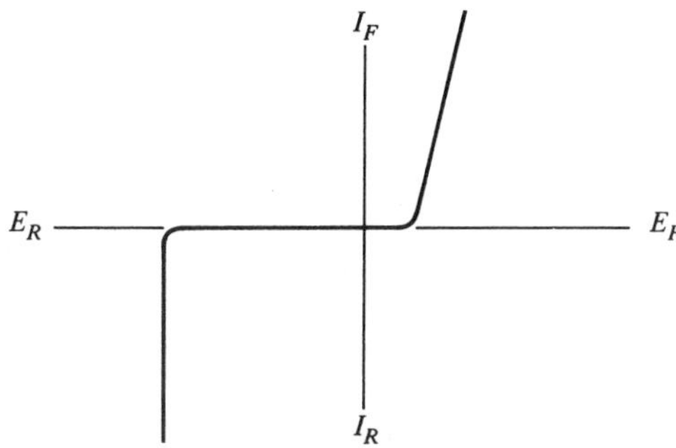

Figure 12.19

13 Simple Meters and Instruments

Someone once stated that you do not really understand something until you can measure and quantify it. In this chapter we shall discuss some of the instruments needed to measure electrical parameters such as voltage, current, resistance, and so forth.

13.1 DC CURRENT METERS

The most basic electrical measuring instrument is the dc current meter movement. The type of instrument shown in Figure 13.1 is known as the permanent magnet moving coil (PMMC), or D'Arsonval movement. In this design a large permanent magnet surrounds a moving coil wound on a jewel-mounted bobbin that is attached to the needle pointer. If an electrical current is passed through the coil, then a magnetic field is created around the bobbin. This field interacts with the magnetic field of the permanent magnet, causing the bobbin to deflect. The amount of deflection is proportional to the electrical current flowing in the coil. If a calibrated scale is positioned beneath the pointer, then you can read the magnitude of the electrical current in the coil.

The moving coil in a D'Arsonval meter movement is mounted on a

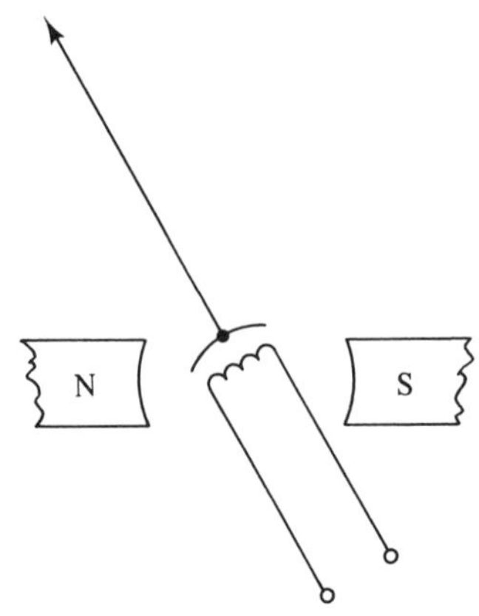

Figure 13.1 Permanent magnet moving coil meter movement.

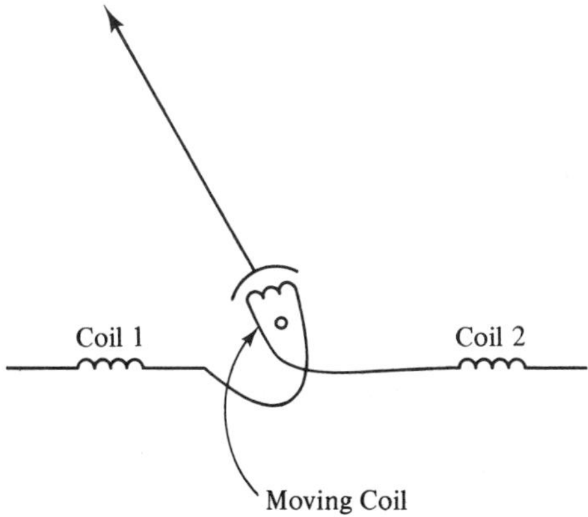

Figure 13.2 Dynamometer meter movement.

pair of jewel bearings to reduce friction and provide support. Although this design is more precise than certain others, it is also relatively fragile. A somewhat more recent, and reportedly tougher design is the *taut-band* movement. It is similar to the D'Arsonval movement, except that the center axis of the cylindrical bobbin is mounted, not on jewel bearings, but on a tightly stretched rubber band.

Another basic type of meter movement is the electrodynamometer, or simply dynamometer. In this type of meter movement the permanent magnet is replaced by an electromagnet consisting of a pair of fixed coils. The basic arrangement is shown in Figure 13.2. The moving coil bobbin is positioned between, and in the mutual magnetic fields of, coils 1 and 2. Current will flow in all three coils. The magnetic field surrounding coil 1 will aid the field generated around coil 2. The moving coil, however, is connected so that its field bucks, or opposes, the other two fields. This will cause the moving coil to deflect an amount proportional to the amplitude of the current flowing in the coils.

This, and other, types of movement may tend to move too easily. This freedom of movement can be damped by placing nonferrous (e.g., aluminum) metal vanes on the moving coil in order to increase air drag.

The meter movement shown in Figure 13.3 is called the *iron vane* movement. The pointer is attached to a movable iron vane that is designed so that it is partially inside a fixed coil when no current is flowing in the windings. When current is passed through the coil, a magnetic field is generated that attracts the iron vane.

The magnetic field surrounding the coil is proportional to the current flowing in the windings. The meter's pointer deflection is proportional to the strength of the magnetic field, so it is also proportional to the cur-

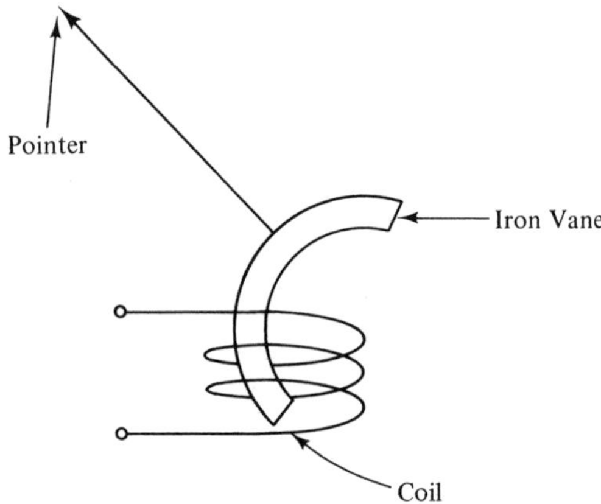

Figure 13.3 Iron-vane meter movement.

rent flowing. The iron-vane movement is used mostly in low-cost instruments, and in some ac applications.

Two movements that work with either ac or dc current are shown in Figures 13.4 and 13.5. The first depends upon thermal expansion of metals, while the second depends upon the thermocouple phenomenon.

The movement in Figure 13.4 uses a resistance element that heats and expands as the current flows through it. A taut thread is attached to a tie-point at one end and a pivoting pointer at the other. As the heated element flexes because of the heat generated by the flow of current, it pulls the thread, which in turn pulls the bottom of the pointer. A spring is used

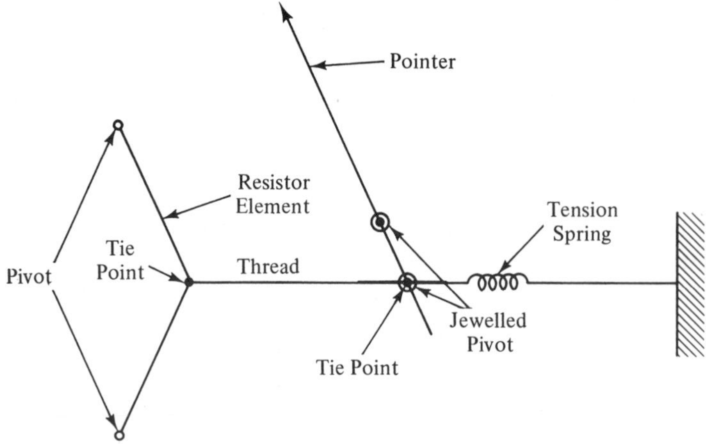

Figure 13.4 Heated wire meter movement.

to provide damping tension, and to return the pointer to zero when the flow of current drops to zero.

The meter movement in Figure 13.5 uses a phenomenon that is called the *thermocouple effect.* When two dissimilar metals are joined to form a "V" junction, a peculiar effect can be noted. When the junction is heated, an electrical potential appears across the open ends. In a thermocouple meter the current is passed through a heating element that is in close proximity to a thermocouple junction. A voltage will appear across points *A* and *B*, and this causes a current to flow in the meter movement.

A typical thermocouple meter will have the heating element thermocouple, and a dc current meter (usually D'Arsonval or taut-band movement) inside the same casing. Most such meters are labelled "RF ammeter" because they respond to ac currents up through much of the radio frequency spectrum. The heating effect is proportional to the rms value of the current, and is reasonably frequency independent—operation to 60 MHz is not uncommon. Many such meters also operate down to dc, and may require some compensation when mounted on ferrous panels.

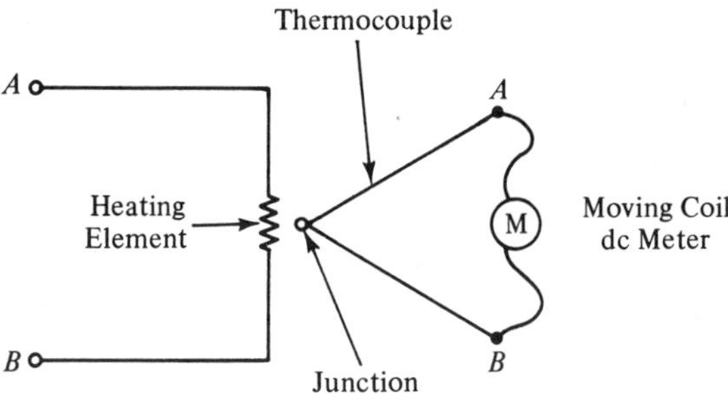

Figure 13.5 Thermocouple meter movement.

DC current meters are manufactured in many different ranges. Some are ammeters, others are milliammeters, and still others are microammeters. Regardless of the range, however, all current meters are connected in *series* with the branch or load to be measured. Figure 13.6 shows the proper way to connect a current meter. It is necessary actually to break the circuit to insert the current meter. A desirable property of all current meters is a low internal resistance. The wire making up the windings of the coil will have a certain dc resistance, ideally as low as possible. Of course, "low" is a relative term. A meter passing dozens of amperes might be poor if it had an internal resistance of as much as 1 Ω. A microammeter, on the other hand, might have an internal resistance in excess of 10,000 Ω and still be considered low.

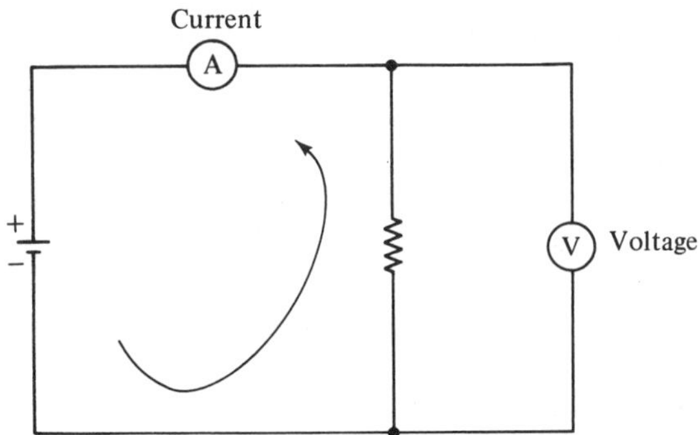

Figure 13.6 Absolute rules: connect a current meter in series with the load and a voltmeter in parallel with the load.

The range of a current meter can be increased by the use of a shunt resistor as in Figure 13.7. Since this is a parallel circuit, current I will break into two components, $I2$ and $I3$. Although most of the current will flow through resistor R_s, the current in the meter will be proportional to the total current. The meter scale is then calibrated to reflect the range of total current $I1$. Current divider equations can be used to compute the value of the shunt resistor, provided that we know the full-scale (f.s.) range of the meter, total current, and the internal resistance of the meter movement.

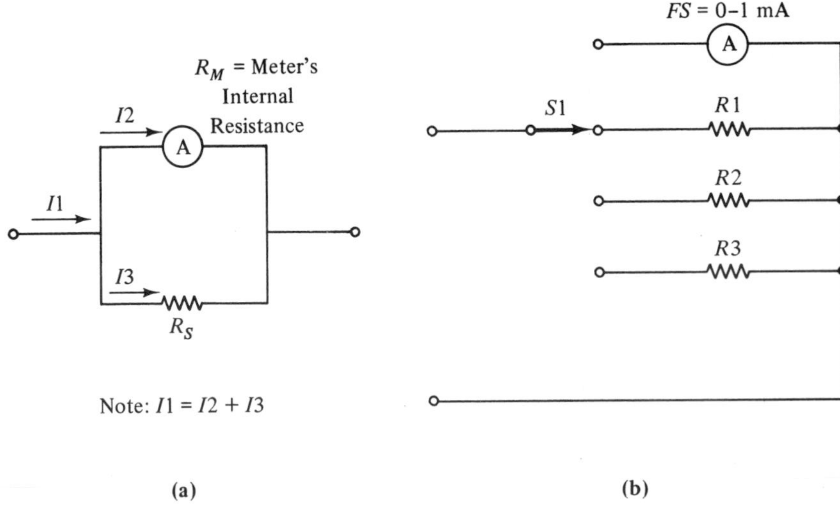

Figure 13.7 **(a)** Shunt resistor increases current range of the basic meter movement, **(b)** Multirange current meter.

Example. We want to read 100 mA f.s. on a meter that has a f.s. of 1 mA, and an internal resistance of 43 Ω. Find the value of the required shunt resistance.

First, compute the current through the shunt resistor. This figure will be the total current minus the f.s. rating of the meter. In this particular case,

$$(100\text{ mA}) - (1\text{ mA}) = 99\text{ mA} \tag{13-1}$$

Using the current divider equation for the shunt branch, we obtain

$$\begin{aligned} 99\text{ mA} &= \frac{(100)R_{\text{meter}}}{R_s + R_{\text{meter}}} \\ 99\text{ mA} &= 4300/(R_s + 43) \\ 99R_s + (99)(43) &= 4300 \\ 99R_s + 4257 &= 4300 \\ 99R_s &= 43 \\ R_s &= 43/99 \\ R_s &= 0.43\ \Omega \end{aligned} \tag{13-2}$$

Example. Assume that the same meter movement as in the above example is to be used in a circuit to measure f.s. 0 to 5 mA. Find the value of the shunt.

The current running through the shunt will be 5 mA − 1 mA = 4 mA, so

$$\begin{aligned} 4R_s &= 43 \\ R_s &= 43/4 \\ R_s &= 10.75\ \Omega \end{aligned} \tag{13-3}$$

A multirange current meter can be constructed by using a circuit such as that shown in Figure 13.7(b). A switch selects the shunt resistor proper for the range desired. One must be cautious when using any current meter, because excess currents will peg the meter (force the pointer hard against the maximum stop) and may well cause permanent damage. This dictum applies to all meters, but is especially critical in the multirange current meter, because it is very easy to forget to set the switch correctly when one is making rapid tests.

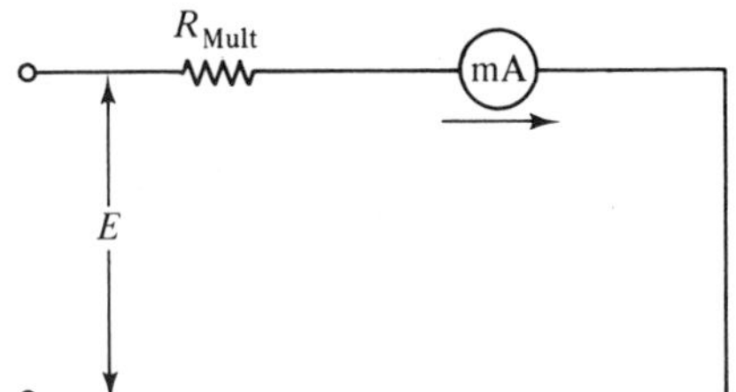

Figure 13.8 Multiplier resistor causes a current meter to measure voltages.

The dc current meter is also used to make a dc voltmeter. We know by Ohm's law that voltage is proportional to the current flowing in a resistance. A series-connected resistor, as in Figure 13.8, converts a milliammeter or microammeter to a voltmeter. We can use Ohm's law to compute the value of this series "multiplier" resistor.

Example. A 0–100-μA movement has an internal resistance of 560 Ω. What value of multiplier resistor is required to make it read 0–100 V f.s.?

$$E = IR$$

$$(100) = (0.0001)(560 + R_{\text{mult}})$$

$$\frac{100}{0.0001} = 560 + R_{\text{mult}} \qquad (13\text{-}4)$$

$$1{,}000{,}000 - 560 = R_{\text{mult}}$$

$$999{,}440\ \Omega = R_{\text{mult}}$$

All voltmeters should have as high an internal resistance as possible. To measure voltage it is necessary to connect the meter in *parallel* with the circuit (see Figure 13.6). A low meter resistance would load the circuit to an extent that would cause excessive errors due to voltage division, and might damage either the meter or the circuit. An indication of the internal resistance is the sensitivity in ohms per volt. In the example above, the total resistance was 1 MΩ and the f.s. voltage was 100 V, so

$$\frac{1{,}000{,}000}{100} = 10{,}000\ \Omega/\text{V} \qquad (13\text{-}5)$$

Generally, the higher the sensitivity figure, the better the meter. A 0–1-mA movement has a sensitivity of 1000 Ω/V, and this is as low as can be ordinarily tolerated. In fact, most electronic applications require

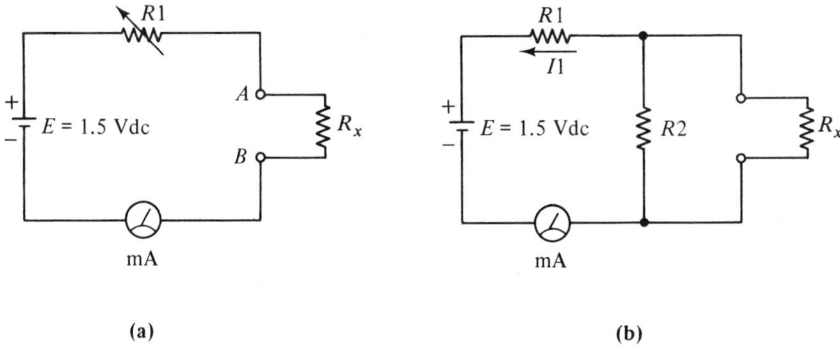

Figure 13.9 **(a)** Series-type ohmmeter, **(b)** Shunt type ohmmeter.

a sensitivity of 20,000 Ω/V or higher. Some transistor circuitry will be disrupted unless the sensitivity is over 100,000 Ω/V.

An *ohmmeter* can also be made by using the simple dc current meter movement. Two different examples are shown in Figures 13.9(a) and 13.9(b). Both are Ohm's law circuits, but one is also known as the "current divider" ohmmeter.

In the circuit of Figure 13.9(a) a battery and a calibration resistor ($R1$) are used to form the ohmmeter circuit. $R1$ also serves to limit the current in the meter movement if the probes (AB) are shorted together. It is adjusted when such a short is present so that the meter reads exactly full scale. When the short is removed, and an unknown resistance (R_x) is substituted, the meter current will be less than full scale by an amount proportional to the value of R_x. The meter scale will, of course, be calibrated in ohms rather than units of electrical current.

An alternate ohmmeter circuit is shown in Figure 13.9(b). It is essentially the same as the previous design, except that resistor $R2$ is placed in parallel with the unknown resistance, across terminals A-B. Current $I1$ will divide between this resistor and the unknown in a manner inversely proportional to the value of the unknown.

13.2 AC METERS

Hot wire and thermocouple meters will work on ac, and give a reading proportional to the rms value of the applied current or voltage. But these meters are not always either the most useful or most sensible choice, so another form is often used. An example of the rectifier type of ac current meter is shown in Figure 13.10(a).

The meter in this circuit is a dc current meter movement and is placed between the (−) and (+) terminals of what appears to be a

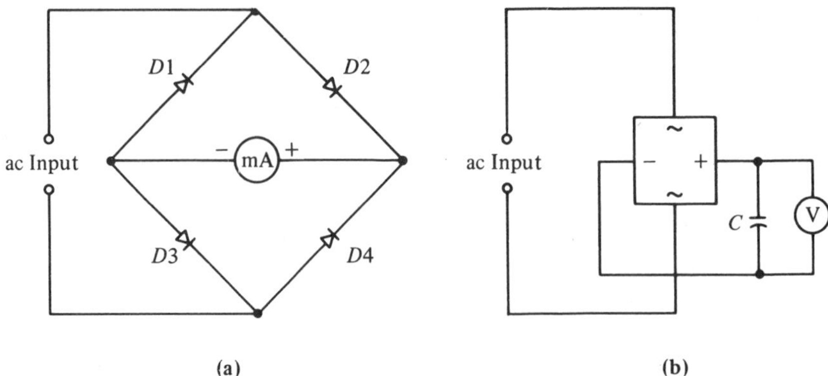

Figure 13.10 (a) An ac meter using individual rectifiers, (b) An ac meter using bridge rectifier.

standard bridge rectifier, such as those discussed in the chapter on power supplies. In most meters of this type, diodes *D*1–*D*4 are low-current, high-frequency types arranged in a single package called an "instrumentation rectifier."

A peak reading ac voltmeter can be made through the simple expedient of placing a capacitor across the dc output terminals of the bridge. The capacitor will charge to the peak voltage of the applied waveform, and this will register on the voltmeter (current meter plus multiplier) in parallel with the capacitor. This meter reads the voltage across the capacitor, which is the peak voltage of the applied waveform.

13.3 THE MULTIMETER

It is simply too much trouble, as well as too costly, to keep on hand one of each meter type that might be needed in day-to-day electronics work. You would need voltmeters, current meters, and ohmmeters in several ranges each. Since all of those instruments are based on a common meter movement with a low full-scale current range, it is possible to construct a single instrument that satisfies all of these functions, over a wide set of ranges, through the use of a proper switching circuit to select appropriate multipliers, shunts, or ohmmeter calibration resistors. Examples of popular multimeters are shown in Figures 13.11(a) through 13.11(c).

The instrument in Figure 13.11(a) is a volt-ohm-milliammeter (usually called "VOM"). It is designed along lines discussed earlier. The main control on the front panel is the range switch, and it selects the appropriate shunts and multipliers. This particular instrument has a long and honorable history in the communications business and is still very

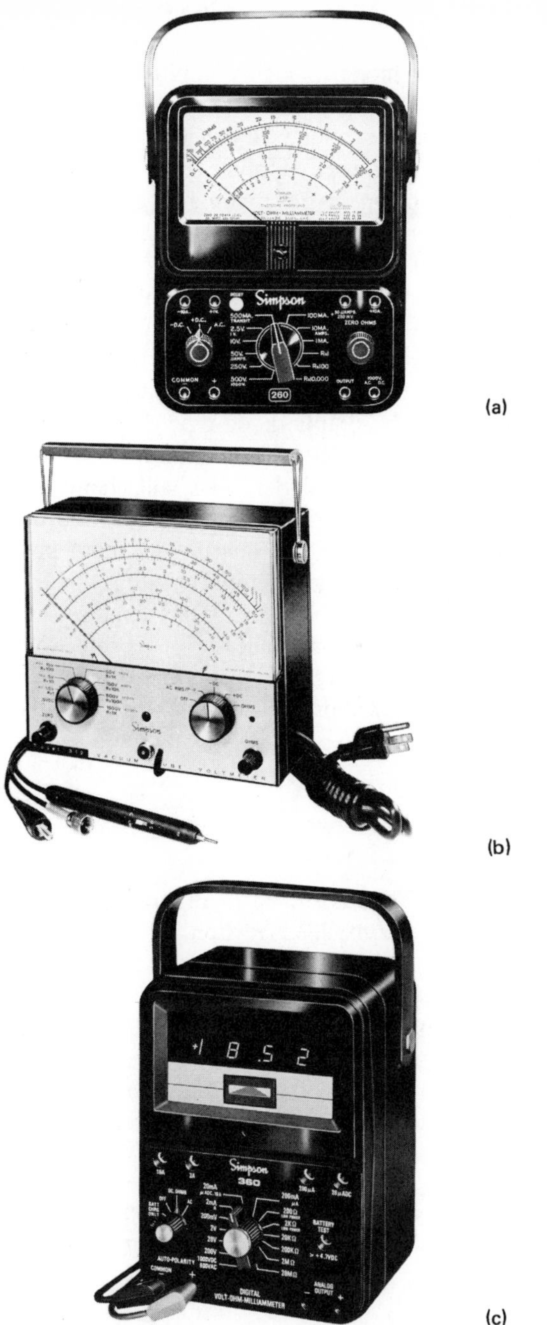

Figure 13.11 **(a)** Volt-ohm-milliammeter (VOM) of classic design. **(b)** Vacuum tube voltmeter (VTVM). **(c)** Modern digital multimeter. (*Courtesy of Simpson Electric.*)

much used, even though more modern, highly sophisticated instruments are available. The only power required for this instrument is a single 1.5-V flashlight battery for the ohmmeter section. All other functions are passive, so they do not require any form of power supply.

The type of instrument shown in the figure has a 50-μA taut-band movement. The sensitivity, therefore, will be a 20 k Ω/V on dc. The ac sensitivity is reduced somewhat because of the loading effect of the rectifier—it is only on the order of 5000 Ω/V. A function not present on all VOM-type instruments is overload protection. Some meters have a pair of diodes across the meter movement. These diodes are in parallel, but are connected oppositely in polarity. The protection circuit in this instrument also includes a reset feature. In the simple diode type of protection circuit, an excess of current will cause a voltage to be generated across the meter's terminals sufficient to forward-bias the diodes. This will clamp the voltage across the meter coil to a safe value. The problem is that the diodes are sometimes destroyed. This means that the instrument must be serviced before it can be placed back into service. Similarly, some meters have a fuse series-connected in the input probe lines. If this fuse blows, the meter will be saved, but again, repairs are necessary. A protection such as that found in the instrument of Figure 13.10(a) features a front panel reset button for instant "repair" without returning the instrument to the manufacturer.

13.4 ELECTRONIC VOLTMETERS

A vacuum tube voltmeter (VTVM) is shown in Figure 13.11(b), and its circuit is in Figure 13.12(a). A simplified version of this type of circuit is shown in Figure 13.12(b). Referring to the latter figure, we see two triode vacuum tubes, $V1$ and $V2$, connected in a bridge circuit. When the current through both tubes is the same, then the current through the meter movement will be zero. $V2$ is biased so that this condition is met when E_{in} is zero. Applying an input voltage to E_{in}, however, unbalances the bridge, causing the cathode voltage of $V1$ to be greater than that of $V2$. This creates a current flow through meter $M1$ that is proportional to the voltage applied to the $V1$ grid.

In the schematic of the Simpson model 312 [Figure 13.12(a)] the two triodes are actually sections of a single type 12AU7 dual-triode tube. This makes it easier to keep the circuit balanced, especially under conditions of thermal change.

The actual meter is designed to provide a certain minimum f.s. range without any additional circuitry. Higher ranges are accommodated by voltage divider $R1$–$R8$ and a range switch. The divider will reduce the

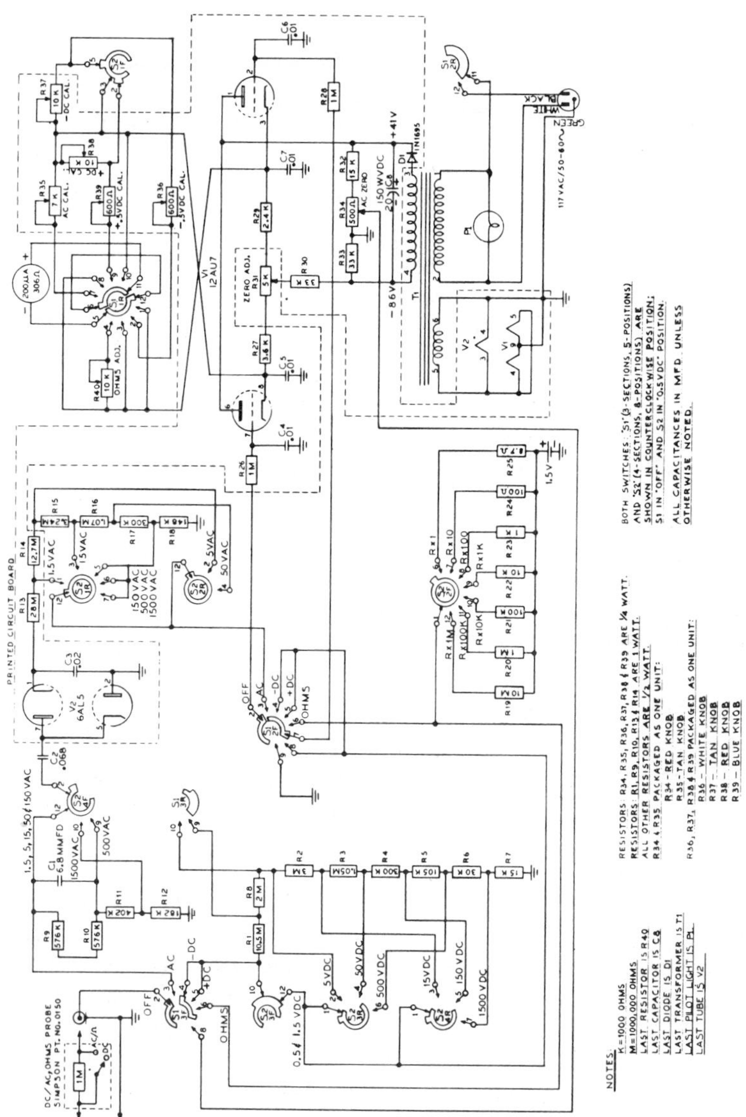

Figure 13.12 (a) Schematic of a VTVM circuit. (*Courtesy of Simpson Electric.*)

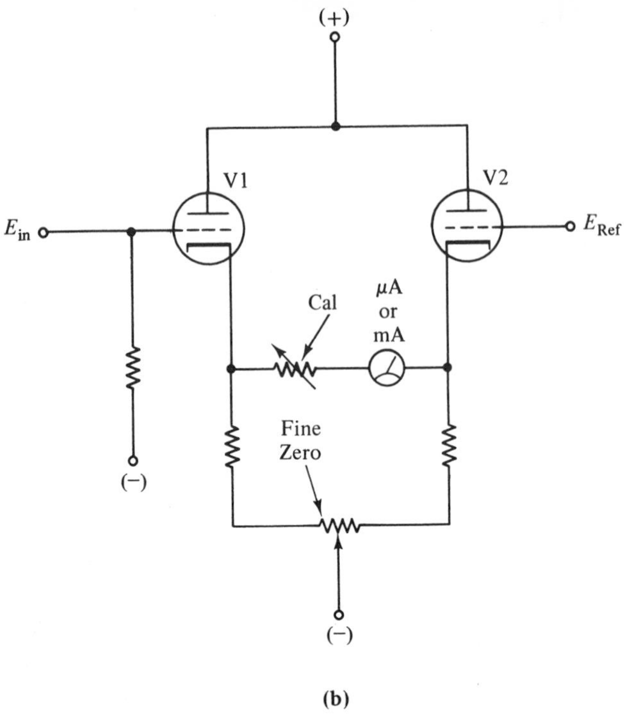

Figure 13.12 (cont.) **(b)** Simplified VTVM schematic.

input potential to the basic range of the meter circuit. The scale calibration, however, is for the higher range.

A modern variation of the VTVM idea is the transistor voltmeter (TVM) in which a junction field effect transistor (JFET) is used in place of the vacuum tube. In addition to the TVM designation, these meters are also sometimes called FETVM.

Selecting a Multimeter. Each class of multimeter has its own distinct set of properties, advantages, and disadvantages. It cannot be said that one particular type is the be-all and end-all, for all applications. The VOM, for example, is very portable, so it is much more independent of the power mains than the other types. Additionally, most will operate on the ohms scale for a year or more on a single size-D or size-C dry cell. Since the battery is used only in the ohmmeter function, its loss does not completely disable the instrument. The classic VOM is also relatively free of the effects of radio transmitters and other energy sources operating nearby—clearly an advantage to a communications technician. In fact, in the vicinity of some transmitters, only a VOM will function properly, so it must be used. However, the relatively low sensitivity of even the best VOMs will load down the circuit and create errors. This becomes especially apparent in transistor circuits, of which all modern communications equipment is designed.

The usefulness of the VOM is restricted to places where ac power mains are easily accessible. The VTVM also does not have a current range, and is subject to some interference by radio transmitters—the probe wires act as an antenna of sorts, so they may pick up signals from local radio transmitters. These signals are impressed on the gate or grid (as the case may be) just the same as the dc being measured. The reading given by the meter will be in extreme error in this case. In fact, some VTVM and FETVM instruments have been known to read upscale all of the time when they are inside a radio transmitter building. The VTVM and FETVM do, however, have an extremely high input resistance that remains constant over a wide range of input ranges. In the typical VTVM (service grade) the input impedance is on the order of 11 MΩ, while that for the FETVM is typically much higher. This is why the VTVM or FETVM is preferred for bench use in a laboratory, workshop, or any other place where ac mains power is easily available. Besides its high input impedance, the VTVM is also relatively tolerant of abuse—such as overvoltage.

The FETVM will exhibit similar or superior input impedance, but is able to work in portable applications that the VTVM cannot handle. The same intolerance for interference exists, however, and the FETVM may tend to be a little less tolerant of voltage excesses. Also, many of these instruments use unusual batteries, so be prepared to keep extras on hand, as they often cannot be obtained at a local all-night drug store when you are working in the field.

Digital readout multimeters (DMM) are more costly than the other types of electronic voltmeter, and are subject to many of the same problems. Despite this fact, they are gaining in popularity, especially since the prices have come down from the kilodollar range a few years ago to less than $200 now.

One advantage to the DMM that must not be underemphasized, however, is that they are very accurate on a dollar-for-dollar comparison, and are provided with nonambiguous displays that require no operator interpretation. The printed analog scales of other types of electronic (and VOM) meters are sometimes difficult to read, and must be interpreted at points between the given calibration points. The DMM reads out in large numerical displays, so it is especially useful where there are inexperienced personnel, or where reading from across the room is required.

It is generally accepted that a properly equipped electronics facility will have at least two different types of multimeter. One should be the classic VOM type of instrument, preferably of high quality. Which of the other types is also selected will be a matter of user's choice. The author prefers the digital types for regular service readings, and an analog type for readings where a control, or tuned circuit, must be adjusted to deliver either a specified voltage value at some point, or either a peak or a null condition. Also needed are several different types of probe. In most cases you will use only a pair of ordinary wires mounted with either alligator clips or test probes at one end. In other cases, however, special probes are required, so they must be supplied. A popular type used in servicing radio transmitters and receivers is the RF voltage or "demodulator" probe.

PROBLEMS

1. A meter movement consisting of a coil on jewel bearings moving in the field of a permanent magnet is called a _______ or a _______.
2. A movement similar to that in Question 1 is mounted on a tight rubber band instead of bearings. This is called a _______ movement.
3. The type of meter shown in Figure 13.13 is a _______.

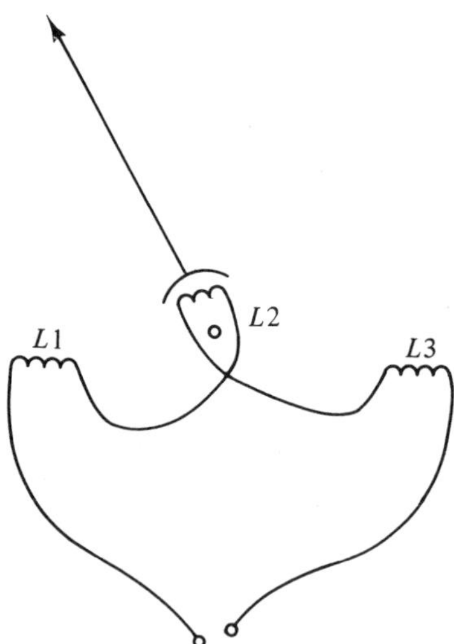

Figure 13.13

4. Most RF ammeters are _______ types.
5. A current meter is connected in _______ with the load.
6. A voltmeter is connected in _______ with the load.
7. A _______ is used to increase the range of a milliammeter.
8. What is the value of a shunt resistor to make a 0–1 milliammeter read 0–50 milliamperes f.s.? The internal resistance of the meter is 34 Ω.

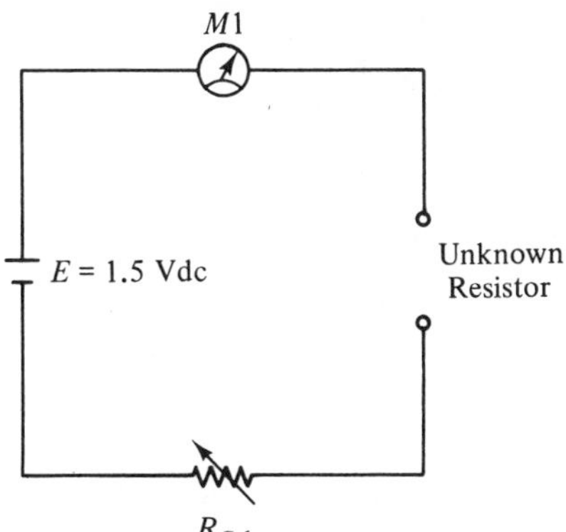

Figure 13.14

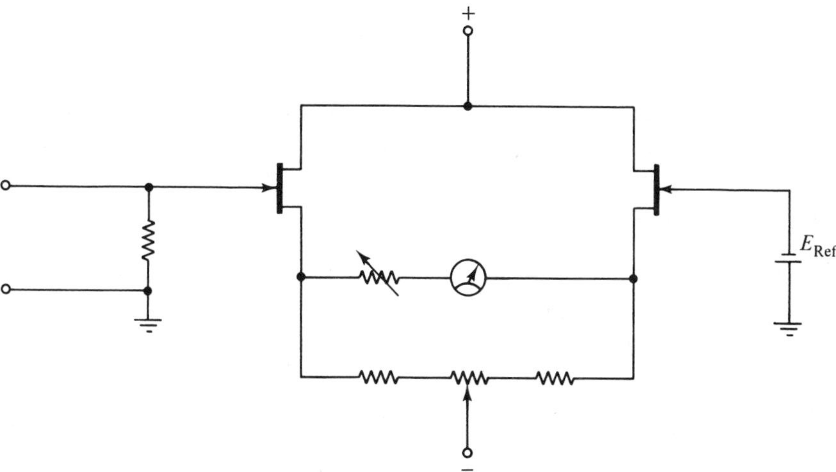

Figure 13.15

9. A ________ resistor is used to make a dc current meter measure voltage.
10. A 0–50 μA movement is to be used to make a 0–5 voltmeter. What value of multiplier resistor is required if the meter's internal resistance is 6200 Ω?
11. What are the units of the sensitivity rating of a VOM?
12. What is the sensitivity of the voltmeter in Question 10?
13. Draw an ohmmeter circuit. (See Figure 13.14.)
14. An ________ is used to make a dc current meter read ac current.
15. The circuit in Figure 13.15 is a ________.
16. The ________ type of multimeter is best suited for use around radio transmitters with high fields.

14
Test Instruments

The simple test instruments of the previous chapter will measure only a limited number of parameters, but there may be several others of interest when one is servicing electronic communications equipment. Those simple meters are critical, to be sure, but other classes of instruments are also needed to complete the job.

14.1 THE OSCILLOSCOPE

Of all classes of electronic test equipment, the most useful is the cathode ray oscilloscope or oscillograph. It is an instrument that draws a picture of a voltage waveform on a screen not unlike the screen of a television receiver—by much the same process.

Allen B. Dumont, father of the cathode ray tube (CRT), invented the basic oscilloscope over forty years ago. The CRT was the basic invention that made the oscilloscope possible, and even it was based upon similar devices used for decades prior to the CRT's introduction by physicists in their laboratories.

Although the original oscilloscope was relatively simple (and simple types can still be purchased new today), its modern counterparts can be among the most complex instruments in your inventory. It is so useful that many technicians and engineers would select the oscilloscope over all other instruments if they were required to use but one single instrument for all of their work.

The internal construction of a typical CRT is shown in Figure 14.1. The basic parts of the CRT are the electron gun, vertical and horizontal deflection plates, an accelerating electrode (an anode), and a phosphor-coated viewing screen. All parts are contained within an evacuated glass envelope.

The electron gun is basically a cathode encloced within a cylindrical electrode that has a small hole in one end. Electrons from the heated cathode (recall thermionic emission) pass through the hole, past some other electrodes, to form a narrow electron beam directed at the phosphor screen at the other end of the glass envelope. The additional electrodes in the gun are those that focus and give initial acceleration to the beam of

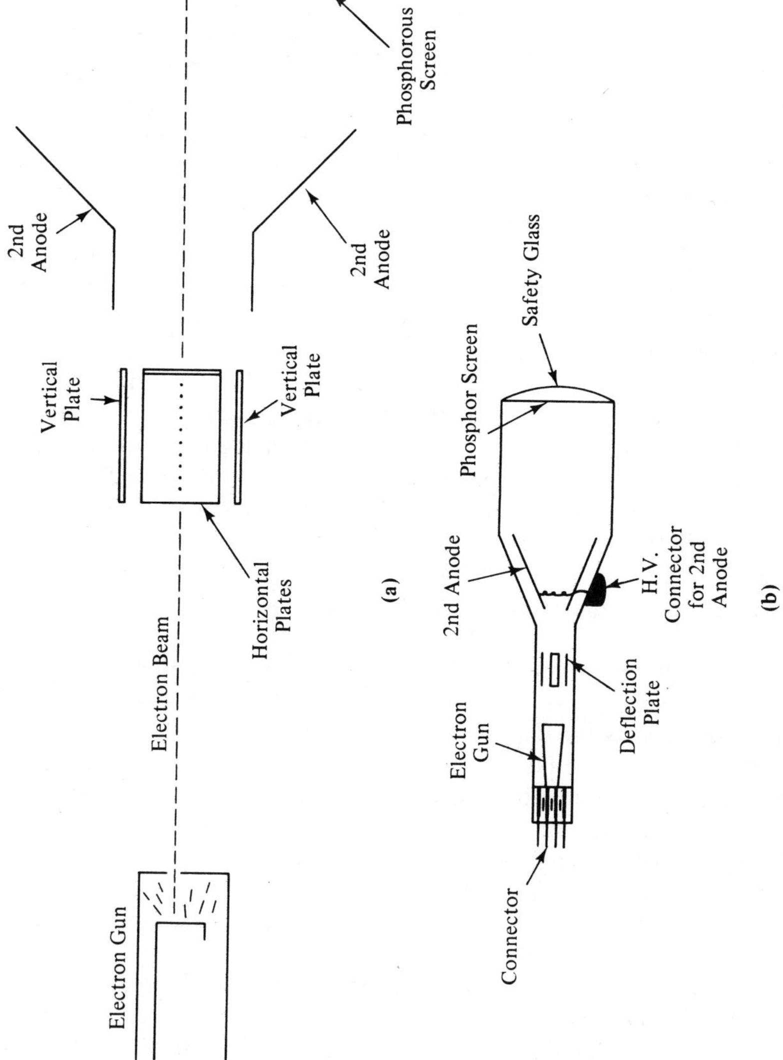

Figure 14.1 Structure of a cathode ray tube (CRT).

electrons. The quality of the oscilloscope is partially dependent upon how well focused the electron beam is, so electron gun design is very critical.

The second anode will have a very high potential—several thousand kilovolts typically—that is positive so that it will accelerate the electrons. This causes them to pick up velocity and, therefore, kinetic energy. The phosphor screen is viewed by the user. When the accelerated electrons strike this screen, they generate a point of light at the point of impact.

A really exhaustive discussion of this phenomenon is beyond the scope of this book, but we can consider a brief description of the mechanism by which light is generated.

The orbital electrons in the atoms of the phosphor material that coats the inside surface of the screen have a certain energy level when at rest. When electrons from the beam strike the screen, they give up their kinetic energy on impact. But since energy must be conserved, the atoms of phosphorous material absorb the energy, although some small amount is given up as heat. When the atoms absorb energy, the energy levels of their orbital electrons are raised, but this is an unstable condition and will not last long. One way of looking at this situation is to think of the atoms taking up positions further away from the nucleus when they absorb the kinetic energy. When the atoms assume their previous energy levels, the electrons in orbit fall back to their rest positions. The extra energy that had been stored in the electrons is then given up in the form of light photons.

If the light beam on the phosphor screen can be moved proportionally to a voltage waveform, then the light pattern on the screen will be the same shape as the applied waveform. This is the job of the vertical and horizontal deflection plates. The vertical deflection plates are mounted so that one is above and another is below the electron beam. The horizontal plates are located to the right and left, on either side of, the electron beam—as viewed from the screen.

The relationship between the voltages applied to the two sets of deflection plates is shown in Figure 14.2, and the block diagram of a simple oscilloscope is shown in Figure 14.3.

Signals to the vertical and horizontal plates usually require some amplification to produce the best deflection. Most oscilloscopes provide high gain amplifiers for this purpose. The gain of the amplifiers is set so that a deflection factor in volts/inch or volts/cm can be used to calibrate the instrument. An input attenuator, as was true in the case of the VTVM, allows higher voltages to produce useful deflections that are on-screen. Since a good oscilloscope will display either ac or dc voltages, the deflection factor can be used to make measurements of the voltage's amplitude. This allows the oscilloscope to function as a voltmeter, if necessary.

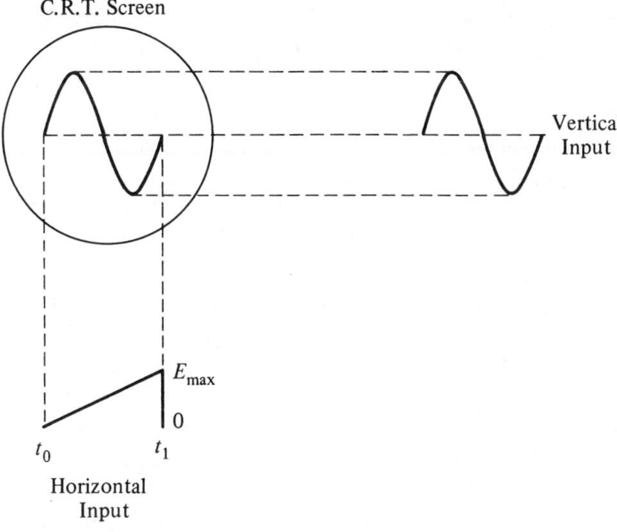

Figure 14.2 Relationship of the horizontal and vertical waveforms creates the waveform on the CRT screen.

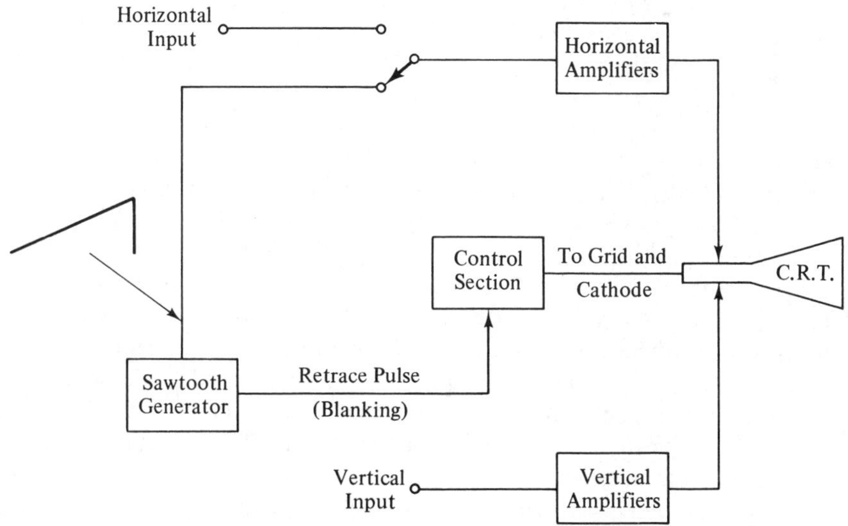

Figure 14.3 Block diagram of a typical cathode ray oscilloscope.

Also provided (see Figure 14.3) are control circuits and a sawtooth waveform generator. The control section sets the CRT beam current, varies the brightness, and so forth. The sawtooth generator provides a ramp voltage to the horizontal deflection amplifier and plates, so the beam can be deflected from left to right. The control circuit biases the horizontal plates so that the beam will be on the left side of the screen when the sawtooth voltage is zero. As the sawtooth waveform voltage rises, the beam will be deflected to the right an amount proportional to the sawtooth voltage.

The sawtooth voltage rises linearly between times t_0 and t_1. Because of this fact, we can calibrate the CRT screen's horizontal axis in units of time. There is a control on the oscilloscope front panel that sets the time base of the sawtooth. Most are calibrated in terms of time, but low-cost oscilloscopes are calibrated in terms of frequency. The CRT screen is divided into divisions of 1 in. or (more commonly) 1 cm each. These have a correspondence to time given by the time-base control that ranges from a fraction of a microsecond to several seconds per division.

The electron beam is deflected left to right by the sawtooth voltage applied to the horizontal plates. At the same time, a sine wave or other waveform is applied to the vertical deflection plates. This will defect the electron beam up and down in response to the applied voltage waveform. The resultant light pattern on the CRT screen has the same shape as the applied waveform.

The light does not fade instantaneously after the electron beam passes, but remains briefly on the screen. This is due to the *persistence* of the phosphorous coating. If the waveform is periodic, then it will repeat itself before the light beam dies away, and this gives the illusion of a constant display. When combined with the natural persistence of the human eye, it makes the display appear to be very steady, when, in fact, it is constantly changing. This is very similar to the manner in which a sequence of still photographs is converted to movement in motion pictures.

In Figure 14.3 we see a blanking pulse applied to the CRT. This pulse is generated at time t_1 (see Figure 14.2) when the sawtooth voltage drops abruptly to zero. Ordinarily, without the blanking pulse, the rapidly falling sawtooth voltage will be seen on the CRT screen in the form of a rapid retrace back to the left side of the screen. Although it is necessary to bring the electron beam back to the left side, this creates an anomoly in the display not due to external input stimulus. The blanking pulse eliminates the problem by cutting off the CRT beam current during retrace, and that extinguishes the light on the screen.

We can make a rough calculation of the frequency of a signal applied to the vertical input by using the oscilloscope time base to measure its period. Recall that the period is defined as the time between the recurrence of the same feature (i.e., the peak, or possibly a certain zero crossing) on sequential waves. We can measure the period by noting how many divisions along the horizontal axis are occupied by the waveform, and then multiplying that figure by the time-base factor.

Example. An oscilloscope time base is set so that the horizontal deflection is 0.1 millisecond (ms) per centimeter. A sine-wave signal is applied to the vertical input, and the resultant CRT trace shows that exactly one cycle occupies 7 cm. What is the frequency of this waveform? (*Note: To find the frequency, first find the period and then take its reciprocal.*)

$$T = 7 \text{ cm} \times 0.1 \text{ ms/cm}$$
$$T = 0.7 \text{ ms}$$
$$T = 0.0007 \text{ s}$$

The frequency, then, is the reciprocal of 0.0007 s, or

$$F = 1/0.0007$$
$$F = 1429 \text{ Hz}$$

In many cases, oscilloscope time-base calibration is in very poor condition, especially if the instrument is more than a few months old. On lower-cost instruments it was never very good. As a result, it is only an approximate measurement. Better precision can be achieved by using a time marker generator to place pulses on the CRT screen. These will occur at fixed intervals, and are generated from a precision crystal oscillator. The time base can be adjusted to display only a given number, say ten, at any given time.

Another method for using an external signal source to measure the frequency of an unknown signal involves generating a pattern called a Lissajous figure. The time-base method is, after all, severely limited by the accuracy of the internal time base of the oscilloscope. It is also true that the internal time base usually does not operate up to the frequency limits of the oscilloscope, so above the time-base range, an external method must be used. In the method using Lissajous figures, we replace the sawtooth with a known signal from a generator.

If an unknown signal is applied to one set of deflection plates (e.g., the vertical), and a known signal from an external calibrated oscillator is applied to the alternate plates, then a pattern similar to those of Figures

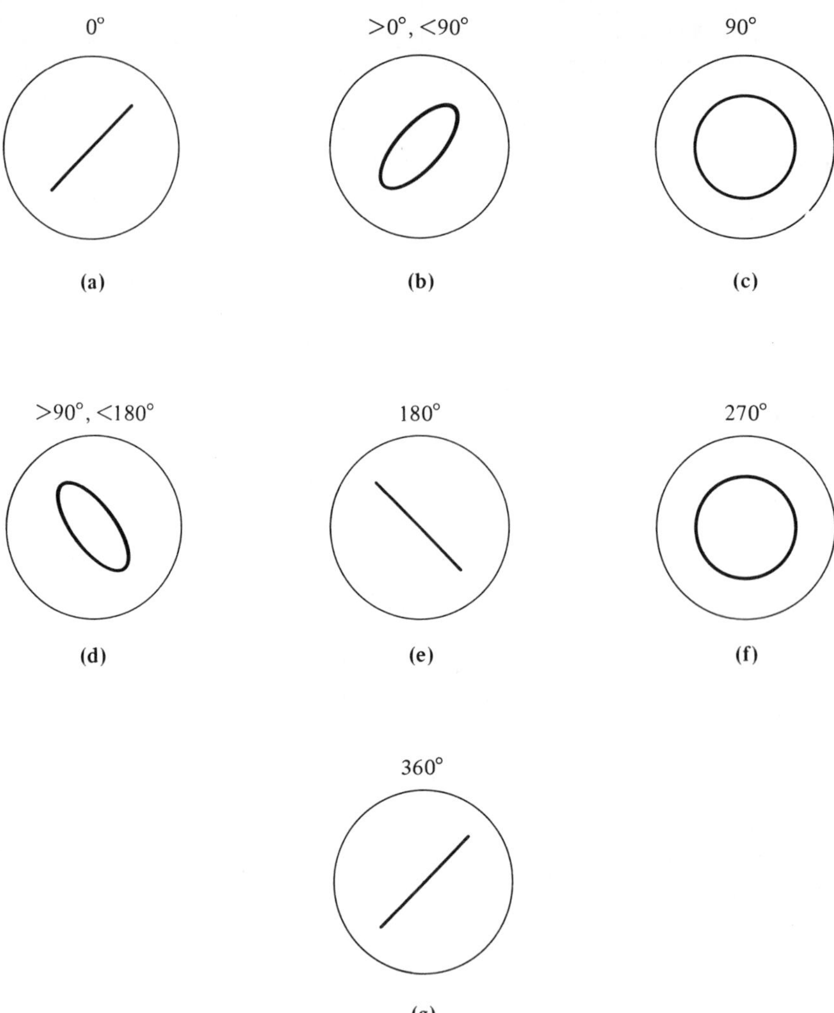

Figure 14.4 Sine wave Lissajous patterns for various phase angles.

14.4 and 14.5 will be created. The pattern in Figure 14.4 exists when the vertical frequency F_v and the horizontal frequency F_h are equal. The only difference between the two frequencies in this particular case is their relative *phase*. If the same, or identical, signals are applied to the two inputs, then the relative phase relationship will be 0 deg. This produces the pattern shown in Figure 14.4(a), a straight line. If both signals are of the same amplitude, then the line will be tilted at an angle of 45 deg from the horizontal axis. Note that the same pattern again appears at 360 deg, because 360 deg on one sine wave is also 0 deg on the next sine wave.

At phase differences greater than 0 deg, the pattern will open up into an ellipse. The "fatness" of the ellipse is proportional to the phase angle. At exactly 90 deg the pattern becomes perfectly circular—the ellipse has reached maximum fatness. As the phase angle increases past 90 deg, the pattern again becomes elliptical, but is of opposite sense. The pattern will become thinner as the phase angle increases, until it is again a straight line at 180 deg [Figure 14.4(e)].

The Lissajous pattern shown in Figure 14.5 results when the two input frequencies are related so that one is an integer multiple of the other. This particular pattern will exist when the horizontal frequency is twice the vertical frequency. The relationship governing this measurement is

$$F_v = \frac{N_h}{N_v} \times F_h \tag{14-1}$$

where F_v is the frequency of the signal applied to the vertical plates.
F_h is the frequency of the signal applied to the horizontal plates.
N_v is the number of loops observed along the vertical edge.
N_h is the number of loops observed along the horizontal edge.

Figure 14.5 Lissajous pattern for a 2:1 frequency ratio.

For the example in Figure 14.5, there are two vertical loops and one horizontal loop, so

$$F_v = \tfrac{1}{2} \times F_h$$

or, as stated above, $2F_v = F_h$.

Oscilloscopes are available in a bewilderingly large variety of types and options. An oscilloscope can cost from a few hundred to a few thousand dollars. Features will, as one wag put it, be able to do everything but tell you when to use it, at frequencies from dc to daylight.

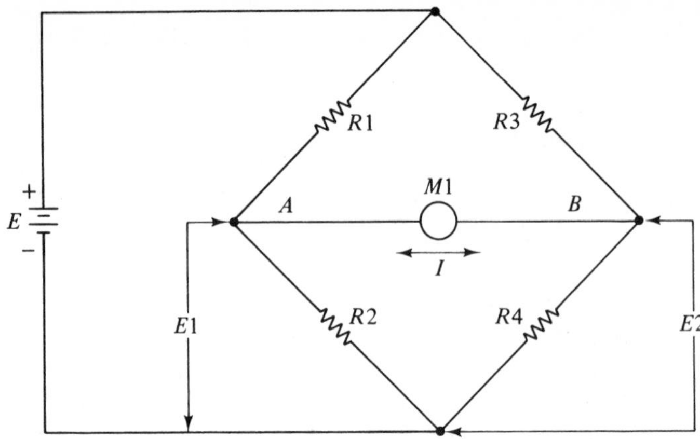

Figure 14.6 Basic dc Wheatstone bridge.

14.2 WHEATSTONE BRIDGE INSTRUMENTS

The basic Wheatstone bridge is shown in Figure 14.6. It consists of two series voltage dividers connected in parallel with each other. Resistors $R1$ and $R2$ form one voltage divider, while resistors $R3$ and $R4$ form the other. The voltage between points A and B in the figure is given by

$$E_{AB} = E\left[\frac{R2}{R1 + R2} - \frac{R4}{R3 + R4}\right] \tag{14-2}$$

When the bridge is in balance, $E1 = E2$, so E_{AB} will equal zero.

Unknown resistances can be measured with the Wheatstone bridge if two of the bridge resistors are fixed, one is the unknown, and the fourth is a variable, calibrated potentiometer or rheostat. When the bridge is in balance, the following ratio holds true:

$$\frac{R1}{R2} = \frac{R3}{R4} \tag{14-3}$$

Let us assume that resistor $R2$ is the calibrated variable resistor and that $R1$ and $R3$ are fixed. $R4$, then, is the unknown. By algebraic manipulation of Eq. (14-3) we get

$$R4 = \frac{R2 \times R3}{R1} \tag{14-4}$$

Since the ratio $R3/R1$ can be computed, and the value of $R2$ can be found from the dial on the potentiometer, the value of $R4$ can be computed. It is usually the practice to make $R1 = R3$, so the ratio will equal unity (1). In that case, the values of $R4$ will be the same as the value of $R2$ when the bridge is nulled. Let us consider an example, however, in which the fixed resistors are *not* equal.

Example. In a certain Wheatstone bridge $R1 = 2000\ \Omega$ and $R3 = 5000\ \Omega$. If the null is found when $R2 = 1200\ \Omega$, what is the value of the unknown?

$$R4 = 1200 \times (5000/2000)$$
$$R4 = 1200 \times 5/2$$
$$R4 = 3000\ \Omega$$

The accuracy of any particular Wheatstone bridge is limited by the accuracy to which the values of $R1$, $R2$, and $R3$ are known, and to the sensitivity of the null indicator. The meter in Figure 14.6 is the principal factor affecting the sensitivity. At null there is no voltage across points A and B, so the meter current is zero. If a sensitive meter movement is used, then the null can be accurately determined. Usually, a 50- or 100-μA movement is used.

AC Wheatstone bridges are those where the excitation voltage source E is an alternating current, and the meter is replaced by some sort of ac null detector. This could possibly be an ac VTVM, a pair of earphones, an oscilloscope, etc. It is also possible that one or more resistors will be reactances (X_c or X_L) or a complex impedance ($R + jX$).

14.3 SIGNAL GENERATORS

There is frequently a need for a locally generated source of signals to bench test, troubleshoot, or adjust electronic equipment. A signal might be needed, for example, to simulate a distant transmitter while a communications receiver is tested. Alternatively, one might require an audio signal to apply to a transmitter's microphone jack to simulate speech from the microphone. The instruments that supply these signals are quite different, but they are all known collectively as *signal generators.*

A signal generator is any device or instrument that contains an oscillator to originate the signal. Furthermore, most signal generators also include an output level control so that the amplitude of the signal can be controlled.

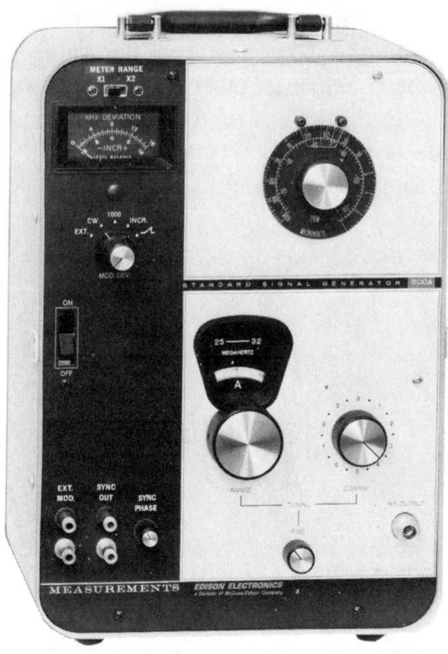

Figure 14.7 Communications type signal generator. (*Courtesy of Edison Electronics.*)

An example of a popular RF signal generator is shown in Figure 14.7. This particular signal generator is often used to test communications equipment, especially in the land-mobile industry. The output frequency is set by the combined efforts of the range switch and two similar controls.

Several different types of signal generators are usually needed. Among these are RF, audio (AF), function, pulse, and any special-purpose generators that might be required for a special application. Examples of the latter are certain communications and navigation equipment in aircraft, and the test simulators needed for FM-stereo receiver servicing. In some cases you will find all, or at least several, of these different instruments in one package, but for the most part separate signal generator packages are the rule.

An audio generator is usually designed to provide sine waves, and possibly square waves, at frequencies between 20 and 20,000 Hz. Output control is relatively precise over a wide range of rms values. This is needed because many audio amplifiers, especially those for hi-fi, require very low-level input signals. There will be either an output meter or a calibrated attenuator that gives the output amplitude in either millivolts-rms or decibels (often of the "VU" or volume units form). Both the dB and VU scales are based on the decibel expression of a ratio between two voltage, current, or power levels. In the case of a voltage or current the ratio is expressed as a number calculated from

$$\mathrm{dB} = 20 \log_{10} (E1/E2)$$

and for power

$$\mathrm{dB} = 10 \log_{10} (P1/P2)$$

Oddly enough, even though the output is a voltage, we use the power version of the decibel. If the meter on the audio generator is calibrated in dB, then the level 0-dB is taken to be equal to 6 mW in a 500-Ω load. If the scale is marked in VU, then we still use the power-decibel form, but the level defined as 0 VU is 1 mW in a 600 Ω load.

In either case, the standard power against which others are measured is plugged into the "P2" expression in the power decibel formula. If the output of the generator is 1 mW and the scale is calibrated in VU, then the formula will evaluate as

$$\mathrm{VU} = 10 \log_{10} (1\ \mathrm{mW}/1\ \mathrm{mW})$$
$$\mathrm{VU} = 10 \log_{10} (1)$$
$$\mathrm{VU} = 0$$

Other output levels are referenced to this point, so the value can be determined from the VU or dB reading. If it is desired to have a voltage reading, then just compute the power and solve for voltage in the formula $E = (PR)^{1/2}$.

The function generator is similar to the audio generator, and is often erroneously labeled as an audio generator. There are, however, some critical differences that make it a much more useful instrument—in many cases. The typical function generator will provide output waveforms of sine, triangle, and square waves at voltages up to 10–15 V rms. Control over the output is usually not as precise as it was in the audio generator, but seems rather coarse by comparison. The frequency range of the function generator is much wider than that of the audio generator. Most function generators have low end frequency limits of at least 1 Hz and upper end limits of at least 20 kHz. There is, though, at least one that has a frequency range from 0.01 Hz to 11 MHz, and most will operate over the range from 0.1 Hz to 100 kHz—even though they are of low cost.

Figure 14.8 shows a modern instrumentation package made by

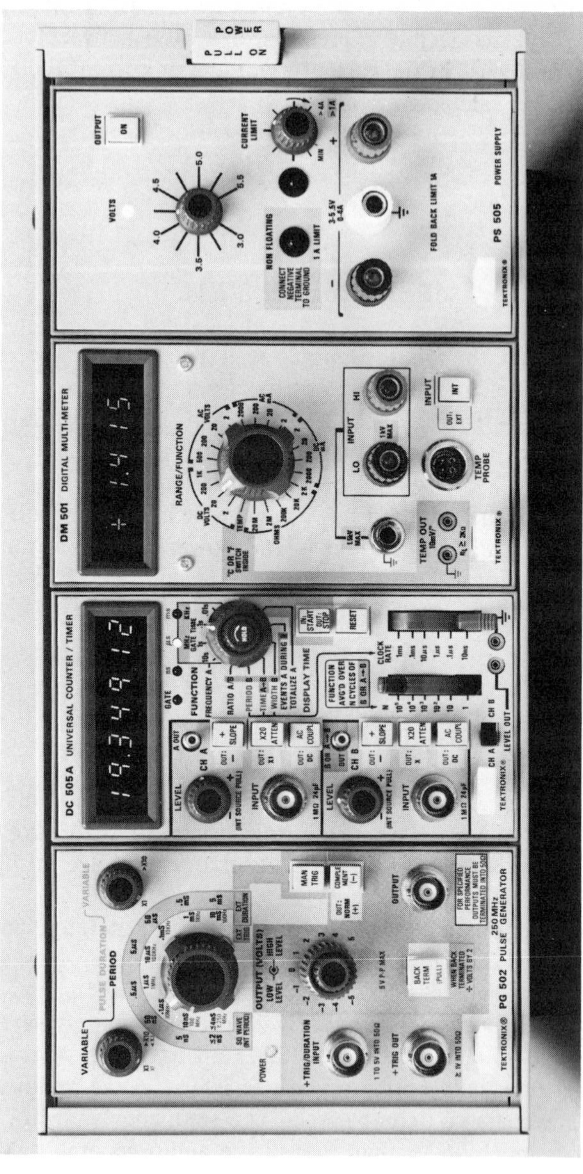

Figure 14.8 Portable instrument pack for the servicer. (*Courtesy of Tektronix, Inc.*)

Tektronix, Inc. (of oscilloscope fame). This package includes a pulse generator that will provide outputs over the range 100 kHz to 250 MHz. The principal difference between the pulse generator and other types, such as the square-wave generator, is that it offers control over both frequency —often called *repetition rate,*—and *duration.* A square-wave output waveform would be perfectly symmetrical, and indeed that is the definition of the square wave. It is also true that the square wave is symmetrical about the 0 V baseline, so its alternate halves will be positive and negative. The pulse generator output may be positive or it may be negative, but at any given time it will be only one polarity. Furthermore, the duty cycle (length of time during each cycle that the output is on) may be considerably less than that of the square wave. In fact, the duty cycle may be only a few percent, in which case there will be a very quick, short-duration pulse, even though the repetition rate has a high frequency.

This may seem like a small thing, but it is critical to the proper testing of some circuits. The physical difference between the square wave and a true pulse is such that they behave differently in some types of circuit. In the chapter on nonsinusoidal waveforms we shall demonstrate that all non-sine waves can be made up from the summation of the large number of harmonically related sine waves. The expression that relates these harmonics and their amplitudes is called the "Fourier series" of the waveform. A treatment of the Fourier series is beyond the scope of this book, but will be given in any good engineering mathematics textbook.

Even though it is an aside, the particular instrumentation package shown in Figure 14.8 should be discussed, because it represents a new departure in portable instrument design. In the past, there was a severe limit on the types of instruments that could be carried on a service call—despite the fact that it is often necessary to have those instruments. The alternatives in the past were none too palatable. One could lug with the ordinarily needed instruments a large truck full of test equipment. Then it became necessary to carry the piece of equipment outside, or to piece-by-heavy-piece lug the test equipment inside to the site. Alternatively, one could take the equipment "to the shop"—always unpopular with customers. Some companies offered instruments packaged in a single case, and that seemed to be the cure. But it soon became apparent that the person who selected what would be in the instrument rarely had a good appreciation of *your* particular needs. In other cases, it was found that the principal function of the test instrument would be well designed and high quality, but the extra add-ons or options were skimpy. Tektronix was a pioneer in the concept of the main-frame oscilloscope in which a single main frame could serve a lot of users. Plug-ins are available that allow the 'scope to become what *you* need. They have extended that concept to include a wide range of instruments that may be plugged into several different main frames—including their oscilloscopes and benchtop and portable mainframe racks. Although only four instruments are shown here, any number may be purchased and used in combination. It is also possible to keep several main frames if you require a lot of instruments at one time. Tektronix makes a variety of their own plug-in modules, but realize that you may have some requirement that they are either ignorant of or see too little market to justify making. For these cases there are blank plug-ins that include the internal printed circuit board.

Special-purpose signal generators are those that are designed to give signals that are peculiar to servicing or testing a specific system or piece of equipment. Avionics, radar, and FM-stereo are examples of areas where a special signal generator might be needed.

14.4 TOTAL HARMONIC DISTORTION (THD) ANALYZERS

The only "pure" electronic waveform is the sine wave. All other electrical waveforms can be made by summing sine waves consisting of a fundamental frequency and its harmonics (f, $2f$, $3f$, $4f$, . . . , nf). The exact shape of any particular waveform is determined by the particular set of harmonics, their amplitudes and relative phase relationships. When a sine wave becomes distorted, that is to say less pure, harmonics are generated. The measure of how much an amplifier or other circuit distorts a sine wave is the number and strength of the harmonics that are generated.

Figure 14.9 shows the block diagram of a total harmonic distortion

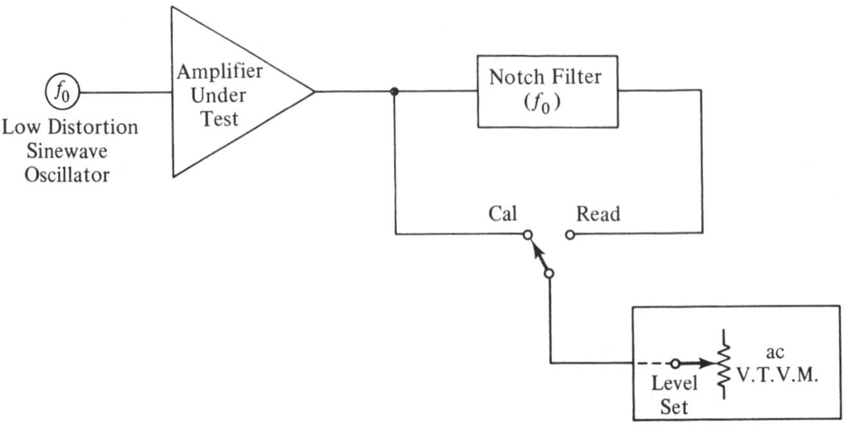

Figure 14.9 Total harmonic distortion analyzer.

(THD) analyzer. Its operation is based on this phenomenon. The signal source is a very low distortion oscillator or audio signal generator. The output level of this generator is set either to some specific value required by the manufacturer of the audio amplifier, or at a point just below the saturation or "clipping" point of the amplifier. In the latter case an oscilloscope must be used to adjust the input signal level until the amplifier output signal just begins to clip. The level is then reduced slightly to remove all traces of clipping.

The output indicator on the THD analyzer is an ac VTVM with special calibration. In addition to the normal rms voltage or dB power calibration, there is also a "percent-THD" scale. There may be two or more such scales to accommodate several ranges. A popular marking is 0–1 for scales of 0–1, 0–10, and 0–100 percent; and 0–3 for scales of 0–3, 0–30 percent.

Operation of the THD analyzer is rather simple, even in the case where it is nonautomatic. When the oscillator output is correctly set to the proper level and test frequency (1000 Hz unless otherwise specified), the switch is set to the "cal" position. The LEVEL SET control is adjusted so that the VTVM reads exactly full scale. This initial adjustment is performed with the range switch set to the 100 percent position, so the meter will read exactly 100 percent when this is done. The switch is then set to the "read" position. This places a notch filter tuned to the oscillator's frequency in the signal path to the meter. This filter is then fine-tuned to obtain the best rejection of the fundamental frequency supplied by the generator. When this is done the fundamental frequency is almost completely nulled out, and only the harmonics are left—it is these that represent the total harmonic distortion. In the first case the VTVM reads the rms value of the total waveform, including both the fundamental and the harmonics. In the second case, however, only the rms value of the harmonics are found. Since the instrument was calibrated to 100 percent in the first case, the pointer will fall back to a point that indicates the percentage of the total represented by the THD—hence %-THD.

PROBLEMS

1. Name the basic elements of the cathode ray tube (CRT).
2. Second anode potentials are typically __________.
3. It is standard practice to apply the unknown waveform to the vertical deflection plates and a calibrated ________ waveform to the horizontal plates.
4. An oscilloscope time base is set to 10 ms/cm. The sine wave on the viewing screen occupies 1.7 cm along the horizontal axis. What is its frequency?

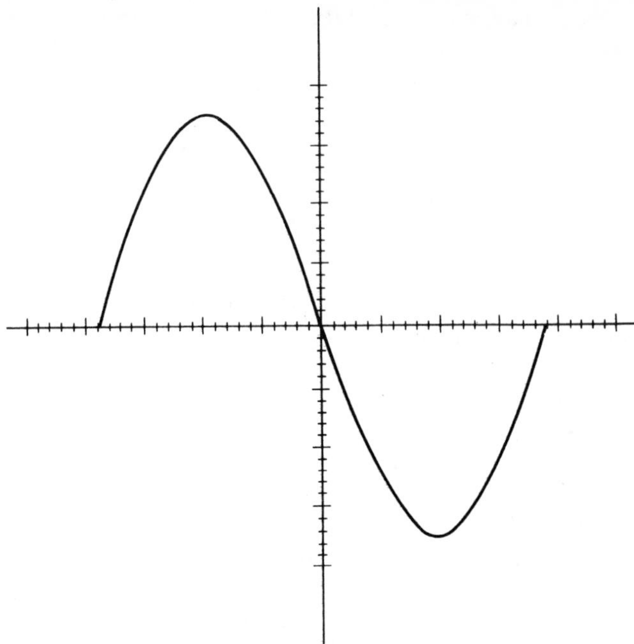

Figure 14.10

5. What is the amplitude in volts of the waveform shown in Figure 14.10 if the vertical input attenuator is set to 5 V/cm?
6. What is the rms value of this waveform?
7. CRT __________ is responsible for the apparent steadiness of the pattern on the viewing screen.
8. A __________ is used to extinguish the CRT beam during retrace.
9. In Figure 14.10 what is the frequency if the time base is set to 1 μs/cm?
10. A ________ pattern will be observed if two harmonically related signals are applied to the vertical and horizontal plates.
11. What is the vertical frequency shown by the Lissajous pattern in Figure 14.11 if the horizontal frequency is 1000 Hz?

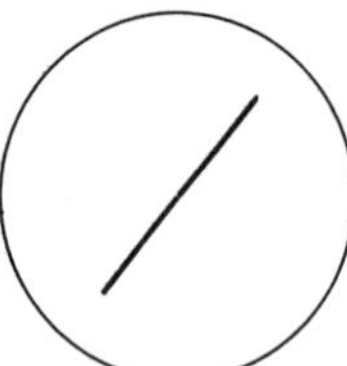

Figure 14.11

12. What is the phase relationship between the vertical and horizontal frequencies in Question 11?

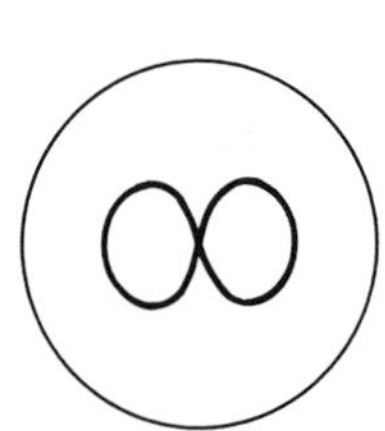

Figure 14.12

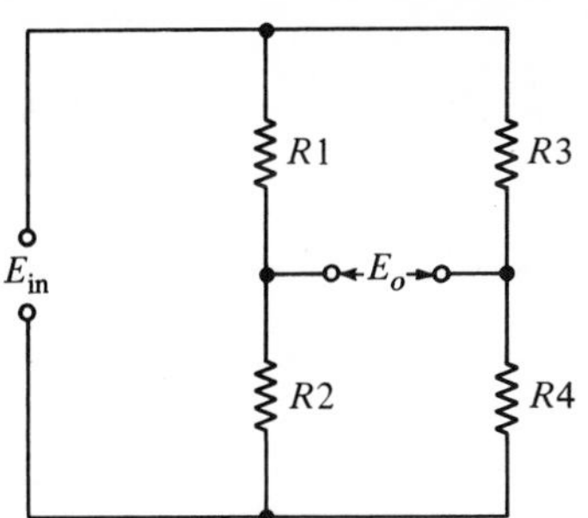

Figure 14.13

13. What is the vertical frequency in Figure 14.12 if a 500-Hz signal is applied to the horizontal plates?

14. The circuit in Figure 14.13 is a ______.

15. Assume that $R1 = 1$ k, $R2 = 4.73$ k, $R3 = 1$ k, and that $E_o = 0$ V. Find the value of $R4$.

15
Frequency Measurement

Most radio communications transmitters must operate on a specific assigned frequency. The Federal Communications Commission specifies the allowable tolerance in output frequency error for each class of service. An AM broadcast station, for example, must maintain its output frequency to within ±20 Hz of the assigned frequency. FM broadcast transmitters, on the other hand, are required to maintain their frequency to within ±2000 Hz of the frequency assigned to them by the F.C.C. Other services each have their own tolerance requirements. Class-D Personal Radio Service (CB) transmitters, for example, must maintain their output frequency to within 50 parts per million (ppm) of the correct channel frequency. Other services have tolerances such as 2.5 ppm or 5 ppm. Measurement of a transmitter's operating frequency is required on a periodic basis in order to insure that the frequency is correct.

15.1 ROUGH METHODS

It is not always true that precision is required in the measurement of frequency. Of course, if you are certifying a transmitter to be officially "on frequency," then a superior method of measurement is required. But for many applications only a rough frequency determination is required. Examples of such cases include determination of the approximate frequency of an unwanted oscillation or other spurious emission in a transmitter, or the carrier frequency during neutralization.

One easy method for measuring frequency is to use a communications receiver covering the band of interest. Such receivers are relatively easy to obtain in the medium wave through shortwave (0.5–30-MHz) region, and only a little more difficult in the VHF and UHF regions. Measurement of frequency is performed by comparing the calibration markings on the receiver dial with the point where the unknown signal is noted.

Even when high-priced, professional-grade receivers are used to make the frequency measurement, accuracy will not be sufficient to satisfy the precision requirements of an official frequency measurement. Thermal drift, component aging, mechanical vibration, and backlash in the dial and tuning mechanisms all seem to conspire to erase whatever precision existed immediately following the last calibration. The receiver is, however, often used in conjunction with other instruments in making very accurate frequency measurements. The difference, of course, is that a comparison is made using the receiver, but against the other instruments—not against the receiver's own calibration.

15.2 ABSORPTION METHODS

The absorption wavemeter is probably the simplest type of frequency meter or indicator. It is also one of the least accurate, but it does have its uses. Two examples of absorption wavemeters are shown in Figure 15.1. Both types consist of a resonant tank circuit made from a fixed inductance and a variable capacitor. The capacitor is ganged to a dial that is calibrated in terms of frequency. The coil in each case is mounted in a manner that allows it to be coupled closely with the circuit being tested. The capacitor, on the other hand, should be shielded from the outside world lest capacitive coupling to nearby objects, and the operator's own hand, detune the circuit and spoil whatever calibration exists. As a result, it is common to find the capacitor mounted inside an aluminum-shielded box. The inductor is then mounted on the outside of the box and is connected to the capacitor through an insulated socket.

The circuit in Figure 15.1(a) is the classic absorption wavemeter. The capacitor, inductor, and lamp form a series-resonant tank circuit, so it will have a low impedance at its resonant frequency. Energy from the tank circuit of the radio transmitter under test is induced into the wavemeter coil. This will set up a current in the wavemeter that causes the lamp to light up. Of course, it takes a fair amount of power to fully light that lamp, so low-current types are often preferred.

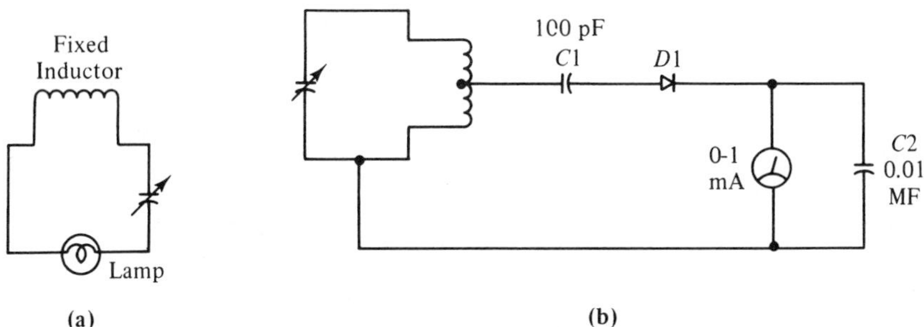

Figure 15.1 **(a)** Simple wavemeter, **(b)** rectified wavemeter.

If the transmitter stage being tested has a plate or cathode milliammeter, then the lamp may be omitted. If the coil of the wavemeter is coupled to the coil of the transmitter's tank circuit, then some of the plate tank energy will be absorbed by the wavemeter. When the two tanks are tuned to the same frequency, this energy absorption increases dramatically. If the wavemeter is tuned across the resonant frequency of the tank, then a slight inflection will be noted on the transmitter milliammeter.

A variation on the wavemeter circuit, and there are many, is shown in Figure 15.1(b). In this case, the tank is used in the parallel resonant mode. Signal from a tap on the coil is coupled through capacitor *C*1 to the diode, where it is rectified. The pulsating dc output waveform is filtered by capacitor *C*2. This produces a steady dc current that is fed to the meter.

The milliammeter in Figure 15.1(b) is deflected an amount that is roughly proportional to the strength of the applied signal. The wavemeter, then, will also function as a relative field-strength meter—useful in certain transmitter tune-up procedures.

The use of a tap on the coil, rather than the entire length, is necessary because of the low impedance of the diode rectifier. You should recall that the maximum power transfer occurs only when the impedances are matched. Furthermore, the low impedance of the diode would load the tank too much if it were connected across the entire coil. This would lower the Q and make the resonant point difficult to read with any accuracy at all. In some cases there is a second coil of a few turns used to drive the diode-filter network. In this case it is acting as a low-impedance transformer.

The absorption wavemeter is a very crude device, no matter how well it is constructed. It is also limited in sensitivity, because it is a passive device. A form of active absorption wavemeter is the "dip oscillator." If an L-C tank circuit is used as the frequency-determining network in a variable oscillator, then a dip oscillator type of wavemeter can be made. Older "dippers" used vacuum tubes in the oscillator, so were usually called "grid dip ocsillators." Modern dip instruments can be called either *base* or *gate dip oscillators,* depending upon whether a bipolar or field effect transistor is used for the oscillator.

A typical grid dip oscillator is shown in Figure 15.2. This circuit is a variable frequency oscillator of a rather ordinary Colpitts design. The inductor is mounted outside the cabinet containing the rest of the circuitry. This is done so that is can be coupled to the circuit under test. The current flowing through the grid resistor is monitored by the microammeter (M1).

The dip oscillator works because energy in its tank circuit coil will be absorbed by any closely coupled external tank that is tuned to the same frequency. Capacitor *C*1 is ganged to a dial that is calibrated in terms of frequency. To operate a dipper, hold the coil close to the tank circuit being

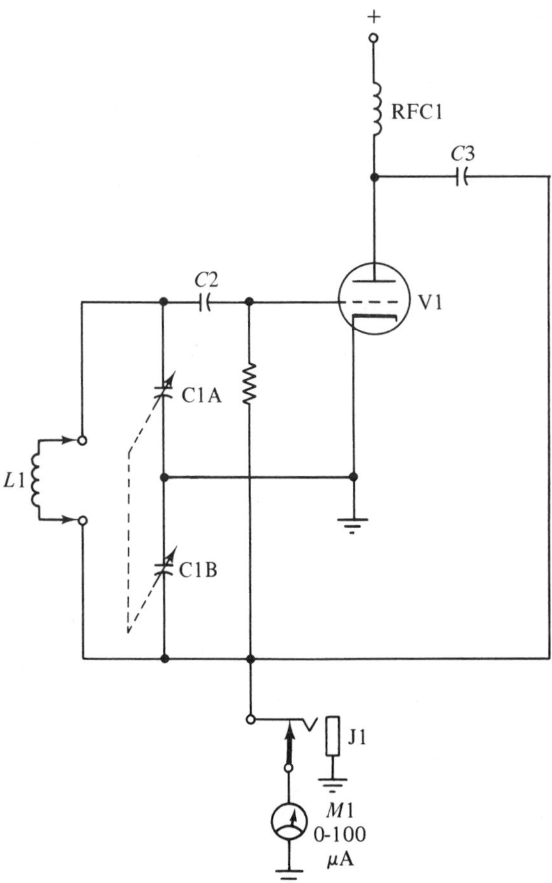

Figure 15.2 Circuit for a grid-dip oscillator.

tested, and slowly tune capacitor $C1$ until a sharp dip is noted in the grid current reading. This indicates that energy has been absorbed from $L1$ by the tank circuit under test. The dial frequency on the dip oscillator is the resonant frequency of the tank circuit.

The chief advantage of the dipper over the simple passive wavemeter is that it is active, so it is therefore more sensitive. This also allows it to test passive, or turned-off, tank circuits. In addition, it allows testing of passive devices such as antennas and resonant cavities that are not normally power generators. The passive wavemeter, on the other hand, can be used to test only those tank circuits that are energized with a fair amount of RF power, several watts or more, at the resonant frequency.

The dip oscillator can also be used with active circuit, just like the wavemeter. In that case the dipper is used as an oscillating detector. A pair of earphones is plugged into jack *J*1, and they take the place of the microammeter. The coil is coupled to the tank under test, and *C*1 is adjusted. When the dipper frequency gets close to the frequency of the signals in the tank, a tone will be heard in the earphones. This is due to a process known as *heterodyning,* which occurs when two different frequencies are mixed together in a nonlinear circuit. There will be four output signals in such a case: the first frequency ($f1$), the second frequency ($f2$), and the sum and difference frequencies ($f1 \pm f2$). In the case of a dipper's being used as an oscillating detector the only output frequency of interest is the difference between the two input frequencies ($f1 - f2$) or ($f2 - f1$). When the two frequencies are close together, this difference is within the range of human hearing. The exact pitch of the beat note thus produced is equal to the difference frequency and is heard in the earphones. As the unknown and dipper frequencies become even closer together, the beat note tone decreases until it is below the range of human hearing. When it is exactly zero, the two signals are said to be in "zero beat." The frequency at which this occurs is the frequency of the signals in the tank under test.

None of these absorption techniques are considered particularly accurate, and are used only for rough, nonprecision work. All of them are subject to the same type of drift as the receiver method, so even good initial calibration soon deteriorates. In addition, they are more sensitive to mechanical shocks and vibration errors. In the case of the oscillating detector there is also a zero beat error due to the fact that the operator cannot hear the beat note once it gets below the range of human hearing, so there is a 30- to 100-Hz uncertainty in dial setting. Because of these facts, and the initially poor calibration suffered by these instruments, none of them are used where precision is a criterion.

Lecher Wires. Lecher wires are a mechanical device used for determining the frequency of signals between 50 and about 500-MHz. Above that limit, similar techniques involving slot lines are used, but the method is essentially the same.

A set of Lecher wires consists of a pair of parallel conductors such as #12 (or larger) solid wires or small-diameter copper tubing. The length of the conductors must be at least one wavelength at the frequency of interest—which explains why the method is not used at frequencies lower than 50 or so megahertz. The wavelength in that range is 6 meters, which turns out to be almost 20 feet. Parallel to the conductors is a measuring stick marked off in units of length—meters, centimeters, and millimeters (or, in a few rare cases, yards and inches).

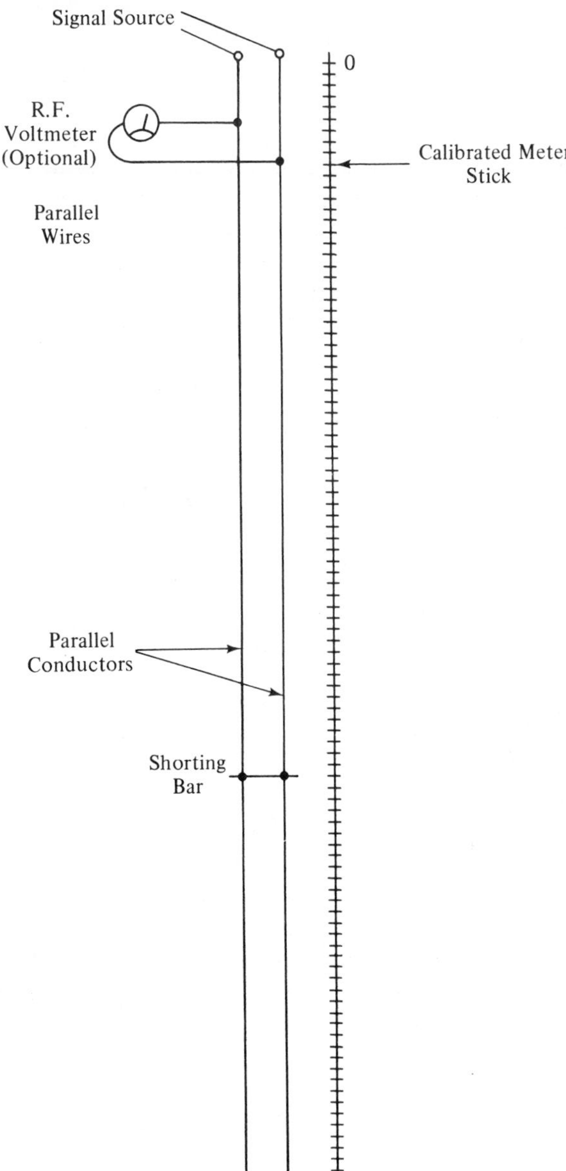

Figure 15.3 Lecher wires.

Some Lecher wires have an RF voltmeter or diode detector to feed a dc voltmeter such as that shown in Figure 15.3. This is not, however, strictly necessary if the transmitter stage being tested is equipped with a dc milliammeter in the plate circuit.

A shorting bar between the two conductors is designed so that it can be moved along the length of the conductors from one end to the other. The effective electrical length of the Lecher wires is the distance from the input end to the shorting bar. When one is performing a frequency measurement, the shorting bar is initially placed at 0 cm, and is then moved slowly down the length of the parallel conductors while the dc milliammeter or the RF voltmeter is monitored. When the shorting bar is a distance down the conductor equal to one-half wavelength of the transmitter's operating frequency, there is a slight rise in the dc plate current reading. The point where this occurs is noted, and the bar is again moved in the same direction. There is a second rise when the short is placed at one full wavelength. Once the wavelength is thus found, it becomes a simple matter to calculate the frequency from the standard formula:

$$F = \frac{C}{\lambda} \tag{15-1}$$

where C is the speed of light (300,000,000 m/s).
F is the frequency in hertz.
λ is the wavelength in meters.

In the case where frequency is in hertz and the wavelength is in meters we can rewrite Eq. (15-1) to include the constant

$$F_{\text{hz}} = \frac{3 \times 10^8}{\lambda_{\text{(meters)}}} \tag{15-2}$$

Since most frequency measurements made on Lecher wires are in the over-50-MHz range, we find that Eq. (15-2) is a little on the clumsy side. We can rewrite the equation to eliminate many of the zeros in the numerator by specifying that frequency is in megahertz instead of hertz. This will cancel out some of the zeros and allow us to write

$$F_{\text{mhz}} = \frac{300}{\lambda_{\text{(meters)}}} \tag{15-3}$$

Another modification of the basic equation will allow calculation of frequency in megahertz when the wavelength is known in inches rather than meters. It is merely necessary to multiply the right-hand side of Eq. (15-3) by 39.37 to obtain the equation

$$F_{\text{mhz}} = \frac{11{,}811}{\lambda_{\text{(inches)}}} \tag{15-4}$$

In those frequent cases where it is required that the half-wavelength be known, simply divide the result of either equation by two.

The accuracy of Lecher wires in frequency measurement can approach something less than 1000 ppm, provided that the operator takes extreme care in observing the peaks in the recorded data. It is desirable to make the measurement at least three times, and then average the results. Tight coupling between the Lecher wires and the transmitter tank can produce a rather broad peak at each halfwave point—because of excessive energy's being induced into the Lecher wires. This will obscure the determination of length, and ruin the measurement. Loose coupling and great care in making measurements is the key to accuracy in the use of Lecher wires to determine operating frequency.

15.3 COMPARISON METHODS

None of the frequency measurement techniques discussed so far satisfies the requirements of the F.C.C. There are, however, several techniques that can yield superior accuracy and *will* measure RF frequency to the specifications.

The use of a *transfer oscillator* is shown in Figure 15.4. In this technique a radio communications receiver is tuned to the unknown signal. A

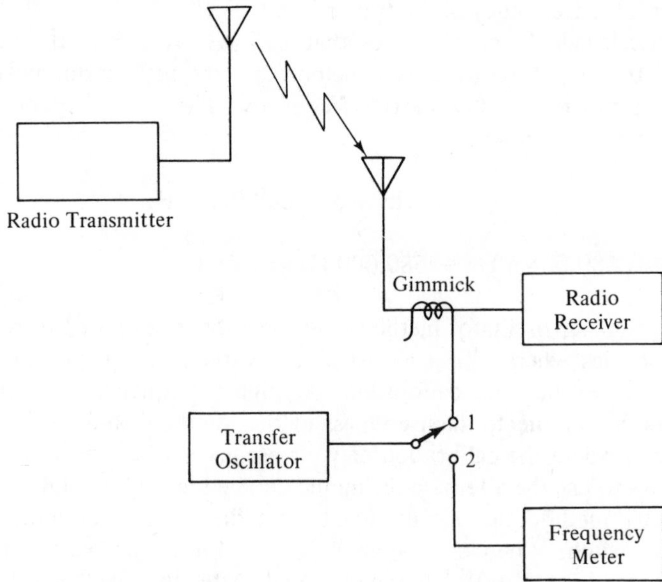

Figure 15.4 Transfer oscillator method of measuring frequency.

stable, low-frequency, well calibrated oscillator is loosely coupled to the receiver through a "gimmick." This is a few turns of wire wrapped around the antenna lead-in wire.

There are several different ways to use a transfer oscillator in making frequency measurements. It is assumed that we know the approximate frequency of the transmitter from information given as to its channel of operation.

In one transfer oscillator technique the oscillator is a precision device operating on a subharmonic of the transmitter frequency. The frequency of the transfer oscillator is adjusted until it zero beats with the unknown signal in the receiver. In this case a harmonic of the transfer oscillator signal beats against the unknown signal. It is, therefore, important to know which harmonic is being used. We can then multiply the transfer oscillator frequency by the harmonic factor to obtain the actual frequency of the transmitter.

Example. It is necessary to measure the frequency of an AM broadcast band transmitter operating on an assigned frequency of 680 kHz. A precision squarewave generator is used as the transfer oscillator. The frequency resolution of the generator is 0.1 Hz. It is found that zero beat occurs when the frequency of the square-wave generator is set to 136,001.1 Hz. What is the frequency of the transmitter?

A quick calculation shows us that 136 kHz is 1/5 of the 680-kHz operating frequency, so we may conclude that the fifth harmonic is beating against the transmitter carrier frequency. The actual operating frequency of the transmitter is

$$136{,}001.1 \text{ Hz} \times 5 = 680{,}005.5 \text{ Hz}$$

The error is $680{,}005.5 \text{ Hz} - 680{,}000 \text{ Hz} = 5.5 \text{ Hz}$

The transfer oscillator method described above is limited to relatively low frequencies where it is easy to obtain variable frequency oscillators that have believable dial calibration. At higher frequencies we run into difficulties that eradicate the usefulness of this simple technique. At higher frequencies, where the calibration of your oscillator is less well behaved, it is necessary to use the alternate technique detailed in Figure 15.4.

In this method the output signal from the transfer oscillator is fed through a switch. When the switch is in position 1, the oscillator is adjusted to zero beat with the unknown signal. After this has been done, the switch is transferred to position 2, and a frequency meter (of which more shortly) is used to read the frequency of the transfer oscillator. Again, we are using a subharmonic of the real frequency, so it is necessary to know which harmonic is actually being used. When frequency is high, it is even more necessary to know which harmonics are involved. In fact, at high frequencies it is usually advisable to use a low-order subharmonic (1/10), or ambiguity can result if two harmonics are audible simultaneously.

Once it is known which harmonic is being used, we can then multiply the frequency meter reading by that factor to obtain the actual operating frequency. This technique is also useful for extending the range of many types of low-cost frequency meter, as well as making it possible to make more precise frequency determinations from less well calibrated transfer oscillators. Several different types of frequency meter will be discussed later in this chapter. The transfer oscillator, even at high frequencies, can be any signal generator that will hold the same frequency for the duration of the test.

A technique related to the transfer oscillator method is detailed in Figure 15.5. Instead of a transfer oscillator, which is a *variable* frequency oscillator, we use a precision quartz crystal oscillator operating on a single standard frequency or several harmonically related standard frequencies. This type of oscillator uses a piezoelectric quartz crystal as the frequency control element in the feedback circuit. In general, crystal oscillators, detailed in Chapter 16, are more accurate and stable than LC or RC types. The primary requirement for the crystal oscillator, outside of accuracy and stability, is that the output waveform have a rich harmonic content. A squarewave meets this requirement, but any irregularly shaped (non-sine) waveform will probably be useful up to the fifteenth or so harmonic—or further.

Examples of crystal oscillators often used as marker oscillators are shown in Figure 15.6. In both cases the frequency divider network is the same, and consists of a cascade chain of type 7490 TTL IC decade dividers. An output selector switch gives you control over output frequency by selecting the proper division ratio to give outputs of 1 MHz, 100 kHz, 10 kHz, or 5 kHz.

Two different types of oscillator are shown in Figure 15.6. The main one is preferred by the author. It uses a special IC device called a "dual voltage controlled oscillator" (Motorola type MC4024). This 14-pin DIP device represents one of the easiest ways to build a TTL-compatible crystal oscillator. The variable capacitor across the crystal is used to set oscillator frequency to the correct value.

An alternate crystal oscillator is shown in Figure 15.6(b). This circuit uses three TTL NAND gates that are part of a single type 7400 digital integrated circuit. Again, a variable trimmer capacitor is used to adjust the frequency of oscillation to the exact value required.

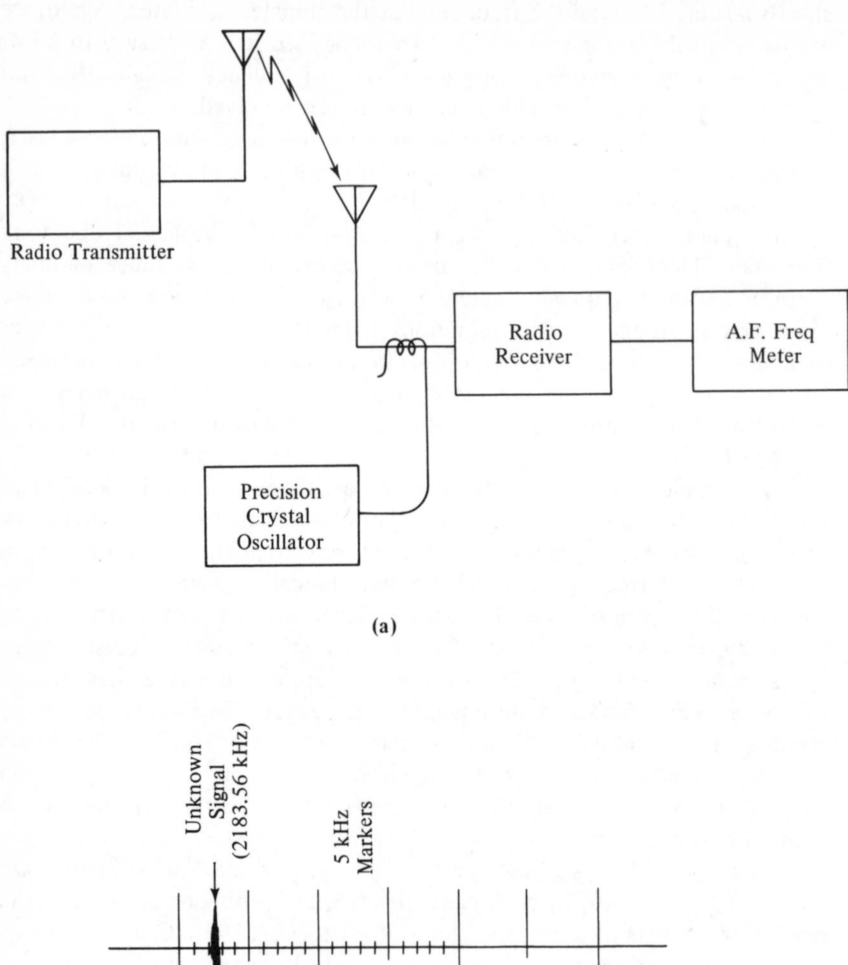

Figure 15.5 (a) Crystal oscillator method of frequency measurement, (b) receiver dial points during frequency measurement.

The crystal oscillators shown in Figure 15.6 can be used for moderately precise applications. When high precision is required, however, a commercially built crystal oscillator can be used instead. A wide variety of such oscillators are sold. Some are in a fancy cabinet complete with

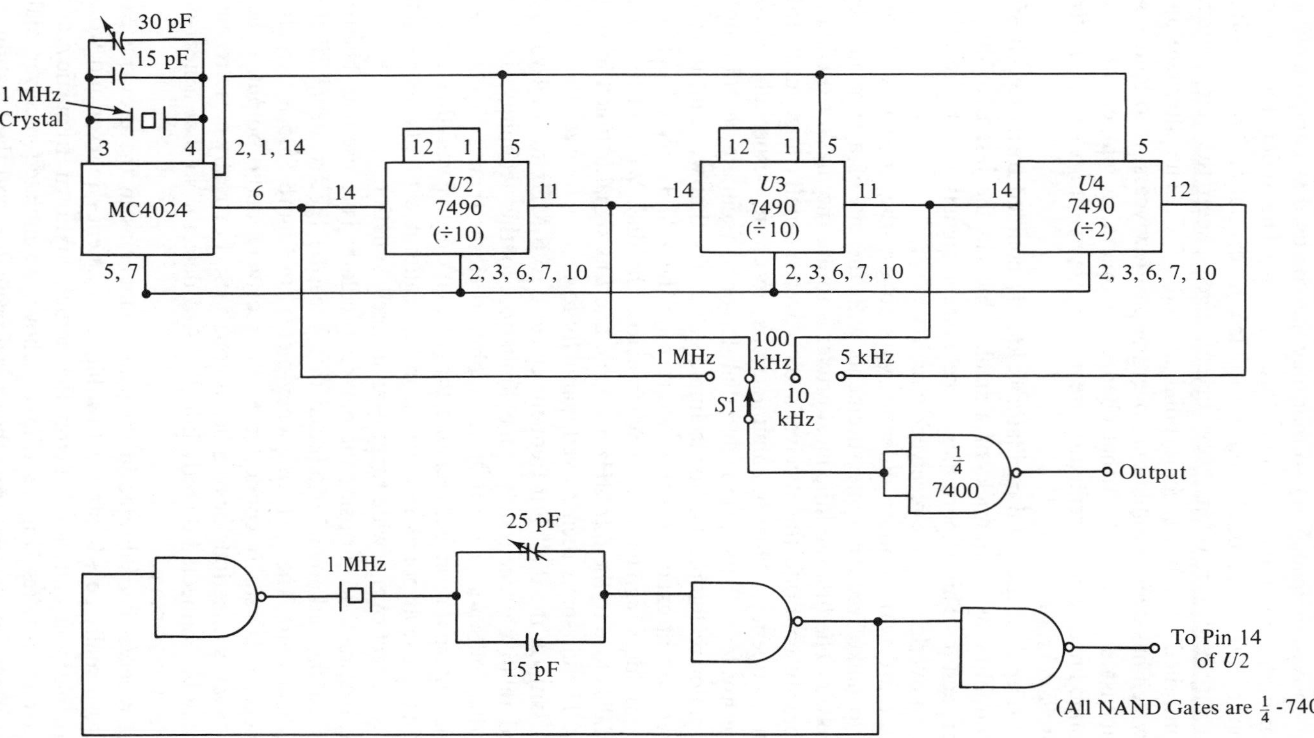

Figure 15.6 Crystal marker oscillator using digital logic ICs for frequency division. (*Inset*) alternate crystal oscillator.

regulated power supply, while others are built into a small package (metal-cased but epoxy-encapsulated) so that they may be used as components in their own right. Two basic designs are evident. The older philosophy (older, but by no means outdated) is to place the crystal and possibly the entire circuit inside an oven. Most crystal ovens keep the temperature inside controlled to some specific point around 75°C. The alternate approach, which has been feasible only over the past few years, is to temperature-compensate the circuit so that changes in operating temperature can be accommodated. Such oscillators are usually *temperature-compensated crystal oscillators,* or *tcxo.*

The output of a crystal oscillator is loosely coupled to the receiver's antenna circuitry by a gimmick, or a small-value (in the less than 40-pF range) capacitor. This superimposes the marker signals on the receiver dial without overloading the receiver's circuitry.

There are two or more different ways to use the crystal oscillator markers to make frequency measurements with the aid of a communications receiver. The first, and the most crude, is to use the marker oscillator to temporarily calibrate the receiver's dial over a small range near the unknown frequency. Most communications receivers, especially those above the toy level, have a movable dial cursor to facilitate recalibration between major realignments. For example, let us say that we want to calibrate a receiver at exactly 6 MHz. We turn on the 1 MHz crystal marker, and that produces signals every 1 MHz across the dial. We find that one of these falls close to the 6.0 MHz marking, and this signal is tuned in very carefully. The cursor is then moved manually to lie exactly over the 6.000 MHz marking on the dial. For frequencies close to 6 MHz the dial will be calibrated relatively accurately. One limitation to this technique is that receiver dial calibrations rarely have resolution closer than 100 Hz, even with visual interpolation between the formal markings. Even that resolution is of little use at points removed from the calibrated points unless dial tracking is perfect over a wide range—an unlikely situation.

The best method for using the marker oscillator is to use it to heterodyne against the unknown signal, and then measure the frequency of the resultant beat note. The "AF frequency meter" in Figure 15.5 is used for this purpose. It is usually connected to the receiver's audio output, either to the speaker connections or to a headphone jack. For really close resolution, it may be connected directly into the AM detector so that a near-dc beatnote can be obtained.

The receiver is calibrated in the same manner as in the previous example. It is usually best to start with a higher frequency marker and work down, so that you can home in on the actual unknown frequency and thereby avoid mistakes. Figure 15.5(b) shows a simulated receiver dial. Also shown are the markers from the crystal oscillator, and the location on the dial of the unknown signal. The generator is first adjusted to produce a 1 MHz output. It is found that the unknown falls between 2 MHz and 3 MHz. The marker generator is then readjusted to produce a 100 kHz output. It is then found that the unknown lies between 2100 kHz and 2200 kHz. Next, the crystal marker is adjusted to produce 10 kHz output signals, and the unknown is noted between 2180 kHz and 2190 kHz. Since the unknown, in this case, falls close to one of the 10 kHz markers, it is unnecessary to go to any lower marker frequency.

Recall, please, that we are looking for a *beatnote.* If the unknown is anywhere near the midpoint between two markers, there will be *two* beatnotes of similar frequency. This ambiguity is cleared up only by going to lower-frequency markers in order to gain resolution. In our present case, however, the unknown is close to one of the 10 kHz points, so no ambiguity exists.

The beatnote produced in the audio output is found to be exactly 3562, measured on the audio frequency meter. This means that the unknown frequency is located at a point 3562 Hz away from the 2180 kHz marker. Since we observe on the receiver dial that the unknown is on the high side of the 2180 kHz marker point, we know that the unknown has a frequency of 2180 kHz + 3562 Hz, or 2,183,562 Hz. Once again, it is desirable, and considered good practice, to measure frequency three times or more, and then average the results. Tune the receiver away from the unknown and then back again to where you think it is centered exactly on the unknown. Then, once again, measure the beatnote frequency. Do this several times and then take the arithmetic average of the results.

The audio frequency meter can be either a *digital frequency counter* (about which more shortly), or an oscilloscope set up with a calibrated audio oscillator. In the latter case, the receiver output is fed to one oscilloscope input, and the audio oscillator is fed to the other. The oscillator is adjusted until the resultant Lissajous figure on the oscilloscope screen is perfectly stationary. If the pattern is either circular, elliptical, or a straight line, then the frequency marked on the oscillator dial is the frequency of the beatnote. If the pattern is multilooped, on the other hand, then apply the Lissajous formula given in the last chapter.

15.4 CALIBRATION OF SECONDARY STANDARDS

Crystal markers or transfer oscillators are of limited usefulness unless there is a method for calibrating their frequencies, or at least for checking that they are on frequency. For those who cannot afford a costly rubidium or cesium beam atomic frequency standard, there are several standard-frequency radio stations operated by the National Bureau of Standards. These are not as good as an atomic standard, but are of sufficient accuracy for many applications. NBS operates two sets of transmitters, located in Hawaii and Fort Collins, Colorado, respectively. Radio station WWV at Fort Collins operates on precise frequencies of 2.5, 5, 10, 15, and 25 MHz, although there is a good possibility that this service will be limited to only a few frequencies after 1977. The station in Hawaii broadcasts the same service on 5, 10, and 15 MHz. These signals are precise to within 1 part in 10^{10} (10,000,000,000). The accuracy is maintained by comparing the frequency to that of an atomic cesium beam oscillator and a clock. An atomic clock oscillates at some natural resonant frequency that is peculiar to the atom being used. The frequency of oscillation is independent of the factors that normally cause errors in electronically generated frequency standards: temperature, vibration, component aging, etc. For the cesium atom the clock oscillator wobbles at 9192.631840 MHz.

The NBS stations also transmit accurate audio tones of 440 Hz and 600 Hz, in addition to both digital (electronic) and voice time-of-day announcements. Another station at the Fort Collins site, WWVB, transmits a precise 60-kHz signal. It is this lower frequency that is usually used for really accurate frequency comparisons.

These stations (WWV, WWVH, and WWVB) are usually received on a quality communications receiver, and the crystal oscillator is zero beat to the station's signal. Except where 60-kHz equipment is available, it is wise to use the highest frequency that produces a strong, readable signal in your area. This will reduce the error in adjustment. Human hearing cannot generally detect tones below about 30 Hz, so when you think that the oscillator is "zero beat," it is actually only within ± 30 Hz if your ears were used to detect the null. Of course, there are some detectors that allow closer setting. An "S" meter on the receiver, for example, will bob back and forth slowly when near zero beat. If the beatnote is 1 Hz, then the meter pointer will waffle back and forth one time per second. If you select a high WWV frequency, the error is reduced. Let us assume a case where it is necessary to adjust a 100 kHz crystal oscillator to WWV, and that only aural zero beat is possible. If the 5-MHz WWV frequency is used to zero the oscillator, we have a standard that is 50 times higher than the frequency of the marker. This means that the fiftieth harmonic of 100-KHz is used to produce the beatnote. The potential error, then, is ± 30 Hz/50, or 0.6 Hz. If the 15-MHz WWV signal were used instead, the error would be ± 30 Hz/150, or 0.2 Hz. It is, however, important to choose a WWV signal that is relatively strong, or other errors will predominate. It is to be noted that "strong" and "audible" are *not* the same thing.

If proper equipment is available, then the 60-kHz WWVB signal can be used for high-precision measurements. This signal is known to produce fewer phase errors at distances removed from the transmitters. The 60-kHz signal can be amplified directly, squared off, and then used as a frequency standard in its own right.

The 60-kHz signal can be used to either zero beat the unknown or to drive electronic phase detector circuits that compare it with other frequencies. In the latter case, a dc voltage proportional to the error between the 60-kHz standard and the unknown is produced. This voltage can be used to drive a paper oscillographic strip chart recorder or a meter movement. In fact, many WWVB comparator receivers use a paper and ink or thermal tip recorder for just such measurements. This allows comparison over time to measure the frequency drift properties of circuits.

15.5 FREQUENCY METERS

A Single Frequency Monitor. Figure 15.7 shows a frequency monitor of a type often found in AM broadcast stations. A circuit called a "mixer" is used to combine two frequencies. Since a mixer is designed to be a nonlinear circuit, the output frequency is the difference beatnote. One input frequency, f_o, is the transmitter frequency. The other is from a precision crystal oscillator operating at a frequency that is 1 kHz below f_o—or at a frequency of (f_o − 1 kHz). When these two signals are combined in a mixer, they form a 1-kHz (1000-Hz) beatnote, provided that both signal sources are precisely on frequency. The circuit in Figure 15.7 uses a 1000-Hz tuned phase detector, or discriminator. If the beatnote is

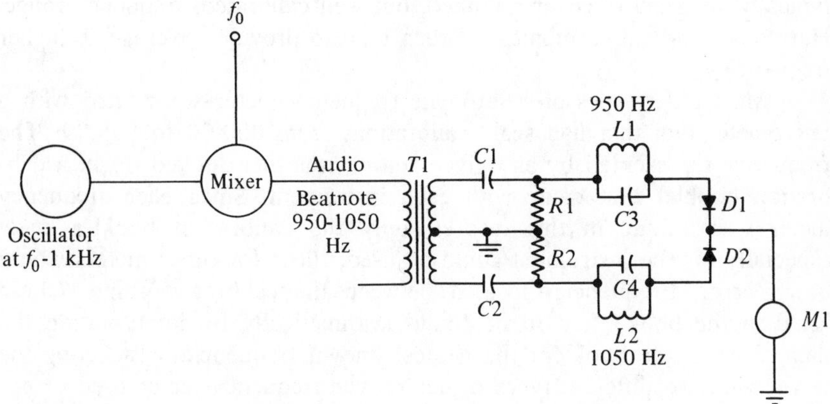

Figure 15.7 Single frequency monitor.

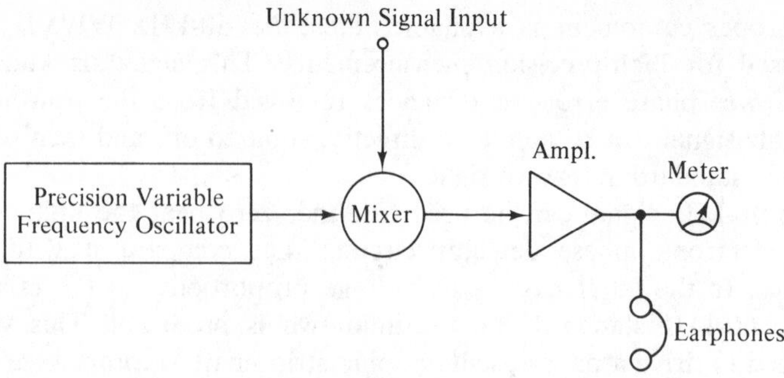

Figure 15.8 Heterodyne frequency meter.

exactly 1000 Hz, then the dc voltages produced by diodes $D1$ and $D2$ are equal, but of opposite polarity. They will, therefore, cancel and produce a net output of 0 VDC. If the beatnote is other than 1000 Hz, then it may be assumed that the frequency f_o is incorrect and the transmitter should be checked by more accurate techniques. In that case, meter $M1$ will deflect an amount proportional to the error. This meter will usually be calibrated in terms of frequency, usually on a ±20-Hz or ±50-Hz scale.

Heterodyne Frequency Meters. The type of frequency meter described in the preceding paragraph is called a "heterodyne frequency meter," but it is only a special case of a much more general class of instruments that also depend upon the heterodyne phenomenon. Figure 15.8 shows the block diagram of a simple heterodyne frequency meter intended for general use. The unknown frequency is heterodyned against the signal from a precision, calibrated variable frequency oscillator. These oscillators are typically designed to cover a limited, but well calibrated, frequency range. Harmonics and subharmonics are then used to provide coverage of higher frequencies.

Most older types of heterodyne frequency meter were fitted with a micrometer dial that had scale calibrations from 000.00 to 999.99. The frequency represented by any given setting was then looked up in a calibration booklet that came with each instrument. Since each frequency meter was unique in this respect, only the calibration booklet made especially for the instrument could be used; those for other meters would be in error. Frequencies located between the calibrated points (those listed in the book) had to be found arithmetically by interpolating the data given in the book for the nearest known frequencies bracketing the unknown. Two different types of heterodyne frequency meter used extensively in communications equipment servicing are shown in Figures 15.9 and 15.10. Both are actually several instruments in one package.

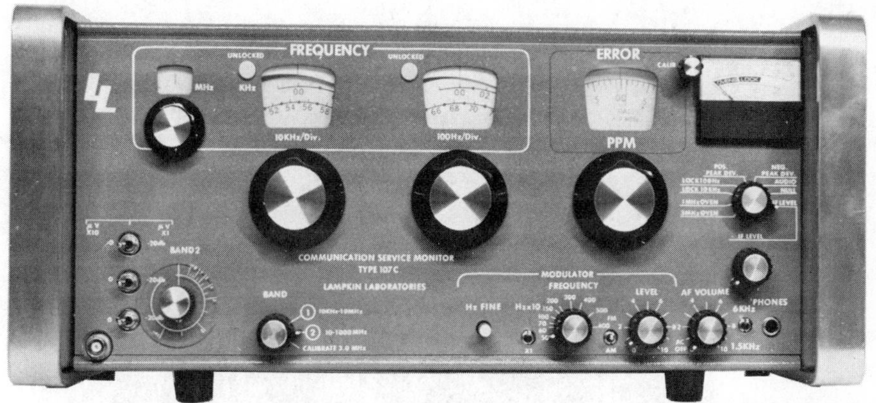

Figure 15.9 Lampkin Model 107C communications frequency monitor. (*Courtesy of Lampkin Laboratories.*)

The instrument shown in Figure 15.9 is the Lampkin Laboratories Model 107-C communications service monitor (CSM). This particular instrument can measure frequencies from 10 kHz to over 1000 MHz, and will also serve as a precision signal generator between 1 kHz and 1000 MHz (1 GHz). The accuracy of the instrument is on the order of 0.5 ppm, so it is accurate enough for all current F.C.C. frequency certification purposes. The generator section also provides modulation that can simulate continuous wave (CW—that is, *no* modulation), AM, or FM transmitters. It may also be operated from any of several optional dc voltages that might normally be found in land mobile, aeronautical, or marine transmitter installations.

One additional, and very useful, feature of the Lampkin model 107-C CSM is the "parts per million (ppm) dial. The transmitter's *assigned* frequency is set by using the three main frequency knobs on the front panel. The error control knob is then adjusted until the frequency meter oscillator is zero beat with the transmitter signal. The erro in transmitter frequency can then be read from the ppm dial. This eliminates the tedious calculation of ppm error required when many other frequency meters are used.

The Cushman Model CE-5 communications monitor is shown in Figure 15.10. In this model, tuning is by switch settings, which control an internal frequency synthesizer. The case shown in the photograph has the frequency meter set to 121.500 MHz. The error between actual and set frequency is read from the meter, calibrated in kHz of error. Again, we have a case where the assigned frequency is set on the switch dials, and the error between it and the actual frequency is read from a dial (or in this case a meter movement).

Figure 15.10 Cushman Model CE-5 communications monitor. (*Courtesy of Cushman Electronics, Inc.*)

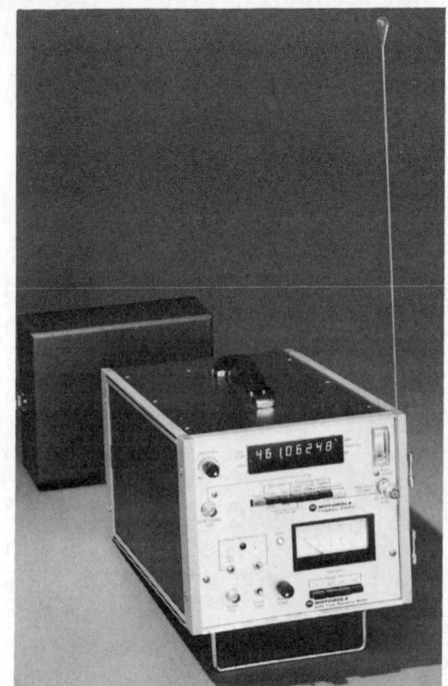

Figure 15.11 Motorola communications monitor. (*Courtesy of Motorola.*)

Digital Frequency Counters. Figure 15.11 shows an example of a communications monitor, this one by Motorola, that uses a digital frequency counter to measure frequency. These devices are not heterodyne or comparison devices, but rather, they count the individual cycles of the input signal on a cycle-for-cycle basis. If the period of time over which the count is made is either 1 second or a decade submultiple of 1 second, then the digital readout will be in units of frequency: hertz, kilohertz, or megahertz.

Until recently, digital frequency and period counters have been extremely high-cost devices and were used only in the most sophisticated communications shops, government installations, or commercial research and development laboratories.

One of the many spinoffs of the space program is an electronics technology industry that can now offer such seemingly exotic, highly sophisticated instrumentation at bargain basement prices. Frequency counters are available today that exceed the abilities and specifications of all but the costliest counters available only a decade ago, but at a small fraction of the old cost. Although the small operation was prohibited by cost from buying those early instruments, almost all can afford the newer types.

The cost of such counters is probably the main outward change in counters resulting from the space effort. Prior to the mid-1970s frequency counters capable of measuring VHF and UHF transmitter frequencies to the accuracy specified by the Federal Communications Commission carried price tags in the range $1800 to $4500. Today, there are several instruments in the same performance class that cost less than $800, while some with lesser performance specifications sell for as little as $100. The cost of the digital counter type of circuitry has dropped so low that many top-end-of-the-line signal generators and radio receivers use digital counters as a dial indicator instead of a mechanical drive indicator.

In this section we are going to examine the inner workings of the typical digital frequency counter and some of the computerlike circuitry that makes the instrument work. Also, we shall try to gain some insight into counter specifications so that you can make a more intelligent purchase decision.

Decimal Counting Units (DCU). The heart of any electronic counter is a digital electronic circuit that accumulates pulses from the outside world, and then drives a readout device that tells the operator how many pulses have been counted. Each one of these circuits counts from zero to nine, then goes back to zero to begin counting again. All such circuits are known collectively as *decimal counting units* or DCU. Several DCUs can be

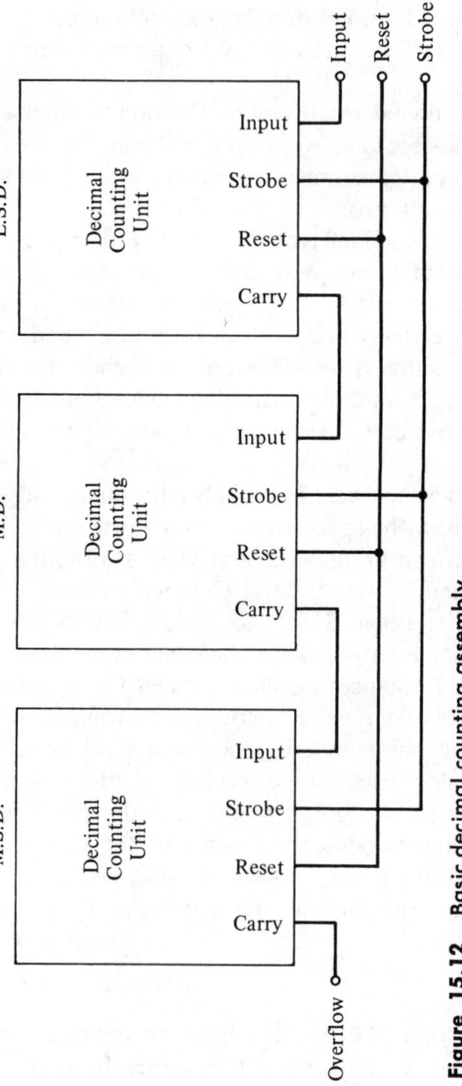

Figure 15.12 Basic decimal counting assembly.

cascaded to provide a much wider count range (i.e., 0–99, 0–999, 0–9999, etc.). A bank of several DCUs in cascade is called a *decimal counting assembly,* or DCA. One DCU is required for every digit of the DCA. (See Figure 15.12.)

One of the factors that previously pushed up the price of counters in past years was that the DCU was made of then very expensive digital logic circuits. Earlier models were transistor designs, whereas some later, and all current, designs use digital integrated circuits (IC). A typical digital counter IC device once cost more than $14 each in quantity purchases, and transistor flip-flop circuits were similarly expensive. The current price on the same or equivalent IC devices is less than a dollar each.

All DCUs require decoding, because the counter IC devices operate in four-bit *binary coded decimal* or BCD. In that number system, four individual "bits" (voltage levels) are presented, each on separate lines, to represent all of the digits between 0 and 9. One popular BCD coding scheme uses the 1-2-4-8 weighting. This is also sometimes referred to as 8-4-2-1 weighting, but it is essentially the same thing. The backwards notation reflects the fact that the most significant bit (8) is usually positioned to the left.

In any binary coding scheme, BCD included, we use two binary digits called 0 and 1 to represent numbers. These binary digits can be represented by voltage levels. For example, it is usual to find OVDC (ground condition) representing the binary 0, and some positive voltage to represent the 1. In most modern cases the 1 is represented by +5 VDC. This level is mandatory in the DTL and TTL (the most common as of this writing) types of digital logic IC, but CMOS and related devices can use any positive voltage between +4 and +18 VDC.

Table 15.1 gives the BCD coding for the ten decimal digits between 0 and 9, if 8-4-2-1 weighting is used.

Figure 15.13 shows the partial schematic of a relatively common DCU that uses transistor-transistor-logic (TTL) integrated circuits. At one time these devices were considerably more expensive than they are today, but now almost any company can afford to incorporate them into a design. In fact, the type 7490 decade counter IC is now considered obsolete, and is even offered for sale to hobbyists and amateurs.

The type of decade counter used in this circuit can count fast enough to follow frequencies up to around 20 MHz, while certain other TTL integrated circuits can count to 50 or even 80 MHz. The internal circuitry of the 7490 contains all of the flip-flops and gates necessary to form a decimal counting unit.

In many older counters, and even a few modern low-cost types, the decade counter BCD output lines feed the decoder directly. This is an

Table 15.1

Decimal	*8421 BCD*
0	0000
1	0001
2	0010
3	0011
4	0100
5	0101
6	0110
7	0111
8	1000
9	1001
10	0001 0000
11	0001 0001
12	0001 0010
13	0001 0110
14	0001 0100
15	0001 0101
16	0001 0110

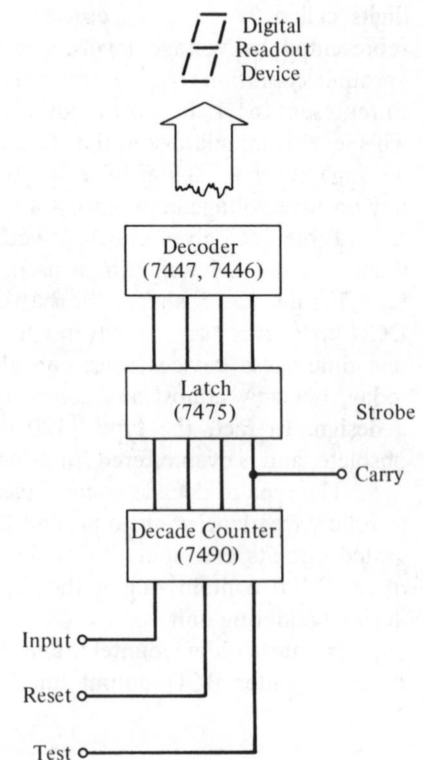

Figure 15.13 The decimal counting unit.

undesirable design, because it produces a rolling display that proves hard to read. You can actually see the digital readout of these instruments change as the count accumulates, much in the same manner as the price accumulates on a gasoline pump.

To keep the display constant and steady, most modern counters, even those of relatively modest cost, use a four-bit memory called a *quad latch* between the counter output and the decoder input. A latch circuit "remembers" the BCD state present on the four input lines that existed when the strobe terminal was enabled (turned on). This design allows the display to be instantly updated at a rate determined by the repetition rate of the display multivibrator, which is set by a control on the front panel. In some low-cost designs the display is also fed by a latching circuit, but the rate is fixed. You can tell whether any particular instrument uses a latch circuit by the way the display operates. If there is a latch in use, the display update will occur all at once. The new digits seem to pop onto the readout precounted. Nonlatched systems will exhibit the rolling symptom.

Frequency Counter Design. Figure 15.14 is the block diagram of a typical medium-cost digital frequency counter. Although this particular design is not found on all counters, it is sufficiently representative to be used for purposes of explanation. The differences between this design and certain others usually involves special features in the special-purpose type of counter, or (in low-cost designs) deletion or automation of some features.

In counter jargon the term *frequency* translates to "events per unit of time" or "EPUT." [Remember that before the general engineering jargon was changed "frequency" was cycles (events) per second (unit of frequency).]

Any EPUT counter requires a *main gate* that allows pulses into the DCA for certain specified lengths of time. The gate is opened and closed by a train of pulses from a *time base circuit*. One use of these pulses is to reset the DCA to zero, and then allow accumulation of pulses from the outside world for a certain time period. Without a main gate and a time base circuit the DCA would continue to accumulate pulses, overflow, then accumulate even more pulses—with no relationship to time.

Period Counter Design. A period counter (see Figure 15.15) is used to measure the amount of time between two successive pulses. This can be accomplished by merely reversing the functions of the input preamplifier and the time base circuit. The main gate flip-flop is enabled by a pulse from the input amplifier, and is then closed by the next pulse. Time base

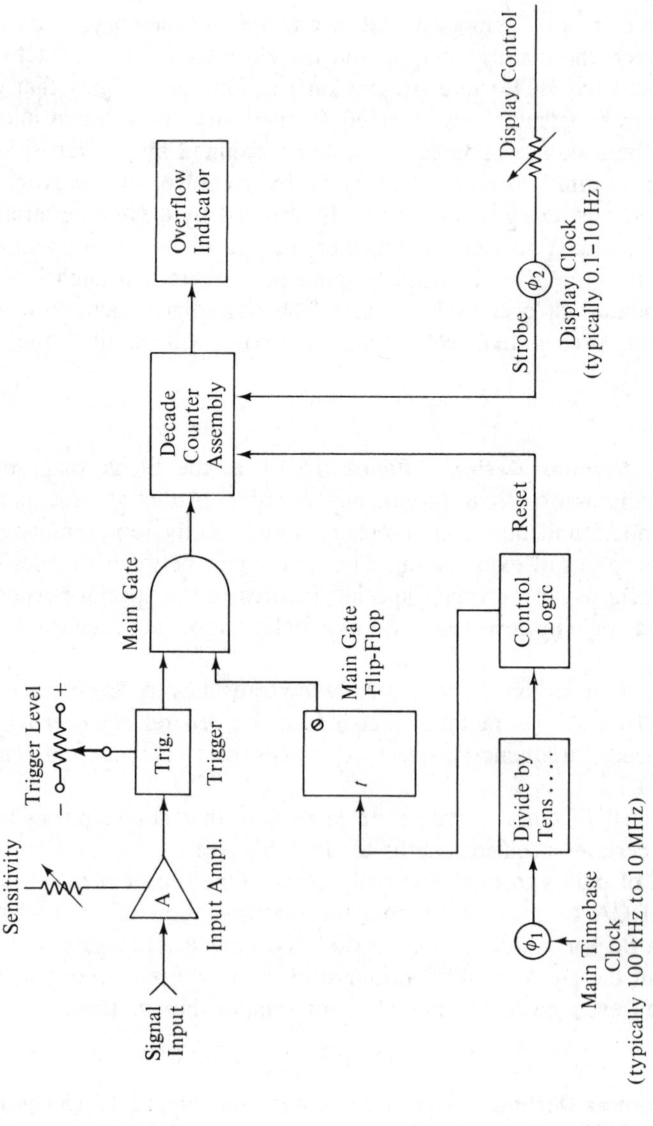

Figure 15.14 Block diagram of a frequency counter.

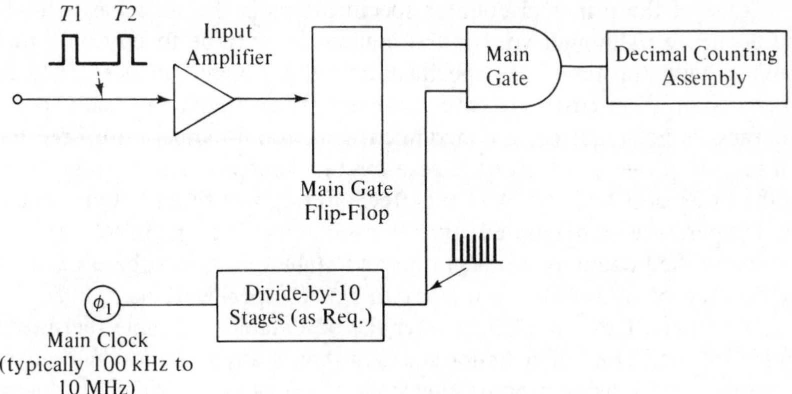

Figure 15.15 Block diagram of a period (time) counter.

pulses are passed through the main gate to the DCA. If a 1000-Hz time base signal is used, the period is measured in milliseconds. Many counters, both period and frequency, allow selection of the time base frequency.

There are many uses for a period counter, other than actually measuring a period. One chief application is in measurement of the frequency of low-frequency (under 100 Hz) signals or higher-frequency signals if improved resolution is required. An example of the latter use is in electronic musical instrument service, in which tones in the kilohertz range are specified to three decimal points of one hertz. In such cases, we simply choose a time frequency high enough to give the desired resolution, and then perform a little arithmetic. The proper relationship is

$$F_{(\mathrm{Hz})} = 1/T_{(\mathrm{sec})}$$

Time Base Circuits. The length of time that the gate stays open is a function of the time base frequency. A time base is a precise crystal-controlled oscillator followed by some TTL decade dividers. In this case these stages are the same type 7490 devices used in the DCU, but without decoding. Typically, 1-MHz oscillators are used, but 3-MHz, 4-MHz, 5-MHz, and 10-MHz types are also occasionally seen.

Some counters provide a switch that allows the user to select time base intervals between 0.1 μs and 10 μs. This is done by selecting the frequency through choice of the proper division ratio. Each 7490 IC produces an output frequency that is 1/10 of the input frequency. A 10-MHz clock input gives 0.1 μs, 1 MHz yields 1 μs, and 1 Hz produces 1-s intervals. Many low-cost counters provide for limited manipulation of the time base through the use of a "Hz/kHz" or "kHz/MHz" switch.

One of the principal counter specifications is the time base stability and accuracy. Although your initial inclination may be to buy only those counters with top time base specifications, this policy can needlessly run up the acquisition cost of your instrument. Where high precision, or top accuracy, is not required, a noncompensated, room-temperature time base will usually prove satisfactory. These circuits can produce stability figures on the order of 5×10^{-6}. A step better, offering five times better stability, are temperature-compensated crystal oscillators (tcxo). In some cases, tcxo-controlled counters are accurate and stable enough to be used in the certification of transmitter frequency to F.C.C. specifications.

Oven-controlled oscillators offer the best stability. Simple thermostat-controlled oscillators offer better stability than many tcxo designs, but not as good as those using proportional control ovens. This design produces a more constant temperature at the crystal chamber. A single-oven proportional control time base can keep the frequency to within $\pm 5 \times 10^{-8}$. The most stable and most accurate counters use double-oven oscillators. These have the actual crystal oven inside an outer oven. Such arrangements are capable of maintaining crystal temperature to within $\pm 0.01\,°C$, producing a frequency stability on the order of 5×10^{-11}. Of course, you should expect a double-oven time base oscillator only in the most expensive frequency and period counters.

Crystal oscillators, even high-grade circuits, always drift in output frequency over a period of time. This slow drift is usually predictable and is expressed as an *aging rate*. This is the principal reason that frequency counters should be sent periodically to the manufacturer, or other metrology laboratory, for a time base recalibration. How often this is required depends upon the time base aging rate and the manufacturer's recommendations.

Keep in mind that even the best counters, with their exceptional stability figures, have an aging rate. Also, their normal stability figures cannot be expected, in most cases, until the instrument has been on for at least 24 hours. Because of this fact, many counters use a special power supply for the time base oscillator. This accomplishes two things: (1) power supply regulation is improved, because loading is essentially constant; (2) the oscillator supply can be left on even when the counter is turned off. If you cannot keep your instrument plugged in (so that its oscillator will run continuously), it may be necessary to buy one with at least one order of magnitude better stability than would otherwise be required. Some battery-operated counters are good in this last respect, because their oscillators can be left running when the counter is not normally plugged in—for example, in the service truck between jobs. The standard of accuracy for a counter is not less than five times, and preferably ten times, the accuracy required of the frequency being measured. For example, a citizens band transmitter must be within ±50 ppm (5×10^{-5}); consequently, a counter useful for CB service should have a time base accuracy not worse than 10 ppm, with 5 ppm preferred.

Trigger Circuits. Most counters are equipped with Schmitt trigger circuits that have both upper and lower hysteresis limits (Figure 15.16). A trigger circuit is one that changes its output state only at certain specific input voltages, the threshold points. An input signal must cross *both* threshold levels if the DCA count is to be affected.

The difference between the threshold limits is called the *hysteresis window*. Its function is to allow only one pulse to be generated for each input cycle. Otherwise, it may prove possible for some nonsinusoidal waveforms to falsely trigger the DCA. The trigger control varies the position of the hysteresis window relative to a minus-zero-positive voltage scale, so that a variety of signals not centered about zero can be counted.

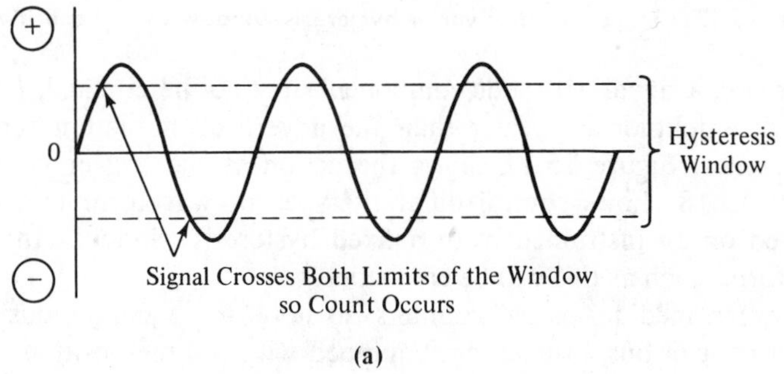

(a)

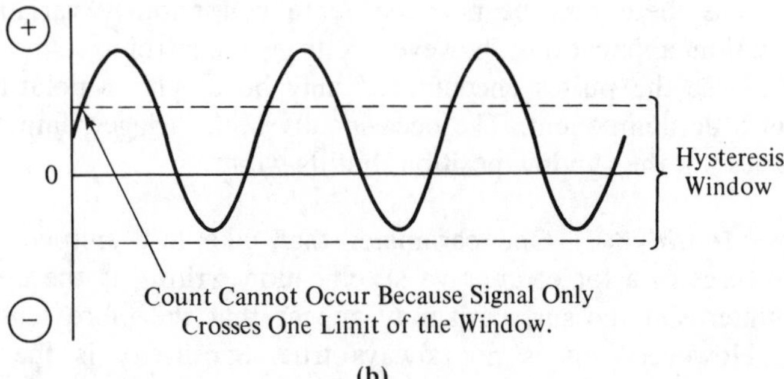

(b)

Figure 15.16 Input signal *must* cross both limits of the counter's hysteresis window or no counting occurs.

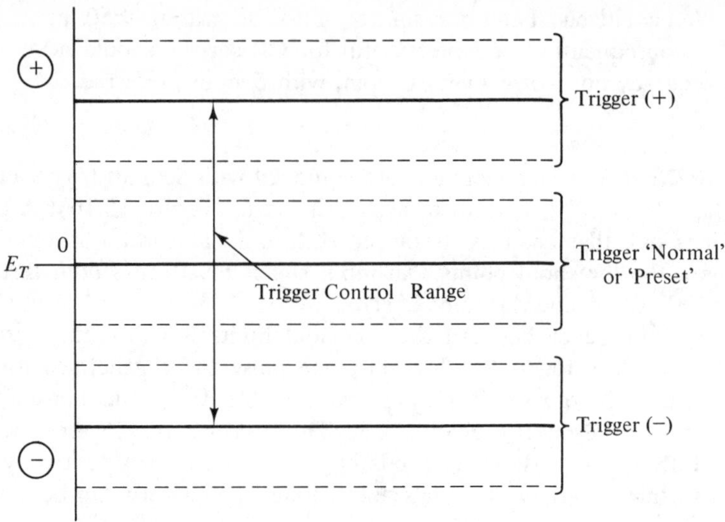

Figure 15.17 Trigger control varies hysteresis window over a specified range.

Otherwise, a signal with a dc component may not be counted, even though its own amplitude is greater than the advertised minimum sensitivity of the counter. Figure 15.17 shows the action of the trigger control, while Figure 15.18 shows several different types of waveform that cannot be counted on an instrument with a fixed hysteresis window. Any count on waveforms such as this will be erroneous.

Some medium-priced counters do not have a continuously variable trigger control but, instead, are equipped with a three-position switch that is typically labeled either "+, 0, −" or "+, preset, −." In many applications this arrangement is less desirable than a continuously variable control, but it is better than no control at all. Besides, for many communications applications there may be no need for a continuously variable control. In television applications, however, a trigger control is almost a necessity, because the pulses encountered may be of either polarity, with or without a dc component. The occasionally seen "trigger amplitude" control varies not the window position, but its width.

Counter Sensitivity. One parameter that, like hi-fi output power, has been subject to a lot of creative specification writing is the sensitivity of the counter. On the surface it may appear that the more sensitivity, the better. However, this is not always true. Sensitivity is the minimum-amplitude input signal that can *reliably* trigger the counter. If the sensitivity is too great, noise may falsely trigger the instrument, but if it is too low, we find that desired signals are ignored.

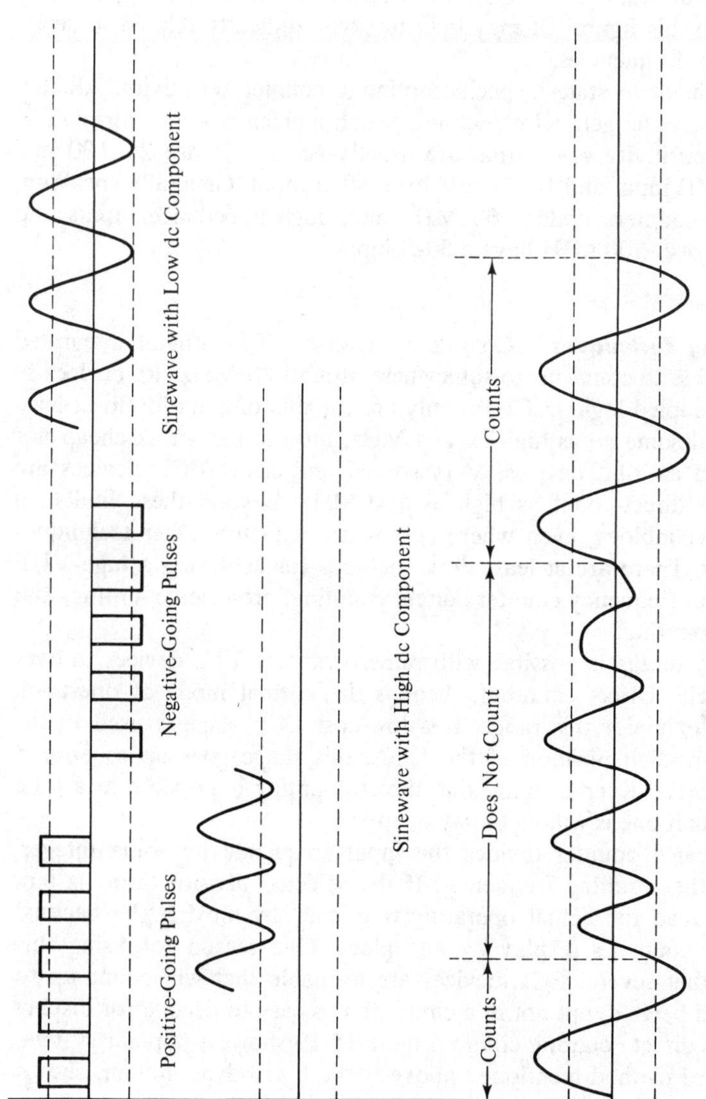

Figure 15.18 Several examples of signals that will not count.

Sensitivity is often expressed in either volts-rms or as a certain pulse amplitude, also in volts. In any event, most trigger circuits have a pulse sensitivity that is 2.82 times higher than the rms figure. If both values are given, be a little wary of the instrument in which the ratio is significantly different from this figure—it may indicate some difficulty related to sensitivity at higher frequencies.

It is difficult to state a specific optimum counter sensitivity. All that is possible are some general guidelines, which incidentally are impedance-dependent. Sensitivity values that are usually acceptable are 25–100 mV rms for a 1-MΩ input and 10–50 mV for a 50-Ω input. Generally speaking, we find that counters under 200 MHz have high impedance inputs and those for use over 200 MHz have a 50-Ω input.

VHF Counting Techniques. Commonly available TTL digital integrated circuits are able to count up to somewhere around 80 MHz. IC devices in the emitter-coupled logic (ECL) family are capable of counting to at least 120 MHz and some go as high as 180 MHz, but are neither as cheap nor as easily used as TTL devices. Very special and costly ECL devices are available that direct-count as high as 500 MHz. Beyond these limits, in the present technology, even where cost is not a factor, other techniques must be used. There are at least three methods for achieving a high-VHF to UHF region frequency counter: direct counting, prescaled counting, and heterodyne counting.

Direct counting is possible with rather ordinary TTL devices to over 50 or 80 MHz. Direct counting, then, is the normal mode of operation for the counter under this range. If a low-cost ECL stage is used in the least-significant-digit position of the DCA, this range goes up to around 120 or 180 MHz. Keep in mind that direct counting is possible to a little over 500 MHz if one is willing to pay the price.

A prescaled counter divides the input frequency by some integer, then counts the resulting frequency. If the selected division ratio is ten, then we can read the actual operating frequency by moving the decimal point on the counter's display by one place. One reason for using this approach is that several ECL devices are available that will count up to 500 MHz and beyond, but not in a circuit that is easy to decode for display purposes in a direct counting circuit. Figure 15.19 shows a popular system.

The third method mentioned above is the heterodyne system, shown in Figure 15.20. In this type of counter, the input frequency is translated to a lower frequency that is within the range of the digital frequency counter. The "local" frequency source can be a separate crystal oscillator, but it is usually a frequency multiplier chain, or phase-locked loop, synchronized to the time base oscillator.

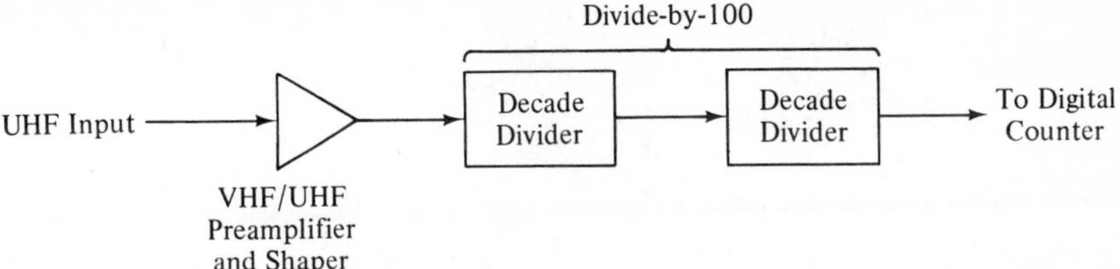

Figure 15.19 Prescaling for VHF/UHF counting.

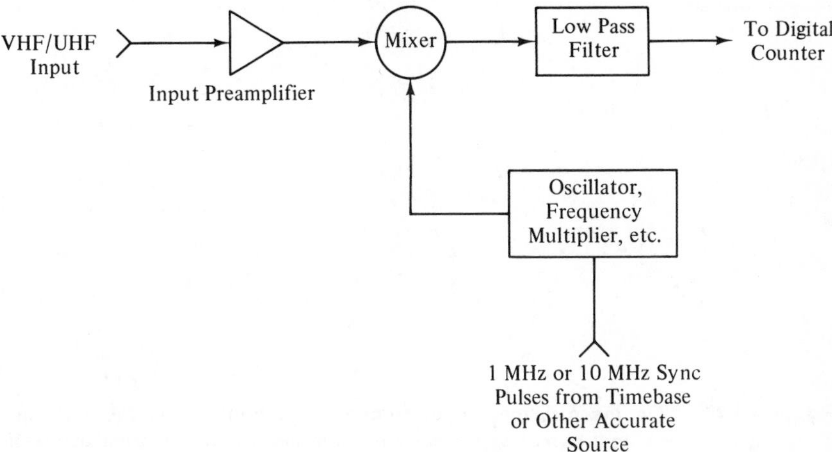

Figure 15.20 Heterodyne counting technique.

If the local frequency source in a heterodyne counter is designed to produce frequencies as high as 400 MHz, and the basic counter is an 80-MHz type, then it is capable of measuring frequencies in the land mobile radio bands up to 480 MHz, because we are actually measuring ($F_{in} - F_{local}$).

Counter Error. All of those pretty digits displayed by an electronic frequency counter may tempt one to make the same error made by students who try to solve science or engineering course problems with a 16-digit calculator while forgetting that only a few digits are significant. Similarly, on a frequency counter only a portion of the display is valid. For all counters in which the main gate circuitry does not synchronize the time base signal with the input signal—and that includes just about all counter designs that you will encounter—the display accuracy is the counter accuracy plus or minus one count of the least significant digit. The overall accuracy is the time base error ± one count.

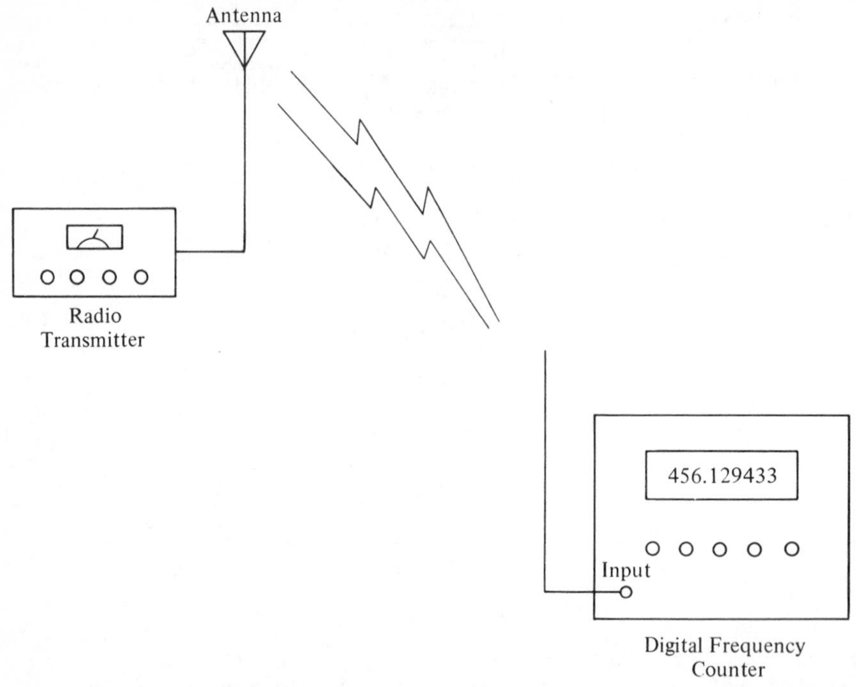

Figure 15.21 "On the air" method of frequency counting (*note: this technique is illegal except on the citizens band and when monitoring on-the-air broadcasting stations.*)

Using a Digital Frequency Counter. The simplest method for checking transmitter output frequency with a digital frequency counter is shown in Figure 15.21. A short whip antenna is connected to the input of the counter through a short piece of coaxial cable. The transmitter is then keyed on, and the signal radiated by the transmitter's antenna is picked up by the whip antenna on the frequency counter. If the frequency counter is close enough to the transmitter antenna (500 ft or less, depending upon power level), sufficient signal will be applied to the input of the counter to cause triggering. The transmitter output frequency is then displayed on the counter readout.

Because the signal radiated in this test may interfere with normal communications on the same channel, it is a proper and legal test only on the citizens band and amateur bands. Even then it is legal only if you listen on the channel to make sure it is free of stations who wish to communicate—before you turn on the transmitter.

To prevent interference with normal communications traffic, it is necessary to measure frequency with a nonradiating load. One version of

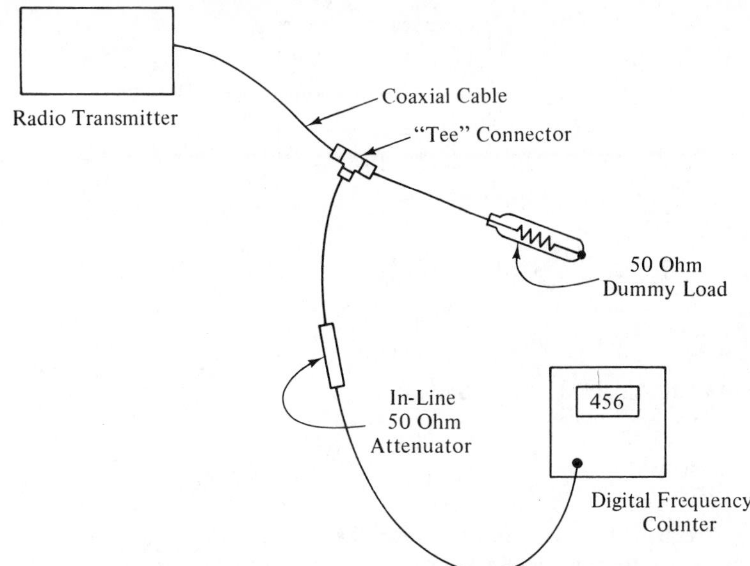

Figure 15.22 Correct method for measuring transmitter frequency with a counter.

this technique is shown in Figure 15.22. Here the transmitter output power is absorbed by a "dummy load." This is a shielded, noninductive, resistor with a power rating that exceeds the maximum power that the transmitter is capable of delivering. A coaxial "tee" connector and a 50-Ω attenuator feeds a portion of the signal to the frequency counter. The attenuator must reduce the power level to a point that can be safely handled by the counter's front-end circuitry. If sufficient attenuation is used, the frequency counter will not be harmed; otherwise damage *will* result.

CAUTION: *Never* feed the output of any radio transmitter directly to a frequency counter, and never connect the frequency counter directly across a dummy load unless *instructed* to do so by the manufacturer.

Another legal method for measuring transmitter output frequency is shown in Figure 15.23. This technique employs a "throughline" RF sampler that picks off a small portion of the transmitter's output signal and routes it to the digital frequency counter. Some counters are equipped with an internal throughline—they are the *only* types where the transmitter output is connected to the counter.

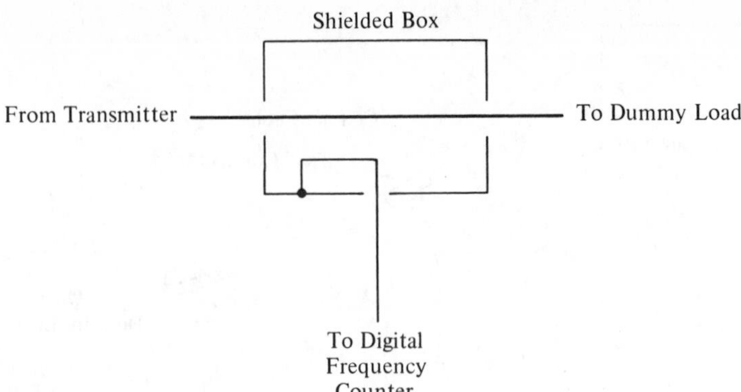

Figure 15.23 Shielded pick-off box.

PROBLEMS

1. A frequency measurement device that consists of a coil, a calibrated variable capacitor, and a lamp in series is called a ________.
2. Lecher wires are used to roughly measure frequency in the ______ range.
3. An absorption wavemeter (may) (may not) use the plate milliammeter of the transmitter being tested.
4. A wavemeter that has a rectifier and meter may also be used as a _______.
5. A _______ oscillator works because the energy from its tank coil will sharply increase when it is coupled to a tank circuit resonant to the same frequency.
6. A dip oscillator is normally used on passive (unpowered) tank circuits. When it is used on active tanks, it is called an __________.
7. A _______ frequency meter zero beats a calibrated signal source with the unknown signal.
8. Draw a block diagram of a simple heterodyne frequency meter. (See Figure 15.24.)
9. A pair of Lecher wires is used to measure the operating frequency of a radio transmitter. The first peak is noted at 32.4 cm and the second is at 64.8 cm. What is the frequency of operation?
10. A crystal oscillator and a receiver are used to measure a frequency near 9 MHz. It is found that a 1112-Hz heterodyne beat note is heard when the receiver is tuned to the unknown below the 9085-kHz marker. What is the frequency?
11. The _______ technique of frequency measurement uses a local subharmonic oscillator to zero beat the unknown. The output of the local oscillator is then measured by an external frequency meter.

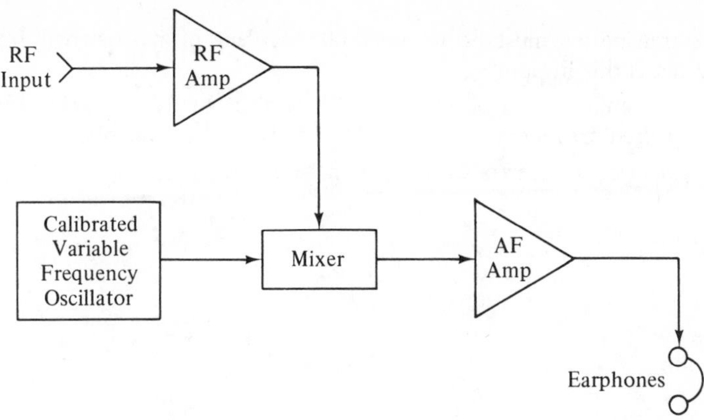

Figure 15.24

12. A transfer oscillator is zero beat with a signal in the 2-MHz range. The fifth harmonic is being used, and the oscillator frequency is found to be 400,136 Hz. The transmitter frequency is ________.

13. A good-quality crystal oscillator will have the following properties: accurate calibration, mechanical and thermal compensation, and an output that is ________.

14. There are two methods for achieving good crystal oscillator stability: ________ and ________.

15. Two types of atomic frequency standard are ________ and ________.

16. When one is using WWV or WWVH it is best to use the ________ channel available, provided that it gives a strong signal in your locality.

17. The frequency of WWVB is ________.

18. What is the maximum error if a 100-kHz crystal is aurally zero beat to 25 MHz WWV?

19. The basic element in a digital frequency counter is the ________.

20. Several DCUs in cascade form a ________.

21. What number is represented by 8-4-2-1 BCD code 1001?

22. Timing of the count is by time base pulses opening and closing a ________.

23. A rolling count or rolling display can be eliminated by using ________ circuits.

24. Another term for frequency counters is ________.

25. In a digital frequency counter the signal amplitude must cross both limits of the ________ for a count to be affected.

26. A counter that works to 80 MHz in the direct mode can be extended to 500 MHz by two methods: ________ and ________.

27. A frequency counter may be connected directly to a transmitter output. True or false?

28. A transmitter must be within 0.005 percent of its assigned frequency. What is this in ppm?

29. A transmitter must be within 0.005 percent of 27,075 kHz. The actual measured frequency is 27,076,020 Hz. Is this within tolerance?

30. Typical counter error is the time base error ________.

16
Oscillator Circuits

An "oscillator" is an electronic circuit that produces a periodic waveform such as a sine wave, square wave, sawtooth, or pulse. Oscillators are used as signal sources in a wide variety of electronic equipment. Although there are many different design variations, there are actually only a few different classes of oscillator circuit.

16.1 OSCILLATION REQUIREMENTS

There are two basic requirements for making an oscillator circuit work. One is positive or "regenerative" feedback, and the other is an overall circuit gain greater than unity. The block diagram serving for all feedback oscillators is the same for the basic feedback amplifier. The only difference is in the phase of the feedback signal. In an amplifier circuit it is necessary to use negative or degenerative feedback. In that case the feedback signal tends to cancel part of the input signal, it is to be hoped to good advantage. In an oscillator, the feedback is *in phase* with the input signal, so the input signal is sustained. In-phase feedback must have a phase angle of either 0 deg or 360 deg with respect to the input signal. Such feedback is also called regenerative—because it helps regenerate the input signal—or "positive" feedback.

16.2 THE ARMSTRONG OR "TICKLER COIL" OSCILLATOR

Figure 16.1 shows one of the simplest and oldest forms of vacuum tube oscillator circuit, the Armstrong oscillator (named after its inventor). The frequency-determining element in this oscillator circuit is an LC resonant tank circuit consisting of $L1$A and $C2$. This circuit is coupled to the amplifier tube ($V1$) in the same manner as might be expected in any tuned amplifier circuit. Feedback from the plate circuit is through a small coil that is coupled to $L1$A. This coil is shown as $L1$B in the figure.

When the power is first applied to this circuit, there is a small rise in vacuum tube plate current. Since this is a *changing* current, the magnetic field surrounding $L1$B is also changing. Flux lines from this magnetic

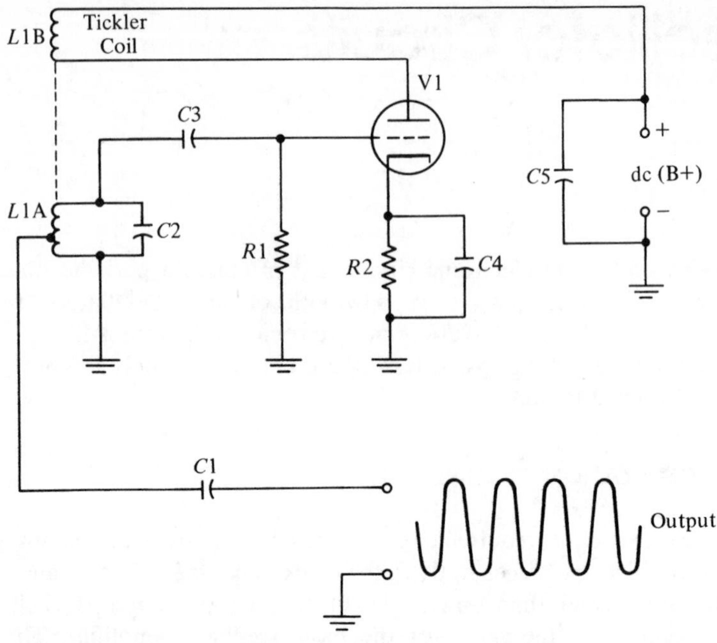

Figure 16.1 Armstrong oscillator.

field cut across the turns of coil $L1$A, inducing a small current in $L1$A. This current effectively "rings" the LC tank circuit and creates an oscillating current in the tank that has a frequency very nearly that of the resonant tank. This signal is coupled through capacitor $C3$ in much the same manner as any other ac signal, and develops a voltage drop across grid resistor $R1$, which typically has a high value.

The signal developed across resistor $R1$ is also impressed across the grid-cathode of the vacuum tube, so it will be amplified. The amplified ac signal then creates a magnetic field of its own in plate coil $L1$B. This is a varying magnetic field, so it also couples to the tank coil, and the process continues. Initial oscillation is established by the variation in plate current during warmup of the tube, and afterwards by the amplified oscillation of the tank circuit.

The operation of the Armstrong oscillator serves to illustrate a basic electrical phenomenon that seems to be at its best when one is dealing with oscillator circuits: LC tank circuit excitation and the flywheel effect. Any time that a varying current is introduced into an LC tank circuit, it creates ringing. Even if the source of energy is only a battery and a momentary contact switch, we see evidence of ringing and flywheel effect. In that case there is a step function applied to the tank. This current charges the capacitor, which then discharges through the inductor, generating a magnetic field around the coil. When the inductor is completely discharged this field can no longer be supported, so it collapses, generating a current in the windings of the coil. This recharges the capacitor, and so on. This type of action creates a sine wave recirculating current and is called the "flywheel effect." If there were no losses in the circuit, the oscillations would continue forever. But perpetual motion does not, alas, exist, so the current dies out at an exponential rate that is dependent upon the nature and value of the losses. There are some losses in the capacitor and flux losses in the coil, but the really major losses are the result of just plain resistance—especially in the windings of the coil.

The oscillations from a straight LC tank circuit are said to be damped, so they decay in the exponential manner shown in Figure 16.2. The positive feedback provided by the tickler coil, however, keeps re-exciting the tank circuit, so the oscillation becomes continuous.

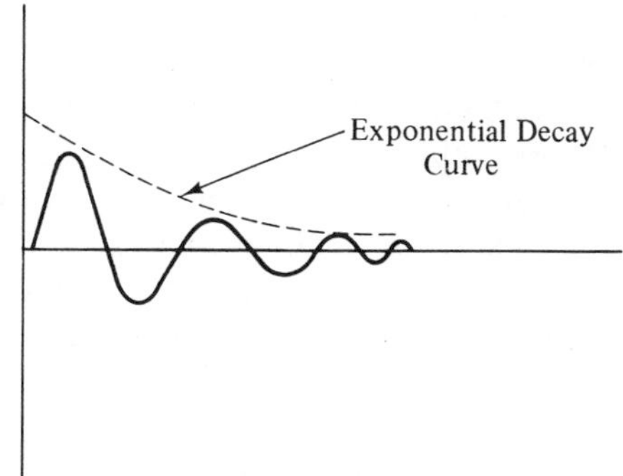

Figure 16.2 Damped ringing oscillation.

Output signal is a sine wave taken from a tap on the coil ($L1$A). This signal is lightly coupled to the next stage through a small-value capacitor, $C1$. It is very important to keep loading of an oscillating tank to a minimum, so it is usually the practice to keep this capacitor very small in value. The amplitude may then be made up in a following buffer stage.

The oscillation of the Armstrong circuit is established and sustained by the feedback provided by tickler coil $L1$B. This coil must be connected into the circuit in such a way that this feedback is positive. Otherwise, the feedback signal would deteriorate the tank circuit oscillation, rather than sustain it. The *sense* of the tickler coil connection, then, is very important in determining whether or not the circuit will oscillate.

The amount of feedback is also important, especially where the frequency stability of the oscillator is important. The degree of coupling between the two coils, $L1$A and $L1$B, is one method for varying this feedback level. Also used is variation of the voltage applied to the plate circuit. In fact, some older circuits used a series-variable resistor between the plate of the tube and the B+ supply. This resistor was usually labeled "regeneration" or "feedback."

Bias on the oscillator tube must be relatively high if the circuit is to be efficient. This bias is supplied by the grid-leak principle so that the tube will be essentially unbiased at initial start-up. This allows a relatively high current to flow in the plate of $V1$ so that oscillation can begin. In fact, this sort of bias is almost necessary if the oscillator is to be self-starting on application of power. Once the oscillations begin, however, the ac signal coupled through capacitor $C3$ develops a negative dc voltage between the grid and the cathode, which biases the tube and effectively controls the operation of the tube. The value of $C3$ and $R1$ must be such that it will produce the highest dc oscillation, without allowing the tube to break into a low-frequency parasitic oscillation. Capacitors $C4$ and $C5$ are bypass capacitors used to provide a low impedance path to ground at the frequency of oscillation, but to block dc potentials.

The Armstrong oscillator can also be made using transistors with but little modification to the basic configuration. One area of change is the coil configuration. In a transistor oscillator we find that the base impedance is much lower than the input impedance of a vacuum tube. The coupling capacitor to the transistor base is, therefore, connected to a tap on $L1$.

16.3 TUNED-GRID, TUNED-PLATE (TPTG) OSCILLATORS

The oscillator circuit of Figure 16.3 is called the "tuned-grid, tuned-plate" oscillator design. Whereas the Armstrong oscillator was an inductive feedback type, this circuit is a capacitive feedback oscillator. The feedback path consists of the internal capacitances of the vacuum tube, or transistor, used as the active device. These are shown in the diagram as C_{gp} and C_{gc}. They are drawn with dotted lines because they are not (or may not be) physically present in the circuit. In most cases the interelectrode capacitances are quite sufficient to sustain oscillation. In fact, there are many RF amplifiers that cannot operate normally without *neutralization* of these capacitances. If a triode or other tube type with high interelectrode capacitances is used in a tuned RF amplifier, it has a circuit not unlike that of Figure 16.3. Unless it is neutralized, however, it may well oscillate rather than amplify.

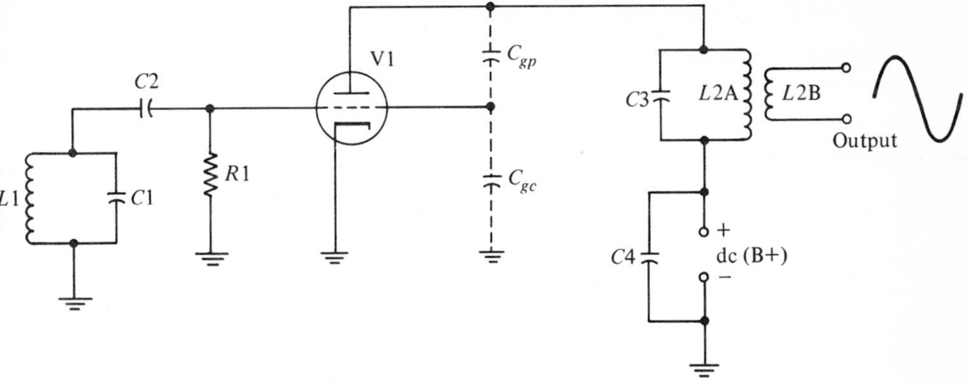

Figure 16.3 Tuned-grid, tuned-plate (TPTG) oscillator.

When power is first applied to the circuit, there is a small increase in plate current, and that tends to shock-excite the tank circuit in series with the plate supply (*L*2A/*C*3). This creates a ringing current in much the same manner as was true in the Armstrong oscillator circuit. The ringing current flowing in the tank circuit creates a voltage drop across the tank circuit. Since bypass capacitor *C*4 has a very low impedance at the tank's resonant frequency, the entire tank voltage is applied across the plate-cathode path of the vacuum tube. This means that the voltage is also across the series capacitor voltage divider consisting of the two major interelectrode capacitances, C_{gp} and C_{gc}. A portion of the total tank voltage, then, is applied across the cathode-grid capacitance, where is can be coupled through capacitor *C*2 to shock-excite the grid tank circuit (*L*1/*C*1). It is necessary that this tank is tuned to exactly the same frequency as the plate tank. Otherwise, the oscillations may well become damped and die out. Tuning accuracy becomes especially important where the two interelectrode capacitances are sufficiently different that only a small portion of the plate tank signal is applied to the grid tank.

Two different situations can arise in response to having the two tanks on slightly different frequencies. One is that the circuit may oscillate at two frequencies—one for each tank. The other possibility is that the circuit may oscillate at the frequency of the tank circuit that has the highest *Q*. The latter is the usual situation.

In some vacuum-tube, and most transistor oscillator circuits, there may be insufficient interelectrode capacitance to sustain oscillation. In these cases there will be a small external capacitor shunting either (or both) tube capacitances. These extra capacitances range from 2 pF to over 100 pF, depending upon the situation.

In the case of Figure 16.3 the output signal is taken from a coupling link on the plate inductor, *L*2A. There are, however, several other methods for obtaining this signal. One is by a tap and series capacitor on coil *L*2A itself, as was the case in the Armstrong circuit.

The TPTG oscillator and the TPTB transistor version have several drawbacks, not the least of which is the necessity of having two LC tank circuits tuned to the same frequency. If it is desired to change frequency, both tanks must be adjusted simultaneously and equally, or the oscillator will cease operating. As a result, it is usually the case that both amateur and commercial communications equipment use either an LC oscillator with a single LC tank, or one of those that has a piezoelectric crystal as the resonating element.

16.4 HARTLEY OSCILLATORS

The Hartley oscillator is a relative of the Armstrong oscillator in that both are inductive feedback types. In the Hartley circuit we find that the tickler coil has been made part of the tank circuit inductance. Examples of Hartley circuits are shown in Figures 16.4(a) and 16.4(b). Both of these circuits use junction field effect transistors as the active element, but the discussion applies to bipolar transistors and vacuum tubes as well.

When the Hartley oscillator of Figure 16.4(a) is first turned on, there is no bias applied to the gate of the JFET. An unbiased gate creates a current surge in the channel of the JFET. Since part of tank coil *L*1 is connected in series with the source-drain current path, this surge generates a changing magnetic field about that portion of the coil. The flux lines from the magnetic field cut across the rest of the turns, and this induces energy into the tank, where is creates a brief oscillation. The oscillatory energy in the tank circuit creates an ac voltage across the tank that can be coupled through capacitor *C*2 to the gate of JFET *Q*1. This voltage accomplishes two things. One is that it establishes the needed bias across the gate-source terminals of the JFET, and second, it is amplified by the JFET. The current in the channel from then on is varying at the same frequency as the oscillations in the tank circuit. The source current also flows through a part of the coil, so it creates a magnetic field that cuts across the rest of the turns. This establishes a sustained oscillation in the tank as long as power is applied. Output signal is usually taken by capacitor coupling from either the top of, or a tap on, tank circuit inductance *L*1. In other cases there may be a coupling link to *L*1 going to the outside world.

The coil in the Hartley oscillator is rarely tapped exactly in the center of its winding. Maximum power output is obtained when the tap is nearer

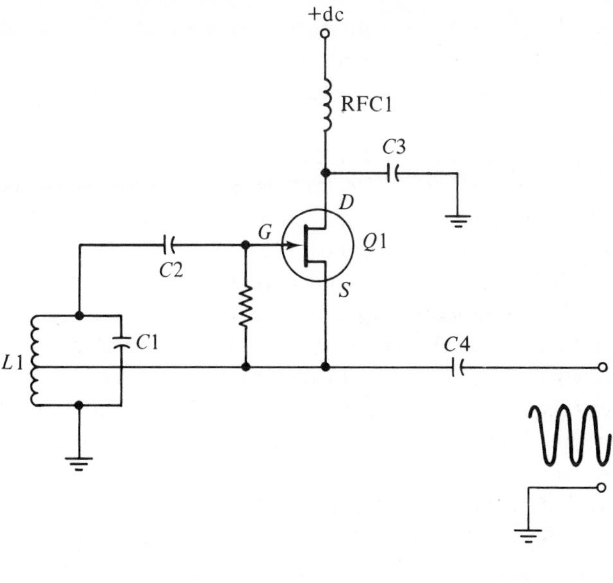

(a)

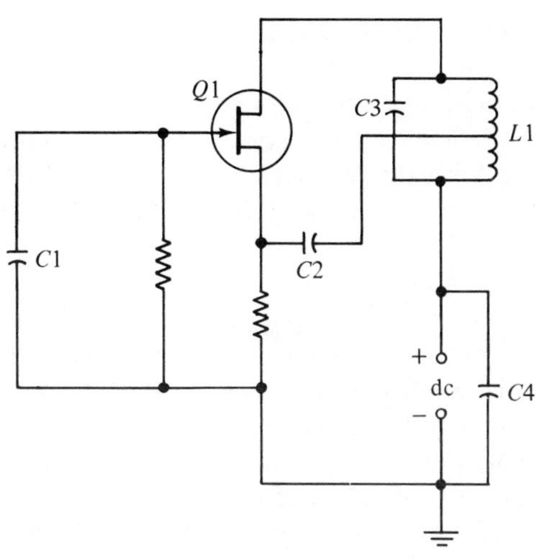

(b)

Figure 16.4 (a) JFET Hartley oscillator with coil in gate circuit, (b) JFET Hartley oscillator with coil in the drain circuit. A *tapped* coil designates the Hartley class of oscillators.

to the gate end of $L1$, whereas the best frequency stability occurs when the tap is nearer to the ground end. In most cases tap placement is a trade-off favoring stability. In other cases there may be a link to $L1$ going to the outside world.

Figure 16.4(b) shows a variation on the Hartley oscillator that is seen occasionally. In this circuit the tank is placed in the drain (or plate, if a vacuum tube is used) and feedback from the tap is applied to the source through low-impedance capacitor $C2$.

In many of the examinations that communications people must pass (such as the F.C.C. commercial radiotelephone and amateur radio exams), you may be asked to identify or draw certain circuits. Among the types most often asked for are the several different types of oscillator presented in this chapter. You will learn certain key identifying features for each type of circuit. The key feature serving to identify the Hartley oscillator is the use of a single tapped coil as both the resonating tank circuit coil and the feedback path. The Armstrong oscillator, on the other hand, is identified by the use of a tickler coil and a single inductance tank circuit. The feature by which you recognize the TPTG oscillator is the two resonant tank circuits tuned to the same frequency—particularly if the interelectrode capacitances are drawn in or there is no neutralization.

16.5 COLPITTS AND CLAPP OSCILLATORS

The circuit shown in Figures 16.5(a) and 16.5(b) is shown as the Colpitts oscillator. This variation uses a tapped capacitor voltage divider instead of a tapped coil to form the feedback path. Operation of the Colpitts oscillator proceeds in much the same manner as for types discussed previously. In general, capacitor $C3$ is much larger than $C4$, but both are part of the overall resonant tank circuit. In this circuit the tank consists of a single inductance, $L1$, and three capacitances ($C1$, $C2$, and $C3$-$C4$).

One reason for the popularity of the Colpitts oscillator in high-frequency and VHF applications is that the total capacitance is made up of capacitors $C1$ through $C4$, inclusive, but mechanical and thermal effects can be largely limited to a single capacitor—$C1$. If the total value of $C1$ is only a small portion of the overall capacitance creating the resonant condition, then changes in $C1$ due to thermal problems have but a small effect on the frequency of oscillation. Capacitors $C2$ through $C4$ can be of whatever temperature coefficient best creates stability in the operating frequency. It is also true that interelectrode capacitances, especially in tubes, have a much smaller effect (about half) on operating frequency during warmup when compared with the performance of the Hartley circuit.

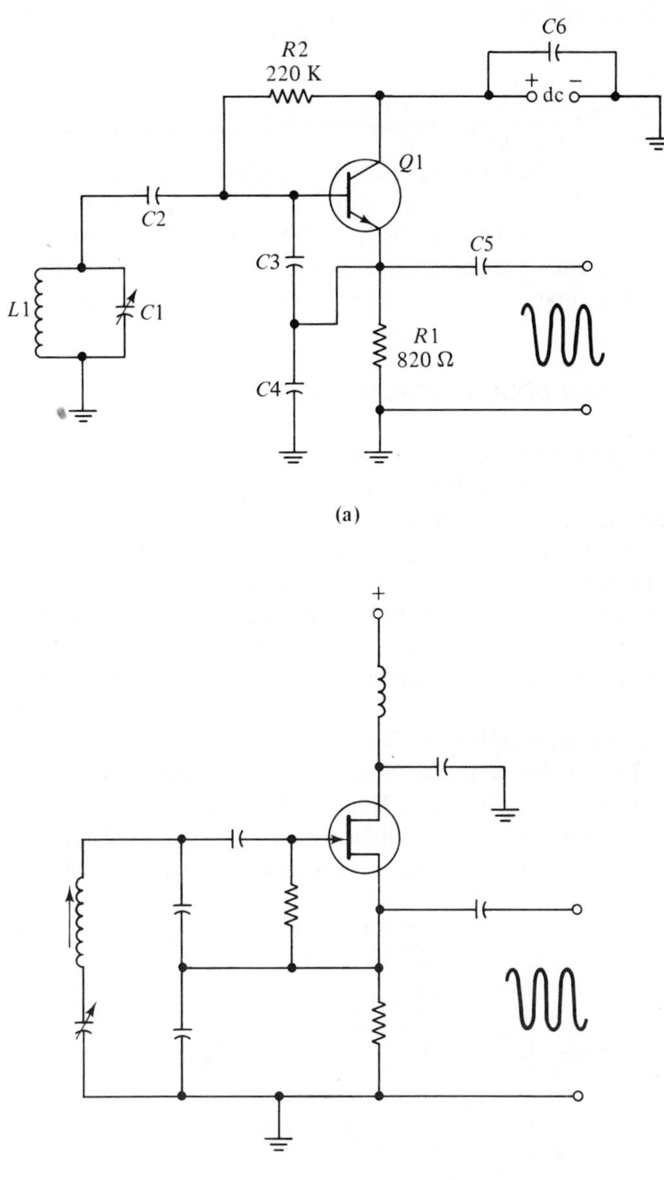

Figure 16.5 (a) Colpitts oscillator (parallel-tuned), (b) series-tuned Colpitts oscillator, also called the Clapp oscillator.

A variation on the Colpitts circuit is shown in Figure 16.5(b). In this circuit we have essentially the same conditions as previously, but the tank is series-resonant. This circuit is often called the "Clapp oscillator," or "series-tuned Colpitts."

When asked to identify an oscillator circuit, look for the peculiar features. Some of these for the Armstrong, TPTG, and Hartley circuits were discussed in the previous section. In the Colpitts and Clapp circuits it is the tapped-capacitor, voltage-divider feedback network that is our clue. If the series-tuned version is not otherwise identified (i.e., in a choice offered in the multiple-choice question), use the "Clapp" name, but if Clapp is not a choice, then use either "Colpitts" or "series-tuned Colpitts."

16.6 ELECTRON-COUPLED OSCILLATORS

Almost every oscillator circuit, even those presented so far, will not operate properly if it is loaded heavily, or if the load is varied over a wide range as the circuit operates. Unfortunately, these conditions can almost be promised to exist in any real electronic circuit. In some cases a separate buffer amplifier is placed between the oscillator and the load that it must drive. The input to this amplifier is designed to lightly and consistently load the output of the oscillator. Variations in external load and heavy load requirements have little or no effect on the stability of the oscillator circuit.

The electron-coupled oscillator (ECO) is an attempt at placing the oscillator and buffer amplifier functions inside the same tube. An example is shown in Figure 16.6. Here we have a tetrode, or more likely a pentode, vacuum tube. The oscillator may be any of the types discussed so far, or most of the types to be discussed subsequently. The oscillator

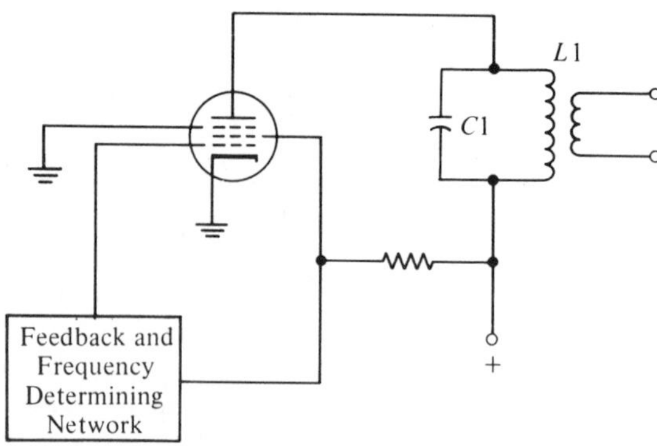

Figure 16.6 Electron-coupled oscillator (ECO).

circuit is formed by the cathode, control grid, and the screen grid. In this circuit the screen grid of the tube acts as the anode of the oscillator; the tube behaves as a triode. The plate of the tube is tuned to the frequency of oscillation. The electron stream that is the oscillator's "anode" current is also the same current that flows to the plate of the vacuum tube. Variations in this electron flow are coupled to the outside world through tank circuit $L1/C1$.

The chief advantages of the electron-coupled oscillator include better frequency stability due to more consistent loading of the oscillator, and far greater available power output compared with the same tube used in a conventional oscillator circuit. Changes in the "external world," even variation of the resonant frequency of the plate tank circuit, have little or no effect on the frequency of oscillation. As a result, the ECO is probably the most commonly found oscillator configuration in older vacuum-tube transmitters. Solid-state oscillator circuits must, however, rely on the use of buffer amplifiers.

16.7 CRYSTAL OSCILLATORS

The use of LC tank circuits is not without problems. The coils and capacitors used in these circuits suffer from instability caused by a number of sources. They drift with changes in temperature, and shift abruptly with changes in the mechanical situation, or vibrations. They are also somewhat difficult to place, and keep, on a specific frequency.

The answer to these problems, where frequency must be kept tightly on one channel, is the use of a piezoelectric crystal as the resonant element controlling oscillator frequency. These devices can be closely calibrated, and they hold their calibrated frequency over a wide range of ambient conditions.

Some crystals, such as natural quartz and some synthetic ceramics, possess the property known as *piezoelectricity*. This phenomenon causes the crystal to generate electricity when it is mechanically deformed, or alternatively, to deform when subjected to an electrical field. Figure 16.7 shows how a crystal might be used in an oscillator circuit. A slab of piezoelectric crystal is cut and mounted between two fixed electrodes. In older units these electrodes were brass plates pressed into place by springs. Modern crystals, however, have the electrodes' vapor deposited onto the actual crystal surface, and then the wires are soldered directly to the silvered surface electrode. The schematic symbol for an electrode is shown in Figure 16.7(b).

If a dc voltage is placed across the pins of Figure 16.7(a), then the crystal element is placed across an electric field. This causes the crystal

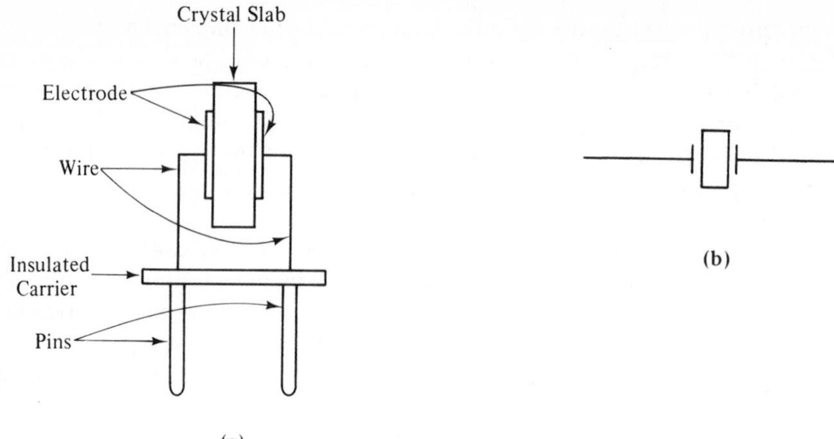

Figure 16.7 Piezoelectric crystal resonator replaces the LC tank circuit in oscillators.

to mechanically deform—it physically changes shape. If the voltage is turned off, then the crystal returns to its original shape. If the polarity of the voltage is then reversed and reapplied, then the crystal again deforms, but in the opposite direction.

If an ac signal voltage is applied to the pins, then we find that the crystal possesses resonance, much like an LC tank circuit. The resonant frequency of any given piece of crystal depends upon several factors, but the most important are the physical dimensions. If an off-resonance ac potential is applied to the crystal, then little activity is noted. The mechanical activity increases rather dramatically, however, if resonance is approached. The activity is maximum, in fact, at resonance.

But so what? Of what possible use is a piece of rock that wiggles when an ac potential is applied? It turns out that this phenomenon is a reversible one. Mechanical deformation produces an output voltage that has the same frequency as the resonant frequency of the crystal. If you place an RF voltmeter or oscilloscope probe across the pins of the crystal assembly, and then remove excitation potentials (ac or dc) you will note that the crystal continues to produce an ac output signal at the frequency of its resonance. This signal dies out in precisely the same manner as the damped oscillation encountered when one is ringing an LC tank circuit. Similarly, if you flex the crystal and let it go (mechanical excitation), it mechanically oscillates back and forth, producing an electrical output that follows this motion. This oscillation is also damped unless it is reinforced like the periodic push one would give a child's swing. When the piezoelectric crystal is used in an electronic oscillator circuit, the feedback of the circuit supplies this needed "push."

The Miller Oscillator. We can make use of the fact that the crystal behaves very nearly like a high-Q LC tank circuit, and make an oscillator with superior performance characteristics. The circuit in Figure 16.8 is called the *Miller oscillator,* and is derived from and related to the TPTG circuit. In this case, however, we have replaced the grid tank circuit with a parallel resonant crystal.

The total dc bias for this circuit is derived from the oscillation of the crystal. If the oscillation is zero, then the bias will also be zero, and the plate current will be high. This plate current change will prove of use in adjusting the Miller oscillator circuit for optimum performance. Of course, we can use the dc grid bias, but that proves to be less desirable, because a voltmeter or oscilloscope probe tends to load the crystal, and that changes its frequency of oscillation.

Tank circuit $L1/C1$ is tuned to a frequency that is slightly higher than the resonant frequency of the crystal. When the circuit is turned on, plate current increases and causes ringing in the tuned circuit. Since capacitor $C3$ has a low impedance at the operating frequency, the voltage generated by the tank oscillations is impressed across the plate-cathode circuit. Here we find the same capacitive voltage divider as in the TPTG: the interelectrode capacitances of the tube. This will impress an ac frequency near resonance across the crystal. When the voltage is applied to the crystal, deformation is caused, and this generates a ringing oscillation in the manner described earlier. The signal voltage thus generated is applied to the grid of the tube, where it is amplified and applied to the LC tank, sustaining oscillation.

Tuning of the plate tank can be a little tricky in this type of circuit.

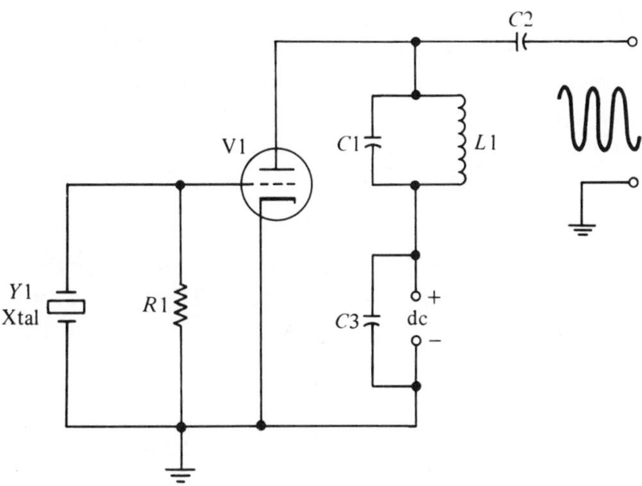

Figure 16.8 Miller crystal oscillator.

If the plate tank is way off resonance *below* the operating frequency, and is then slowly tuned so that its frequency is increased, we note that there is no output and that the plate current is maximum. When the resonant point is reached, however, oscillations begin and an output signal is noted. The current in the plate circuit drops to a *minimum.*

If this same procedure is followed with the plate tank off resonance *above* the operating frequency, then a very different behavior is noted. The oscillation begins slowly, and the plate current drops gradually as the tank frequency is varied. When resonance is passed, the plate current suddenly increases to a maximum and the oscillations cease. The proper operating point is usually specified by the equipment manufacturer to be between 25 and 75 percent of the maximum plate current on the high side of resonance.

Factors Affecting Crystal Oscillators. There are several factors that determine the frequency of oscillation in a crystal oscillator circuit. We have already noted that the physical dimensions are one such factor. Also of importance is the angle of cut from the original piece of crystalline quartz. A natural quartz crystal, the best type for radio transmitter frequency control, is a pointed hexagonal prism shape. Two axes are assigned designations in the plane sliced so that a hexagonal slab is obtained. The *X*-axis is that axis from one point on the hexagon to the point (there are six points in a *hex*agon) exactly opposite. The *Y*-axis is that which is between the midpoints of the two opposing flat sides of the hexagon.

Besides the *X*-cut and *Y*-cut crystal, we find that there are also some cut at odd angles from the main axis of the prism. These cuts are designated by letters such as *AT, CT, Z,* and *BT*. The angle of cut determines the physical dimensions that are required for any given operating frequency of oscillation. It also determines the temperature coefficient. Although crystals vary under temperature less than LC tank circuits, they do change some small amount. The temperature coefficient is usually given in units of parts per million per °C (ppm/°C or $p/10^6/°C$).

Example. A certain crystal has a temperature coefficient of −50 ppm/°C. It is to be operated on a frequency of 2184 kHz. If it is exactly on frequency at a temperature of 60°C, what frequency will it produce if the temperature is increased to 80°C?

$$\frac{-50\text{ ppm}}{°\text{C}} \times (80 - 60°\text{C}) = -1000\text{ ppm} \qquad (16\text{-}1)$$

There will be a -1000 ppb change in the frequency of operation. Since we have an assigned frequency of 2184 kHz, this is the same as 2.184 MHz, megahertz being equal to *millions* of hertz. The actual frequency shift converts to a change of

$$(-1000)\ (2.184) = 2184 \text{ Hz} \qquad (16\text{-}2)$$

The new operating frequency will be

$$2{,}184{,}000 - 2184 \text{ Hz} = 2{,}181{,}816 \text{ Hz} \qquad (16\text{-}3)$$

Example. A 1.2-MHz transmitter must be kept within ±20 Hz of its assigned frequency. The crystal in the oscillator has a temperature coefficient of -15 ppm. If the temperature of the crystal changes from 50°C to 60°C, will the transmitter still be within tolerance? Let us see:

$$(-15 \text{ ppm})\ (60 - 50°\text{C})\ (1.2 \text{ MHz}) = -180 \text{ Hz} \qquad (16\text{-}4)$$

No, the transmitter will *not* remain on frequency. This leads us directly to one technique for keeping a transmitter on the correct frequency: the crystal oven.

A crystal oven is a heated chamber that is controlled by either a thermostat or a proportional control circuit. Typical radio crystal ovens keep the temperature within a few tenths of a degree centigrade at some specified oven temperature that is usually between 75°C and 80°C. If the crystal in the above example had been in an oven that kept the temperature within ±0.1°C, would it have been on frequency?

$$(-15 \text{ ppm})\ (0.1°\text{C})\ (1.2 \text{ MHz}) = -1.8 \text{ Hz} \qquad (16\text{-}5)$$

Clearly, then, the transmitter with the crystal oven is better able to stay on frequency. This is the reason that most broadcasting stations and those radiotelephone transmitters that have tight frequency tolerances are generally designed with a crystal oven to warm the "rock."

Trimming Crystal Frequency. Figure 16.9 shows several ways to effect minor changes in the operating frequency of a crystal. The first two occur because a crystal is slightly sensitive to the capacitance into which it operates. The capacitance seen by the oscillating crystal can be changed by placing a small trimmer in parallel [Figure 16.9(a)] or series [Figure

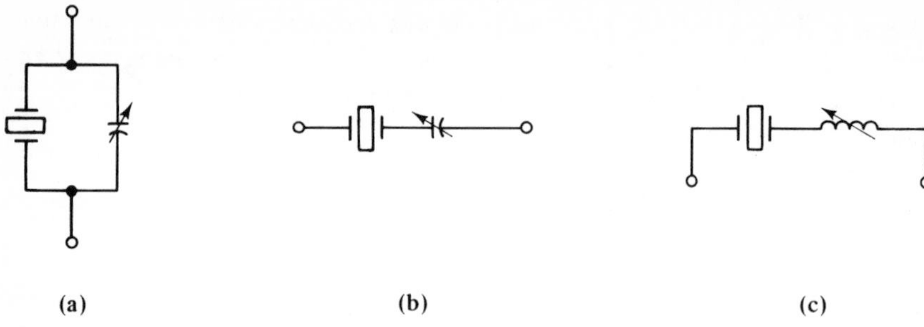

Figure 16.9 Methods for creating small changes in the oscillating frequency of a crystal (**a**) parallel capacitor, (**b**) series capacitor and (**c**) series inductor.

16.9(b)] with the crystal in the circuit. A third method is to place a series inductor [Figure 16.9(c)] or a resonant LC tank circuit in parallel with the crystal. These last two techniques, however, reduce the thermal stability to a point that is on a par with some LC tank circuits, destroying the usefulness of the crystal. This is why that technique is not too popular, except at relatively low frequencies where reasonably stable LC tank circuits are easier to build.

Other Circuits. Two additional crystal oscillator circuits are shown in Figures 16.10 and 16.11. The former is called the *Pierce oscillator,* and the latter is a crystal-controlled version of the *Colpitts oscillator* that you studied earlier.

In the Pierce crystal oscillator circuit we have a crystal between the drain and gate of a junction field effect transistor (JFET). These can also be produced by using bipolar transistors (collector to base) or vacuum

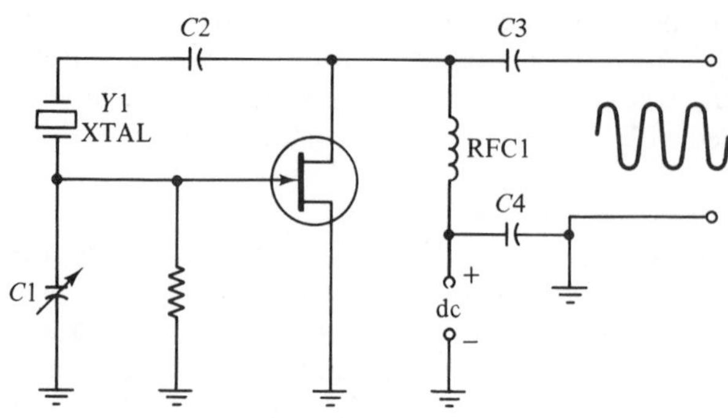

Figure 16.10 Pierce crystal oscillator.

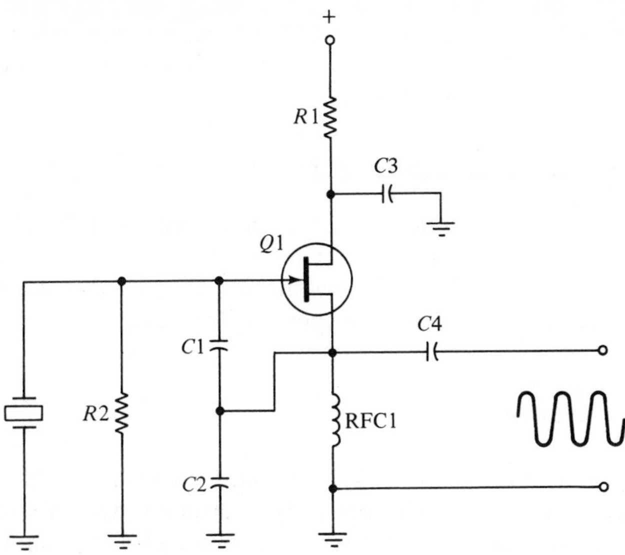

Figure 16.11 Colpitts crystal oscillator.

tubes (plate to grid). In this circuit we can see the use of a series capacitor to make minor frequency changes.

The Pierce oscillator has been popular chiefly because it requires no LC tank circuits. The limitation, however, is that it can operate only at very low power levels, or damage may result to the crystal. In vacuum-tube circuits it is necessary to keep plate potentials low so as not to "cook" the crystal. A more satisfactory arrangement may be the crystal Colpitts oscillator.

16.8 VHF-UHF OSCILLATORS

UHF and VHF frequencies pose special problems for the designer of oscillator circuits. Crystals cannot be used directly, because they are too thin at those frequencies. If the crystal slab it too thin, then it may fracture, or suffer other damage under *normal* operating conditions. Similarly, it becomes difficult to use LC oscillators because stray capacitances and inductances in the rest of the circuit would be greater than the lumped component values supposedly used to control the frequency. There are, fortunately, several techniques for either eliminating or alleviating these problems.

The *ultraaudion* is a Colpitts-type oscillator, but it may appear in the schematic to have only inductance in its tank circuit. The interelectrode capacitances form the resonating and feedback capacitances. This type of oscillator is especially popular in television receiver tuners. The inductor in such a circuit may be an actual coil at some frequencies in the lower end of the VHF-UHF range, but as the frequency of operation is increased, it begins to look less and less like an inductor. In the 200 MHz to 600 MHz range the inductor may even look like a hairpin (half-turn coil). At still higher frequencies the inductor may be a flat piece of wire whose length sets the inductance value. Also used at those frequencies is the resonant cavity. This is a hollow metallic cylinder that has dimensions that are quarter-wavelength at the operating frequency.

16.9 RC OSCILLATORS

There are three categories of RC-controlled oscillator: relaxation, phase shift, and multivibrator. Of these, the relaxation type is probably the simplest, so we shall study it first. An example of a relaxation oscillator is shown in Figure 16.12.

This type of oscillator circuit is built around certain properties of the neon glow lamp. These devices are diode lamps (two pronglike electrodes in the same glass envelope) and are filled partially with neon gas. At a certain voltage, usually in the 40–75-V range, the gas in these lamps ionizes, and light is produced. An ionized gas is a good conductor of electricity, while the un-ionized gas is a good insulator.

The voltage across the neon glow lamp in Figure 16.12 is controlled by the charge stored in capacitor *C*. When the capacitor charge reaches the ionization potential, also called the "firing voltage," of the neon lamp, the gas fires and begins to conduct electric current. The voltage waveforms in the circuit are shown in Figure 16.12(b). If there were no lamp in the circuit, then the voltage across the capacitor (E_c) would continue to rise in the exponential manner shown by the dotted line. But in this case, the firing potential of lamp *I*1 is less than the total supply voltage, so the E_c rise will be interrupted at some intermediate point, E', the firing potential. If the capacitor value is relatively small, then the voltage across it may drop all the way to zero when *I*1 fires. But a neon glow lamp requires a certain minimum voltage, less than the firing voltage, to keep the gas ionized. If the capacitor voltage drops below this point, then the lamp resistance rises to a very high value, because the gas inside is no longer in an ionized state. In that case, the capacitor voltage will not drop all the way back to zero, but only to some specific voltage less than E'.

The oscillation frequency of the neon-glow-lamp relaxation oscillator is dependent upon several factors: the values of *R* and *C*, the firing potential of the particular bulb used, the quenching (turnoff) potential of the

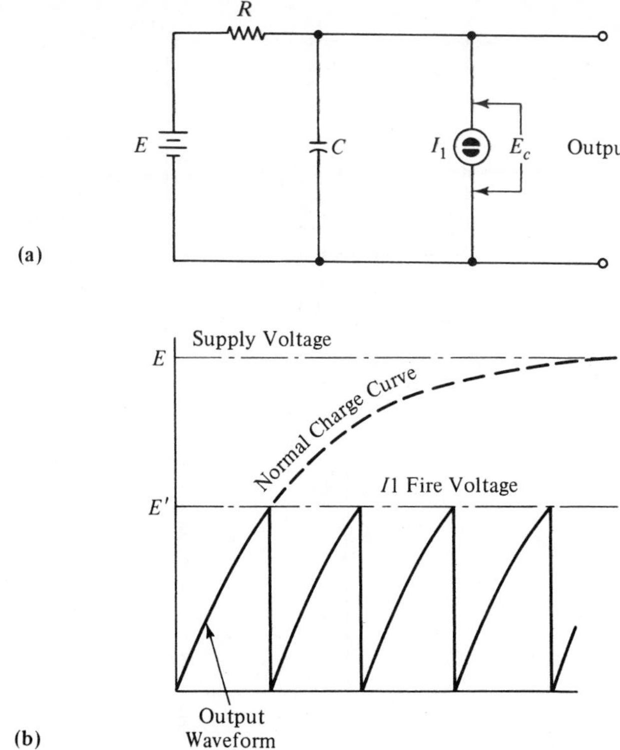

Figure 16.12 **(a)** Neon-lamp relaxation oscillator and **(b)** relaxation oscillator waveforms.

bulb, and the value of the supply voltage *E*. The waveform will be a semi-sawtooth, in that the rising edge will have a curve characteristic of capacitor charging. A nearly linear rise can be generated by replacing the resistor with a *constant current source* (CCS). A CCS can be approximated by making the resistor *R* very high. This may not, however, always be compatible with the requirements of the operating frequency.

Two additional forms of relaxation oscillator are shown in Figures 16.13(a) and 16.13(b), respectively. The circuit in Figure 16.13(a) uses a special gas-filled triode tube called a *thyratron*. At some particular plate-cathode potential the resistance of this tube suddenly decreases, in much the same manner as the neon lamp. The specific voltage required to fire the thyratron is set by the potential applied across the grid-cathode. Figure 16.13(b) shows the unijunction transistor relaxation oscillator. Since this circuit was also presented in Chapter 10, we shall not again discuss its operation.

Several different types of phase shift oscillators are shown in Figures

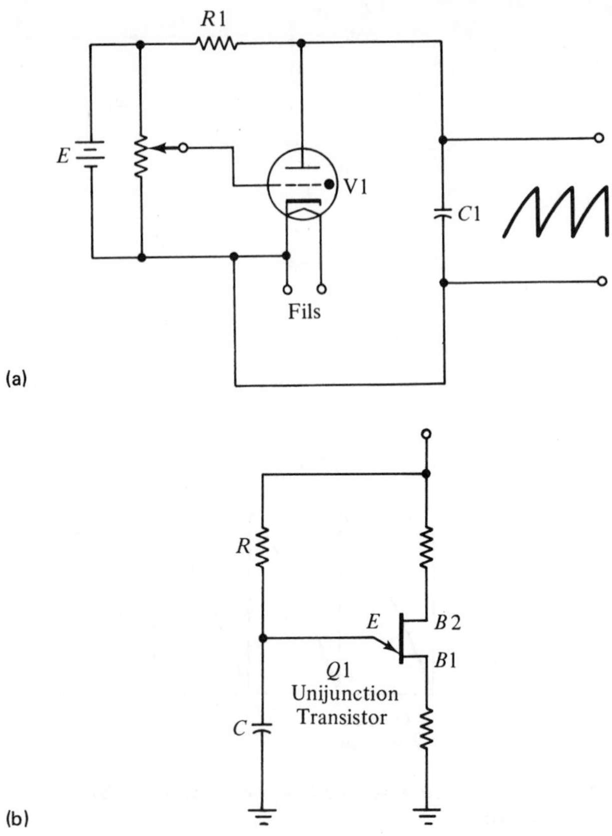

Figure 16.13 **(a) Thyratron relaxation oscillator and (b) unijunction transistor relaxation oscillator.**

16.14 through 16.16. Most of these can be built by using either the devices shown, or almost any vacuum tube, transistor, or linear integrated circuit.

The classic RC phase shift oscillator is shown in Figure 16.14. Recall that the criterion for oscillation includes an in-phase feedback signal. The drain of the JFET is normally 180 deg out of phase with the gate signal. If this signal were fed back directly, then the circuit would be degenerative (it would have negative feedback) and no oscillation would occur. In this case, however, the feedback network consists of three RC combinations in cascade: $C1-R1$, $C2-R2$, and $C3-R3$. It is usually the practice to also specify that $R1 = R2 = R3$ and $C1 = C2 = C3$, although this is not strictly necessary.

Each of these three RC networks gives a 60 deg phase shift at some single frequency. The total phase shift around the feedback loop at that frequency is 360 deg—just as required to sustain oscillation. It gets this value of shift from the 180 deg of the amplifier and the sum of the RC phase shifts (3 × 60 deg = 180 deg). This results in positive, or regenerative feedback, so the stage will oscillate. At all other frequencies, the feedback has some other phase relationship, so it is degenerative—and no oscillations occur. Only at the single frequency where the combined phase shift of $R1$–$R3$/$C1$–$C3$ is 180 deg will we see oscillation. In some cases one or more feedback resistors will be made variable so that the oscillation frequency may be trimmed to some precise value. Output signal is usually taken from the drain and the source resistor is bypassed. The reactance of the bypass capacitor should be not greater than one-tenth of the value of $R4$ at the frequency of oscillation.

In the circuit of Figure 16.15 we introduce an amplifier device called an *operational amplifier,* or "op-amp," for short. This is a special breed of linear IC that has found applications in all manner of electronic circuits, including those of interest in communications electronics. For our present limited purposes we may define an operational amplifier as a device that has an extremely large gain when there is no feedback. The properties of the circuit with feedback are dependent almost entirely upon the characteristics of the feedback network. In general, there are two inputs on the typical op-amp. The inverting input [designated by a (−) sign] produces an output that is out of phase with the input signal. The other input [designated with a (+) sign] gives an output that is in phase with the input signal, so it is called the noninverting input. If the same signal were simultaneously applied to both inputs, they would have equal but opposite effects on the output, and so would cancel. In that case the output would be zero. The gain of an op-amp with feedback is set by the

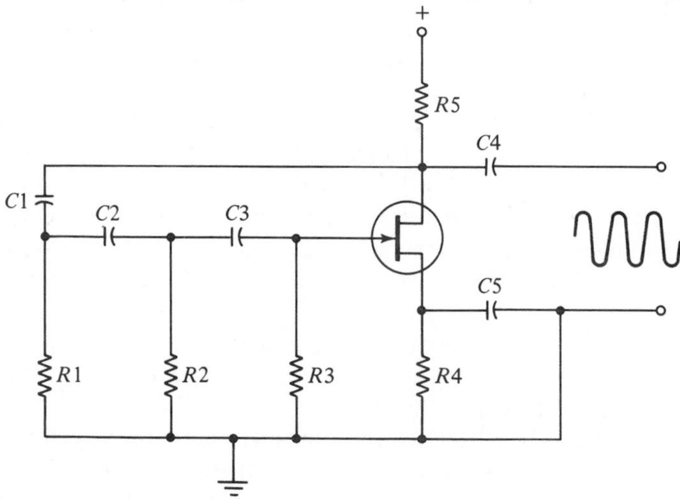

Figure 16.14 Phase shift oscillator.

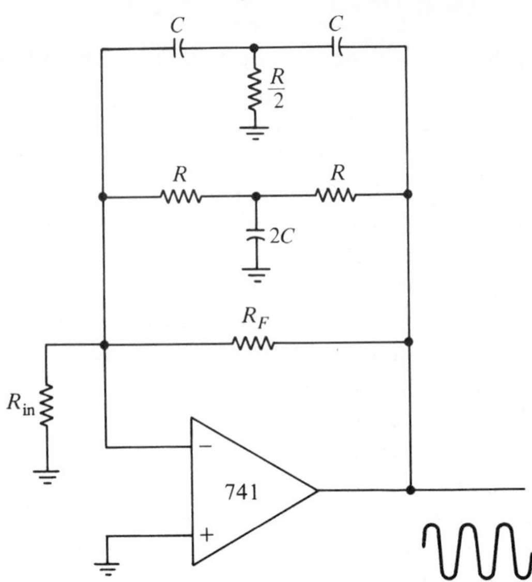

Figure 16.15 Twin-tee oscillator.

feedback loop, but the output voltage is the product of this gain figure and the *difference* between the voltages applied to the two inputs. This makes the op-amp a *differential amplifier*—its output is proportional to the difference between two input potentials.

In the circuit of Figure 16.15 we have an operational amplifier connected with a *twin-tee* RC phase shift network in the negative feedback loop. At some frequency approximately equal to $1(2\pi RC)$ the phase shifts of the two parts of the network combine to produce a total phase shift of exactly 180 deg. This, added to the 180-deg phase shift provided by the op-amp's inverting configuration, produces the 360-deg phase shift required for oscillation.

A variation, also built around the operational amplifier is the Wein bridge oscillator of Figure 16.16. At some specific frequency, again approximately given by $1(2\pi RC)$ the phase shift is 360 deg, so oscillation occurs. At all other frequencies the phase shift will be other than 360 deg, so the feedback will be degenerative, despite being applied to the noninverting input. The amplitude stability of this oscillator is improved by the use of a variable resistance element in the negative feedback path. In this case the element is an ordinary low-current incandescent lamp.

One last method for generating a sine wave is first to generate a square wave, and then pass it through a sharp roll-off low-pass filter that has a cutoff frequency between the fundamental frequency of the square wave and the second harmonic. The filter will cut out all of the harmonics, leaving a relatively pure sine wave signal output. This method is often

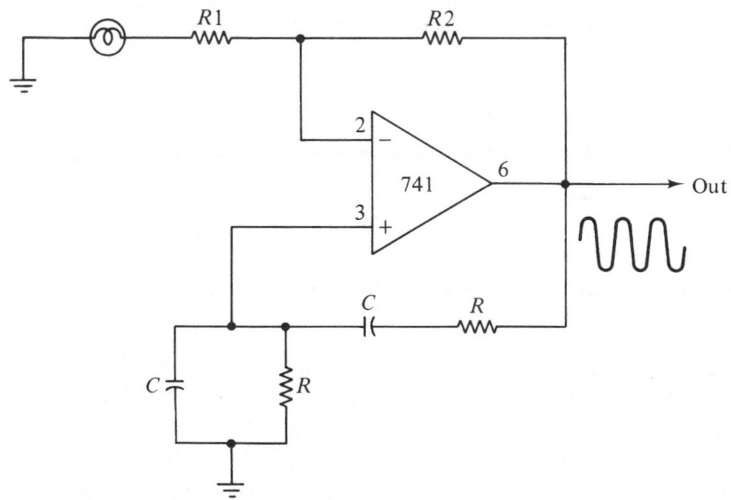

Figure 16.16 Wein bridge oscillator.

done because it is possible to create constant-amplitude square waves much more easily than it is to create constant-amplitude sine waves.

Two of the many different types of square-wave generator circuit are shown in Figures 16.17 and 16.18. The circuit in Figure 16.17 is known as an *astable multivibrator*. Operation is similar to several other oscillator circuits. When power is first applied, the collector currents of the two

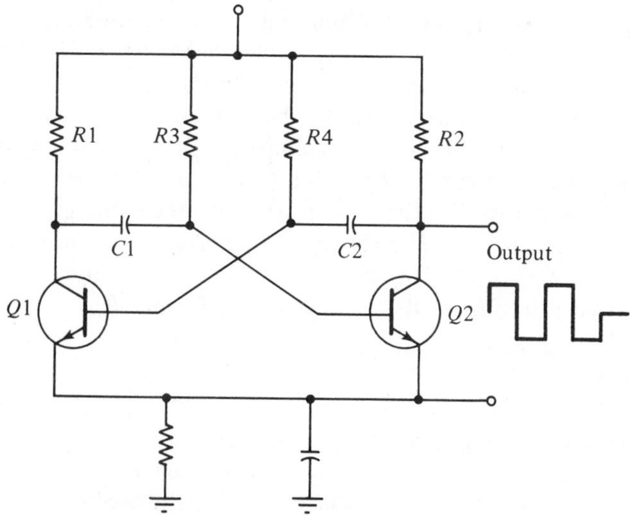

Figure 16.17 Cross-coupled multivibrator.

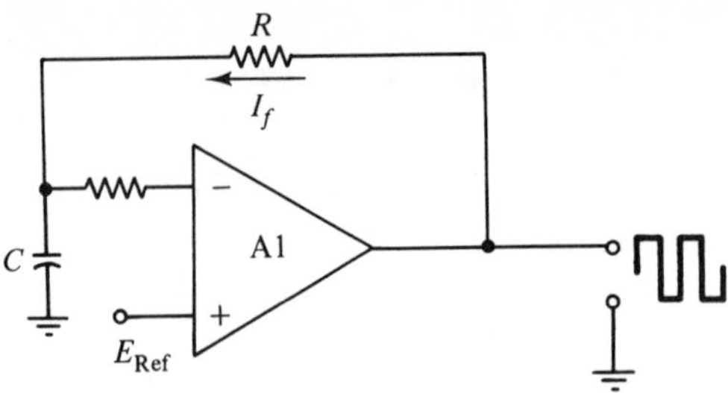

Figure 16.18 Simple operational amplifier multivibrator.

transistors do not increase at precisely the same rate. Let us say, for example, for the sake of discussion, that the collector current of transistor $Q1$ increases faster than that of $Q2$. This differential current creates a small surge that is coupled through capacitor $C1$ to the base of transistor $Q2$. This small pulse is then amplified in $Q2$, and appears as a large pulse at the collector. It is then coupled through capacitor $C2$ back to the base of transistor $Q1$. Here the pulse is again amplified, and appears at the collector of $Q1$. The signal at the $Q1$ collector is then passed back to the base of $Q2$ via capacitor $C1$. After a few cycles of oscillation, we find the action sustained, and both $Q1$ and $Q2$ alternately turn each other on and off. When the collector of $Q2$ is saturated, the output waveform goes down, but when the $Q2$ collector is cut off, the waveform goes to some positive value.

A slightly different approach is shown in the operational amplifier square-wave generator of Figure 16.18. Recall that the output voltage of an op-amp is dependent upon the difference between two input voltages. In this circuit one input is connected to a reference voltage. The other input is connected to a capacitor that is charged by the op-amp output voltage through feedback resistance R. When the reference potential is first applied at circuit turn-on, the output voltage snaps up to some maximum value. This creates current I_f in resistor R, and that charges capacitor C. When the charge across C is the same as the reference voltage, the op-amp output snaps back to zero. The capacitor then discharges through resistor R and the load resistance. This circuit produces a nonsymmetrical output square wave at a frequency determined by R, C, and E_{ref}.

PROBLEMS

1. Two criteria for oscillation are __________.
2. An LC oscillator characterized by a tickler coil between the collector and an LC tank in the base is called an __________ oscillator.
3. What phase angle will yield regenerative feedback?

4. A tank circuit shock-excited by a step-function dc potential will exhibit _______.
5. Ringing is an oscillatory tank circuit current that will diminish _______ with time because of circuit losses.
6. What are two methods for varying regeneration effects in an Armstrong oscillator circuit?
7. An oscillator employing two resonant LC tank circuits, one in the plate and the other in the grid, is called _______.
8. The TPTG oscillator uses the _______ of the tube as a feedback voltage divider network.
9. Identify the circuit in Figure 16.19.

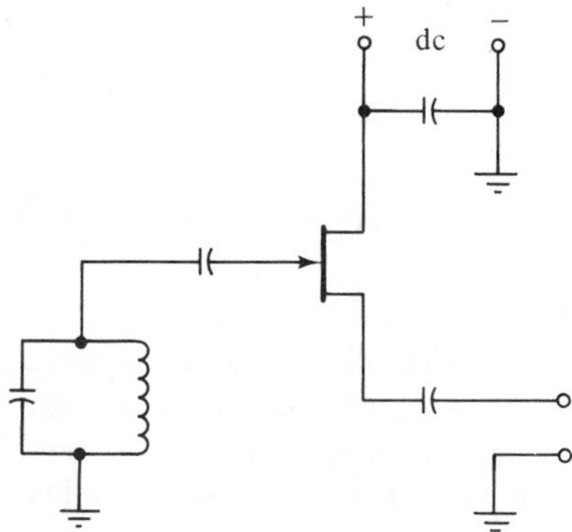

Figure 16.19

10. The Hartley oscillator uses an _______ feedback voltage divider.
11. Identify the circuit in Figure 16.20.

(*Note:* We are asking you only to *identify* these circuits—on an examination you may be asked to draw them, so be very familiar with all aspects of each class of oscillator circuit.)

12. The _________ oscillator is popular for use in HF and VHF applications because thermal capacitance changes have a minimal effect on operating frequency.
13. A Colpitts oscillator using a series-tuned LC tank circuit is sometimes called a _______ oscillator circuit.
14. In an electron-coupled oscillator (ECO) the anode of the oscillator is actually the _________ structure of the tube.
15. The electron-coupled oscillator serves as an oscillator and a _________ in one tube.
16. A _______ crystal can be used instead of an LC tank.
17. A piezoelectric element will generate electricity when it is _________.
18. A piezoelectric element will mechanically deform when an _______ is applied across its faces.

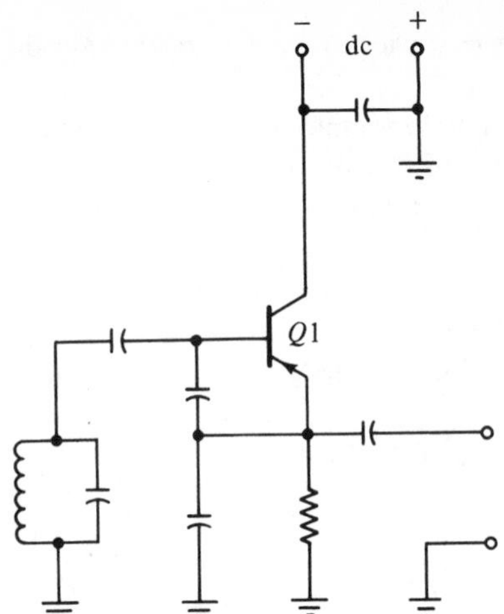

Figure 16.20

19. A piezoelectric crystal will ring in response to either mechanical or electrical stimuli. True or false?
20. Identify the circuit in Figure 16.21.
21. A Miller oscillator is a piezoelectric version of the ________ circuit.
22. A crystal resonant to 9862 kHz has a temperature coefficient of −150 ppm/°C. If the crystal is calibrated at 25°C, and the temperature increases to 60°C, what is the frequency of operation?

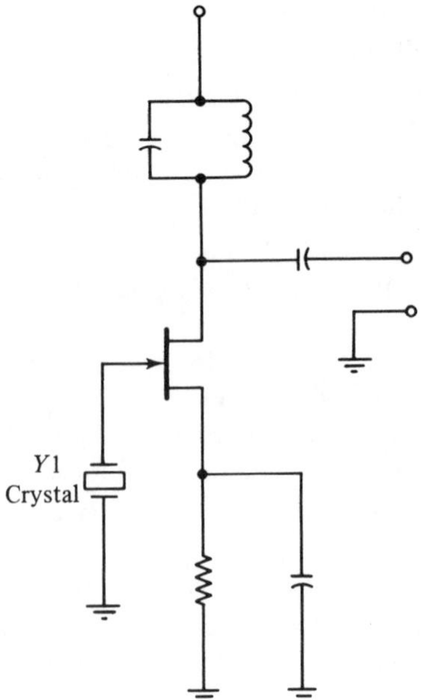

Figure 16.21

23. A small variable _______ in parallel with the crystal will allow minor trimming of the operating frequency.

24. A _______ oscillator is a version of the Colpitts used in VHF-UHF applications, where the interelectrode capacitance of the tube is part of the tank.

25. A sawtooth waveform can be generated by a capacitor, a resistor, and a _______ lamp.

26. A _______ transistor can also generate a sawtooth.

27. The circuits in Questions 25 and 26 are _______ oscillators.

28. An _______ multivibrator will generate square waves.

17
Audio Amplifiers

Audio amplifiers have certain properties and characteristics that make them best suited for the amplification of signals between frequencies of about 20 to 30 Hz on the low end and around 20 kHz on the high end. Many of these properties are shared by all amplifiers in general. Other things, however, are unique to audio amplifiers. Vacuum tubes are somewhat neglected in this treatment because they are of decreased importance in currently available communications equipment. If you are interested in studying vacuum tube amplifiers, we recommend either reading between the lines and drawing conclusions appropriate to tube designs, or consulting an older textbook in the library.

17.1 SOLID-STATE BIASING IN AUDIO AMPLIFIERS

One of the most important aspects of the solid-state audio amplifier is to understand the methods used by circuit designers to achieve proper biasing of the transistors. By now, most of us are familiar with the more or less standard transistor biasing arrangement. A few of these are shown in Figure 17.1. These circuits, and close variations on them, are used in most types of audio amplifier circuits.

Dual-supply Biasing. A biasing circuit that may not be so universally recognized, but is being used more and more, is the dual supply design shown in Figure 17.2. It can be identified by the fact that the ground, or "common" if you prefer, is not returned to either positive or negative sides of the power supply. The circuit in Figure 17.2(b) more nearly represents the type of power supply that is typically used in dual-supply amplifier circuits. In most applications the ground, usually the chassis, floats at the electrical midpoint between the two supplies, or in some cases nearer one supply than the other (electrically, of course).

One of the principal advantages of the dual supply circuit is increased voltage swing in the output. Another claimed advantage is superior thermal stability. This can mean a lot in an amplifier that has marginal heat sinking, is inside of a closed equipment cabinet, or is installed in

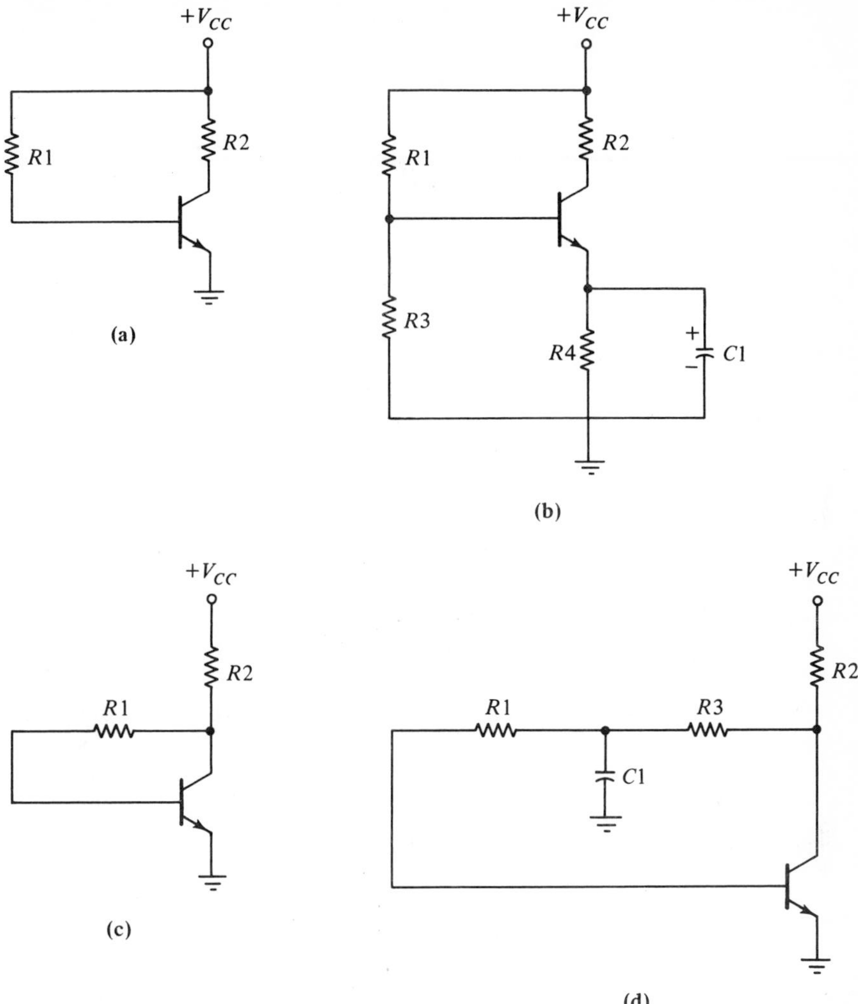

Figure 17.1 Standard transistor biasing circuits.

something like a mobile communications equipment where the temperature will vary over a wide range. A third advantage, especially for fixed base-station locations, is that the dual supply amplifier tends to cancel out power supply ripple components that might otherwise show up as a hum on the output.

Another type of circuit frequently seen in audio amplifiers is the Darlington amplifier or Darlington pair. An example of this transistor configuration is shown in Figure 17.3. Notice that the collectors of the

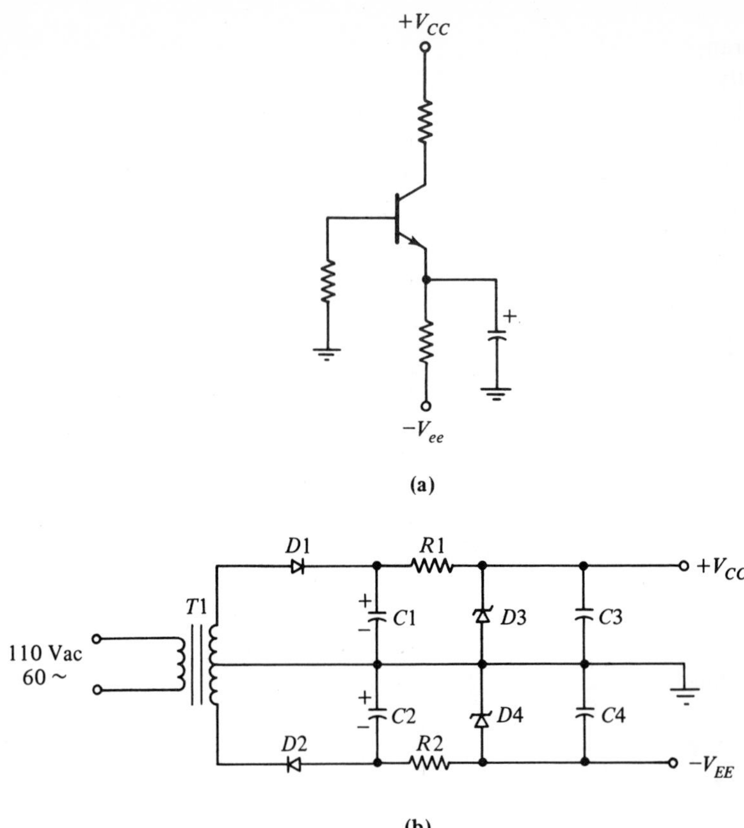

Figure 17.2 (a) Dual supply biasing and (b) dual supply.

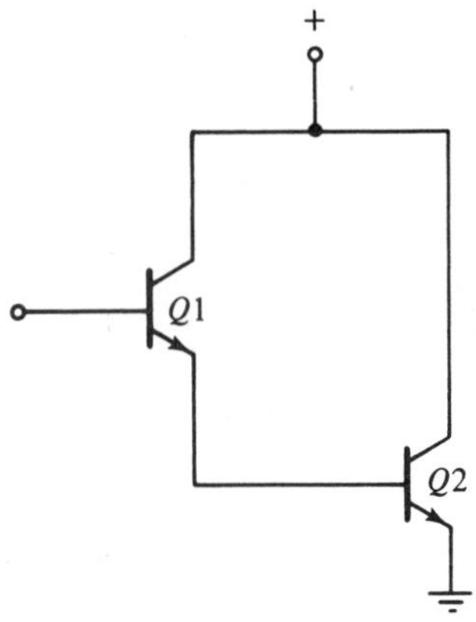

Figure 17.3 Darlington amplifier or "Darlington pair."

two transistors are tied together, and that the emitter of the input transistor directly drives the base of the output transistor. The emitter of the output transistor is used as the "emitter" for the pair, while the base of the input transistor serves as the "base" for the pair.

The Darlington pair produces a much higher input impedance than does a single transistor. It also produces a higher overall beta figure. The beta of a Darlington pair is the product of the individual beta figures for $Q1$ and $Q2$. Although any two transistors may be used in the Darlington pair, it has become standard practice to use identical transistors. In that case the beta of the pair is merely the $(h_{fe})^2$ of a single transistor. Some manufacturers offer Darlington pair transistors under the heading of "super beta" transistors. RCA also offers an integrated circuit with a pair of Darlingtons connected to a common collector terminal. This is their device type CA3036.

17.2 AUDIO POWER AMPLIFIERS

Single-ended—transformer-coupled. One of the oldest designs in both solid-state and vacuum-tube amplifiers is the single-ended, transformer-coupled stage. In most solid-state designs, though, the transformer may actually be an inductor or autotransformer such as that shown in Figure 17.4. By itself this type of stage is not very good; it has a lot of distortion and is limited in frequency response. With the use of feedback, however, much improvement is shown.

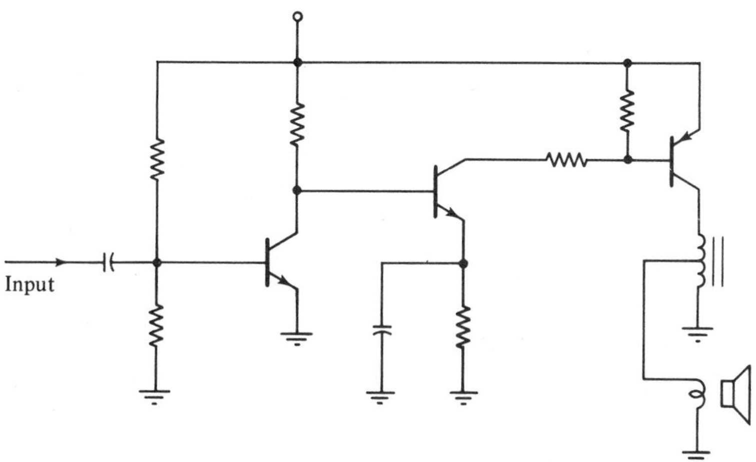

Figure 17.4 Class A audio power amplifier with autotransformer output circuit.

Feedback. There are several different types of feedback used in audio amplifier circuits. One of these, shown in Figure 17.5(a), is called the "second-collector-to-first-emitter" system. With the correct value components, this circuit can make a relatively mediocre audio power amplifier sound almost like high fidelity. The importance of the feedback path

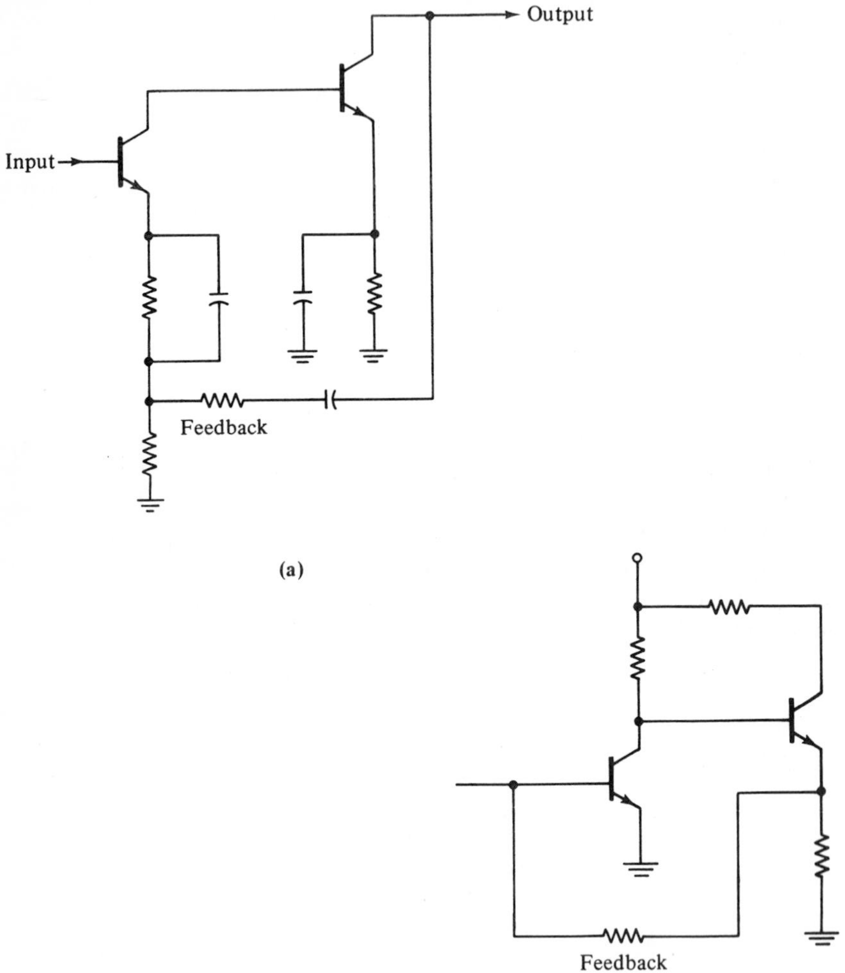

Figure 17.5 **(a)** Second-collector-to-first-emitter feedback and **(b)** second-emitter-to-first-base feedback.

can be seen when certain defects occur. An open or shorted capacitor, or a changed resistor value, will create problems that range from a mildly irritating distortion to a type of thermal runaway that will completely destroy the output transistors.

Figure 17.5(b) shows a second widely used feedback system. This one has been dubbed the "second-emitter-to-first-base" system. This circuit proves popular because it requires only a single resistor to implement.

Push-pull Power Amplifiers. The push-pull circuit is widely preferred over many other types, especially over single-ended designs. They offer superior power handling ability and overall performance. Figure 17.6 shows the standard audio push-pull amplifier, which has been used in almost every audio application from throwaway portable transistor radios to moderately expensive high fidelity and communications equipment. It is, however, far from efficient when compared with certain other push-pull designs of more recent vintage.

The heart of this circuit is two transformers, *T*1 and *T*2. Input transformer *T*1 has a center-tapped secondary, while the output transformer *T*2 has a center-tapped primary. In a manner of speaking, this circuit operates much like the full-wave power supply of a previous chapter. On one-half of the audio input cycle, the base of transistor *Q*1 is driven positive, while the base of *Q*2 is driven negative. This action is due to the relative phase of the two ends of the *T*1 secondary with respect to the center tap. This center tap is grounded for ac through capacitor *C*1.

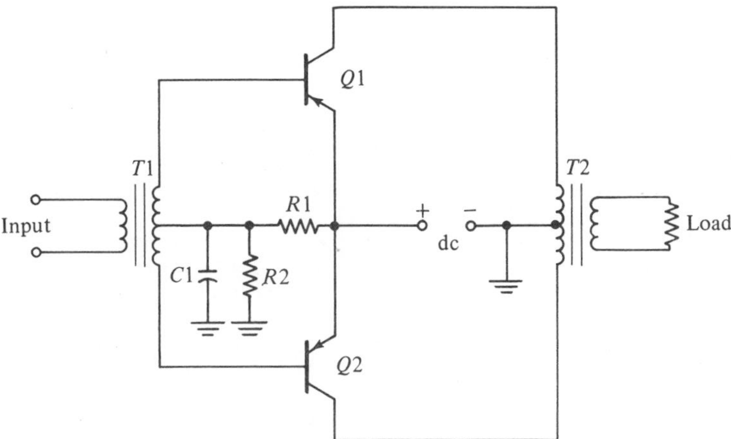

Figure 17.6 Transformer-coupled push-pull power amplifier.

The value of $C1$ is selected to have a low impedance at the lowest frequency of operation. On this half of the cycle $Q1$ (which is a *PNP* type) is biased less hard than $Q2$, so $Q2$ contributes the greater part of the output signal. On the second half of the input signal alternation, the directly opposite situation occurs, and $Q1$ is supplying the output. The two halves of the output signal are rejoined at the secondary of transformer $T2$.

The circuit in Figure 17.7 is a more recent addition to the family of push-pull, solid-state amplifiers. It is often called the "split-secondary" or "totem pole" circuit. The series connection of two identical power transistors and the use of a split-secondary interstage transformer are the two main identifying features of this circuit. Note that there is no output transformer.

One feature that all push-pull amplifiers have in common is the necessity of phase-splitting the input signal to supply two signals that are 180 deg out of phase to drive the two halves of the push-pull amplifier circuit. In older designs, both tube and transistor, this was accomplished by either a center-tapped or split-secondary transformer. In the latter case

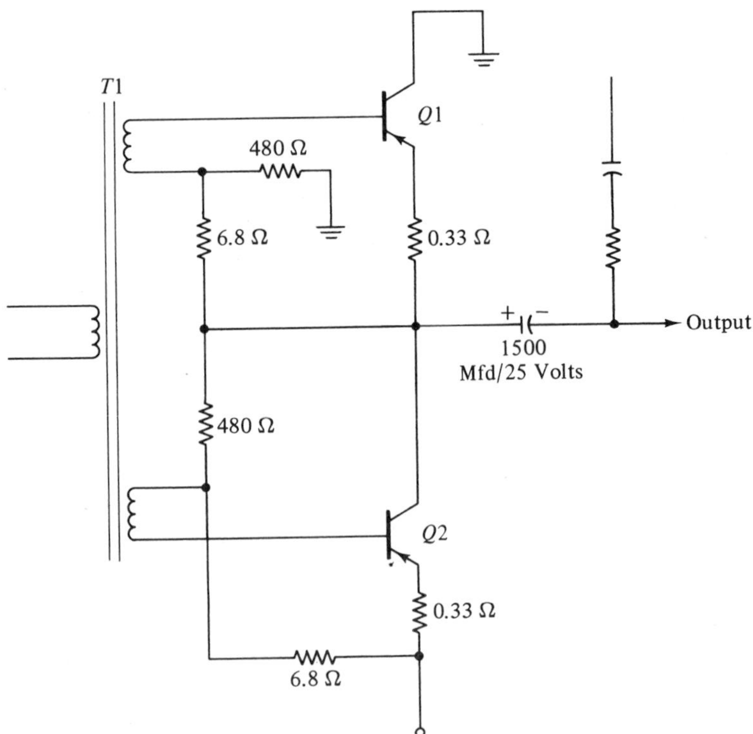

Figure 17.7 Split-secondary or "totem pole" power amplifier.

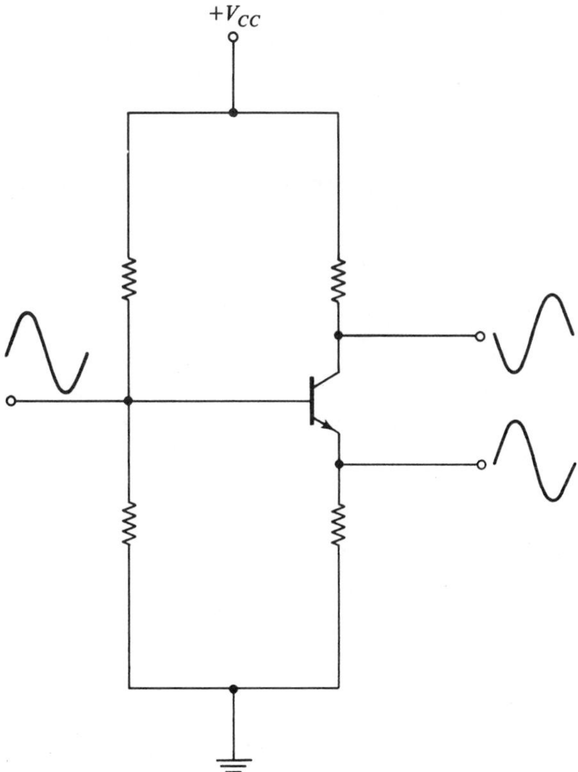

Figure 17.8 Transistor phase inverter circuit.

the two transformer secondaries were connected to the bases of their respective transistors in the opposite sense so that one would be going positive while the other was going negative. In many modern designs, however, the interstage transformer was left out entirely. Omitting it reduces cost, and often improves the frequency response. Some other means of phase-splitting must be provided, however.

The transistor phase inverter, like its vacuum-tube predecessors, is one often used replacement for the interstage transformer. An example is shown in Figure 17.8. In this circuit the collector and emitter resistors are balanced so that the same signal voltage is developed. But the emitter signal is in phase with the input signal, and the collector signal is out of phase. Because of this action we have equal-amplitude, but opposite-polarity, signals at the two outputs of the phase inverter. The collector signal is used to drive one transistor in a push-pull pair, while the emitter signal is used to drive the base of the other transistor.

Another method for producing the opposite-polarity drive signals is

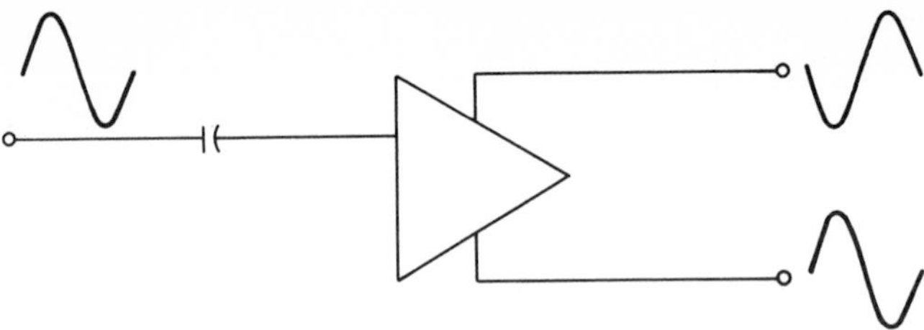

Figure 17.9 Integrated circuit phase inverter.

to use an integrated circuit that has two outputs that are 180 deg out of phase. Such an IC device can be used to drive the transistors of a push-pull pair. An example of this circuit is shown in Figure 17.9.

Designers have another technique for accomplishing phase inversion that is often more economical than any other. It is a circuit that is called the "complementary symmetry" amplifier. This design is shown in Figure 17.10 in simplified form. This design takes advantage of the fact that *PNP* and *NPN* transistors require signals of opposite polarity in order to perform the same function.

Notice that the bases of the two transistors are fed essentially in parallel, and that the load, minus and output transformer, is connected to the electrical midpoint of the two series-connected transistors. The single-supply version of this circuit (as shown) requires a capacitor to block dc from getting to the load. Dual-supply versions frequently have no such capacitor. This circuit is also sometimes called the "emitter follower power amplifier." Resistor *R*1 and the two diodes are used to overcome a phenomenon called "crossover distortion." Transistors require a certain bias,

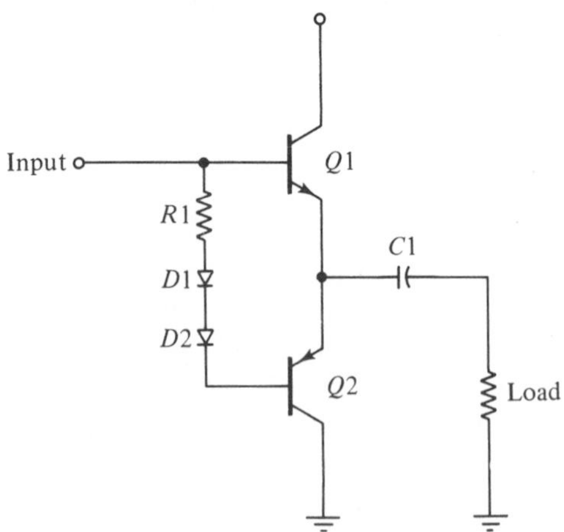

Figure 17.10 Complementary symmetry power amplifier.

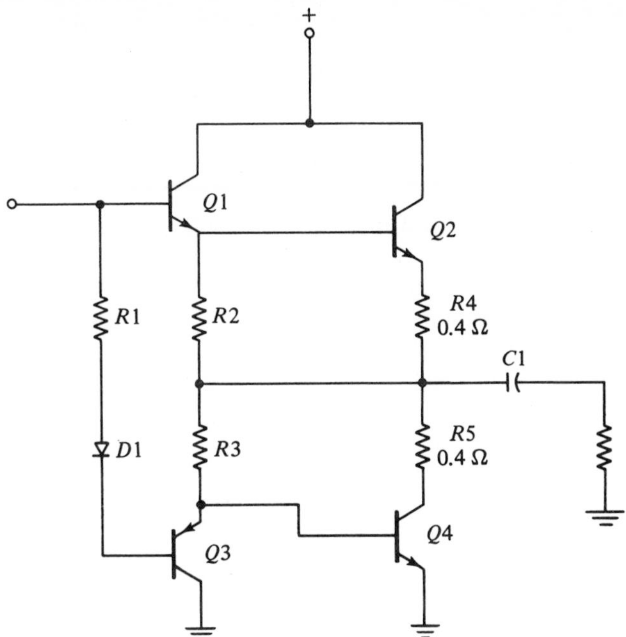

Figure 17.11 Quasi-complementary power amplifier.

and at audio signal levels lower than this voltage the transistors do not amplify properly—linearity suffers. This would create a certain amount of distortion at the zero crossing baseline between the two halves of the input cycle. The resistor and diodes create a small amount of forward bias that effectively eliminates this problem.

The one big disadvantage of the complementary symmetry power amplifier is that it can be expensive to find exactly matched complementary pairs of power transistors—especially at high-power levels. These transistors must be electrically identical except for polarity. Only a few types have this property, and as power levels increase even fewer numbers are available.

It is, however, relatively easy to find complementary pairs at low- and medium-power levels. It is even easy to find replacement transistors not supplied by the original equipment manufacturer. This becomes especially true at power levels of only a few watts.

This situation has led to an interesting modification of the classic complementary symmetry power amplifier circuit. The push-pull amplifier of Figure 17.11 employs the so-called "quasi-complementary" configuration. In this circuit the identical output transistors (usually *NPN* types) are connected in the totem-pole manner, while the drivers are in complementary symmetry.

PROBLEMS

1. Two advantages claimed for the dual supply biasing are ________ and ________.
2. What is the overall beta of a Darlington pair if the beta of $Q1$ is 50, and the beta of $Q2$ is 100?
3. _______ feedback is used to improve stability and reduce distortion in some audio amplifiers.
4. A ________ push-pull amplifier uses two identical, but opposite-polarity power transistors.

18
Radio Frequency Amplifiers

An RF amplifier is designed to amplify signals in the range above approximately 20,000 Hz. In most, but not all, cases the RF amplifier is designed to pass just one frequency, or a small band of frequencies. Before going too far into the tuned amplifier case, however, let us first consider the broadband or wideband amplifier.

There are a number of applications that require an amplifier capable of amplifying a wide range of frequencies simultaneously. Certain of the amplifier stages in your television receiver, the so-called "video amplifiers," are an example of this class. Master TV antenna systems, where one antenna feeds television signal to an entire apartment building or other facility, often require an amplifier capable of handling all of the VHF and UHF frequencies at one time. These broadband amplifiers must operate almost equally well from 54 MHz to over 800 MHz. Another class of wideband amplifier is the modern solid-state linear power amplifier used in some mobile communications equipment. These provide output power levels of 20 W to around 200 W over a range of 1 MHz to 30 MHz.

18.1 WIDEBAND AMPLIFIERS

Figure 18.1 shows examples of broadband amplifiers that might commonly be found. The circuit in Figure 18.1(a) shows a junction field effect transistor (JFET) used in the grounded gate mode. This configuration is analogous to the grounded base circuit in transistor equipment and the grounded grid in vacuum tube circuits. Input and output coupling to this circuit is in the form of trifilar wound transformers. Each of these has three windings that are closely spaced on the powdered iron or ferrite core material. It is usually the practice to wind these transformers in such a way that all three windings are adjacent to each other. In fact, sometimes it is the case that the three wires forming the windings are twisted together before being wound on the core. In most instances we find that the two transformers are wound on toroid (doughnut-shaped) cores. This is done because the toroid core is unique in that the magnetic field is almost entirely contained within the core; there is little flux leakage. This limits the possibility that stray magnetic fields will couple to other circuits, or between input and output.

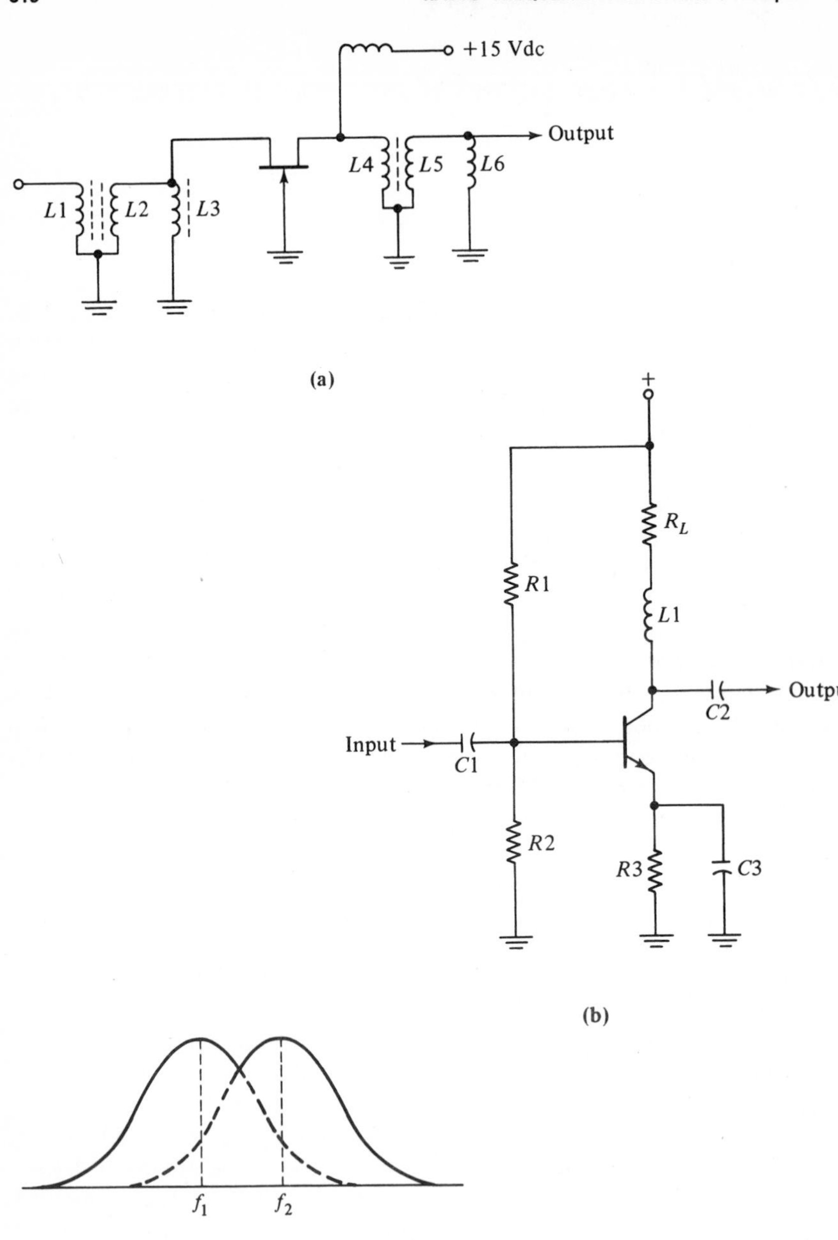

Figure 18.1 (a) Broadband RF amplifier using transformer coupling. (b) Resistance-coupled wideband amplifier using a *peaking coil* to improve high frequency response. (c) Tuning circuits of a stagger-tuned wideband amplifier are adjusted to slightly different frequencies so that their response curves overlap.

Standard resistance-coupled amplifier stages such as those we studied in the section on audio amplifiers are also made into wideband configurations with but little modification. There are, however, a few problems that must be solved. It is, for example, necessary to use a transistor with a very high gain-bandwidth product in the wideband amplifier. Also, the types of capacitors that may be used are limited. All capacitors have properties other than capacitance, and these can tend to limit the high-frequency response of the circuit in which they are used. Certain aluminum electrolytics, for example, operate properly only to frequencies of a few hundred kilohertz (or less). If the desired range of operation is less than this, then simple RC wideband amplifiers can be made by using the standard techniques of the audio amplifier and an appropriate transistor type.

One problem besetting the design of RC-coupled wideband amplifiers is a phenomenon called the "Miller effect." There is an apparent "amplification" of input capacitance in both tube and transistor amplifiers equipped with resistive plate or collector loads. For simplicity we shall consider only the case of the vacuum-tube amplifier. The input capacitance seen by the signal source is given by

$$C_{\text{in}} = C_{gc} + C_{gp} (A_v + 1) \tag{18-1}$$

Example. We have a vacuum tube that has a grid-to-plate capacitance of 0.6 pF and the grid-to-cathode capacitance of 12 pF. If the voltage gain of the RC amplifier using this tube is 1500, what is the Miller effect capacitance seen by the input signal source?

$$C_{\text{in}} = 0.6 + (12)(1500 + 1)$$

$$C_{\text{in}} = 0.6 + 18{,}012 \text{ pF}$$

$$C_{\text{in}} = 18{,}013 \text{ pF} = 0.018\ \mu\text{F} \tag{18-2}$$

The larger capacitance seen by the input signal tends to shunt more of the higher frequencies to ground than the lower frequencies. This creates a gain that is effectively lower for high frequencies than it is for low, and makes it difficult to achieve a flat response from a conventional RC amplifier stage.

Figure 18.1(b) shows a wideband amplifier that is designed to eliminate the droop in frequency response at high frequencies. This stage is a relatively simple *NPN* transistor circuit, but there is an inductance, called a "peaking coil," in the collector circuit. The value of this coil is low, so it has little reactance at low frequencies. In those ranges the amplifier acts much like any other bipolar transistor, common-emitter

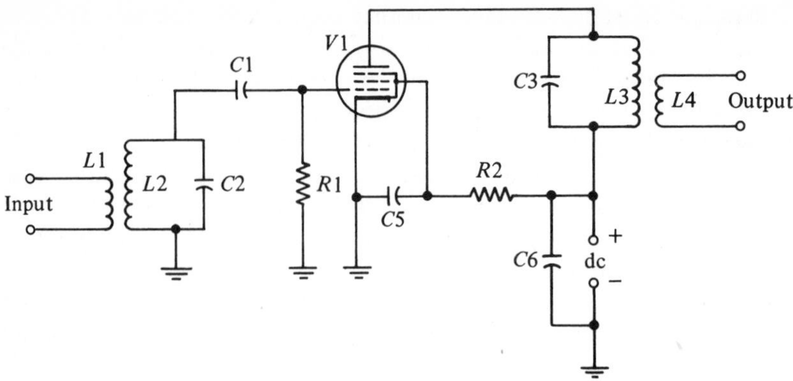

Figure 18.2 Vacuum tube tuned RF amplifier.

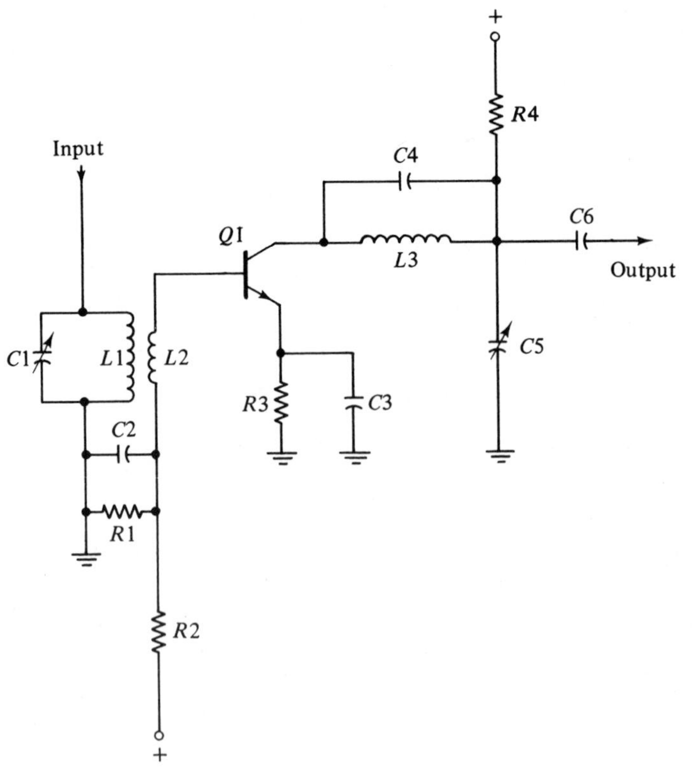

Figure 18.3 Transistor tuned RF amplifier.

amplifier with a load resistance of R_L. At higher frequencies, however, the reactance of $L1$ becomes larger and is then an appreciable portion of the total load. At these frequencies the inductive reactance of $L1$ must be taken into account.

The load seen by high-frequency signals is approximately equal to the quantity $(R_L + X_L)$. Since X_L increases with frequency, we find that the load impedance also increases with frequency. This allows a greater voltage to be dropped across the total load, and that overcomes the effects of high-frequency rolloff.

One last method for broadbanding an amplifier is shown in Figure 18.1(c). In this case we see a tuned circuit at the input and output ports of the amplifier stage (see also Figures 18.2 and 18.3). If we want to increase the bandwidth of the stage, it is possible to "stagger-tune" the input and output tanks. That is to say that we tune them to slightly different frequencies. In Figure 18.1(c) the two tanks are tuned to $F1$ and $F2$, respectively. Each tank exhibits the normal bell-shaped resonance curve, but their frequency response domains overlap. This creates the dip in the middle of the curve, or double-humped curve, as it is sometimes called. The depth of the dip is usually specified as not more than 10 percent of the total amplitude. If the individual tanks are not overcoupled, and their resonant points are judiciously selected, then it becomes relatively easy to obtain 3-dB bandwidths on the order of 6 to 10 MHz. This technique is employed extensively in certain amplifier stages of the usual television receiver.

18.2 TUNED RF AMPLIFIERS

Most radio frequency amplifiers are tuned to a specific frequency or narrow band of frequencies. There are two basic classes of tuned RF amplifier, small signal and power. Small-signal RF amplifiers are normally found in radio and television receivers, and in the low-level stages of certain types of radio transmitter.

The small-signal amplifier is normally operated in Class A mode. Examples of these circuits are shown in Figures 18.2 through 18.4. At low frequencies, from around 20 kHz to under 1 MHz, tuned circuits tend to be very narrow. At those frequencies it is fairly easy to achieve well-behaved, high-Q resonant tank circuits. At higher frequencies, though, coils become lower Q and are harder to manage. Capacitors will also become less than ideal at those frequencies. While the low-frequency tank circuit was happy with insulators such as paper, Bakelite, and plastics, the higher-frequency tank circuit finds them too lossy. As frequency increases, it is necessary to use ceramic, steatite, and certain highly specialized plastics as insulators.

One factor in the increased use of high, very high and ultrahigh frequencies (HF, VHF, and UHF, respectively) is the development of materials that would resonate at those wavelengths without presenting an excessive loss factor. In the 1930s few commercial stations operated above 25 MHz, and only a few amateur researchers dared go as high as 50 or 100 MHz. In fact, it was these amateurs who pioneered the world above 25 MHz (12 meters). But today commercial use is made of frequencies up into the "microwave" region—up to around 25 GHz (1 gigahertz = 1000 MHz).

The small-signal RF amplifier is usually Class A and may take the form shown in Figure 18.2. Bias to this stage is by the grid leak action of resistor *R*1 and capacitor *C*1. The input circuit is tuned by the LC tank circuit consisting of coil *L*2 and capacitor *C*2. This is a high-impedance tank, as befits the impedance situation of the vacuum-tube grid. If a low-impedance driver source is used, however, there would be a poor match, so a link couple is formed by making a transformer primary consisting of a few turns of wire. The output side of the RF amplifier is also tuned, this by *L*3/*C*3. The plate tank is bypassed around the power supply by capacitor *C*6. This places the tank essentially across the entire plate-to-cathode path of the tube, allowing a high-voltage swing. Since the vacuum tube being used is a pentode, there is little need for neutralization. The interelectrode capacitances do not affect the stability as much as they would in a triode or tetrode tube.

Figure 18.3 shows a bipolar transistor version of the small-signal RF amplifier. The base circuit is tuned by tank circuit *L*1/*C*1, but in this case the secondary is not tuned and the primary is tuned. This is due to the fact that the base input impedance of the transistor is small, so a step-down input transformer is required. The collector tuning is a little different, in that there are actually two tanks using a single inductance. The main tuning tank consists of capacitor *C*5 and inductor *L*3. This circuit is tuned to the same frequency as the input tank. Coil *L*3 is also used in conjunction with capacitor *C*4 in a parallel resonant tank. This combination is a kind of wavetrap that is used to suppress unwanted nearby signals. There might be a case where a local source of interference is close enough in frequency to the desired frequency that it will override the weaker, but wanted, signal. A parallel resonant wavetrap such as *L*3/*C*4 attenuates signals at its resonant frequency, so this will reduce the amplitude of the unwanted signal.

The circuit in Figure 18.4 is a bipolar transistor, common-base, RF amplifier that is popular in equipment designed to operate at frequencies over about 100 MHz or so. The input tank circuit actually uses two separate capacitances. *C*3 is a variable capacitor that is used to trim the tank

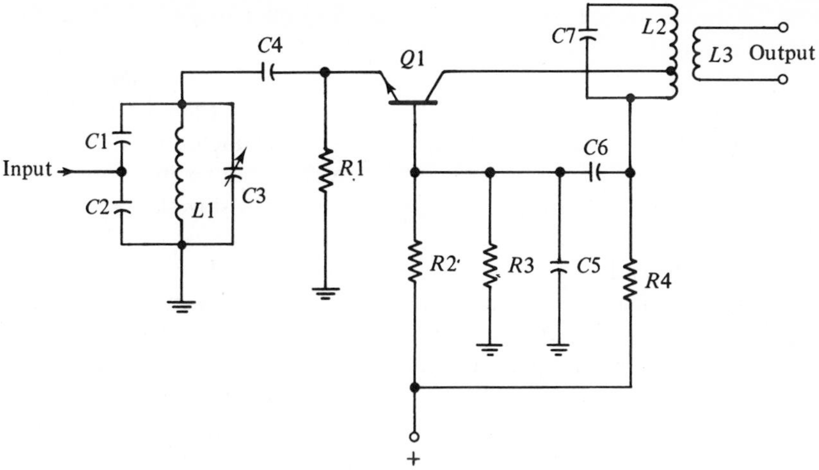

Figure 18.4 Grounded-base tuned RF amplifier.

frequency to optimum. Capacitors *C*1 and *C*2 are used to match the impedance of the input source. They form a voltage divider circuit that matches the impedance of the tank circuit to that of the antenna or other driving source.

The output tank circuit in Figure 18.4 is similar to those in other circuits, except that the transistor collector is connected to a low-impedance tap on the coil, rather than to one end, as has been the case previously. This matches the low impedance of the transistor's collector. The interelectrode capacitance of the grounded base amplifier, like that of the grounded grid or grounded gate configurations, is minimized so that neutralization is not usually required.

18.3 NEUTRALIZATION TECHNIQUES

At various points in our discussions we have used the term *neutralization*. You are probably asking just what it is and why it seems so necessary. The interelectrode and stray capacitances are sometimes sufficient to cause regeneration (positive feedback) that leads to oscillation and instability of the stage. The frequency of the oscillation is normally close to the frequency of the RF amplifier, but it may also be at some remote and seemingly unrelated frequency. In the latter case it is called a "parasitic oscillation." In *all* cases, however, these spurious signals interfere with normal operation and must be suppressed. In some instances, especially when the affected stage is in a radio transmitter or is the first RF amplifier in a receiver, the spurious signal is radiated into the air and may cause severe interference with other stations.

There are various techniques for ridding ourselves of these oscillations. We have discussed the use of grounded grid (or base or gate) amplifiers and pentode vacuum tubes. But tubes have all but faded from the scene, and it is not always best to try operating a bipolar or field effect transistor in the common-base or common-gate configurations. Also, we would not want to operate triode or tetrode vacuum tubes in the common-cathode configuration without some means of suppressing the regenerative effect, because the stage will operate as a TPTG oscillator. The answer lies in *neutralizing* the effects of the interelectrode capacitances.

All neutralization circuits involve the creation of some degenerative, or "negative," feedback to counteract the positive feedback through the interelectrode capacitances. The simplest type of neutralization is the "losser resistor." This is a noninductive, carbon-composition resistor placed in series with the grid connection of the vacuum tube. The losser resistor develops a degenerative voltage drop that effectively counteracts much of the regenerative energy that is coupled into the grid circuit from the plate circuit. In many cases this loss is sufficient to prevent oscillation.

When the losser resistor is not enough, then some other technique must be employed. Among those commonly found are the plate (or "Hazeltine"), grid (or "Rice"), inductive, and direct methods.

The Hazeltine or plate circuit is shown in Figure 18.5. This circuit is also called the "bridge neutralization" method in some texts. Recall that the problem is the grid-to-plate capacitance (C_{gp}) feeding back a portion of the plate energy to the grid. The purpose of any neutralization scheme is to feed back another signal voltage that is of opposite polarity so that the positive and negative feedback voltages effectively null (cancel) each other. This is accomplished by neutralization capacitor C_n and the tapped plate inductor $L1$. As far as the plate signal is concerned, the whole of $L1$

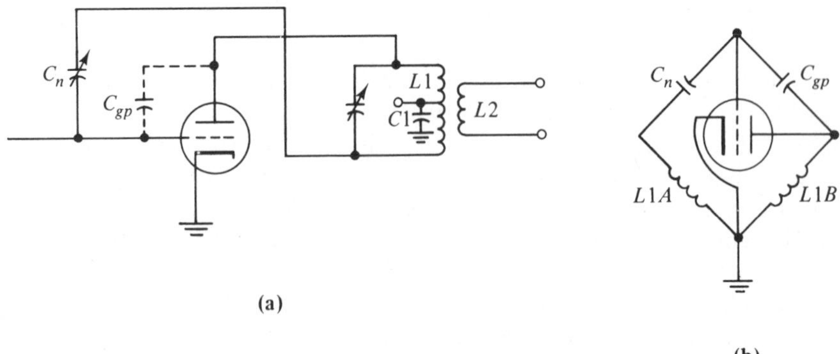

Figure 18.5 Hazeltine neutralization: (a) actual circuit and (b) equivalent circuit.

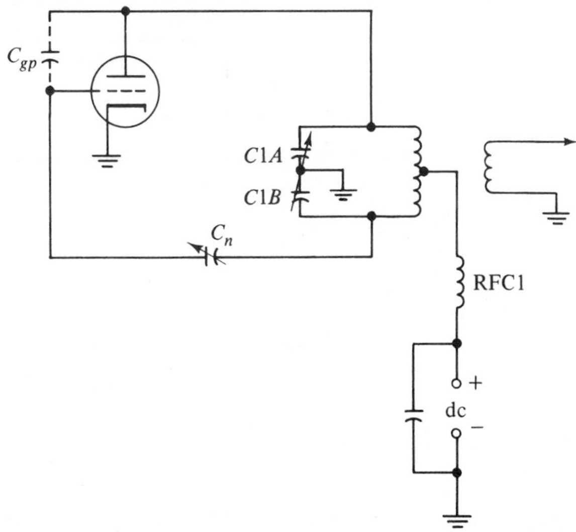

Figure 18.6 Alternate Hazeltine circuit uses tapped tank capacitor instead of the tapped coil of the previous example to establish the zero RF potential reference.

is used to tune the tank to resonance, but the tap on $L1$ is bypassed to ground for RF through power supply decoupling capacitor $C1$. This places the center tap of $L1$ at an RF potential of 0 V. In that case the potentials at the opposite ends of the coil have equal amplitudes but opposite phase relationships. Capacitance C_{gp} feeds back the RF voltage at the plate end of the coil to the grid. Similarly, neutralization capacitor C_n feeds back equal, but oppositely phased, signal voltage from the other end of $L1$. This signal cancels the regenerative feedback signal through C_{gp}, provided that $C_n = C_{gp}$. The equivalent circuit is shown in Figure 18.5(b), and this more clearly illustrates why this is called a "bridge neutralization" technique.

A variation on the Hazeltine circuit is shown in Figure 18.6. Here we have a two-section variable capacitor resonating coil $L1$. The tap on $L1$ is connected to an RF choke ($RFC1$), so it is *not* at an RF potential of 0 V. The type of capacitor used is a "split stator," and is equivalent to having two identical variable capacitors ganged to the same shaft. The junction between the two capacitors is connected to the rotor plates and is grounded. This places the rotor plates at a potential of 0 V (RF). Again we have a neutralization capacitance equal to the interelectrode capacitance of the tube so that the degenerative signal will cancel out the regenerative.

An example of grid or "Rice" neutralization is shown in Figure 18.7.

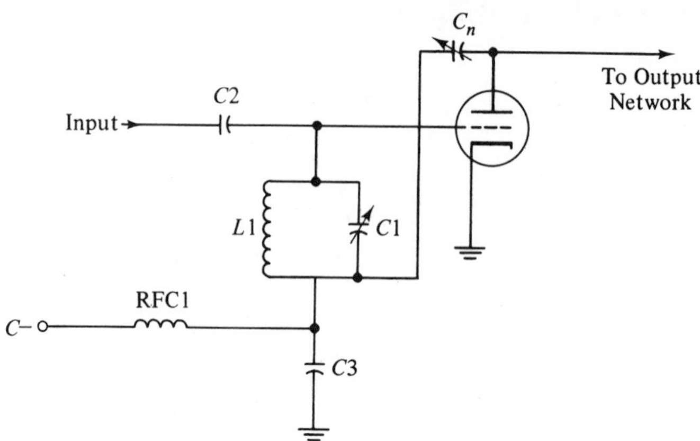

Figure 18.7 The grid neutralization, or "Rice" circuit.

There are actually two variations on the grid neutralization circuit. In one there is a tapped grid inductor; it operates in much the same manner as the Hazeltine circuit described above. The version shown in Figure 18.7, however, does not use a tapped coil, but is capacitive. This circuit is popular in low-power, high-frequency radio transmitters, such as those using the type 6146 vacuum tube. In some amateur radio transmitters using this tube the neutralization capacitance is merely a short length of solid hook-up wire (3–5 cm in length) passed through the chassis. One end is connected to the grid tank, while the other is placed close to the vacuum tube, parallel to the anode structure.

Inductive neutralization is shown in Figure 18.8. In this circuit there are a few turns of wire around each tank coil to form a small step-down transformer. The respective senses of these coils are opposite, so the feedback voltage has the opposite phase as the interelectrode capacitance voltage, which will produce the desired cancellation. These coils may be either fixed or variable. In the latter case there is sometimes a mechanical method for varying the physical coupling between either tank coil and its feedback link.

Direct neutralization uses an inductance connected between the plate and the grid. In actual circuits, there is a capacitor in series with the inductor to prevent the high dc plate potential from getting onto, and affecting, the grid. It is necessary that this capacitor have a relatively high value so that it will not resonate at any frequency that is near the stage's operating frequency. Its only purpose is to block dc, not to tune the coil to any specific frequency. We shall cover the procedures for neutralizing the RF power amplifier in the chapter on radio transmitters and their adjustment.

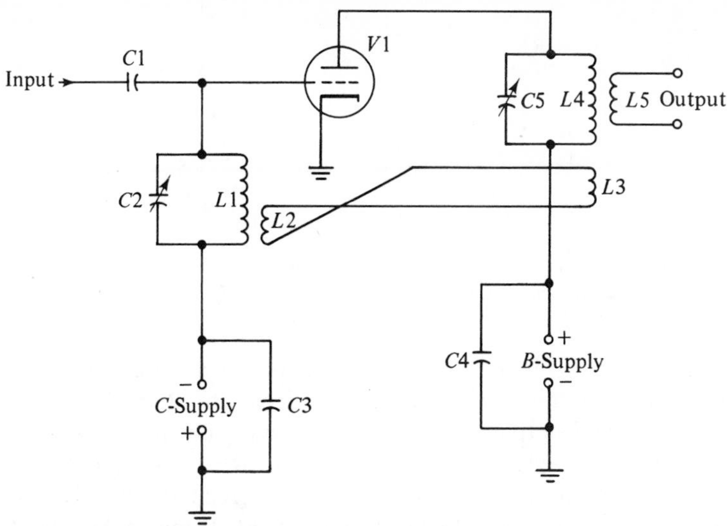

Figure 18.8 Inductive neutralization.

18.4 RF POWER AMPLIFIERS

Although most small-signal RF amplifiers are operated in the class A mode, this is not the case for power amplifiers. Single-ended RF power amplifiers are almost universally Class C, while push-pull types are either Class B or Class AB. There are actually two different breeds of RF power amplifier, linear and nonlinear. The linear amplifier is never operated in Class C.

Those power amplifiers that are operated Class C are used in radiotelegraph (CW) transmitters, or in those classes of radiotelephone transmitter that use either frequency modulation or high-level amplitude modulation. (Plate modulation of the final stage is generally considered to be most effective.) The Class C vacuum tube amplifier is usually operated with a bias that is two to five times cutoff, and is driven with a high-amplitude signal.

Examples of solid-state power amplifiers are shown in Figures 18.9 and 18.10. In the example of Figure 18.9 we have a single-ended transistor circuit that should seem familiar. Since this is not a Class A stage, there is no bias resistor network. In some cases the input transformer secondary, *L*2, would be connected directly to the base of the transistor, but in this case a series resistor is added. The voltage drop through this resistor is of a polarity that slightly reverse-biases the transistor, forcing it to operate Class C.

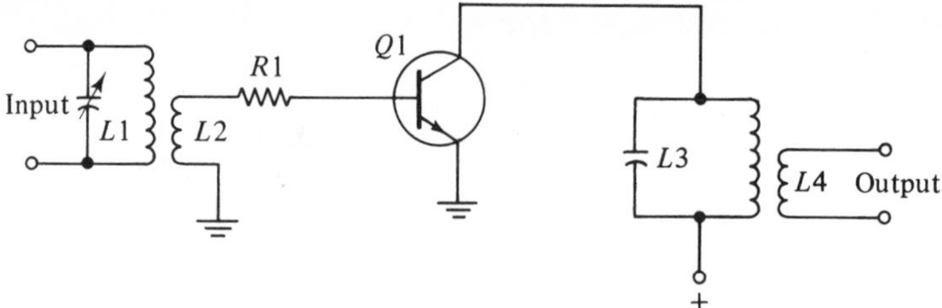

Figure 18.9 Transistor RF power amplifier uses a resistor in series with the base signal circuit to develop bias.

The circuit in Figure 18.10 is a VHF power amplifier using a single transistor such as the 2N6084 or a type from the 2N5590-series. Note that the input and output networks are considerably more complex than they were in the previous example. Also, the RF choke (*RFC*1) in the base circuit is a little unusual. In this type of circuit the "choke" is actually several tiny cylindrical ferrite beads threaded onto a length of #14 solid wire. At VHF and UHF frequencies such beads act as an RF choke, yet are free of the problems of wirewound chokes at those frequencies. This type of power amplifier is very representative of the power amplifier stages found in land and marine mobile VHF-FM radiotelephone transmitters, and it will probably be seen in other types of equipment as well in the very near future.

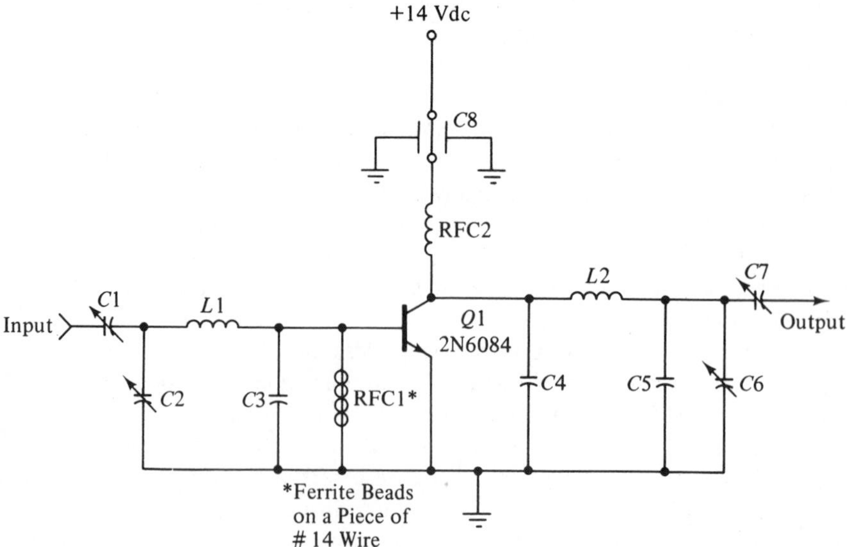

Figure 18.10 Typical VHF transistor power amplifier for mobile communications service.

Solid-state power amplifiers operated in the high-frequency and lower VHF ranges are often linear designs, and may not be tuned to any specific frequency, but rather are broadbanded. A great deal of progress has been made over the past few years in the design of broadband, toroid transformers that are able to handle significant amounts of power in the 1–30-MHz range. It is often the case that the only tuned circuits in these amplifiers are low-pass filters in the output that are needed to keep harmonics caused by any possible nonlinearity from radiating into the air.

Although solid-state power amplifiers are gaining fast, the vacuum tube is still the device of choice at high-power levels. We shall, however, in all probability see transistor designs improve at the high-power end of the power range. Only a few years ago transistors were useful only in power amplifiers that generated less than 10 W of RF power. Today, there are many amplifiers in production, not just in the laboratory, that produce power output levels in the 100–500-W range. At least one is in existence that produces power in the kilowatt range. The vacuum tube is, however, still "king" in the above-500-W range.

Figure 18.11 shows a popular vacuum-tube power-amplifier design built around the grounded-grid principle. A family of triodes such as the older 811A and newer types such as the 3-500Z, 3-1000Z, etc. are especially suited to zero-bias grounded-grid operation. The input and output

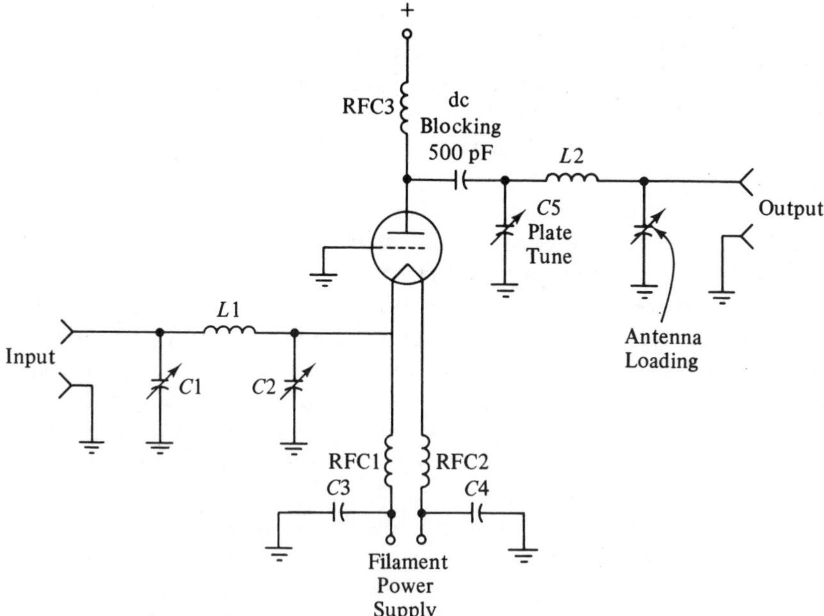

Figure 18.11 Grounded-grid RF power amplifier.

tank circuits are of a type known as "pi-networks." This circuit is used to match a high-impedance load, such as the plate resistance of a vacuum tube, to a low-impedance load, such as a 50-Ω antenna. In the case of the output network, the first capacitor, *C*5, is used to resonate the network to the frequency of the current pulses in the plate of the amplifier tube. The second capacitor (*C*6) is used to adjust the coupling between the amplifier and its load. The RF choke is used to pass dc from the power supply, yet at the same time prevent the RF signal pulses at the plate from entering the supply lines. Similarly, the two chokes in the filament circuit are used to keep RF drive signal from getting into the filament supply. Optimum performance occurs when these chokes are wound on the same core, so *RFC*1 and *RFC*2 are, therefore, usually bifilar wound.

Tuning a power amplifier is relatively simple. The pi-network, and other parallel resonant tanks, present a high impedance at the resonant frequency. Since the dc plate current pulses in this amplifier class are at this frequency, we find that little current flows when the tank is tuned to the same frequency as the pulses. Tuning, then, is done with a milliammeter in the dc plate supply. When capacitor *C*5 is tuned to resonance, the reading on the meter will be minimum.

The plate tuning capacitor must be adjusted initially with the coupling capacitor adjusted to its loosest (lowest capacitance) position. After the initial dipping of the plate current with the plate tuning capacitor (*C*5), the capacitance of loading capacitor C6 is adjusted to a slightly higher value. This increases the coupling between the final amplifier tube and the load, and this necessitates the readjustment of *C*5 to a new minimum plate current. This minimum will be slightly higher than the first minimum. The load-dip procedure is repeated until the plate current is approximately 75–80 percent of its off-resonance (maximum) value. This figure is given with the assumption (not always valid, but generally so) that it is within the tube's operating characteristic. Also, it is very important that the loading procedure be done in small steps. When the loading capacitor is adjusted to increase the plate current, make it a small adjustment.

An alternative method used in some low-power tube and most solid-state transmitters is to use an RF output meter and then tune for maximum output. It must be pointed out that this method is safe only when the maximum safe output level for that transmitter is known and can be recognized. Otherwise, someone may attempt to adjust the transmitter until no further output is obtained. Such a procedure could easily damage the transmitter, so it must be avoided. If the coupling is adjusted until it is too tight, then there will be no dip noted, or possibly a very broad dip, in the plate current reading.

The dc power input to the plate of a vacuum-tube amplifier is given by the product of the plate current in amperes and the plate-to-cathode voltage. The overall efficiency is the relationship

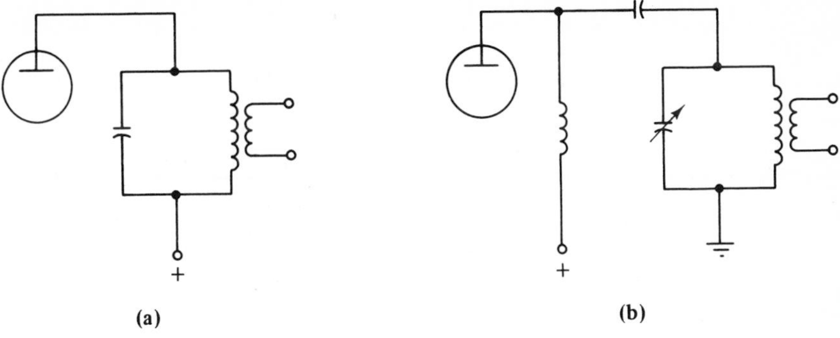

Figure 18.12 (a) Series-feed and (b) shunt-feed.

$$\text{Eff}(\%) = \frac{\text{RF power output}}{\text{dc power input}} \times 100 \qquad (18\text{-}3)$$

The difference between the dc power consumed from the power supply and the RF power delivered to the load is dissipated in the form of heat in the plate structure of the tube, or in the collector of a transistor. It is critical that his figure be less than the heat dissipation rating of the tube or transistor being used; otherwise destruction of the device can be expected.

18.5 POWER FEED SYSTEMS

There are two recognized methods for applying dc power to the amplifier stage. These are illustrated in Figure 18.12. The method shown in Figure 18.12(a) is called *series-feed,* while that in Figure 18.12(b) is called *shunt-feed,* or *parallel-feed.* The method used for determining which is being used in any particular case, even when the tank circuit does not take the form shown here, is to note whether the dc plate current flows through the tank inductor. In a series-fed system the dc plate current *does* flow through the inductor, but in a shunt-fed system it does not.

18.6 COUPLING METHODS

It is very rare to find tubes or transistors operated directly into their respective loads without some form of coupling. Although there are a few transistors operating in the common collector (emitter follower) configuration that require little or no impedance matching, it is usually the case that some sort of tuning will be required. Several of the possible variations in coupling networks for RF amplifiers are shown in Figure 18.13.

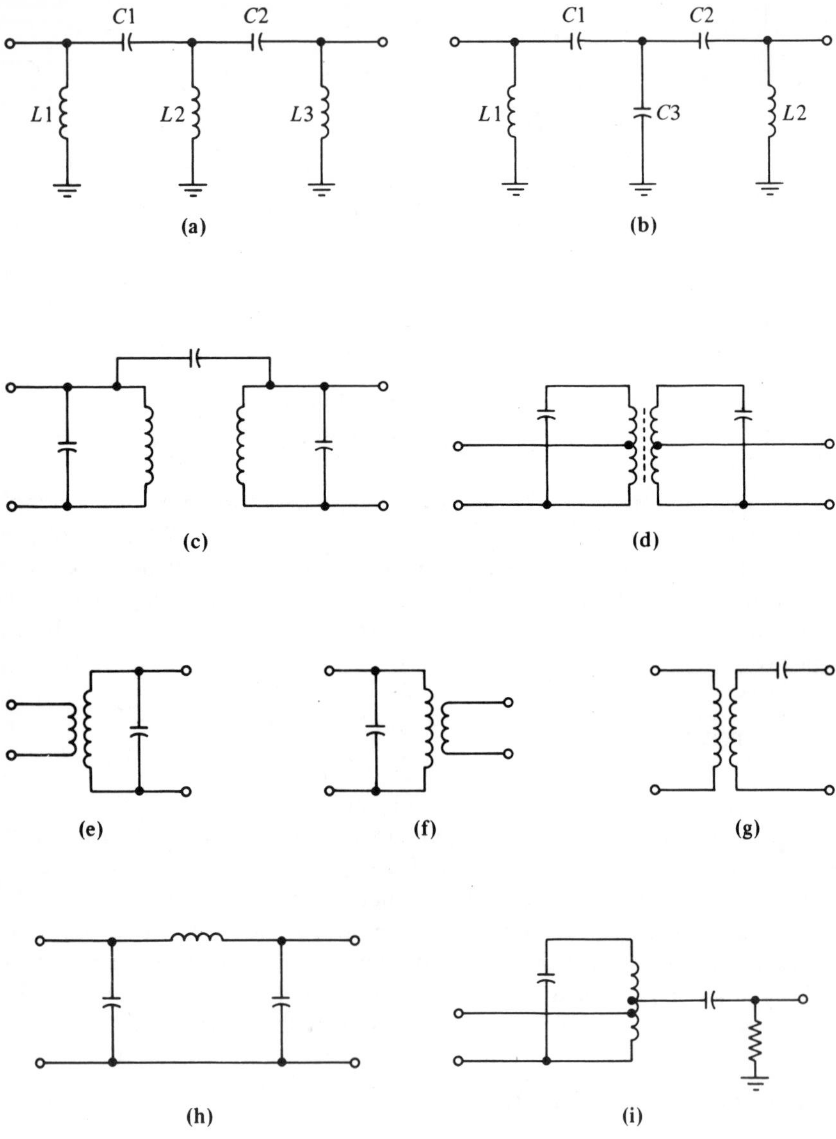

Figure 18.13 RF amplifier coupling circuits.

The two coupling circuits in Figures 18.13(a) and 18.13(b) are actually variations on the same idea. In both cases we develop the signal across a mutual reactance that is part of both input and output circuits. In the case of Figure 18.13(a) the input tank consists of $L1/C1$, and the output tank is $L2/C2$. Coil $L2$ is a small-value inductance that is part of both tank circuits and serves to transfer energy between them. In the circuit of Figure 18.13(b) this same function is performed by capacitor $C3$.

The circuits in Figures 18.13(c) through 18.13(h) are related to each other. In the case of Figure 18.13(c) we have a standard tuned transformer modified by a coupling capacitor. In the standard circuit there is no capacitor, and the bandwidth of the circuit depends almost entirely upon the coefficient of coupling between the primary tank coil and the secondary tank coil. The capacitor serves to make the tuned transformer a little more broadbanded.

In Figure 18.13(d) we see the standard tuned transformer, in which the input and output connections are made to taps on the inductor. This is done to match lower impedance levels, while the level of impedance in the tank is retained. This method is seen in almost all transistor RF small-signal amplifiers and in certain power amplifiers. A variation on this theme is to use a tapped resonating capacitor instead of a tapped inductance. In general, the tapped inductor is used in series-feed circuits and the tapped capacitor is used in parallel-fed applications.

The circuits in Figure 18.13(e) and 18.13(f) use untuned windings for either primary or secondary. The other winding in each case *is* tuned, however. In many cases this is the only type of tuned circuit, but in others a pair of tanks is connected together in such a way that their untuned links are in parallel. This would be the circuit that would be formed if the secondary of Figure 18.13(f) were used to drive the primary of Figure 18.13(e).

A minor variation is shown in Figure 18.13(g). Here we have a tuned transformer in which the secondary is series-resonant and the primary is parallel resonant. It is used mostly where it is necessary to prevent dc from entering the winding. A related circuit is that of Figure 18.13(h), in which only one tank is used and the capacitor is connected to a tap on the coil that best matches the load impedance. The other tap on the inductor is used to match the input circuit.

Coupling should be variable wherever the RF amplifier is to feed a load that may vary. This is the case of the amplifier stage that feeds the final amplifier or antenna in many radio transmitters. The coupling should also vary if it is to be used as a method for varying the bandwidth of the circuit. In the case of the RF transformer designs it is necessary to physically move the primary and/or secondary windings of the coil with respect to each other.

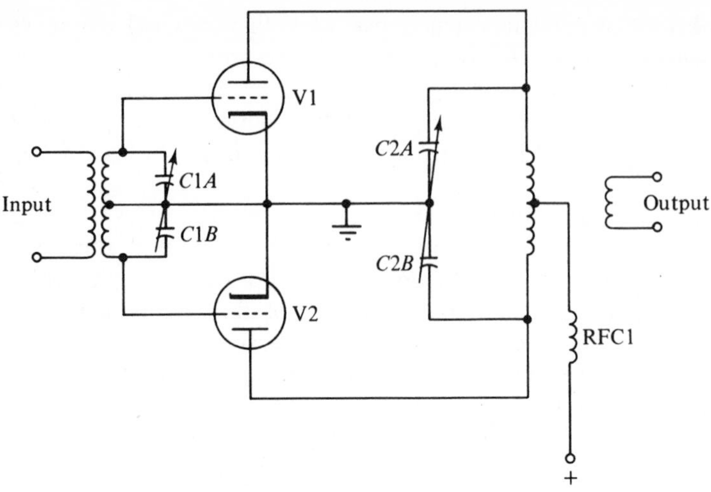

Figure 18.14 Push-pull RF power amplifier.

18.7 PUSH-PULL RF POWER AMPLIFIERS

The only way to make an RF amplifier that is both linear and reasonably efficient is to use the push-pull configuration, an example of which is shown in Figure 18.14. If a single-ended amplifier stage is to be operated in a linear manner, then it must operate Class A, and that limits its maximum efficiency to around 30–45 percent. The heat generated by this type of amplifier is high and must be dissipated in some manner or damage to the amplifier may result. The input and output tank circuits both use tapped inductors and tapped capacitors, although in some cases the input capacitor is not tapped. Again, as in neutralization circuits, a split-stator variable capacitor is used in this application. Most RF power amplifiers are Class B, Class AB_1, or Class AB_2—and these must be push-pull.

PROBLEMS

1. A ______ vacuum-tube RF amplifier may not require neutralization, even though the tube is a triode or tetrode.
2. The Miller effect can be described mathematically as ________.
3. If the grid-cathode capacitance is 22 pF and the grid-plate capacitance is 152 pF, what is the effective input capacitance? (The gain is 200.)
4. Stray magnetic fields are reduced when tank circuit inductors are wound on a ______ form.

5. A wideband RF voltage amplifier is RC coupled, but may use _______ coils to enhance high-frequency response.
6. _______ and _______ are used as high-frequency insulators.
7. _________ tuning is sometimes used in wideband, bandpass amplifiers.
8. Most small-signal RF amplifiers operate in Class _______.
9. _______ vacuum tubes frequently operate as RF amplifiers without neutralization.
10. All neutralization methods are essentially _______ feedback circuits, and are used to counteract the effects of ___________.
11. A _______ resistor is a simple and often effective means of neutralization.
12. Plate neutralization is also called the _______ circuit.
13. Grid neutralization is also called the _______ circuit.
14. In most neutralization circuits $C_n =$ _______.
15. Two other neutralization methods are the _______ and _______.
16. Most radiotelegraph and FM-radiotelephone transmitters use Class _______ amplifiers in the final stage.
17. Class-C RF power amplifiers are normally biased_______ to _______ times cutoff.
18. In some VHF/UHF RF amplifiers _______ are used as RF chokes.
19. An RF final amplifier has a parallel resonant plate tank. At resonance, I_p is _______.
20. In a properly tuned RF power amplifier employing a pi-network plate tank, I_p will usually be _______ percent to _______ percent of its off-resonance value.
21. An RF amplifier has 1000 VDC applied to the anode. When it is properly tuned, $I_p = 100$ mA. An RF watt-meter shows that it is delivering 60 W to the antenna. What is the percentage of efficiency?
22. In Question 19, how much heat is dissipated in the tube anode?
23. In _______-feed RF power amplifiers the dc plate current flows through the tank inductor.
24. What are some amplifier classes that might be found in linear, push-pull, RF amplifier service?

19
Amplitude Modulation and Single Sideband

A radio carrier signal is of little use unless it conveys some form of information. Although its mere existence or nonexistence is technically considered to be "information," this is hardly useful in the broader context of communication. "Modulation" is the variation of some property of the radio carrier (i.e., amplitude, frequency, or phase) in a manner that conveys information. This definition is also occasionally called the superposition of "intelligence" on the carrier.

It is relatively easy to modulate the amplitude, frequency, or phase of an RF carrier with an audio signal. In this chapter we shall consider ordinary amplitude modulation and some more efficient variations called "double sideband suppressed carrier" (DSBSC) and "single sideband suppressed carrier" (SSBSC). Incidentally, it is common to hear these referred to as simply "DSB" and "SSB," respectively. In the next chapter we shall consider both basic forms of angular modulation, frequency (FM), and phase (PM).

19.1 THE MODULATION CLASSIFICATION SYSTEM

The Federal Communications Commission (F.C.C.) and the communications engineering profession have adopted a classification system for specifying radio modulation systems. Each class is assigned an alphanumeric code by which is it designated. Table 19.1 gives some of the more common classes.

Table 19.1

Designation	*Type of Modulation*
AØ	Unmodulated carrier
A1	Radiotelegraphy, on-off CW
A2	Tone modulated (AM) radiotelegraphy
A3	Full amplitude modulation with carrier and both sidebands
A3a	AM, reduced carrier but both sidebands
A3j	SSBSC
A3h	SSB, full carrier

Table 19.1 (cont.)

A3b	Independent sideband, AM
A4	Slow scan television
A5C	Normal television video, vestigial sideband (AM)
F1	Frequency shift keyed telegraphy
F2	FM tone telegraphy
F3	Radiotelephone, FM or PM
F4	FM facsimile
F5	TV sound (FM)
PØ	Pulsed radar

19.2 SIMPLE AMPLITUDE MODULATION

In ordinary amplitude modulation (A3) an audio modulating signal is superimposed on a radio frequency carrier. This situation is shown in Figure 19.1, where the RF signal, audio signal, and the modulated RF carrier are drawn on a common time scale.

The audio modulating signal will be added to the RF signal in such

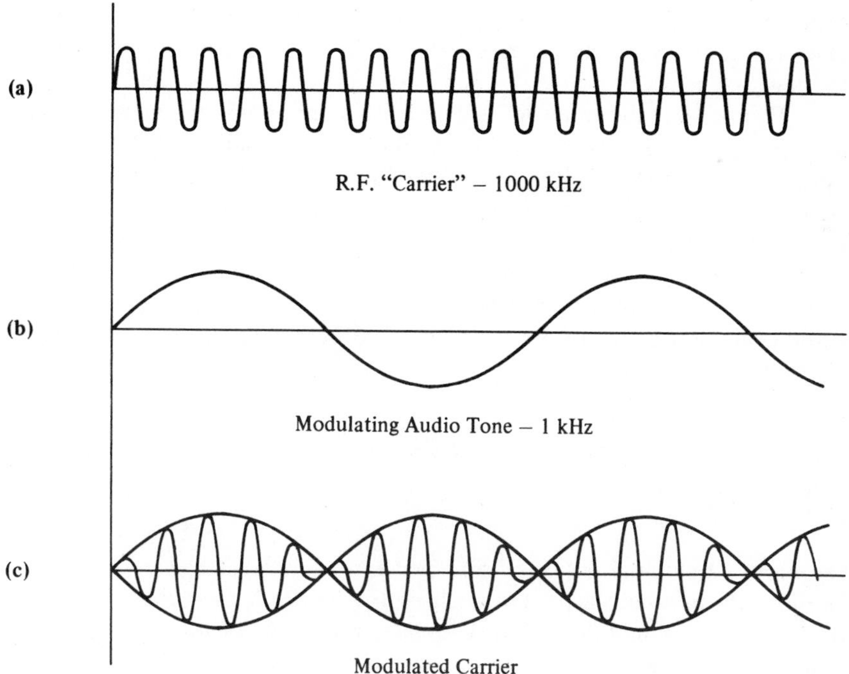

Figure 19.1 Amplitude modulation waveforms.

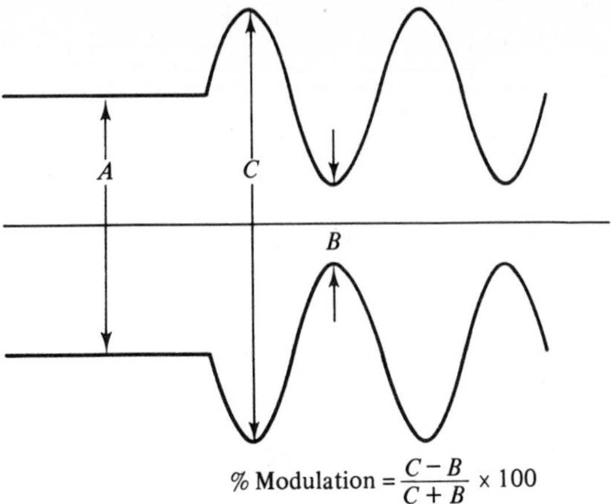

Figure 19.2 The modulated waveform showing method for determining percentage modulation.

a way that the two signals algebraically add. At 100 percent modulation the positive peaks of the audio causes the amplitude of the RF carrier [Figure 19.1(a)] to double [Figure 19.1(c)], whereas on negative audio peaks the RF carrier drops to zero amplitude. At lesser modulation percentages the addition of the two waves is less than complete, so the carrier does not quite double on positive audio peaks, nor does it drop to zero on the negative peaks.

Figure 19.2 shows an RF carrier that is amplitude-modulated by an audio sine wave. In our discussions in this text we shall obey the convention of considering only the sine wave case, because it is, at once, both simpler and representative of the situation when speech or other complex waveforms are applied.

Section A of the waveform in Figure 19.2 represents the amplitude of the unmodulated carrier. Section C shows the effect of the positive audio peak, and B that of the negative audio peak voltage. The percentage of modulation is given by

$$\text{Percentage of modulation} = \frac{C - B}{C + B} \times 100 \qquad (19\text{-}1)$$

Example. Examination of a sine wave modulated RF carrier on an oscilloscope produces a pattern such as Figure 19-2, in which amplitude $B = 0$, and the amplitude of C is greater than that of A. Find the percentage of modulation.

From Eq. (19-1)

$$\text{Percentage of modulation} = \frac{C - B}{C + B} \times 100$$

$$\text{Percentage of modulation} = \frac{1 - 0}{1 + 0} \times 100$$

$$\text{Percentage of modulation} = 100\%$$

Example. When the audio signal in the previous example is reduced, it is found that amplitude C is twice as large as B. In this case we can say that $C = 1, B = ½$. Find the percentage of modulation.

$$\text{Percentage of modulation} = \frac{C - B}{C + B} \times 100$$

$$\text{Percentage of modulation} = \frac{1 - 0.5}{1 + 0.5} \times 100$$

$$\text{Percentage of modulation} = \frac{0.5}{1.5} \times 100$$

$$\text{Percentage of modulation} = 33\%$$

Sidebands. Amplitude modulation is a mixing process in which heterodyning plays a big part. The frequencies produced in the output are the modulating audio frequency (F_{af}), radio carrier frequency (F_{rf}), and the sum and difference frequencies ($F_{rf} \pm F_{af}$). Since the output circuit contains an RF tuned tank circuit, only F_{rf} and the sum/difference frequencies will pass. The audio signal is filtered out and rejected.

The output spectrum of a standard amplitude-modulated transmitter operating on a carrier frequency of 1000 kHz is shown in Figure 19.3. Since the audio signal is very much lower than the RF signal, the sidebands ($F_{rf} \pm F_{af}$) are close enough to the carrier to pass through the output tank circuit. The upper sideband (USB) is the sum frequency ($F_{rf} + F_{af}$), while the difference frequency ($F_{rf} - F_{af}$) is the lower sideband (LSB).

The case shown in Figure 19.3 represents a 1000-Hz audio signal modulating a 1000-kHz radio signal. The upper sideband is, then, found on a frequency of (1000 kHz + 1 kHz) or 1001 kHz. The lower sideband appears at (1000 kHz – 1 kHz) or 999 kHz. This signal occupies a bandwidth of the difference between upper and lower sideband limits, or 1001 – 999 = 2 kHz. We can claim, then, that the bandwidth of the

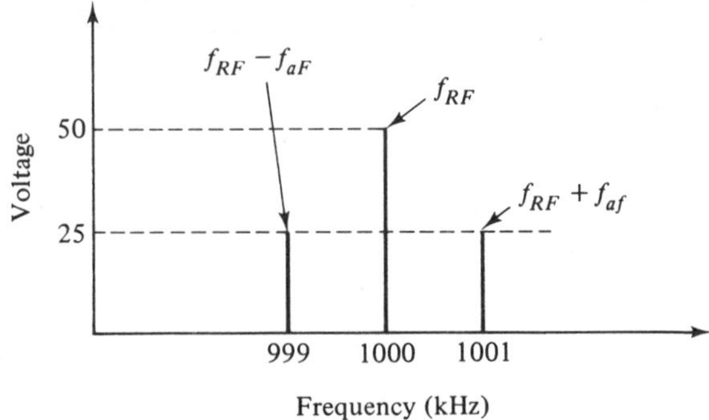

Figure 19.3 Generation of sidebands in AM.

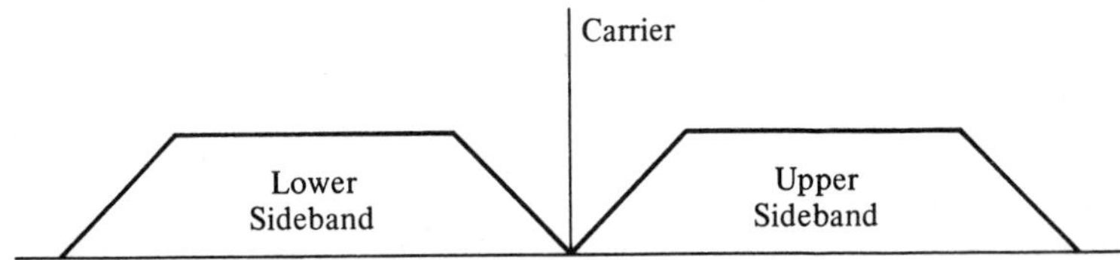

Figure 19.4 Relationship of the sidebands to the carrier when complex modulating waveforms such as speech or music are used.

regular A3 amplitude-modulated signal is *twice* the frequency of the modulating audio signal.

Speech or music waveforms are a very complex mixture of assorted sine waves at different frequencies. Even a seeming monotone voice is actually such a waveform, in which the timbre or pitch is determined by the number and relative strengths of the constituent frequencies. This is why a note played on one instrument sounds different from the same note played on a different instrument. An "A above middle C," for example, sounds different when played on a piano than when played on a trombone.

If such a waveform is used to modulate a radio signal, there will be one sideband pair generated for each frequency present in the audio signal. This creates sidebands that cover a spectrum centered about the carrier (see Figure 19.4). The total bandwidth of this spectrum is *twice* the highest modulating frequency, or

$$\text{B.W.} = 2F_{(\text{af}-\text{max})} \tag{19-2}$$

Example. Find the bandwidth that must be allowed for an amplitude-modulated broadcast transmitter in which the highest modulating frequency allowed by the regulations is 5000 Hz.

$$\text{B.W.} = 2F_{\text{max}}$$

$$\text{B.W.} = (2)(5000\ \text{Hz})$$

$$\text{B.W.} = 10{,}000\ \text{Hz} = 10\ \text{kHz}$$

19.3 TYPES OF AMPLITUDE MODULATION

Variation of an RF carrier by an AF signal requires that the RF power be changed in a manner proportional to the amplitude of the audio signal. Figure 19.5 shows a method by which this may be accomplished. Vacuum tube *V*1 is the RF power amplifier stage. The modulated stage may be operated Class C for best efficiency. In most cases the modulated RF amplifier is also the final amplifier; that is, it is the stage feeding power directly to the antenna. If it is *not* the final amplifier, then all RF power amplifier stages following the modulated stage must be linear amplifiers.

In the circuit of Figure 19.5 we have an example of *plate* modulation. Although other elements of the vacuum tube may be modulated (see Figure 19.6), plate modulation is usually considered most effective.

Most of the components used in this stage are the same as those

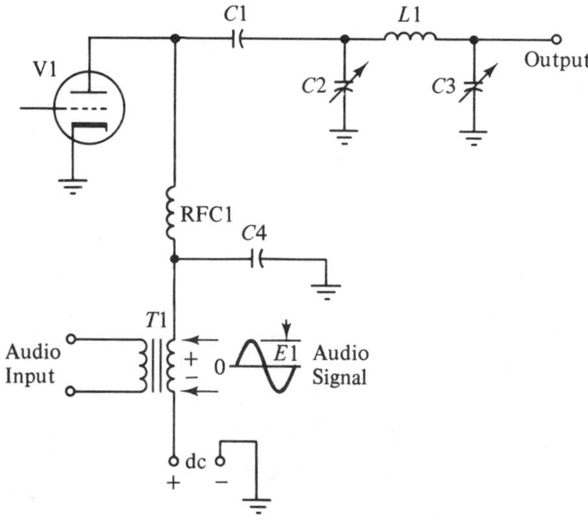

Figure 19.5 Plate modulation.

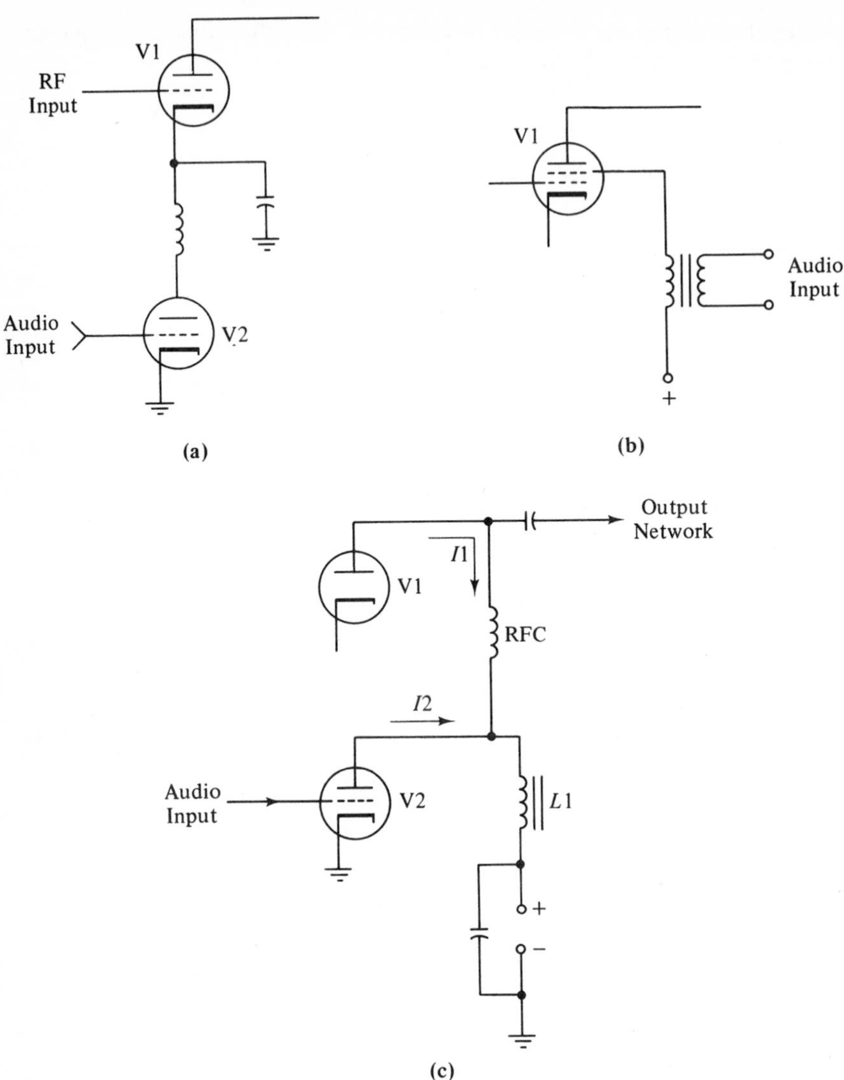

Figure 19.6 (a) Cathode or series modulation, (b) screen modulation and (c) Heising or constant current modulation.

found in any RF power amplifier stage. *C*2/*C*3/*L*1, for example, form a pi-network output tank, while *C*1 is used to prevent high-voltage dc on the plate of *V*1 from appearing at the output. RF choke *RFC*1 is used to prevent RF signal from the plate getting into the power supply. Capacitor *C*4 is for decoupling any residual RF that passes through the RFC. This makes the L-section combination $C4/RFC1$ act like a low-pass filter that passes frequencies from dc through audio, but attenuates ac signals in the RF range.

Transformer $T1$ is called the "modulation transformer," and it is responsible for superimposing the audio signal onto the RF signal. The primary of this transformer is driven by an audio power amplifier. The purpose of $T1$ is mostly impedance matching between the plate resistance of the RF power amplifier and the audio source. The power level of the audio source has to be sufficient to create a certain peak voltage, given as $E1$ in Figure 19.5.

On positive audio peaks the audio voltage will add with the dc power supply voltage, so the actual voltage applied to the plate of $V1$ is their sum—$E_{dc} + E1$. On negative audio peaks the plate voltage on $V1$ will be their difference, or $E_{dc} - E1$. For 100 percent modulation by a symmetrical sine wave the value of $E1$ must be equal to E_{dc}. If this is true, then the plate voltage on $V1$ will exactly double at the positive audio peak and drop to zero on the negative audio peak.

A certain minimum amount of audio power is required to produce the desired voltage effects. At 100 percent modulation we can find this power from the familiar power equation $P = E^2/R$.

Example. A 100-W transmitter uses 750 VDC on the plate and a plate current of 133 mA. How much audio power is required for 100 percent modulation?

First find the plate resistance of the final amplifier tube.

$$R_p = E_{dc}/I_p$$

$$R_p = 750/0.133$$

$$R_p = 5600\ \Omega$$

The modulator must deliver a power level that will develop a peak voltage equal to E_{dc} across a 5600-Ω load. We can use the power equation to find the power required of the audio modulator.

$$P_{af} = E^2/R_p$$

where P_{af} is the audio power.
E is the rms voltage across the secondary of transformer $T1$.

$$E = 0.707E_{dc} = 0.707(750)$$

$$E = 530\text{ V}$$

so

$$P_{af} = (530)^2/5600$$

$$P_{af} = 280{,}900/5600$$

$$P_{af} = 50 \text{ W}$$

The peak power in the modulated envelope is four times the unmodulated power. Consider the situation on positive audio peaks at 100 percent modulation. When $E1 = E_{dc}$, the plate voltage will be $2E_{dc}$. Twice the plate voltage will draw twice the plate current (by Ohm's law), so by the normal power equation:

(A) $$\text{If } P_{\text{unmod}} = I_p \times E_{dc}$$

(B) $$\text{then } P_{\text{mod}} = (2I_p)(2E_{dc})$$

$$P_{\text{mod}} = 4I_pE_{dc}$$

Substituting (A) into (B), we obtain

$$P_{\text{mod}} = 4 \times P_{\text{unmod}} \tag{19-3}$$

Keep in mind, though, that this is *peak* power, not average power.

The audio power requirements can also be found from a simplified formula:

$$P_{af} = \tfrac{1}{2} m^2 P_{dc}$$

where P_{af} is the audio power in watts.
P_{dc} is the dc input power, in watts, drawn by the RF power amplifier.
m is the decimal expression of the desired modulation percentage (i.e., 0.5 for 50 percent, 1 for 100 percent, etc.).

Example. A transmitter has a dc input power of 450 W. How much power is needed to modulate the amplifier 75 percent?

$$P_{af} = \tfrac{1}{2}(0.75)^2(450)$$

$$P_{af} = 127 \text{ W}$$

Several other amplitude modulation circuits are shown in Figure 19.6. These are all considered less desirable than plate modulation, but are often used in low-cost transmitters for economic reasons.

The circuit shown in Figure 19.6(a) is called "cathode" or "series" modulation. Here we have an audio power amplifier tube connected with its plate-cathode path in series with the plate-cathode path of the RF power amplifier tube. An LC low-pass filter places the cathode of *V*1 at ground potential for RF signals, but maintains a high impedance to dc and audio frequency ac signals. For reasons that should be now obvious, this circuit is also called "series modulation."

Audio modulator tube *V*2 can be treated as an electronically variable resistor. It operates in Class A, and is driven by other Class A stages that are called either *audio drivers* or *audio preamplifiers*. Such stages are also known as speech amplifiers in radiotelephone transmitters. These stages pick up and amplify the tiny audio voltage variations produced by the microphone, phonograph cartridge, tape head, or other audio transducer.

Consider the case when a sine wave modulating signal is applied to the grid of vacuum tube *V*2. On positive alternations of the audio sine wave *V*2 conducts harder, so its plate resistance is lowered. Similarly, on negative audio peaks *V*2 conducts less, so its plate resistance increases. Although this resistance variation causes the plate current of *V*1 to vary, the positive and negative excursions are approximately equal, so the plate milliammeter will not vary or fluctuate during modulation.

Cathode modulation has the advantage of being low-cost, but it is not without drawbacks. Among these are lower overall RF efficiency compared with that attainable in plate modulation. Also, it is necessary to use approximately twice the dc plate potential that would be required if *V*1 were plate-modulated. In a cathode modulation scheme the plate voltage divides between the two tubes.

Any element of the vacuum tube will prove amenable to modulation under the correct set of circumstances. It is possible to use all three grids, as well as the plate and cathode, as the modulated element. In Figure 19.6(b) we see an example of screen grid (g2) modulation. Although variations exist, we have shown here a transformer version of the screen modulator. Note that the screen voltage and power levels tend to be less than those in the plate, so a screen modulation transformer is much smaller than a plate transformer.

Vacuum tube *V*1 is the Class C RF power amplifier. The secondary of the modulation transformer is in series with the screen grid $B+$ supply. In most cases, the $B+$ supply is lower than it would be normally if plate modulation had been used instead.

Both suppressor grid and control grid modulation are known, but are rarely used. Both types have the advantage of requiring very little power from the modulator. The control grid modulation method is also called *efficiency modulation,* because the efficiency of the RF amplifier varies with the amplitude of the modulating signal.

One last form of amplitude modulation is called the *Heising system,* or *constant current modulation system.* This is shown in Figure 19.6(c). Although Heising modulation is a variation on plate modulation, it is not as efficient, and cannot obtain full, 100 percent modulation. This circuit operates on the principle of current division. The dc plate currents of both *V*1 and *V*2 pass through the high-inductance series choke. The inductance of this choke tends to smooth out current variations; hence the current in *L*1 is always constant and is equal to $(I1 + I2)$.

Modulator tube *V*2 can be considered as a Class A amplifier functioning as an electronically variable resistor. The plate resistance of *V*1 varies with the audio waveform at its grid. When the input audio signal is positive, the plate resistance of *V*2 drops, increasing current *I*2. Since the total current is constant, an increase in *I*2 has to decrease current *I*1—having the effect of starving *V*1. Alternatively, on negative audio peaks the plate resistance increases, thereby reducing *I*1. This will, of course, cause an increase in *I*2, because we are dealing with a constant-current system.

19.4 MODULATION PROBLEMS

There are several difficulties associated with amplitude modulation systems. Perhaps the most critical is overmodulation, the bane of CBers using power microphones. If excessive modulating signal is used, then the RF amplifier tube may be cut off during part of the negative audio peak. Recall that the audio modulating voltage should be such that the plate potential on the RF amplifier tube drops to exactly zero at the negative audio peak. In that condition $E_{dc} - E1 = 0$. This is shown in Figure 19.7(a). If this is the case, then 100 percent modulation is obtained. But if the situation in the modulated stage more nearly resembles that in Figure 19.7(b), then overmodulation will result. In this case the peak audio voltage is greater than the dc plate potential, so the voltage on the plate will be negative during part of the negative alternation of *E*1. This will cut off the RF amplifier tube and create distortion.

An overmodulated AM transmitter generates spurious sideband frequencies called "splatter." These sidebands can and will interfere with stations on adjacent channels, so they are illegal. Some transmitters, especially recent-vintage CB transmitters, use a limiter circuit in the modulator to prevent the application of an audio signal capable of overmodulating the carrier.

In contrast to overmodulation and its attendant problems is undermodulation of transistorized RF power amplifiers and those vacuum-tube power amplifiers where a tetrode is used.

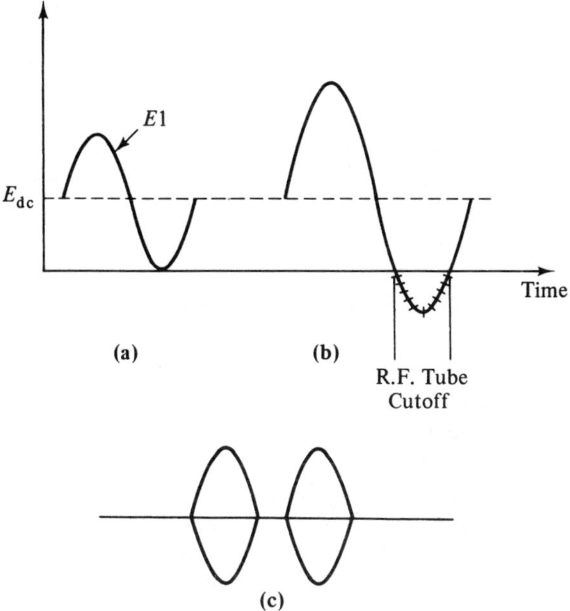

Figure 19.7 (a) Condition for 100% modulation, (b) condition for overmodulation and (c) modulated waveform for overmodulation.

It is very difficult to 100 percent-modulate a transistor RF power amplifier. In order to get modulation approaching 100 percent, it is often necessary to simultaneously modulate both the final RF amplifier and the driver stage in transistor transmitters. This requirement and problems associated with the use of bulky transformers make series modulation a desirable approach in transistorized equipment. The emitters of both final amplifier and driver transistors are connected to the collector of a modulator transistor.

In vacuum-tube stages using a tube with a screen grid, it is often found to be necessary to modulate the screen grid and the plate simultaneously. This can be accomplished through any of several means. In some cases the screen is self-modulated by an audio choke placed in series with the dc supply feeding the screen grid. Fluctuations in the screen current caused by the modulation process create a large audio frequency voltage drop across the series choke.

Another method for modulating the screen grid is to use a plate modulation transformer that has a tertiary winding. This is a second secondary winding, and it is placed in the circuit in series with the screen's dc supply. On one alternation of each audio sine wave the tertiary voltage is series-aiding, while on the other alternation it is series-opposing.

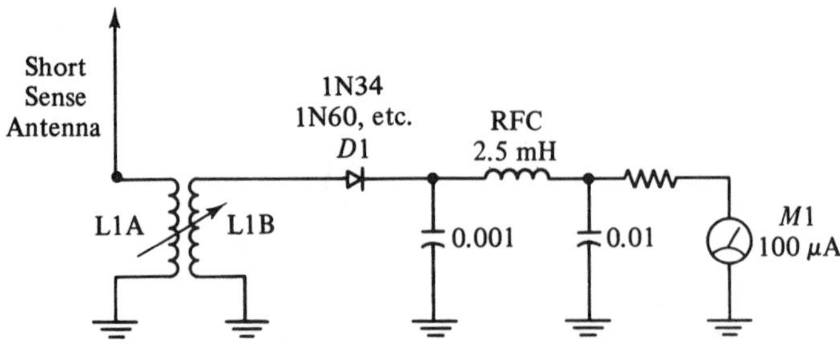

Figure 19.8 Carrier shift meter for detecting modulation symmetry.

Checking Modulation. The modulation on any radiotelephone transmitter should be checked regularly so that distortion and adjacent channel interference can be prevented.

Figure 19.8 shows a simple modulation monitor that may be home-brewed, and is useful for checking the modulated envelope for carrier shift —a phenomenon caused by having a dc component or other lack of symmetry in the modulating signal. Coil *L*1 is used as an RF pickup. Signal developed across this coil is rectified by diode *D*1. The low-pass filter component values are selected so that they produce no smoothing action at audio frequencies, yet will attenuate those signals at the RF carrier frequency. The coupling between *L*1 and the transmitter's RF tank is adjusted under modulated conditions to produce a convenient deflection on meter *M*1. Commercial carrier shift meters have a mark or "green zone" to which the meter is set. If the modulation is symmetrical and is free of distortion, then the meter will remain at the same point. If the modulating signal develops assymmetry, where the positive and negative halves of the sine wave are unequal, then the meter pointer will change position. The carrier shift meter is really not a good check of modulation purity or percentage, but it will show gross changes that could get the broadcaster in trouble with the F.C.C. It is, therefore, used extensively as a monitoring technique.

The best method for checking modulation is use of an oscilloscope. A small pickup coil dangled on the end of a short piece of coaxial cable will pick up the modulated RF envelope if placed near the plate tank coil in the transmitter. If the other end of the coaxial cable is applied to the vertical input of an oscilloscope, and the oscilloscope's horizontal sweep is adjusted to display several complete cycles at the modulating frequency, then the modulated envelope will be shown on the CRT screen (see Figure 19.1(c) or Figure 19.2.)

The above procedure can prove very dangerous to both personnel and equipment if the plate tank coil is accidentally touched. A superior

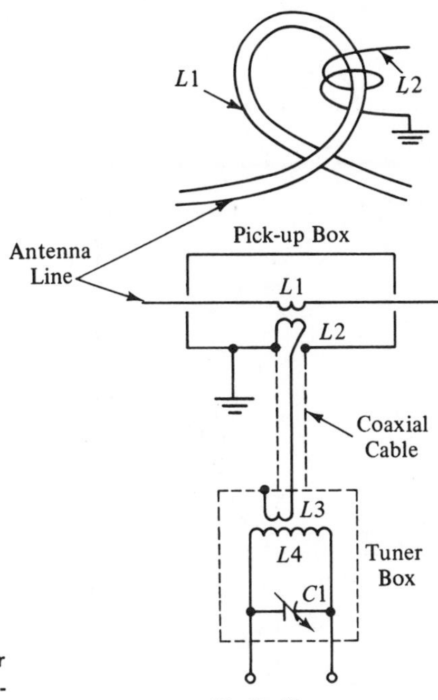

Figure 19.9 RF pickup box for modulation measurement.

alternative is the RF pickup box shown in Figure 19.9. The actual pickup box is inserted into the transmission line between the transmitter and the antenna.

Transformer $L1/L2$ consists of s single turn in both the primary and secondary. Coil $L1$ is part of the antenna line and should be made of at least #12 or #14 solid bus wire at power levels of 1000 W or less. It is formed into a single loop, as shown in Figure 19.9(b). Coil $L2$ is a single turn of #22 *insulated* hookup wire.

The two ends of the antenna line are terminated in female coaxial connectors such as the BNC or SO-239. The output to the tuner box is also through coaxial cable, but for most purposes BNC connectors are best here.

The tuner box may be unnecessary in some cases. If the oscilloscope is sensitive enough at the operating frequency of the radio transmitter, then apply the signal directly to the vertical amplifier, and delete $L3/L4/C1$. The tuner box, however, allows the use of low-frequency oscilloscopes in this test—especially if the vertical (Y) and horizontal (X) deflection plates are directly accessible. Where the vertical amplifier deflection sensitivity is insufficient, this will permit at least some display amplitude.

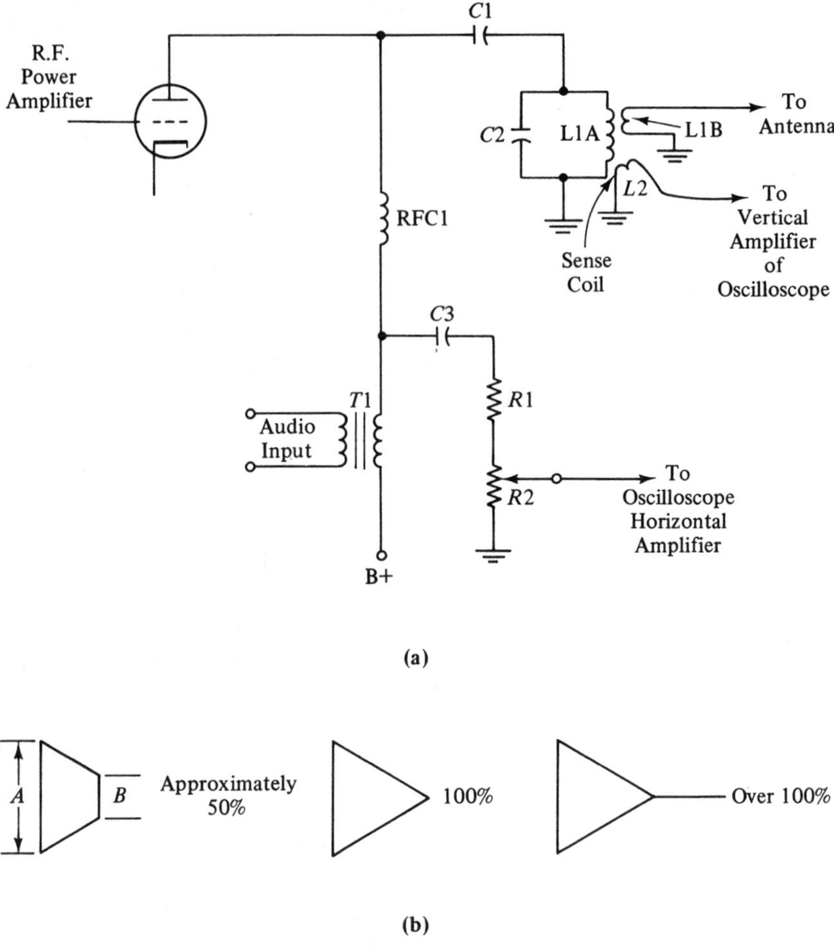

Figure 19.10 (a) Circuit for performing trapezoidal display modulation measurements. (b) Trapezoidal patterns for undermodulation, 100% modulation, and overmodulation.

The display of the modulation envelope is particularly useful in checking for modulation symmetry and overmodulation—shown by "flat topping" of the envelope's shape at peaks.

The trapezoidal method of checking amplitude modulation is shown in Figure 19.10. A sample of the modulating signal is taken from the secondary of the modulation transformer, and is applied to the horizontal input of the oscilloscope. At the same time, a sample of the RF modulated envelope is applied to the vertical input. This will produce a pattern such as those in Figure 19.10(b).

The percentage of modulation may be found from the trapezoid by using the following formula:

$$\text{Percentage of modulation} = \frac{A + B}{A - B} \times 100$$

You are advised to memorize this relationship and the patterns characteristic of 50 percent, 100 percent, and over 100 percent modulation. Also on some examinations is that for 0 percent modulation, which is merely a single vertical line.

19.5 DOUBLE AND SINGLE SIDEBAND

Single sideband (SSB) transmitters have almost completely replaced conventional amplitude-modulated (AM) equipment in most types of communications. Amateur radio and point-to-point commercial radiotelephones are almost all SSB, and have been for years. Citizens band (see Figure 19.11) and the medium wave (2–3 MHz) marine band equipment has been making the changeover. Under proposed rules, the CB will go over to all SSB in the next few years, just as the marine frequencies are already using that mode.

Single-sideband suppressed carrier (SSBSC), the correct name for this mode (SSB is also used, but is vernacular), is a form of amplitude modulation in which the RF carrier and one of the two identical sidebands are removed.

Consider the voltage-vs.-frequency plot of an AM signal (refer to Figure 19.3) when it is modulated 100 percent by a sine wave audio signal. Three distinct output frequencies are generated by this modulation process: the RF carrier plus sum and difference signals. Suppose, as illustrated in Figure 19.3, that a 1000-kHz RF carrier is modulated by a 1-kHz audio signal. The output spectrum for this transmitter is a 1000-kHz carrier, a 1001-kHz sum signal, and a 999-kHz difference signal, called upper sideband (USB) and lower sideband (LSB), respectively.

One of the principal problems with the effectiveness of the conventional method of amplitude modulation is that most of the available RF power is in the carrier. Most of the RF power in an AM transmitter is *wasted* in transmitting the unnecessary carrier and two identical sidebands. Because all of the information transmitted in an AM signal is transmitted in both sidebands, only a single sideband is necessary to convey the message. For a transmitter that is 100 percent modulated by a sine wave, the voltage vectors that represent the USB and LSB (Figure 19.3) are each

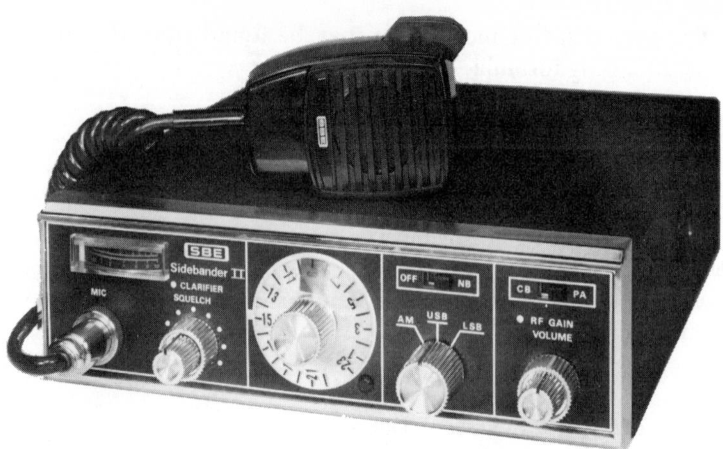

Figure 19.11 Single-sideband (SSB) citizens band transceiver. (*Courtesy of SBE.*)

only 50 percent of the carrier voltage amplitude. Since power is proportional to the square of the voltage, only $(\frac{1}{2})^2$, or ¼ of the total power, is in each sideband. This can be interpreted as using only one-fourth of the total power output to transmit usable information; the other three-fourths of the RF power is wasted in transmitting a useless carrier and a redundant sideband.

There are two basic forms of transmission in which there is a greater conservation of power. In the *double sideband suppressed carrier* (DSBSC) type of transmitter the carrier is suppressed by a method to be examined shortly, the output spectrum consists of the sidebands, and there is no carrier. Figure 19.12 shows the spectrum output for these various types of amplitude modulated system. In all cases the sidebands represent speech or other multiple frequency modulating voltages, rather than a single sine wave. In Figure 19.12(a) we see the standard AM signal with full carrier. This is the type of output spectrum that one would expect from an AM broadcast or standard CB transmitter. The DSBSC signal in Figure 19.12(b) shows the effect of suppressing the carrier. In this case the total available power developed by the transmitter is used to transmit the information. True, the sidebands are still redundant, but the DSBSC signal is greatly improved over the standard AM signal.

The SSB signals [Figures 19.12(c) and 19.12(d)], on the other hand, concentrate *all* of the available RF power into one sideband. In the case of Figure 19.12(c) the upper sideband (USB) is transmitted, while in Figure 19.12(d) the lower sideband (LSB) is transmitted.

Another advantage of the SSB mode is the fact that SSB signals, being carrierless, disappear when no audio is present to be transmitted. By

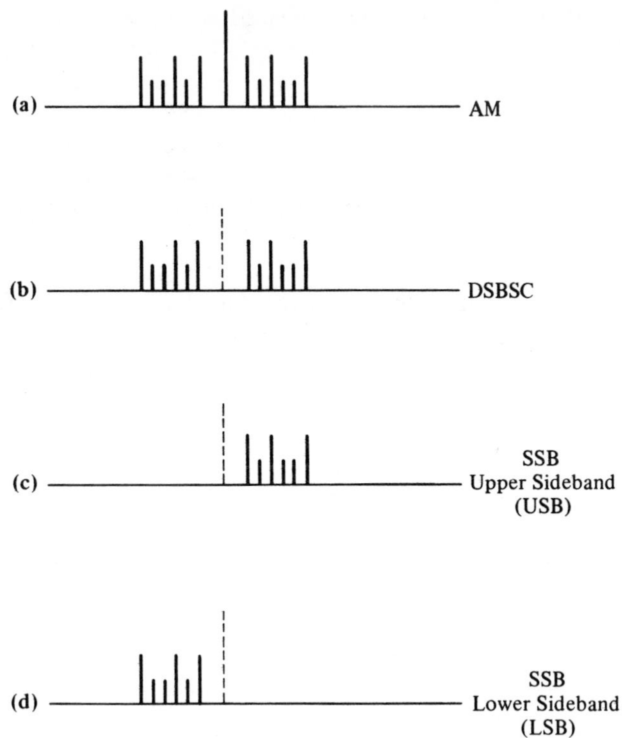

Figure 19.12 **(a)** Double-sideband with carrier (regular AM). **(b)** Double-sideband, suppressed carrier (DSBSC). **(c)** Single-sideband suppressed carrier (SSB or SSBSC) using the upper sideband (USB). **(d)** Single-sideband suppressed carrier (SSB or SSBSC) using lower sideband (LSB).

way of contrast, an AM signal has a carrier that *will* be transmitted under no-audio conditions and can, therefore, interfere with other stations.

Another advantage of SSB—and this can be very important on today's crowded frequency spectrum—is that the SSB signal requires only one-half the bandwidth of an AM signal with the same modulating signal. This, in fact, is the basis for the erroneous claim by some CB manufacturers whose SSB CB transceivers were said to "effectively have 46 channels," instead of the normal 23 allowed at that time. (There are 40 Class D CB channels at this writing.) What they were referring to was that each channel could be made to operate either USB or LSB, so the channels could be called 1-USB, 1-LSB, 2-USB, 2-LSB, etc.

Radiotelephone voice communications channels are usually limited in audio frequency response to about 300–2500 Hz. These frequencies (see Figure 19.13) form sidebands spaced up to ±2500 Hz from the carrier. The total required spectrum for an AM transmitter, then, is twice the bandwidth of a comparably modulated SSB system. Because the low-frequency end of the audio passband drops off below 300 Hz, there will be a 600-Hz guardband (2 × 300 Hz) between the lower and upper sidebands.

If receivers of adequate selectivity are used, it is possible for SSB stations to occupy the same channel (have the same carrier frequency) so long as one uses USB and the other LSB. Because the requirements for selectivity are so stringent, the selectivity filters for an SSB receiver are usually either piezoelectric or mechanical in nature. Such filters at the usual IF frequencies will have very steep passband slopes (see Chapter 21).

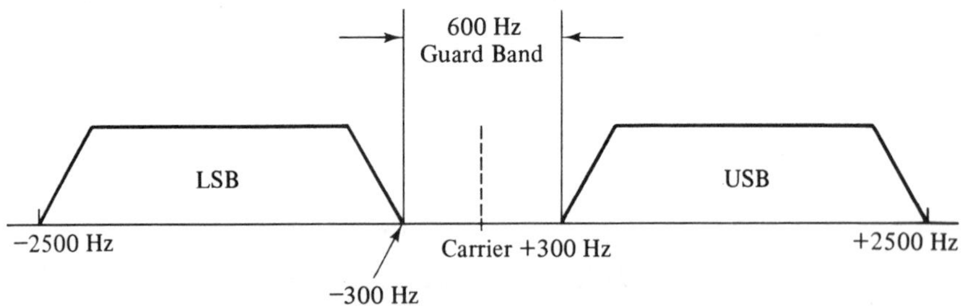

Figure 19.13 Spectrum occupied by a typical AM transmitter. The same carrier frequency can theoretically be used by *two* different SSB transmitters if one is using USB while the other uses LSB.

Generating the SSB signal. There are two basic methods for generating the SSB signal: phasing and filtering. Because it is the most often used, and easiest to implement, the filter method will be discussed first. Figure 19.14 shows the block diagram of a typical filtering-type SSB transmitter. The heart of the system is a stage called a *balanced modulator,* which is used to cancel the carrier when no audio signals are present. A balanced modulator will produce a double-sideband suppressed carrier (DSBSC) signal output only when an audio signal is applied at the input.

In this type of transmitter the output of the balanced modulator is fed to a highly selective RF filter (again, it will be mechanical or piezoelectric) that removes the unwanted sideband. There are two different philosophies for producing the respective sideband outputs. In one case, there are two filters, and only one carrier frequency. The USB is selected by having the center of the filter's passband approximately 1.25 kHz above the carrier frequency. If the filter is adequately selective, then the lower sideband and the carrier residue will be rejected. The LSB is similarly

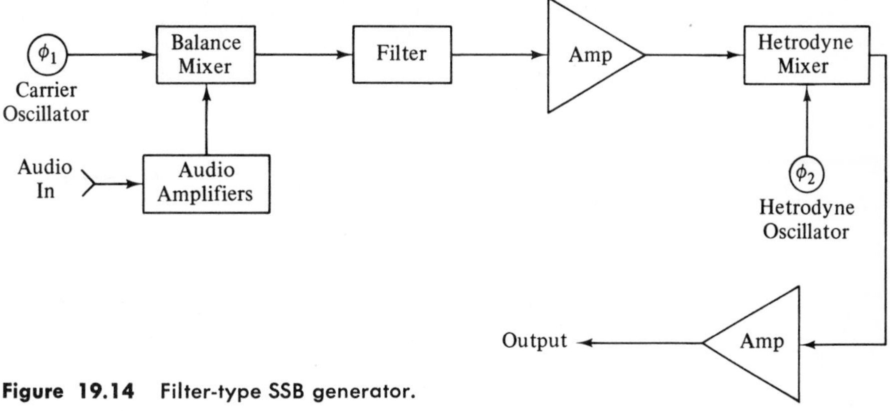

Figure 19.14 Filter-type SSB generator.

selected by using a second filter that has a center-passband frequency approximately 1.25 kHz *below* the carrier frequency. In the other method for sideband selection, there is but one crystal or mechanical filter, and the carrier frequency is shifted above or below the filter's passband. In that system the center passband frequency of the filter is the same as the channel frequency that is usually identified as the carrier. If the USB is desired, a signal is generated at a frequency that is 2.5 kHz *below* the carrier frequency. This serves as a pseudo-carrier, and is cancelled out by the balanced modulator. Similarly, when the LSB is to be transmitted, the pseudo-carrier frequency will be 2.5 kHz *above* the carrier.

In some designs the stage following the filter is an RF amplifier. This, in turn, is followed by a heterodyne mixer stage that is used to convert the signal to the desired RF channel frequency. This is done because it is too costly and too inconvenient to generate the SSB signal on every frequency on which the transmitter must operate. Instead, the usual practice is to generate the SSB signal at some fixed frequency (e.g., 455 kHz, 9 MHz, 3385 kHz) and then to heterodyne it to the correct operating frequency. Following the mixer is a cascade chain of RF amplifiers and the power output stage. All of these, despite the low efficiency, *must* be linear amplifiers, or a distorted output will result.

The DSB and SSB transmitter must, like all low-level modulated transmitters (a stage prior to the final is the modulated stage. A high-level modulation system uses the final amplifier as the modulated stage), uses the linear amplifiers after the generator. Power output from an SSB transmitter is usually expressed in "watts-PEP," which stands for "peak envelope power." Although space limitation prevents a complete discussion of the meaning of PEP, it is usually safe to say that PEP is approximately twice the dc input power to the final amplifier when the transmitter is modulated by ordinary speech with a 50 percent (assumed) duty cycle.

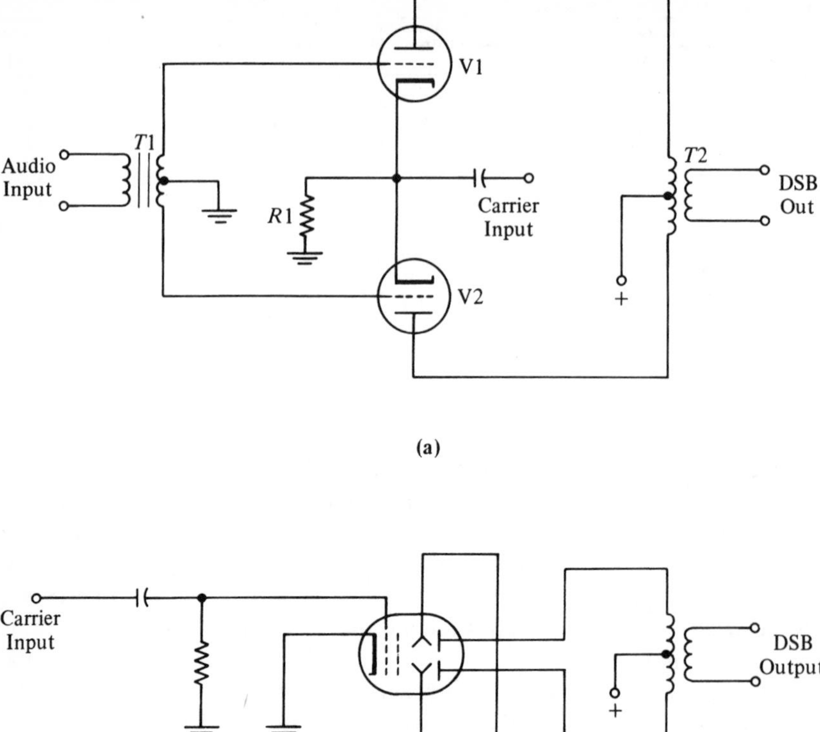

(a)

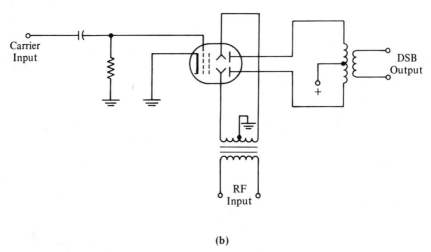

(b)

Figure 19.15 Balanced modulators **(a)** dual-triode and **(b)** beam-shift switching tube such as the 7360.

Balanced Modulators. The balanced modulator stage needed to produce the DSBSC signal must have a zero signal output when there is no modulating audio voltage present at the input. Many such circuits operate as either series or shunt switches that are electronically "toggled" by the audio signal.

Figure 19.15(a) shows an older vacuum-tube type of balanced modulator that uses a pair of triodes. Notice that the audio signal drives the grid's push-pull in a common-cathode configuration. The RF carrier signal, on the other hand, drives the cathodes in parallel in a grounded-grid configuration. When there is no audio present, the RF flowing in the plates of *V*1 and *V*2 produces equal but opposite currents in the primary of transformer T2. Consequently, without a modulating signal applied to the grids, the output is zero, because these currents produce mutually cancelling magnetic fields.

When the audio signal is present, the circuit becomes unbalanced. As the audio becomes more positive, the grid of *V*1 will become more positive and that of *V*2 will become more negative, in typical push-pull fashion. Because this increases *I*1 and decreases *I*2, a changing magnetic field is produced and induces a signal in the secondary. On the negative half-cycle of the audio signal the opposite situation exists, and *I*2 will be greater than *I*1.

Figure 19.15(b) is another form of balanced modulator using a vacuum tube, in this case a special beam-switching type called the 7360. This tube has a single cathode and control grid structure that is common to a *pair* of anodes. Electrons can be diverted to one anode or the other by application of a positive voltage to the proper deflection plate. When the two deflection plates are at the same potential, equal currents flow in the two plate circuits, and the same cancellation occurs as in the previous circuit. Applying an audio signal to the deflection plates, however, switches the beam back and forth from one plate to the other at a rate established by the modulating signal. This circuit, like the one discussed in Figure 19.15(a), produces zero output when no audio is present, and a DSBSC output when there is audio.

Figure 19.16 shows simple balanced modulators based on diode switching. Both vacuum-tube and solid-state types are known, but the latter predominate in modern equipment. Diodes *D*1 and *D*2, in Figure 19.16(a), are a matched pair connected so that there is no output signal when only the carrier is present. A positive-going audio signal will forward-bias diode *D*2 and reverse-bias *D*1, allowing current *I*1 to flow. On the negative half-cycle the situation reverses, and diode *D*1 conducts while *D*2 is cut off, allowing current *I*2 to flow. Capacitor *C*2 and resistor *R*1 are used to balance the circuit under no-audio conditions. This pair of controls can be adjusted while signal amplitude is monitored at the next, or any following, stage, and the controls *R*1 and *R*2 are adjusted to produce a null.

Another, more complex version of the diode balanced modulator is shown in Figure 15.16(b). This is the circuit used in much commercial equipment. One model is equipped with this circuit, and uses the RCA type CA3019 quad-diode integrated circuit for *D*1–*D*4. This approach makes use of the inherently close match and thermal tracking of the IC diodes. One version of this type of circuit is found in small metal cases

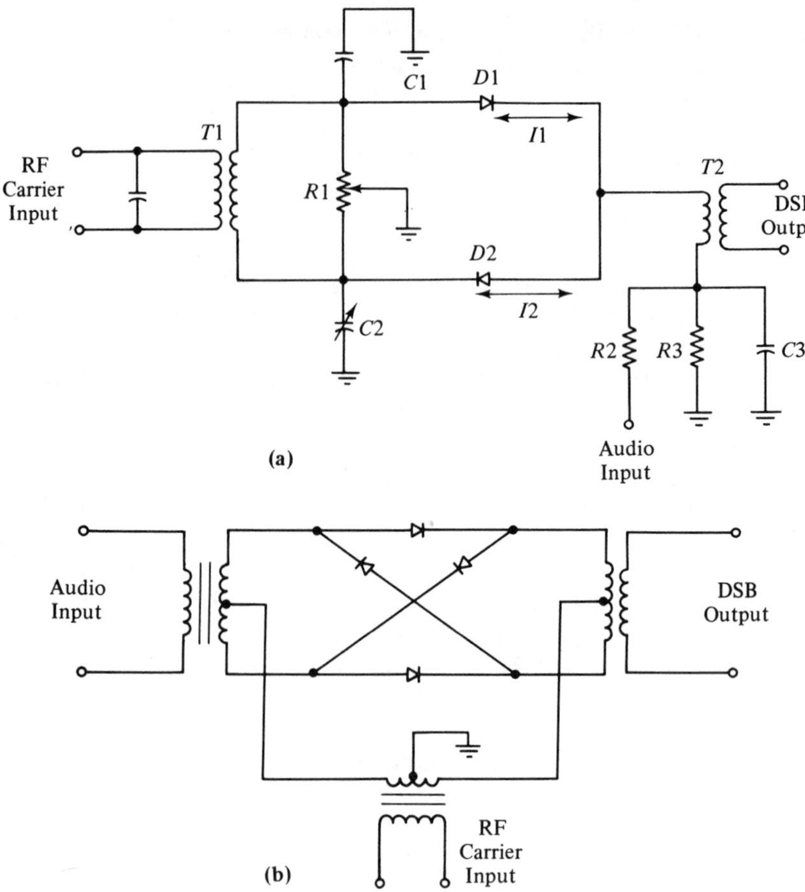

Figure 19.16 **(a) Simple diode balanced modulator. (b) Bridge type balanced modulator.**

measuring about ¾ in. × ⅜ in. each of which contains four hot-carrier diodes and a toroidal RF transformer. Such circuits, called *double-balanced mixers,* can be made into balanced modulators by the addition of an external audio transformer.

SSB Receivers. The subject of radio receivers will be covered in detail in Chapter 21, so only a brief description will be given here of the SSB receiver. The carrier rejected at the transmitter is not as useless as we originally led you to believe; it is necessary to recover the information in the sideband that is transmitted. In normal AM detectors the modulated signal is passed through a nonlinear stage (such as a simple solid-state

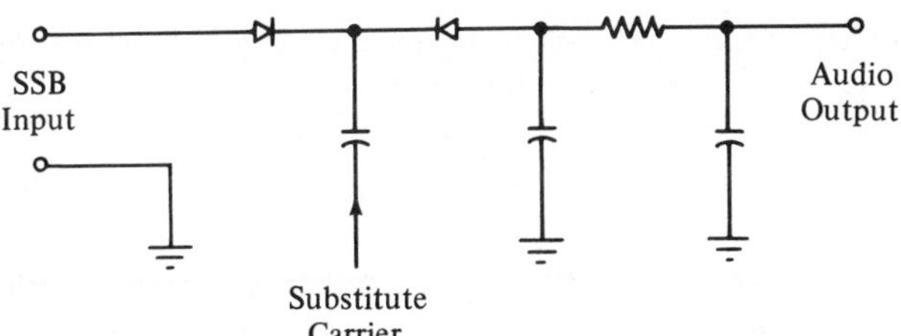

Figure 19.17 Simple product detector for SSB demodulation.

diode), and the carrier heterodynes with the sidebands. The difference frequency is the audio signal. In the SSB receiver a local beat frequency oscillator (BFO) is used to provide a surrogate carrier at the detector. Figure 19.17 shows one method for such a *product detector* to demodulate the SSB information.

Testing of the SSB transmitter is pretty much the same as testing any AM transmitter. In most cases the RF pickup box and an oscilloscope are used. In SSB transmitters, however, it is necessary to use a *two-tone* audio modulating signal to simulate the performance under speech conditions. It is usual to find 1800 Hz and 800 Hz as the two modulating tones. In many cases a modulation monitor oscilloscope, such as the Heathkit SB-610, is used—and it contains the two-tone generators. This oscilloscope, although designed for higher powers, is usable down to the 5-W power limit of CB transmitters.

PROBLEMS

1. "Modulation" is the _______ of an RF carrier to transmit _______ or _______.
2. Three basic parameters or properties of the RF carrier can be varied in a modulation system: _______, _______, and _______.
3. Ordinary AM, with both carrier and sidebands, is designated a type _______ emission.
4. A transmitter produces modulation described as 10A3. The highest audio frequency transmitted is _______.
5. SSBSC is also denoted as _______ modulation.
6. DSBSC is also denoted as _______ modulation.
7. If an RF carrier is 100 percent modulated by a sine wave, then the carrier output power will be _______ on the negative peak of the modulating audio signal.
8. The sidebands are the _______ and _______ frequencies produced by a mixing process in which the RF carrier and modulating audio are combined.

9. A 10,000-kHz radio carrier is modulated by a 5-kHz audio tone. What is the frequency of the upper sideband?
10. In the previous problem the lower sideband is at ________.
11. The bandwidth of an A3 signal using the modulating tone in the previous two problems would be ________.
12. In 100 percent, sine wave, plate modulation, the potential applied to the plate of the modulated stage will be ________ on positive audio peaks and ________ on negative audio peaks.
13. How much power is required to plate-modulate a transmitter that has a plate potential of 1250 V and a plate current of 100 mA? Assume that 100 percent modulation is required.
14. What is the peak power of a carrier that is 100 percent modulated by a sine wave if the unmodulated power is 1000 W?
15. How much power is required to 50-percent modulate a transmitter that has a dc input power to the plate of 100 W?
16. Series modulation is also called ________ modulation.
17. Control grid modulation is also called ________ modulation.
18. The Heising system of modulation is also called ________.
19. Overmodulation is permissible if a power microphone is used. True or false?
20. The screen grid is sometimes modulated by a ________.
21. The ________ system of checking modulation percentage on an oscilloscope uses a sample of the modulated envelope and a sample of the modulating audio to drive the plates of the oscilloscope.
22. The DSBSC signal is generated in a ________.
23. The carrier in an SSB signal is ________.
24. An SSB transmitter has a dc input power of 1000 W. What is the approximate PEP?
25. A type of balanced modulator using the hot-carrier type of diodes is the so-called ________.

20 Frequency Modulation

The first radiotelephone transmitters were amplitude-modulated because AM is easy to implement, even if primitive electronic components are used. But there are problems associated with AM radiotelephones, one of which is noisy reception. Frequency modulation (FM) was invented prior to the Second World War as an answer to the problems of AM, but it was not until after the war—many years by some accounts—that FM finally came into its own. Most FM transmitters operate in the VHF/UHF region, and it took advances in the engineering art to make these frequencies commercially exploitable.

20.1 FM BASICS

Frequency modulation is a process of varying a radio carrier (i.e., modulation) in which the *frequency* of the carrier is changed in a manner proportional to the applied audio signal. The amplitude of the RF carrier remains constant, but the frequency is varied. In this chapter we shall discuss the elements of FM transmitter theory, but you should also read Chapter 21 soon after reading this one in order to get an appreciation of how FM receivers work.

Figure 20.1 shows the graph of the frequency spectrum of an FM signal. Also shown is the sine wave used to modulate the RF carrier. When the modulating voltage is zero, then the carrier frequency is F. As the modulating voltage increases in the positive direction, however, the carrier frequency begins to increase also, until it reaches a new frequency F_h. This frequency is attained by the carrier at the instant the audio sine wave reaches its peak (E_{peak}). After the modulating voltage passes the peak, however, the carrier frequency decreases until it is again at frequency F when the audio sine wave is at zero crossing. The polarity of the sine wave then reverses, and the amplitude begins to increase in the negative direction. As its amplitude increases with negative polarity, the frequency of the carrier begins to decrease until it reaches a minimum at F_L just as the audio sine wave reaches its negative peak. The FM modulator continues to sweep the oscillator of the transmitter through the frequencies from F_L to F_h as the modulating voltage oscillates back and forth between its negative and positive peaks.

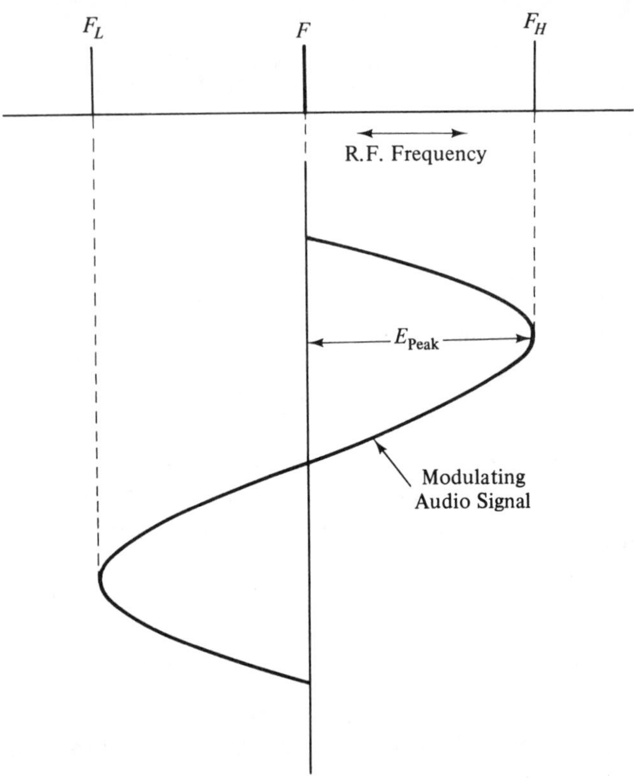

Figure 20.1 Relationship of the modulating audio waveform to the frequency of the radio carrier in FM systems.

There are several basic concepts peculiar to FM systems, and these are often misunderstood. Among these are *deviation* and *frequency swing*. Also confusing to many students are the terms *deviation ratio* and *modulation index*. Let us first tackle the first pair of similar terms.

Deviation is the change of frequency between the unmodulated carrier frequency F and either upper or lower frequency limit (F_h or F_L, respectively). Obviously, then, there may be *two* deviation figures in some cases. Any given FM signal may have both positive and negative deviation figures. The positive deviation is $(F_h - F)$, while the negative deviation is given by $(F - F_L)$. These figures are also sometimes given as $\pm\Delta F$ (read "plus or minus delta F"). The negative and positive deviation figures are identical *only* when the modulating audio signal is perfectly symmetrical about the zero baseline. A pure sine wave, which has no dc offset component, produces equal positive and negative deviation figures. The units of deviation are units of frequency.

Frequency swing is the total carrier frequency shift between the lower frequency extreme F_L and the upper frequency extreme F_h. This can be defined mathematically as $(F_h - F_L)$. If the modulating signal is perfectly symmetrical, then the frequency swing is exactly 2 ΔF. In other words,

$$(F_h - F_L) = (F_h - F) + (F - F_L) = 2\,\Delta F \tag{20-1}$$

The other two similar terms that seem to cause confi sion are *deviation ratio* and *modulation index.* The deviation ratio is the ratio of the maximum allowable deviation to the maximum allowable modulating frequency. The modulation index, on the other hand, is the ratio of the maximum allowable deviation and the *actual modulating frequency* at any given instant. In other words,

$$\text{D.R.} = \frac{\text{maximum allowed deviation}}{\text{maximum allowable audio frequency}} \tag{20-2}$$

$$\text{M.I.} = \frac{\text{maximum allowable deviation}}{\text{actual modulating frequency (instantaneous)}} \tag{20-3}$$

Example. Consider an FM broadcast transmitter. The F.C.C. allows deviation of ±75 kHz, and modulating audio frequencies up to 15 kHz. Assume that a 1-kHz sine wave is used to modulate this transmitter. Find the deviation ratio and the modulation index.

$$\text{D.R.} = (75\text{ kHz})/(15\text{ kHz}) = 5 \tag{20-4}$$

$$\text{M.I.} = (75\text{ kHz})/(1\text{ kHz}) = 75 \tag{20-5}$$

The only time that deviation ratio and modulation index are equal is when the transmitter is *being modulated* by an audio signal of the maximum allowable frequency. In the case of the FM broadcast transmitter of the example, this occurs when the audio signal is 15 kHz, and in that case

$$\text{D.R.} = \text{M.I.} = 5 \tag{20-6}$$

One Hundred Percent Modulation in FM Systems. In an AM transmitter we can see some specific physical parameters that can be used to define the occurrence of 100 percent modulation. When the audio power causes

Figure 20.2 VHF-FM marine radiotelephone transceiver. (*Courtesy of Ray-Jefferson.*)

Figure 20.3 Amateur VHF-FM transceiver. (*Courtesy of The Heath* Co.)

the RF envelope to double in amplitude on positive audio peaks and drop to zero on negative audio peaks, we say that 100 percent modulation exists. If these limits are exceeded, then bad things occur—splatter (spurious sidebands that interfere with other channels) and distortion increase dramatically. In FM transmitters, however, there is no such easily discerned property, so FM modulation percentage is defined arbitrarily, or so it seems. The FM broadcast transmitter, for example, is considered "100 percent modulated" when the deviation is ±75 kHz. The sound channel of the television signal is considered to be 100 percent modulated with a deviation of only ±25 kHz. Similarly, the standard narrow band FM used in landmobile, marine, and some amateur radio FM transmitters (Figures 20.2 and 20.3, respectively) are 100 percent modulated with only 5-kHz deviation.

20.2 FM MODULATORS

Before discussing the various techniques for generating frequency-modulated RF signals, we should be sure that it is understood that there are two closely related forms of modulation that are generally called FM: frequency and phase. The receiver and most stages of the transmitter will treat these two types as equivalents, but when discussing the modulator we find that they are different enough to warrant separate treatment. Frequency modulation, also called *direct FM,* is a system in which the actual frequency is varied, whereas phase modulation (*indirect FM*) has constant frequency and the *phase* of the RF carrier is varied.

The simplest form of frequency modulation (direct FM) is shown in Figure 20.4. In this circuit the microphone is a type called a *capacitance microphone*. Such a microphone has two opposing plates, forming a capacitor. One is rigid and forms part of the case. The other is a thin diaphragm, and it varies mechanically as sound waves impinge upon it. This will change the spacing between the two plates, so therefore it varies the capacitance in step with the audio signal. In Figure 20.4 the capacitance microphone is made part of the LC tank circuit in an oscillator circuit. As the sound waves cause the capacitance of the microphone to vary, the frequency of the oscillator also varies. This is, however, an inflexible and not very good system. Its main applications seem to be in the

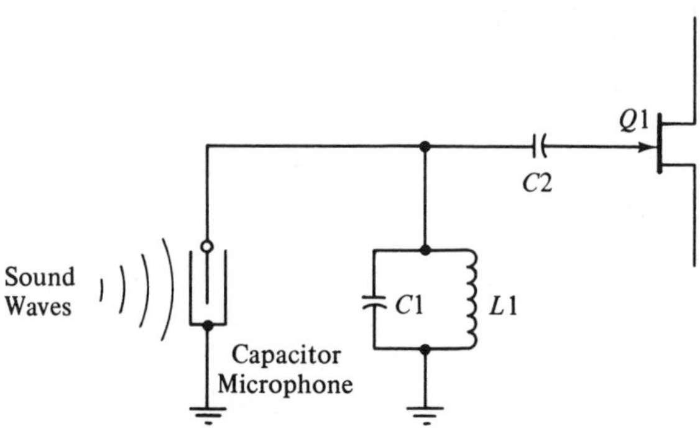

Figure 20.4 Generation of FM by capacitance microphone.

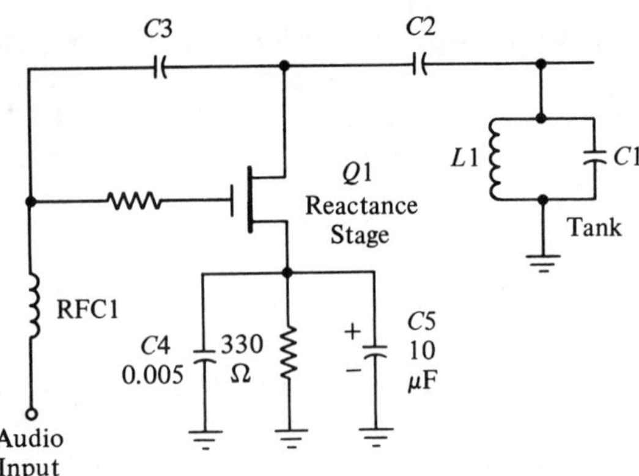

Figure 20.5 Generation of FM by reactance stage across the oscillator tank circuit.

form of so-called "wireless microphones" and in the high-quality recording microphones that take advantage of the high audio frequency response attainable with capacitor microphones.

A more viable method of attaining direct FM is shown in Figure 20.5, where a reactance stage is connected in shunt with the oscillator tank circuit. This stage will *simulate* an electronically variable capacitance by having the drain voltage and current vectors out of phase in the same manner as a capacitor circuit (E lags I).

Figure 20.6 shows the type of direct-FM modulator that seems most popular in modern equipment. Here we have a crystal oscillator that has a special diode, called a *varactor,* in series with the piezoelectric crystal. This type of diode has a very special property: its junction capacitance varies with applied voltage. All *PN*-junctions exhibit some capacitance because the positive and negative carriers on opposite sides of the junction tend to simulate capacitor plates. When a low reverse bias potential is applied across the diode junction, the carriers are in close proximity (the depletion zone is narrow), so capacitance is high. When the reverse bias potential is increased, however, the depletion zone widens and the capacitance drops.

Diode $D1$ in Figure 20.6 is biased to a point that will prevent forward bias of the PN junction at any audio amplitude that is likely to be found.

You should recall that a variable capacitance across a crystal changes its resonant frequency slightly. This is the action that is seen in this circuit. The audio signal causes the capacitance of diode $D1$ to vary proportionally, and that causes the frequency also to vary proportionally to the applied audio.

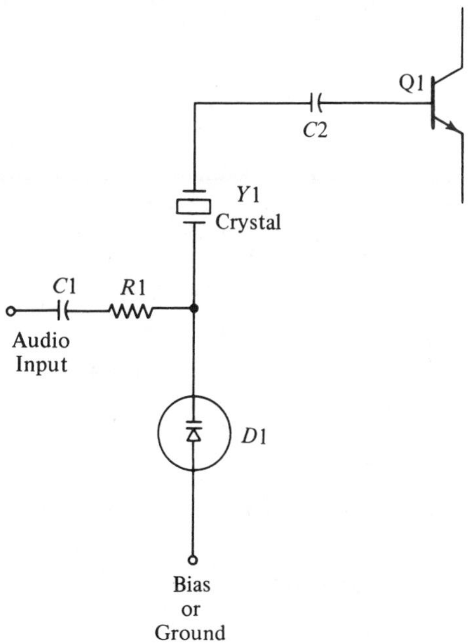

Figure 20.6 Use of a varactor (variable capacitance) diode in series with the crystal in the transmitter oscillator to generate FM signal.

Phase modulation is probably the most common form of FM. It is not actually "FM," but the habit of calling it by that name has become fixed in the jargon of the industry. Besides, the receiver and most transmitter stages recognize the PM signal as if it were FM, so no harm is done. A typical reactance modulator for the generation of phase modulation is shown in Figure 20.7.

The phase modulator is placed so that it shunts the signal line between the oscillator that generates the carrier and the stages that follow. Two vector components of the signal at the drain of $Q1$ are a direct signal through capacitor $C3$ and the phase-shifted signal through $Q1$. This signal is shifted 180 deg, but its amplitude will vary as the audio signal varies. This will add with the shifted signal through $C3$ to vectorially combine and produce phase variations in the output RF signal that are proportional to the audio variations. The advantage of this type of modulator is that the frequency control stage precedes it, so it can be a crystal oscillator. This may seem less a factor in modern equipment, where a varactor can be used, but in older designs, when the PM system became popular, it was difficult to obtain both deviation and the frequency stability of the carrier required both by good engineering practice and the rules of the F.C.C.

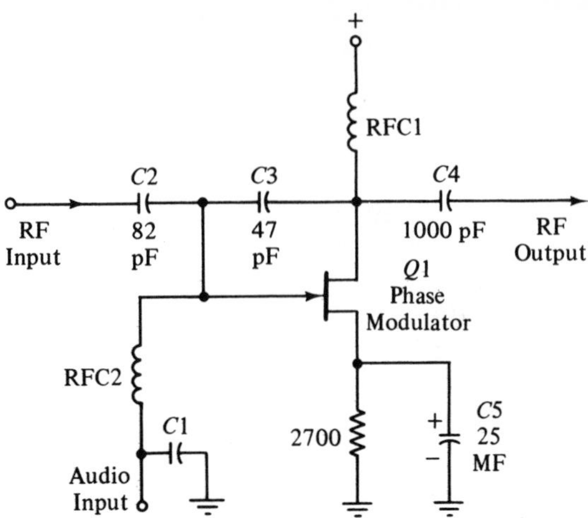

Figure 20.7 Phase modulation generated by a reactance modulator.

20.3 A "TYPICAL" FM TRANSMITTER

The block diagram for a typical FM-VHF transmitter is shown in Figure 20.8. This circuit is representative of a large class of FM/PM transmitters covering all technologies from vacuum tubes to monolithic integrated circuits.

The RF signal is generated in a high-stability crystal oscillator of the type studied in an earlier chapter. The output signal from this stage is fed to a reactance modulator, where it is combined with the signal from the audio stages to produce a phase-modulated output.

The audio section consists of three basic parts; microphone, speech amplifiers, and a clipper/filter. The microphone picks up the sound wave variations in the air and converts them to an equivalent audio signal voltage. The speech amplifiers build up this signal to a point where it can drive the modulator directly. Following the speech amplifiers is the clipper/filter. This consists of an amplitude limiter that prevents the application of an excessive audio voltage to the reactance modulator—it "clips" the amplitude when it exceeds the threshold set by the "deviation" control. The filter is a low-pass audio filter that reduces the harmonics generated in the audio waveform by the clipping process.

The phase-modulated signal is usually generated at a low frequency, and is then multiplied in frequency doubler and tripler stages until it is on the operating frequency. In the transmitter of Figure 20.8 the multiplication factor of the signal is $2 \times 3 \times 2 \times 2$, or $\times 24$. The output frequency will be 24 times the oscillator frequency. Similarly, the deviation

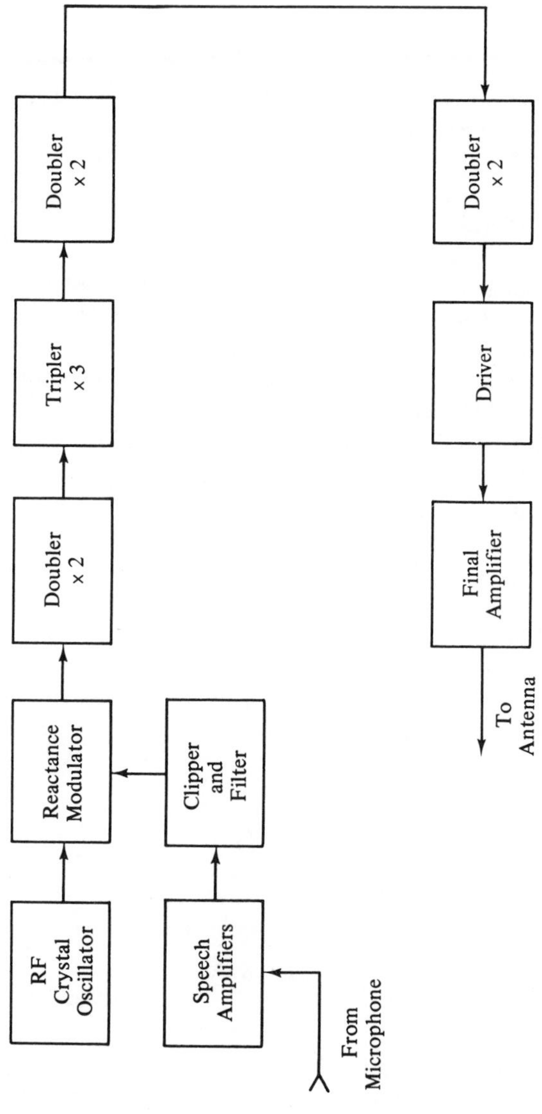

Figure 20.8 Block diagram of a typical FM/PM transmitter.

produced by the modulator is also multiplied by a factor of 24. The last two stages are tuned to the operating frequency and are Class C power amplifiers.

Example. An amateur radio transmitter is to operate on a frequency of 146.94 MHz, and is to have a deviation of ±5 kHz. The bandwidth of the audio speech amplifiers is 300–3000 Hz, and a 1-kHz sine wave is used to modulate the transmitter. Find the frequency of the crystal oscillator, the deviation that must be produced by the reactance modulator, and the D.R. and M.I. figures.

1. The operating frequency is 146.94 MHz, so the crystal frequency is this divided by the multiplication factor, or 146.94 MHz/24 = 6.1225 MHz = 6122.5 kHz.
2. The deviation is 5 kHz, so the reactance modulator must produce a deviation of 5 kHz/24 = 0.2083 kHz = 208.3 Hz.
3. D.R. = 5/3 (kilohertz) = 1.67.
4. M.I. = 5/1 = 5.

21 Receivers

Radio signals are electromagnetic waves and will remain so unless a means is provided for taking them from the air and recovering the information or supposed "intelligence" carried by the signal. A radio receiver is a device that performs that chore. It picks up the electromagnetic wave in the air on an antenna, amplifies and processes the signal, and then demodulates it to retrieve the information contained in the modulations.

21.1 EARLY RECEIVERS

Early radio receivers consisted of an antenna, a chain of cascaded RF amplifiers, and a detector. The antenna in those models was usually a long piece of wire outside of the building. The signal from the antenna is coupled to the input of the receiver and fed to an RF amplifier in the manner of Figure 21.1. This creates an electrical signal in the tank circuit that has the same frequency and amplitude variations as the original radio wave in the air. This electrical signal is amplified by a chain of from one to five RF amplifiers before being fed to a detector that actually removes the information content. In some cases such a detector is a simple diode rectifier, but in others it is a "regenerative detector." This latter circuit uses the Armstrong oscillator with a feedback control, often a variable resistor in the stage's $B+$ supply, that can be adjusted to keep the stage barely on the verge of oscillation. In fact, this was once the best and most sensitive method for detection. Regenerative receivers are still available today, even though the design has been supplanted with more modern ideas. The regenerative detector is popular as kits marketed for the youthful hobbyist.

One failing of the *tuned radio frequency* (TRF) receiver just described is that it must be tuned very carefully. All of those tuned RF amplifiers must be tuned to the same frequency, and the tuning must "track." (The stages must be tuned to the same frequency on both ends of the dial.) It is quite a problem to get several RF tanks to tune so that they track nicely; there are too many variations. Also a problem is the fact that the high gain used in these receivers causes many of them to become oscillators, and that destroys any possible reception.

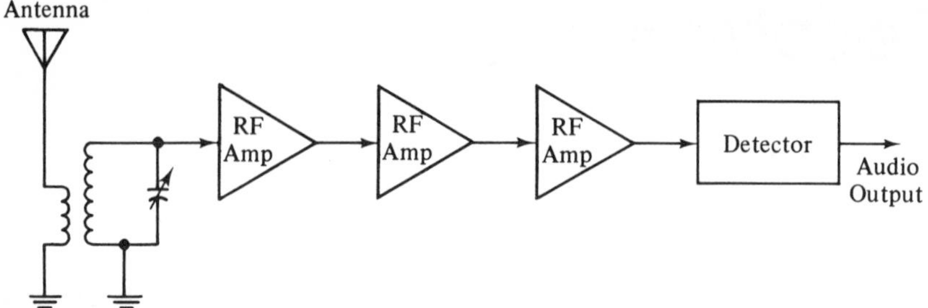

Figure 21.1 Block diagram of the *tuned radio frequency* (TRF) radio receiver.

On the other end of the complexity range among early radio receivers was the crystal set—still popular with hobbyists as a "first project." Figure 21.2 shows a typical crystal set. In the simplest case all that is needed is the diode detector and the earphones, but that is not too practical unless it is located near a high-power transmitter antenna. In this case, a tuned tank circuit is used to select the desired signal. A degree of "amplification" is gained by connecting the antenna and ground terminals to opposite ends of a primary winding consisting of a few turns of wire around the ground end of coil $L1$b. The antenna should be at least 50 ft long, and preferably longer, unless there are stations nearby. A diode detector is connected to an impedance-matching tap on the tank coil, although in some designs it is connected to the top of the coil. This diode is the actual demodulation detector. In early crystal sets, those made before World War I, a natural semiconductor crystal of the mineral galena was used for this purpose. Unfortunately, those crystals (which resembled a chunk of rock) were not usable as a detector at all points on their bodies, so a "cat's whisker" probe consisting of a fine piece of wire and a support was moved about by the operator to find a point that would result in radio reception. Needless to say, it was a difficult process that required no small amount of tenacity. In World War II American G.I.'s found similar properties in heat-blued (not the painted blue type) razor blades issued by the U.S. Army. Many a "foxhole radio" was constructed from these razor blades and bits of wire, earphones and other parts "requisitioned" for the purpose. In modern crystal sets (modern in the crystal set world means those made since World War II) the detector is a 1N34- or 1N60-type solid-state diode.

We shall use this description of the crystal set to introduce the concept of demodulation, even though subsequent paragraphs will make you think that that is a little like putting the cart before the horse. Figure 21.2(b) shows the waveforms associated with almost any radio receiver, but particularly the lowly crystal set. The first waveform is an audio signal that is amplitude-modulating the radio carrier. This is the signal existing

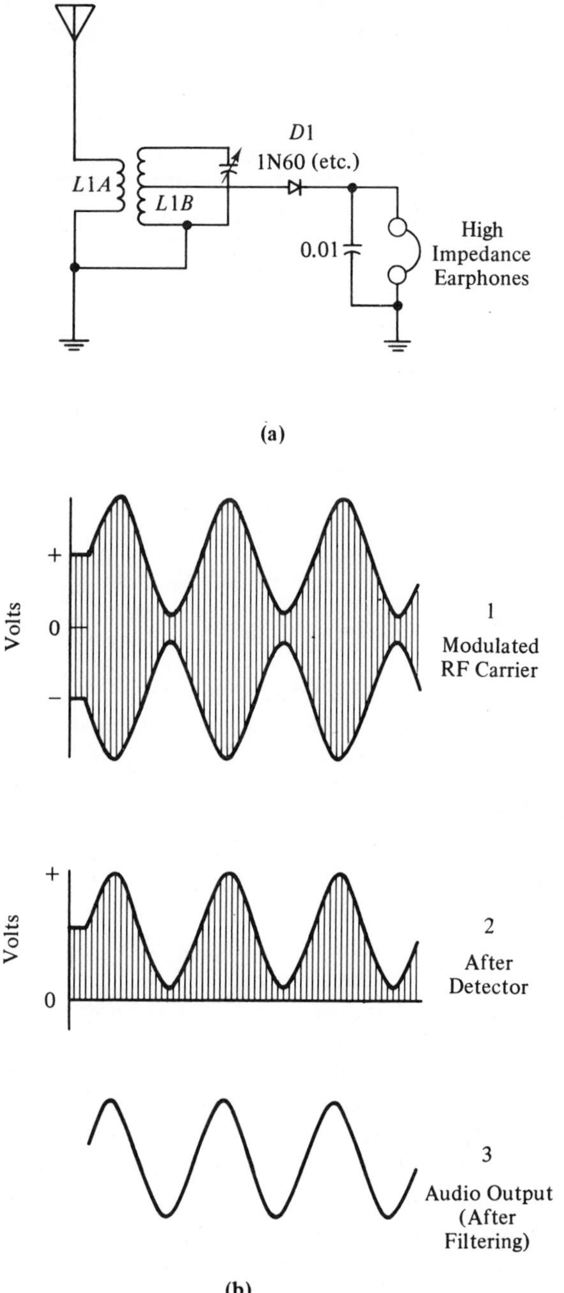

Figure 21.2 **(a)** The simplest tunable radio—the crystal set. **(b)** (1) modulated RF waveform (2) following detection (3) recovered audio after filtering.

in the tank circuit of the crystal set and amplified by the RF amplifier of the TRF radio. The diode detector is basically a rectifier, so its output (the second waveform) is a dc signal that varies at the same rate and in the same manner as the modulating signal. The capacitor across the earphones in the crystal set is used to remove the RF variations that form the diode's output pulsations. This capacitor is given a value that is large enough to filter out the RF signal, but is not high enough to attenuate the audio signals. If the earphone is a standard 2000-Ω high-impedance type, then the capacitive reactance of the filter at the RF frequency should be less than 200 Ω—following the 1/10 rule. The recovered audio, less the RF component, is shown in the final waveform. This is applied to the earphones and is heard by the listener. "Sophisticated" crystal sets sometimes follow the diode with an audio amplifier so that it can drive a loudspeaker. We normally think of crystal sets as having a very limited reception range, but in the pioneer days of radio communications and broadcasting reception up to 1000 miles or more was noted.

21.2 THE SUPERHETERODYNE RECEIVER

There are severe problems associated with both of the receiver types we have discussed thus far. To say the least, those radios were less than "optimum" appliances. The crystal set was very easy to tune, but it had a tremendous lack of sensitivity. The TRF, on the other hand, took advantage of electronic amplification, but was very touchy, and was a bit of a bother to tune correctly. One of the worst problems was the fact that it would not track from one end of the dial to the other because of all of those RF tank circuits. It was also noted, once the shortwaves began to be used, that these receivers were much less sensitive and selective on the high end of the dial than on the low. Also, the TRF radio would frequently act as a TPTG oscillator, and break into a howl whenever a station was encountered (heterodyne beats).

These problems were alleviated or even solved completely by the superheterodyne design. Actually, the "super . . ." part of that designation is more a creation of advertisers than of engineers, but the heterodyne part is very descriptive of the process used in this type of receiver. In the superheterodyne receiver the RF signal is frequency-translated to a lower frequency. The advantage of this is that it is easier to obtain a lot of amplification at low frequencies, while the desired degree of selectivity is maintained. Radio frequency amplifier-type circuits are much better behaved at low frequencies than at higher frequencies.

Heterodyning. The purpose of heterodyning is merely the mixing together of two signals in a *nonlinear* device. If this is done there will be additional signals created at the output. Assume that two frequencies, $f1$ and $f2$, are mixed together in a nonlinear stage. The frequencies at the output are $f1$, $f2$, and $(f1 \pm f2)$. This can be seen on the piano, or almost any other musical instrument. Pick a note in the middle of the keyboard, any note. Strike its key and listen to the tone. Next, strike a nearby key and note the difference in pitch. Finally, strike both keys at the same time. You should be able to hear a mixture of both keys plus additional tones not present with either key alone. One of these, the *difference frequency,* has a low pitch. If two keys are slightly different, this pitch is a very low frequency variation that almost seems like a variation in loudness. In fact, this is how you tune a musical instrument. A pitch pipe or oscillator that is on exactly the correct frequency is beat, or "heterodyned" against the corresponding key or string on the instrument. The pitch of the string's vibrations are then varied to a point where the beatnote variations become lower and lower in frequency. When the string is exactly in tune, the variations will disappear altogether because $(f1 - f2 = 0)$.

Figure 21.3 shows a receiver designed along the lines of the classic superheterodyne. It consists of the following stages: RF amplifier, oscillator/mixer, IF amplifier, detector, audio amplifier, and automatic gain control (AGC).

The RF amplifier is of classic design much like those used in the TRF radio receivers. They are tunable over a certain range or "band" of frequencies. The RF amplifier does not have too much selectivity because of the nature of high-frequency tank circuits. Gain of the RF amplifier, as well as its selectivity, is kept at a minimum. In fact, some low-cost receivers do not have RF amplifiers. This class includes almost all low-cost home table-model AM radios. Deleting the RF amplifier causes other problems, however, so better receivers retain it.

The heterodyning is done in a stage called the oscillator-mixer. The mixer is the nonlinear stage discussed above, while the oscillator (also called the "local oscillator" or "L.O." in jargon) is used to select stations. Some receivers combine the two functions into one stage called a "converter."

The greatest amount of gain and selectivity is found in the intermediate frequency (IF) amplifier. This amplifier will normally be a low-frequency RF-type amplifier. In home radios and low-cost communications receivers a popular IF frequency is 455 kHz, while standard practice in automobile radios is to use 262.5 kHz as the IF.

In the early days of radio almost all IF frequencies were low because of the fact that selectivity was easier to obtain with tank circuits in the

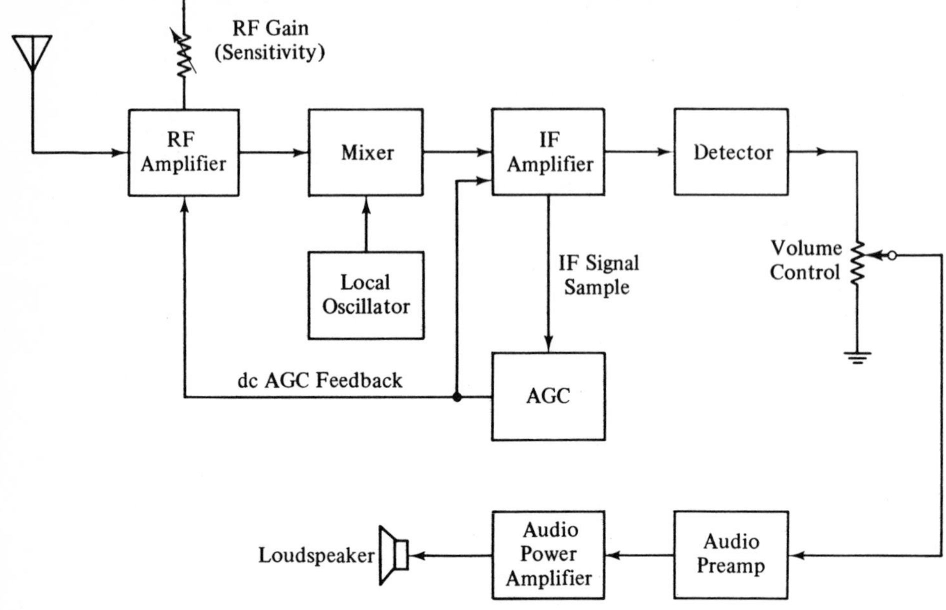

Figure 21.3 Block diagram of the superheterodyne receiver.

50-kHz to 500-kHz range. Today, though, you find communications receivers with IFs of 9 MHz and higher, because crystal filters now make selectivity at those frequencies easier to obtain. In these cases the IF may well be above the operating frequencies. FM radios typically have 10.7-MHz IFs because they have never required selectivity, except in the case of the FM communications (as opposed to broadcasting) receivers.

The detector may be a simple envelope detector such as that discussed in the section on the crystal set, or it may be a product detector for single sideband. It may also be an FM detector. There are several integrated circuit detectors that will accommodate all three types of signal. Whatever the design specifics, however, all detectors have one function: demodulation of the carrier to retrieve the information.

The local oscillator in a receiver may be either fixed frequency (in which case it will be crystal-controlled), or a variable-frequency type. It may be any of the types of oscillator discussed in an earlier chapter. The important thing is that it be stable, and that its dial drive be calibrated accurately for frequency.

Several different types of mixer circuit are shown in Figure 21.4. In all cases there are two inputs, one each for RF and L.O. There will also be one output, for the IF. The IF amplifiers that follow the mixer will accept only one frequency, so only one of the mixer products will appear

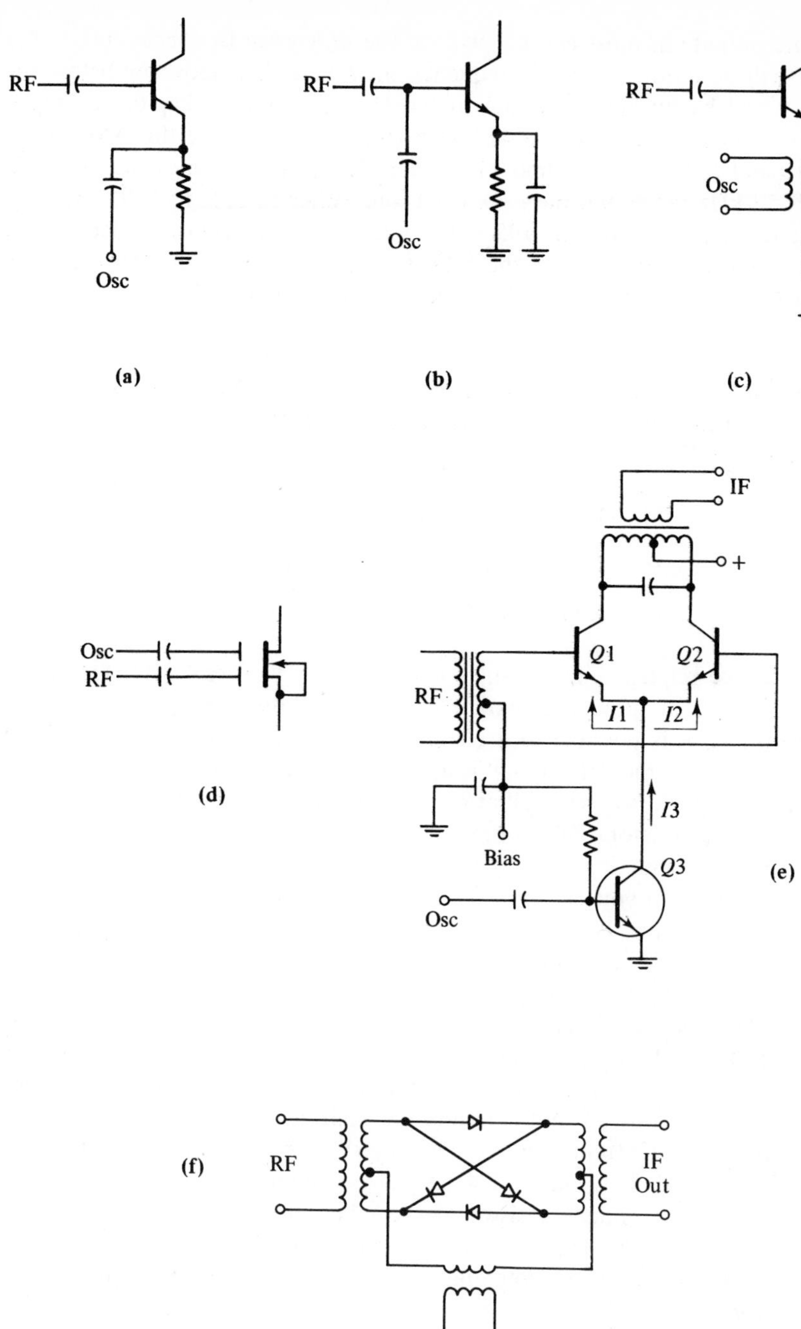

Figure 21.4 Receiver mixer circuits.

at the output. In most cases it will be the *difference* frequency ($f1 - f2$) that will be used. The L.O. frequency must be either above or below the RF signal by an amount equal to the IF frequency. Take, for example, the case of a receiver with a 455-kHz IF designed to tune the AM broadcast band (540 kHz to 1650 kHz). The RF amplifier tunes the 540-kHz to 1650-kHz range, but the L.O. must tune either 85 kHz to 1195 kHz, or, as is the normal situation, 995 kHz to 2105 kHz. In AM broadcast band and in most other receivers the L.O. frequency is above the RF, but it is possible to find receivers in which the L.O. is below the RF.

Example. A superheterodyne receiver is tuned to 14.2 MHz. What is the L.O. frequency if the IF is 3.3 MHz and the L.O. is on the high side of the RF signal?

$$\text{L.O.} = \text{RF} + \text{IF}$$

$$\text{L.O.} = 14.2\ \text{MHz} + 3.3\ \text{MHz}$$

$$\text{L.O.} = 17.5\ \text{MHz}$$

Three related mixer designs are shown in Figures 21.4(a) through 21.4(c). All of these use bipolar transistors. Although an *NPN* type is shown here, it is possible to use transistors of either polarity. In this type of mixer stage the RF signal is normally lower in amplitude than the oscillator signal, so the oscillator tends to alternately saturate and then cut off the transistor. This is precisely the sort of nonlinear operation that will create the mixing action. If you recognize this as being similar to modulation, then you are very observant. The process is almost identical, except that the amplitude modulation stage is a special case in which one frequency is very much higher than the other. In that situation the mixer products show up as sidebands.

The principal difference between these stages is the method for injecting the local oscillator signal. In all three cases the RF signal is applied to the base and the stage is operated in the common emitter configuration. Also, in all three circuits the collector contains a tank that is resonant at the IF frequency so that only the difference component ($f1 - f2$) is extracted. In Figure 21.4(a) the oscillator signal is connected in parallel with the emitter resistor of the mixer transistor. On positive excursions of the L.O. signal, therefore, the emitter voltage will rise to a point close to the base potential; which will, of course, turn off the transistor. On negative excursions the polarity of the L.O. signal subtracts from the dc emitter bias, and makes the stage think that the base-emitter voltage is much greater because the emitter is at a negative potential. High base-emitter voltage causes the stage to saturate.

The design of the circuit in Figure 21.4(b) causes the oscillator signal to inject into the mixer in parallel with the RF signal. On positive excursions of the L.O. signal the transistor's base is much higher than the emitter, so the stage saturates. Alternatively, on the negative swing of the L.O. signal, the base-emitter voltage is zero or negative, so the stage is cut off. The circuit of Figure 21.4(c) is similar in operation to that of Figure 21.4(a), but the signal is injected via a transformer so that it is in series with the dc bias on the emitter.

Junction field effect transistors (JFET) operate in a manner not too much unlike their bipolar cousins, and some of the same techniques are used for the injection of the L.O. signal. A dual-gate MOSFET, though, may be used in a manner such as that shown in Figure 21.4(d). Here the RF signal is applied to gate 1 and the L.O. signal to gate 2. The high-amplitude L.O. signal cuts off, then saturates, the MOSFET on alternate halves of each cyclic excursion.

A differential amplifier is used as the mixer in Figure 21.4(e). This type of amplifier consists of two identical, and closely matched, transistors connected with their bases and collectors in push-pull and their emitters tied together. The common emitter terminal draws its current from a constant current source (CCS), transistor $Q3$. When there is no L.O. signal at the base of transistor $Q3$, the bias circuit causes $Q3$ to operate at some quiescent point. In that condition current $I3$ is the constant regardless of the amplitude of the RF signal. It is also true, by Kirchoff's current law, that $I3 = I1 + I2$. Consequently when the RF signal causes $Q1$ to turn on and $Q2$ to turn off, $I1$ becomes larger and $I2$ becomes smaller. This makes the $Q1$-$Q2$ differential collector voltage larger than if the same transistors had been used in a normal RF amplifier stage. When used as a mixer stage the base of $Q3$ is driven between cutoff and saturation by the L.O. signal. The differential amplifier type of mixer has not been exceptionally popular in the past, but recent designs show more usage because there are several mixer/amplifier integrated circuits available that are based on this circuit. RCA offers the most commonly found devices in this area.

One last mixer type is the diode circuit shown in Figure 12.4(f). This circuit uses the balanced modulator concept, except that all of the transformers operate at RF and IF frequencies. Several manufacturers offer double balanced mixers such as this in small, hermetically sealed metal cans. Most of them may be operated over an extremely wide frequency range—on the order of at least 0.1 MHz to 500 MHz.

A converter circuit is one in which the functions of mixer and local oscillator are combined in a single tube or transistor. An example of a bipolar transistor converter stage is shown in Figure 21.5. To the RF signal this stage looks much like any ordinary mixer stage. The RF signal is applied to the base of a common emitter transistor. The local oscillator

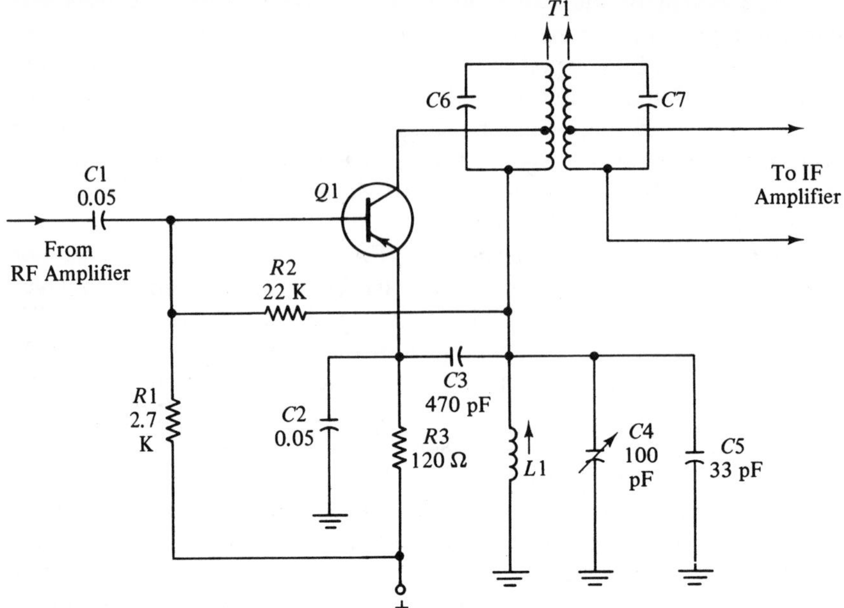

Figure 21.5 Converter stage combines functions of the local oscillator and mixer.

consists of the same transistor, plus coil *L*1 and capacitors *C*2, *C*3, *C*4, and *C*5. Main tuning control is the function of capacitor *C*4, which is a large variable type. The portion of the IF transformer secondary that is in series with *L*1 has but little effect on the overall operating frequency, provided that the tap is low on the primary winding. Although the RF signal would like to see this stage as a Class A amplifier, which it would indeed be if the oscillator were not running and the collector were tuned to the RF frequency instead of the IF, the action of the L.O. is to alternately cut off and then saturate the transistor. The dc bias between the emitter and base terminals of the transistor might suggest that the transistor is permanently cut off if measured while the oscillator is running. DC values close to 0VDC are common, and even where higher potentials are encountered they are rarely as high as the 0.6–0.7 V normally expected in a forward-biased transistor.

Most IF amplifiers are merely RF amplifiers fixed-tuned to the IF frequency. Most use separate tuned tank circuits at the input and output sides of the amplifier. An example is shown in Figure 21.6(a). In most cases the collector and base terminals of the transistor are connected to taps on the respective transformer coils for purposes of impedance matching. Other than that, the stage is a rather ordinary Class A amplifier

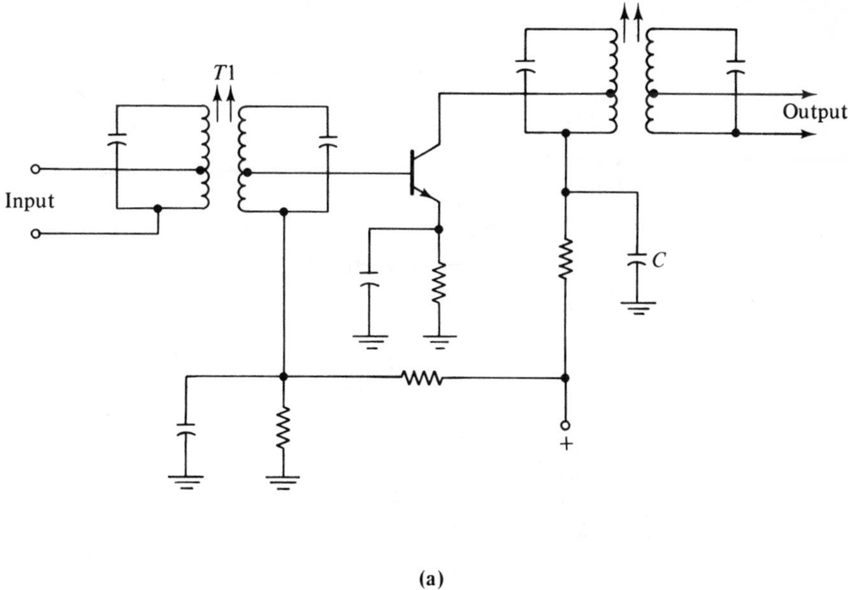

(a)

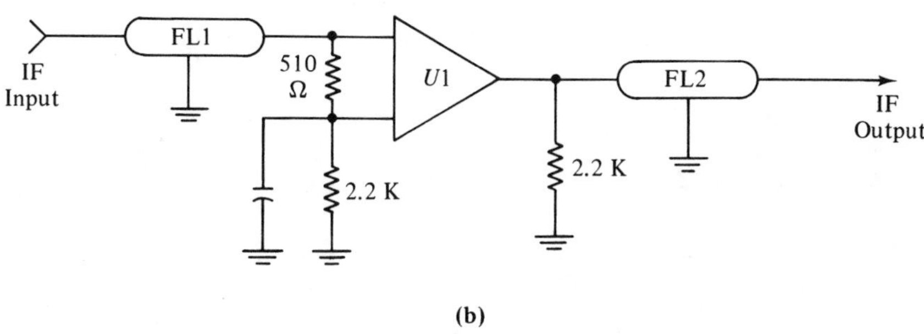

(b)

Figure 21.6 (a) Intermediate frequency (IF) amplifier. (b) Integrated circuit IF amplifier using crystal filter resonators in place of tuned transformers.

tuned to the IF frequency. Use of multiple tank transformers makes the selectivity very good compared with high-frequency RF amplifiers. In some cases the IF transformer may not use a tuned secondary, but in most tuning is the rule. It is also possible to find IF stages that have several tuned Class A stages in cascade.

In more recent designs we find the use of synthetic, monolithic, crystal filters in place of the IF transformers. Although transistors may be

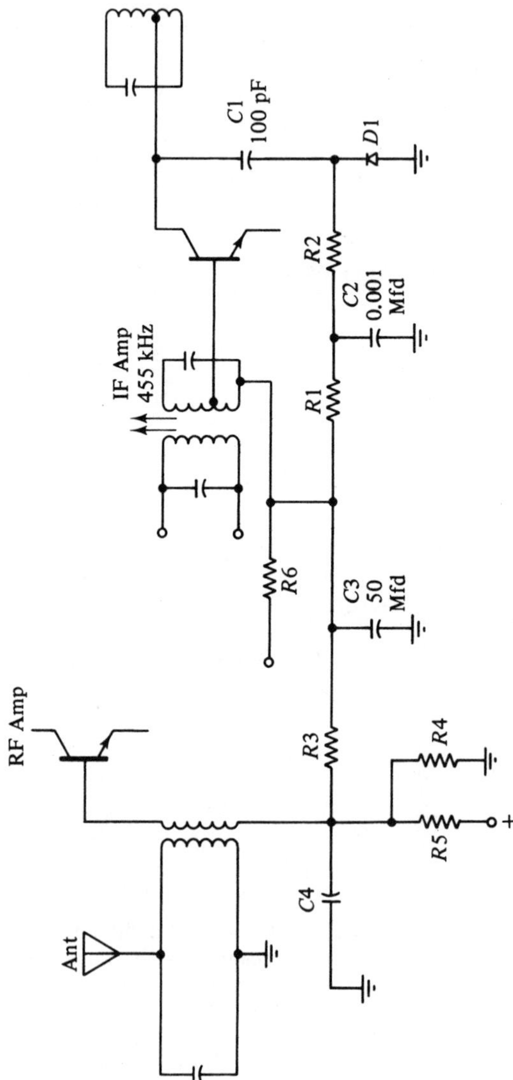

Figure 21.7 Automatic gain control (AGC), also called automatic volume control (AVC).

used, these are normally found in stages using integrated circuits as the amplifier. An example is shown in Figure 21.6(b). The crystal filter resonators are used in preference to transformers, because they can be made with very narrow bandwidths—much more so than most LC tanks. The crystal filter is capable of much higher *Q* figures than the LC version. Recall that a piezoelectric crystal element is actually a form of tank circuit, so the device is very frequency selective. There are some receiver designs in which the only high-grade filter is used at the output of the mixer. The amplifier to follow is a wideband, Class A cascade stage.

The automatic gain control, or AGC (also sometimes called "automatic volume control" or AVC), is used to smooth out variations in signal loudness as the radio is tuned across the band. There is a tremendous variation in the strength of radio signals picked up by the antenna. If there were no AGC circuit, the listener would turn up the volume to hear a weak station, then would be blasted out of the room when he tuned in a very strong station. Alternatively, the listener would turn down the gain to keep that from happening, and would then miss weaker stations. The job of the AGC is to increase the RF and IF amplifier gain on weak signals, and then decrease it on strong signals. An example of a simple AGC circuit is shown in Figure 21.7. A small sample of the signal at the collector of the IF amplifier transistor is tapped off by a small-value capacitor. This signal is applied to a rectifier diode that is of the same type as that used in the detector. This will create a negative dc potential with a value proportional to the amplitude of the IF amplifier signal.

Bias to the RF and IF amplifier transistors comes from two sources. Each transistor has its own regular bias network such as that found in all tuned, Class A, amplifier stages. This is the function of $R4$ and $R5$ for the RF amplifier and $R6$ in the IF amplifier. The second source of bias is the voltage developed across diode $D1$. The effect of this latter potential is to buck the normal bias voltage. A strong input signal creates a high bucking voltage, so the gain of the two stages is reduced.

Although AGC systems can be quite good, they often lack adequate dynamic range for some communications receivers. In those cases a separate bias adjustment may be provided for the RF amplifier (see Figure 21.3). This control may be labeled "RF gain" or "sensitivity."

Detectors. Figure 21.8 shows a simple AM detector. This is the same sort of envelope detector as that found in the crystal set of Figure 21.2. Of course, instead of a tunable RF tank we have, instead, a fixed tuned IF transformer. The principle, however, is the same. Following the diode detector is a pi-section "tweet filter." This is a low-pass audio filter that passes only audio signals between dc and a few kilohertz. This is used to prevent adjacent channel stations from interfering with each other. In the AM broadcast band, for example, stations transmit only sidebands out to 5 kHz from the carrier, and channels are spaced 10 kHz apart. If two signals on adjacent channels are mixed together with sufficient relative amplitudes, then a 10-kHz beatnote will be present in the output of the detector. The low-pass filter reduces its amplitude, while passing audio signals up to 5 kHz unattenuated.

Radiotelegraph and single sideband transmissions cannot successfully be demodulated in an envelope detector. Low-cost communications and shortwave receivers may use an oscillating IF amplifier stage as the detector. In those radios the last IF amplifier is allowed to oscillate at a frequency that is a few hundred hertz away from the normal IF frequency. The oscillation and the IF signal beat together in the AM detector following the IF amplifier to form a beatnote equal to the difference between the two frequencies.

Most modern SSB receivers, however, do not depend upon an oscillating detector. For best demodulation, and elimination of the "Donald Duck" quality of the SSB transmission, it is necessary to reinsert the carrier at the receiver. This carrier must be nearly identical to the original. Because of this requirement, most SSB receivers use a product detector. Most such detectors are equipped with a crystal-controlled *beat frequency oscillator* (BFO) that produces two frequencies, one each for USB and LSB. The product detector more nearly resembles the heterodyne mixer type of circuit, except that the output circuit is an audio low-pass filter.

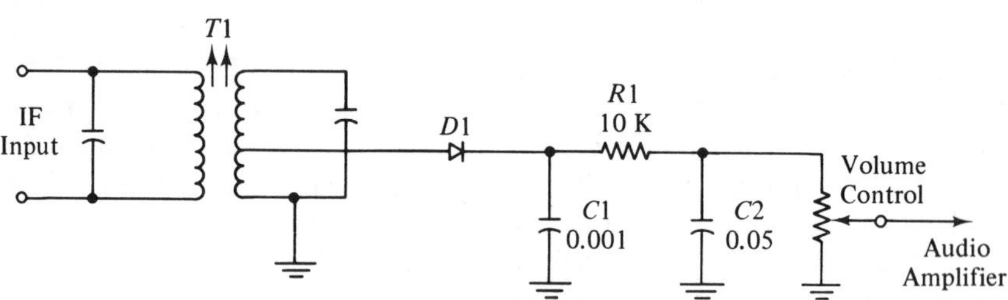

Figure 21.8 Envelope detector for AM demodulation.

Superheterodyne Problems. Two main problems exist in superheterodyne design: tracking and image rejection. Tracking refers to the ability of the RF and L.O. tank circuits to keep tuned to the same channel. This is made even more difficult because the RF and L.O. tanks are tuned to different frequencies. This problem is alleviated, and in many respects cured, by the use of different values of tuning capacitor for the L.O. and RF tanks.

Images are spurious signals picked up due to heterodyning. The IF amplifier does not care whether the RF signal is above or below the local oscillator signal, so long as the difference between them is equal to the IF frequency. If the RF amplifier is sufficiently broadbanded, then an image frequency may also be picked up and converted to the IF. This image has a frequency equal to the RF ± twice the IF. For example, let us assume that a 2-MHz signal is being received on a receiver equipped with a 455-kHz IF amplifier. Let us further stipulate that the L.O. frequency is above the RF. This means that the L.O. will operate on a frequency of 2455 kHz. The difference frequency is the L.O. − RF, or 455 kHz. But a signal at 2910 kHz also heterodynes with the L.O. in the mixer and produces a 455-kHz difference frequency.

There are several approaches to reduction of the image response of a superheterodyne. First, it is necessary to have an RF amplifier ahead of the mixer. This adds a measure of selectivity before the mixer receives the image frequency. It is also preferable to have a relatively high IF. The 455-kHz figure so often quoted works reasonably well for receivers up to around 10 MHz, but is less than desirable at higher frequencies because the selectivity of tuned tank circuits at those frequencies broadens enough to accept and pass the image frequency. It is applied, amplified, to the mixer and an image response is created. True, the amplitude of the image is not as great as when the receiver is actually tuned to that frequency, but it is usually great enough to cause interference. Most modern communications receivers use high IF frequencies in order to improve image rejection. IF frequencies in the neighborhood of 3 MHz, 9 MHz, or 10.7 MHz are no longer uncommon, because crystal filters provide decent selectivity at those frequencies—something not always attainable with LC filters.

Older communications receiver designs used double- or even triple-conversion schemes to eliminate the image response problem. An example of a double-conversion receiver is shown in Figure 21.9. The "front end" consists of stages very similar to the front end of the single-conversion receiver just studied. The IF frequency, however, tends to be higher, something over 1500 kHz in most cases. A low-gain IF amplifier passes the signal on to a second mixer that heterodynes the high-IF with a signal from a local oscillator. This produces a difference frequency in the 50-kHz to 500-kHz range. The low-IF stages provide the bulk of the gain and selectivity—consistent with the properties of low-frequency tank circuits.

Another approach to double- and triple-conversion receiver design is shown in Figure 21.10. Although the basic technique applies to either type, we shall discuss the circuit in terms of the triple-conversion design in an effort to be complete. This type of radio receiver uses what is called the "variable IF" technique. The front end consists of an RF amplifier

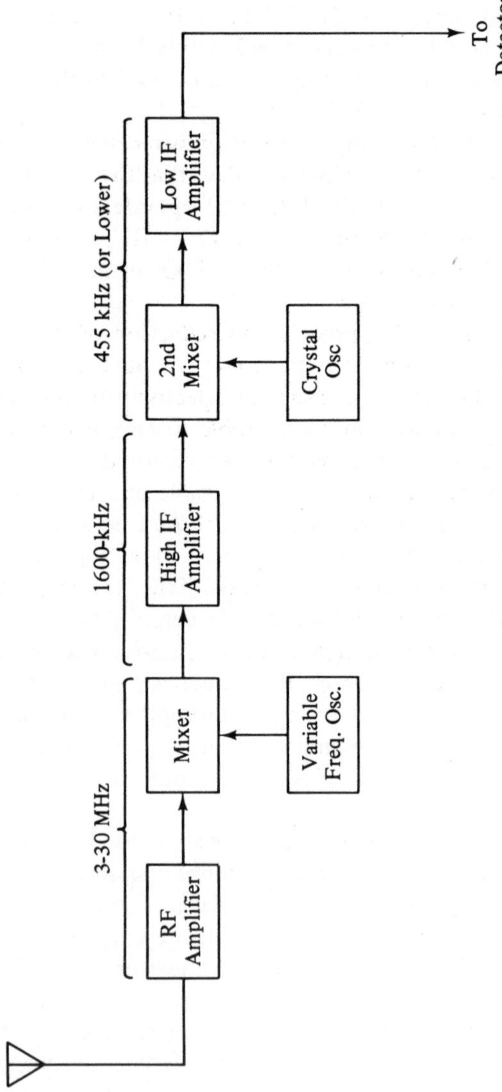

Figure 21.9 Dual-conversion superheterodyne receiver.

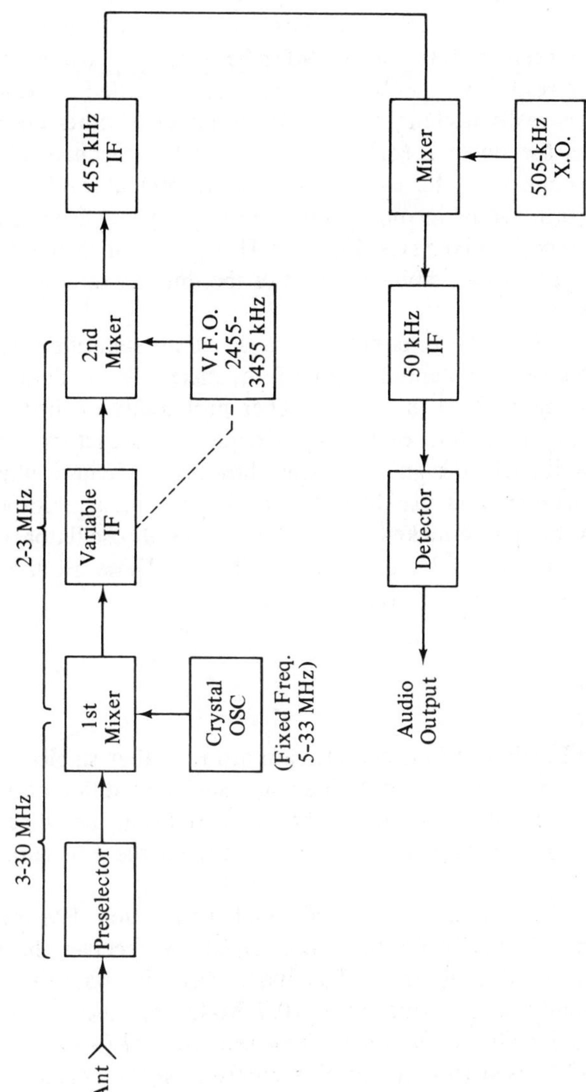

Figure 21.10 Triple-conversion superheterodyne receiver.

called a "preselector" because it is usually tuned separately from the main tuning dial. The first mixer heterodynes the RF signal (3 MHz to 30 MHz in our example) with a fixed frequency signal from a crystal oscillator. There is one crystal for each band covered. The particular crystal frequencies lie between 5 MHz and 33 MHz because they are above the RF signals in their respective bands. The next stage is called a "variable-IF" amplifier, but is really nothing but the RF amplifier of other designs. This amplifier tunes the range 2 MHz to 3 MHz and is mechanically ganged to the tuning control in the variable frequency oscillator (VFO). These two controls form the main tuning knob on the receiver front panel. The output of the second mixer is a 455-kHz IF signal, which is heterodyned down to 50 kHz by the combined efforts of the third mixer and a 505-kHz local oscillator.

This type of design is popular because of its superior stability and precise dial calibration potential at high frequencies. In the double-conversion design of Figure 21-9 there is a higher probability of drift and other problems due to the nature of the high-frequency oscillators used in the L.O. The variable-IF design is fading, however, because ultramodern communications receivers use high IFs to improve image response and the L.O. can be phase-locked to a stable crystal oscillator/frequency divider chain that can resolve to as little as 10 Hz. These are the so-called phase-locked loop (PLL) receivers.

21.3 FM RECEIVERS

Frequency modulation (FM) receivers are always either single- or double-conversion superheterodynes, but there are sufficient differences to warrant separate coverage. We shall not, however, reinvent the wheel, as they say, but we shall elaborate the differences between the FM superhet and the others.

A block diagram of the typical single-conversion FM receiver is shown in Figure 21.11. In the main portion of the receiver the only two differences worthy of note are the fact that a cascade chain of several IF amplifiers (usually on a frequency of 10.7 MHz) are used, and we have a feedback circuit called an *automatic frequency control* (AFC).

The AFC is used to keep the FM receiver on the correct frequency despite the fact that the local oscillator wants to wander in frequency. In early FM receivers this drift was so pronounced that some cheap models changed station just because a person approached the case—body capacitance created the shift. AFC works because all FM detectors (of which more later) produce a dc output voltage that is proportional to the error in center frequency. If the L.O. is tuned so that the receiver's front end is

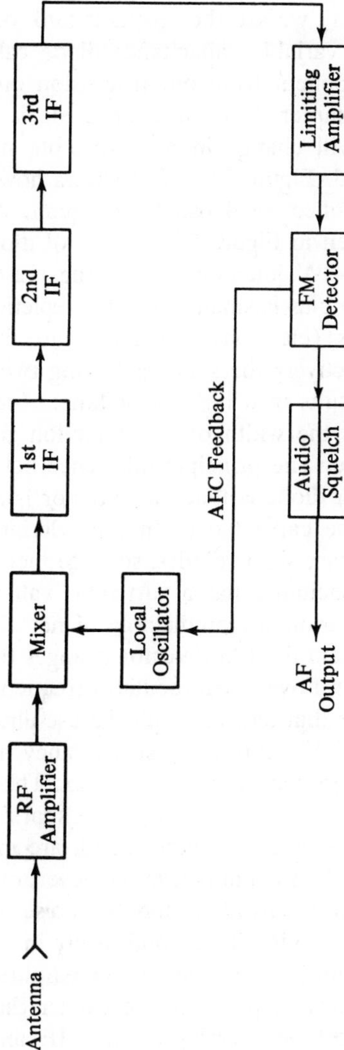

Figure 21.11 Typical FM communications receiver.

centered exactly on the FM carrier's center frequency, then the dc voltage will take on some specific value, in most cases 0 VDC. Figure 21.12 shows how the local oscillator of an FM receiver uses this dc feedback control voltage to keep the receiver on frequency.

In Figure 21.12(a) we see the resonant tank of the local oscillator. Diode *D*1 is a special variable capacitance diode called a *varactor.* You should recall this component from our discussion on direct-FM modulators in the previous chapter. The varactor diode is designed so that its junction capacitance will change in a predictable manner with changes in reverse bias potential. Figure 21.12(b) shows how this diode might be used in a crystal-controlled local oscillator circuit. A view of how such a diode operates is given in Figure 21.12(c). All diodes exhibit a certain capacitance across the *PN* junction due to the existence of a depletion zone. When the reverse bias is small, then the depletion zone is also small and the charge carriers (electrons and holes) are in close proximity to each other. This is effectively the same as having two conductive surfaces close together, so it results in a high capacitance. Increasing the reverse-bias potential increases the width of the depletion zone and thus lowers the junction capacitance. The principal difference between a varactor and a regular semiconductor diode is that the varactor is specially designed to enhance and control the capacitance. In fact, designers try to minimize the capacitance in ordinary signal diodes, so as to increase switching speed. In the varactor the capacitance has a particular value at a given reverse-bias potential, and is reasonably predictable, if not altogether linear. The dc feedback potential from the FM detector changes the bias on the varactor, and this effects control over local oscillator frequency.

Noise is one factor that tends to limit the usefulness of a communications system. AM and CW receivers must use fancy noise elimination circuitry, some of which can become quite complex. The nature of this noise is mostly impulses of RF energy generated from sparking electrical sources and lightning. FM receivers, on the other hand, are much touted as being "free of impulse noise." This claim is true, however, only under the proper set of circumstances. It seems that impulse noise tends to amplitude-modulate the RF carrier, so it will respond nicely in an AM receiver. The FM receiver, though, does not depend upon amplitude variations. It is variations in the frequency or phase of the carrier that convey the information. One purpose of the seemingly extra IF amplification and the limiter stage is to build up the signal amplitude as much as possible, then clip off the positive and negative peaks. Figure 21.13 shows graphically how a limiter stage reduces noise in the FM receiver output. The limiter can be likened to a window through which the signal must pass on its way to the detector. The noise-ridden peaks are clipped off, leaving a relatively noiseless signal to be applied to the demodulator.

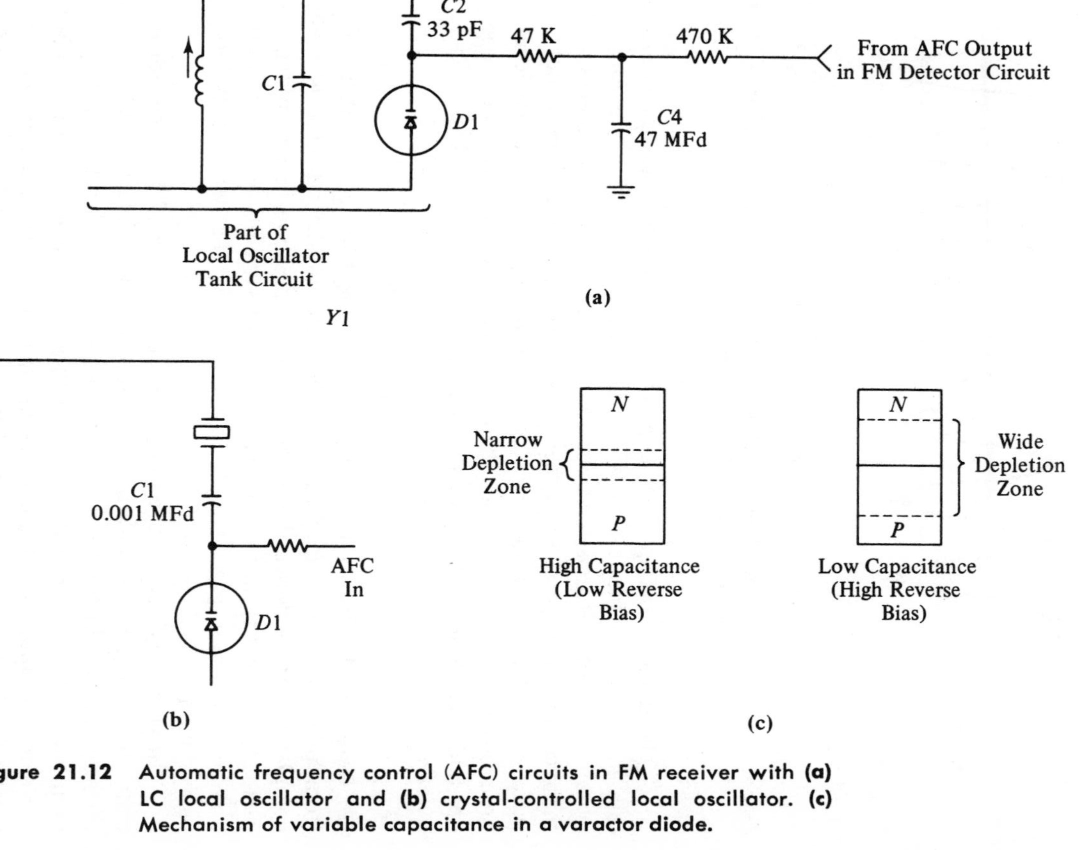

Figure 21.12 Automatic frequency control (AFC) circuits in FM receiver with **(a)** LC local oscillator and **(b)** crystal-controlled local oscillator. **(c)** Mechanism of variable capacitance in a varactor diode.

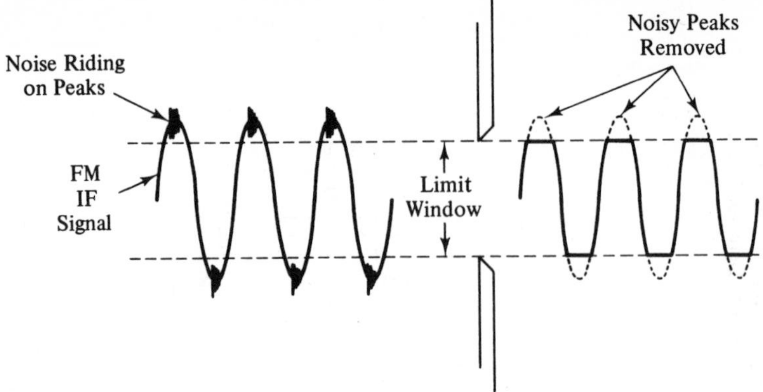

Figure 21.13 FM is more free of noise than AM because a limiter circuit clips off the noisy peaks of the incoming signal.

The signal at the antenna terminals of the receiver must have a certain minimum amplitude that will cause substantial clipping before the system is capable of noise-free reception. This level causes "quieting" in the receiver. Between stations there is a high noise level. This is not impulse noise, but is instead a hiss or "white noise." As the signal level is brought up greater in amplitude than the noise, the signal/noise ratio goes up, and this causes the *apparent* noise level to go down. This is called *quieting*.

FM Detector Circuits. Of all properties of the FM receiver that differ from other types of superhet, only the detector/demodulator is really completely unique. Since the nature of the modulation in FM systems is radically different from the modulation in AM systems, one would expect a radically different process in demodulation—one that would sense angular variations.

In years past there were only two widely regarded FM detector circuits: the Foster-Seeley discriminator and the ratio detector. While both of these are still in wide use, other designs are seen far more frequently than was previously the case. Some of these are brand new, while others are merely adaptations of older designs that have been made either technically feasible or more economical by recent advances in semiconductor technology.

Review of Fundamentals. In frequency modulation systems the carrier frequency of a radio transmitter is varied by an audio modulating voltage. Figure 21.14 shows the relationship between carrier frequency and that modulating voltage.

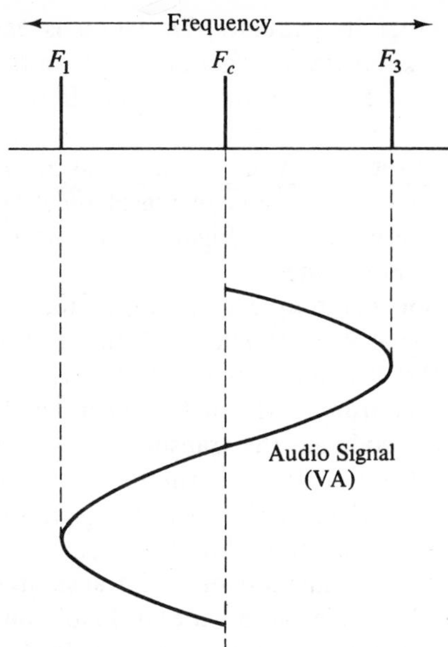

Figure 21.14 Relationship of the FM frequency extremes to the amplitude of the modulating audio signal.

When the value of the audio sine wave is zero, the transmitter frequency is at f_c. As the audio signal voltage increases in the positive direction, the carrier frequency increases until frequency $f2$ is reached at the time that the audio voltage reaches its positive peak. The carrier frequency then begins to decrease back toward f_c as the audio voltage also decreases in amplitude toward zero. On negative-going excursions of the audio signal voltage the carrier frequency decreases to $f1$.

The "true FM" transmitter modulating action previously described is not found often in actual use, because of the difficulties in designing "true FM" transmitters that meet the accuracy and stability requirements of the government. Most "FM" transmitters use phase modulation, which to the receiver is functionally equivalent—or almost so. In that system of modulation, the carrier frequency is held constant while its phase is varied by the audio modulating signal. This approach allows the use of a highly stable oven or temperature-compensated crystal oscillator for frequency control. Phase variations occur in the reactance modulator that follows the crystal oscillator.

As pointed out in the last chapter, and reiterated here for emphasis, there are several concepts in FM that are often confused. For example, "deviation" and "frequency swing" are often confused. Deviation is the amount of frequency change of the carrier between its unmodulated frequency f_c and either of its extremes. Deviation is expressed in units of frequency—hertz or kilohertz. Frequency swing, on the other hand, is the *total* frequency change between lower and upper frequency extremes ($f2 - f1$) and is a measure of the channel width occupied by the transmitter. The relationship between frequency swing and deviation is dependent upon the positive-negative symmetry of the modulating signal. For a perfectly symmetrical sine wave, as in Figure 21.14, deviation is exactly one-half of the total frequency swing.

Neither deviation nor frequency swing is affected by the frequency of the modulating signal in a straight or "true" FM system. That is not true, however, of the PM modulator, which has a 6 dB/octave rising (preemphasis) characteristic. FM, on the other hand, is essentially flat; all audio frequencies modulate the transmitter the same amount for any given amplitude. In the true FM transmitter the audio frequency determines only the rate at which the carrier swings through its range. Only the amplitude affects the amount of deviation.

Full, 100 percent modulation of AM transmitters occurs when the audio signal causes the carrier amplitude to double on positive peaks and drop to zero on negative audio peaks. "One hundred percent modulation" of an FM transmitter, on the other hand, is a matter that is specified more arbitrarily. In the 88-MHz to 108-MHz FM broadcast band, 100 percent modulation is defined as a deviation of ±75 kHz. The TV sound carrier is fully modulated with only ±25 kHz deviation. Keep in mind that there is no fundamental difference between these carriers; they are merely in different services. The reason that they are 100 percent modulated at different deviation figures is a matter of convention only. Incidentally, the VHF/UHF landmobile, marine, and most amateur equipment is 100 percent modulated with a deviation of only ±5 kHz.

Until recently, when the specifications were changed to accommodate Dolby and other noise-reduction systems, the typical FM broadcast transmitter gave a great deal of preemphasis to the upper audio frequencies in an effort to improve the signal-to-noise ratio (SNR) at the receiver end of the system. The receiver detector circuit included a 75-μs RC network that provided deemphasis and reestablished the proper frequency response of the audio amplifiers.

Slope Detection. Figure 21.15 illustrates a crude but effective method for FM demodulation, which is shown here mostly to show one of the primary requirements of any FM or PM detector: a frequency response at the receiver IF frequency that varies as a function of input frequency. This method, called "slope detection," requires a receiver with a relatively narrow passband. The center of the carrier is tuned in so that it lies on the

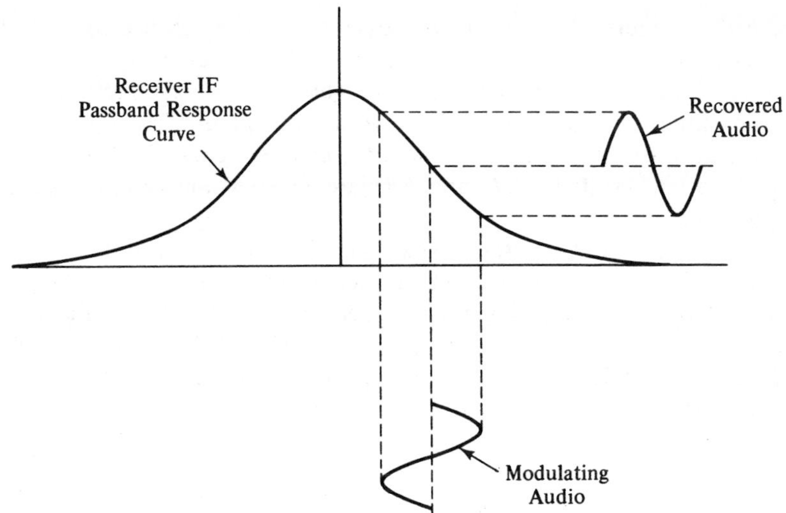

Figure 21.15 Slope detection of FM signal.

downslope of the IF amplifier response curve. The incoming signal then sees an IF amplifier frequency response that varies as the carrier frequency varies.

Foster-Seeley, or "Classic," Discriminators. Figure 21.16(a) shows the circuit of the Foster-Seeley discriminator that has been used for many years in a wide variety of FM receivers. Note that the RF choke, $L1$, is common to both the primary and secondary windings of transformer $T1$. In fact, it is in series with the secondary and in parallel with the primary. If you doubt this last statement, examine Figure 21.16(b). This common connection of $L1$ allows the usage of its voltage and current as references. When the IF signal applied to the primary of $T1$ is unmodulated, it will be at a frequency equal to the resonant frequency of the $T1$ secondary tank circuit. This causes the voltages across $Ls1$ and $Ls2$ to be equal. Currents $I1$ and $I2$ are also equal. Since these currents flow in opposite directions, however, they tend to cancel each other, and that makes the output voltage zero.

Figure 21.17(a) shows the voltage and current vector relationships in the discriminator when the frequency of the input signal increases above f_c. Because the secondary tank circuit takes on inductive properties, secondary current I_s lags behind voltages $E1_{s1}$ and $E1_{s2}$ by 90 deg. Since the voltages and currents in an inductive circuit are out of phase, they must be added vectorially to find the resultant. The voltage vectors are labeled $Ed1$

and $Ed2$ in Figure 21.17(a). In this case, the voltage applied to diode $D1$ is greater than the voltage applied to diode $D2$, so current $I1$ is greater than $I2$. Under these circumstances, the currents no longer totally cancel and an output voltage is generated. Similarly, in Figure 21.17(b), we see the situation existing when the carrier decreases below f_c. The relationships between resultants $Ed1$ and $Ed2$ are reversed and vector $Ed2$ predominates.

Figure 21.18 shows the typical voltage-vs-frequency response curve of a typical discriminator. Part of the technician's task in alignment of an FM detector is to place f_c right at the zero crossover point on this curve. The bandwidth of this circuit must be such that the expected deviation (75, 25, or 5 kHz) will not drive the signal into the nonlinear regions of the curve.

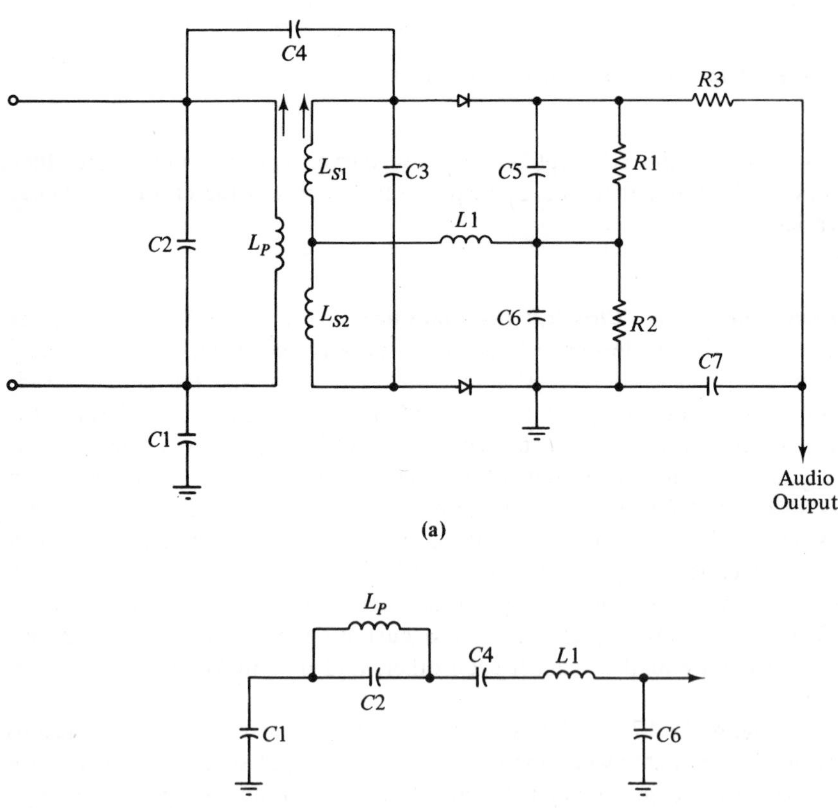

Figure 21.16 Discriminator type FM demodulator. **(a)** Entire circuit. **(b)** Partial equivalent circuit.

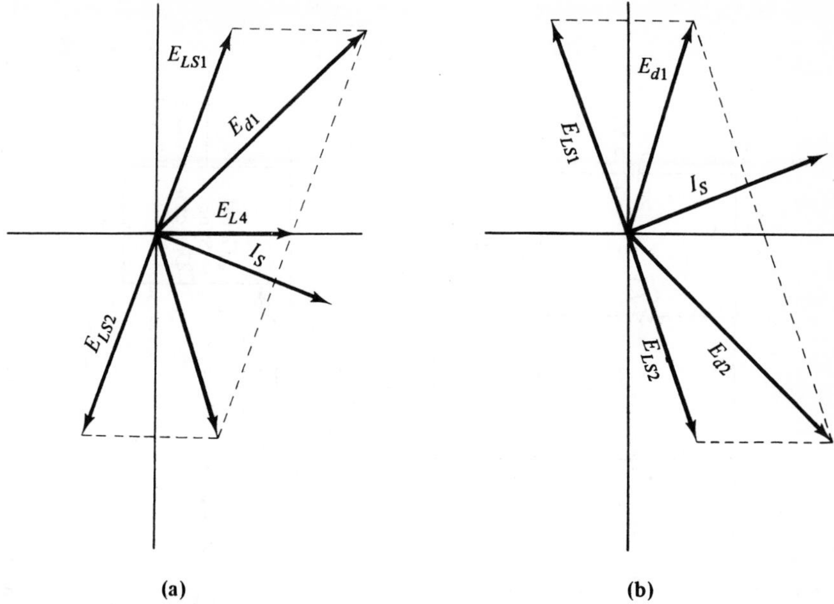

Figure 21.17 Vector diagram of the signals in the discriminator.

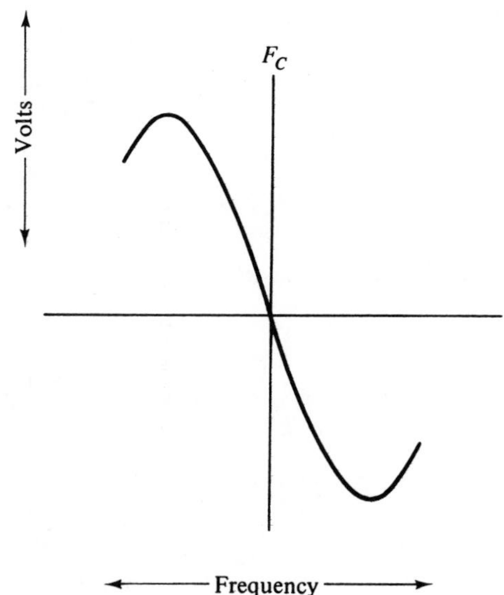

Figure 21.18 Discriminator "S" curve.

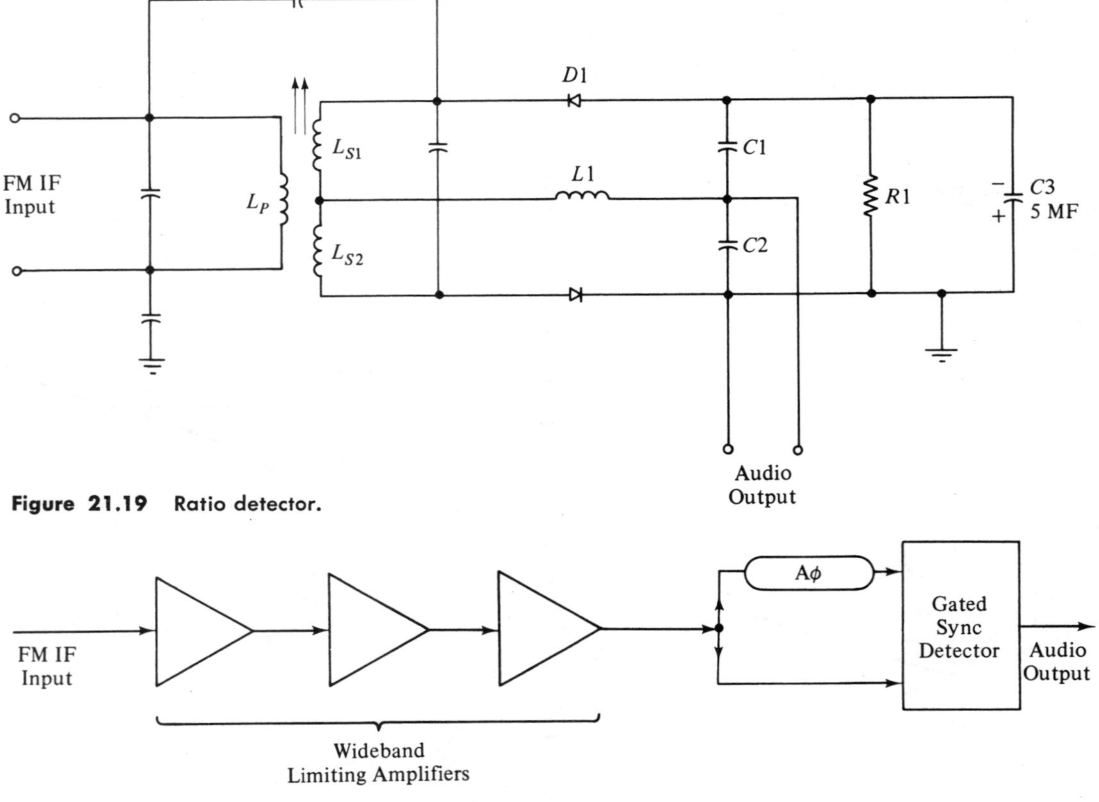

Figure 21.19 Ratio detector.

Figure 21.20 Block diagram of the integrated circuit quadrature FM detector.

Ratio Detectors. Figure 21.19 shows a typical *ratio detector* circuit. The major difference between this circuit and the Foster-Seeley discriminator is that the diodes are reversed. The diodes in the ratio detector circuit are in series, and that allows the voltages across capacitors *C*1 and *C*2 to add rather than cancel. When the input signal is at its unmodulated frequency, voltages across these two capacitors are equal. When the carrier is deviated to a higher frequency, however, the voltage across *C*2 increases, and that across *C*1 drops. Exactly the opposite occurs when the deviation is in the other direction: *Ec*1 rises and *Ec*2 drops. This, of course, results in a dc voltage that varies in amplitude as the modulation on the carrier causes the frequency to deviate above and below f_c.

Capacitor *C*3 has two functions: (1) it stabilizes the voltage across series capacitor combination *C*1/*C*2 so that the ratio can be taken; (2) it suppresses any amplitude modulation, including noise, that may be riding on the carrier waveform. It is this last function that makes it possible for ratio-detector-equipped receivers to function without a limiter.

IC Quadrature Detectors. Integrated circuit (IC) technology has revived a type of FM detector once used extensively in vacuum-tube TV receivers, but otherwise little used: the quadrature detector. Once popular in circuits using the 6BN6 gated-beam vacuum tube, the quadrature detector has made a comeback in the form of several IC devices. Examples are the Motorola MC1357P and the uLN2111 by others. This is one type of detector that was made economically possible by advances in semiconductor technology.

Figure 21.20 shows the block diagram of a typical IC quadrature detector. The input stages form a high-gain, wide-band, limiting amplifier whose output is a series of varying-period square pulses. These are fed to two places: to one input of the gated synchronous detector, and to a quadrature (i.e., 90 deg) phase shift network external to the IC. The output of this network is brought back inside of the IC, as shown in Figure 21.21, and is used to drive the alternate input of the gated detector. This detector produces output pulses with constant amplitude, but with periods that vary with the modulating frequency. These are then integrated in a low-pass filter to produce the audio signal.

The integrated circuit quadrature detector has been used extensively in car radios, hi-fi, and communications receivers over the past several years. Be aware, though, that an IC in the detector circuit does not automatically indicate that it is a *quadrature* circuit. A number of semiconductor manufacturers offer IC devices that contain the last several IF amplifier stages and the diodes needed to make either ratio detector or discriminator circuits. One popular type of this class is the RCA CA3043.

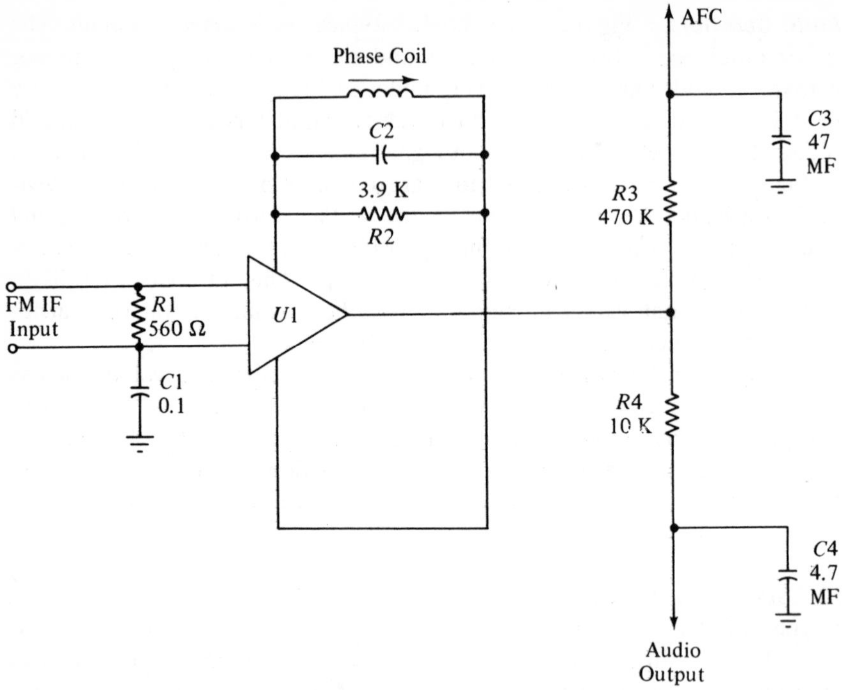

Figure 21.21 IC quadrature detector circuit.

Phase-locked Loop (PLL) Detectors. Although developed in the decade 1930–1940, when oddly enough it was an AM detector, the PLL has only come into its own as a viable product with the invention of PLL integrated circuits. Figure 21.22 shows the block diagram of a typical PLL FM detector. Although the same PLL is used for other purposes as well, here we shall describe the circuit action as if it were designed exclusively for FM detection.

A phase detector in the chip receives two inputs: one from the FM IF amplifier and the other from an internal voltage-controlled oscillator (VCO). When the carrier is unmodulated, the frequency of the VCO is equal to the IF frequency. This makes the output of the phase detector zero. As the IF signal deviates, this equality is lost, and a dc error signal voltage is developed that is proportional to the frequency difference between IF and VCO frequencies. This error voltage is passed through a low-pass filter that removes any residual RF voltages present, and then to a dc amplifier (DCA). The output of the DCA controls the VCO frequency. This pulls the VCO to the new frequency from the IF amplifier. Since the IF signal is deviating about the center frequency, the VCO will

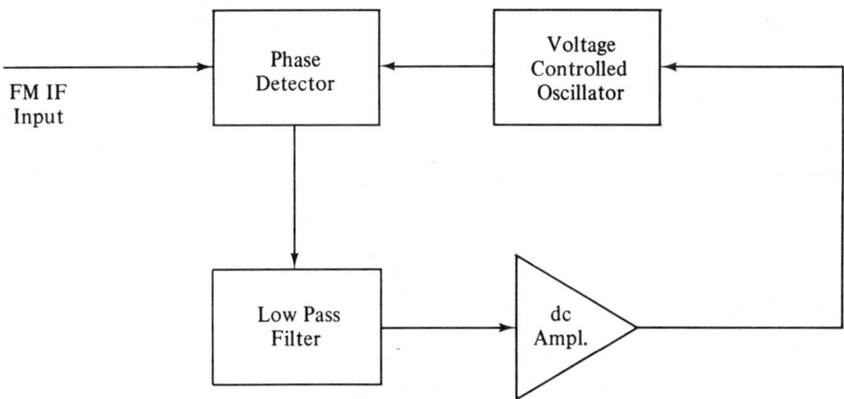

Figure 21.22 Phase locked loop FM detector (block diagram).

always be trying to catch up. The control voltage will be continuously varying at the rate of the audio that modulated the carrier. This voltage is the recovered audio.

Figure 21.23 shows an actual PLL IC FM demodulator using the Signetics type 560B device. IF signal is coupled to the IC via capacitor *C*7 and pin 12. The frequency of the VCO is set to its approximate range by capacitor *C*4. Since the internal resistances of any IC device normally vary ±20 percent, this capacitor will likely be a variable type. The input signal level required for proper operation must be between 2 mV and 15 mV. Below the lower limit the PLL may have difficulty tracking the IF signal, while above the upper limit the AM suppression is lost. RC

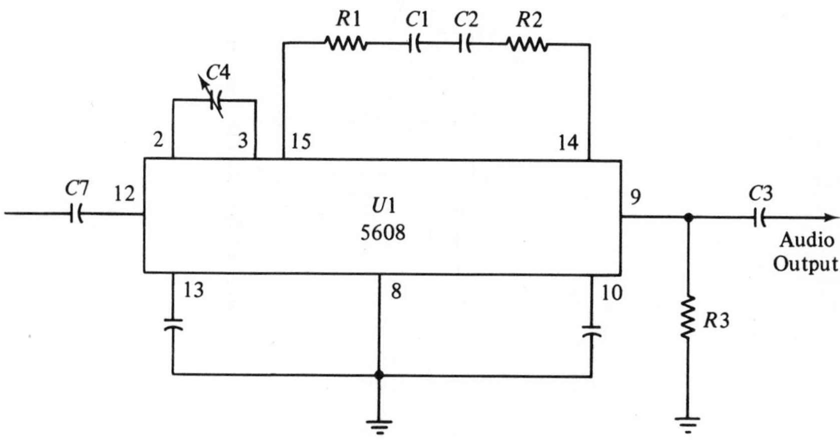

Figure 21.23 Circuit for a PLL FM detector.

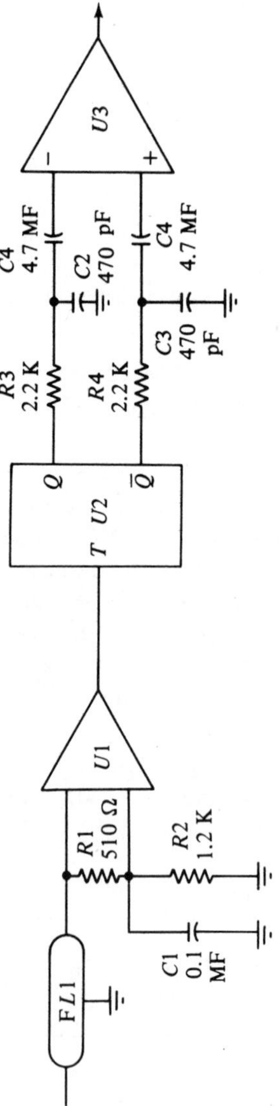

Figure 21.24 Coilless or "digital" (pulse counting) FM detector.

networks $R1/C1$ and $R2/C2$ form the low-pass filter between the phase detector and the dc amplifier. The output signal is obtained from pin 9, and is coupled through RC network $R3/C3$ to the following circuits. The function of capacitor $C6$ is deemphasis. It has a value selected to give the required deemphasis when the internal resistance at pin 10 is 8 kΩ. In actual practice, though, the internal resistance will vary 20 percent, so a 0.001-μF capacitor is usually deemed adequate.

Digital (Pulse-counting) Detectors. Figure 21.24 shows a "coilless" FM detector which, until recently, was restricted mostly to the demodulation of audio subcarriers in FM telemetry applications. At least one manufacturer of high-quality FM broadcast tuners, however, uses this type of circuit in a receiver design. $FL1$ is a bandpass filter which must be either a LC or ceramic piezoelectric type. Integrated circuit $U1$ contains the gain stages and a limiting amplifier. IC $U2$, however, is a special TTL digital logic type called a *retriggerable monostable multivibrator,* or *one-shot*. This IC produces a single pulse every time it is triggered by an input pulse from $U1$. These pulses have constant amplitudes and durations; only their repetition rates vary with the deviation of the IF signal. There are two complementary outputs from $U2$, designated Q and $\overline{Q}$ (read "not Q"). Each of these opposite outputs is fed to an RC integrator that averages the signals to obtain a push-pull audio signal, which in turn is fed to an audio amplifier that has differential inputs.

PROBLEMS

1. A type of detector used in crystal sets used the mineral __________.
2. A class of detector based on the Armstrong oscillator is the __________ detector.
3. When the stages preceding the detector are all tuned RF amplifiers the radio is a ________ type.
4. The ________ type of radio receiver uses a local oscillator to beat against the RF signal to produce a third frequency.
5. The third frequency in the superheterodyne is called ________.
6. AGC stands for __________.
7. Images can occur in a superheterodyne receiver, and usually appear at a frequency of ________ the IF above or below the actual frequency.
8. A receiver has an IF of 455 kHz and is tuned to 1200 kHz. If the L.O. is above the RF, then it is operating at a frequency of __________.
9. SSB and CW (radiotelegraph) signals are demodulated by using a ________ detector.
10. Name several types of FM detector.

22 Radio Transmitters

Although radio transmitters exhibit wide variations in design, there are certain commonalities that make them similar to each other. We shall treat radiotelegraph and all forms of radiotelephone transmitters as simple outgrowths and extensions of the basic design discussed in Sec. 22.1.

22.1 MOPA AND MOBPA DESIGNS

Figure 22.1 shows the block diagram for the two basic types of radio transmitters. The type shown in Figure 22.1(a) is the most basic and is called the *master oscillator power amplifier* (MOPA), while that in Figure 22.1(b) is the master oscillator *buffer* power amplifier (MOBPA).

The MOPA forms the basis for many low-power amateur and marine transmitters, but it is used mostly in radiotelegraph applications. In this class of transmitter the radio signal is generated by the master oscillator, although when we study more modern designs you will see that the term "master oscillator" is actually somewhat anachronistic.

In the simple MOPA transmitter the master oscillator is either a fixed-crystal oscillator or a variable-frequency oscillator (VFO), but in this instance let us consider the case of a crystal oscillator that is in the electron-coupled circuit configuration. This type of stage is designed so that it has adequate power to directly drive the power amplifier stage. An example is shown in Figure 22.2.

In the circuit of Figure 22.2 an RF signal from the crystal oscillator is developed across the RF choke, forming the plate load of the M.O. tube ($V1$). The signal is coupled through capacitor $C4$ to the grid of the power amplifier tube $V2$, which is tuned to resonance by tank circuit $L1/C10$. The output circuit that feeds power to the antenna is a pi-network, such as that studied in Chapter 18.

Metering of two parameters is sufficient to allow proper tune-up of the MOPA transmitter: the $V2$ grid and plate currents. These are monitored by meters $M1$ and $M2$, respectively. In most low-power transmitters $M1$ and $M2$ are actually the same meter, and a "grid-plate" switch is provided that selects which current is measured.

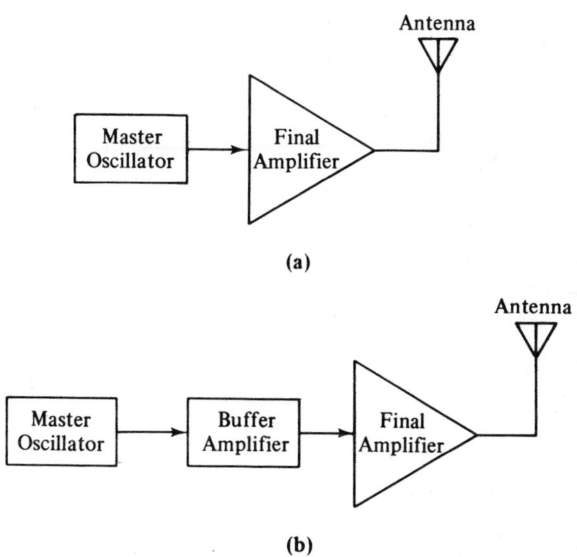

Figure 22.1 (a) Master oscillator power amplifier (MOPA) transmitter and (b) master oscillator *buffer* power amplifier (MOBPA) transmitter.

MOPA Tune-up. The tune-up instructions for any given transmitter may differ from those given below by some small amount, but these are adequate for most cases.

1. Set *C*8 to minimum capacitance (lightest loading), *C*7 and *C*10 to maximum capacitance.
2. Apply power and adjust *C*7 for a minimum current reading on *M*2.
3. Adjust *C*10 for maximum grid current (*M*1).
4. Readjust *C*7 for minimum plate current (*M*2).
5. Adjust *C*8 for a 10–20 percent increase in plate current (*M*2).
6. Readjust *C*7 for minimum plate current (*M*2).
7. Repeat steps 5 and 6 until *M*2 reads approximately 75–80 percent of its off-resonance value (step 2) unless instructed by the manufacturer to stop at some other value.

This procedure works for most MOPA transmitters designed according to good engineering principles. Some have an additional switch called "tune-operate" and a control labeled "drive level." The tune-operate switch is set to "tune" as a part of step 1. It is usually designed to lower

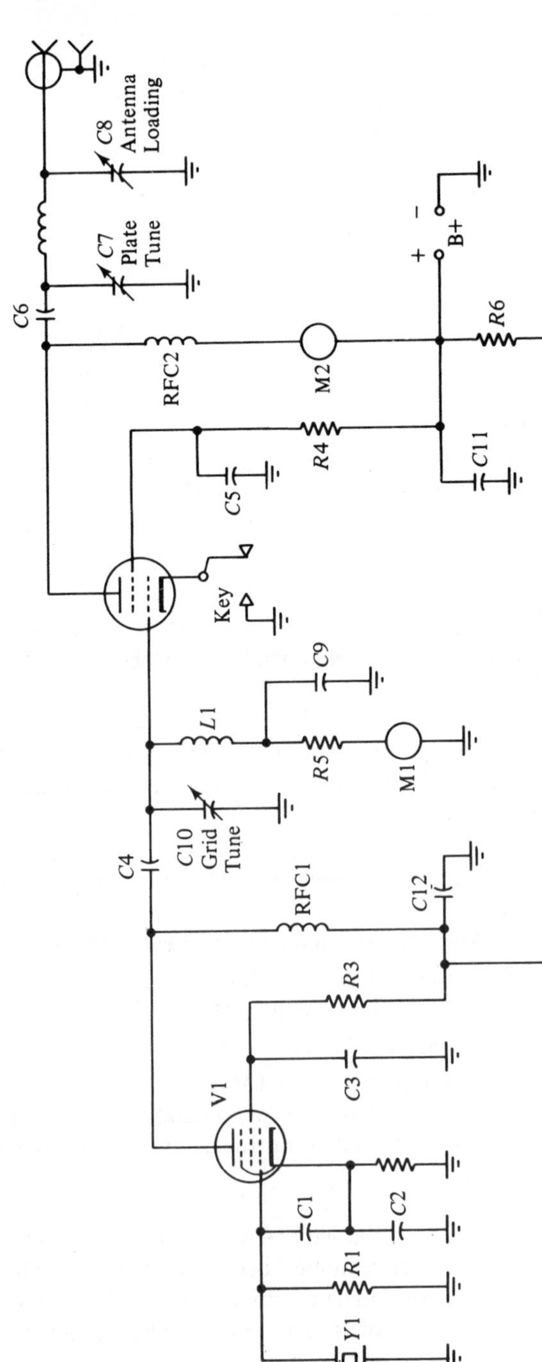

Figure 22.2 A simple MOPA radiotelegraph (CW) transmitter.

the screen grid voltage of the power amplifier tube (*V*2) so that the off-resonance current existing at the beginning of step 2 is limited to a value that will not damage the tube. After the grid current is peaked in step 2 and the plate current is at minimum, then we place the T-O switch in the operate position and continue to tune the transmitter. The difference now is that the situation is controlled.

The drive control sets the signal level developed by the amplifier section of the master oscillator (*V*1) and is used to vary either the plate or screen potential of that tube. Once step 7 is completed, reduce the grid current (*M*1), using the drive level control to the current specified by the manufacturer of either the transmitter or the final amplifier tube.

The MOBPA transmitter is essentially the same as the MOPA design, except that a buffer amplifier is placed in cascade between the output of the master oscillator and the final amplifier. In most cases the MOBPA can be tuned by using the same procedure as the MOPA, except that step 3 should be extended to include peaking of the grid current (*M*1) by the buffer tuning controls. In a few MOBPA transmitters a separate plate milliammeter is provided for the buffer, so we can dip the tuning control of the buffer using the correct meter as an indicator.

The circuit in Figure 22.2 shows a telegraph key in series with the cathode of final amplifier *V*2. In an actual radiotelegraph transmitter there might be any of several keying schemes, of which cathode is the simplest. Other keying methods will be discussed shortly.

22.2 FREQUENCY MULTIPLIER STAGES

At frequencies over 10 MHz to 12 MHz crystals become too thin for safe operation. They will prove very fragile and break easily. In this same range, or lower, LC oscillators become very difficult to stabilize and control. To counteract these defects some transmitter designs are equipped with frequency multiplier stages. The actual signal is developed at a low frequency, where oscillator designs are easier to tame, and is then multiplied upwards to the correct operating frequency. The frequency of the crystal oscillator, in such a transmitter, operates on a *subharmonic* of the actual operating frequency.

Several approaches to frequency multiplication are used, but not all are equally desirable. All of them, except the passive diode type, operate either Class B or Class C because those classes are nonlinear, so they have large amounts of harmonic energy in their output waveforms. An output tank circuit is tuned to the desired harmonic of the input frequency. Two examples of frequency multiplier stages are shown in Figure 22.3.

The circuit in Figure 22.3(a) is a passive multiplier in which an

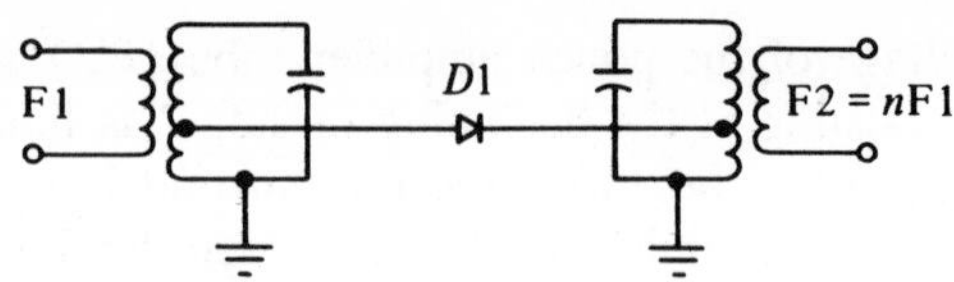

(a)

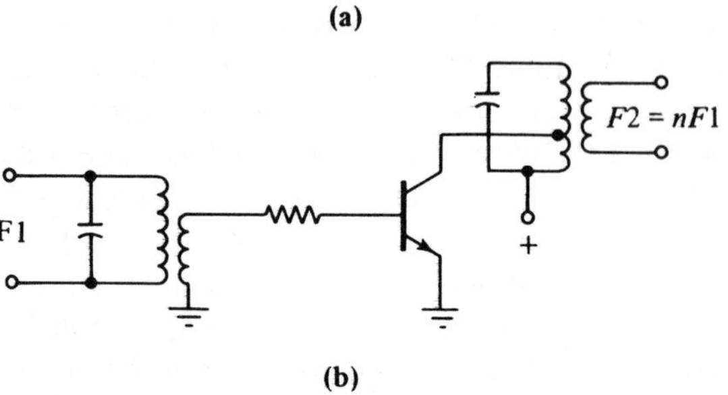

(b)

Figure 22.3 Frequency multiplier stages (a) diode and (b) transistor.

ordinary diode is the nonlinear element. This is an example of a *passive* frequency multiplier. The diode acts as a halfwave rectifier to the RF sine wave delivered to its input by the preceding stage. The halfwave output waveform, of course, is nonlinearly related to the input, so there are lots of harmonics. The desired harmonic ($f2$) is selected by the output tank circuit, the other harmonics being rejected. The "flywheel effect" in this tank will change the halfwave pulsations back into sine waves, with a frequency of $f2$.

Figure 22.3(b) shows a common form of transistor multiplier that might be found in almost any solid-state radio transmitter. Note that there is no dc bias on this stage, but that a series resistor is in the base circuit. This will cause $Q1$ to operate Class C, which is rich in harmonic output. Again the desired harmonic is selected by an output tank and the others are rejected.

It is generally not feasible to produce a multiplier that has a high order of multiplication, because the energy content of higher harmonics will be too low. This would necessitate the use of extra amplification, which presents certain problems. As a result, most transmitter multipliers are either doublers, triplers, or (and these are rare) quadruplers.

A doubler is a stage in which the output frequency is two times the input frequency ($f2 = 2f1$). A similar definition holds for the tripler, which has an output frequency that is three times the input frequency ($f2 = 3f1$), and so on. If it is necessary to obtain orders of multiplication higher than three or four, then it is necessary to cascade multiplier stages that produce an output that is the desired frequency. The output frequency multiplication factor is the *product* of the individual factors.

Example. Two stages such as those shown in Fig. 22.3(b) are connected in cascade. The first is a doubler and the second is a tripler. What is the output frequency if the input frequency is 12 MHz?

$$\begin{aligned}(2) \times (3) \times (12\text{ MHz}) &= f_{\text{out}} \\ (6) \times (12\text{ MHz}) &= f_{\text{out}} \qquad (22\text{-}1) \\ 72\text{ MHz} &= f_{\text{out}}\end{aligned}$$

In many transmitters there are several multiplication stages. Even the MOPA transmitter [Figure 22.1(a)] may use frequency multiplication. The master oscillator tube, for example, may be an electron-coupled type in which the oscillator (using the screen grid as a pseudo-anode) operates at a frequency that is a subharmonic of the frequency to which the tank in the plate is tuned. In a few cases, the grid of the final amplifier ($V2$ in Figure 22.2) is tuned to $f1$ and the plate is tuned to $f2$. This last case is an example of multiplication in the final amplifier stage, and is generally not considered satisfactory, since some of the supposedly suppressed harmonics could easily find their way into the antenna and be radiated.

In the typical MOBPA transmitter, on the other hand, multiplication is usually done in the buffer amplifier stages, of which there may be more than one.

Frequency multipliers should not be confused with frequency translators such as might be found in a single sideband transmitter. Translator stages are heterodyne mixers. The multiplier cannot be used following any amplitude- or pulse-modulated stage, or the modulation will be lost because of stage nonlinearity. If a transmitter uses low-level modulation, as do almost all SSB transmitters, then the stages following must be linear, at least insofar as the shape of the waveform is concerned. The typical SSB signal is generated at a fixed frequency and is then heterodyned to the desired operating frequency.

22.3 MASTER OSCILLATORS

Although the term "master oscillator" was once almost universally appropriate when transmitter designs were discussed, modern design techniques have made it less so. In fact, some classes of transmitter, including almost all CB types, use several oscillators to produce the desired output frequency. In the older context, prior to the 1970s, the M.O. was a crystal or variable-frequency oscillator of the type discussed in Chapter 21.

Today's commercial and CB transmitters, though, use one of several techniques that fall broadly under the heading "frequency synthesis" in place of the old master oscillator. Several different types of frequency synthesizer are known, and these fall into the categories: filter, crystalplexers, and phase-locked loops (PLL).

In the filter type of synthesizer (a type that is no longer popular) a quasi-white noise spectrum of pulses is generated that consists of a fundamental, such as 1000 kHz, and as many subharmonics as necessary. A typical filter-type synthesizer might have a 1000-kHz fundamental mixed with subharmonics of 100 kHz, 10 kHz, 1 kHz, and 100 Hz. LC or RC filter circuits are used to select the harmonic of these components that will generate the correct operating frequency when mixed together. Let us consider as an example a transmitter operating on a frequency of 2562 kHz. A 2000-kHz filter selects the second harmonic of the 1-MHz fundamental, another selects the fifth harmonic of the 100-kHz source, another the sixth harmonic of 10 kHz, and finally the second harmonic of 1 kHz. These are heterodyned together, and a final filter tuned to 2562 kHz selects the desired product. The filter method was expensive enough that it was used only on the most expensive laboratory equipment. The filter type of frequency synthesizer was also found to be difficult to control. As the LC filters detuned over time, more and more spurious frequencies would show up in the output—making for an illegal transmitter.

Somewhat better are the crystalplexers, an example of which is shown in Figure 22.4. In this case we have two crystal oscillators mixing to form various frequencies, although more oscillators may be used in any given design.

Notice in the example of Figure 22.4 that oscillator 1 produces output frequencies between 36 MHz and 37 MHz in steps of 100 kHz. The second oscillator produces output frequencies between 11 MHz and 14 MHz in 1-MHz steps. When their difference ($f2 - f1$) is selected as the output, we generate 40 output frequencies from only 14 crystals (4 of $f1$ and 10 of $f2$). We could also add another 40 channels by changing the filter to cover the 47-MHz to 50-MHz band so that the sum frequency ($f1 + f2$) is selected instead of the difference. Note that in each case the sum and difference signals are removed from either $f1$ or $f2$ sufficiently to prevent leakage of these frequencies through the bandpass filter.

The crystalplexer form of frequency synthesizer has been popular for the control of 27-MHz CB transmitters, certain commercial transmitters, and 2-meter band amateur transmitters. In the case of the CB transmitter the crystalplexer has proved popular because it allows control

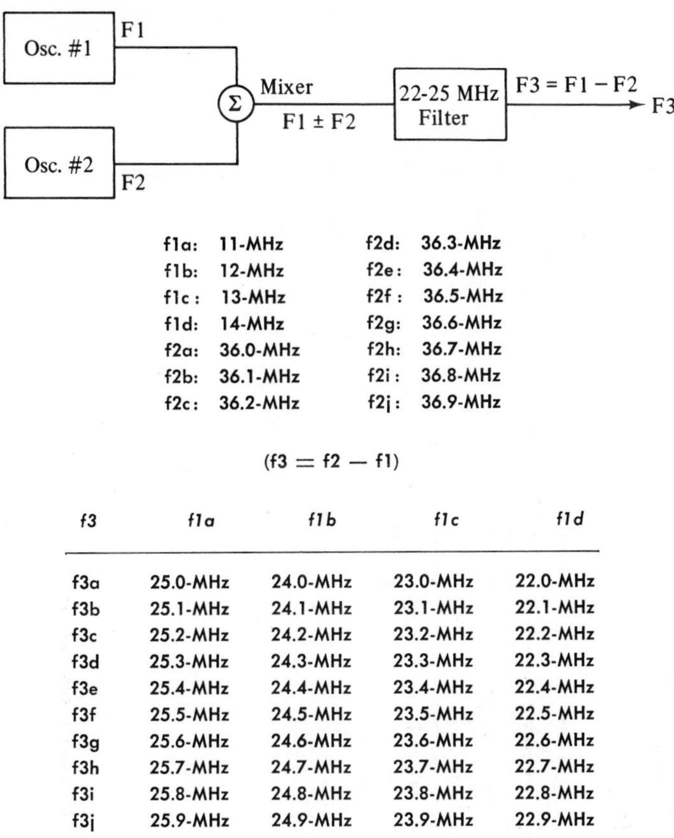

f1a:	11-MHz	f2d:	36.3-MHz
f1b:	12-MHz	f2e:	36.4-MHz
f1c:	13-MHz	f2f:	36.5-MHz
f1d:	14-MHz	f2g:	36.6-MHz
f2a:	36.0-MHz	f2h:	36.7-MHz
f2b:	36.1-MHz	f2i:	36.8-MHz
f2c:	36.2-MHz	f2j:	36.9-MHz

(f3 = f2 − f1)

f3	*f1a*	*f1b*	*f1c*	*f1d*
f3a	25.0-MHz	24.0-MHz	23.0-MHz	22.0-MHz
f3b	25.1-MHz	24.1-MHz	23.1-MHz	22.1-MHz
f3c	25.2-MHz	24.2-MHz	23.2-MHz	22.2-MHz
f3d	25.3-MHz	24.3-MHz	23.3-MHz	22.3-MHz
f3e	25.4-MHz	24.4-MHz	23.4-MHz	22.4-MHz
f3f	25.5-MHz	24.5-MHz	23.5-MHz	22.5-MHz
f3g	25.6-MHz	24.6-MHz	23.6-MHz	22.6-MHz
f3h	25.7-MHz	24.7-MHz	23.7-MHz	22.7-MHz
f3i	25.8-MHz	24.8-MHz	23.8-MHz	22.8-MHz
f3j	25.9-MHz	24.9-MHz	23.9-MHz	22.9-MHz

Figure 22.4 Heterodyne or "crystalplexer" frequency synthesizer.

of 23 channels with only a few crystals. More recently, however, 40-channel CB transmitters and certain VHF transmitters use the phase-locked loop (PLL) technique, an example of which is shown in Figure 22.5.

The PLL consists of a voltage-controlled RF oscillator (VCO), a crystal reference oscillator, a phase detector, a low-pass filter, a dc amplifier (DCA), and a divide-by-*N* frequency divider/counter.

The VCO is a special oscillator in which the output frequency is a function of some dc control voltage ($E1$) applied to an appropriate point in the circuit. This oscillator usually operates on the transmitter's assigned frequency or on some predetermined subharmonic of that frequency. 146-MHz amateur transmitters, for example, could use a frequency-determining

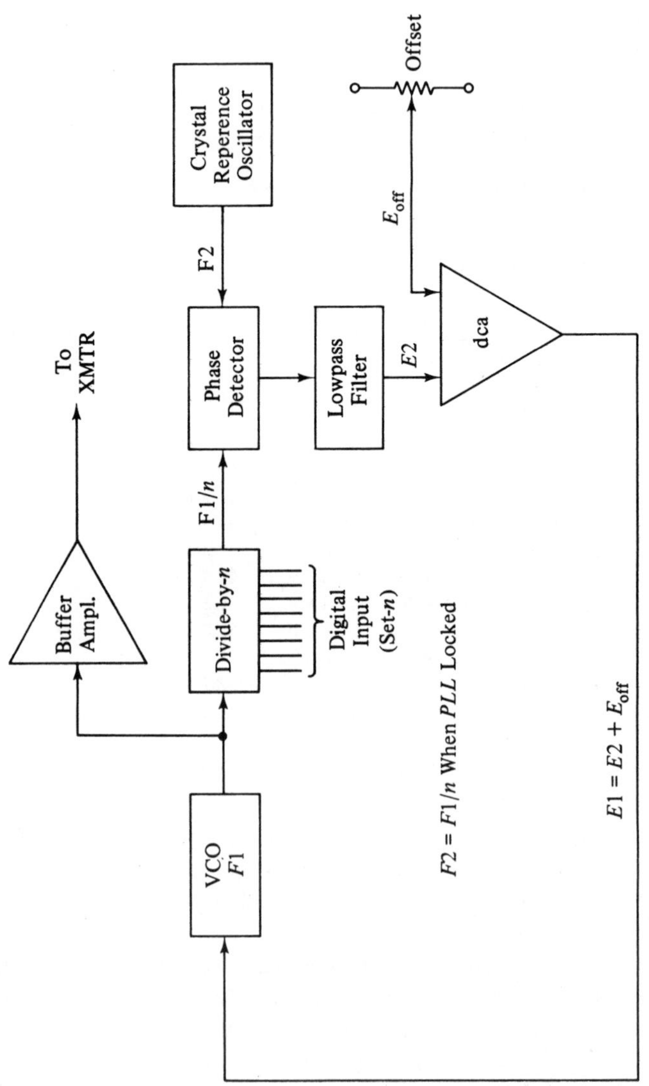

Figure 22.5 Phase locked loop (PLL) frequency synthesizer.

circuit (M.O. or synthesizer) at 12 MHz followed by multipliers with a factor of $\times$ 12. We shall consider as our example such a transmitter to be operated on 25-kHz increments between 145.8 MHz and 147 MHz.

The crystal reference oscillator is a low-frequency, stable crystal oscillator that operates at a frequency equal to the channel spacing, in this case 25 kHz. Although it may tend to complicate frequency modulation, generating the VHF signal directly without multiplication results in a purer output.

The phase detector is a comparison circuit that will generate a dc output that is proportional to the frequency difference between two input signals. The low-pass filter following this stage removes any residual input signal ($f1$ or $f2$) that might remain. The dc amplifier (DCA) scales the dc output to the range required of $E1$ by the VCO.

The real heart of the PLL is the divide-by-N counter (N is any integer). This circuit will divide the output of the 145.8–147 MHz VCO by the integer set by manipulating its digital control inputs (these set N). Table 22.1 gives the values for N required to produce a 25-kHz output to the phase detector from the VCO.

Table 22.1

f_0	N	
145.8	5832	
145.825	5833	
145.85	5834	
145.875	5835	
.	.	
.	.	(25-kHz increments)
.	.	
147.00	5880	

Let us assume that the transmitter is set to a frequency of, say, 145.8 MHz, and that we want to change to a frequency of 145.875 MHz. Initially, then, the control inputs ("set N") will see a digital word representing the division ratio "5832." When the operator changes the channel (usually by a switch on the front panel) the digital word representing N is changed. In this case we want to go from 145.8 MHz ($N = 5832$) to 145.875 MHz ($N = 5835$). When this change is made the counter output no longer equals 25 kHz, so the phase detector output is no longer 0 VDC. This generates a change in $E1$, which in turn shifts the frequency of the VCO. This change continues until the VCO is on a frequency of 145.875 MHz, which, when divided by the new value of N (5835), equals 25 kHz. This makes $f1/N = f2$, so the circuit stabilizes at 145.875 MHz, and the new output frequency is created.

The stability of the PLL synthesizer is essentially that of the crystal oscillator. Also, trimming the crystal frequency sets the output frequencies to the correct point over the entire band.

22.4 RADIOTELEGRAPH KEYING

Radiotelegraph operators transmit international Morse code by turning the carrier of the transmitters on and off with a telegraph key to form the dots and dashes. In this section we consider some of the more popular types of keying circuit used in these transmitters.

The simplest form of keying, introduced briefly in Figure 22.2, uses a telegraph key connected in series with the cathode of the final amplifier stage. When the key is open, the dc plate current is interrupted, so no power output is created. Dots and dashes may be sent by closing the telegraph key.

A somewhat similar system connects the cathodes of the master oscillator and the power amplifier together, and keys them both simultaneously. This is to eliminate a phenomenon called "backwave." When only the final amplifier is cathode-keyed, the oscillator signal appearing at the final amplifier grid is capacitively coupled to the plate circuit, although it is not amplified. From the plate circuit it is coupled through the output network to the antenna, where it is radiated. You hear a backwave on a radiotelegraph signal as a weaker signal between the dots and dashes when the transmitter should be turned off altogether.

"Cathode keying" may suffice for simple amateur transmitters, but it is not altogether desirable. It can be dangerous to the operator if the key is connected directly to the cathode. When the key is up, the transmitter plate voltage appears across the telegraph key contacts, where it can possibly cause a shock to the operator. In some transmitters a mechanical relay is used in which the key energizes the relay, and the relay contacts turn on and off the cathode circuit.

Figure 22.6(a) shows an example of *grid block* keying. The grid of the final amplifier tube and possibly the oscillator is biased past cutoff by a negative C-supply. This keeps the transmitter cut off. When the telegraph key is closed, however, point A is grounded and the bias is removed. In some designs resistor $R2$ is used to keep the bias from dropping to zero. It will perform this function because the voltage at point A will be $(R2/(R1 + R2))$ times C−.

A variation on the blocked grid scheme is shown in Figure 22.6(b), and is called "differential keying." A problem called "chirp" is created when the oscillator and final amplifier are keyed simultaneously because the surge of current into the power amplifier temporarily creates a heavy

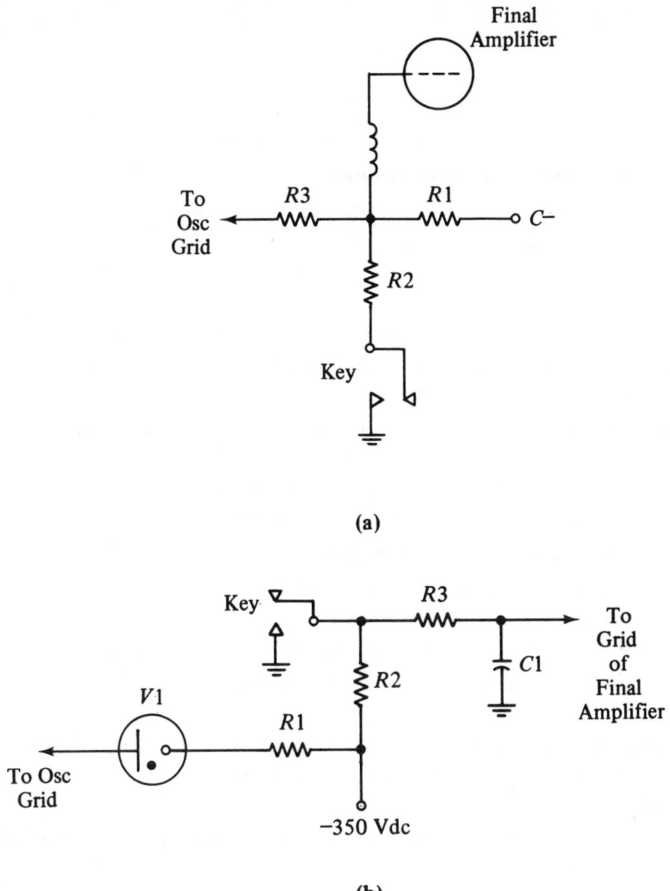

Figure 22.6 Radiotelegraph transmitter keying methods **(a)** grid block keying and **(b)** differential keying.

load on the power supply. A differential keyer turns on the oscillator a few milliseconds before turning on the final amplifier. This allows the final amplifier to remain off until the oscillator has stabilized.

When the key is up, gas regulator tube $V1$ is turned on and passes a current to the grid of the oscillator tube. This biases the oscillator tube off, so it will not produce a signal. The negative supply also charges capacitor $C1$ and is applied to the grid of the final amplifier, cutting it off. When the key is closed, $V1$ extinguishes almost immediately, and that turns on the oscillator. The grid voltage on the final amplifier, however, does not diminish to zero rapidly, because it depends upon the time constant of $R3/C1$.

PROBLEMS

1. MOPA stands for __________.
2. The capacitance of the loading capacitor in the output network of a MOPA or MOBPA transmitter should be set initially to its __________ value when the transmitter is tuned.
3. The plate current of the final amplifier stage is adjusted to __________ by capacitor $C7$ during tune-up.
4. An alternative method might be to adjust the power output to __________ by using the tuning controls.
5. A transmitter has three doublers and a tripler in a cascade chain following a 6.132-MHz oscillator. What is the operating frequency?
6. Deviation in an FM or PM transmitter is also multiplied by the frequency multiplier stage. In other words, if the transmitter in Question 5 had been FM, and was deviated 5 kHz at the output, the oscillator deviation would be 5000 Hz/24 = 208 Hz. Find the output deviation if the oscillator deviation is 450 Hz at 1000 Hz.
7. A transistor multiplier stage is generally ________-biased.
8. Three types of frequency synthesizers are __________, __________, and __________.
9. A heterodyne frequency changer is called a __________.
10. Any frequency changer following a low-level modulated stage must be a __________.
11. A PLL transmitter has channels spaced 10 kHz. What is the division ratio of the divide-by-N counter if the operating frequency is 166.12 MHz?
12. ________ keying is used to turn on the oscillator just before the final amplifier is turned on.

23
Basic Radio Antennas

The antenna is the device that actually radiates the electromagnetic signal into the air. It is generally conceded in electronic communications circles that the antenna is the most important link—over power output, especially. The antenna can make or break a radio station, yet only real professionals seem to pay much attention to the details of the antenna system.

23.1 BASIC FORMS

There are actually only two basic forms of radio antenna, although many variations exist. These are shown in Figures 23.1(a) and 23.1(b). The type shown in Figure 23.1(a) is called the hertz antenna. It is characterized by a signal source (the transmitter) placed at the center of the radiator that is half-wavelength. Although vertical antennas of this design exist, most are placed horizontally. The other basic form is the Marconi antenna of Figure 23.1(b). In this case we have a quarter-wavelength radiator mounted vertically. The generator is placed between the radiator and the ground.

One principal difference between these two classes of antenna is in the polarization of the radiated electromagnetic wave. All electromagnetic fields have two components that are perpendicular to each other: a magnetic field and an electric field. The polarization of the electromagnetic

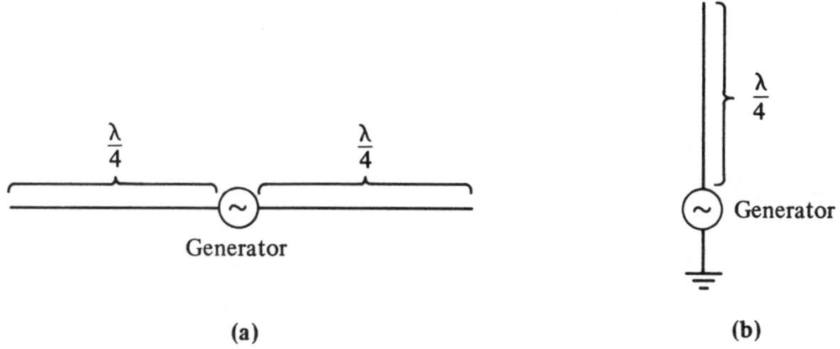

Figure 23.1 Basic antenna forms **(a)** halfwave hertz and **(b)** quarterwave Marconi.

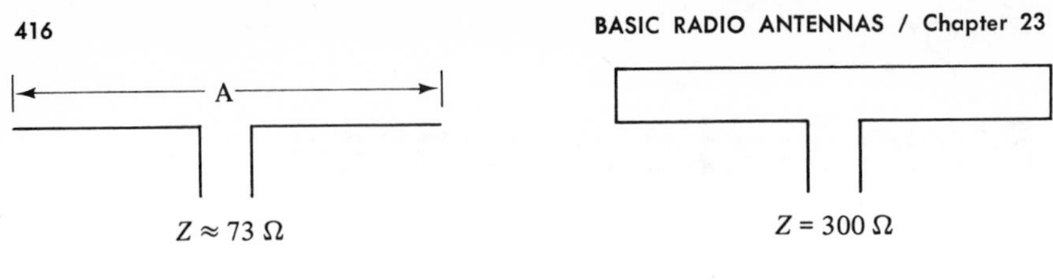

Figure 23.2 Dipole antennas (a) simple dipole and (b) folded dipole.

field is the polarization of the electric field. In the case of the hertz type of antenna the electric field is horizontal (parallel to the conductor), while in the case of the Marconi antenna the electromagnetic field is vertical—again parallel to the conductor. In both types of antenna the direction of propagation is perpendicular to the radiating conductor.

Dipoles. The hertzian antenna is the basis for the dipole antenna shown in Figure 23.2. The type of antenna shown in Figure 23.2 is known as the simple dipole, and consists of two quarter-wavelength radiators fed in the center by a transmission line from the transmitter. The nominal impedance at the center of the dipole is given as 70 Ω, but that is only when the antenna is in free space, away from any conductive surfaces that could affect the antenna. In reality the center impedance of dipole antennas mounted close to the earth's surface vary from around 25 Ω to around 120 Ω.

The dipole shown in Figure 23.2(b) is the so-called "folded dipole" in which a second half-wavelength conductor is paralleled with the main conductor. This type of antenna has an impedance of approximately 300 Ω. The purpose of the folded dipole is to make the antenna less responsive to small changes in frequency. The antenna is designed to operate only at a single frequency, but the folded dipole configuration supposedly can tolerate a larger frequency change before the effects of off-resonance become too serious.

The length of the antenna (either case) is given by the formula

$$L_{\text{feet}} = \frac{492}{F_{\text{mhz}}} \qquad (23\text{-}1)$$

in free space and by

$$L_{\text{feet}} = \frac{468}{f_{\text{mhz}}} \qquad (23\text{-}2)$$

closer to the earth.

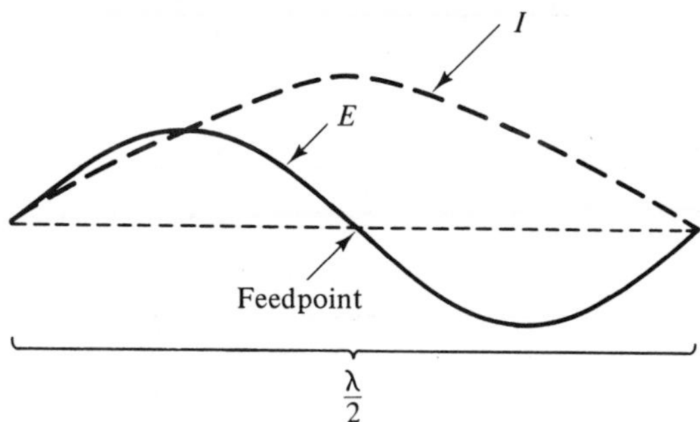

Figure 23.3 Current and voltage distribution along a halfwave antenna radiator.

These two formulas both express the half-wavelength, but Eq. (23-2) is used in real problems because it approximates the required length by taking into account the effects of the ground and surrounding objects. It must be realized, though, that any given antenna will have a length that is slightly different from this, so a means will be provided to compensate for errors. Such means will be discussed in the section on antenna matching.

The voltage and current distribution along the halfwave antenna is shown in Figure 23.3. Notice that the voltage is at a minimum and the current is a maximum at the feedpoint (center). This tells us that the impedance of the antenna varies along its length, and is minimum at the feedpoint. Most matching systems make use of this fact.

The radiation patterns of several basic types of antenna are shown in Figure 23.4. The pattern in Figure 23.4(a) is omnidirectional in that it sends signal equally in all directions. It is characteristic of the vertical

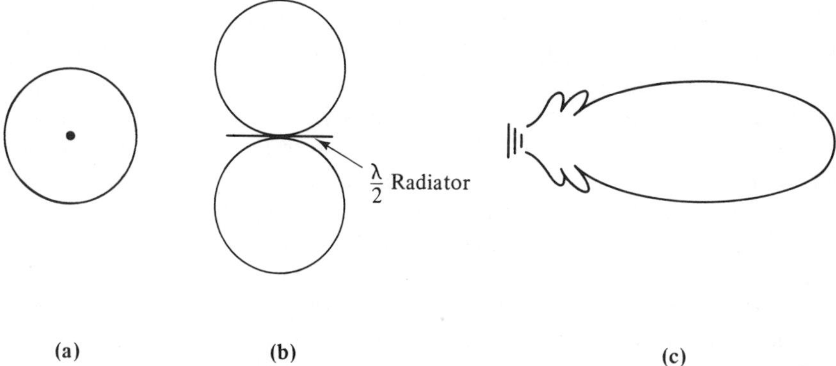

Figure 23.4 Common antenna radiation patterns viewed from above **(a)** vertical, **(b)** dipole and **(c)** yagi.

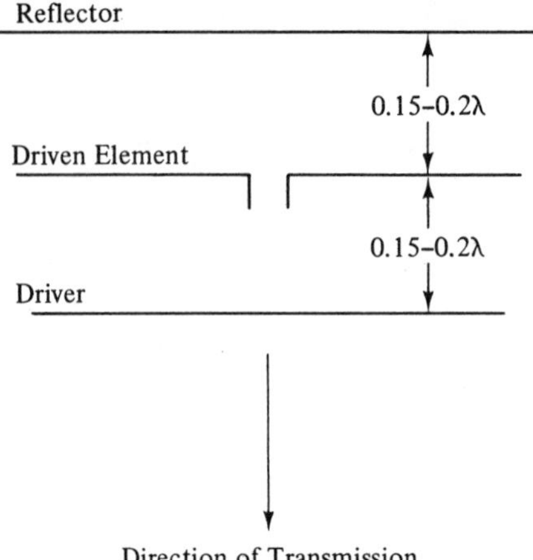

Figure 23.5 Yagi or parasitic array antenna.

(Marconi) radiator. The figure-eight pattern of Figure 23.4(b) is that of the dipole. The basic dipole sends signal in both directions perpendicular to the radiator. The dipole produces equal field strengths in both of these directions, and neither direction is preferred.

A highly directional pattern [Figure 23.4(c)] can be produced from a half-wavelength radiator by placing parallel parasitic elements as in Figure 23.5. These elements are also approximately half-wavelength, but the *reflector* is about 3–5 percent *longer* than the driven element, while the director is about the same amount shorter than the driven element. That driven element is nothing but a dipole, and is connected via a transmission line to the transmitter output. The effect of the parasitic elements is to act as kind of a lens—they direct all energy from the transmitter into a single direction. This has the effect of seeming to increase power. It actually does increase the field strength at a receiver located in the direction of the main lobe [see Figure 23.4(c)], but power is not increased.

Antenna gain figures are usually quoted in decibels. These ratings are labeled *forward gain*. Since the field intensity at the receiver location is greater than that of a dipole fed with the same transmitter (in which case all of the energy is divided into two directions), the gain is the decibel representation of the power produced by the parasitic beam (or yagi) of Figure 23.5 relative to that of the dipole. Also sometimes given is the gain over "isotropic," but that is based not on real measurements but on theoretical concepts. The isotropic gain of any antenna tends to be a couple of decibels higher than its gain over a dipole. Although there are valid engineering reasons for using the isotropic gain in analysis, one can see why the advertising departments of antenna companies like to quote the isotropic figure instead of the "dipole-gain."

The *effective radiated power* (ERP) of an antenna-transmitter system is the apparent power if the antenna gain is taken into consideration. For example, let us say that a transmitter delivers 5000 W to the antenna, and that the antenna gain is 4.5 dB. What is the ERP?

$$\begin{aligned} 4.5 &= 10 \log_{10} (x/5000) \\ 0.45 &= \log_{10} (x/5000) \\ 10^{0.45} &= 10^{\log (x/5000)} \\ 2.82 &= x/5000 \\ \text{ERP} &= x = 14{,}100 \text{ Watts} \end{aligned} \tag{23-3}$$

This is to say that a dipole would require a power level of over 14 kW to produce the same field strength at a given distance as the beam antenna (with a 4.5-dB gain) generates with only 5 kW.

Antenna Length. The length of a transmitting antenna is critical to proper operation and is based on the well-known equation for almost all wave phenomena, namely

$$\text{Wavelength} = \frac{\text{wave velocity}}{\text{frequency}} \tag{23-4}$$

In the case of radio waves, we are dealing with electromagnetic phenomena, so we find that the velocity, 300,000,000 m/s, is that of light. The formula reduces to the following when all of the corrections for conversion from meters/second to feet are taken into account

$$\text{Wavelength} = \frac{984}{\text{frequency (MHz)}} \tag{23-5}$$

and for half-wavelength,

$$L_{(\text{feet})} = \frac{492}{F_{\text{MHz}}} \tag{23-6}$$

This formula works for antennas that are at least several wavelengths above the earth's surface, and far from any other surroundings. The version of the equations using the 492 and 984 factors are called the "free space" equations for antenna length. Closer to the earth's surface, however, a modification is used for almost all practical antennas. For most the equation is

$$L_{feet} = \frac{468}{F_{MHz}} \tag{23-7}$$

Example. Find the length of a halfwave antenna located close to the earth's surface if the resonant frequency is to be 14.2 MHz.

$$\begin{aligned} L &= 468/14.2 \\ L &= 33 \text{ ft} \end{aligned} \tag{23-8}$$

Antenna Fields. Figure 23.6 shows a halfwave radiator and the field lines that surround it. The rules regarding these lines are the same as the rules for any electrical conductor in which an oscillatory current is flowing, so you may wish to review the appropriate earlier chapters. The magnetic field lines never intersect the conductor, and are in the form of concentric circles around the conductor. The electric field lines, on the other hand, are parallel to the conductor, and can be expected to intersect. These are

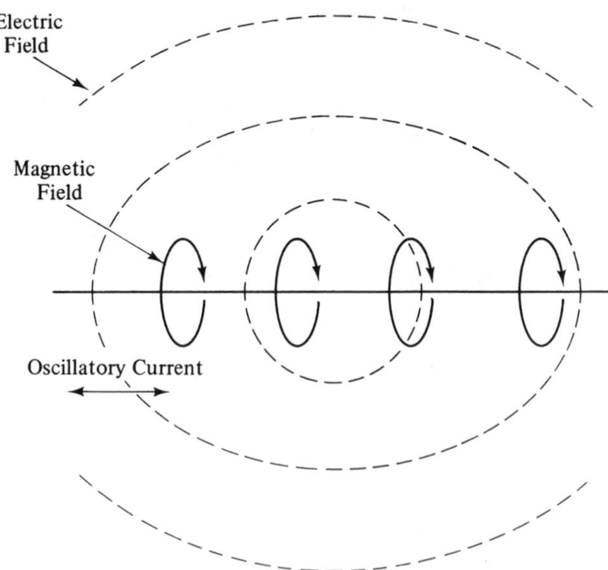

Figure 23.6 Distribution of electric and magnetic fields.

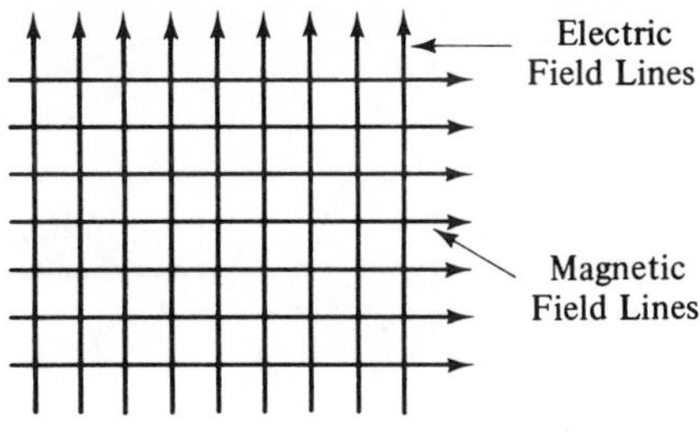

Figure 23.7 Electric and magnetic fields appear perpendicular to each other when viewed at the wavefront a long way from the antenna.

the field lines that go to make up the polarization of the electromagnetic wave radiated from the antenna. Figure 23.7 shows how they might look at a great distance from the antenna. Imagine the antenna as a point source of electromagnetic waves in far space (i.e., it is said to be *isotropic*). The wavefront radiated from such a source is spherical, and can be imagined to expand as in the manner of a perfect balloon. If you were to examine a small section of the expanding front of this electromagnetic sphere in a way that would allow you to see the force field lines, they would appear as in Figure 23.7. There would be two distinct and mutually perpendicular sets of lines, one vertical and the other horizontal. If the antenna that radiated these waves were vertical, then the electric field lines would be vertical and the magnetic would run horizontally. If, on the other hand, the antenna had been horizontally polarized, then the magnetic lines would be vertical and the electric field would be horizontal. A rule of thumb is that the electrical field lines are the factor that determines polarity. Horizontal electric lines mean a horizontally polarized antenna, and vertical electric lines mean vertically polarized antennas.

23.2 RADIO SIGNAL PROPAGATION

Radio signals travel in essentially straight lines, so how are communications possible beyond the horizon? If the rectilinear propagation were all there is to the story, then communications would indeed be limited to line of sight (as it is in the VHF/UHF range). But radio waves are subject to all phenomena that also affect light (another type of electromagnetic waves of much greater frequency than radio waves). Of these, reflection and refraction are the most important for long-distance high-frequency communications.

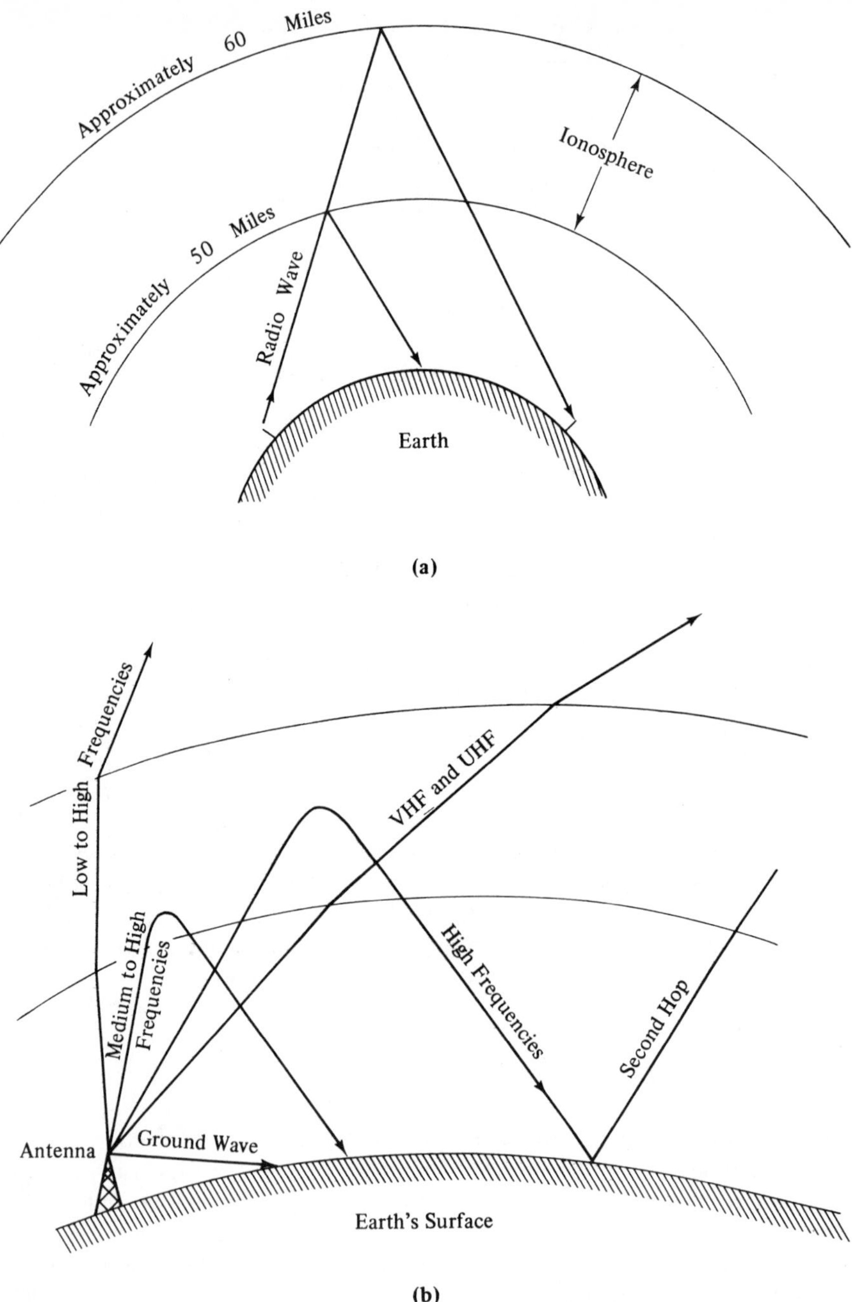

Figure 23.8 **(a)** Reflection of the radio wave in the ionosphere and **(b)** behavior of different frequencies in communications.

Figure 23.8 shows how radio waves propagate through reflection and refraction—the phenomenon known as "skip."

The earth's atmosphere becomes thinner at upper levels, and in between it is variable in the manner of a gradient. Although the atmosphere is broken up into "layers" that are given designating letters (*e*1, *e*2, *f*1, *f*2, etc.), it is really a continuum that is denser near the earth's surface and almost a vacuum in near-space. The letters designate rough zones that seem to possess similar properties with respect to the way a radio wave behaves.

When a radio wave leaves an antenna on the earth's surface, it travels in straight lines. A component traveling along the surface of the earth is called the *ground wave* and is used for local (up to 200 miles) communications. The ground wave is attenuated by ground absorption somewhat, and will not travel much past the horizon.

The *sky wave* is those components of the radio wave that leave the antenna at some angle greater than 0 deg (horizontal), and these are used for long-distance communications and intercontinental broadcasting. Figure 23.8(a) shows how the radio waves become skip signals. They leave the antenna at some angle greater than 0 deg and enter the ionosphere, where they are bent. At some critical angle (different for each frequency) the wave is bent enough to cause the phenomenon of total internal reflection, and the wave is bent back toward the earth's surface. The difference in effect due to frequency is shown in Figure 23.8(b). The rules governing radio propagation are so complex that only a brief description is possible. You will often see texts with some form or another of the standard wisdom regarding which frequencies are usable at which distances, but these are always incorrect. The truth is that the situation changes hourly on any given day. The best that radio communicators can do is predict a probability of communicating with any given area of the world on any specific frequency. In fact, propagation prediction is a valid subspecialty of communications engineering.

The amateur radio bands provide a good example of how variable the matter of radio propagation can be. In *general,* the 20-m and 15-m bands provide long skip to other continents during daylight hours, while the 40-m and 80-m bands are useful for shorter ranges, under about 300 miles. At night, however, the situation changes. As the sun goes down, so does the level of ionization in the atmosphere. When this happens, the maximum frequency at which useful skip occurs drops (the maximum usable frequency is often abbreviated muf). After local sunset you will begin to hear signals from long distances on 40- and 80-meter bands, and nothing on the upper bands (20, 15, and 10 meters). Sometime in the wee hours of the morning, before local sunrise, you can even hear signals from other continents on the 40- and 80-meter bands. Europe from North

America is not at all uncommon on either band (especially 40 meters), and even Australia/Asia is frequently heard. In fact, there are many radio broadcasters in Europe (and Radio Moscow's blockbuster signal) that use 40-meter bands for international broadcasting to North America in the early evening hours to midnight.

23.3 TRANSMISSION LINES

The transmission line carries the power generated by the transmitter to the antenna, where it can be radiated into space. In the simplest case the transmission line could be a single piece of ordinary electrical wire, but that is not usually the case. Several types of radio transmission line are shown in Figure 23.9.

The type of transmission line shown in Figure 23.9(a) is called *open line* or *flat line*. It consists of a pair of conductors parallel to each other, held apart by insulators. All transmission line types have a *characteristic impedance* (usually symbolized by Z_o), also called the *surge impedance*. The idea of surge impedance is a little difficult, because it is difficult to measure and put a number on. If an impulse were to be applied to one end of a transmission line, it would be treated as if the line had impedance made up of units of inductance and capacitance. In fact, the surge impedance is defined as the square root of the quotient L/C, or $(L/C)^{1/2}$, where L and C are the inductance and capacitance per unit of length. Z_o tends to acts like an impedance that is resistive, and will limit the amount of current that a line will accommodate for any given voltage level. Another way to define Z_o, although not altogether accurate, is to say that it is the value of the resistance terminating one end that will absorb all of the power supplied by a generator at the other end. For open, or flat, lines, the surge impedance is given by

$$Z_o = 276 \log \frac{d}{r} \tag{23-9}$$

where d is the center-to-center spacing of the two conductors.
r is the radius of the conductors.

It is interesting to note that most open line is designed to have either a 300-Ω or 600-Ω surge impedance.

A related form of transmission line is the ribbon line of Figure 23.9(b). This is like open line, except that the insulator is a rubber or vinyl plastic and runs the length of the line. This makes the dielectric properties of the line more important. Almost all ribbon line has a surge impedance of 300 Ω, and is used extensively in older television antenna installations.

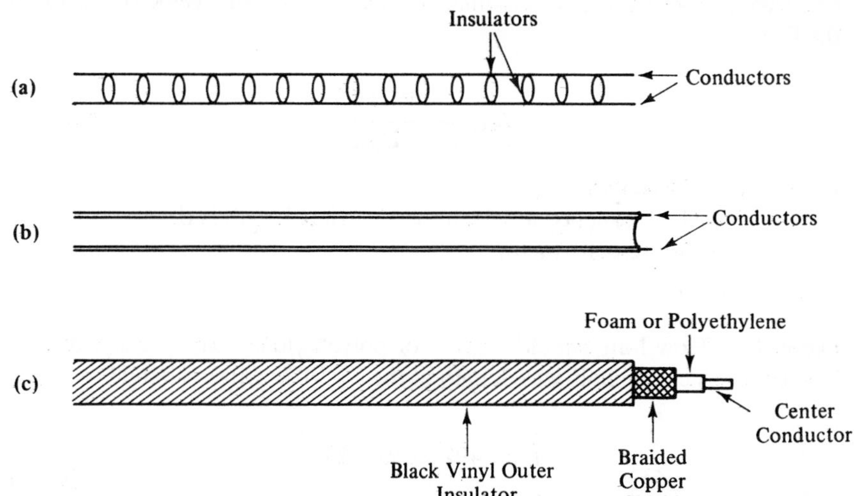

Figure 23.9 Types of antenna transmission line.

Most modern communications systems use the type of transmission lines shown in Figure 23.9(c)—coaxial cable. This type of line consists of two conductors, a center conductor and an outer shield, separated by an insulator of polyethylene or foam. The outer shield is insulated from the environment by a vinyl jacket.

Coaxial cable is considered unbalanced, whereas the other two categories are balanced. The coaxial type has many advantages, such as relatively good freedom from noise pickup and the ability to be installed in almost any environment. Coax can be twisted or even tied in a knot without substantially affecting its ability to perform its job. Twin lead and open lead, on the other hand, are extremely sensitive to that sort of abuse and will give only deteriorated performance under those conditions.

Signals do not propagate along a transmission line with the same velocity factor that they have in free space. The speed of a radio wave in free space, you should recall, is on the order of 300,000,000 m/s. It will be only a fraction of that velocity in a transmission line. Typically, it will have a velocity of $0.82c$ in twin lead and either $0.8c$ (foam) or $0.66c$ (polyethylene) for coaxial cable, where c is the velocity, given above, in free space. The decimal fraction that applies to each type of transmission line (0.82, 0.8, 0.66) is called its *velocity factor*.

In most cases the antenna transmission line can have any length that is convenient or necessary. It need only be long enough to couple the transmitter to the antenna. There are cases, however, where it is desirable to have a transmission line that is a particular length. In the event, the halfwave formula must be modified to account for the velocity factor of the line:

$$L_{\text{feet}} = \frac{492(V)}{F_{\text{mhz}}} \tag{23-10}$$

where L is the length.
F is the frequency at which the electrical length is desired.
V is the velocity factor.

Example. How long should a piece of polyethylene coaxial cable be if it is to be an electrical half-wavelength at the 27-MHz citizens band?

$$L = 492(0.66)/27$$
$$L = 12 \text{ ft} \tag{23-11}$$

Standing Waves. When a load at one end of a transmission line (such as an antenna) does not accept all of the power placed on the line by the generator at the input end of the line, the unabsorbed power is reflected back down the line toward the source. This reflected power sets up standing waves on the line (see Figure 23.10). Both voltage and current waves exist, but they are offset from each other so that one will go through its positive peak as the other goes through a negative peak. The diagram in Figure 23.10(a) shows the situation when the line is not terminated, so that all of the incident power is reflected back toward the source.

The situation in Figure 23.10(b) is that existing when the line is terminated in a resistive impedance. The *standing wave ratio* of the line is defined in terms of either voltage or current peaks.

$$\text{VSWR} = \frac{E_{\text{max}}}{E_{\text{min}}} \qquad \text{ISWR} = \frac{I_{\text{max}}}{I_{\text{min}}} \tag{23-12}$$

where you will designate the voltage SWR as "VSWR" and the current SWR as "ISWR." In most practical cases it is VSWR that we are measuring.

In a perfect antenna system where the output impedance of the source, the surge impedance of the transmission line, and the feedpoint impedance of the antenna are all equal, the VSWR will be 1:1, because $E_{\text{max}} = E_{\text{min}}$, and the line is said to be *flat*.

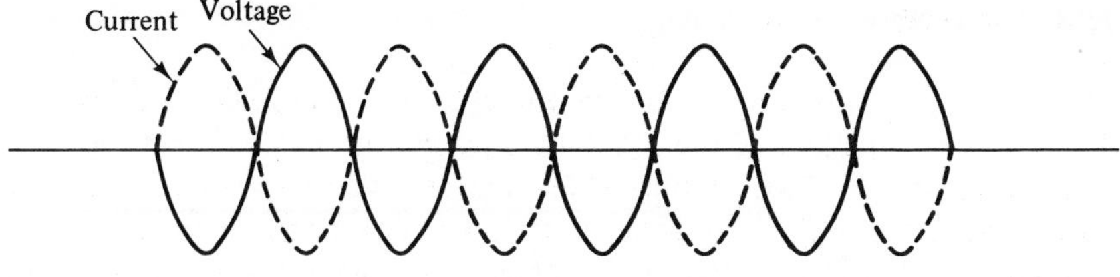

Open Circuit (Total Reflection)

(a)

Standing Waves on a Transmission Line

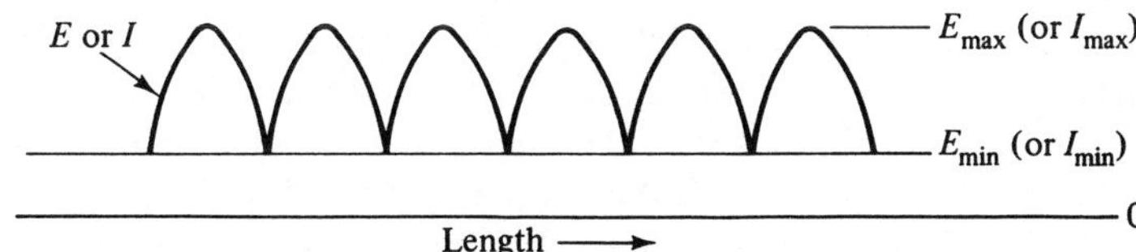

Terminated in a Resistive Load

(b)

Figure 23.10 Distribution of current and voltage along a transmission line that is **(a)** open-circuited and **(b)** terminated in a resistive load.

The mismatch between the transmission line and the antenna will affect the SWR. In fact, one can also define the SWR in terms of impedance:

$$\text{VSWR} = \frac{Z_o}{Z_L} \quad \text{or} \quad \frac{Z_L}{Z_o} \tag{23-13}$$

(whichever results in a number greater than unity)

where Z_o is the surge impedance of the transmission line.
Z_L is the resistive impedance of the antenna or load.

Example. A vertical antenna is erected, and Wheatstone bridge measurements of its feedpoint impedance are made. It is found that the value of Z_L is 32 Ω resistive. RG-8/U coaxial cable with a surge impedance of 52 Ω is used as the transmission line. What is the expected SWR?

$$\text{SWR} = Z_o/Z_L = 52/32 = 1.63{:}1 \tag{23-14}$$

23.4 ANTENNA MATCHING

Much of the activity with regard to antennas and radio station construction involves reduction of the SWR by appropriate matching between the antenna and the feedline. A high SWR indicates that an amount of power is being reflected back toward the transmitter. This power is wasted, since it is not radiated. By matching the antenna to the transmission line we are able to reduce the power lost.

Before dealing with matching techniques, let us put to rest one matter that many amateurs, CB operators, and even a few professionals believe concerning the reduction of SWR. Most CB operators believe that the SWR can be reduced by trimming the length of the transmission line, usually a coaxial cable. This is utter nonsense and will not affect the operation of the system one little bit. The reason for this belief is an understandable, if somewhat undeserved, dependence on the low-cost SWR meter normally used for antenna work. All of these are simple voltage bridge circuits, so they are dependent upon the voltage level that exists on the line at the point where the measurement is taken. But the antenna itself does not particularly care how long the line is, so most installers use a convenient length. The typical SWR meter, though, cares very much. If you move the SWR meter along the line (effectively the same thing as trimming the length and measuring at the feed end), you will note that the SWR seems to vary. The only place in the system where the SWR meter reading actually measures the SWR correctly is at the feedpoint of the antenna and at halfwave intervals along the line back from the feedpoint. This latter stipulation is merely the result of the impedance situation's repeating itself every half wavelength along the line. The length of line that will give this situation is determined by the $492(V)/F$ formula for the electrical length of transmission line.

Rule. If you are working on an antenna that has a high SWR, and want to reduce it, do not ever cut the line for minimum SWR. This is a fool's method and produces no useful result. Instead, try to match the line impedance using techniques given in this section.

Radiation Resistance. The radiation resistance of an antenna is the resistance determined by the power level radiated and the line current. It can be defined as

$$R = \frac{P_{\text{radiated}}}{I^2_{\text{line}}} \tag{23-15}$$

or $$R = \frac{E}{I} \tag{23-16}$$

In the second instance the voltage and currents are measured usually at the feedpoint. For most antenna types the voltage is at a minimum and the current is maximum at this point.

For the simple dipole that we studied earlier the radiation resistance is theoretically 73 Ω, but again this is only in free space. Closer to the earth's surface the impedance will vary from around 50 Ω to over 120 Ω, depending upon how close to the ground the antenna is physically placed and the existence of surrounding structures. Vertical antennas will have radiation resistance values from around 30 Ω to around 65 Ω, with 52 Ω being the theoretical free space resistance. Mobile vertical antennas may have a radiation resistance as low as 5 Ω to 12 Ω. Do not mistake the radiation resistance for ohmic resistance, caused by the nature of the conductors making up the antenna. These are typically less than 1 Ω, even in fairly long low-frequency antennas. In the event that a long antenna is constructed of wire, it is wise to reduce the ohmic resistances by the use of a large-diameter wire conductor. Ohmic losses in the form of heat occur if the ohmic resistance is not minimized.

Antenna Matching with Stubs. A stub is an open or shorted (see Fig. 23.11) section of transmission line that has a certain electrical wavelength. Stubs have certain properties that make them useful for a wide variety of applications. A quarter-wave shorted stub, for example, will have a dc (ohmic) resistance of near zero, certainly under 1 Ω, yet it appears as a parallel resonant tank at its open end—it has a high impedance at the resonant frequency. A halfwave shorted stub, as shown in the figure, will have the same impedance at the short as exists at the antenna feedpoint. If we want to match 600-Ω open line it is a simple matter to find a point somewhere between the antenna feedpoint and the short that has an impedance of 600 Ω. As a practical matter, of course, stubs are limited to the higher frequencies, because the length of a halfwave stub can be considerable below about 15 MHz.

The feedpoint impedance of the halfwave antenna should be 73 Ω, but seldom is. We can drive a halfwave antenna (or any other length for that matter) using an open line or twin lead and a technique called "delta matching." This is shown in Figure 23.12, and gets its name from the fact that it results in a configuration that resembles a triangle—the Greek letter delta. The conductors of the transmission line are spread apart and connected to points symmetrically displaced from the center that exhibit an impedance equal to that of the transmission line, usually 600-Ω open line.

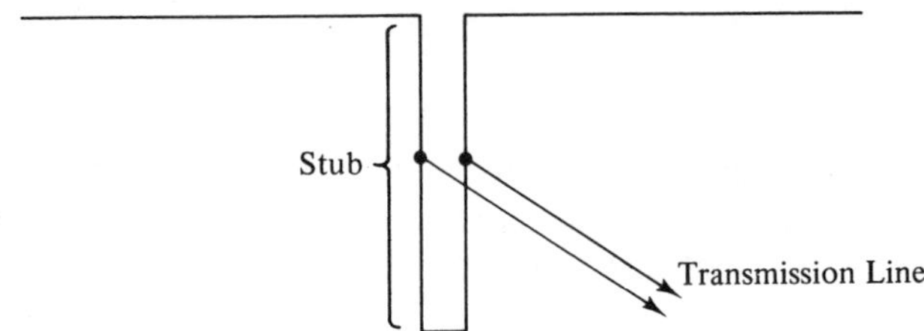

Figure 23.11 Matching stub.

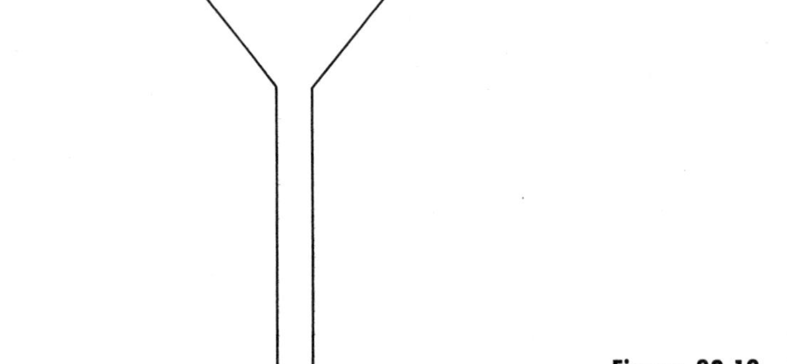

Figure 23.12 Delta match.

Two additional matching methods are shown in Figure 23.13. The method in Figure 23.13(a) is called the "gamma" match and is popular with parasitic beam antennas such as the yagi. In this method the center of the coaxial cable is connected to the center of the antenna's driven element and the braid is connected to a point, through a capacitance, that has an impedance equal to that of the coaxial cable surge impedance.

The use of a simple transformer is shown in Figure 23.13(b). This approach has been made easier in recent years because of the availability of broadbanded toroidal transformer core material. The turns ratio of the transformer is adjusted to provide a match between the feedpoint impedance of the antenna and the surge impedance of the transmission line.

Antennas are purely resistive at their feedpoint only when the excitation frequency is the same as the resonant frequency of the antenna as defined by length. At frequencies higher than resonance the antenna is too long, so it will appear to be inductive at the feedpoint. In that case the impedance is not purely resistive, but is complex. Similarly, when the antenna is connected to a source that has a frequency below resonance it is too short. In this case the antenna will appear to be capacitive. For the antenna that is too long we are able to compensate by connecting, in series with the radiator, a certain capacitance. The reactance of the matching capacitor must be the same as the reactive component of the feedpoint

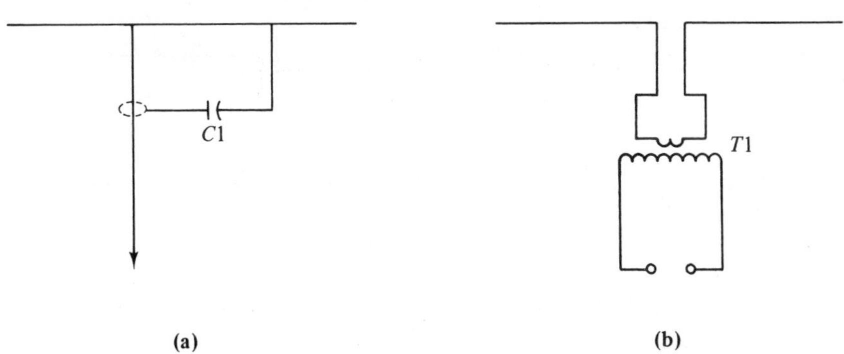

Figure 23.13 (a) Gamma match and (b) transformer match.

impedance. Similarly, if the antenna is too short, as is often the case at medium wave and the lower end of the shortwave spectrum, then a series inductance can be used to restore the impedance to a purely resistive state.

Figure 23.14 shows the use of capacitance and inductance elements to make antenna tuners. The circuit in Figure 23.14(a) is the L-section coupler, and is used to feed single-wire antennas. The radiator is a single piece of wire. One end is connected to the output of the coupler, and the other end is suspended from an insulator. To be most effective, the wire should be run in a straight line, and should have a length greater than quarter-wave. This last is not an absolute, and it is possible to construct antennas of the "long wire" variety that are considerably shorter than quarter-wave, but only at the expense of effectiveness.

A variation is shown in Figure 23.14(b). Here we have a low-impedance (low-Z) transformer primary connected to the coaxial cable from the transmitter, and a series-resonant secondary. Recall that a series-resonant tank circuit has a low impedance, so this circuit will match Lo-Z inputs.

A balanced version of the same circuit is shown in Figure 23.14(c), and is used to feed antennas driven from open line or twin lead. Also of the balanced variety, but for high impedance (Hi-Z) cases, is the parallel resonant circuit of Figure 23.14(d).

Figure 23.14(d) is the universal transmatch and is used by many manufacturers, especially in amateur radio. The energy from the transmitter is applied across a split stator capacitor/inductor tank circuit. This circuit is useful for adjusting the match over a limited range.

Balun Coils. The balun (i.e. *bal*anced-*un*balanced) coil is shown in Figure 23.15. This is usually implemented in the form of a toroidal transformer in modern antenna systems, but in the past more ordinary designs

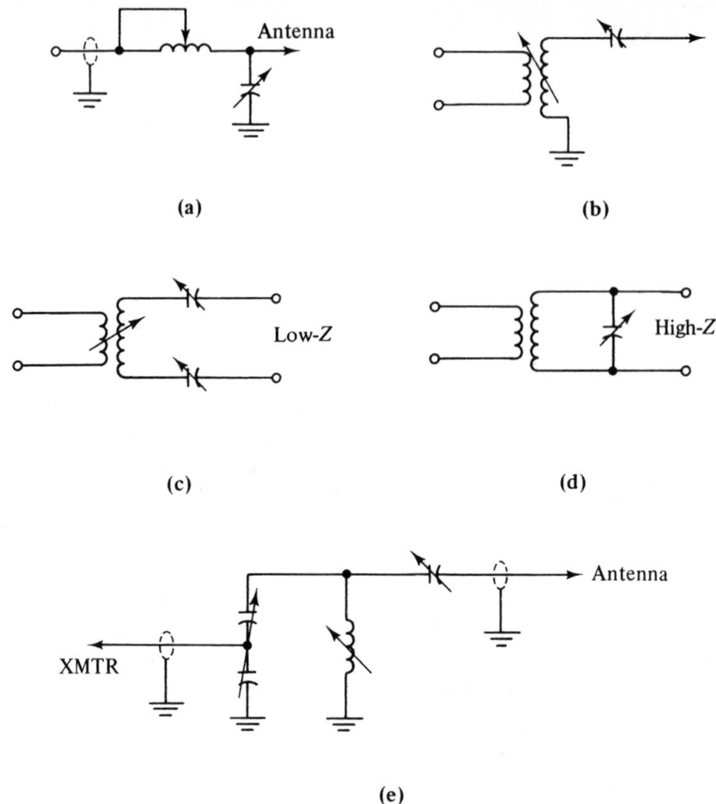

Figure 23.14 Various antenna matching networks.

were used. The coils of the balun transformer are wound over a common core, and are bifilar. That is to say that all three wires are placed in touching proximity and then treated as a single wire when the winding is done. The configuration in Figure 23.15(a) is used when one wants no impedance transformation, but merely to convert from an unbalanced feed line, such as coaxial cable, to a balanced antenna that has the same feedpoint impedance. A case where this might be done is in feeding a dipole antenna at the center. The secondary of the balun is placed at the feedpoint, and the coaxial cable is connected to the unbalanced input. This supposedly reduces radiation from the feedline and makes the currents in the respective halves of the dipole equal to each other.

The same use can be made of the configuration in Figure 23.15(b), but a 4:1 impedance transformation takes place. This circuit could be used to feed a 300-Ω folded dipole with 75-Ω coaxial cable.

A method for feeding vertical antennas is shown in Figure 23.16.

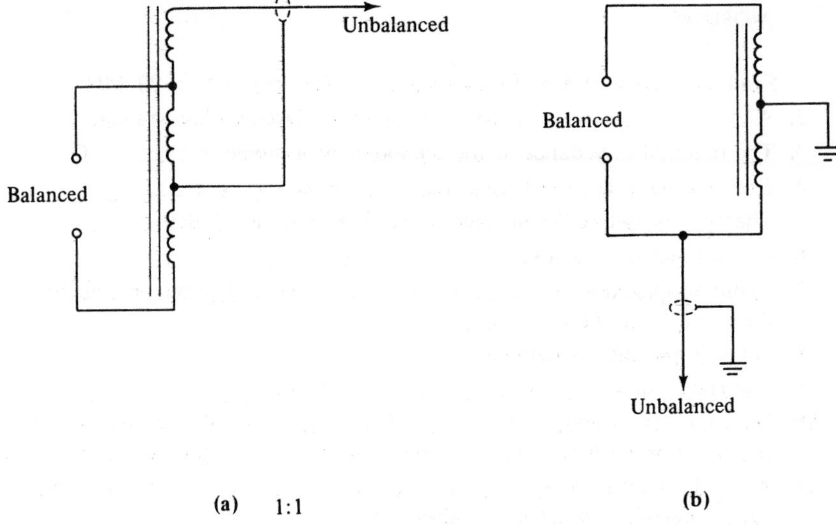

Figure 23.15 (a) 1:1 and (b) 4:1 balanced-unbalanced (balun) transformers.

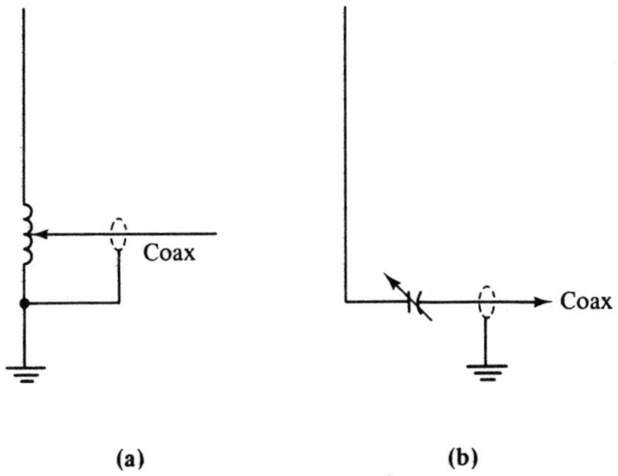

Figure 23.16 Resonating a vertical radiator that is (a) too short or (b) too long for the frequency.

Ordinarily, the feedpoint impedance of a vertical is low, on the order of 30–50 Ω, so coaxial cable can be used directly. If the feedpoint impedance is 30 Ω, and the surge impedance of the coaxial cable is 52 Ω, the SWR is only 1.7:1. Generally speaking, SWR figures less than 2:1 can be tolerated, the massive and expensive efforts of CBers to obtain 1:1 notwithstanding.

PROBLEMS

1. Find the length of a halfwave antenna to be operated on 23 MHz.
2. A __________ antenna is an example of a Marconi class system.
3. The nominal impedance at the feedpoint of a dipole is ________ Ω.
4. The nominal feedpoint impedance of a folded dipole is _______.
5. The figure-eight radiation pattern is characteristic of the __________.
6. Parasitic elements cause an antenna to have __________.
7. Radio propagation is caused by refraction and reflection phenomena in the ionosphere. True or false?
8. Surge impedance is defined as __________.
9. The surge impedance of flat line is found from __________.
10. Find the actual length of a piece of foam coaxial cable if the operating frequency is 20 Mhz, and the cable is used as a quarter-wave stub.
11. A dipole with a feedpoint impedance of 120 Ω is connected to a 72 Ω coaxial feedline. What is the SWR?
12. An antenna is ____________ above its resonant frequency.

A
Answers to Chapter Questions

CHAPTER 1

1. There is no electrical charge on a neutron—it is electrically neutral.
2. The proton carries a charge of +1 unit and the electron carries a charge of −1 unit.
3. Static.
4. Repel, attract.
5. Voltage.
6. $R = \rho L/A = ((9.56)(10))/(1.5) = 64$ ohms.
7. Most metals (silver, copper, gold, aluminum, iron, steel, etc.), most acids, many salts.
8. Porcelain, ceramics, Bakelite, plastics, nylon, rubber, dry wood, and pure water. (Does that last one surprise you? Ordinary water is not pure H_2O, but contains many impurities—metals, salts, organic material. It is the impurities in tap and rain water that cause dangerous currents to flow.)
9. 6.28×10^{18}.
10. $I = Q/t = 10/1 = 10$ amperes.
11. 1000.
12. 1500 μA.
13. 20 mA.
14. The ohm.
15. The mho.
16. $$2500\ \mu\text{mho} \times \frac{1\ \text{mho}}{10^6\ \mu\text{mho}} = 0.0025\ \text{mho}$$

    so $R = 1/G = 1/0.0025 = 400\ \Omega$.
17. 0.01
18. $E = IR = (0.25)(1000) = 250$ V.
19. $$R = \frac{E}{I} = \frac{150\ \text{V}}{0.05\ \text{A}} = 3000\ \Omega.$$
20. Gold.

21. $I = \frac{E}{R} = \frac{1000}{10{,}000} = 0.1$ A.

22. $E = IR = (0.12)\ (50) = 6$ V.

23. 1000 Ω, 10 percent.

24. 150,000 Ω (150 k), 5 percent.

25. 39,000 Ω (39 k).

26. Yes.

Discussion: When there is no color band in the fourth place on the standard resistor body, the tolerance is assumed to be ±20 percent, which for a 47-k resistor is ±9.4 k. A measured resistance of 45,803 Ω is certainly within the range 47,000 ± 9400 Ω.

CHAPTER 2

1. Watt.
2. One.
3. $P = EI = (100)\ (0.68) = 68$ W.
4. $I = P/E = 90/560 = 0.161$ A.
5. $P = E^2/R = (80)\ (80)/120 = 6400/120 = 53$ W.
6. $P = I^2R = (0.15)\ (0.15)\ (560) = 12.6$ W.
7. $P = I^2R = (0.05)\ (0.05)\ (1.2 \times 10^4) = 30$ W.
8. 400 Ω.
9. 14 Ω.
10. 50 Ω.
11. 2445 Ω.

Discussion: *Step 1.* Find the resistance of parallel combination $R1$, $R2$, $R3$. Call this R_a ($R_a = 545$ Ω).

Step 2. Find the resistance of parallel combination $R5$, $R6$, $R7$. Call this R_b ($R_b = 400$ Ω).

Step 3. Find the total resistance by adding the series combination $R_a + R_b + R4 + R8 = 545 + 400 + 500 + 1000 = 2445$ Ω.

12. 50 Volts.

Discussion: By Kirchoff's voltage law $E_t = E1 + E2 + E3$, so

$$E_t - E1 - E3 = E2$$
$$(100) - (20) - (30) = E2$$
$$(100) - (50) = E2$$
$$50 = E2$$

13. 50 mA.

Discussion: We know the resistance of, and voltage drop across, resistor *R*2. We can, therefore, compute the current flowing in *R*2. Since this is a series circuit, the same current will also flow in resistor *R*3.

14. $P = EI = (20)\ (0.05) = 1$ W.

15. $E_{AB} = (100)\ (R2/(R1 + R2)) = (100)\ (300/800) = 37.5$ W.

16. $E_{R1} = 100 - 37.5 = 62.5$ V.

17. 68.4 mA.

18. $120 - 68.4 = 51.6$ mA.

19. Series.

20. 3 Ω.

21. Parallel (also called "shunt" by some).

22. High.

23. Series.

24. Low.

25. NO!

CHAPTER 3

1. False.

2. Gilbert of ampere-turn.

3. Permeability.

4. μ (lowercase Greek letter "mu").

5. Reluctance.

6. Maxwell.

7. $H = F/L = 250/4 = 62.5$ ampere-turns/in.

8. *B-H* curve.

9. Permeance per unit of volume.

10. Hysteresis.

CHAPTER 4

1. 60 Hz.

Discussion:

$$\frac{1800 \text{ rev}}{\text{min}} \times \frac{1 \text{ min}}{60 \text{ sec}} \times \frac{2 \text{ cycle}}{\text{rev}} = \frac{60 \text{ cycles}}{\text{s}}$$

2. $E_{\text{p-p}} = 2 \times E_{\text{peak}} = 2 \times 140 = 280$ VAC (p-p).

3. $E_{rms} = (0.707)\ (E_{peak}) = (0.707)\ (140) = 99$ V.
4. $E_{peak} = 1.414 E_{rms} = (1.414)\ (250) = 354$ V.
5. 100 V.
6. 69.5 V.

Discussion: $e = E \sin 0$, but $E = 1.414 \times E_{rms}$, so
$e = (70.7)\ (1.414) \sin 136 = 100 \sin 136 = (100)(0.6946)$
$= 69.5$ V

7. $e = (150)\ (\sin 64) = (150)\ (0.8988) = 135$ V.
8. $F = 1/P = 1/0.150 = 6.7$ Hz.
9. $F = 1/1.5 \times 10^{-4}$ s $= 6667$ Hz.
10. $P = 1/60 = 0.0167$ s $= 16.7$ ms.
11. $P = 1/1000 = 0.001$ s $= 1$ ms.
12. 90 deg.
13. $1500\ \mu s \times \dfrac{1\ ms}{1000\ \mu s} = 1.5\ ms$
14. Positive peak.
15. Negative peak.
16. Peak-to-peak.
17. rms voltage.
18. Average voltage.
19. 180.
20. 360.

CHAPTER 5

1. Inductance is a property of electrical conductors, related to the magnetic field surrounding the conductor, that tends to oppose *changes* in the flow of current.
2. Concentric.
3. It will automatically assume a polarity that opposes changes in the primary current.
4. Counter electromotive force, or CEMF.
5. True.
6. Henry.
7. 1 V.
8. *L*.
9. 460 μH.

Discussion:

$$L_{\mu H} = \frac{r^2 n^2}{9_r + 10w} = \frac{(1)^2(150)^2}{(9)\ (1) + (10)\ (4)} = \frac{22{,}500}{49} = 460\ \mu H$$

10. 63.2

11. $T = L/R = 2/100 = 0.02$ s.

12. Five.

13. $T = L/R = (0.1)/(10^4) = 1 \times 10^{-5}$ s.

14. Energy $= \frac{1}{2}LI^2 = (\frac{1}{2})\,(5)\,(3)^2 = (\frac{1}{2})\,(5)\,(9) = 22.5$ J.

15. Joules are the same as "watt-seconds."

16. The RL circuit is opened.

17. Into adjacent turns of the same coil.

18. Into the turns of a nearby coil.

19. 9.8 μH.

Discussion:
$$m = (0.05)\,((1.5 \times 10^{-4})\,(2.5 \times 10^{-4})^{1/2})$$
$$m = (0.05)\,(1.95 \times 10^{-4})$$
$$m = 9.8\ \mu\text{H}$$

20. Zero.

21. $L_t = L1 + L2 = (200\ \mu\text{H}) + (1000\ \mu\text{H}) = 1200\ \mu\text{H}$.

22. 1.78 mH.

Discussion:
$$L_t = L1 + L2 + 2m = L1 + L2 + 2(k(L1 \times L2)^{1/2})$$
$$L_t = (200) + (1000) + 2(0.65(200 \times 1000)^{1/2})$$
$$L_t = 1200 + 2(290)\ \mu\text{H}$$
$$L_t = 1780\ \mu\text{H} = 1.78\ \text{mH}$$

23. 75 μH.

24. 50 μH.

Discussion:

$$L_t = \cfrac{1}{\cfrac{1}{150} + \cfrac{1}{150} + \cfrac{1}{150}} = \frac{1}{0.02} = 50\ \mu\text{H}$$

25. The ohm.

26. X_L.

27. 3140 Ω.

Discussion: $X_L = 2\pi fL = (2)\,(3.14)\,(1000)\,(0.5) = 3140\ \Omega$

28. 63 Ω.

Discussion: $X_L = (2)\,(3.14)\,(10^5)\,(1 \times 10^{-4}) = 63\ \Omega$

29. 0.32 A.

Discussion: $I = E/X_L = (10)/((2)\,(3.14)\,(5000)\,(0.001)) = 0.32$ A

30. $2\pi f$.

31. 90 deg.

32. Lags.

33. 510 Ω.

Discussion: $Z = (R^2 + X_L^2)^{1/2} = (100^2 + 500^2)^{1/2} = 510\ \Omega$

34. 2200 V.

Discussion:

$$E_s = \frac{E_p N_s}{N_p} = \frac{(110)\ (2000)}{(100)} = 2200\ \text{V}$$

35. 24 A.

Discussion:

$$I_s = \frac{I_p N_p}{N_s} = \frac{(1.2)\ (1000)}{(50)} = 24\ \text{Amps.}$$

36. 2500 Ω.

Discussion: $Z_p = Z_n(N_p/N_s)^2 = (100)\ (5)^2 = (100)\ (25) = 2500\ \Omega$

37. Flux linkage, copper, external induction, hysteresis, eddy currents.

38. Copper losses.

39. Laminated, as opposed to solid, soft-iron core.

40. Grounded electrostatic, or "Faraday," shield.

CHAPTER 6

1. Electrostatic field.

2. Energy storage capability.

3. Farad.

4. 10^{-12}.

5. 400 J.

Discussion: $e = \frac{1}{2} CV^2 = (\frac{1}{2})\ (1.6 \times 10^{-5})\ (7070)^2 = 400\ \text{J}$

6. 25 μF.

Discussion: $C = 2e/V^2 = (2)\ (50)/(2000)^2 = 2.5 \times 10^{-5}\ \text{F} = 25\ \mu\text{F}$

7. 1800 pF.

Discussion: We may assume that dry air is used as the dielectric because none was specified.

$$C = kKA/d = (0.225)\ (1)\ (400)/(0.05) = 1800\ \text{pF}$$

8. $T = RC$, where T is time in seconds, R is the resistance in ohms, and C is the capacitance in farads.

9. 63.2

10. 36.8

11. $T = RC = (10^4)\ (0.1 \times 10^{-6}) = 1 \times 10^{-3}\ \text{s} = 0.001\ \text{s} = 1\ \text{ms}.$

12. $T = RC = (1 \times 10^{-6}) \times (1 \times 10^{6}) = 1$ s.
13. $T = RC = (100)\ (100 \times 10^{-6}) = 0.01$ s = 10 ms.
14. $C_t = C1 + C2 + C3 + C4 = (0.01) + (0.02) + (0.1) + (0.01) =$ 0.14 μF.
15. 0.005 μF.
16. 2 × 600 WVDC = 1200 WVDC
17. Ohm.
18. X_c.
19. 16,000 Ω.

    Discussion:

$$X_c = \frac{1}{2fC} = \frac{1}{(2)\ (3.14)\ (10{,}000)\ (0.001 \times 10^{-6})} = 16{,}000\ \Omega$$

20. Leads.
21. 16,000 Ω.
22. $Z = (600^2 + 100^2)^{1/2} = 608\ \Omega$.
23. 1000 Ω.

CHAPTER 7

1. $Z = 103\ \Omega$.

    Discussion: Z $= (R^2 + (X_L - X_e)^2)^{1/2} = (100^2 + (75 - 50)^2)^{1/2} =$ 103 Ω)

2. 14 deg.

    Discussion: $\theta = \arctan (25/100) = 14$ deg.
3. Inductive.
4. 25 Ω.
5. 0.097 A.

    Discussion: $I = E/Z = 10/103 = 0.097$ A
6. $E = IR = (0.097)\ (100) = 9.7$ V.
7. $E = IX_c = (0.097)\ (50) = 4.85$ V.
8. $E = IX_L = (0.097)\ (75) = 7.3$ V.
9. 79 W.

    Discussion: $P_{\text{true}} = EI \cos \theta = (100)\ (100/100) \cos 38 = 79$ W
10. Power factor = cos θ, so P.F. = 0.788.
11. 100 – j75.
12. 500 + j(450 – 400) = 500 + j50.
13. Susceptance.
14. $B = 1/X$.

15. Admittance.
16. $Y = 1/Z$.

CHAPTER 8

1. $X_L = X_c$.
2. 21,268 H.

Discussion: $f = 1/(2)\ (3.14)\ (0.1 \times 5.6 \times 10^{-10})^{1/2} = 21{,}268$ H

3. 2.25 mHz.

Discussion: $f = 1/(2)\ (3.14)\ (5 \times 10^{-5} \times 1 \times 10^{-10})^{1/2} = 2{,}250{,}000$ Hz $= 2.25$ mHz

4. 1 kΩ, $\theta = 0$ deg.

Discussion: In a resonant circuit the reactances are equal, so they will cancel out, leaving only the resistance.

5. Parallel.
6. Infinity.
7. Series.
8. Maximum.
9. Minimum.
10. Maximum.
11. 10.5 kΩ.

Discussion:

$$Z = \frac{X_c X_L}{X_L - X_c} = \frac{(525)\ (500)}{525 - 500} = 10{,}500\ \Omega$$

12. 23 dB.

Discussion: dB $= 10 \log_{10} (1000/5) = 10 \log_{10} (200) = 23$ dB

13. -10 dB.

Discussion: dB $= 10 \log_{10} (50/500) = 10 \log_{10} (0.1) = -10$ dB

14. $A_v = E_{out}/E_{in} = 10.00/0.1 = 100$.
15. 40 dB.

Discussion: dB $= 20 \log_{10} (100) = 20(2) = 40$ dB

16. dB $= 20 \log_{10} (I1/I2)$.
17. 1 mW (0.001 W).
18. 10 μW.

Discussion:
$-20 = 10 \log_{10} (P1/0.001)$
$-2 = \log_{10} (P1/0.001)$
antilog $(-2) = P1/0.001$
$0.01 = P1/0.001$
$(0.01)\ (0.001) = P1 = 0.00001$ W $= 10\ \mu$W

19. 3.
20. 20.
21. *C*.
22. *B*.
23. *A*.
24. 3.
25. "Figure of merit."
26. $Q = X_L/R = 2000/100 = 20$.
27. B.W. $= F_r/R = 10^7/500 = 20$ kHz.
28. $Q = F_r$/B.W. $= 455/25 = 18$.
29. $Q = F_r$/B.W. $= 10^6/(5 \times 10^3) = 200$.

Discussion: Be sure that both frequencies are expressed in the same units, i.e., hertz, kilohertz, or megahertz.

30. A single frequency.
31. Frequencies higher and lower than a selected pair of cutoff frequencies.
32. Frequencies higher than the selected cutoff frequency.
33. Frequencies lower than a selected cutoff frequency.
34. Constant-*k*, pi-section, low-pass filter.
35. *m*-derived, pi-section, low-pass filter.
36. Constant-*k*, pi-section, high-pass filter.
37. Constant-*k*, *T*-section, high-pass filter.
38. *m*-derived, pi-section, high-pass filter.
39. 3-element, pi-section, bandpass filter.
40. *L*-section, high-pass filter.
41. *L*-section, low-pass filter.
42. $X_L X_c$.
43. Nulls.
44. Steep.
45. Wavetraps.
46. Bandwidth.

CHAPTER 9

1. Electrons.
2. Edison effect.
3. Space charge.
4. Thermionic emission.
5. Diode.
6. Fleming.
7. Plate, anode.
8. Only one direction.

9. Will *not*.
10. Indirectly heated.
11. Thoriated (thorium oxide coated) tungsten.
12. Filament.
13. Plate-cathode path.
14. False.
15. $R_p = E_B/I_P = 150/0.012 = 12.5\ \text{k}\ \Omega$.
16. Triode.
17. Triode.
18. Lee Deforest.
19. Grid, or "control grid."
20. Between the cathode and the plate.
21. Cutoff.
22. $E_c = 0$.
23. Distortion, or lack of.
24. Close spacing between the cathode and control grid.
25. Tetrode.
26. Screen grid, accelerator grid.
27. Positive.
28. Acceleration.
29. True.
30. Secondary emission.
31. Reverse.
32. Suppressor grid.
33. Pentode.
34. Between screen and plate.
35. Very high amplification factor, and very low interelectrode capacitance.
36. $50\ \text{k}\ \Omega$ to $1\ \text{M}\ \Omega$.
37. Remote cutoff, sharp cutoff.
38. Variable-mu pentode.
39. $(5500)\ (1.2) - 2500 = 6600 - 2500 = 4100$ W.
40. $\dfrac{2500 \times 100}{6600} = 38$ percent.
41. Plate dissipation.
42. Water jacket.
43. Amplification factor.
44. $-E_c = E_B/u = 350/200 = -1.75$ V.
45. $R_p = E_B/I_p = 200/0.0012 = 167$ k.
46. $g_m = \Delta i_P/\Delta e_c = 0.005/0.25 = 0.02$ mho $= 20{,}000\ \mu$mho.
47. $g_m = u/r_p = 200/1.5 \times 10^5 = 1300\ \mu$mho.

48. $I = I_p + I_{scr} = 0.005 + 0.0005 = 0.0055$ A, so by Ohm's law, $E = IR = (0.0055)\ (150) = 0.83$ V.

49. $R = E/I = (250 - 175)/(0.0005) = 150\ \text{k}\ \Omega$.

CHAPTER 10

1. Galena.
2. Silicon (Si) and germanium (Ge).
3. Tetravalent.
4. Covalent.
5. Pentavalent.
6. Arsenic, phosphorous, antimony.
7. Electrons.
8. True.
9. Boron, aluminum, indium.
10. Holes.
11. A hole is a place in a crystal lattice structure where an electron is supposed to be, but is not.
12. Opposite.
13. +1.
14. Forward.
15. Depletion zone.
16. High.
17. Leakage.
18. True.
19. True.
20. 0.2–0.3.
21. 0.6–0.7.
22. Reverse bias.
23. *A* is the base and *B* is the emitter.
24. *NPN*.
25. *PNP*.
26. Base.
27. *PNP* used in a negative ground configuration.
28. *NPN*.
29. 1 to 5.
30. Current.
31. Thermal stability.
32. Alpha gain.
33. Alpha = 0.9/0.99 = 0.91.

34. $I_b = I_c/\beta = 0.100/60 = 1.7$ mA.
35. $B = \alpha/1 - \alpha = 0.95/1 - 0.95 = 19$.
36. $\alpha = \beta/1 + \beta = 150/1 + 150 = 150/151 = 0.99$.
37. AC beta gain, or h_{fe}.
38. 3 dB, or $0.707h_{fbo}$.
39. Lower.
40. 3 dB.
41. $F_t = G \times \beta$. So $G = F_t/\beta = 100$ MHz/5 MHz $= 20$.
42. Unity (1).
43. Emitter.
44. Beta, or h_{fe}.
45. Voltage.
46. 430.
    Discussion: $A_v = (R_L)\ (h_{fe})/R_e) = 430$
47. 150 kΩ.
    Discussion: $Z_{in} = R_e \times h_{fe} = (150)\ (1000) = 150{,}000\ \Omega$
48. Collector.
49. Slightly less than unity.
50. Approximately $h_{fe} + 1$.
51. 180 deg. out of.
52. In phase.
53. In phase.
54. Emitter follower.
55. Impedance matching, buffering.
56. Alpha = unity.
57. High-voltage.
58. JFET.
59. Depletion zone.
60. High.
61. Negative.
62. Pinch-off.
63. $g_m = \Delta I_{ds}/\Delta E_g = 0.001/0.5 = 0.002$ mho $= 2000\ \mu$mho.
64. Pentode.
65. Many megohms.
66. MOSFET, IGFET.
67. Depletion, enhancement.
68. Off.
69. Substrate.
70. Reverse-biased.
71. Zener diode.
72. Various names often given are *zener knee, zener voltage,* or *zener point.*

73. Static electricity.
74. JFET, diode-clamped MOSFET.
75. Zener.
76. Tunnel.
77. Relaxation.
78. Zener.

CHAPTER 11

1. Infinite.
2. 360.
3. 180.
4. Approximately 120.
5. 360, 180.
6. (38) (100)/(150) = 25 percent.
7. Class A.
8. Heat.
9. Equal to E_c.
10. 50.
11. Voltage.
12. Power amplifiers.
13. High-mu.
14. Does not.
15. Does.
16. Flywheel effect.
17. Negative.
18. Degenerative.
19. $A_v = \dfrac{A_{\text{vol}}}{1 + (A_{\text{vol}})B} = \dfrac{1000}{1 + (1000)\,(0.01)} = 91.$
20. 16:1.

    Discussion: $N_n/N_s = (Z_p/Z_s)^{1/2} = (2500/10)^{1/2} = 16$
21. Resistance.
22. Coupling.

    Discussion: $C2$ blocks the high dc potential on the plate of $V1$, but allows the signal to pass. The high dc potential would bias the following tube into hard conduction.
23. Bypassing the power supply.
24. One-tenth.
25. ½ B+.

CHAPTER 12

1. Rectifier.
2. Passes current in only one direction.
3. Pulsating.
4. 60 Hz.
5. 120 Hz.
6. Center-tapped.
7. Halfwave.
8. Fullwave bridge rectifier.
9. Twice.
10. The same as any fullwave rectifier—120 Hz.
11. Peak reverse voltage (P.R.V.) or peak inverse voltage (P.I.V.).
12. High forward voltage drop, long warm-up time, and limited power range.
13. Mercury vapor.
14. Low forward voltage drop, high current capability, high peak forward voltage.
15. Low p.i.v., generation of hashlike noise.
16. These form a hash reduction filter (lowpass).
17. Filter circuit.
18. R.F. $= 1/416RC = 1/(416)(100)(1000 \times 10^{-6}) = 0.02$.
19. $R = E/I = 1.36/0.56 = 2.4\ \Omega$.
20. $E_o = (E)(R_L)/(R_s + R_L) = (1.36)(20)/(2.4 + 20) = 1.21$ V dc.
21. $\% = ((E - E_o)/(E)) \times 100 = (1.36 - 1.21)(100)/(1.36) = 11$ percent.
22. 10.
23. Pi-section *RC* filter.
24. $1/(10^5 C1C2R1R_L) = 1/(10^5(20 \times 10^{-6})(4 \times 10^{-6})10^3(5 \times 10^3) =$ 0.003.
25. 0.0008.
26. Changes in current.
27. $1/(1.3 \times 10^6 \times 10 \times 4 \times 10^{-6}) = 0.02$.
28. Mercury vapor, or halfwave, rectifiers.
29. The high rate of current change at the beginning of each hump creates a voltage spike because of inductive kick.
30. $L = R_L/1000 = 3300/1000 = 3.3$ H.
31. 1500 Ω.
32. 7.7 μF [use Eq. (12.10)].
33. 0.005.

    Discussion: First calculate X_L and X_c.

    $X_L = 2(3.14)(120)(8) = 6032\ \Omega$

    $X_c = 1/(2)(3.14)(120)(4 \times 10^{-6}) = 332\ \Omega$

Next, use Equation (12.13).

$$\text{R.F.} = \frac{1.4X_{c1}X_{c2}}{X_L R_L}$$

R.F. = ((1.4) (332) (332))/((6032) (5000))
R.F. = 0.005

34. Swinging choke.
35. Low.
36. Oil-filled, aluminum, and tantalum electrolytics.
37. 20 μF.
38. $3 \times 450 = 1350$ WVDC.
39. Zener.
40. Cold-cathode, or gas-filled, tube.
41. $V_z - X_{be} = (5.6 - 0.6) = 5.0$ V.
42. Zener diode.
43. 105 V.

CHAPTER 13

1. PMMC, D'Arsonval.
2. Taut-band.
3. Electrodynamometer, or, simply, dynamometer.
4. Thermocouple.
5. Series.
6. Parallel.
7. Shunt resistor.
8. 0.69 Ω.
9. Multiplier.
10. $E = IR$
    $5 = (0.000050)\ (6200 + R)$
    $10^5 = 6200 + R$
    $93{,}800 = R$
11. Ohms per volt or Ω/V.
12. 100,000 Ω/5 V = 20,000 Ω/V.
13. See Figure 13.14 on page 221.
14. Instrumentation rectifier.
15. Transistor voltmeter.
16. VOM.

CHAPTER 14

1. Electron gun, focusing electrodes, accelerating electrodes, vertical and horizontal deflection plates, and a phosphor-coated viewing screen.

2. Several kilovolts.
3. Sawtooth.
4. (10 ms/cm) × (1.7 cm) = 0.017 s
   $F = 1/t = 1/0.017 = 59$ Hz
5. 7 × 5 V/cm = 35 V (p-p).
6. (35 V/2) × 0.707 = 12.4 V rms.
7. Persistence.
8. Blanking pulse.
9. 7.5 cm × (1 μs/cm) × (1 s/10^{-6} μs) = 7.5 × 10^6 s
   $F = 1/t = 1/7.5 \times 10^{-6} = 133{,}000$ Hz
10. Lissajous.
11. 1000 Hz.
12. 0 deg or 360 deg.
13. $F_v = (N_h/N_v) \times F_h = (2/1) \times 500 = 1000$ Hz.
14. Wheatstone bridge.
15. 4730 Ω.

CHAPTER 15

1. Wavemeter.
2. 50–500 MHz.
3. May.
4. Relative field strength indicator.
5. Dip.
6. Oscillating detector.
7. Heterodyne.
8. See the figure.
9. $F = 300/L = 300/0.648$ m = 463 MHz.
10. 9085 kHz – 1.112-kHz = 9,083,888 Hz.
11. Transfer oscillator.
12. 2,000,680 Hz.
13. Rich in harmonics.
14. Oven, tcxo.
15. Rubidium, cesium.
16. Highest.
17. 60 kHz.
18. 25,000/100 = 250 times, so ±30 Hz/250 = 0.12 Hz.
19. Decimal counting unit, or DCU.
20. Decimal counting assembly, or DCA.
21. 9.

22. Gate.
23. Latch.
24. Events per unit of time, or EPUT counters.
25. Hysteresis window.
26. Heterodyning, prescaling.
27. FALSE!
28. 50 ppm.
29. Yes.
30. One count of the least significant digit.

CHAPTER 16

1. Positive feedback, gain greater than unity.
2. Armstrong.
3. 360 deg or 0 deg.
4. Ringing.
5. Exponentially.
6. (1) Varying the coupling between the tickler coil and the coil in the tank circuit; (2) varying the dc plate (collector, drain) potential.
7. Tuned-plate, tuned-grid, or TPTG.
8. Interelectrode capacitances C_{gp} and C_{gc}.
9. It is a Hartley oscillator.
10. Inductive.
11. It is a Colpitts oscillator.
12. Colpitts, Clapp.
13. Clapp.
14. Screen grid.
15. Buffer amplifier.
16. Piezoelectric.
17. Mechanically deformed.
18. Electric field.
19. True.
20. It is a Miller oscillator circuit.
21. TPTG, TDTG, TCTB.
22. 9810.2 kHz.

    Discussion: (−150 ppm/°C) (60 − 25°C) = −5250 ppm change, so
    (−5250 ppm) (9.862 MHz) = −51.776-kHz change.
    (9862 kHz) − (51.776 kHz) = 9810.2 kHz.

23. Capacitor.

24. Ultra audion.
25. Neon glow.
26. Unijunction.
27. Relaxation.
28. Astable.

CHAPTER 17

1. Increased output voltage swing, better thermal properties.
2. $50 \times 100 = 5000$.
3. Negative or degenerative.
4. Complementary symmetry.

CHAPTER 18

1. Grounded-grid.
2. $C_{in} = C_{gc} + C_{gp}(A_v + 1)$.
3. $C_{in} = 22$ pF + (152 pF) (200 + 1) = 30,570 pF = 0.031 μF.
4. Toroid.
5. Peaking.
6. Steatite, ceramic.
7. Stagger.
8. A.
9. Pentode.
10. Negative, interelectrode capacitance.
11. Losser.
12. Hazeltine.
13. Rice.
14. C_{gp}.
15. Inductive, direct.
16. C.
17. 2, 5.
18. Ferrite beads.
19. Minimum.
20. 75, 80.
21. $(60)/(1000 \times 0.1) = 60/100 = 0.6$ or 60 percent.
22. (1000 V) (0.1 A) − (60 W) = (100 − 60) W = 40 W.
23. Series.
24. Class B, Class AB_1, and Class AB_2.

CHAPTER 19

1. Variation, intelligence, information.
2. Amplitude, frequency, phase.
3. A3.
4. 5 kHz.

   Discussion: The number preceding the type of modulation specification (A3) denotes the maximum allowable bandwidth. Since this is a standard A3 AM transmitter, the bandwidth is twice the maximum allowable audio modulating frequency, or 10 kHz/2 = 5 KHz.

5. A3j.
6. A3a.
7. Zero.
8. Sum, difference.
9. 10,000 kHz + 5 kHz = 10,005 kHz.
10. 10,000 kHz − 5 kHz = 9995 kHz.
11. 10 kHz.
12. $2 \times E_{dc}$, 0.
13. Approximately one-half of the dc input power, or ½ (1250) (0.1) = ½ (125 W) = 62.5 W.
14. 4000 W.
15. $P_{af} = \frac{1}{2}(0.5)^2(100) = (\frac{1}{2})(\frac{1}{4})(100) = (\frac{1}{2})(25) = 12.5$ W.
16. Cathode.
17. Efficiency.
18. Constant-current modulation.
19. False; overmodulation is never permitted.
20. Series choke or tertiary winding on a plate-modulated transformer.
21. Trapezoid.
22. Balanced modulator.
23. Suppressed or nulled out.
24. 2 kW.
25. Double-balanced mixer.

CHAPTER 21

1. Galena.
2. Regenerative.
3. TRF.
4. Superheterodyne.

5. Intermediate frequency, or IF.
6. Automatic gain control.
7. Twice.
8. 1655 kHz.
9. Product.
10. Discriminator, ratio-detector, PLL, pulse counting, quadrature, etc.

CHAPTER 22

1. Master oscillator power amplifier.
2. Minimum.
3. Minimum.
4. Maximum.
5. $2 \times 2 \times 2 \times 3 = 24$, so $6.132 \times 24 = 147.168$ MHz.
6. 450 Hz $\times$ 24 = 10.8 kHz.
7. Self.
8. Filter, PLL, crystalplexer.
9. Frequency translator.
10. Frequency translator.
11. 166.12 MHz/10 kHz = 166.12 MHz/0.01 MHz = 16,612.
12. Differential.

CHAPTER 23

1. $L = 468/23 = 20.3$ ft.
2. Vertical, long-wire, etc.
3. 70–73.
4. 300 Ω.
5. Halfwave dipole.
6. Forward gain.
7. True.
8. $(L/C)^{1/2}$.
9. $Z_o = 276 \log_{10} (d/r)$.
10. $L = 492(0.8)/20 = 19.7$ ft.
11. 120/72 = 1.67:1.
12. Inductive.

B
Some Questions For You

(Answers will be found at the end of this appendix.)

1. A unit of electrical current is a
   A. Volt
   B. Henry
   C. Coulomb
   D. Milliampere

2. Which is the correct formula?
   A. $R = E/I$
   B. $E = R/I$
   C. $I = ER$
   D. $R = EI$

3. Which of the following is a bipolar transistor?
   A. MOSFET
   B. IGFET
   C. *PNP*
   D. JFET

4. The rms value of a sine wave is given by:
   A. 0.707 peak
   B. 0.636 peak
   C. 1.414 peak
   D. 0.5 peak

5. A 100-V rms ac signal has a peak-to-peak voltage of:
   A. 141 V
   B. 70.7 V
   C. 200 V
   D. 282 V

6. How much current is drawn by a 110-V, 60-W lamp?
   A. 0.55 A
   B. 0.8 A
   C. 1 A
   D. 1.8 A

7. The circuit is correct as shown in Figure B.1.
   A. True
   B. False

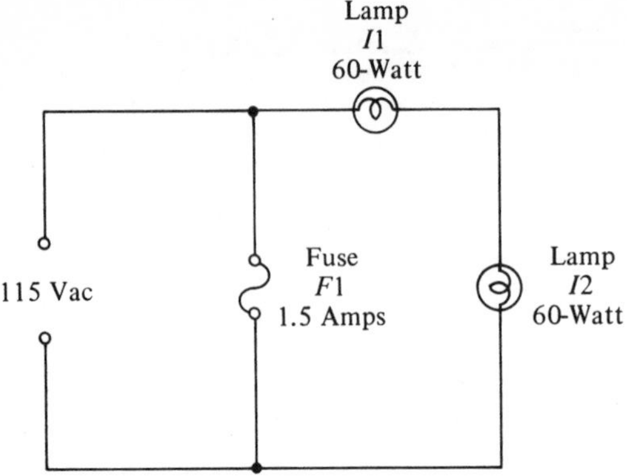

Figure B.1

8. A unit of capacitance is a
   A. Henry
   B. Gilbert
   C. Farad
   D. Microvolt
9. What are the values and tolerances of a carbon resistor that has the following color bands: red-violet-orange-gold?
   A. 12 k, 20 percent
   B. 27 k, 5 percent
   C. 127 k, 10 percent
   D. 47 k, 5 percent
10. What is the value of *I*2 in Figure B.2?
   A. 1.5 A
   B. 3.9 A
   C. 2 A
   D. 3.4 A

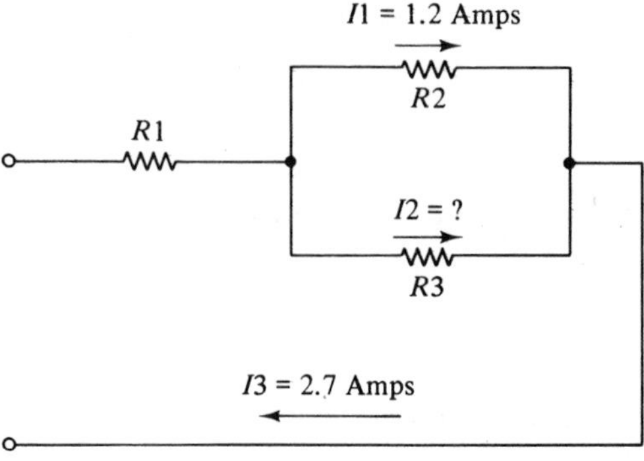

Figure B.2

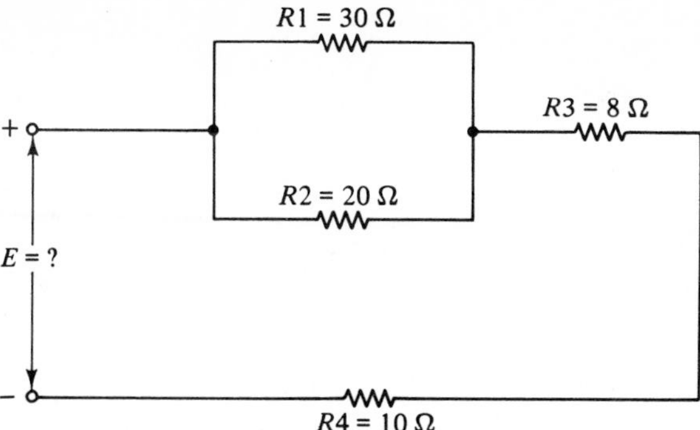

Figure B.3

11. What is the value of E in Figure B.3?
A. 10 V
B. 20 V
C. 30 V
D. 40 V

12. A 200-Ω resistor passes a current of 0.5 A. How much power is dissipated?
A. 100 W
B. 200 W
C. 5 W
D. 50 W

13. A 10-V dc potential is applied across a 50-Ω load resistor. How much power is dissipated?
A. 5 W
B. 2 W
C. 500 W
D. 0.2 W

14. A current of 0.5 A flows in a 10-Ω resistor. What is the voltage drop across the resistor?
A. 20 V
B. 10 V
C. 7.5 V
D. 5 V

15. AC power mains in the United States are said to be "115 V ac." What type of ac measurement does this figure represent?
A. Peak
B. rms
C. Peak-to-peak
D. Average

16. A unit of inductance is a
A. Gilbert
B. Gauss
C. Henry
D. Farad

17. A "microfarad" is _________ F.
    A. 0.000001
    B. 0.0001
    C. 0.00001
    D. 1,000,000
18. A type of solder appropriate for electronic work is
    A. 60/40 resin
    B. 60/60 resin
    C. 60/40 acid
    D. 50/50 plain core
19. The meters are connected correctly as shown in Figure B.4.
    A. True
    B. False
20. What is the total capacitance of the circuit shown in Figure B.5?
    A. 10 μF
    B. 20 μF
    C. 40 μF
    D. 5 μF

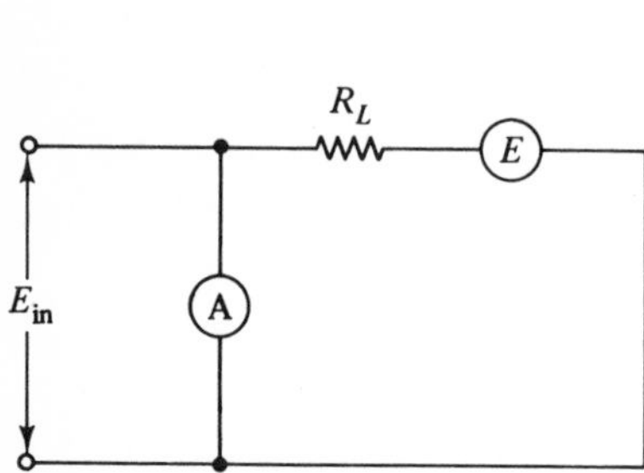

Figure B.4

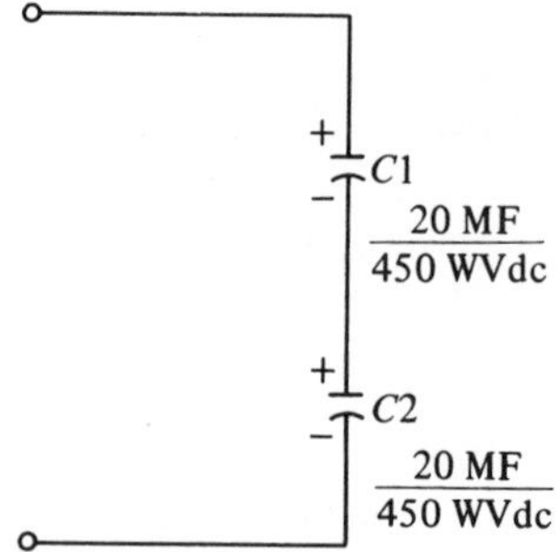

Figure B.5

21. What is the working voltage of the combination in Figure B.5?
    A. 250 V
    B. 450 V
    C. 900 V
    D. 750 V
22. What is the capacitance of the combination in Figure B.6?
    A. 0.0018 μF
    B. 0.022 μF
    C. 2020 μF
    D. 2200 pF

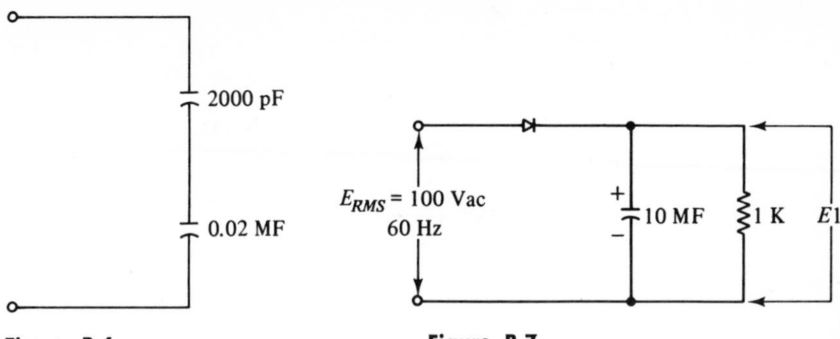

Figure B.6

Figure B.7

23. A resistor used to make a current meter operate on a higher current scale is called a(n) ________.
A. Multiplier
B. Adder
C. Shunt
D. Absorber

24. A resistor such as that described in Question 23 is connected in ________ with the meter.
A. Series
B. Parallel

25. A current of 0.05 A flows in a 47-Ω, ½-W resistor. Is this safe?
A. Yes
B. No

26. *E*1 in Figure B.7 has a value of:
A. 100 VDC
B. 125 VDC
C. 182 VDC
D. 141 VDC

27. A 1000-Hz signal is applied to a 100-mH choke coil. What is the inductive reactance?
A. 100 Ω
B. 628 Ω
C. 1201 Ω
D. 975 Ω

28. What is the capacitive reactance when a 1-MHz signal is applied to a 100-pF capacitor?
A. 10 k
B. 1.59 k
C. 2 k
D. Less than 1 Ω

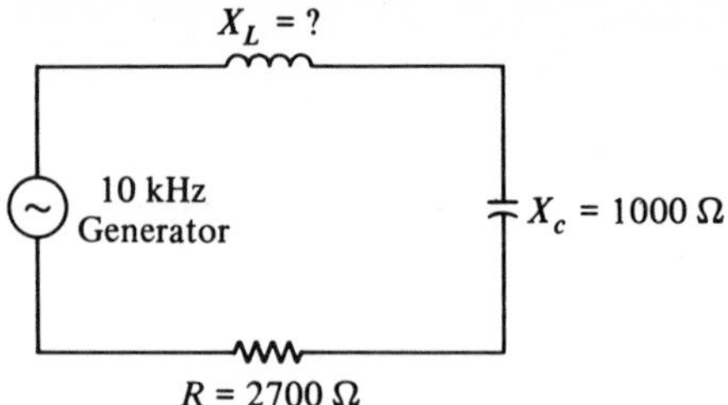

Figure B.8

29. The circuit in Figure B.8 is series-resonant at 10 kHz. What is the value of X_L?
A. 1000 Ω
B. 3900 Ω
C. 1700 Ω
D. 2700 Ω

30. What is the impedance of the circuit in Figure B.8?
A. 700 Ω
B. 3700 Ω
C. 1700 Ω
D. 2700 Ω

31. What current flows in the circuit of Figure B.8 if the rms output of the generator is 10 V?
A. 1 mA
B. 2.7 mA
C. 3.7 mA
D. 2.5 mA

32. Which graph in Figure B.9 represents the frequency response of the circuit in Figure B.8?
A.
B.
C.
D.

33. The impedance of a parallel resonant circuit is ________ at its resonant frequency.
A. Maximum
B. Minimum
C. Unimportant
D. Moderate

34. What is the approximate resistance across terminals *A*-*B* in Figure B.10?
A. 8.2 k
B. 11 k
C. 10 k
D. 12.5 k

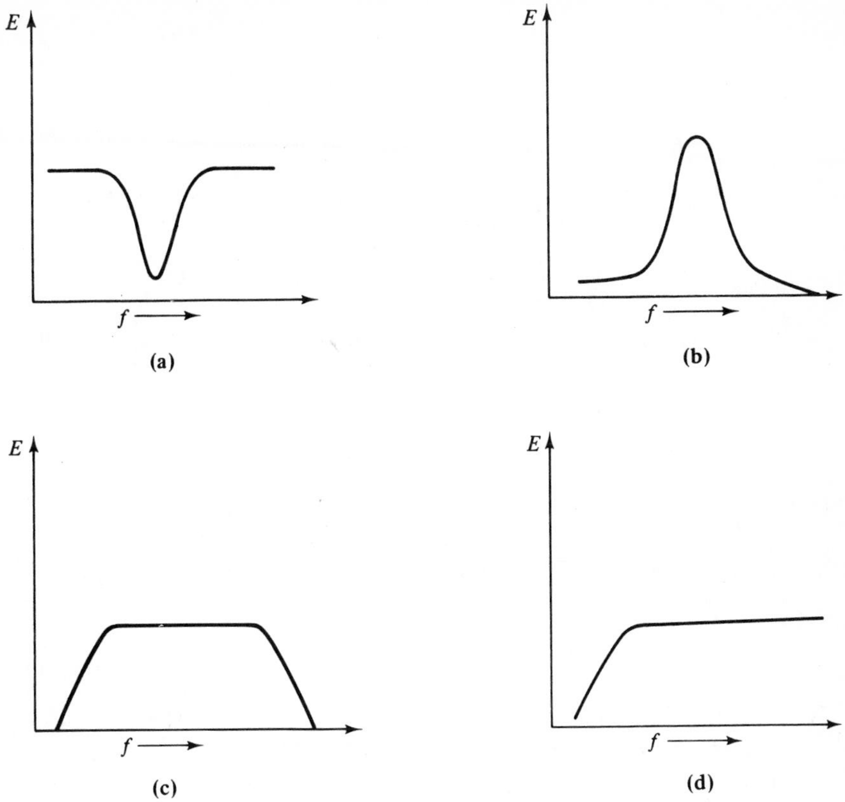

E f

(a)

E f

(b)

E f

(c)

E f

(d)

Figure B.9

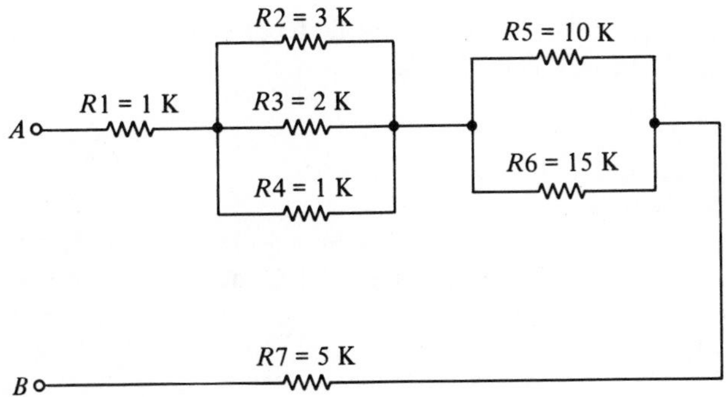

Figure B.10

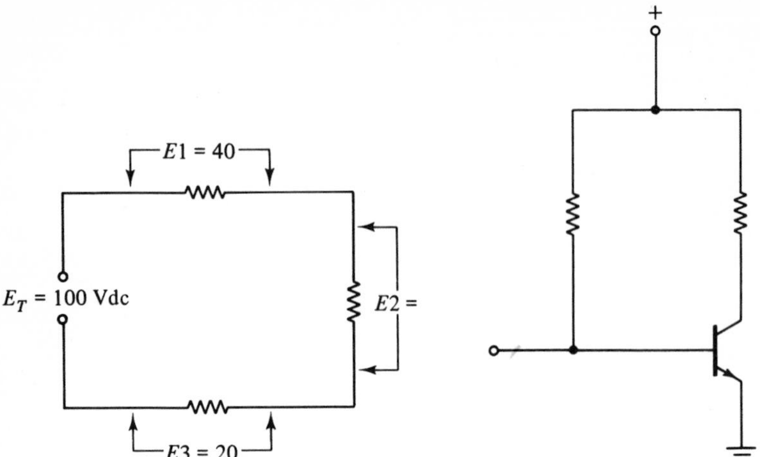

Figure B.11

Figure B.12

35. What is the value of $E2$ in Figure B.11?
A. 20 V
B. 40 V
C. 60 V
D. 80 V

36. If the transistor in Figure B.12 is normally biased, and is made of silicon, what voltage would you expect between emitter and base?
A. 1 V
B. 0.2 V
C. 0.7 V
D. 0.3 V

37. The transistor in Figure B.13 is correctly biased.
A. True
B. False

38. Which of the following equations best represents Kirchoff's current law for junction A in Figure B.14?
A. $I1 = I2 + I3$
B. $I2 + I1 - I3 = 0$
C. $I1 + I3 - I2 = 0$
D. $I2 = I1 + I3$

39. There is a series circuit consisting of a 50-Ω and a 60-Ω resistor. If the voltage applied to this circuit is 100 VDC, how much power is dissipated by the 60-Ω resistor?
A. 50 W
B. 75 W
C. 25 W
D. 30 W

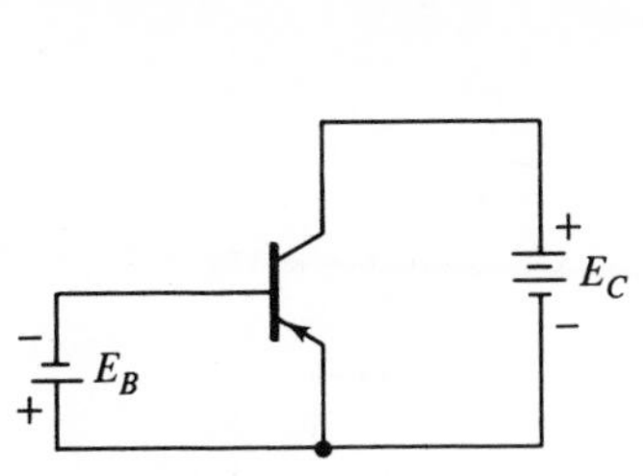

Figure B.13

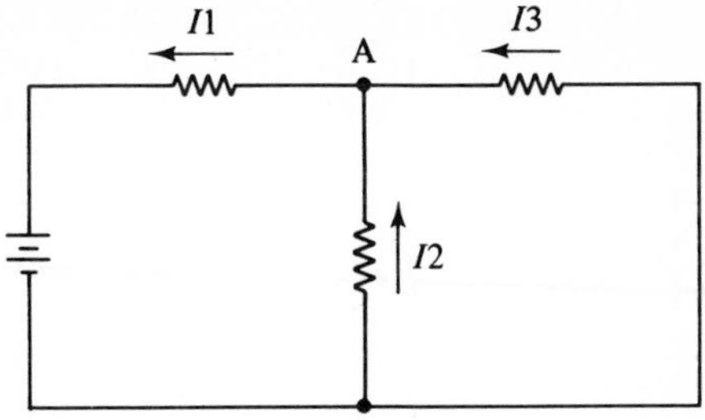

Figure B.14

40. A series circuit consists of a 25-Ω and a 60-Ω resistor. If 25 VDC is applied across the circuit, how much voltage is dropped across the 60-Ω resistor?
A. 16.1 V
B. 11 V
C. 17.6 V
D. 9.2 V

41. The lamp in Figure B.15 normally draws 600 mA. The circuit in the figure is appropriate.
A. True
B. False

42. Examine Figure B.16 *closely*. What is the approximate voltage that will be read on the meter?
A. −11 VDC
B. +6 VDC
C. −6 VDC
D. 0.7 VDC

43. The circuit in Figure B.17 is biased to operate as a Class A amplifier. What will happen to the voltage at point *A* if switch *S*1 is closed?
A. Stays the same
B. Increases
C. Decreases
D. Zero

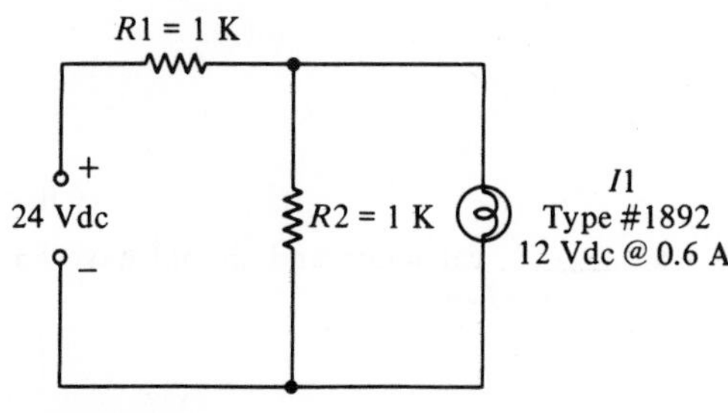

Figure B.15

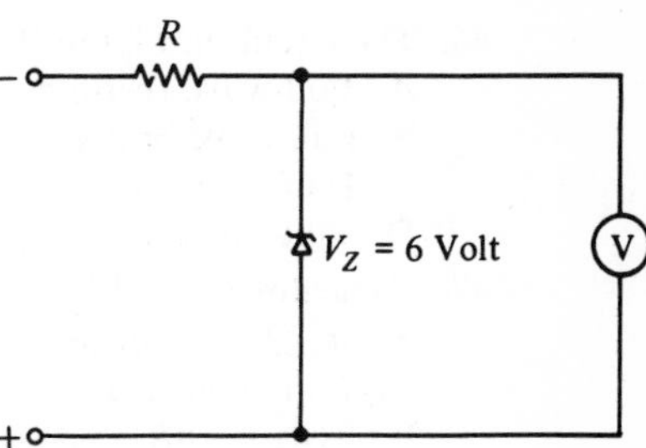

Figure B.16

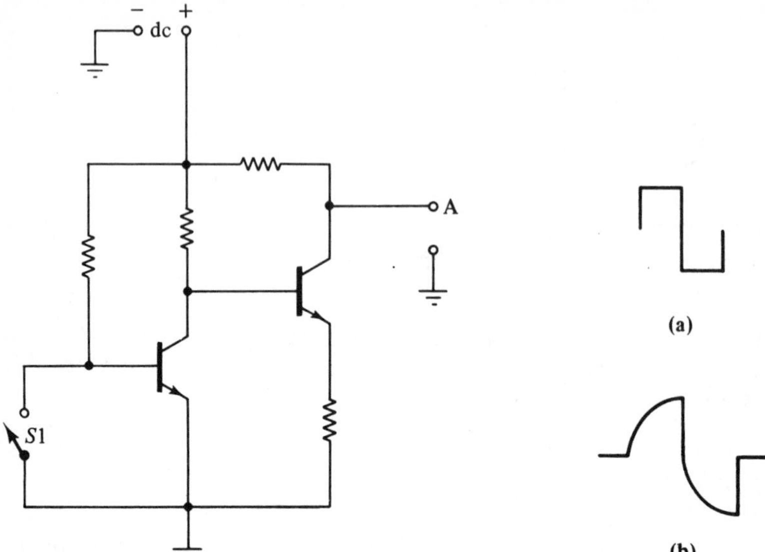

Figure B.17

Figure B.18

44. Signal A is found at the input of a circuit, while signal B is the output. What can be said about the frequency response of the circuit? (See Figure B.18.)
   A. High-frequency rolloff
   B. Low-frequency rolloff
   C. Mid-frequency rolloff
   D. Low-frequency attenuation

45. Which type of capacitor is most suitable for use as a bypass capacitor in a 10.7-MHz amplifier?
   A. Aluminum electrolytic
   B. Disc ceramic
   C. Paper or mylar
   D. Oil-filled

46. The circuit in Figure B.19 is a
   A. Full-wave rectifier
   B. Full-wave bridge
   C. Half-wave bridge
   D. Full-wave ring

47. Capacitor $C1$ in Figure B.20 is a _______ capacitor and should have an X_c of _______ or less.
   A. Coupling, $R/10$
   B. Bypass, $10R$
   C. Bypass, R
   D. Bypass, $R/10$

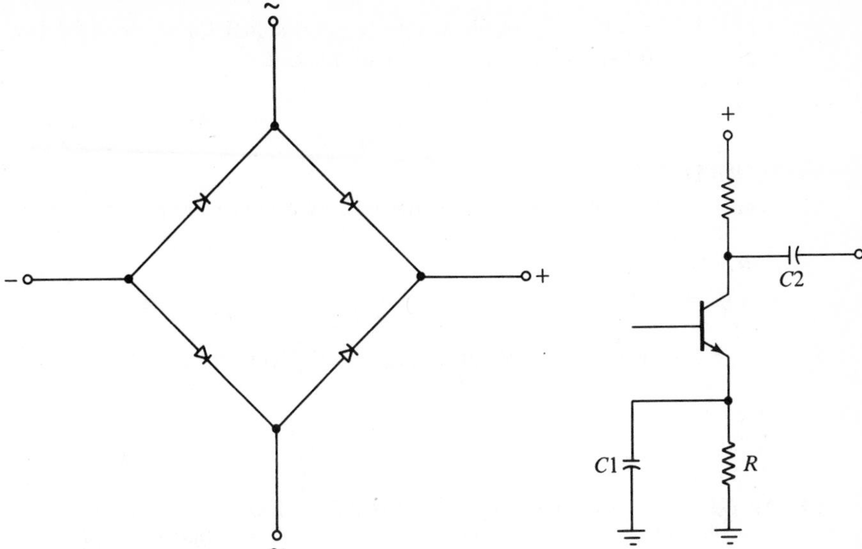

Figure B.19

Figure B.20

48. The circuit in Figure B.21 is an example of a
    A. Pulse generator
    B. Capacitor limit regulator
    C. Relaxation oscillator
    D. Indicator lamp
49. The device in Figure B.22 is a(n) ________.
    A. IGFET
    B. SCR
    C. MOSFET
    D. JFET
50. The waveform across the capacitor in Figure B.21 is roughly a
    A. Square wave
    B. Pulse
    C. Sawtooth
    D. Sine wave

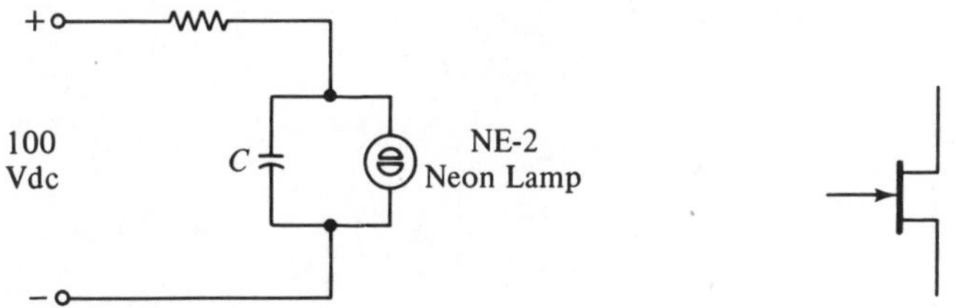

Figure B.21

Figure B.22

51. Which of the following probes would be most suited for observing a fast rise-time, 750-kHz, square wave on an oscilloscope?
A. 10 ×
B. 1 ×
C. Demodulator
D. RF Detector

52. What type of oscilloscope would be used to view a transient waveform?
A. Dual-beam
B. High-frequency
C. Storage
D. *X-Y*

53. How much current will flow in resistor *R*2 of Figure B.23?
A. 91 mA
B. 67 mA
C. 23 mA
D. 133 mA

54. An *NPN* transistor has a current of 0.005 A flowing in the base circuit, and 1800 mA flowing in the collector circuit. What is the approximate h_{fe} (beta) of this transistor?
A. 360
B. 180
C. 28
D. 100

55. A transistor has a collector current of 220 mA and an emitter current of 198 mA. What is the approximate alpha?
A. 220
B. 0.9
C. 0.5
D. 72

56. A *PNP* power transistor has a collector current of 1.2 A, and an emitter current of 1.15 A. What is the approximate h_{fe}?
A. 23
B. 100
C. 0.9
D. 86

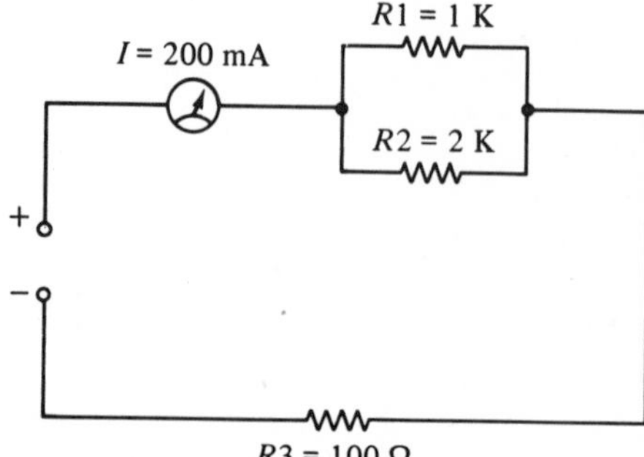

Figure B.23

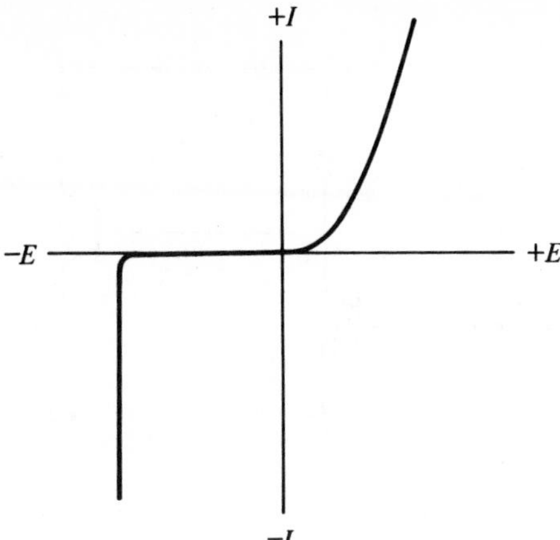

Figure B.24

57. Which type of *NPN* transistor is *most suited* for replacement of a series-pass +200 VDC regulator transistor?
A. Mesa
B. Planar
C. Epitaxial
D. Silicon

58. Consider the graph in Figure B.24. This is the characteristic curve of a __________.
A. Zener diode
B. Tunnel diode
C. SCR
D. Triac

59. Which of the following might be used to tune a resonant tank?
A. Varistor
B. UJT
C. Varicap
D. LED

60. What will probably happen to *Q*2 if *Q*1 shorts collector to emitter in Figure B.25?
A. Nothing.
B. It opens.
C. It saturates.
D. It is destroyed.

61. An open-circuited power supply measures 15.6 VDC. When it is connected to a normal load, this voltage drops to 14.4 VDC. What is the percentage of regulation?
A. 7.7 percent
B. 0.8 percent
C. 5 percent
D. 10 percent

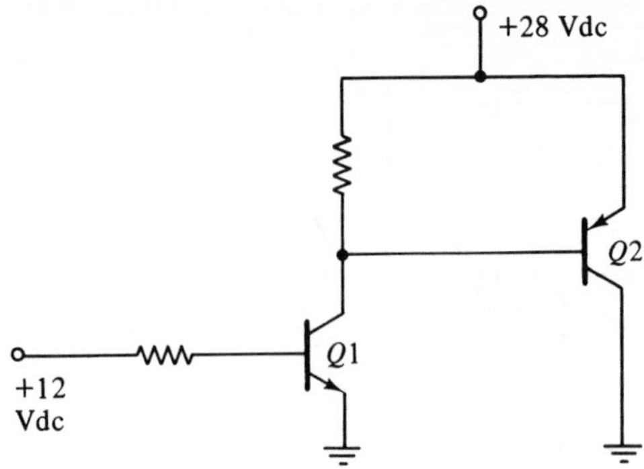

Figure B.25

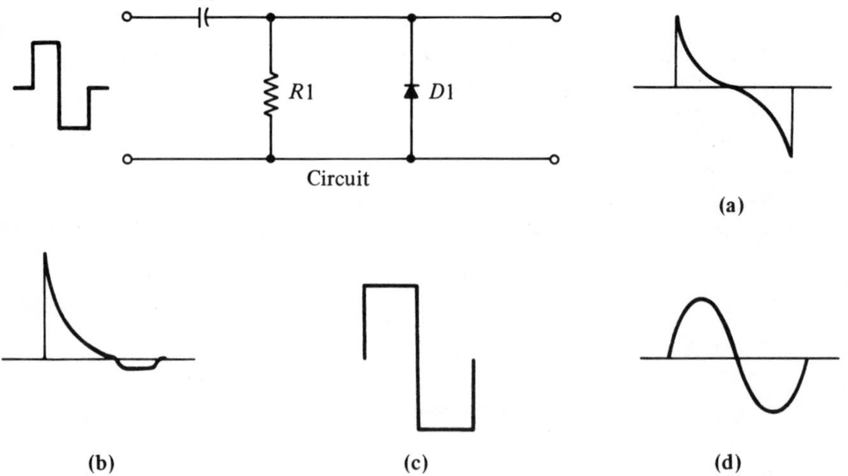

Figure B.26

62. Which waveform would you expect at the output of the circuit in Figure B.26? (Assume that $T = RC$ is short relative to the period of the input waveform.)

A.

B.

C.

D.

63. The circuit in Figure B.27 is a(n)

A. Pulse shaper

B. High-pass filter

C. Differentiator

D. Integrator

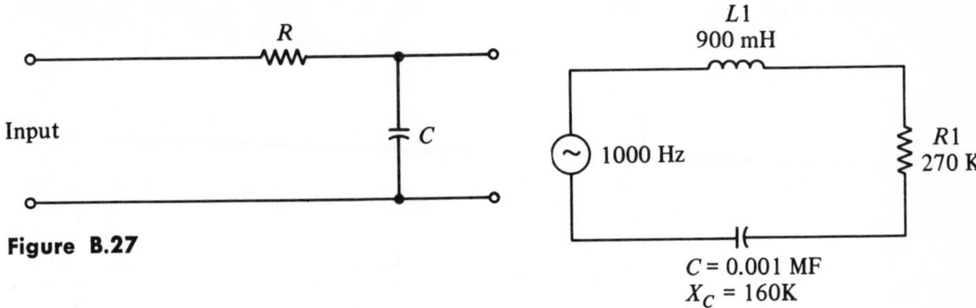

Figure B.27

Figure B.28

64. What is the impedance of the circuit in Figure B.28?
A. 311 k
B. 506 k
C. 21 k
D. 270 k

65. A transformer has a turns ratio of 20:1. A 10-Ω load resistor is connected across the secondary. What is the reflected impedance across the primary?
A. 200 Ω
B. 8 k
C. 3 k
D. 4 k

66. The circuit in Figure B.29 is a(n)
A. Hartley oscillator
B. Colpitts oscillator
C. Armstrong oscillator
D. Pierce oscillator

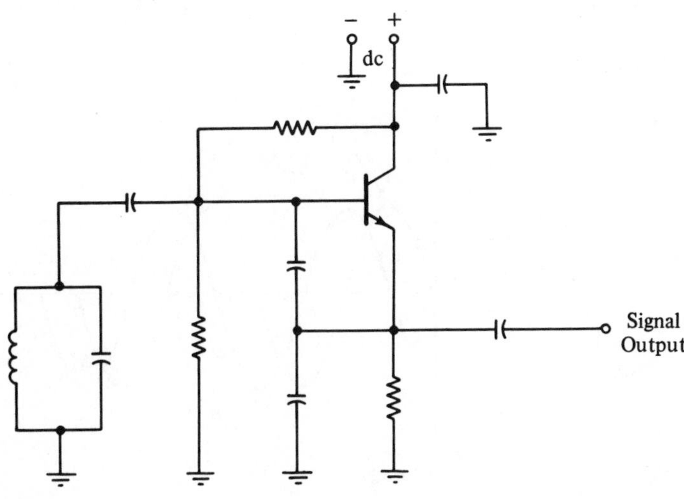

Figure B.29

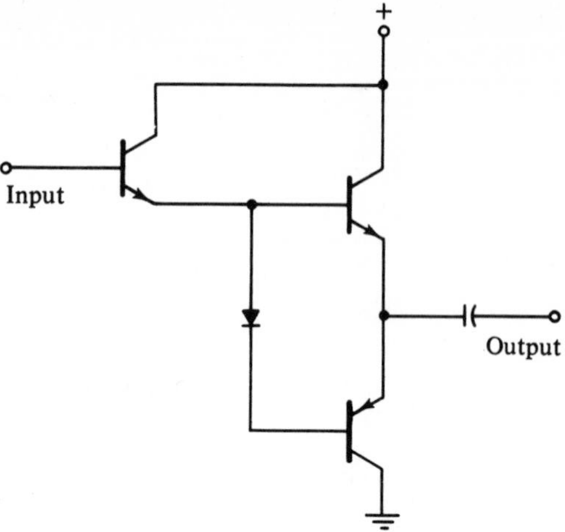

Figure B.30

67. The circuit in Figure B.30 is a(n) ______.
   A. Totem pole
   B. Emitter follower
   C. Complementary symmetry amplifier
   D. Class C amplifier
68. What is the phase angle of the Lissajous figure in Figure B.31?
   A. 90–180 deg
   B. 45–90 deg
   C. 180–270 deg
   D. 270–360 deg
69. The waveforms shown in Figure B.32 represents a(n) ______ circuit.
   A. Capacitive
   B. Inductive
   C. Resistive
   D. Resonant

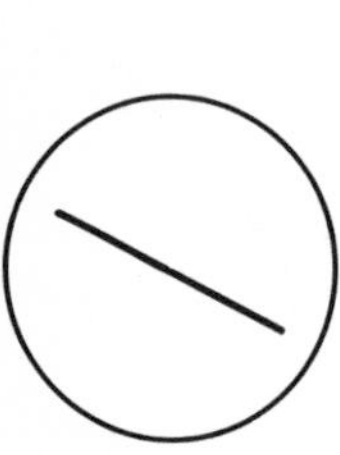

Figure B.31

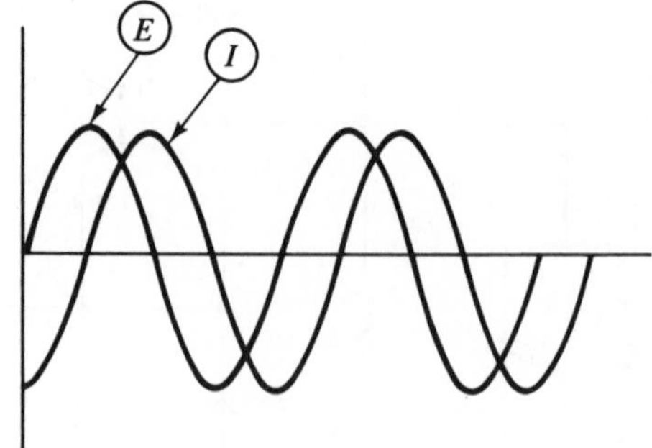

Figure B.32

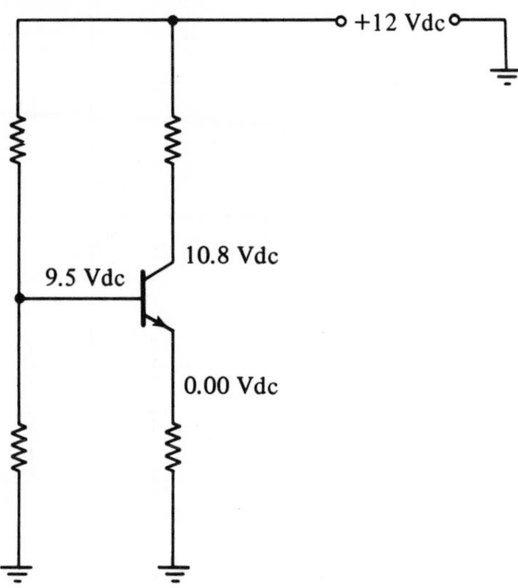

Figure B.33

70. A 100-Ω resistor and a capacitor with an X_c of 75 Ω are connected in a phase shift circuit. What is the phase angle?
A. 60 deg
B. 45 deg
C. 42 deg
D. 37 deg

71. What is the Q of a tuned circuit that is resonant at 2700 kHz, and has a bandwidth of 25 kHz?
A. 120
B. 60
C. 1000
D. 45

72. The voltages shown in Figure B.33 were actually measured. What, if any, defect exists?
A. None
B. Open-collector junction
C. Open-emitter junction
D. Shorted collector

73. A 100-pF capacitor and a 10-μH coil are connected in parallel. At what frequency is impedance the greatest?
A. 5033 kHz
B. 10,560 kHz
C. 6.04 MHz
D. 1.2 MHz

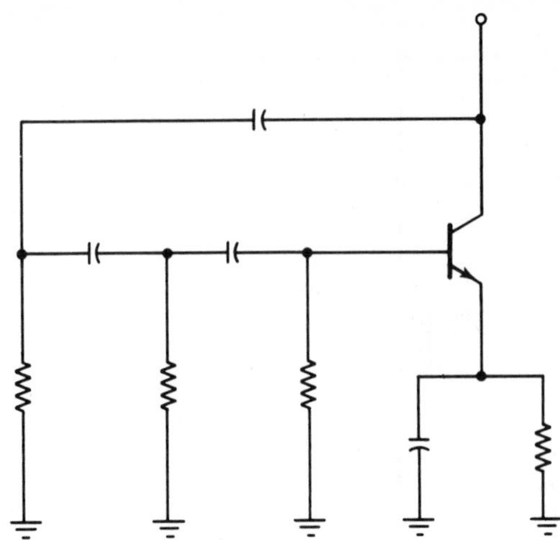

Figure B.34

74. What is the circuit in Figure B.34?
A. Hartley oscillator
B. Relaxation oscillator
C. RC phase shift oscillator
D. Sawtooth generator

75. What is the output waveform of the circuit shown in Figure B.35?
A. Sine wave
B. Sawtooth
C. Square wave
D. Trapezoidal

76. What is always a requirement when one is mounting power transistors?
A. Tighten screws as much as possible
B. Use of mica insulators
C. Use of silicone grease
D. Measure collector or case temperature

77. In the 1-2-4-8 BCD code a number is represented by the word 1001. What is this in decimal?
A. 6
B. 5
C. 4
D. 9

78. A frequency must be measured to within ±0.005 percent. What is the minimum accuracy required of the frequency counter?
A. 50 ppm
B. 100 ppm
C. 5 ppm
D. 1 ppm

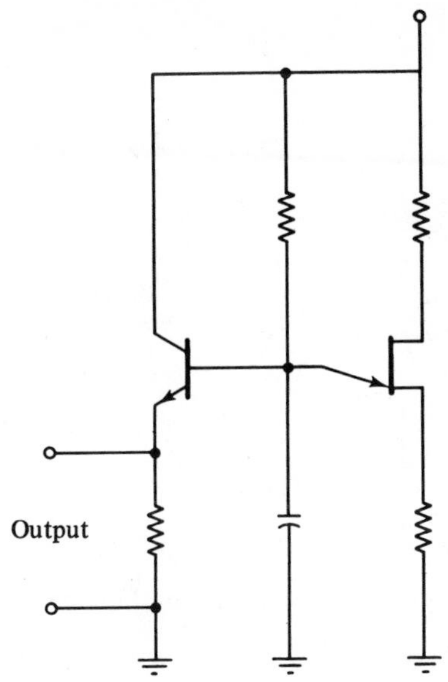

Figure B.35

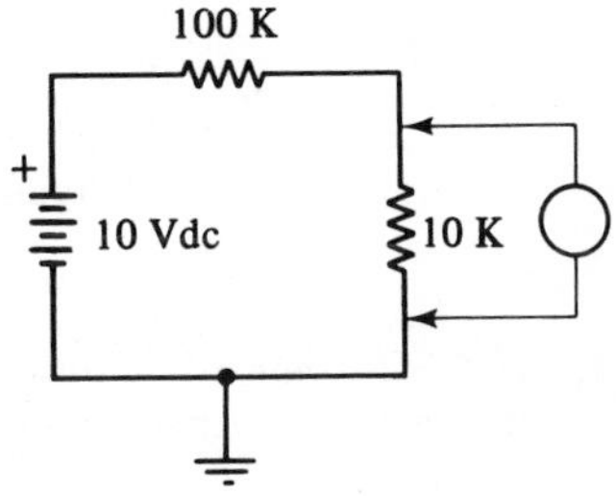

100 K

10 Vdc

10 K

Figure B.36

79. It is necessary to measure the dc bias on the screen grid of an RF power amplifier tube. What is the most desirable form of instrument for this purpose?
A. VOM
B. VTVM
C. RF Volter
D. FETVM

80. The voltmeter in the circuit in Figure B.36 has a sensitivity of 1000 Ω per volt. Will this measurement be valid?
A. No
B. Yes

81. How much current is drawn by the meter in Figure B.36 if +1.5 VDC is applied and the full-scale range is 0–3 V?
A. 1 mA
B. 300 μA
C. 0.5 mA
D. 0.250 mA

82. The circuit in Figure B.37 is a(n)
A. *PNPN* switch
B. Darlington amplifier
C. Doherty amplifier
D. Emitter follower

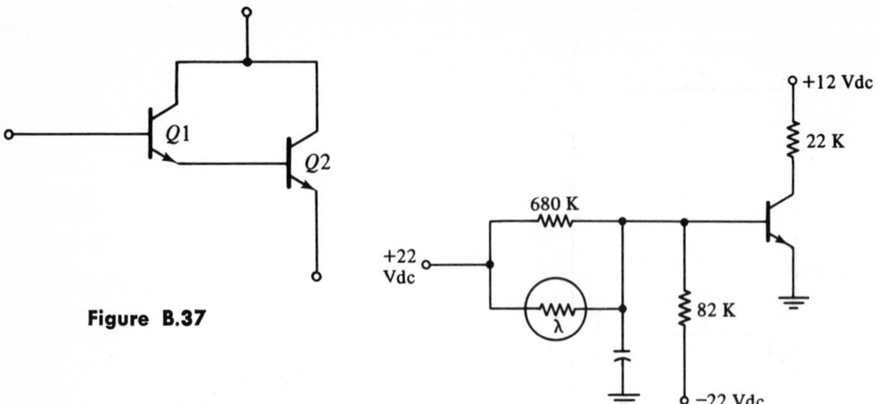

Figure B.37

Figure B.38

83. If $Q1$ in Figure B.37 has a beta of 50, while $Q2$ has a beta of 75, what is the beta of the combination?
A. 3750
B. 125
C. 25
D. 50

84. When light falls on the photocell in Figure B.38 transistor $Q1$ will be:
A. Destroyed
B. Turned off
C. Turned on
D. Reverse-biased

85. What will the voltmeter in Figure B.39 read?
A. 0 VDC
B. −15 VDC
C. −20 VDC
D. −5 VDC

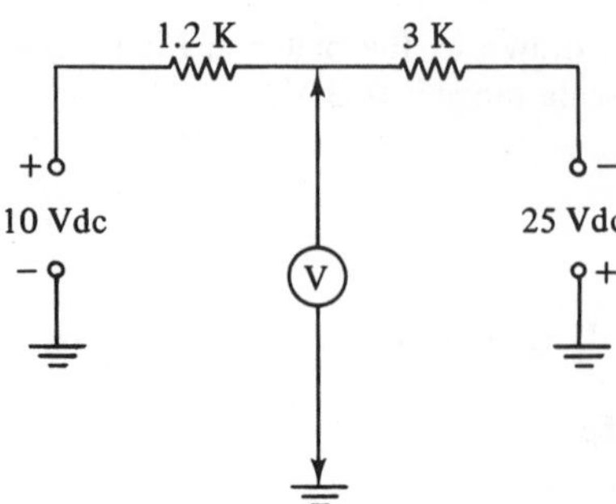

Figure B.39

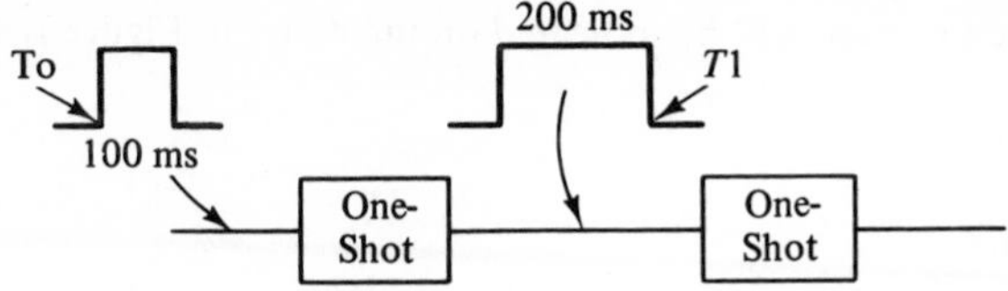

Figure B.40

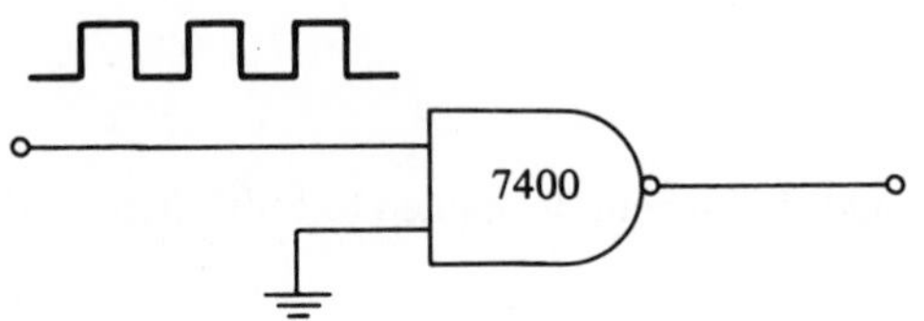

Figure B.41

86. Both of the one-shot multivibrators shown in Figure B.40 are trailing-edge triggered. What is the time interval between t_o and t_1?
A. 100 ms
B. 300 ms
C. 50 ms
D. 75 ms

87. What is the output of the circuit shown in Figure B.41?
A. +5 VDC
B. Pulses
C. Square waves
D. 0 VDC

88. What is the circuit in Figure B.42?
A. Balun bridge
B. Resistance meter
C. Hay/Schering bridge
D. Wheatstone bridge

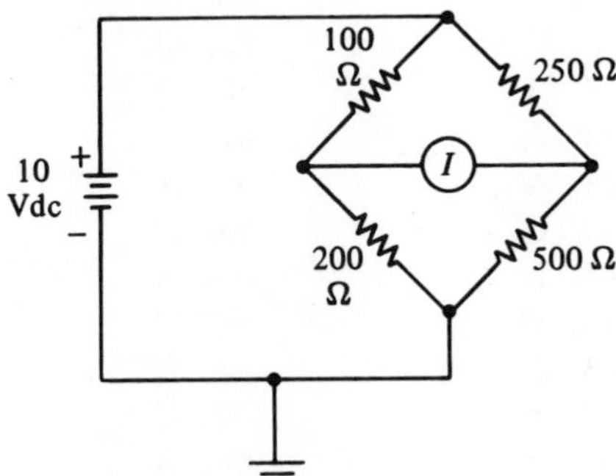

Figure B.42

89. How much current will be indicated on the meter in Figure B.42?
A. None
B. 450 mA
C. −0.45 mA
D. 4.5 mA

90. A ni-cad battery has a rating of 4 A/h. What is a safe charging current for a fully discharged cell?
A. 4000 mA
B. 1 A
C. 400 mA
D. 40 mA

91. How long should the current be applied to fully charge a discharged ni-cad cell?
A. 1 hr
B. 4 hr
C. 10 hr
D. 14 hr

ANSWERS TO QUESTIONS

1. D
2. A
3. C
4. A
5. D
6. A
7. B
8. C
9. B
10. A
11. C
12. D
13. B
14. D
15. B
16. C
17. A
18. A
19. B
20. A
21. B
22. A
23. C
24. B
25. A
26. D
27. B
28. B
29. A
30. D
31. C
32. A
33. A
34. D
35. B
36. C
37. B
38. A
39. A
40. C
41. B
42. D
43. C
44. A
45. B
46. B
47. D
48. C
49. D
50. C
51. A
52. C
53. B
54. A
55. B
56. A
57. C
58. A
59. C
60. D
61. A
62. B
63. D
64. A
65. D
66. B
67. C
68. A
69. B
70. D
71. A
72. C
73. A
74. C
75. B
76. C
77. D
78. C
79. A
80. A
81. C
82. B
83. A
84. C
85. A
86. B
87. A
88. D
89. A
90. C
91. D

Index

Key Formulas Index